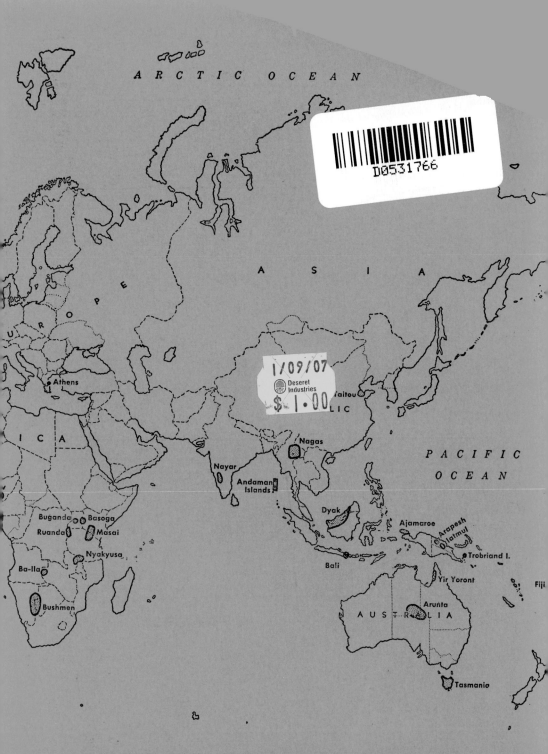

ARCTIC OCEAN

EUROPE

ASIA

ICA

Athens

Nayar

Andaman
Islands

Nagas

Waitou

LIC

Dyak

PACIFIC

OCEAN

Buganda Basoga
Ruanda   Masai
Nyakyusa
Ba-Ila
Bushmen

Bali

Ajamaroe Arapesh
          Iatmul
          Trobriand I.

Yir Yoront

Arunta

AUSTRALIA

Fiji

Tasmania

ANTARCTIC OCEAN

SCALE IN MILES
0   500   1000   1500   2000   2500   3000

EXPLORING THE WAYS OF MANKIND

EXPLORING THE WAYS OF MANKIND

WALTER GOLDSCHMIDT
University of California, Los Angeles

HOLT, RINEHART and WINSTON, Inc.

FOR: KARL

AND

MARK

Preface

This book does two things at the same time: it provides an introduction to the basic concepts and understandings of the science of anthropology, and it gives us a knowledge of our own social milieu in terms of those understandings. To serve both these masters at once is not difficult, for the best way to learn new concepts is through familiar examples. A physicist illustrates the principles of optics by reference first to the mirrors and lenses of everyday experience, and then on the basis of these demonstrates the uses and variance of these familiar phenomena. In like fashion anthropology provides a particularly happy subject for such dual purpose, for it deals both with the familiar and the exotic; it provides special insights into our own social environment. The challenge offered by an introduction to the subject therefore lies in providing the reader with an anthropological viewpoint and at the same time using that viewpoint to illuminate for him the everyday events of his own experience. *Exploring the Ways of Mankind* takes up this challenge. I sincerely believe that any person coming fresh to anthropology who reads this book through will have a new and more accurate understanding of the world he lives in, of his own personal environment, and thus of himself. He will also have a knowledge of the anthropological discipline.

Anthropology treats with human beings in their ordinary activities of getting food, taking wives, rearing children, working together, worshiping gods, and the like. It deals with them as members of the variety of peoples that are to be found throughout the world—whether they be primitive hunters eking out a living on the Kalahari desert, or modern man in Suburbia. It treats them comparatively, so that the student can find out what aspects of human behavior are universal and timeless, what are unique and variant. In order to understand mankind, and in order to understand ourselves, it is necessary to appreciate the various ways in which mankind has met the familiar challenges of life. It is also fun. For there is an eternal fascination in learning how different people go about the business of satisfying their desires.

The plan of this book is simple. Human social and cultural behavior is discussed under thirteen separate topics. Each section has a brief introduction and a group of readings taken from the literature of anthropology and sociology. These readings fall into three categories: (1) general discussion of the topic, (2) illustrations taken from primitive or exotic societies, and (3) illustrations from modern American or contemporary Western civilization. Usually there are more than one to each category, and they do not necessarily appear in that order.

This constant interweaving between the general and the specific, between the familiar and the exotic, between ourselves and others gives texture and variety; it also leads to interesting surprises. When we see a description of the modern suburban family and the Chinese family side by side, we learn how variantly the common domestic scenes can be played. We learn not only that there are different ways of doing things, but also that each has its values and creates its own problems. Above all, we see the common core of humanity that underlies the differing cultural modes. Again, when we examine next to one another the disruptive effects of technological change among the stone-age Australians and in a modern small city, we realize how similar the problems can be in diverse cultural situations. Thus, as these comparisons develop, we learn that though man's world is not uniform and simple, neither is it chaotic, and we begin to appreciate the scientific and comparative approach to human behavior. Concept and general understanding are given reality through the specific, concrete materials derived from scholarly reporting; yet examples are not sufficient in themselves, they must serve to illuminate general principles which, in turn, can be applied to new experiences.

The major advantage of the approach used here is that a scholarly understanding of familiar events of everyday life emerges from the data. It has other advantages as well. It gives the reader an opportunity to become familiar with the materials of the social sciences. He becomes acquainted with some of the most important ethnographic and sociological monographs, which he may later examine in greater detail. He senses how raw data shape the ideas of scholars.

A further advantage of this mode of presentation is that the reader becomes acquainted with eminent scholars in the field through their own writing. Essays were not selected simply because of the distinction of the writers, but it is natural that these writers are heavily represented for the very qualities that made them important. Such early scholars as Tylor, Morgan, Cooley, Weber, and such modern intellectual leaders as Kroeber, Kluckhohn, and Mead are here to be read at first hand.

Finally, the use of separate essays gives change of pace. Each item is different in style and in content. One turns from a general statement and analytic treatment to a descriptive presentation of case material. At one point the familiar is seen with new eyes; at another the exotic is examined in relation to the familiar. The academic presentation of theories in one essay is followed by a sprightly description in the next.

Yet it must be emphasized that this is not just a book of readings; not a mere collection of essays; the volume has a central theme. Its content is determined by the elements necessary to that controlling theme, and the essays represent the best writings relevant to that purpose. They are directly in their author's words; they have been edited only in the sense that materials extraneous to the purposes of this book have been deleted. Thus they efficiently express the ideas and understandings of the several authors as they impinge on the intellectual problems which the book addresses.

The book's thirteen sections have been arranged in sequence. The basic concept of anthropology—*culture*—is the subject of the first section. This concept illumines all human behavior and distinguishes the human mode of life from that of other beings. The second and third sections deal with man's two special gifts: language, which is truly *the* human attribute, and man's dependence upon tools and technical knowledge, which are learned ways of satisfying his needs. These are parts of culture, to be sure, but they are crucial to man's way of life. Then we take up education, the learning processes by which culture is transmitted—for culture, as we shall see, is learned behavior. Since the most fundamental learning takes place in the context of the family, we are next introduced to the nature and multiform patterns of family life.

The organization of social systems is discussed in the succeeding three sections under the headings of Groups, Status and Role, and Authority, and the reader becomes aware of anthropology's second major concept—*society*—in its chief ramifications. These are followed by four sections dealing with man's most noble attributes: Values, Religion, Ethics, and Art. The final section is a summary, pointing up the universal and the diverse elements in human behavior as they are found among living social systems.

Exploring the Ways of Mankind is a second edition. The first, under the title *Readings in the Ways of Mankind,* was published by the Fund for Adult Education in 1957 for use in discussion groups and has had a wide circulation, though it was not available through normal bookselling channels. The present edition, built on the same structure, is much changed. The introductions to each of the sections are new, three additional sections are included (only about half the essays in this edition appeared in the earlier one), and the brief headnote to each essay is an added feature.

The book has a longer history. In 1951 I was asked to develop a series of radio shows, *The Ways of Mankind,* designed to introduce basic concepts in social anthropology. Two units of thirteen half-hour dramas were recorded; they are available in album form for use in classrooms, discussions, and the like. The scripts for the first series were published by Beacon Press. The effectiveness of these materials for educational purposes has been recognized by a number of groups, and the Fund for Adult Education has sponsored their use throughout the United States. It was for this purpose that the first edition of this book was prepared.

Exploring the Ways of Mankind is designed so that it may be used in conjunction with Album I of *The Ways of Mankind.* It covers the same set of thirteen topics and includes readings that are relevant to the content of these dramatizations, along with other materials. Hearing these presentations will help the reader to sense the meanings and appreciate the nuances of each subject covered. Yet, at the same time, the book stands on its own; it does not require the use of the recordings nor does an understanding of the content rest on them in any way.

The human scene is an exciting one, and the study of human behavior is fascinating. The author has endeavored to preserve that feeling of excitement and fascination without sacrificing scientific accuracy in exploring the ways of mankind.

W. G.

Los Angeles, California
March, 1960

Acknowledgments

Many persons deserve gratitude for their special contributions to this book. First and foremost are the authors of the essays and their publishers, who have kindly granted permission for the use of their materials. Wherever possible, the authors have been contacted and it is gratifying to know that all gave their permissions most generously. Individual appreciation is expressed in the introduction to their respective contributions.

I wish to express a particularly warm thanks to those who helped and encouraged me during the years since this endeavor began, in the form of *The Ways of Mankind* radio project. Chief among these are my own family—my wife, Gale Goldschmidt, and two sons, Karl and Mark—whose response to and suggestions for the dramatic treatments were of great importance to me. For the present book, I am deeply indebted to a number of my colleagues and students in the Department of Anthropology and Sociology at The University of California, Los Angeles, not only for their encouragement but for their useful and generous advice. Among these I wish to note especially Professors Ralph L. Beals, Donald R. Cressy, Richard Hill, Harry Hoijer, Richard T. Morris, Raymond Murphy, and Councill Taylor. Among the students who have been specifically helpful are Robert Edgerton, S. Chadwick Oliver and H. Clyde Wilson and my former student Edgar V. Winans. I want also to thank Mrs. Betty Bell, Editorial Assistant for the *American Anthropologist,* and Mrs. Anne Cook, of the Institute of Industrial Relations, for their valuable editorial services, and Miss Ursula Finken for her patient and efficient secretarial work. The staff of Henry Holt and Company deserves my gratitude for seeing a difficult manuscript rapidly through press.

Because this work emerges out of the background of *The Ways of Mankind* radio project, there is a deeper and older level of indebtedness. C. Scott Fletcher, President of the Fund for Adult Education, originally made this project possible, and to him, to G. H. Griffiths, and to Glen Burch I express my gratitude. The late Robert Redfield, Robert Meynard Hutchins Distinguished Service Professor at The University of Chicago, originally conceived the idea for such a program. He and the remainder of my advisory committee, Ralph L. Beals, Margaret Mead, Cora Du Bois, and A. L. Kroeber have my sincerest thanks. The program was sponsored by the National Association of Educational Broadcasters, and I am indebted to the members of this committee, George E. Probst, Richard Hill, Harold B. McCarty, Seymour Siegel and Parker Wheatley, and to Ralph Lowell, Miss Ruth Perkins and William Harley who had various official roles. The more intimate involvement with my working colleagues on the programs make for a particular debt, and among these I should mention Andrew Allan, who produced the shows, Lister Sinclair, Len Peterson, Eugene S. Hallman and George Salverson, who wrote them, and Lucio Agostini, who composed and directed the music.

Charles Nelson has been helpful in preparing the special discussion-group edition.

Above all, this book owes a debt to that tradition of scholarship which, over the past century, has accumulated a great world literature on human behavior and which has created a scholarly discipline to give this literature meaning. The essays printed here are a sample of this heritage.

Contents

INTRODUCTION

The Cultured Animal

One of the most exciting things about this world is its variety, and of these variations none is more interesting than those displayed by man in different parts of the world. Ever since travelers have returned from strange lands—whether they be Herodotus returning from Egypt, Marco Polo from China, Columbus from America, or Cook from the South Seas—they have returned with tales of the peculiar manners, customs, and appearance of the people they saw. Dress, architecture, religion, beliefs, customs, and the very form and features of these strange peoples always have a fascination for those who remain at home. Travel books continue among the most popular in our libraries. Everyone is interested in the different ways people have worked out the common problems of satisfying their material needs, organizing their social life, and embellishing their daily existence with the arts.

Philosophers, noting the great variety of human types and human behavior, have long tried to explain why these differences exist. The task has been taken over by the social sciences and, in keeping with the dominant scientific mode of thought, social scientists have endeavored over the past century to bring some order into the accumulating evidence of human similarities and differences, and to evaluate the various explanations that have been set forth. Thus the basic question to which anthropology has addressed itself from the beginning is: how can we explain the uniformity and diversity of human behavior?

The quest for an answer to this problem has led scholars into many paths of inquiry; has taken them by dog sled to the Arctic ice cap to examine the Eskimo, has led them down into the caves of France and Spain to view the products of paleolithic artists, has brought them into the modern factory, has sent them to the jungles of Sumatra with tape recorder and field glass to investigate the behavior of the great apes, and has led to innumerable tables of measurements of the human head and body parts. It has, in fact, gone into every quarter of the globe and every aspect of human behavior and physique. For the laboratory of anthropology is man himself, and the understanding of human behavior requires that we investigate every facet of his being in every possible manifestation.

No final and complete answer can be given nor is one likely to be found. But the problem is outside the hands of the philosopher who erects idea systems and is in the hands of the scientists who accumulate evidence and test their hypotheses as best they can in terms of actual events, and with as much control as possible. They have found that no single explanation, no simple "monolithic" theory, will serve to account for the divergent ways of mankind. Anthropology is, and must be, a many-faceted subject. Significantly it is recognized in scholarly circles as being at one and the same time a biological science, a social science, and a part of humanistic studies.

Among such monolithic theories, the oldest and most popular have been biological. That is, peoples have tried to account for the differences in behavior in terms of the hereditary difference of the populations. The biological aspects of human differences have led to one major field of anthropology, generally called physical anthropology, which has sought to describe and classify physical variation among people. Human populations do differ in hereditary biological traits. Characteristics of body build, skin color, the distribution, texture, and color of hair, facial features, head size and shape, and many minor descriptive elements have different distributions over the face of the earth. On the basis of such characteristics, it is possible to classify people into separate races. Races are categories of people who share a pattern of detailed features of the kind enumerated above. But since populations of divergent races can and do interbreed, no race is pure, and all populations show a range of variation. The function and distribution of these physical characteristics are appropriately the subject matter of the biological aspects of anthropology.

As we are interested in understanding the variation in human behavior patterns rather than the physical features themselves, the question becomes: do these variations in bodily structure reflect variations in hereditary temperament, intelligence, or other attributes which might account for differences in patterns of behavior? The evidence leads to an almost certain *no*.

What are the evidences? Chief among them is the fact that there are wide ranges of variation in cultural behavior among peoples having the same racial features, and similarities among people of divergent physical attributes. The Utes of Utah and Nevada were among the most primitive people in North America. A people speaking a closely related language and racially indistinguishable were the Aztecs; thus, some of the most primitive and the most advanced of native American peoples were both members of a single physical type. In Asia, so-called Mongoloids gave us the philosopher Confucius, the military despot Gengis Khan and the Siberian shaman. While European culture has flourished for several millennia and has been responsible for creating elaborate arts, masterful engineering, and complex societies, the Australian aborigines who are predominantly of the same basic racial stock live in a traditional stone-age mode of life. Contrariwise, while the inhabitants of northern Europe were living in circumstances not unlike some of the peoples of North America, life in southeastern Asia was highly civilized. In parts of Mexico, Guatemala, and Peru, the Indians had much more advanced arts and architecture than our ancestors in North Europe who were their contemporaries. Despotic kingdoms have existed among all races and in all the major continents.

The world has offered us a natural laboratory for further exploration of this relationship. We discover that people have changed their mode of life in a few generations' time—and it is impossible for biological change to take place so fast. Perhaps no example is better than that of the Japanese, whose rapid industrial development is well-known, though the adjustment of many peoples to Western civilization, especially in America, offer examples which we know more intimately. The simple fact is that differences in mode of behavior do not correlate with racial characteristics.

All this does not mean that physical anthropology is not a useful and important subject. Its former interest in racial classification has been superseded by other more important contributions. One of these is the age-old interest in fossil men and the evolutionary development of man himself. The second is the study of human genetics in relation to the inheritance of physical features and the evolutionary processes. The third is the study of the functional characteristics of body traits— the advantages and disadvantages of such features as skin color, hair distribution, nose form, and aspects of body build. Out of the study of man as a biological animal—which is the province of physical anthropology—we are therefore beginning to appreciate how man has evolved into his present form, to comprehend the function of the body in response to different environmental and dietary situations and the nature of individual differences among men. One ironic conclusion is that man's cultural behavior appears to have been more influential in determining physical attributes in man than the physical attributes have been in determining the differences in culture. For the development of tools, cooking, clothes, and the like have rendered certain physical features obsolete and made others advantageous.

What emerges from our concern with the physical characteristics of humanity is this: culture builds upon the potentials of the human body and the human mind, it must operate in terms of those drives and physiological characteristics that the human animal is heir to; man's nature therefore sets the potentialities and limitations on his mode of life. Cultures cannot disregard the given facts of biology; on the other hand, these facts of biology cannot account for the differences in human behavior and patterns of life as they are found among the various primitive and civilized peoples. It does not provide the basis for understanding the difference between one mode of life and another. It stands like a constant in an equation, influencing the final answer but not in itself differentiating.

A second popular monolithic explanation for the variety of human behavior is environmental. In its simple form the notion that the environment determines the behavior of a population, is no more than an elaboration of the popular and erroneous phrase: "Necessity is the mother of invention." To be sure, man everywhere lives in an environment, and the natural resources available to him, the climatological conditions to which he must adjust, and the effective techniques which can be employed all have an influence upon his behavior. But this is not to say that they determine his behavior. Here, again, the evidence is clear. A single area may at one time be occupied by people with one mode of life and at a subsequent period (without environmental change) be inhabited by people with an entirely different pattern of existence. The remarkably productive irrigated agriculture of modern California follows by but a century the Indians who lived by hunting, fishing, and gathering wild fruits and vegetables—a totally different culture. The environment has not changed; what has changed is the technical equipment of the two civilizations which enable a different kind of exploitation of the same environment. There are few places on the face of the earth for which a similar kind of differential cannot be demonstrated to have taken place.

The popular notion remains that the temperament of a people is determined by the climate; that the dourness of the Scot and the volatility of the Italian derive from the gloom and fog in one area and the sunshine and warmth in the other. But such a correlation cannot be sustained when we examine the world-wide distribution of human behavior.

This does not mean that the anthropologist can disregard geography as a factor in human difference. Each environment offers opportunities and places limitations. The degree to which a people can take advantage of the opportunity and overcome the limitations rests upon the technical accomplishments that it has at its command and upon other parts of its cultural apparatus. Therefore, the way in which a people will utilize a territory depends in large measure on its existing cultural characteristics. All this means that man's relationship to his environment is a two-way street; that the circumstances of geography influence his culture, but the culture in turn influences geography.

The modern concept of ecology expresses far better the relation between man and his environment than did the older environmental determinism. Ecology is the study of the relationship between an animal and its environment, including other life forms, and its own manner of utilizing that environment. Since man utilizes his environment through his cultural equipment, the study of human ecology involves itself inevitably with a recognition of the tools and techniques that a particular people has at its disposal.

Other simple explanations have been set forth: theories evoking economic determinism, instinct, Freudian psychology, and the like have contributed to a general understanding, but they are not in and of themselves sufficient.

The concept of culture offers the key to the understanding of human behavior, according to modern anthropology. We have already had to introduce the word, but must briefly set forth its meaning here, reserving a detailed discussion for the first section of this book.

If we say that a person is behaving in a particular way because of his culture, we are asserting that he has been conditioned to this behavior through living in a social environment in which the mode of behavior is general for his age and sex; that he is following traditional forms of response to the problems of everyday life; that the attitudes of those around him have set, for him, his way of dealing with his world. These are not all exactly the same thing, but they point out that culture is learned behavior, that it is shared by a population, and that the individual, though neither an automaton nor a slave to the cultural expectations, is nevertheless subtly and continuously influenced by those around him to act in conformity to established precedents.

This can apply, as we shall see, to anything that a person does, for nothing escapes the pervasive influence of culture. It applies to the kind of foods that will cause him to salivate, the manner in which he will secure these foods, the way he expects others to treat him as well as the way he will treat others, the kind of person he will seek for a wife, the gods he will supplicate and the form of that supplication. We need not go on. No man is born without entering into a cultural environment, and no person can escape the pervasive influence of his culture except by going to another—and even this is never a total escape, because the attitudes and feelings will persist without his own awareness of them.

The anthropologist, therefore, says that the differences in behavior between the Eskimo, the Chinese, the French and ourselves is a difference in culture. That is to say, the variety of human activities reported by Herodotus, Marco Polo, Columbus, Cook and all those other travelers, missionaries, and anthropologists who have described how people behave in different parts of the world, are variations brought about by differences in culture.

By now you must certainly believe that either we have a new simplistic explanation or that this is no explanation at all. For either we must set culture up as a single positive force—like race or economic determinism—or we must explain why cultures themselves differ. If we must do the latter, have we gained anything by adding this new factor, culture?

We have. For culture offers us a basis of variation that (1) is not biological and yet (2) is still an intimate part of man rather than some outside force, like environment or spirits. Yet, explaining the variation in behavior in terms of culture does not take us very far; it has, in fact, merely allowed us to ask the right questions.

In order to understand how culture makes for human variation, we must, so to speak, take the concept apart. We must see its component elements as they operate, sometimes uniformly for all people, sometimes variantly. There are several elements here:

1. Culture is the material means by which the human animal gains his livelihood; it is useful to man's continued life on earth.

2. Culture is learned behavior; it is acquired by each organism in the process of growing up.

3. Culture is shared behavior; it is the behavior characteristic of a population.

4. Culture is based upon customs; there is always a strong traditional element in the way people do things.

5. Culturally established behavior must take into consideration three aspects of human circumstances which cannot simply be overlooked, though they may be variantly met: (a) man's biological needs and characteristics not only for sustenance and comfort but also for self-expression, understanding, and whatever psychological elements may be found to characterize humanity, (b) environmental circumstances out

of which living must be obtained, and (c) the requirements of orderly social arrangements so that people can continue to live and work in reasonable harmony and gain the benefits of cooperative action which culture makes possible.

Now this traditional, shared, learned behavior that supplies man's physical, emotional, and social needs is itself a kind of growing thing. The culture of a people in a given time and place is a product of its own historical development, adjusted to environmental circumstances and the needs of the people as individuals and as a group. The knowledge that man has gained in times past and the successful or satisfying modes of behavior grow with the accumulation of human experience. This element of growth applies particularly to those aspects of culture which serve practical ends (mostly technical knowledge, but, as we shall see, other parts of culture, too), for with them man increases his numbers, his material well-being and his security. Some of this growth of knowledge is useful in adjusting to peculiar environmental necessities—snowshoes for example—but others have a wider range of applicability. Occasionally such a development can be thought of as a major breakthrough to whole new potentialities, as with agriculture, irrigation, and the use of steam power.

When Western civilization burst out of Europe with the age of exploration, it found peoples at various levels of cultural development. Some, like ourselves, had had the benefit of the accumulated knowledge of mankind, while others, for one reason or another not in the main stream of cultural growth, did not inherit such knowledge but remained more or less in the conditions of life that characterized earlier stages of cultural evolution. This divergence accounts for many of the differences between one culture and another and is the basis for the classification of cultures into economic types, since the mode of livelihood influences all aspects of culture. This is by no means the only source of culture variance, but it is one of the most important and certainly the most fundamental. The magnitude of this source of variation is discussed in detail in the section on technology and its implications delineated throughout the volume.

The level of technical development cannot account for all of cultural variation. Special historical backgrounds, special environmental circumstances, and many other factors are also influential in setting the character of a society at any particular time. The interplay among the elements that constitute culture, already set forth, must also be recognized. In short, culture is a phenomenon so complex that it is shaped by many forces. Yet, in turn, it shapes the individual to imperfect conformity.

The concept of culture, defined and delimited in the first section, underlies the remainder of the volume. For each section takes up a separate aspect of human activity and shows the kinds of uniformity and variety which it displays. It is the ultimate aim of this work to show how cultures operate, and how, in their operation they set life-patterns for their participants.

The concept of society is a kind of counterpart to the idea of culture, and it is necessary also that we have an understanding of what the sociologists mean by the term and how it relates to and differs from the concept culture. Society is the organization of men into functioning groups, the patterned and established on-going relations among peoples who view themselves as forming an entity. The manner of organization is set by culture, but the fact of organized action and the interplay of persons is societal. No culture can exist except as it is embodied in a society of men; no society can operate without cultural directives. Like matter and energy, like mind and body, they are interdependent and interacting yet express different aspects of the human situation.

Living together, daily interaction, cooperation for mutual benefit, the stresses and strains inherent in the constant interaction, and the modes of coping with potential conflict may be seen as societal matters. For everywhere men live in society, and everywhere they must maintain sufficient harmony to supply their mutual needs and acceptable wants. This fact of social life is a second element that runs through the volume.

As we open with the concept of culture, we close with a discussion of society. In the section on groups we introduce society formally, and develop its implications in subsequent sections. For all societies have certain organizational features in common (though they differ in details), which the recurrent problems of social existence call forth.

Exploring the Ways of Mankind is therefore devoted to examining the many aspects of culture and society and, by examining the variety of ways by which man has met the conditions of life, to come to a broader understanding of human behavior. It presents the separate facets of human behavior while recognizing the interrelationships among the parts. In dealing with culture and society in their variant manifestations, it focuses attention upon the core elements in human behavior as these appear in group situations.

It does not—and cannot—cover every aspect of anthropology and sociology. Anthropology consists of a number of fields or subdisciplines: physical anthropology, linguistics, archeology, folklore, and the like. None of these are entirely left out of the discussion, but they are related at all times to the central concepts of culture and society which offer the key to understanding the ways of mankind.

I.

CULTURE

The Essence of Human Life

Cultures are many, though man is one. Each people has its own set of solutions to the universal needs of man's physical and social life. The manner in which it meets these challenges is its culture. For men everywhere must satisfy basic animal wants; men everywhere must live together in social groups and work out means of cooperative action; men everywhere must communicate among their fellows—and they do all these things through established patterns of behavior handed down from the past and modified to meet new circumstances.

Very nearly every act of every human being is to some extent affected by the culture to which he is accustomed. In saying this, we are not denying that man is an animal and has animal needs and appetites which he must satisfy. Rather, we are saying that man, alone among all living things, interprets these basic demands according to custom, and that when man eats or sleeps or fights or loves, he is doing so in accordance with patterned expectations set up for him by his fellow man. Aside from actions of the basic autonomic system such as heartbeat, breathing and blinking (and occasional idiosyncratic behavior), nothing man does is freed from the pervasive influence of culture, and even these may be influenced by culturally established responses—for example, his reactions to a pretty girl (as viewed by his culture).

Consider the matter of eating. Man, like every living thing, must transfer matter into energy; he must eat. An unusually wide range of substances can be digested, but everywhere man has set up preferences and rejections, so that some items are a luxury while others are disgusting. In response to cultural dictates, the human animal may starve rather than eat tabooed food. In no culture is eating merely the gobbling of digestible substances; it is a cultural act, culturally defined. Man is conditioned to eating at certain times of the day and becomes hungry at the hour of his habituation, though some peoples eat but twice daily while others four or five times; he is accustomed to certain instruments for eating, and it was as important for a Fiji Islander to eat his cannibal feast with a special fork as it is for a modern American to distinguish his salad fork from his dinner fork. Eating, that basic animal attribute, is culturally defined the world over. The same may be said for mating. It may be said for every physiological act, within the broad limits set by human physiology. Man's behavior may be said to be channeled by the culture into which he is born. This is truly his unique characteristic.

No other animal may be said to have culture, though many of them have some of the more specific characteristics that are a part of our culture. Human beings build shelters the world over, though some are exceedingly crude while others are highly elaborate. Many animals also build shelters—birds, bees, beavers and hosts of others. But the pattern of building among other animals is not learned as part of a tradition; rather it is an inherited response. We can see this best with insects: a swarm of bees or ants builds its edifice without ever having seen a model or communicated with a creature that has seen one. The same is true of other animal construction. If you had crossed the American continent with Lewis and Clark, you would have noted a variety of Indian house types as you moved from one region to another—wigwam, earth-lodge, tepee—but the beaver dams would have been uniform. Man has learned a variety of adaptive ways to shelter himself from cold and rain; the beaver has an innate response as a part of his make-up. We need not multiply examples: the difference between man and other animals is that man has culture and animals do not.

Culture includes the whole gamut of behavior, knowledge, and thought. It includes modes of making implements, weapons, and other material things; the customary pattern of social interaction, from patterned ways of training infants to the manner of mourning the dead; it includes the wisdom of the sages and inconsequential animal fables; it includes religious beliefs and magical formulae; it includes even the patterns of emotional responses and feeling. In short, whatever aspects of life are influenced by customary procedures are contained in the broad concept of culture.

We may find it hard to accept the concept that our sentiments of love and hate, and the stimuli which evoke them, are culturally determined. But this also is true. We know that the Balinese shout and sing at funerals, while the Karankawa Indians of southern Texas weep copiously at greeting a friend—but are perhaps less surprised at the latter when we remember our own custom of women weeping at weddings.

We must remember that the learning of our culture is an extremely subtle process, that much of it is transmitted without premeditation both on the part of those who have it and those who are receiving it. We know only dimly some of the processes by which attitudes and sentiments are conveyed, but we know that they are conveyed and that the people in one culture will tend to respond to things quite differently from another. Culture is not merely a bag of customs; it is an orientation to life.

Culture is learned behavior, but not all learning is culture. Learning is of course common in animal life; even earthworms have learned to run a simple T maze. All animals presumably respond to stimuli, make associations between events, and direct future actions accordingly. But the degree to which human life is governed by learned behavior is infinitely greater than among other beings. More important, however, is the degree to which man is consciously taught. And, finally, as we shall see in subsequent sections, the fact that this teaching is not merely by precept but through language makes for profound differences between human and nonhuman behavior patterns. For the moment, however, we must note merely that these facts tend to give to culture, as distinct from animal learning, a high degree of detail and at the same time a wholeness, a unity of pattern.

If we are to understand the phenomenon of culture, we must keep in mind an important attribute of human life. All of us enter our culture by way of the womb; all of us grow up into it through stages of infancy and childhood. We are therefore subjected to a period of many years when perforce we must passively accept the patterns of behavior which are already established and current among the people who are our seniors. It is in this process of growing up into an ongoing system that the individual acquires his culture; it is in this context that culture is learned and through this mechanism that it continues.

And it is in this sense that culture is the pattern of behavior that is shared by a group, a society. The shared aspect of culture is an important attribute, and must be appreciated if we are to understand the cultural mode of life. Each society has its own ways of doing things, and it is this commonality that is an important attribute of culture. This does not mean that everyone in a culture behaves exactly alike. Men act differently from women, the old act differently from the young, the chief from the ordinary man, the priest from the layman. But each is acting in terms of the cultural definition of his role (a point to which we will return later in this book); each is acting in accordance with the patterned expectation of those around him. How the group is defined will in part be a product of the very culture itself, but that there is always a large group that shares these patterns of behavior and thought is universal.

Let us pause for a moment over the word "expectation." For culture is not merely behavior but is also a set of anticipations, of expectations and presumptions about the behavior of others. If man is to work out cooperative life on the basis of learned rather than innate responses, he must have some reasonable assurance that his fellow men will behave in prescribed ways. Therefore he comes to have in his mind a pattern of how the world, and especially the social world, ought to operate. He may expect a certain amount of deviance and be able to accommodate it, but this deviance cannot be chaos. In our mind we carry, as it were, a sort of blueprint for total behavior of our society—or as much of it as we need to be cognizant of. We can, with these normal expectations, chart our own course through the maze of social interactions, just as we drive a car by anticipating that by and large other drivers will behave according to the rules—though we watch out for the erratic drivers.

Culture is also patterned. By this we mean that the totality of behavior, knowledge, and belief shared by a people has a kind of internal consistency. It is not merely the conglomeration of customs and ideas to which a people has fallen heir, even though it is accurately said that a people inherits its culture out of the past. For, though culture is handed down, the heirs are not merely passive recipients, taking whatever is given and leaving it untouched and undirected. Two factors tend to give unity to culture: The first is that certain situations demand certain responses. For instance, when the Plains Indians acquired the horse, they developed not only the trappings necessary for horsemanship, but they adopted hosts of institutions with respect to hunting, warfare and other social regulations that their new mobility made possible or necessary. The second is a human tendency to give a kind of logical consistency to events. To give a trivial example: people accustomed to driving cars in the United States usually stay on the right, even when they are walking, as part of their patterned response. In the broader arena of social action, we find the same notion of carry-over from one situation to another so that, for instance, the attitudes a child develops toward his father will tend to be carried into all relations with senior males. Nowhere is this patterning, this internal consistency, greater than in the realm of language.

When a child uses *comed* or *bringed* for the past tense of *come* or *bring,* he is not merely committing a common childish error, he is demonstrating the human tendency to see the pattern of events and to respond consistently; only later does he learn the distinction between regular and irregular verbs.

This illustration makes a further point: there is a constant pressure to consistency and patterning in human behavior, but not all elements are orderly—the pattern is not perfect in its symmetry. A living culture, like a living language, is always somewhat out of joint with the times. The more so in a modern, complex, and rapidly changing culture such as our own. Such exceptions should not obscure the fact that there is a strong tendency toward consistency and pattern in cultures.

We have now seen that culture is the mosaic of learned behavior, knowledge and belief shared by a group, passed on from generation to generation, modified to meet circumstances, having a measure of internal consistency in response to the external pressures of efficiency and the human tendency to render the world orderly; that it ranges the full arc of human action and thought, including not only beliefs and emotional responses but also the patterns of expectations that each individual has regarding each other.

1. *Culture as a Mode of Life.*

Man has been a successful animal. In the past half million years he has increased from probably a few thousand individuals to over two billion. For a good part of that time, his career was doubtful. While neither in total bulk nor in total numbers does he outdistance all rivals, in terms of his control of events and in terms of dispersal over the globe, he has no equal. The success of this newcomer among living species must be attributed to culture. Though many of man's woes and much of his travail can be laid at the door of this unique human characteristic, we must also appreciate its virtues.

It is through culture that man has developed the material accoutrements with which he wrests his livelihood. As a naked animal bereft of tools and weapons, man is no tower of strength. Unprotected from the elements, with weak claws, short teeth and but two legs, he is neither remarkably fierce nor remarkably swift. But by extending his capacity through the use of tools he has overcome his natural handicaps and is to be reckoned a formidable foe of all his fellow creatures. (In terms of his phylogenetic history he may have actually lost some of his physical powers as a result of the substitution of cultural attributes, but this is not susceptible to proof at present.)

Tool-using is of course a part of culture. It is not merely the fact that a stick or a stone is used that is involved here, for many birds and mammals use them. It is, rather, the fact that man shapes these tools according to prescribed fashion and learns precisely how to use them, being taught by his elders. It is man's capacity to pass on experience and therefore to accumulate knowledge that gives him his strength. This knowledge has grown through time, for once a device is found or invented, it is passed on to others.

Thus, through the ages man has stored knowledge and passed it on, and as every new element appears it becomes part of his stock in trade, as it were, increasing the human capacity to cope with environment. While half a million years (the length of time which we think culture has existed) seems a long time, no other animal has changed his capacity so much in so short a time.

Thus the cultural mode of life has had the potentialities for rapid growth that has led man from being a creature of the forest into modern industrial life. It has also made him highly adaptable. Leave him naked and arm him with a poisoned blow gun, and he survives in the jungles of South America. Wrap him in the skins of other animals and arm him with a bow, and he lives on the Arctic ice cap. And this he has done for himself, repeatedly, and in all environments (today, even in the Antarctic). For since culture is learned, it can be adapted to needs as they arise. Though this adaptation is neither automatic nor perfect, it is repetitive and adequate. As we examine subsequent sections in this book we will discuss some of the concomitant aspects of this adaptation, will learn that it is not merely a matter of adding this feature, changing that one and dropping a third, but that it involves quite extensive adjustment. Culture, as Tylor said, "is that complex whole . . ." and if it is a complex whole, its adjustment must also be complex.

2. *Culture and the Individual.*

The individual does not choose his culture, any more than he chooses his parents. He is born to it. (Of course, a few persons in the modern world renounce their heritage, insofar as they can, and adopt a new country and culture.) Therefore what the individual is, what he does, what he wears, what he yearns for and cherishes and what he rejects and despises, is set for him by his culture.

This is not to say that man is a plastic lump, shaped in any way at all. As an animal, and a very complicated one at that, he has certain needs and certain limitations; he has also certain tendencies of proclivities. But within this broad range of possibilities, and within his individual capacities or talents, he is made by his culture. Beethoven may have had musical talent, but his music built on the technical and artistic accomplishment of Western civilization and particularly on the high value placed upon music in contemporary Germany. Edison might have been creative in other settings, but he not only built upon an elaborate technology, he was supported by a heightened interest in mechanical gadgets that are a part of the American pattern of life. When we say that a man is shaped by his culture, we do not reduce him to an automaton but merely recognize that he is constantly influenced not only by the grosser aspects of his civilization, but by the subtle and pervasive forces of his social environment.

The grosser aspects we understand clearly enough. That man learns to use the tools around him, accepts customs of eating, dressing, and social intercourse is so much a matter of observation that we need not labor the point. But culture is, as we have insisted, not merely a matter of customs and paraphernalia, it is also shared systems of attitudes and feelings. These are often so subtle that we cannot accept the notion that they are taught or directly imitated. To see this point, we must travel in our minds across cultural boundaries. A trip through Europe exemplifies the difference in national cultures. While not every Frenchman is volatile, every Englishman reticent nor every German efficient, we recognize these adjectives as appropriate to their several national temperaments. We need not concern ourselves here with how these differences of culture arose; we are concerned now with how they are communicated, how they are passed on.

Earlier writers noting these differences thought of them as being biological, used the biological term race, and let it go as a matter of inheritance. We know that it is not biological, but cultural (that is, learned) behavior. Yet the French don't teach their children to be volatile and the English reticent in social behavior, nor many of the other elements in their characteristic social poses and psychological orientation to life. Since these attitudes and orientations lie very deep, since they organize the personality attributes of the individual, we cannot think of them as merely being an imitation of the world around them. Rather, we must presume that these characteristics are responses to the typical, or usual, life experiences of the individual—life experiences which are brought about by growing up in that particular kind of culture. Since they lie deep, they must to a considerable extent be formulated early in individual experience, and reinforced by many recurrent aspects of life.

Influenced by Freudian theory, some anthropologists and psychologists have sought the explanation in early infantile experience, such as feeding, toilet training, weaning, and handling. Others feel that the general emotional tone of infantile experience, the patterned expectations and responses that are set up in the early years of life are responsible.

At any rate, we must appreciate that, though an infant is neutral culturally at the moment of birth, he is very early drawn into the basic psychological modes of his culture through the characteristic elements of his early, culturally conditioned experiences. It is a point to which we will return in the section on education.

3.   *Unity and Variation in the Meaning of Culture.*

Most of what has already been said is recognized by all students of anthropology as the characteristics of culture. Not all scholars emphasize the same aspects of culture, and the readings which follow demonstrate some of the more particular ways through which culture can be viewed.

E. B. Tylor was the first to formulate the concept of culture in the more or less modern anthropological sense. He saw in the concept an organizing principle for understanding the varieties of behavior found in all parts of the world, and believed that through the analysis of culture we could understand why different people behave in the many different ways that they do. It is no wonder that Tylor is often called the father of anthropology. He believed that there was a progressive evolution in culture from the simple to the complex, and that certain laws of development and certain patterns of association between cultural elements could be uncovered. Anthropologists are not all agreed that such laws can be found, though many of them are working on the problem. We must remember that in the mid-nineteenth century, culture was viewed largely as a collection of customs, skills, and beliefs, and that the notion of pattern and the subtle orientation to behavior was not yet being considered.

A. L. Kroeber, whose long creative life as an anthropologist makes him undisputed dean of American anthropology, writes in a more contemporary vein. After eighty years of scholarly research, anthropologists fully recognize the complexity of their subject matter and the difficulty of reducing social behavior to any clearly defined sets of principles. Kroeber accepts the philosophical notion that there are several separate "levels" in nature: the physical, the biological, and the psychological. To him, culture is to be seen as a fourth level, operating beyond the biological and the psychological; it is a plane that is peculiarly human, to which he has given the term *superorganic*.

The selection by Ruth Benedict discusses some aspects of a particular culture. Benedict believes that each culture is characterized by a central, perduring theme which she calls pattern, and that one can only understand a culture in terms of such a dominant theme. She is illustrating the point here with the culture of the northwest coast of North America, concentrating on the Kwakiutl tribe. She believes that the dominant pattern of a culture not only suffuses the culture itself, but also affects the individual participant. Robert Lynd, who as a young man studied Muncie, Indiana ("Middletown"), much as an anthropologist studies a tribe, endeavors to set forth the themes of modern American culture, based upon this experience and, of course, extensive reading.

The final selection, by Edward Sapir, involves a very different view of culture—one that comes much closer to the popular meaning of the word than does the prevalent anthropological usage. Yet not quite, for Sapir is not talking about the loss of arts and literature, he is not making a judgment about the relative merits of modern versus native music; he is, rather, concerned with the loss of cultural commitment or the involvement with any culture whatever.

Sapir's view raises an important point of another kind: The relative value of cultures. All of us are brought up in a culture and most of us accept the assumptions, the subtle orientation or basic patterns of our own way of life. It can hardly be otherwise nor, as Sapir indicates, should it be. But if we are committed to a culture, we tend to view alternate ways not only as foreign but as inferior, wrong, or perhaps disgusting. The anthropologist cannot carry his prejudices into the field; he examines cultures without judgment. Can we properly view some cultures as better and others as worse? The question should best be held for the time, since a deeper knowledge of all aspects of culture is required before a meaningful answer can be achieved. The point here is only that we should, like all anthropologists, withhold judgment.

Despite the variations in emphasis with respect to the meaning and nature of culture, the central point remains: Man everywhere lives in a cultural world which sets his life patterns; man is born with the potential for culture, but cultures themselves differ. Man is one but cultures are many.

1. The Science of Culture

EDWARD B. TYLOR

Edward Burnett Tylor is often called the father of anthropology. Though not trained in the universities of England, he lectured at Oxford University from 1883 until near the end of his life, and organized the School of Anthropology there. He became interested in primitive customs, toured Mexico and wrote a book on ancient and modern Mexico which was published in 1861.

It is appropriate to start our exploration with these few pages which include the first effort to define the word *culture* and a clear call for a scientific understanding of cultures. Tylor was certainly not the first to investigate primitive peoples nor to try to generalize about human behavior, but he was one of the first to use the methods of science in such study—he even applied statistical techniques in some of his work. He recognized the complexity of the problem, and his bold aim set forth in this article has not yet been fulfilled. Anthropologists are still working along the broad outlines he sets for them here.

The selection is from the opening pages of Tylor's classic and most important work *Primitive Culture*, Volume I, Chapter 1, pp. 1–9. New York: Henry Holt and Company, 1871.

Culture or Civilization, taken in its wide ethnographic sense, is that complex whole which includes knowledge, belief, art, morals, law, custom, and any other capabilities and habits acquired by man as a member of society. The condition of culture among the various societies of mankind, in so far as it is capable of being investigated on general principles, is a subject apt for the study of laws of human thought and action. On the one hand, the uniformity which so largely pervades civilization may be ascribed, in great measure, to the uniform action of uniform causes; while on the other hand its various grades may be regarded as stages of development or evolution, each the outcome of previous history, and about to do its proper part in shaping the history of the future. . . .

Our modern investigators in the sciences of inorganic nature are foremost to recognize, both within and without their special fields of work, the unity of nature, the fixity of its laws, the definite sequence of cause and effect through which every fact depends on what has gone before it, and acts upon what is to come after it. They grasp firmly the

Pythagorean doctrine of pervading order in the universal Kosmos. They affirm, with Aristotle, that nature is not full of incoherent episodes, like a bad tragedy. They agree with Leibnitz in what he calls "my axiom, that nature never acts by leaps," as well as in his "great principle, commonly little employed, that nothing happens without its sufficient reason." Nor, again, in studying the structure and habits of plants and animals, or in investigating the lower functions even of man, are these leading ideas unacknowledged. But when we come to talk of the higher processes of human feeling and action, of thought and language, knowledge and art, a change appears in the prevalent tone of opinion. The world at large is scarcely prepared to accept the general study of human life as a branch of natural science, and to carry out, in a large sense, the poet's injunction to "Account for moral as for natural things." To many educated minds there seems something presumptuous and repulsive in the view that the history of mankind is part and parcel of the history of nature, that our thoughts, wills, and actions accord with laws as definite as those which govern the motion of waves, the combination of acids and bases, and the growth of plants and animals. . . .

"One event is always the son of another, and we must never forget the parentage," was a remark made by a Bechuana chief to Casalis the African missionary. Thus at all times historians, so far as they have aimed at being more than mere chroniclers, have done their best to show not merely succession, but connection, among the events upon their record. Moreover, they have striven to elicit general principles of human action, and by these to explain particular events, stating expressly or taking tacitly for granted the existence of a philosophy of history. Should any one deny the possibility of thus establishing historical laws, the answer is ready with which Boswell in such a case turned on Johnson: "Then, sir, you would reduce all history to no better than an almanack." That nevertheless the labors of so many eminent thinkers should have as yet brought history only to the threshold of science, need cause no wonder to those who consider the bewildering complexity of the problems which come before the general historian. The evidence from which he is to draw his conclusions is at once so multifarious and so doubtful, that a full and distinct view of its bearing on a particular question is hardly to be attained, and thus the temptation becomes all but irresistible to garble it in support of some rough and ready theory of the course of events. The philosophy of history at large, explaining the past and predicting the future phenomena of man's life in the world by reference to general laws, is in fact a subject with which, in the present state of knowledge, even genius aided by wide research seems but hardly able to cope. Yet there are departments of it which, though difficult enough, seem comparatively accessible. If the field of inquiry is narrowed from History as a whole to that branch of it which is here called Culture, the history, not of tribes or nations, but of the condition of knowledge, religion, art, custom, and the like among them, the task of investigation proves to lie within far more moderate compass. We suffer still from the same kind of difficulties which beset the wider argument, but they are much diminished. The evidence is no longer so wildly heterogeneous, but may be more simply classified and compared, while the power of getting rid of extraneous matter, and treating each issue on its own proper set of facts, makes close reasoning on the whole more available than in general history. . . .

A first step in the study of civilization is to dissect it into details, and to classify these in their proper groups. Thus, in examining weapons, they are to be classed under spear, club, sling, bow and arrow, and so forth; among textile arts are to be ranged matting, netting, and several grades of making and weaving threads; myths are divided under such headings as myths of sunrise and sunset, eclipse-myths, earthquake-myths, local myths which account for the names of places by some fanciful tale, eponymic myths which account for the parentage of a tribe by turning its name into the name of an imaginary ancestor; under rites and ceremonies occur such practices as the various kinds of sacrifice to the ghosts of the dead and to other spiritual beings, the turning to the east in worship, the purification of ceremonial or moral uncleanness by means of water or fire. Such are a few miscellaneous examples from a list of hundreds, and the ethnographer's business is to classify such details with a view to making out their distribution in geography and history, and the relations which exist among them.

2. Central Elements in Kwakiutl Culture

RUTH BENEDICT

The Kwakiutl Indians of British Columbia are one of the thousands of tribes and peoples of the world—and one of the best known, for they were intensively studied by Franz Boas over a period of forty years. We offer a brief description of their customs here as an example of the life-ways of primitive man; a sample of the subjects of anthropological enquiry, and as an example of culture. Of course, only a few of the details can be given, but they are enough to show: (1) the wide range of subjects anthropology must cover, (2) the kind of details that make up the culture of people, and (3) something of the spirit of Kwakiutl life.

Though based upon the work of Boas, the selection was written by Ruth Benedict, one of his students. She is chiefly known for her interest in the patterning of culture, the tendency of the different aspects of life to share a central emotional tone. This point she developed in *Patterns of Culture* (Chapter IV, "The Northwest Coast of America"), Boston: Houghton Mifflin Company, 1934, pp. 160–180, from which this selection is reprinted by permission of and arrangement with Houghton Mifflin Company, the authorized publishers, and Routledge & Kegan Paul Ltd., London.

The Indians who lived on the narrow strip of Pacific seacoast from Alaska to Puget Sound were a vigorous and overbearing people. They had a culture of no common order. Sharply differentiated from that of the surrounding tribes, it had a zest which it is difficult to match among other peoples. Its values were not those which are commonly recognized, and its drives not those frequently honored.

They were a people of great possessions as primitive peoples go. Their civilization was built upon an ample supply of goods, inexhaustible, and obtained without excessive expenditure of labor. The fish, upon which they depended for food, could be taken out of the sea in great hauls. Salmon, cod, halibut, seal, and candlefish were dried for storage or tried out for oil. Stranded whales were always utilized, and the more southern tribes went whaling as well. Their life would have been impossible without the sea. The mountains abutted sharply upon their shore territory; they built upon the beaches. It was a country wonderfully suited to the demands they put upon it. The deeply indented coast was flanked with numberless islands which not only trebled the shoreline, but gave great sheltered areas of water and protected navigation from the unbroken sweep of the Pacific. The sea life that haunts this region is proverbial. It is still the great spawning ground of the world, and the tribes of the Northwest Coast knew the calendar of the first runs as other peoples have known the habits of bears or the season for putting seed into the earth. Even in the rare cases when they depended upon some product of the earth, as when they cut the great trees that they split into boards for their houses or hollowed with fire and adzes for canoes, they held close to the waterways. They knew no transportation except by water, and every tree was cut close enough to a stream or inlet so that it could be floated down to the village.

They kept up constant intercommunication by means of seagoing canoes. They were adventurous, and expeditions pushed far to the north and south. Marriages, for persons of prestige, were arranged with the nobility of other tribes, and invitations to great feasts, the potlatches, were sent hundreds of miles up the coast and answered by canoe-loads of the distant tribes. The languages of these peoples belonged to several different stocks, and it was necessary therefore for most people to speak a number of unrelated languages. Certainly the differences in language formed no obstacle to the diffusion of minute details of ceremonial or of whole bodies of folklore the fundamental elements of which they shared in common.

They did not add to their food supply by means of agriculture. They tended small fields of clover or cinquefoil, but that was all. The great occupation of the men, aside from hunting and fishing, was woodworking. They built their houses of wooden planks, they carved great totem poles, they fashioned the sides of boxes of single boards and carved and decorated them, they dug out seagoing canoes, they made wooden masks and household furniture and utensils of all kinds. Without metal for axes or saws they felled the great cedars, split them into boards, transported them by sea without any use of the wheel to the villages and made of them their great many-family houses. Their devices were ingenious and admirably calculated. They guided accurately the split of the logs into planks, raised tremendous tree trunks as houseposts and house-beams, knew how to sew wood through slanted awl-holes so that no sign of the joining remained upon the surface, and out of single cedars constructed canoes capable of navigating the open sea and carrying fifty or sixty men. Their art was bold and exotic, and as competent as any that a primitive people has achieved. . . .

The tribes of the Northwest Coast had great possessions, and these possessions were strictly owned. They were property in the sense of heirlooms, but heirlooms, with them, were the very basis of society. There were two classes of possessions. The land and sea were owned by a group of relatives in common and passed down to all its members. There were no cultivated fields, but the relationship group owned hunting territories, and even wild-berrying and wild-root territories, and no one could trespass upon the property of the family. The family owned fishing territories just as strictly. A local group often had to go great distances to those strips of the shore where they could dig clams, and the shore near their village might be owned by another lineage. These grounds had been held as property so long that the village-sites had changed, but not the ownership of the clam-beds. Not only the shore, but even deep-sea areas were strict property. For halibut fishing the area belonging to a given family was bounded by sighting along double landmarks. The rivers, also, were divided up into owned sections for the candlefish hauls in the spring, and families came from great distances to fish their own section of the river.

There was, however, still more valued property that was owned in a different fashion. It was not in the ownership of the means of livelihood, however far that was carried, that Kwakiutl proprietorship chiefly expressed itself. Those things which were supremely valued were prerogatives over and above material well-being. Many of these were material things, named house-posts and spoons of heraldic crests, but the greater number were immaterial possessions, names, myths, songs, and privileges which were the great boast of a man of wealth. All these prerogatives, though they remained in a blood lineage, were nevertheless not held in common, but were owned for the time being by an individual who singly and exclusively exercised the rights which they conveyed.

The greatest of these prerogatives, and the basis of all others, were the nobility titles. Each family, each religious society, had a series of titular names which individuals assumed according to their rights of inheritance and financial ability. These titles gave them the position of nobility in the tribe. They were used as personal names, but they were names that according to tradition had not been added to nor subtracted from since the origin of the world. When a person took such a name he assumed in his own person all the greatness of his ancestors who had in their lifetime borne the name, and when he gave it to his heir he necessarily laid aside all right to use it as his own.

The assumption of such a name did not depend on blood alone.

In the first place, these titles were the right of the eldest born, and youngest sons were without status. They were scorned commoners. In the second place, the right to a title had to be signalized by the distribution of great wealth. The women's engrossing occupation was not the household routine, but the making of great quantities of mats, baskets, and cedar-bark blankets, which were put aside in the valuable boxes made by the men for the same purpose. Men likewise accumulated canoes, and the shells or dentalia they used as money. Great men owned or had out at interest immense quantities of goods, which were passed from hand to hand like bank notes to validate the assumption of the prerogatives. . . .

Every individual of any potential importance, male or female, entered this economic contest as a small child. As a baby he had been given a name which indicated only the place where he was born. When it was time for him to assume a name of greater importance, the elders of his family gave him a number of blankets to distribute, and upon receiving the name he distributed this property among his relatives. Those who received the child's gifts made it a point to repay him promptly and with excessive interest. Whenever a chief who was one of these beneficiaries distributed property at a public exchange soon after, he gave the child treble what he had received. At the end of the year the boy had to repay with one hundred per cent interest those who had originally financed him, but he retained the remainder in his own name and this was the equivalent of the original stock of blankets. For a couple of years he distributed these, and collected interest, until he was ready to pay for his first traditional potlatch name. When he was ready, all his relatives gathered and all the elders of the tribe. In the presence of all the people and before the chief and the old men of the tribe his father then gave up to him a name which designated his position in the tribe. . . .

It was this game of validating and exercising all the prerogatives and titles that could be acquired from one's various forebears, or by gift or by marriage, which chiefly engrossed the Indians of the Northwest Coast. Everyone in his degree took part in it, and to be shut out from it was the chief stigma of the slave. Manipulation of wealth in this culture had gone far beyond any realistic transcription of economic needs and the filling of those needs. It involved ideas of capital, of interest, and of conspicuous waste. Wealth had become not merely economic goods, even goods put away in boxes for potlatches and never used except in exchange, but even more characteristically prerogatives with no economic functions. Songs, myths, names of chiefs' house-posts, of their dogs, of their canoes, were wealth. Valued privileges, like the right to tie a dancer to a post, or to bring in tallow for the dancers to rub on their faces, or shredded cedar bark for them to wipe it off again, were wealth and were passed down in family lines. Among the neighboring Bella Coola, family myths became such exceedingly valued and cherished property that it became the custom for the nobility to marry within the family so that such wealth should not be dissipated among those not born to hold it. . . .

This primary association of wealth with the validation of nobility titles is, however, only a part of the picture. The distribution of property was rarely so simple as this. The ultimate reason why a man of the Northwest Coast cared about the nobility titles, the wealth, the crests and the prerogatives lays bare the mainspring of their culture: they used them in a contest in which they sought to shame their rivals. Each individual, according to his means, constantly vied with all others to outdistance them in distributions of property. The boy who had just received his first gift of property selected another youth to receive a gift from him. The youth he chose could not refuse without admitting defeat at the outset, and he was compelled to cap the gift with an equal amount of property. When the time came for repayment if he had not double the original gift to return as interest, he was shamed and demoted, and his rival's prestige correspondingly enhanced. The contest thus begun continued throughout life. If he was successful he played with continually increasing amounts of property and with more and more formidable rivals. It was a fight. They say, "We do not fight with weapons. We fight with property." A man who had given away a copper had overcome his rival as much as if he had overcome him in battle array. The Kwakiutl equated the two. One of their dances was called "bringing blood into the house," and the hemlock wreaths the men carried were said to represent heads taken in warfare. These they threw into the fire, calling out the name of the enemies they represented and shouting as the fire flared up to consume them. The wreaths, however, represented the coppers they had given away, and the names they called out were the names of the rivals whom they had vanquished by the distribution of property. . . .

. . . All the motivations they recognized centered around the will to superiority. Their social organization, their economic institutions, their religion, birth and death, were all channels for its expression. As they understood triumph, it involved ridicule and scorn heaped publicly upon one's opponents, who were, according to their customs, also their invited guests. At a potlatch the host's party carved mocking life-sized figures of the chief who was to receive the copper. His poverty was symbolized by his protruding ribs, and his insignificance by some undignified posture. . . .

The whole economic system of the Northwest Coast was bent to the service of this obsession. There were two means by which a chief could achieve the victory he sought. One was by shaming his rival by presenting him with more property than he could return with the required interest. The other was by destroying property. In both cases the offering called for return, though in the first case the giver's wealth was augmented, and in the second he stripped himself of goods. The consequences of the two methods seem to us at the opposite poles. To the Kwakiutl they were merely complementary means of subduing a rival, and the highest glory of life was the act of complete destruction. It was a challenge, exactly like the selling of a copper, and it was always done in opposition to a rival who must then, in order to save himself from shame, destroy an equal amount of valuable goods.

The destruction of goods took many forms. Great potlatch feasts in which quantities of candlefish oil were consumed were reckoned as contests of demolition. The oil was fed lavishly to the guests, and it was also poured upon the fire. Since the guests sat near the fire, the heat of the burning oil caused them intense discomfort, and this also was reckoned as a part of the contest. In order to save themselves from shame, they had to lie unmoved in their places, though the fire blazed up and caught the rafters of the house. The host also must exhibit the most complete indifference to the threatened destruction of his house. Some of the greatest chiefs had a carved figure of a man upon the roof. It was called the vomiter, and a trough was so arranged that a steady stream of the valuable candlefish oil poured out of the figure's open mouth into the house fire below. If the oil feast surpassed anything the guest chief had ever given, he must leave the house and begin preparations for a return feast that would outstrip the one given by his rival. If he believed that it had not equalled a feast that he had previously given, he heaped insults upon his host, who then took some further way of establishing his greatness.

For this purpose the host might send his messengers to break in pieces four canoes and bring the pieces to heap upon the fire. Or he might kill a slave. Or he might break a copper. . . .

The behavior which was required of the chief was arrogant and tyrannical to a degree. There were necessarily cultural checks upon too despotic an interpretation of a chief's role. He was not free to destroy property to the utter impoverishment of his people or to engage in contests which were ruinous to them. The great social check that acted to keep his activity within limits they phrased as a moral tabu: the tabu on overdoing. Overdoing was always dangerous, and a chief must keep within bounds. These boundaries exacted by custom allowed . . . many extreme courses, but the check was always in readiness if a chief overreached his claims on tribal support. Good fortune, they believed, abandoned the man who went too far, and he was no longer supported by his followers. Society set limits, though the limits seem to us fantastic.

3. Elements of the American Culture

ROBERT S. LYND

Robert S. Lynd's study of "Middletown" was the first scientific effort to describe the American culture—so successful that the book is still in print after about thirty years. Since then, numerous efforts have been made to describe American villages and cities from the standpoint of the anthropologist—some of which will be the basis for future selections.

Lynd is Professor of Sociology at Columbia University; his original Middletown study and the follow-up study ten years later had the collaboration of his wife. The present selection is taken from a book written during World War II; it is a call upon the social scientists to use their knowledge for human betterment. Here he is setting forth the general features of the American culture; he is aware of the wide variation which actually exists in our heterogeneous country, but is convinced that certain general characteristics exist.

The selection is excerpted from Chapter 3 entitled "The Pattern of American Culture" in *Knowledge for What?* Princeton, N. J.: Princeton University Press, 1945, pp. 56–101, and is reproduced with the kind permission of the publisher and author.

One must . . . tread warily in attempting to characterize so complex a thing as the patterning of a culture. And this is particularly true in the case of our American culture, which stresses individualism, professes to run under *laissez-faire,* relates to a wide geographical region, and includes such extremes as New York City and the Tennessee Mountains. To be sure, central tendencies are observable, but they are at best only tendencies in a wide and irregular distribution, and they may not even be counted upon to take the form of a comfortably smooth Gaussian curve. Furthermore, the emphasis in one institutional area, such as the family or religion, may conflict with that of another area, such as business. Rather, therefore, than resort to such over-all characterizations of pattern as Nietzsche's "Apollonian," and "Dionysian" or Spengler's "Apolinian," "Faustian," and "Magian," the method will here be employed of describing a number of outstanding related characteristics of the contemporary American culture pattern. . . .

1. *The process of patterning is basically casual.* Believing as we do in *laissez-faire,* the patterning of our culture has been left largely to chance. There are exceptions. Our written Constitution, inherited from the eighteenth century, is anything but casual, and its rigidity has created special problems as it has been employed in the fluidity of subsequent circumstances. Other minimum elements of deliberately designed pattern have been introduced by law. A pattern of religious observance has been taken over largely from the European background of the culture. Beyond such minima, our American culture tends to inch along into change, assuming such islands of patterning as it manifests largely as a kind of afterthought adaptation to the exigencies of specific situations thrust upon it by events. Casual fluidity is the "American way" and by long habituation "feels right."

This orientation makes sense to Americans because of their strong traditional commitment to three assumptions . . . :

a. That people are rational, can and do know what is best for them, are free to choose, and will accordingly choose wisely.

b. That "the greatest good to the greatest number" occurs when individual enterprise is left free from controls in the interest of any type of planned pattern.

c. That any design and unity in pattern which is useful can be depended upon to develop automatically under the frictions of competing individual self-interests. . . .

2. Growing directly out of this casualness is the related aspect of the pattern which may be described as *the grossly uneven relative organization, or structuring, of the several functional areas of living.* Every culture develops its institutional structure around certain persisting life-

activities of human beings: in getting a living, cohabiting with the other sex and making a home, training the young in their rôles, and carrying on common activities in governance, in play, in religion, and so on. It is to the relative degrees of supporting institutional structure around each of these persisting human activities that reference is here made. All of the functional areas of living are constantly interacting, and if one area is strongly organized and another weakly, this institutional situation invites the riding down of the weaker by the stronger. A case in point is the overbearing elaboration of the institution of war in our present world, which tends to render all the rest of our living insecure. Or one may point to the coercion of our high school curriculum by the authoritative structure of university education. . . .

Within the general framework of devotion to *laissez-faire* individualism, our American culture has tended to make the following sub-assumptions regarding the process by which its structural form grows:

a. It is assumed that as individuals feel the strain of trying to do any over-complicated thing alone, they will recognize, as free, rational persons, the need to join with their fellows and do something about it.

b. It is assumed that when the institutional structure supporting one area of behavior, such as getting a living, becomes over-developed and begins to unbalance and to distort the rest of living, individuals will be aware of this and will automatically redress the balance. . . .

It is this structural distortion, with the elements so unequal and out of balance that the sheer preservation of the going system becomes a monopolizing preoccupation, that presents one of the most striking aspects of our culture. To the resulting general sense of strain may be traced the compulsive overemphasis upon aggression rather than affectionate mutuality, upon action rather than upon repose, and upon doing rather than feeling. . . .

3. The pattern of culture *stresses individual competitive aggressiveness against one's fellows as the basis for personal and collective security.* Each man must stand on his own feet and fight for what he gets—so runs the philosophy of the culture—and in this way the common welfare throughout the entire culture is best achieved. In addition to thus explaining away the obvious crudities of aggression by identifying the latter with the common good, sheer anarchy is prevented by certain established rules of combat. If one dislikes the presence of a competitor's store across the street, one may not assault or threaten him, kill him, blow up his shop, or slander him, though one may ruin him and deprive him of his livelihood by underselling him, by buying up

the property on which his store is located and forcing him out, or by other devious means within the ample armory of business competition.

Cultures differ in the rules of the game by which the individual acquires status. Broadly speaking, they tend to emphasize one or the other of two means: status by ascription (e.g., by reason of birth into a given family), and status by achievement. Our culture stresses the latter, leaving the outcome almost entirely up to unremitting individual effort. This forces upon the individual in our culture a restless ambivalence between his deep need to be affectionately and securely accepted by those about him as the person that he is, regardless of what he manages to achieve, and the cultural demand that he stick out his chest, square his jaw, and force those about him to yield him what he wants. The most clearly patterned path out of this ambivalence is through concentration upon the achievement of success measured in terms of money. With the culture so little structured to encourage other lines of action, and with the need for security so great in a society of untied-in, offensive-defensive individuals, this general emphasis upon aggression involves a belittling of other paths to status. The shifting, anonymous world of the city mutes one's importance as a person by the peremptory demand that one demonstrate again and again what one can do in this artificially narrowed world of striving for pecuniary success. This is apparent on every hand. Veblen described the prevalence of "conspicuous consumption" in his *The Theory of the Leisure Class.* People who meet in crowds, touch, and carom apart, must accept and reject each other rapidly by obvious tags. Under these circumstances, the subtle, sensitive, and highly individuated person tends to become an isolate. The range of socially viable personality organizations is narrow, and even such relationships as marriage or friendship are not unaffected by demands for that kind of status which only the job can yield.

Over against any such summary characterization of American culture as this must be set the manifest fact that most of us Americans are not super-aggressors, most of us are not successes-in-a-big-way, and life consists for most people in just living along. This "just living along" quality is a large part of American culture. But its numerical predominance does not render it either emotionally predominant or entirely emotionally self-contained. It represents, rather, in American life an enforced second-best, a coming to terms with the situation in which one finds oneself caught. At every point our young, optimistic culture thrusts forward its gains rather than its costs and losses. It plays up in print and symbol the pace-setting ways of life. . . .

4. Growing directly from the preceding is the marked presence in the culture of *extreme differences in power*. This appears in many ways: in the dominance of urban industrial areas over rural areas in such matters as important tariffs; in the ability of business pressure-blocs to prevent the passage of legislation manifestly in the public interest. . . .

In a culture which prizes "equality" as one of its foundation assumptions, this habitual and widespread tolerance of extremes of inequality in power requires the disguise of a formula. Two such convenient formulae are in wide use:

a. The disparities at any given moment are regarded either as but temporary differences in a general progress in which "tomorrow can be different," or as due to the deliberate volition of the parties concerned—i.e., one has worked harder, or saved harder, or elected to be more enterprising and farsighted than the other. . . .

b. The second formula invoked to justify a special but crucial disparity in size and power, i.e., that between the individual and the corporation, is the convenient legal fiction which views a corporation as a person. . . .

5. The pattern of our culture is one of *great individual mobility,* both horizontal and vertical, and consequently one in which *human beings tend to put down shallow roots.* This mobility involves positive gains in the access it gives to wider and more varied experience. But it is controlled primarily by the main chance to perform the instrumental activity of making more money, rather than by the varied needs of the whole personality. As machinery has taken over more and more of the learned skills of the worker, he has become increasingly a standard interchangeable part in the productive process, and his tie to a special craft, factory, or city has been attenuated. The individual in our culture is tending increasingly to "travel light"; he encumbers himself with fewer children, moves his place of residence more frequently, commits himself irrevocably to fewer things, often avoids making friendships with those who may become liabilities, and he even seeks subtly to disencumber himself from in-laws and the now vanishing lateral kinship degrees. . . .

6. It is a pattern of *increasingly large population masses, held together principally by the tie of the individual to his job, and with attenuated sentiments of community in feeling and purpose.* Ours is a culture of increasing mass-living in urban units. The portion of the total population of the United States living in urban places with 8,000 or more population has risen from 3 percent in 1790, to 7 percent in 1830,

to 16 percent in 1860, to 33 percent in 1900, and to 49 percent in 1930. . . . [Current estimates indicate that about two thirds of our population is "urban" by census definition.]

While this growing urbanization derives predominantly from economic causes, such as the concentration of industry in the "easy labor market" which a dense population affords and the resulting multiplication of retailing and other service activities among such a dense population, the growth of cities has also been influenced by other factors. Urban living represents the most favorable environment for those wishing to benefit by the resources of the culture. On the personal side, the city presents the opportunity for rich, selective acquaintanceship in the pursuit of personal growth. On the material side, the overhead cost of providing desirable modern services—from labor-saving utilities to schools and the arts—can best be borne when widely shared. . . .

Many of those who migrate to our larger cities pride themselves on the fact that "Now, thank God, I don't *have* to know my neighbors, go to Rotary, belong to a church, or participate in an annual Community Chest drive!" And the big city does little to disabuse them of this attitude. Individuals can and do live comfortably in our large cities with no formal ties between themselves and the structures of the culture save the money tie between them and their jobs. One may or may not elect to exercise one's political right to vote; one may or may not own property, marry, or belong with anybody else to anything; but one must tie into the structure to the extent of getting money regularly. The culture puts an extreme reliance upon this money nexus between the individual and his job to hold the culture together. . . .

7. The culture is patterned *to point life into the future.* The rhythms of tension and release within the individual organism orient living toward many short-run future consummations. One moves recurrently away from hunger toward food, away from fatigue toward rest, and so on. These raw physical drives become overlaid in every culture by a more or less elaborate congeries of institutionalized motivations toward future consummations. These may involve becoming more popular, more successful, richer, more skilled, better informed, and so on, through scores of specific wants. Each of us grows up in a world of people exhibiting such motivations. We learn those that feel best in terms of our unique personality organization and environment or that we are coerced into accepting, and we live these private versions of orientation toward desired consummations back into the culture.

Thus every culture involves some tilt into the future. But cultures vary widely in the number of these future desiderata, the length of the chains of tension-sustention involved before the patterned goal is achieved, and in the relative preponderance of emphasis upon present, as over against future, consummations. Our own culture, as a relatively young culture that grew up with the Industrial Revolution in an unusually rich physical setting, has gambled heavily on the future and written it into our institutional forms and the private lives of all of us. This gamble may have been largely justified during the expanding phase of our economy, but it also operates to confuse realism with hope.

It has been remarked that the Industrial Revolution gave the Western World the option of having more leisure, more babies, or a higher standard of living—and it "chose" to trudge up the long sandy slope represented by the last of these. This choice was rendered more or less inevitable by its past experience: by the historic prominence of scarcity as an inveterate enemy of men living in northern climates where winters are long and the earth's yield often niggardly or precarious; by the Christian emphasis upon the future; by the stern Puritan emphasis upon developing one's character through careful, thrifty stewardship; by the enthusiastic endorsement by capitalism of unceasing individual acquisitiveness; by the frontier tradition of a world to conquer, in which one was endlessly building a better tomorrow out of a crude present. The nineteenth century's discovery of the doctrine of evolution gave a thumping endorsement to this devotion to "progress," while the stupendous technological inventions completed the process of hypnosis. Ours was a culture which appeared to have the world by the tail with a downhill drag. . . .

8. The pattern *places strong emphasis upon children, and, in adult life, upon youth in women and the years of greatest energy output in men.* Activities tend increasingly to be structured according to age groups. Whole-family work and recreation have given way to specialized groupings cross-cutting the population by age-level. Certain age-periods occupy preferred positions, the years of youth and early middle life being most highly valued. The care and nurture of children is a major concern, and institutions for their education are second only to economic institutions in cultural emphasis. The stress upon mobility rather than upon deep-rooted continuity, upon action and scientific technique rather than wisdom, upon change rather than growth, upon winning and holding status rather than receiving it freely granted at the hands of one's fellows, tends to displace men and women of advanced years in favor of their juniors. In such a culture "venerability" has lost its meaning

and old age its function. Even in the professions gray hairs are becoming a liability to a man, while the rise of beauty parlors and growing cosmetic sales are evidences of the battle women are fighting to postpone becoming "motherly looking." . . .

9. The character of the culture *encourages considerable (and possibly increasing) conflict between the patterned rôles of the two sexes.* As already pointed out, growing urbanization is forcing a separation of the worlds of job and of home; and the job world tends to run under rules of its own, largely divorced from the rest of living. This entails not merely a division of labor, but a basic split in the structure of values by which men and women live. The fact that many women are going into jobs and professions means less the merging of the patterns of the two sexes than the adoption of a difficult dual pattern by these women; for the demands upon them to be feminine remain, even though they must live during their hours of work by the values of the men's world. Both sexes accept the traditional assumption of the culture that, fundamentally, the values for which the home stands—sympathy, understanding, mutuality, gentleness, treating persons as persons, cooperation rather than aggression—are ultimate and therefore more important. But the job world of the men, operating as it does to such a degree independently of the rest of the culture, demands more and more channeling of the personality into impersonality and aggressive dominance. The rôle of the male in the family is also constricting as the separateness of his job world diminishes his activities as parent. The status of the father as a family member is narrowing to that of "a good provider." At the same time, increased popular awareness of the importance of good, positive sex-adjustment—an awareness heightened by the relaxing of religious condemnations of sex, the rise of mental hygiene, fiction written under the Freudian influence, and the great lovers on the cinema screen—has strengthened the demand on the male that he play an emotionally more subtle rôle as husband and lover. Likewise, new knowledge is making fresh demands of him to be an active, constructive person as a parent; which demands neither his training nor his time and energy resources help him to meet. The result is an intermittent sense of personal inadequacy in a situation from which, biologically and emotionally, he should draw strength and security. . . .

At no point more than in the family are the disjunctions of our culture and the worlds of different values they embody more directly and dramatically in conflict. Rich familial and marital adjustments are at best difficult of achievement because of the subtleties of personality demands. These adjustments are rendered more complex in our culture by the lack of strong, clear institutional structure supporting family life. As a result, family members are thrown back upon each other as a small group of over-dependent personalities who must work out a common destiny in a family situation which has lost many of its functions and, hence, forces them to rely overmuch upon intimacy. When the values of a culture are split into two sharply conflicting systems, with each sex assigned the rôle of carrying one system, the family becomes perforce, as Horney points out, the battleground not merely for the resolution of differences among the individual personalities of family members but also for the attempted resolution of the larger conflicts of the entire culture. Too little stress has been laid upon this toll which the casualness of our culture exacts of persons at the point of greatest potential richness in personal intimacy.

10. It is a pattern that *assumes that achievement of man's values will follow automatically from material advancement.* Our national history, as already pointed out, has happened to coincide with an era of amazing advance in material prosperity. As men have devoted themselves to business and industry, unparalleled wealth has resulted, and a share of this wealth has gone into a very tangible increase in the general level of welfare. Through the bottleneck of the price-system we have managed to get better medical care, better education, better housing, more leisure, less heavy toil in the home, and many other desirable things. Nobody planned all this, and apparently there had been no great need to plan, for these things seemed just to happen. They happened, in fact, because of our rich natural resources, the discovery and swift development of machine technology, and the presence of a vast frontier to settle and develop; but, to the average citizen, it seemed enough to say that they happened because men had been left free to make money. . . .

11. Growing out of all the preceding, a final characterization of our culture pattern runs somewhat as follows: It is a pattern of *markedly uneven change, of unprecedented rapidity in some traits and of marshalled resistance to change in others, and tolerating at many points extreme disjunctions and contradictions.* Our culture has grown up during one of the eras of most rapid cultural change in the history of the Western World. The pace has been set by scientific discovery and by technological invention. With the process of change ruled by private enterprise, unchecked by any clear philosophy of control in the public interest, it has been a helter-skelter affair. The accumulated momentum of change in certain areas is such that we now have no option but to

recognize the need for extensive accompanying change in the many areas of life upon which changes already accepted impinge. The problem that confronts us is what to do about the confusions created by the unevenness of the process of adjustive change throughout the whole field. For we exhibit marked hospitality to certain types of change—for instance in our technologies—while the strain of adjustment to these large and rapid changes makes us conservatively resistant to undergoing the tension of change at other points; and we also complicate the situation by leaving interested private power-blocs free to obstruct needed change at many points. The resulting disjunctions and contradictions within the culture are humanly costly; but we excuse ourselves from recognizing the need to do anything about this situation because of our optimistic belief that "things are getting better" and "all these things will straighten themselves out in time."

4. Culture and the Levels of Knowledge

ALFRED L. KROEBER

Alfred L. Kroeber sees culture as the "highest" level of natural phenomena appropriate for scientific study. Elsewhere he has called it "the super-organic," for it is based upon, yet is outside of and beyond the organic realm. Thus he places the subject of anthropology in the natural order of the world and relates the science of anthropology to other sciences. Furthermore, Kroeber believes that culture operates according to its own laws, that it has a kind of force of its own, and that cultural events cannot be "explained" with biological or psychological causes. The course of human history is the product of these cultural forces, and the individuals who "make history" are made by their cultural environment.

Kroeber is the dean of American anthropologists; his work with California and other American Indians is balanced with a detailed study of the regularities in history, *Configuration of Culture Growth,* and a wide variety of special and general essays. Having taken his Ph.D. degree under Franz Boas at Columbia in 1901, he came to the University of California where he taught until his retirement. The present essay is taken from a lecture given in 1948 at a University of Chicago symposium on education; was first published in the

Journal of General Education (volume III, 1949) and is reprinted in *The Nature of Culture* (Chapter 14, pp. 118–135), Chicago: The University of Chicago Press, 1952. It is reprinted here with the kind permission of The University of Chicago Press and the author. Copyright 1952 by The University of Chicago.

I propose to discuss the concept of culture—its origin and validity, its use and limitations. Like every concept, this one is a tool; and as a tool the concept of culture is two-edged. It ties some phenomena and interpretations together; it dissimilates and distinguishes others—about which more later.

Like all important ideas, that of culture was the realization of many minds, and it developed gradually. There are still great civilized nations—the French, for instance—who refuse to admit the word "culture" into their intellectual vocabulary. On the other hand, the ancients knew, and modern primitives are aware of, some of the phenomena of culture—as, for instance, distinctive customs. "We don't do that way, we do like this"—such a statement, which every human being is likely to make at some time, is a recognition of a cultural phenomenon.

Phenomena have a way of occurring composite in nature, intricately blended. Their qualities, still more their conceptualized general aspects, can be extricated only gradually from the welter of appearances. Until well into the nineteenth century and in certain situations and contexts until today, the concept of culture has remained unextricated from that of society. When Comte founded sociology and coined its name more than a century ago, he stamped on it the impress of the social. But his famous three stages of mythology, metaphysics, and positivism are stages primarily of ideology, and therefore of culture. Only incidentally are they stages of specifically social or interpersonal relations. . . .

When so original and penetrating a thinker as Durkheim hypostasized society as that by which early groups were impressed, which they worshiped, and thus originated religion, he put forth a view which has generally seemed farfetched and, to many, mystical. But as soon as we substitute for his nondifferentium of "society" the customs and beliefs which hold together primitive societies and seem to help them to survive —in another word, their "culture"—then the Durkheim interpretation begins to assume reasonableness. It seems fair to assume that that is what Durkheim "meant," what he would say today.

That nondifferentiation of the two aspects should continue up to a certain point is expectable, since culture by definition includes, or at least presupposes, society. As something shared and supraindividual, culture can exist only when a society exists; and, conversely, every human society is accompanied by a culture. This converse, to be sure, is not complete: it applies only to *human* societies. In principle, however, the limitation is extremely important. The existence of cultureless or essentially cultureless subhuman societies, especially the highly elaborate ones of the social insects, serves as an irrefutable touchstone for the significant discrimination of the concepts of the social and the cultural: they *can* exist separately. At any rate, one of them does exist separately. . . .

The word "culture" in its modern scientific sense, as, for instance, any anthropologist would use it with assurance that every other anthropologist would know what he meant, and not something else—this modern meaning of "culture" is . . . recent. The first definition of "culture" in this broad but definite sense of its current social science usage— as distinct from cultivation and refinement, from nurture, from agriculture and pearl culture and test-tube cultures—the first definition I have found in an English dictionary dates from the late twenties. The first deliberate usage in a book was by Tylor when in 1871 he published *Primitive Culture* and formulated that most-quoted of definitions of culture which begins: "that complex whole which includes. . . ."

. . . Just as culture presupposes society, so society presupposes persons. It is an assemblage of individuals—plus something additional —that something which we and termite societies share. Well, here, then, are three elements or sets of factors: culture, society, persons, each resting upon, or preconditioned by, the next. In fact, we can immediately go one step further and separate persons into bodies and minds as two aspects which in some situations at least it is profitable to deal with separately—in all strictly psychological situations, for instance. That the separation is warranted, when it is useful, is clear not only from the current distinction of biological science from psychology but also from the fact that plants, though possessing somas, are generally conceded as showing no evidence of having psyches.

So now we are already facing four superposed aspects—four "levels," let us call them: body, psyche, society, culture. By now it is obvious where the line of thought is leading us; the next step prefaces the inorganic as underlying the somatic, the psychic, the social, and the cultural. . .

It has become customary of late to designate these hierarchical planes as "levels of organization" and, alternatively, as "dimensions." . . .

However, it is necessary not to confound "levels of organization" with "levels of abstraction." It is true that, while we are focusing on cultural aspects, we are in a technical sense "abstracting" from the organic and physical aspects pertaining to the same phenomena. "Abstracting" here means removing our consideration from, ignoring; it is temporary, shifting, reversible. But cultural phenomena are *not* more abstract than physical or organic phenomena in the sense of being more abstruse, rarefied, unconcrete, or conceptualized. The surge of anger is as concrete a phenomenon as is a contracted eyebrow or a constricted blood vessel. The custom of headhunting or of catching the bride's bouquet is certainly thoroughly concrete. It is only culture as a generalized concept that is abstract; but so are society, psyche, body, matter, and energy abstract. What is much more significant than abstractness is that cultural phenomena occur organized on different principles from social phenomena, social phenomena from psychic, and so on down the series.

What is clearest about the levels is that certain properties or qualities of the phenomena of each are peculiar to it. Presumably this is due to a difference in arrangement or organization. That which is specifically characteristic and distinctively significant of phenomena of a level is intelligible only in terms of the other phenomena, qualities, or regularities of that same level. The most characteristic qualities or phenomena are never explained by what we know of another level: they are not really reached by other-level knowledge, especially when the levels are well separated. The findings of a study of lower-level phenomena do indeed *apply* to those of higher level, but they apply with decreasing significance. . . .

This does not mean that a new entity is hypostasized as the unique substance of each level. Life, mind, society, and culture are not outside matter and energy, not outside space and time and free of them. They are in and of nature with matter and energy. They are different organizations of matter and energy, if one will, which physicists and chemists cannot, in virtue of their physical and chemical methods, deal with fruitfully; and similarly all the way up the scale. . . .

. . . It is cultural phenomena—or, let us say, phenomena organizable in cultural terms and relations—that constitute the very top level of our hierarchy. If it seem rash to affirm this when the concept of culture is of as recent emergence into consciousness as we have seen it to be, we can modify the statement to say: culture is the top level recognized to date. Personally, I would not have the glimmering of a suspicion as to what a level of organization higher than that of culture might be like. Yet a future generation may see more clearly. For the present, however, let us examine the consequences of this top-level position of our subject matter.

First of all, while culture is underlain and preconditioned by social and psychosomatic factors, the enormous influence of culture on the behavior and activity of individual men and of men in groups has become fully recognized. So heavy is this overlay that "human nature," as that which is biologically given before culture begins to operate, has receded into a remote background in the social sciences and is maintained by biologists as a citadel of principle rather than with specific effectiveness. . . .

Second, it is reasonable to assume that the findings of the top level will differ considerably in kind from those of the bottom levels. All our experience to date corroborates this. The revolutionary extension of physicochemical science by speculation and devised trial during the last fifty years centers around subatomic particles. In the same half-century we have also become much more aware and informed of the domain of culture. But this better understanding of culture has given no sign, until now, of including anything corresponding to the subatomic particles or the geneticists' genes. There is nothing in sight which suggests that we shall discover in culture any invariable elemental units, or even definite relations of integral number of fixed association. . . .

What evidently takes the place of the formulation of law, in intellectual operations on the cultural level, is the recognition of significances, including values. . . .

. . . We must also expect to discover in our material little of causality in the sense of the physicist's causality. We must be ready, where we get further by it, to ignore and suppress the individual, who from the angle of the understanding of culture is perhaps more often irrelevant and distracting than helpful. The ordering or relating which yields understanding in the study of culture is basically best defined, perhaps, as a process of perceiving significant interrelations of forms as forms. . . .

. . . Today we think in terms of inventors. But the discoveries and inventions of other lands, of the past, of our own Middle Ages, are anonymous. Metal-working, blacksmithing; plows, screws, shears; stirrups, horseshoes, harness, wheels, axles; clocks, levels, lamps, candles; glass and pots; fertilizing, irrigating, castrating, riding—the whole basis of mechanical civilization has no personally known authors. They were never recorded or have been long forgotten, because they did not matter.

When finally this condition changes and legend or history gives us, first, imagined inventors and then documentarily authenticated ones, a strange persistence of the ancient condition nevertheless continues. The inventors now come in contemporary pairs or triplets or teams of competitors. Wallace synchronizes with Darwin, Leverrier with Adams, DeVries with Correns and Tschermak; Langley's flight with Wright's; Bell anticipated Gray by a day; Fulton contests with Symington, Fitch, Rumsey, and Stevens. That the making of inventions is normally multiple and simultaneous is by now a fairly well-established fact. From the angle of the individual, the inventors operate independently. From that of the culture, it is the trend, the antecedents, the moment, that unite to force the invention; within its setting it has become, as it were, inevitable; which person is the vehicle of discovery matters little to the society and to the growth of the culture.

Another long-noted phenomenon points the same way, if one will see it so. This is the clustering of great men in certain epochs of certain civilizations and their rarity elsewhere. Nothing now known in biological heredity, nothing in the laws of chance, can account for these tremendous variations in the frequency and intensity of genius. The only explanation yet advanced which is not wholly speculative or arbitrary sees a correlation between realized genius and opportunity given by stage of a civilization's development—the stage where its productive cultural patterns are defined and mature but where their inherent potentialities have not yet begun to be exhausted. By this view, it is the phase of developing culture patterns that is primarily determinative of greatness and fineness of human achievement; geniuses are the index of such development of pattern. What we are wont to call "great men" are those among many more individuals of above-average ability who happen to get born in a time and place and society the patterns of whose culture have formed with sufficient potential value and have developed to sufficient ripeness to allow the full capacities of these individuals to be realized and expressed. This is not really a revolutionary view. It should not even be disturbing to anyone who has apprehended the strength and fulness with which culture holds us all. It ought certainly not upset him who has read and absorbed Sumner's *Folkways* of more than forty years ago and has made the inevitable short extrapolation from the folk to the sophisticates and has realized that we are all in the grip of our ways and our mores—in the grip of our culture.

I have just spoken of greatness and fineness, of potential and realized achievements. Therewith we are plumb in the field of that which the scientist has long said is not for him to touch: values—human values which are cultural values, whether moral, aesthetic, sensory, intellectual, or what not.

One must grant that human cultural values have nothing to do with physics, have no place in it or in any science that models itself on the plan and rules of physics. But how is it possible, without the most sterile stultification, to make intellectual study of social man who is cultural man, and yet permanently to leave out of consideration his product, culture, and that essence of culture, its forms and its values? . . .

Cultural values, along with cultural forms and cultural content, surely exist only through men and reside in men. As the products of human bodies and minds and their functionings and as a specialized extension of them, cultural values thus form a wholly "natural" part of nature. Here the concept of the hierarchy of levels helps. Not only are the levels separated into steps; their superposition one on the other also ties them together, though not into an undifferentiated unity.

Values, like all sociocultural manifestations, are largely superpersonal. That is, far more of any individual's values are instilled into him from outside, directly or indirectly from his society, than he produces within and by himself. Hence values participate in what used to be called the "collective" or "mass" origin—what I prefer to call the "essential anonymity" of origin—of phenomena like customs, morals, ideologies, fashions, and speech. Sumner's "folkways" excellently conveys this same quality except for its false implication that there also exists a social intelligentsia exempt from being folk. It is possible to exalt collectivity into something self-containedly mystical, as shown by the example of Jung and perhaps of Durkheim. But it is not necessary to be mystical in dealing with collectivity, and we shall therefore assume that we are concerned with the collective only as something completely in relation with the remainder of nature.

Now the collective or anonymous, being everybody's, is also nobody's: there is a quality of the impersonal about it. The things that are everyone's enter individuality more diffusely than those which a person has sweated out for or by himself. These latter he is likely to prize, almost certain to be well aware of, and to have a conscious history and highlighted reasons for, whether these reasons be true or false. But what he shares with the collectivity is more massive and extensive, often more firmly rooted, and also more obscure; it tends to be less in the focus of consciousness. Hence what has been called the "covertness" of many patterns of culture; they have been set aside from the overt patterns as "configurations" by Kluckhohn. "Covertness" here does not imply intent of concealment, as it does so often in interpersonal motivations, rather only lack of awareness. It is probably a case of cultural forms being relatively more and less in focus of awareness along a sliding scale partly of occasion and partly of generic situation. Thus rules of conduct, which serve as protections to personality, are likely to be formulated with awareness and explicitness, though also subject to attempted warpings by self-interest. At the other end of the scale, rules of grammar in speech, which normally serves to connect personalities when they feel relaxed and in least need of protection, are unformulated, except as a result of the highly sophisticated curiosity of linguists, and can properly be described as having grown up both anonymously and unconsciously. Breaches of grammatical rules, though instantly observed, are ordinarily not resented, because they invade nothing particular to the individual, but are accepted with tolerance, amusement, or contempt.

Allied to this unawareness or unconsciousness of cultural form and organization is the irrationality of much of the collective in culture. "Irrationality" is what it is sometimes called. I have used the term myself. It covers a variety of happenings in culture which have in common a factor of inconsistency. The totality of a situation or way of doing comes out less regular and less coherent than it might have been under rational planning. Daylight saving; the letter *Double-U* after *U* and *V;* mannered mediaeval instead of classic Roman script; ideographs when an alphabet is available; the spellings "ought" and "eight"; the plural "oxen" instead of "oxes," will serve as examples. The point, of course, is that such irregularities and inefficiencies *were* not thought out but are the result of long and complex histories, with quite different factors often impinging successively. Established individual habits, prestige values, change in one part of a system with lag in another, actual economic cost, mere inertia or nostalgia—all sorts of reasons, mostly rational enough in the concrete situation, have been at work; and the resulting system shows the effect of compromises and patches. Any fool could devise a more consistent system than exists, but even a despot rarely can institute one. In one sense the outcome is "irrational" indeed, in that the institution lacks the full reasonableness which its defenders claim for it. Actually, it rather is nonrational, and only partly that. Most strictly, it is that the institutional pattern is irregular, not wholly consistent.

These considerations rather foreshadow what might be said of the integratedness of the cultures of particular societies. Cultures tend toward integration and, in the main, largely achieve some degree of it, though never total integration. This latter is an ideal condition invented by a few anthropologists not well versed in history. It is hard to imagine any historian—other than a propagandist—bringing himself to advance such a claim as the complete integration of any culture, in the face of his professional experience.

That values constitute an essential element of cultures leads to another consideration. A first account of a new culture, having necessarily to seize and portray the values which help to give it organization and orientation, is likely to emerge as a somewhat idealized account, since the values of the culture are reflected in the society's ideals. Of course, no society is ideal in its behavior. The society aims to conform to the value standards; but we are all more or less lazy, mean, self-centered, cowardly, spiteful, motivated by personal interest. There is thus an unavoidable gap between the ideal or "pure" picture of the culture and the actuality of how this ideal is lived out by the average adherent of the culture. The psychologically minded analyst of behavior, the student of personality and culture, for whom culture is less an end than a take-off of interest, will accentuate the actuality; and between personality stresses and strains, traumas and frustrations, the ideal values of conduct which the "culturologist" has built up into such gleaming, streamlined patterns will emerge tarnished and battered or even cracked. This is a difference to be aware of without worrying too much over it. He who is really interested in the phenomena of culture knows that their ideal values always suffer in actual human living of them. But, at the same time, he knows that in apprehending cultures the most essential thing to apprehend is their values, because without these he will not know either toward what the cultures are slanted or around what they are organized. . . .

. . . It cannot be doubted that single individuals occasionally affect the stream of culture perceptibly: Napoleon with his Code, Caesar on the Calendar, Shi Hwang-ti with the Burning of the Books, Copernicus with his revolution—not to mention religious leaders. Even suborganic influence on culture must be admitted: catastrophes that wipe out one society, obliterating its culture, but spare another, leaving its culture intact; changes in climate favorable to prosperity and increase of particular populations, with consequent dominance of their cultures over those of disadvantaged peoples. It is evident that the greater the number and variety of these subcultural causes, the greater the variability or "plasticity" of cultural phenomena is likely to be.

Of course, the total outcome is not utter cultural randomness but only a high degree of what may properly be called plasticity; and this for the following reason.

Predominantly it will be the psychosomatic actions of human beings that contain the immediate causality of cultural phenomena. But human beings, with their extraordinarily high symbolizing faculties, which means cultural faculties, are always culturalized. That is, they are culturally determined—and heavily determined—by the time they reach the age at which they become potential causes of culture. What is therefore operative is a powerful system of circular causality. The human beings who influence culture and make new culture are themselves molded; and they are molded through the intervention of other men who are culturalized and thus products of previous culture. So it is clear that, while human beings are always the *immediate* causes of cultural events, these human causes are themselves the result of antecedent culture situations, having been fitted to the existing cultural forms which they encounter. There is thus a continuity of indirect causation from culture event to culture event through the medium of human intermediaries. These intermediaries are concerned, first of all, with relieving their own tensions and achieving their personal gratification; but in so doing they also transmit, and to some degree modify, the culture which they carry because they have been conditioned to it. In a sense, accordingly, a kind of cultural causality is also operative. However, compared with the immediate efficient causality of men on culture, the causation of culture on culture is indirect, remote, and largely a functional relation of form to form. At any rate, as long as one's interest is in what happens in culture, it is the cultural antecedents that become significant. The human transmitters and carriers and modifiers are likely to average pretty much alike. As causes they tend to average uniform and constant, except so far as cultural exposure has differentiated them.

The inquirer, if his interest is really in culture, tends therefore to omit the human agents. He operates *as if* individual personalities did not have a hand in cultural events. In the main he is justified in this procedure. He is certainly justified in proportion as his view is long-range. On telescopic inspection of the greater cultural currents, even the greatest and most influential personalities shrink to minuteness.

As the range contracts and the segment of culture examined begins to be minute, the role of individuals, under the microscopic dissection being carried on, looms correspondingly larger. Here is an equally legitimate method of study; but, of course, it yields results of a quite different order. It gives insight into the interaction of persons and culture: on how individuals get caught in the net of their culture; of how some kinds of them stretch the net or tear rents in it; how others, meanwhile, are weaving new ranges of mesh. The value of such studies is as examples of the close-up mechanism of the change which culture is always tending to undergo. An additional value is in the illumination thrown on the reactions of human beings, viewed as integral personalities, to their enveloping culture. These are certainly fields of knowledge. But they are obviously different from straight culture history or from the analytic comparison of cultural forms and values as such. . . .

The problem remains unresolved of how far general forms, therefore recurrent forms, can be demonstrated in culture. . . . There is also no agreement as yet as to the most general forms among which the totality of culture could be distributed, so far as recurrences or regularities do hold water. The earliest such attempts took the shape of stages and suffered from intellectual naïveté. There was the hunting-herding-farming stage sequence; the mythologic-religious-positive one; even the chipped stone-polished stone-bronze-iron classification. . . .

Finally, there is the question of how far the maximum nexuses or totalities which we call "civilizations" show recurrences in their developmental phases—in other words, show a recurrent pattern of growth. If they do, empirically, show such a recurrent pattern, civilizations would provide an actual and natural segmentation which would help us to organize intellectually the otherwise variably tossing and endlessly stretching sea of the variable continuum of culture as a whole. There is a growing recognition of the probable reality of such segmentation, as well as of its specific limits and inclusions—in other words, of what each civilization takes in.

As to what is at work in the formation of these great units, however, there is wide divergence. Spengler sees immanent predestination, Toynbee moral free will, Sorokin a pendulum beat between sensate and ideational proclivities. This area of inquiry will unquestionably undergo considerable further cultivation, if for no other reason than that our thinking of history has until recently been too ethnocentrically weighted, too "auto-culturo-centric," for the large problems in this area to be effectively conceived or framed.

The question remains whether the concept of culture will serve as a mechanism for integrating more closely the several social sciences. The answer is both Yes and No. There is no doubt that cultural aspects can be recognized and followed through all human areas commonly recognized as social. Economics and government *are* only segments of culture. The data of formal sociology are so intertwined with cultural ones that subjects like family, kinship, associations, the state, are claimed and treated equally by sociologists and by cultural anthropologists. Formal history, even at its most biographical, cannot wholly avoid institutional implications; and, at the opposite end of its range, history is institutional, and thus *de facto* cultural. Psychology can pretty much eliminate cultural factors by narrowing its analysis and by holding the cultural factors constant in selective experiment. Yet, as soon as it rewidens its activity to take in total personalities, a flood of cultural considerations inevitably pours in on it.

However, what all this means is that, if one is interested in cultural manifestations, one can recognize them and deal with them selectively in every scientific study that has man for its subject. And such a selective pursuit will yield certain understandings unattainable by any other and less differentiated method. But it *is* selective; that is a fact that must not be forgotten. There are other bases of selection, and each has its own kind of fruitfulness. Economic theory, though validated by empirical techniques rather than derived from them, seems reasonably to satisfy economists and is not likely to be given up by them for any more generalized theory of culture. Historians presumably will continue to prefer their accustomed mixed diet of events, persons, and institutional forms, with its maximum of adherence to raw phenomena, opportunities for stirring dramatic representation in narrative, and minimum necessity of generalization—and then generalization merely as incidental commentary. We have already considered the trans-level or interlevel studies of fields like personality in culture, which, though still groping and unsure of method and occasionally confusing hope with fulfilment, are certainly legitimate and to be counted on to grow.

In summary, it is evident that the cultural approach, now that it is well isolated and developed, will continue to be used because it yields distinctive results. Yet it is equally clear that the cultural approach is not exclusively valid within the area of superorganic phenomena; nor, of course, is it a panacea. It is a selective approach, fruitful because of its selectiveness, but, for the same reason, not unlimited in its scope.

5. Culture, Genuine and Spurious

EDWARD SAPIR

Edward Sapir's quite different approach to culture is frankly an essay in discontent—discontent at the social patterns that underlie nihilism, existential philosophy and the "beat generation"—though written thirty-five years ago. Sapir asks us to evaluate culture, but neither according to our own culturally induced tastes and prejudices nor according to its material and mechanical attainments. Rather, he would have us examine cultures for the degree to which they provide satisfactory life modes for the participants, the degree to which there is a wholeness and unity and a sense of meaning and purpose. Sapir believes that there is no adequate "patterning" to our own culture, and he views this with alarm. It is not the usual anthropological approach, which tends merely to describe and analyze, but it is one which makes us look deep into ourselves as individuals as well as into our culture.

Sapir was primarily a linguist, one of the most influential in America. He was also a pioneer in examining the relation of the individual to his culture, which we will examine in the section on education. He received his doctorate from Columbia University in 1909 and taught at the Universities of Toronto and Chicago until he was appointed Sterling Professor of Anthropology and Linguistics at Yale University in 1931. The present essay was first published in the *American Journal of Sociology*, Volume 29, 1924, and appears in a volume of essays entitled *The Selected Writings of Edward Sapir in Language, Culture, and Personality* (David Mandelbaum, editor), University of California Press, Berkeley, (pp. 308–331), 1949. It is published by kind permission of the University of Chicago Press. Copyright 1924 by The University of Chicago.

. . . We may accept culture as signifying the characteristic mold of a national civilization, while from a second conception of culture, that of a traditional type of individual refinement, we will borrow the notion of ideal form. Let me say at once that nothing is farther from my mind than to plead the cause of any specific type of culture. It would be idle to praise or blame any fundamental condition of our civilization, to praise or blame any strand in the warp and woof of its genius. These conditions and these strands must be accepted as basic. . . . In other words, a genuine culture is perfectly conceivable in any type or stage of civilization, in the mold of any national genius. It can be conceived as easily in terms of a Mohammedan polygamous society, or of an American Indian "primitive" non-agricultural society, as in those of our familiar occidental societies. On the other hand, what may by contrast be called "spurious" cultures are just as easily conceivable in conditions of general enlightenment as in those of relative ignorance and squalor.

The genuine culture is not of necessity either high or low; it is merely inherently harmonious, balanced, self-satisfactory. It is the expression of a richly varied and yet somehow unified and consistent attitude toward life, an attitude which sees the significance of any one element of civilization in its relation to all others. It is, ideally speaking, a culture in which nothing is spiritually meaningless, in which no important part of the general functioning brings with it a sense of frustration, of misdirected or unsympathetic effort. It is not a spiritual hybrid of contradictory patches, of water-tight compartments of consciousness that avoid participation in a harmonious synthesis. If the culture necessitates slavery, it frankly admits it; if it abhors slavery, it feels its way to an economic adjustment that obviates the necessity of its employment. It does not make a great show in its ethical ideals of an uncompromising opposition to slavery, only to introduce what amounts to a slave system into certain portions of its industrial mechanism. Or, if it builds itself magnificent houses of worship, it is because of the necessity it feels to symbolize in beautiful stone a religious impulse that is deep and vital; if it is ready to discard institutionalized religion, it is prepared also to dispense with the homes of institutionalized religion. It does not look sheepish when a direct appeal is made to its religious consciousness, then make amends by furtively donating a few dollars toward the maintenance of an African mission. Nor does it carefully instruct its children in what it knows to be of no use or vitality either to them or in its own mature life. Nor does it tolerate a thousand other spiritual maladjustments such as are patent enough in our American life of today. It would be too much to say that even the purest examples yet known of a genuine culture have been free of spiritual discords, of the dry rot of social habit, devitalized. But the great cultures, those that we instinctively feel to have been healthy spiritual organisms, such as the Athenian culture of the Age of Pericles and, to a less extent perhaps, the English culture of Elizabethan days, have at least tended to such harmony.

It should be clearly understood that this ideal of a genuine culture has no necessary connection with what we call efficiency. A society may be admirably efficient in the sense that all its activities are carefully planned with reference to ends of maximum utility to the society as a whole, it may tolerate no lost motion, yet it may well be an inferior organism as a culture-bearer. It is not enough that the ends of activities be socially satisfactory, that each member of the community feel in some dim way that he is doing his bit toward the attainment of a social benefit. This is all very well so far as it goes, but a genuine culture refuses to consider the individual as a mere cog, as an entity whose sole *raison d'être* lies in his subservience to a collective purpose that he is not conscious of or that has only a remote relevancy to his interests and strivings. The major activities of the individual must directly satisfy his own creative and emotional impulses, must always be something more than means to an end. The great cultural fallacy of industrialism, as developed up to the present time, is that in harnessing machines to our uses it has not known how to avoid the harnessing of the majority of mankind to its machines. The telephone girl who lends her capacities, during the greater part of the living day, to the manipulation of a technical routine that has an eventually high efficiency value but that answers to no spiritual needs of her own is an appalling sacrifice to civilization. As a solution of the problem of culture she is a failure—the more dismal the greater her natural endowment. As with the telephone girl, so, it is to be feared, with the great majority of us, slave-stokers to fires that burn for demons we would destroy, were it not that they appear in the guise of our benefactors. The American Indian who solves the economic problem with salmon-spear and rabbit-snare operates on a relatively low level of civilization, but he represents an incomparably higher solution than our telephone girl of the questions that culture has to ask of economics. There is here no question of the immediate utility, of the effective directness, of economic effort, nor of any sentimentalizing regrets as to the passing of the "natural man." The Indian's salmon-spearing is a culturally higher type of activity than that of the telephone girl or mill hand simply because there is normally no sense of spiritual frustration during its prosecution, no feeling of subservience to tyrannous yet largely inchoate demands, because it works in naturally with all the rest of the Indian's activities instead of standing out as a desert patch of merely economic effort in the whole of life. A genuine culture cannot be defined as a sum of abstractly desirable ends, as a mechanism. It must be looked upon as a sturdy plant growth, each remotest leaf and twig of which is organically fed by the sap at the core. And this growth is not here meant as a metaphor for the group only; it is meant to apply as well to the individual. A culture that does not build itself out of the central interests and desires of its bearers, that works from general ends to the individual, is an external culture. The word "external," which is so often instinctively chosen to describe such a culture, is well chosen. The genuine culture is internal, it works from the individual to ends.

We have already seen that there is no necessary correlation between the development of civilization and the relative genuineness of the culture which forms its spiritual essence. This requires a word of further explanation. By the development of civilization is meant the ever increasing degree of sophistication of our society and of our individual lives. This progressive sophistication is the inevitable cumulative result of the sifting processes of social experience, of the ever increasing complication of our innumerable types of organization; most of all of our steadily growing knowledge of our natural environment and, as a consequence, our practical mastery, for economic ends, of the resources that nature at once grants us and hides from us. It is chiefly the cumulative force of this sophistication that gives us the sense of what we call "progress." Perched on the heights of an office building twenty or more stories taller than our fathers ever dreamed of, we feel that we are getting up in the world. Hurling our bodies through space with an ever accelerating velocity, we feel that we are getting on. Under sophistication I include not merely intellectual and technical advance, but most of the tendencies that make for a cleaner and healthier and, to a large extent, a more humanitarian existence. It is excellent to keep one's hands spotlessly clean, to eliminate smallpox, to administer anesthetics. Our growing sophistication, our ever increasing solicitude to obey the dictates of common sense, make these tendencies imperative. It would be sheer obscurantism to wish to stay their progress. But there can be no stranger illusion—and it is an illusion we nearly all share—than this, that because the tools of life are today more specialized and more refined than ever before, that because the technique brought by science is more perfect than anything the world has yet known, it necessarily follows that we are in like degree attaining to a profounder harmony of life, to a deeper and more satisfying culture. It is as though we believed that an elaborate mathematical computation which involved figures of seven and eight digits could not but result in a like figure. Yet we know that one million multiplied by zero gives us zero quite as effectively as one multiplied by zero. The truth is that sophistication, which is what we ordinarily mean by the progress of civilization, is, in the long run, a merely quantitative concept that defines the external conditions for the growth or decay of culture. We are right to have faith in the progress of civilization. We are wrong to assume that the maintenance or even advance of culture is a function of such progress. A reading of the facts of ethnology and culture history proves plainly that maxima of culture have frequently been reached in low levels of sophistication; that minima of culture have been plumbed in some of the highest. Civilization, as a whole, moves on; culture comes and goes. . . .

It is perhaps the sensitive ethnologist who has studied an aboriginal civilization at first hand who is most impressed by the frequent vitality of culture in less sophisticated levels. He cannot but admire the well-rounded life of the average participant in the civilization of a typical American Indian tribe; the firmness with which every part of that life—economic, social, religious, and aesthetic—is bound together into a significant whole in respect to which he is far from a passive pawn; above all, the molding role, oftentimes definitely creative, that he plays in the mechanism of his culture. When the political integrity of his tribe is destroyed by contact with the whites and the old cultural values cease to have the atmosphere needed for their continued vitality, the Indian finds himself in a state of bewildered vacuity. Even if he succeeds in making a fairly satisfactory compromise with his new environment, in making what his well-wishers consider great progress toward enlightenment, he is apt to retain an uneasy sense of the loss of some vague and great good, some state of mind that he would be hard put to it to define, but which gave him a courage and joy that latter-day prosperity never quite seems to have regained for him. What has happened is that he has slipped out of the warm embrace of a culture into the cold air of fragmentary existence. What is sad about the passing of the Indian is not the depletion of his numbers by disease nor even the contempt that is too often meted out to him in his life on the reservation, it is the fading away of genuine cultures, built though they were out of the materials of a low order of sophistication.

We have no right to demand of the higher levels of sophistication that they preserve to the individual his manifold functioning, but we may well ask whether, as a compensation, the individual may not reasonably demand an intensification in cultural value, a spiritual heighten-

ing, of such functions as are left him. Failing this, he must be admitted
to have retrograded. The limitation in functioning works chiefly in the
economic sphere. It is therefore imperative, if the individual is to preserve his value as a cultured being, that he compensate himself out of
the non-economic, the non-utilitarian spheres—social, religious, scientific, aesthetic. This idea of compensation brings to view an important
issue, that of the immediate and the remoter ends of human effort.

As a mere organism, man's only function is to exist; in other words,
to keep himself alive and to propagate his kind. Hence the procuring of
food, clothing, and shelter for himself and those dependent on him constitutes the immediate end of his effort. There are civilizations, like that
of the Eskimo, in which by far the greater part of man's energy is consumed in the satisfaction of these immediate ends, in which most of his
activities contribute directly or indirectly to the procuring and preparation of food and the materials for clothing and shelter. There are practically no civilizations, however, in which at least some of the available
energy is not set free for the remoter ends, though, as a rule, these
remoter ends are by a process of rationalization made to seem to contribute to the immediate ones. (A magical ritual, for instance, which,
when considered psychologically, seems to liberate and give form to
powerful emotional aesthetic elements of our nature, is nearly always
put in harness to some humdrum utilitarian end—the catching of rabbits
or the curing of disease.) As a matter of fact, there are very few "primitive" civilizations that do not consume an exceedingly large share of
their energies in the pursuit of the remoter ends, though it remains true
that these remoter ends are nearly always functionally or pseudo-
functionally interwoven with the immediate ends. Art for art's sake may
be a psychological fact on these less sophisticated levels; it is certainly
not a cultural fact.

On our own level of civilization the remoter ends tend to split off
altogether from the immediate ones and to assume the form of a spiritual
escape or refuge from the pursuit of the latter. The separation of the
two classes of ends is never absolute nor can it ever be; it is enough to
note the presence of a powerful drift of the two away from each other.
It is easy to demonstrate this drift by examples taken out of our daily
experience. While in most primitive civilizations the dance is apt to be
a ritual activity at least ostensibly associated with purposes of an economic nature, it is with us a merely and self-consciously pleasurable
activity that not only splits off from the sphere of the pursuit of immediate ends but even tends to assume a position of hostility to that sphere.

In a primitive civilization a great chief dances as a matter of course, oftentimes as a matter of exercising a peculiarly honored privilege. With us the captain of industry either refuses to dance at all or does so as a half-contemptuous concession to the tyranny of social custom. On the other hand, the artist of a Ballet Russe has sublimated the dance to an exquisite instrument of self-expression, has succeeded in providing himself with an adequate, or more than adequate, cultural recompense for his loss of mastery in the realm of direct ends. The captain of industry is one of the comparatively small class of individuals that has inherited, in vastly complicated form, something of the feeling of control over the attainment of direct ends that belongs by cultural right to primitive man; the ballet dancer has saved and intensified for himself the feeling of spontaneous participation and creativeness in the world of indirect ends that also belongs by cultural right to primitive man. Each has saved part of the wreckage of a submerged culture for himself. . . .

The transformation of ends is of the greatest cultural importance because it acts as a powerful force for the preservation of culture in levels in which a fragmentary economic functioning of the individual is inevitable. So long as the individual retains a sense of control over the major goods of life, he is able to take his place in the cultural patrimony of his people. Now that the major goods of life have shifted so largely from the realm of immediate to that of remote ends, it becomes a cultural necessity for all who would not be looked upon as disinherited to share in the pursuit of these remoter ends. No harmony and depth of life, no culture, is possible when activity is well-nigh circumscribed by the sphere of immediate ends and when functioning within that sphere is so fragmentary as to have no inherent intelligibility or interest. Here lies the grimmest joke of our present American civilization. The vast majority of us, deprived of any but an insignificant and culturally abortive share in the satisfaction of the immediate wants of mankind, are further deprived of both opportunity and stimulation to share in the production of non-utilitarian values. Part of the time we are dray horses; the rest of the time we are listless consumers of goods which have received no least impress of our personality. In other words, our spiritual selves go hungry, for the most part, pretty much all of the time.

There is no real opposition, at last analysis, between the concept of a culture of the group and the concept of an individual culture. The two are interdependent. A healthy national culture is never a passively accepted heritage from the past, but implies the creative participation of the members of the community; implies, in other words, the presence of cultured individuals. . . .

It is only an apparent paradox that the subtlest and the most decisive cultural influences of personality, the most fruitful revolts, are discernible in those environments that have long and uninterruptedly supported a richly streaming culture. So far from being suffocated in an atmosphere of endless precedent, the creative spirit gains sustenance and vigor for its own unfolding and, if it is strong enough, it may swing free from that very atmosphere with a poise hardly dreamed of by the timid iconoclasts of unformed cultures. Not otherwise could we understand the cultural history of modern Europe. Only in a mature and richly differentiated soil could arise the iconoclasms and visions of an Anatole France, a Nietzsche, an Ibsen, a Tolstoi. In America, at least in the America of yesterday, these iconoclasms and these visions would either have been strangled in the cradle, or, had they found air to breathe, they would have half-developed into a crude and pathetic isolation. There is no sound and vigorous individual incorporation of a cultured ideal without the soil of a genuine communal culture; and no genuine communal culture without the transforming energies of personalities at once robust and saturated with the cultural values of their time and place. . . .

The individual self, then, in aspiring to culture, fastens upon the accumulated cultural goods of its society, not so much for the sake of the passive pleasure of their acquirement, as for the sake of the stimulus given to the unfolding personality and of the orientation derived in the world (or better, a world) of cultural values. The orientation, conventional as it may be, is necessary if only to give the self a *modus vivendi* with society at large. The individual needs to assimilate much of the cultural background of his society, many of the current sentiments of his people, to prevent his self-expression from degenerating into social sterility. A spiritual hermit may be genuinely cultured, but he is hardly socially so. . . .

No greater test of the genuineness of both individual and communal culture can be applied than the attitude adopted toward the past, its institutions, its treasures of art and thought. The genuinely cultured individual or society does not contemptuously reject the past. They honor the works of the past, but not because they are gems of historical chance, not because, being out of our reach, they must needs be looked at through the enshrining glass of museum cases. These works of the past still excite our heartfelt interest and sympathy because, and only in so far as, they may be recognized as the expression of a human spirit warmly akin, despite all differences of outward garb, to our own. This is very nearly equivalent to saying that the past is of cultural interest only when it is still the present or may yet become the future. Paradoxical as it may seem, the historical spirit has always been something of an anticultural force, has always acted in some measure as an unwitting deterrent of the cultural utilization of the past. . . . We know immensely more about Hellenic antiquity in these days than did the scholars and artists of the Renaissance; it would be folly to pretend that our live utilization of the Hellenic spirit, accurately as we merely know it, is comparable to the inspiration, the creative stimulus, that those men of the Renaissance obtained from its fragmentary and garbled tradition. . . .

To summarize the place of the individual in our theory of culture, we may say that the pursuit of genuine culture implies two types of reconciliation. The self seeks instinctively for mastery. In the process of acquiring a sense of mastery that is not crude but proportioned to the degree of sophistication proper to our time, the self is compelled to suffer an abridgment and to undergo a molding. The extreme differentiation of function which the progress of man has forced upon the individual menaces the spirit; we have no recourse but to submit with good grace to this abridgment of our activity, but it must not be allowed to clip the wings of the spirit unduly. This is the first and most important reconciliation—the finding of a full world of spiritual satisfactions within the straight limits of an unwontedly confined economic activity. The self must set itself at a point where it can, if not embrace the whole spiritual life of its group, at least catch enough of its rays to burst into light and flame. Moreover, the self must learn to reconcile its own strivings, its own imperious necessities, with the general spiritual life of the community. It must be content to borrow sustenance from the spiritual consciousness of that community and of its past, not merely that it may obtain the wherewithal to grow at all, but that it may grow where its power, great or little, will be brought to bear on a spiritual life that is of intimate concern to other wills. Yet, despite all reconciliations, the self has a right to feel that it grows as an integral, self-poised, spiritual growth, whose ultimate justifications rest in itself, whose sacrifices and compensations must be justified to itself. The conception of the self as a mere instrument toward the attainment of communal ends, whether of state or other social body, is to be discarded as leading in the long run to psychological absurdities and to spiritual slavery. It is the self that concedes, if there is to be any concession. Spiritual freedom, what there is of it, is not alms dispensed, now indifferently, now grudgingly, by the social body. That a different philosophy of the relation of the individual to his group is now so prevalent, makes it all the more necessary to insist on the spiritual primacy of the individual soul. . . .

It is in the New World, perhaps more than in any other part of the globe, that the unsatisfactory nature of a geographically widespread culture, of little depth or individuality to begin with, is manifest. To find substantially the same cultural manifestations, material and spiritual, often indeed to the minutest details, in New York and Chicago and San Francisco is saddening. It argues a shallowness in the culture itself and a readiness to imitation in its bearers that is not reassuring. Even if no definite way out of the flat cultural morass is clearly discernible for the present, there is no good in basking forever in self-sufficiency. It can only be of benefit to search out the depths of our hearts and to find wherein they are wanting. If we exaggerate our weakness, it does not matter; better chastening than self-glorification. We have been in the habit of giving ourselves credit for essentially quantitative results that are due rather to an unusually favoring nature and to a favoring set of economic conditions than to anything in ourselves. Our victories have been brilliant, but they have also too often been barren for culture. The habit of playing with loaded dice has given us a dangerous attitude of passivity—dangerous, that is, for culture. Stretching back opulently in our easy chairs, we expect great cultural things to happen to us. We have wound up the machinery, and admirable machinery it is; it is "up to" culture to come forth, in heavy panoply. The minute increment of individuality which alone makes culture in the self and eventually builds up a culture in the community seems somehow overlooked. Canned culture is so much easier to administer.

Just now [1924] we are expecting a great deal from the European war. No doubt the war and its aftermath will shake us out of some part of our smugness and let in a few invigorating air currents of cultural influence, but, if we are not careful, these influences may soon harden into new standardizations, or become diluted into another stock of imitative attitudes and reactions. The war and its aftermath cannot be a sufficient cultural cause, they are at best but another set of favoring conditions. We need not be too much astonished if a Periclean culture does not somehow automatically burst into bloom. Sooner or later we shall have to get down to the humble task of exploring the depths of our consciousness and dragging to the light what sincere bits of reflected experience we can find. These bits will not always be beautiful, they will not always be pleasing, but they will be genuine. And then we can build. In time, in plenty of time—for we must have patience—a genuine culture—better yet, a series of linked autonomous cultures—will grace our lives. And New York and Chicago and San Francisco will live each in its own cultural strength, not squinting from one to another to see which gets ahead in a race for external values, but each serenely oblivious of its rivals because growing in a soil of genuine cultural values.

II.

LANGUAGE

Man's Peculiar Gift

If culture is seen to be the unique characteristic of man, language must be viewed as the particular human gift that makes culture possible. For without the human capacity to communicate intricate patterns of thought—to re-create experience in words—culture could not exist. There are some who believe that it is language which is the truly distinguishing feature of man, and that culture is a mere by-product of this human attribute.

However that may be, this much is true: All mankind has language, and man alone among the known creatures of the world is endowed with speech. Let us consider the second point first.

Many animals make sounds, and through sounds convey meaning. Any dog owner will assure you that his pet has a considerable vocabulary of barks, growls and whines. When my own dog barks at the door because I haven't responded to his whining request for entry, I know the sound as distinct from his bark at the postman. I have no doubt that the tone is different, and I am willing to believe it is purposely so. He successfully communicates this and other things to me. Animals do the same thing in nature. Crows caw a signal of danger, crickets chirp their readiness to mate. The gibbon, that agile little ape from Southeastern Asia, has been studied in his natural habitat by Clarence R. Carpenter, who learned to differentiate nine separate vocalizations used to communicate diverse matters. Why are these sounds not language?

They are not language because language is not merely a vocal action pertaining to the immediate situation. A knocking at the door, a howl of pain, or a grunt of satisfaction—though each conveys unmistakable meaning to others—is not language. Language involves the communication of ideas; the placement, through sounds, of objects and actions in a context of time, place, and circumstance. My dog cannot say: "Let me back in when I have finished the bone," nor can the gibbon mother warn her offspring to avoid a tiger, if and when one comes along. All that either can do is to express immediate states of readiness, awareness, or emotion. They cannot communicate the relationship between things and events, they cannot express the conditional, the possible, the future, or the past. (There is some exception in the "dancing" of bees, which indicates direction and distance to food, but this appears to be highly limited, is done with gestures rather than vocalization, and is far remote from anything involving the vertebrate animals.)

Why man should be so endowed and other animals not is a moot point. Presumably it reflects a development in the brain; it is a true differential in capacity. Efforts to teach animals to vocalize experience have regularly failed. One scientist spent six months trying to teach an orangutan to talk, and she seemed to have learned to say "cup" for water and "papa" for her teacher. Then she died—presumably not from mental exhaustion. Two young psychologists had a chimpanzee live with them and grow up with their baby. The chimpanzee learned everything during the first year faster than the baby did—except speech. Apes have the physical equipment to make the complex sets of sounds that constitute human speech: larynx, tongue, palate, and lips; they can and do make a variety of sounds. But they do not make regular sets of sounds so as to form words and sentences. Though one student claims that they do not speak because they have nothing to say, this seems unlikely (at least it isn't true for man). We can only conclude that man has some mental ability that he shares with no other living creature.

But all mankind can speak. No tribe or people, however crude their culture in other respects or however mean their circumstances, lacks a language. Furthermore, though the languages are constructed on very different principles and use quite different sets of sounds, there is no evidence that some languages are poorer or more primitive than others. To be sure, our language has more words than primitive languages, for we have more things to name and have inherited a rich storehouse through writing, adopting many words from foreign tongues. But every language develops words for new objects or events as they occur; vocabulary reflects culture by providing labels for what it knows and what is important to it, but any language is capable of communicating, one as adequately as another, that which its speakers want to say.

This is not to say that all languages are alike—as all of us know to our dismay. Yet the languages with which most of us are familiar are closely related and have similar characteristics in structure and vocabularly that are not shared by the languages of the Orient, Africa, native America and elsewhere. Languages differ not only in the sounds employed and vocabulary, but in their basic structure. They all share only the following broad characteristics: They are constituted of a set of sounds made with the mouth and larynx; a small number (fifteen to fifty) of separate sounds are recognized and these combine in limited ways; they form into unit utterances which we call words and into larger units of meaning that we call sentences; the relation between these standard units in speech communicates the relation between the elements spoken about (which we call grammar and syntax). Though made up of finite units and observing limited rules of combination, the possibilities of combination are virtually infinite. The sounds selected, the manner of combination and the principles of grammatical structure vary widely. Some of these characteristics are illustrated in the essay by Harry Hoijer which appears in this section.

The essential ingredient of human speech, as Leslie White states, is the capacity for symbolization. It is perhaps in this ability that the human brain is to be seen as distinctive. Symbolization affects all aspects of human culture, especially social and religious life, but it is nowhere so elaborately developed or centrally important as in that primary element of culture, language. In order that set sound patterns have meaning, they must be symbols for "events" in the external world, and speech is the manipulation of these symbols in such a manner that they create for the speaker and for the listener a more-or-less accurate representation of the relationship between these events in space and time. Since events are infinitely complex, it requires a limitless system, and even then we know, often to our dismay, how inadequate words are to express our feelings and our perceptions. It is this inadequacy of language (which presents in a linear form events which in reality are multidimensional) that makes us say that languages are *equally* capable of expressing our thoughts, but not that they are fully capable of doing so.

Languages are symbolic because the word does not stand for a single event or thing, but for a category of events or things. The word *tree* stands for a wide variety of plants; the word *oak* for a broad class of trees and the word *black-oak* for all oaks of a particular species. Only the proper name, such as *Founder's Tree,* stands for a single item. The same can be said for acts, as well as for things. We distinguish between *go* and various manners of going, such as *walk* or *run*. The capacity to abstract classes or categories of events is essential to the communication process, and our speech tends to divide and to combine the infinite variety of events in the real world into a series of discrete units—units which do not really exist as such, but which we perceive. Accuracy in language involves selecting the words that convey precisely the class of events to which we intend to refer—neither so narrow as to eliminate some that are relevant, nor so broad as to include others that are not. Scientific language requires that this rule be observed with great accuracy; in consequence, to the layman it sometimes sounds like jargon. Significantly, a first step in scientific understanding is the classification of things or events into entities that are meaningful in their proper relationship to nature, as the Linnaean classification of life or the periodic table of chemistry.

Since languages differ, and since the symbolic representation of words must inevitably classify events, it follows that languages classify events differently. This means that a person learning one language tends to perceive unities of a different kind from those who have learned another. As this does not apply only to things and actions, but to such metaphysical categories as time, space, and causation, it follows that language is not only a way of communicating among people but it is also a way of perceiving and conceiving the world. We will not give examples here, for several are offered in the readings which follow. But it is of primary importance that we appreciate this very subtle role that language plays in shaping our way of behaving and feeling; how crucial a part of culture language is; how fundamental to culturally established life-orientations.

Perhaps we can best see this by reminding ourselves of how we learn our mother tongue. We begin to learn to speak at a very early age, long before we have had many experiences in the real world, long before we can develop any theories about the way things are. We learn our speech from those who are already in our society—and they in turn learned to speak in the same way. This means not only that the speaker of a language always adopts forms already in existence, but also that in many instances he experiences events vicariously through language before he experiences them directly. His mode of understanding experience is thus set for him by the very structure of the language which he has already learned. We can see this in problems of zoological classification, when detailed knowledge enables us to separate the bat from the bird and the whale from the fish—supplying a scientific biological classification for the older one of flying animals, swimming animals, and so on.

In simple matters of classification this problem can be readily perceived and compensated for. But the important thing is that it also pervades the subtler aspects of our speech and therefore of our thinking. Let us consider an example. A fundamental distinction of English grammar (and all Indo-European languages, to which family English belongs) is that between nouns and verbs. Nouns are things and verbs are actions, and the naive speaker assumes that these are two separate categories of "events," as the modern linguist says. We cannot speak a grammatical sentence in English without recognizing this distinction, for our grammar requires a subject (which must be a "thing") and a predicate (which must be an "act"). But consider the word *wave*. Taken alone, its role is not known. When we say: "the wave laps over the rocks," it is a thing. When we say: "the flag waves," it is an action. Yet in both cases, the word applies to an undulating movement; in both cases it is an action, but in one we treat the action as if it were a thing. The point is not that we are unaware that a wave is a series of undulating movements; rather, it is that we treat the world as if there were two fundamental and separate categories of events because the spirit of our language requires that we do, and that it takes a real effort to see the world otherwise. In this connection we must not forget the controversy among physicists between wave and particle theories of light. We must also be aware that not all languages make this classification of events into two discrete categories.

Language, then, is an elaborate structure of vocal symbolization, capable of infinite variation, through which ideas, understanding and feelings are communicated, and through which we tend to perceive the events of the world. As the linguist and anthropologist Edward Sapir has said: "The world in which different societies live are distinct worlds, not merely the same world with different labels attached."

Language is also something more; or rather, language performs another function. We translate experience into language, and through language we communicate experience to others. In this way language serves as a kind of storehouse for human experience. A person discovers that in a drought water may be found underground at certain kinds of places. Though he may be dead before the next severe drought, if he has imparted this wisdom to others, his decendants can benefit from his experience. They need not have seen the original action. In this way human knowledge can be stored and transmitted; man is the only animal capable of this means of accumulating experience. (Apparently verbalization makes memory easier—at least for man: the Singhalese drummers of Ceylon learn their complicated rhythms by translating them into verbal forms, which are more easily communicated and memorized.)

It is in this storehouse of language that much of culture is preserved, and all men, everywhere, have a vast fund of knowledge and tradition which they preserve through the ages. It is this capacity which has made possible the gradual accumulation of knowledge and the progressive evolution of man's culture—which is discussed in the next section.

In recent years, speaking in terms of human history, man has added an important element to his capacity for speech: writing. It should be clear that language is not dependent upon writing (which was not invented until 99 percent of man's history on earth had elapsed), though there is a popular tendency to confuse the two—probably because of the manner in which they are placed together in our schooling. Writing at its best is but inadequately represented speech. Though it suffers from the absence of adequate tonal representations, gestures and other accompaniments of spoken language, it has the great advantage of being durable. The durability of writing makes it possible for man to store far more knowledge than is possible through memory alone. Anthropologists are frequently surprised at the feats of memory achieved by natives who have no writing, yet all this memory can be but an infinitesimal part of the knowledge accumulated in a good encyclopedia. The discoveries that led to the development of writing have made possible the great advances in technical knowledge of modern man, and thereby gave rise to the great spurt of growth in culture in the last three or four of the thousand millennia that man has existed on the earth. But we must not forget that writing is merely a way of transmitting and storing up language, just as language is a way of transmitting thought.

6. Symbol, the Basis of Language and Culture

LESLIE A. WHITE

Leslie A. White sees symbolizing not only as the feature in the human intellect which makes language possible, but also as the very basis of the cultural mode of existence. Though other animals make and respond to vocalizations (see pp. 90–95), these are so limited in character as to be an entirely different thing. Presumably, this capacity to symbolize is a quality of the human intellect that marks man off from all other animals. It clearly is essential to language, which in turn is essential to culture. Here White is developing the concept of the symbol.

White is Professor of Anthropology at the University of Michigan. He received his doctoral degree from the University of Chicago in 1927; has worked intensively with the Indians of the Southwest, but is chiefly interested in the theory of cultural evolution. His latest work is *The Evolution of Culture* (McGraw-Hill). The present essay was originally published in the *Philosophy of Science* (Volume 7, pp. 451–463, 1940) and reappears in Leslie A. White, *The Science of Culture, A Study of Man and Civilization,* New York: Farrar, Straus and Co., 1949, copyright 1949 by Leslie A. White. Used by permission of the publishers Farrar, Straus and Cudahy, Inc., and the author.

In July, 1939, a celebration was held at Leland Stanford University to commemorate the one hundredth anniversary of the discovery that the cell is the basic unit of all living tissue. Today we are beginning to realize and to appreciate the fact that the symbol is the basic unit of all human behavior and civilization.

All human behavior originates in the use of symbols. It was the symbol which transformed our anthropoid ancestors into men and made them human. All civilizations have been generated, and are perpetuated, only by the use of symbols. It is the symbol which transforms an infant of *Homo sapiens* into a human being; deaf mutes who grow up without the use of symbols are not human beings. All human behavior consists of, or is dependent upon, the use of symbols. Human behavior is symbolic behavior; symbolic behavior is human behavior. The symbol is the universe of humanity.

The great Darwin declared in *The Descent of Man* that "there is no fundamental difference between man and the higher mammals in their mental faculties," that the difference between them consists *"solely* in his [man's] almost infinitely larger power of associating together the most diversified sounds and ideas . . . the mental powers of higher animals do not differ *in kind,* though greatly *in degree,* from the corresponding powers of man" (chs. 3, 18; emphasis ours).

This view of comparative mentality is held by many scholars to-day. . . .

That there are numerous and impressive similarities between the behavior of man and that of ape is fairly obvious; it is quite possible that chimpanzees and gorillas in zoos have noted and appreciated them. Fairly apparent, too, are man's behavioral similarities to many other kinds of animals. Almost as obvious, but not easy to define, is a difference in behavior which distinguishes man from all other living creatures. I say "obvious" because it is quite apparent to the common man that the non-human animals with which he is familiar do not and cannot enter, and participate in, the world in which he, as a human being, lives. It is impossible for a dog, horse, bird, or even an ape, to have *any* understanding of the meaning of the sign of the cross to a Christian, or of the fact that black (white among the Chinese) is the color of mourning. No chimpanzee or laboratory rat can appreciate the difference between Holy water and distilled water, or grasp the meaning of *Tuesday, 3,* or *sin.* No animal save man can distinguish a cousin from an uncle, or a cross cousin from a parallel cousin. Only man can commit the crime of incest or adultery; only he can remember the Sabbath and keep it Holy. It is not, as we well know, that the lower animals can do these things but to a lesser degree than ourselves; they cannot perform these acts of appreciation and distinction *at all.* It is, as Descartes said long ago, "not only that the brutes have less Reason than man, but that they have none at all." . . .

A symbol may be defined as a thing the value or meaning of which is bestowed upon it by those who use it. I say "thing" because a symbol may have any kind of physical form; it may have the form of a material object, a color, a sound, an odor, a motion of an object, a taste.

The meaning, or value, of a symbol is in no instance derived from or determined by properties intrinsic in its physical form: the color appropriate to mourning may be yellow, green, or any other color; purple need not be the color of royalty; among the Manchu rulers of

China it was yellow. The meaning of the word "see" is not intrinsic in its phonetic (or pictorial) properties. . . . The meaning of symbols are derived from and determined by the organisms who use them; meaning is bestowed by human organisms upon physical things or events which thereupon become symbols. Symbols "have their signification," to use John Locke's phrase, "from the arbitrary imposition of men."

All symbols must have a physical form otherwise they could not enter our experience. . . . But the meaning of a symbol cannot be discovered by mere sensory examination of its physical form. One cannot tell by looking at an *x* in an algebraic equation what it stands for; one cannot ascertain with the ears alone the symbolic value of the phonetic compound *si;* one cannot tell merely by weighing a pig how much gold he will exchange for; one cannot tell from the wave length of a color whether it stands for courage or cowardice, "stop" or "go"; nor can one discover the spirit in a fetish by any amount of physical or chemical examination. The meaning of a symbol can be grasped only by non-sensory, symbolic means. . . .

We define a *sign* as a physical thing or event whose function is to indicate some other thing or event. The meaning of a sign may be inherent in its physical form and its context, as in the case of the height of a column of mercury in a thermometer as an indication of temperature, or the return of robins in the spring. Or, the meaning of a sign may be merely identified with its physical form as in the case of a hurricane signal or a quarantine flag. But in either case, the meaning of the sign may be ascertained by sensory means. The fact that a thing may be both a symbol (in one context) and a sign (in another context) has led to confusion and misunderstanding.

Thus Darwin says: "That which distinguishes man from the lower animals is not the understanding of articulate sounds, for as everyone knows, dogs understand many words and sentences," (ch. III, *The Descent of Man*). . . .

The man differs from the dog—and all other creatures—in that *he can and does play an active role in determining what value the vocal stimulus is to have, and the dog cannot*. The dog does not and cannot play an active part in determining the value of the vocal stimulus. Whether he is to roll over or go fetch at a given stimulus, or whether the stimulus for roll over be one combination of sounds or another is a matter in which the dog has nothing whatever to "say." He plays a purely passive role and can do nothing else. He learns the meaning of a vocal command just as his salivary glands may learn to respond to the sound of a bell. But man plays an active role and thus becomes a creator: let *x* equal three pounds of coal and it does equal three pounds of coal; let removal of the hat in a house of worship indicate respect and it becomes so. This creative faculty, that of freely, actively, and arbitrarily bestowing value upon things, is one of the most commonplace as well as *the* most important characteristic of man. Children employ it freely in their play: "Let's pretend that this rock is a wolf."

The difference between the behavior of man and other animals then, is that the lower animals may receive new values, may acquire new meanings, but they cannot create and bestow them. Only man can do this. To use a crude analogy, lower animals are like a person who has only the receiving apparatus for wireless messages: he can receive messages but cannot send them. Man can do both. And this difference is one of kind, not of degree: a creature can either "arbitrarily impose signification," can either create and bestow values, or he cannot. There are no intermediate stages. This difference may appear slight, but, as a carpenter once told William James in discussing differences between men, "It's very important." All *human* existence depends upon it and it alone. . . .

All culture (civilization) depends upon the symbol. It was the exercise of the symbolic faculty that brought culture into existence and it is the use of symbols that makes the perpetuation of culture possible. Without the symbol there would be no culture, and man would be merely an animal, not a human being.

Articulate speech is the most important form of symbolic expression. Remove speech from culture and what would remain? Let us see.

Without articulate speech we would have no *human* social organization. Families we might have, but this form of organization is not peculiar to man; it is not *per se,* human. But we would have no prohibitions of incest, no rules prescribing exogamy and endogamy, polygamy or monogamy. How could marriage with a cross cousin be prescribed, marriage with a parallel cousin proscribed, without articulate speech? How could rules which prohibit plural mates possessed simultaneously but permit them if possessed one at a time, exist without speech?

Without speech we would have no political, economic, ecclesiastic, or military organization; no codes of etiquette or ethics; no laws; no science, theology, or literature; no games or music, except on an ape level. Rituals and ceremonial paraphernalia would be meaningless without articulate speech. Indeed, without articulate speech we would be all but toolless: we would have only the occasional and insignificant use of the tool such as we find today among the higher apes, for it was articulate speech that transformed the non-progressive tool-using of the ape into the progressive, cumulative tool-using of man, the human being.

In short, without symbolic communication in some form, we would have no culture. "In the Word was the beginning" of culture—and its perpetuation also.

To be sure, with all his culture man is still an animal and strives for the same ends that all other living creatures strive for: the preservation of the individual and the perpetuation of the race. In concrete terms these ends are food, shelter from the elements, defense from enemies, health, and offspring. The fact that man strives for these ends just as all other animals do has, no doubt, led many to declare that there is "no fundamental difference between the behavior of man and of other creatures." But man does differ, not in *ends* but in *means*. Man's means are cultural means: culture is simply the human animal's way of living. And, since these means, culture, are dependent upon a faculty possessed by man alone, the ability to use symbols, the difference between the behavior of man and of all other creatures is not merely great, but basic and fundamental.

The behavior of man is of two distinct kinds: symbolic and non-symbolic. Man yawns, stretches, coughs, scratches himself, cries out in pain, shrinks with fear, "bristles" with anger, and so on. Non-symbolic behavior of this sort is not peculiar to man; he shares it not only with the other primates but with many other animal species as well. But man communicates with his fellows with articulate speech, uses amulets, confesses sins, makes laws, observes codes of etiquette, explains his dreams, classifies his relatives in designated categories, and so on. This kind of behavior is unique; only man is capable of it; it is peculiar to man because it consists of, or is dependent upon, the use of symbols. The non-symbolic behavior of *Homo sapiens* is the behavior of man the animal; the symbolic behavior is that of man the human being. It is the symbol which has transformed man from a mere animal to a human animal. . . .

As it was the symbol that made *mankind* human, so it is with each member of the species. A baby is not a *human* being until he begins to symbol. Until the infant begins to talk there is nothing to distinguish his behavior qualitatively from that of a very young ape, as *The Ape and the Child* showed. As a matter of fact, one of the impressive results of this fascinating experiment by Professor and Mrs. Kellogg was the demonstration of how ape-like an infant of Homo sapiens is before he begins to talk. The baby boy acquired exceptional proficiency in climbing in association with the little chimpanzee, and even acquired her "food bark"! The Kelloggs speak of how the little ape became "humanized" during her sojourn in their home. But what the experiment demonstrated so conclusively was the ape's utter inability to learn to talk or even to make *any* progress in this direction—in short, her inability to become "humanized" at all.

The infant of the species *Homo sapiens* becomes human only when and as he exercises his symbol faculty. Only through articulate speech—not necessarily vocal—can he enter the world of human beings and take part in their affairs. The questions asked earlier may be repeated now. How could a growing child know and appreciate such things as social organization, ethics, etiquette, ritual, science, religion, art and games without symbolic communication? The answer is of course that he could know nothing of these things and have no appreciation of them at all. . . .

Children who have been cut off from human intercourse for years by blindness and deafness but who have eventually effected communication with their fellows on a symbolic level are exceedingly illuminating. The case of Helen Keller is exceptionally instructive, although those of Laura Bridgman, Marie Heurtin, and others are very valuable also.

Helen Keller was rendered blind and deaf at an early age by illness. She grew up as a child without symbolic contact with anyone. Descriptions of her at the age of seven, the time at which her teacher, Miss Sullivan, came to her home, disclosed no *human* attributes of Helen's behavior at all. She was a headstrong, undisciplined and unruly little animal.

Within a day or so after her arrival at the Keller home, Miss Sullivan taught Helen her first word, spelling it into her hand. But this word was merely a sign, not a symbol. A week later Helen knew several words but, as Miss Sullivan reports, she had "no idea how to use them or that everything has a name." Within three weeks Helen knew eighteen nouns and three verbs. But she was still on the level of signs; she still had no notion "that everything has a name."

Helen confused the word signs for "mug" and "water" because, apparently, both were associated with drinking. Miss Sullivan made a few attempts to clear up this confusion but without success. One morning, however, about a month after Miss Sullivan's arrival, the two went out to the pump in the garden. What happened then is best told in their own words:

> I made Helen hold her mug under the spout while I pumped. As the cold water gushed forth, filling the mug, I spelled "w-a-t-e-r" into Helen's free hand. The word coming so close upon the sensation of cold water rushing over her hand seemed to startle her. She dropped the mug and stood as one transfixed. A new light came into her face. She spelled "water" several times. Then she dropped on the ground and asked for its name and pointed to the pump and the trellis, and suddenly turning round she asked for my name . . . *In a few hours she had added thirty new words to her vocabulary.*

But these words were now more than mere signs as they are to a dog and as they had been to Helen up to then. They were *symbols*. Helen had at last grasped and turned the key that admitted her for the first time to a new universe: the world of human beings. Helen describes this marvellous experience herself:

> We walked down the path to the well-house, attracted by the fragrance of the honeysuckle with which it was covered. Someone was drawing water and my teacher placed my hand under the spout. As the cool stream gushed over one hand she spelled into the other the word *water,* first slowly, then rapidly. I stood still, my whole attention fixed upon the motion of her fingers. Suddenly I felt a misty consciousness as of something forgotten—a thrill of returning thought; and somehow *the mystery of language was revealed to me.* I knew then that "w-a-t-e-r" meant the wonderful cool something that was flowing over my hand. That living word awakened my soul, gave it light, hope, joy, set it free!

Helen was transformed on the instant by this experience. Miss Sullivan had managed to touch Helen's symbol mechanism and set it in motion. Helen, on her part, grasped the external world with this mechanism that had lain dormant and inert all these years, sealed in dark and silent isolation by eyes that could not see and ears that heard not. But now she had crossed the boundary and entered a new land. Henceforth her progress would be rapid.

"I left the well-house," Helen reports, "eager to learn. Everything had a name, and each name gave birth to a new thought. As we returned to the house every object which I touched seemed to quiver with life. That was because I saw everything with the strange new sight that had come to me."

Helen became humanized rapidly. "I see an improvement in Helen from day to day," Miss Sullivan wrote in her diary, *"almost from hour to hour*. Everything must have a name now . . . She drops the signs and pantomime she used before as soon as she has words to supply their place . . . We notice her face grows more expressive each day . . ."

A more eloquent and convincing account of the significance of symbols and of the great gulf between the human mind and that of minds without symbols could hardly be imagined.

The natural processes of biologic evolution brought into existence in man, and man alone, a new and distinctive ability: the ability to use symbols. The most important form of symbolic expression is articulate speech. Articulate speech means communication of ideas; communication means preservation—tradition—and preservation means accumulation and progress. The emergence of the faculty of symboling has resulted in the genesis of a new order of phenomena: an extra-somatic, cultural order. All civilizations are born of, and are perpetuated by, the use of symbols. A culture, or civilization, is but a particular kind of form which the biologic, life-perpetuating activities of a particular animal, man, assume.

Human behavior is symbolic behavior; if it is not symbolic, it is not human. The infant of the genus *Homo* becomes a human being only as he is introduced into and participates in that order of phenomena which is culture. And the key to this world and the means of participation in it is—the symbol.

7. The Nature of Language

HARRY HOIJER

All languages have structure, involving limited number of sounds, limited arrangements of sounds, unit expressions of meaning, and orderly arrangements of parts. All languages select a small number out of the infinite possible forms that utterances might take. The structure of a language at any one time and place tends to be consistent, though obviously it varies from place to place and from time to time. This essay sets forth the features that characterize all languages and shows how they operate; it also indicates in what ways they vary.

Harry Hoijer is Professor of Anthropology at the University of California, Los Angeles. He studied anthropological linguistics under Edward Sapir at the University of Chicago, receiving his doctorate in anthropology in 1931. His research has been chiefly with the structure of Navaho and related members of the Athapascan family of languages, but he has published widely on anthropological and linguistic subjects.

Language is so much a part of our daily activities that some of us may come to look upon it as a more or less automatic and natural act like breathing or winking. Of course, if we give the matter any thought at all, we must realize that there is nothing automatic about language. Children must be taught their native tongue and the necessary training takes a long time. Language is not something that is inherited; it is an art that can be passed on from one generation to the next only by intensive education.

It is difficult to realize the enormously important role that language plays in our social behavior. What would a society without language be like? It would of course have no writing or other means of communication by words, for all these are ultimately dependent on spoken speech. Our means of learning would therefore be greatly restricted. We should be obliged, like the animals, to learn by doing or by observing the actions of others. All of history would disappear, for without language there would be no way of re-creating past experiences and communicating them to others. We should have no means of expressing our thoughts and ideas to others or of sharing in the mental processes of our fellowmen. Indeed, it is very likely that we should not think at all. Many psychologists maintain that thought itself requires the use of language, that the process of thinking is really talking things over with ourselves.

A society lacking language would be incapable of engaging in any but the simplest of co-operative enterprises. An individual or group of individuals would have no way of planning such activities, of explaining them to others, or of directing the actions of the participants in co-operative enterprises toward the common goal. Each individual would be to a large extent dependent on his own strength and ability since he would lack the means of securing the help of others.

Most important, a society lacking language would have no means of assuring the continuity of behavior and learning necessary to the creation of culture. Human society, without culture, would be reduced to the level of present-day ape societies. Apes have a bodily structure very like our own. Like humans, they learn readily from experience and by observing and imitating the actions of others. A number of experimenters have shown that apes not only learn to use tools but also invent them. Despite, however, the fact that individual apes learn easily and, as individuals, show remarkable progress in the acquisition of knowledge, apes as a species have never developed a culture.

There are two reasons for this. Lacking language, the apes have no way of continuing in word and thought their separate experiences in the use of tools and techniques. When an ape has disposed of a problem the knowledge he has derived from that experience remains static. He may remember it when and if another problem of the same sort arises, but he does not in between times mull over his knowledge and devise means of applying it to further problems. Man does. His overt experiences with practical problems are, like those of the ape, separate and distinct. But because man possesses language, he can continue his problem-solving activities beyond the actual physical experience and so develop, in thought and discussion, new applications of his knowledge and improved means of solving problems. In short, by reason of language, man's experiences are continuous, not discontinuous as among apes, and so show far more rapid development.

Secondly, man's possession of language enables him to share the experiences and thoughts of his fellows and to re-create his personal experiences for their benefit. An ape's knowledge, acquired through experience and observation, is his alone, except in so far as he can demonstrate it in physical activity so that it may be acquired by another ape. No matter how skillful an ape may become in the use of tools and techniques, his offspring will be obliged to begin their learning as he began his, by experience and observation. The learned ape cannot communicate his knowledge and so enable his successors to build upon it. Culture among men reveals progress. Each generation takes over, by word of mouth and tradition, the accumulated knowledge of their predecessors, add their own contributions as drawn from their experiences and observations, and pass the whole on to succeeding generations. This cumulative aspect, which differentiates human cultures from the kind of knowledge current in animal societies, is made possible by language.

The Antiquity of Language

Studies of the skeletal and cultural remains of ancient man have shown that the first human beings came into being about one million years ago. Man's early cultures were very simple and crude and we know only a portion of their material remains, the tools and implements made of materials tough enough to withstand the passage of time. It is highly significant, however, that these early traces of man's cultures reveal a cultural continuity through time. As we study the several chronological phases of culture in any given area of the world, there is revealed a slow but steady advance both in the number of tools made and in the complexity of their manufacture. The men of successive generations did not begin anew each generation to fashion their cultures but built upon the techniques which had been discovered in the past and transmitted to them by their ancestors.

The fact that the history of man's cultures shows a continuous and cumulative development extending from their earliest beginnings to the present means of course that man has possessed language as long as he has possessed culture. Language must be as old as the oldest of man's cultural artifacts; it began when culture began and has developed continuously ever since.

This inference as to the age of language is amply borne out by other observations which may be made on modern languages. First, it is clear that all human societies have possessed a language for as long as we have known them; there is no group of men anywhere, today or in the past, who lack this important aspect of culture. Secondly, we may also observe that modern languages are very numerous and exceedingly diverse. The precise number of distinct languages spoken today cannot even be estimated, but we know that there are several thousand. Some of these are historically related to one another; that is, they are clearly derived from a single earlier tongue. Languages so derived are said to belong to the same linguistic family or stock, and there are hundreds of such stocks in the world today. Most of these stocks show no resemblance whatsoever to each other, because, as we may almost certainly assume, all traces of common origin have long since disappeared.

The universality of language and the amazing diversity of modern idioms can only mean that language is very old. Studies of languages known for centuries through the medium of written records reveal that languages change with relative slowness. Thus, though English and German have certainly been separate languages for well over 2000 years, they still retain many obvious similarities in both vocabulary and grammar which point clearly to their common origin. The enormous diversity of modern languages, then, must have taken a very long time to achieve.

A third and final evidence as to the antiquity of language is found in the fact that known languages, ancient or modern, cannot be classed in terms of their level of development. There are neither primitive languages nor highly developed ones, if we take into account only their structural features.

Thus, all the languages we know possess a well-defined system of distinctive speech sounds. These are finite in number, are carefully distinguished from one another, and are put together to form words, phrases, and sentences in accordance with definite rules. In this respect, there is no real difference between the languages of people who possess very simple and crude cultures and those of the highly civilized peoples of Europe and America.

Similarly, all human groups, regardless of the crudity of their culture, have a vocabulary sufficiently detailed and comprehensive to meet every need likely to arise. Languages vary, of course, in the size of their vocabularies, but this variation is cultural, not linguistic. The language of a people having a relatively simple or undeveloped culture may have a smaller vocabulary than one belonging to a group with a relatively complex and highly developed culture. It is notable, however, that the vocabulary of any group, however simple its culture, appears to be indefinitely expansible. As new cultural items are invented or borrowed, the vocabulary increases or changes to meet the new requirements imposed upon it.

Finally, all languages possess a definite and clear-cut system of grammar. Grammar may briefly be defined as the meaningful arrangement of sounds or combinations of sounds to produce words, phrases, and sentences. Well-defined rules governing such arrangements are found in all languages, whether they are spoken by the pre-literate Pygmies of the Congo forest or the culturally advanced groups of modern Europe.

The basic similarities mean, of course, that language has so long been a human possession as to have developed to about the same level among peoples the world over. There remain today no traces of an earlier and cruder stage of linguistic development.

The Origin of Language

Spoken languages obviously leave no trace in the ancient deposits which mark the history of man's cultures. Written records of human languages began only a few thousand years ago; before that time no human group possessed the technique of writing. It is evident, then, that we have no direct evidence as to the origin of language or of the long period of history that elapsed between its beginnings and the first written records. The problem of the origin of language will never therefore be solved in the sense that we shall know directly the circumstances under which language arose or be able to trace in terms of specific historical events the course of its development.

Many theories have been advanced as to the origin of language. Most of these, however, are based on two central hypotheses: the interjectional and the sound imitative or onomatopoeic theory of the origin of language.

Interjectional theories maintain, in general, that interjections or involuntary cries, because these are a good deal alike in all modern tongues, form the earliest stratum of words used by man. All other forms, it follows, must have been derived from these in one or other manner. Sound imitative theories look to words like *bow wow, meow, choo choo,* or *ding dong,* and similar attempts by men to imitate animal cries and noises as marking the beginnings of language. From such imitations of sounds encountered in his environment, man formed the hundreds of languages we now find spoken.

Both hypotheses fail to solve our problem, however, largely because they fail to account for true linguistic forms. Neither involuntary cries nor sound imitative words are as such true linguistic forms. An involuntary cry is really part of an individual's response to strong stimuli. The involuntary ejaculation of surprise is not the same as the conventional word written *Oh!* because the former represents part of the response itself and does not, like the conventional *Oh!,* symbolize the response of surprise. True linguistic symbols, such as words, are all conventional and arbitrary, and their meanings must be learned by speakers. No one learns an involuntary cry; a baby may cry out long before it learns to speak.

Sound imitative words must similarly not be confused with attempts to reproduce sounds characteristic of man's environment. A word like *ding dong,* for example, is a conventionalized representation of the sound of a bell, not necessarily self-evident to anyone except a speaker of English who has learned to associate the sound *ding dong* with the ringing of bells. To understand how languages came into being we must know how man came to establish his arbitrary or conventional habits of associating speech sounds with experience. This is not explained by the sound imitative hypothesis which points out merely that men sometimes name things and actions by the noises they make and that on occasion such names become truly a part of language.

It follows, then, that a useful theory of linguistic origins must be based on a more careful analysis and study of modern tongues. Such studies, as we have suggested, reveal that the elements of speech, such as words, phrases, and sentences, are arbitrary symbols. By this we mean symbols which are themselves no part of the reality or experience symbolized. Thus, for example, the particular succession of sounds which make up the word *horse* have no necessary relation to the class of animals symbolized by it. There is, in short, nothing horse-like about the word *horse;* it is simply that speakers of English have learned to associate the sounds written *horse* with a given class of animal, just as they have learned to associate the forms *dog* and *cat* with wholly different groups of animals.

The fact that linguistic symbols are nearly all arbitrary in nature emphasizes the social aspect of language. Languages are always associated with groups of individuals; they never belong exclusively to a single individual. An individual acquires his language from the group with which he lives. If he deviates widely in speech from other members of the group, he runs the risk of being misunderstood or of not being understood at all. *Horse* is not just a word peculiar to an individual speaker of English, it is a word used and understood in much the same way by all English-speaking peoples.

Languages function in human societies primarily as a means of communication and co-operation. By means of language an individual is able not only to re-create his own personal experiences and so share them with others, but he is also able to co-ordinate his labors with those of others. A group of men can thus work together in a task too heavy or too complex to be undertaken by any one of them singly. To exemplify this point, let us imagine that a man, hunting alone, manages to kill an animal too large for him to handle. He leaves the dead animal and returns to his encampment or village. There he tells the others what he has done and secures their assistance. They return to his kill with him and assist him to skin the game, cut up the meat, and carry it back to camp. During the whole of this procedure, one individual may take charge, indicating in words the task each is to perform, so that the separate acts of each man will assist rather than obstruct the total performance.

Contrast the action we have just described with a similar incident among, let us say, a pack of wolves. Here, too, we have a social group albeit one composed of animals who lack language. When one of the wolves makes a kill alone, he will eat as much as he can; he will not be concerned or able to inform the pack of his feat. But should the other wolves come upon him as he makes the kill or while he is eating the carcass, they will certainly join him uninvited. Each wolf will get as much as he can and if there is not enough to go around, the weaker wolves will get none at all. The actions of the wolves in disposing of the meat will be separate and individual, with no co-ordination or co-operation whatsoever.

It is probable that the ancient animals from whom man evolved lived in groups very similar to those of present-day animals. Their behavior was only in a small degree co-ordinated. Each worked for himself alone, with the exception that the very young had to be cared for by an adult. On occasion, however, necessity must have enforced some degree of co-operation and co-ordinated effort. Man's primitive ancestor was not a formidable animal in comparison with many others who shared his environment. He must often have had to defend himself against stronger predatory animals and he probably discovered very early that such defense was more effective if undertaken in co-operation with his fellows. When such co-operative enterprises increased in frequency, the habit pattern built up may easily have led to co-operation under other circumstances, such as, for example, the hunting of large animals for food. Even wolves hunt together and, while so doing, correlate their efforts, at least to some degree.

The development of co-operative labor did not alone bring about language, however. Many insect groups are effectively co-operative without language. But co-operation among insects is evidently on a different basis than among men. Unlike the social insects men are not born to a given role in their social groups. Men must learn to adapt their behavior to the roles provided by the society, and language provides a vital tool to this kind of learning.

How and in what way man's animal ancestors came to employ language as an aid in co-operative labor we shall never know. We may safely assume, however, that man's primitive ancestor could and did make noises and perhaps the noises which accompanied the task undertaken together came slowly to symbolize the several actions and ends involved in such tasks. In any case, it appears to be fairly certain that language arose as a result of men learning to work together toward a common end. For whatever reasons, man's primitive ancestors were obliged to acquire such learning, and so they, alone of the animals, stumbled upon the tool, language, which more than any other makes co-operative and co-ordinated activity effective.

The Structure of Language

Languages, like many other cultural phenomena, cannot be observed or studied directly. Just as we can decribe a method of making baskets only by observing the actions of individuals who are weaving them, so can we describe a language only by observing the speech behavior of those who use the language.

Individual acts of speech are called utterances. These are complete in themselves and consist of a flow of speech sounds uninterrupted by the speech of another individual. Some utterances may be quite short, like *Oh!, Come!, Who?,* or *John.* Others are longer: *John runs, I see a man,* or *The man we saw yesterday is dead.* Still others may be very long, examples of these are found in speeches, lectures, or sermons. A first step in studying a language is then to collect utterances, as many as possible, from native speakers of the language.

Once this has been done, it soon becomes obvious that utterances differ not only in length but also in structure. Some of them consist of a single unit which cannot be interrupted without considerable change in meaning. If, for example, we say *John runs?,* it is evident that the forms *John* and *runs* are interdependent. To stop after we have said *John* is like playing an unresolved chord on the piano; the listener awaits impatiently the completion of the utterance. We can of course say *John? Runs?* but here we create a new meaning, quite different from that of *John runs? . . .*

The total stock of words possessed by a language is called its vocabulary or dictionary. Languages differ as to the size of their vocabularies. In general the size of a vocabulary is directly related to the culture of a speech community. If the culture is complex, as among most English-speaking peoples, the vocabulary may be very large and contain numerous highly technical sub-divisions. In a simple and relatively uniform culture, such as that of the Polar Eskimo, the vocabulary will be correspondingly smaller and contain fewer technical aspects. It should not be assumed, however, that so-called primitive peoples have very small vocabularies. We frequently hear, for example, of very primitive folk whose languages possess at most only a few hundred words. This is obvious nonsense for even the simplest culture requires a far greater number of words merely to enumerate the many objects and acts dealt with in the course of every-day occupations.

When we examine the vocabulary of a language and compare the words it contains with one another we soon discover that words, like sentences and utterances, also vary in size and complexity. Take for example English pairs like *dog, dogs; work, worker; black, blackish; combine, recombine; do, undo. Dogs* is obviously derived from *dog* by the addition of *-s, worker* from *work* by adding *-er, blackish* from *black* by adding *-ish, recombine* from *combine* by adding *re-,* and *undo* from *do* by adding *un-*. Each of the added elements conveys meaning: *-s* denotes the plural, *-er* means 'one who,' *-ish* means 'something like' (that is, a blackish object is one which is colored something like one which is black), *re-* means 'to do something again' (in this case, to combine again), and *un-* conveys a negative or opposite meaning (to undo a knot is the opposite or negative of 'doing' or tying a knot). These added elements are not words, however, because they are never spoken alone but always in combination with some other form (either a whole word or part of a word). Some words may contain more than one such element, each adding a measure of meaning to the completed word. Thus, the word *ungentlemanly* is formed by adding *un-* (not) to *gentlemanly. Gentlemanly,* in turn, consists of *gentleman* plus the ending *-ly,* meaning 'in such and such a way or manner.' Finally, *gentleman* is itself composed of *gentle* plus *man* though the meaning of the combination is no longer the same as the sum of the meanings of its two constituent parts.

Words and parts of words like *dog, -s, work, -er, combine, re-, black, -ish, do,* and *un-* are called simple linguistic forms or morphemes. Some morphemes, like *dog* and *work,* may be pronounced alone; these are called free morphemes. Others, like *-ish* and *un-,* are never pronounced alone and are therefore called bound morphemes. Combinations containing more than one morpheme, such as *dogs* or *worker,* are complex linguistic forms. Complex linguistic forms also include phrases, sentences, and utterances, however. Words having more than one morpheme are usually described as derived words or derivations.

Languages differ greatly in word structure. In some of them, Chinese is a good example, most words have but one morpheme; derivations are extremely rare. In others, like English, there may be many single morpheme words plus a large number of words having two or three morphemes and a smaller number having more than three morphemes. Languages like Navaho or Eskimo are found at the opposite extreme in so far as word structure is concerned for here we may find large numbers of so-called polysynthetic words possessing as many as eight or ten or even more morphemes. . . .

Languages differ widely in grammar. In English sentences of the type *he runs,* for example, the verb *runs* has an ending *-s* because the pronoun is singular and third person. With pronouns like *I, you, we,* and *they,* we use *run,* not *runs.* Similarly, we say *a man runs* but *men run.* Grammarians express this rule of grammar by saying that third person forms of present tense verbs must agree in number with the pronoun or noun which precedes them. If the noun or pronoun is singular, the verb is also (as in *he runs, a man runs*) but when the noun or pronoun is plural, so also is the verb (*they run, men run*).

In German, however, the matter of grammatical agreement between pronoun and verb in the present tense is more complicated. Here, very often, we find a different verb form for every pronoun as in *ich laufe* 'I run,' *du läufst* 'you run,' *er läuft* 'he runs,' and *wir laufen* 'we run.'

Similar differences occur in English and German nouns. In English, the definite article *the* is used before almost any noun, as in *the man, the woman,* and *the maiden.* The German definite article, however, is different in each of these cases: *der Mann* 'the (masculine gender) man,' *die Frau* 'the (feminine gender) woman,' and *das Mädschen* 'the (neuter gender) maiden.'

A final step in understanding linguistic structure is to compare morphemes with one another. Such comparison reveals that morphemes are composed of distinctive sounds called phonemes. Thus in English it is obvious that the morphemes *cat* and *pat* are alike except for the initial phoneme, that *cat* and *cot* differ only in their medial phoneme, and that *cat* and *cap* are distinguished by their final phonemes. *Cat,* then is composed of three phonemes and any change in any one of them will change *cat* to some other English morpheme or to an English-like nonsense word (for example *cet*).

The same thing is true of all other languages, that is, in all languages morphemes are built up of one or more phonemes. Languages vary greatly, however, in the complexity of their morphemes and in the kinds of phonemes they may employ. In some languages, morphemes may be very simple, in others the average morpheme may include a relatively large number of phonemes. Similarly, the kinds of phonemes employed, even in languages closely related may be quite different in pronunciation. Thus the German phoneme written *ch* (as in *buch* 'book,' or *lachen* 'to laugh') is quite unknown in English; our closest sound is *h,* a very weak imitation of the harsher German *ch.*

The number of phonemes employed in a language is usually quite small, rarely exceeding thirty. These are of course used over and over again to produce a great variety of morphemes. The following English morphemes illustrate this point; the eighteen morphemes listed employ only six phonemes: *man, map, mat, mass, nan, pan, tam, sam, pat, pap, gnat* (pronounced *nat*), *sap, tap, sat, nap, pass, tan, tat.*

It may be noted, however, that not all the possible combinations of the six phonemes are actually employed in English. Thus combinations like *san, tas,* and *nam* have no meaning in English; they are English-like nonsense words. Other combinations, like *psa, pnt, nmt,* or *psn,* however, are not at all like English words; indeed, all of them involve habits of pronunciation so different from those employed by a speaker of English that he would regard the forms as wholly unpronounceable.

It is clear, then, that the phonemes of a language must be combined according to definite rules. Each language has such rules of combination which are observed strictly by those who speak the language as a mother tongue, and which may differ markedly from the rules characteristic of other languages.

Linguistic Change

From what has been said about linguistic structure we might easily get the idea that the habits of speech characteristic of a given community always remain the same. This is not true, however. All languages are in reality undergoing constant change. . . .

The discovery that languages change led to a method of classifying languages. English, as we have seen, does not really refer to only one language but to a whole group of languages or dialects broadly alike but differing in many details of pronunciation, grammar, and vocabulary. Linguists express this by saying that the modern English languages are descendants of a single common ancestral English and so belong to a single 'family' of languages. Each of the modern idioms is the ancestral English plus those changes in pronunciation, grammar, and vocabulary peculiar to the area in which it is spoken. Actually, of course, this statement is not precisely accurate historically for we know that the older forms of English were also dialectically divided. Some of the modern dialects may have developed from one dialect of the early period, others from quite a different one. . . .

A linguistic stock . . . is a group of modern and ancient tongues between which there exist a large number of similarities and systematic differences in pronunciation, grammar, and vocabulary, too great to be explained by chance or borrowing. The member languages of such a stock are said to be derived from a single ancestral form, usually called the prototype language of the group. Thus, the languages of the Germanic stock, such as English, German, Dutch, Swedish, Norwegian, Danish, and a number of less important idioms, are modern descendants of a theoretical or assumed language called Proto-Germanic. We have no records of Proto-Germanic for our written records do not go back far enough in time.

In a few rare instances, however, we may verify an historical classification of this type. Thus, for example, we note that French, Spanish, Italian, Roumanian, and a number of other languages exhibit the same kind of similarities and systematic differences found in the Germanic group. They are for that reason classed as members of the Romance stock and are said to be derived from a language called Proto-Romanic.

But here we have historical records which confirm, in part at least, the inferences drawn from our comparison of the modern languages. These reveal that Latin, once spoken only in the city of Rome and its environs, was spread throughout much of southern and western Europe by the developing Roman Empire. When first established, these outlying colonies spoke much the same language as Rome. Each of the colonies and Rome, however, modified their Latin in the course of time and since they were more or less isolated from one another these changes were largely independent of each other. As time went on, the changes became progressively greater until today the modern Romance tongues are not only different from Latin but also differ markedly from each other. Such resemblances as still exist between the Romance languages are due to the fact that all of them are connected by a continuous tradition to Latin. Spanish, Italian, French, Portuguese, Roumanian, and the other Romance languages are, then, modern versions of Latin, each characteristic of the population of a particular region in Europe. . . .

8. Communication among the Lower Primates

CLARENCE R. CARPENTER

Apes and monkeys communicate with one another by the use of vocal sounds. The sounds they use have significance to the one who uses them and to their fellows who hear them. In this they are like languages. The limitations of these vocal patterns are clear; nor do we find any evidence of syntax of "symboling" of the kind that exists in all human languages. Considering that the gibbon, one of the four great apes, is about as close biologically to man as any living thing, the great gulf between its use of sound and that of the most primitive known man is indeed remarkable.

The essay that follows is by Clarence R. Carpenter who recorded the vocalizations of gibbons in the field while studying their social behavior in their native Siamese jungle. Carpenter, who is Head of the Department of Psychology and Director of Instructional Research Project in Closed-circuit TV at Pennsylvania State University, made a similar study of howler monkeys in Panama. He is currently devoting himself to the study of human communication as it takes place in motion pictures and television. The essay here is taken from "A Field Study in Science of the Behavior and Social Relations of the Gibbon (*Hylobates Lar*)," *Comparative Psychology Monographs,* Volume 16, No. 5, 1940, and is reproduced by kind permission of the publisher and author.

. . . Clearly the only way that an observer has of arriving at the meaning or function of a gesture or pattern of sound produced by an animal is to use the response of associated animals as an indicator. The situation in which the call is given and the response made must also be considered and interpreted. Technically, the problems of studying vocal expressions in primates and their stimulus values may be stated as follows: 1. To describe the stimulus situation in which the vocal pattern occurs, i.e., the specific patterns of stimuli which call forth the vocalization, 2. To describe and measure the sound patterns produced, 3. To describe the responses of associated animals of the same and of other groups including groups of other species. . . .

In order to study more completely and objectively the vocalizations of gibbons, recording equipment was used in the Siamese study. A Presto

Recorder with play-back attachment, high fidelity recording head, batteries (two 12 volts), transformer, semi-portable parabolic reflector, a directional microphone and 300 feet of cable comprised the essential equipment for making recordings on double-face acetate disks. This equipment was set up in the forest near feeding places, abode trees and trails where gibbon groups had been observed repeatedly. The reflector and microphones could be shifted about a 300-foot radius from the machine and were placed as near as possible and directed toward the known location of gibbons; it was necessary only to wait until calls began to start making recordings. Once I mounted the parabolic reflector on the top of a precipitous cliff face about 100 feet high and directed it out over the forest for picking up calls from several groups located in the valley below. At another time the reflector and microphone were so placed as to have a cliff act as a kind of sounding board to reflect and amplify the sound patterns. It was found possible by using the equipment described above to record most of the *distant sound responses* or vocalizations of gibbons.

Limitations of the procedure involved: 1. Extreme difficulty in handling the rather complex equipment with native laborers as assistants, 2. Impossibility of making recordings of *low volume sounds* such as the intra-group vocalizations, 3. Difficulty of analyzing the sounds once they had been recorded. . . .

The table lists nine types of the more prominent and more easily differentiated sound patterns produced by gibbons. In all probability, further study will more clearly define these types, differentiate others and show sound qualities which are common to some of them. Their functions are extremely difficult to infer and controlled laboratory experiments are urgently needed for further analysis. The fact is clear that these vocalizations as well as other sound patterns not only express excitement in an individual but also they have communicative, signaling value or instrumental value. . . .

In gibbons as well as in howler monkeys, the prominent type of calls by which the two species are best known, have been found to function in *competitive situations*. The barking roars of howlers, like the Type I . . . series of calls made by gibbons, are produced when two or more groups come together, compete for food or for their established territory. In most situations where rhesus monkeys would fight or make bluffing, driving attacks, howlers, gibbons and siamangs roar or call back and forth between competing groups. Vocalizations of the kind

Vocalization of the Gibbon

Type	Stimulus Situations	Subjects	Vocal Pattern
I	a. During travel of group from focus of Territory b. Another nearby group c. Following Type III calls in alarm situations	Adult males or adult females, more frequently the latter, usually individually	A series of hoots with rising inflection, rising pitch, increasing tempo with climax followed by 2 or 3 notes of lower pitch. Duration 12-22 seconds
II	a. Early morning b. Sometimes while group is moving	Adult males	Single discrete calls, a series but may be repeated over and over. Similar to beginning notes of Type I calls
III	When group is surprised by a hunter, observer or possible enemy	Adult males, adult females, and juveniles, often together	A loud, high pitched note. A shout. Repeated but not in original series
IV	When a member of a group gets lost. Toward the end of a period of alarm calls when group is scattered	Adult males, adult females, juveniles	Single note with rising inflection. Seems questioning at times
V	Not known	Adult males, adult females	High pitched, distinctive. Several seconds duration. Given in series of 3 to 12
VI	When a group is closely pressed by observer or hunter and greatly annoyed	Adult males, adult females	Deep throated growl
VII	Play situation or when making friendly approach	Young animals	Little chirp or squeal
VIII	Disturbed situation, confinement in captivity	Young animals	Fretting cry
IX	During group progression	Adult leading	Chatter or series of clucks

mentioned are clearly observed to act as buffers to fighting, and actually substitute for fighting as a secondary means of inter-group social control. In addition to the fact that these loud sounds have stimulus values which cause withdrawal, loud sounds may produce startle and avoid-

in Their Native Habitat

Animals Responding	Responses	Probable Functions
Other groups or individuals of same group	Other groups: same vocalizations; at times withdrawal. Same group: Same vocalizations, orientation, rapid swings on high pitched climax	Exploration. Defensive actions. Protection of territory
Animals in neighboring groups	Other groups: similar calls, simultaneously or alternately	Localizes group in its territory. Avoids conflicts
Mainly in same group but also in nearby groups	Similar calls with avoidance behavior	Alarm, warning defensive
Same group	Assembly, searching	Keeps group together and directs attention
Most groups of same region	Similar calls	Not known
Same group	Aggressive behavior typical of rage response	Defensive
Play associates. Mother	More play, embracing and greeting behavior	Facilitates play, encourages or stimulates approach
All animals present		Begging
Same group	Following	Means of directing group progression

ance responses. In all probability these particular sounds are sometimes reinforced by actual fighting.

When a group of gibbons, e.g., Group 2, encroaches on the territory of Group 1, what the animals are observed to do is first to call, to answer call for call and then when rushed, to retreat toward the heart of their own territory, the less dominant Group 2 giving ground. With greater motivation the groups may come together and fight. . . .

I have observed a fact which I am not able to interpret to my satisfaction, namely, that when Type I calls are given in a situation involving competition between groups, the sound patterns function as defense or aggressive behavior. When, however, a group is alone and well fed, its members may give Type I calls repeatedly and for long periods among themselves. The latter calling seems to be an expression of excess energy, a type of vocal play (it may correspond to human singing), hence it may be concluded that many of the stereotyped vocalizations of primates are *multivalent* i.e., the same sound patterns have several different stimulus values in different situations. Though the sound patterns remain the same, its motivation and biological functions vary, within limits, from one situation to another.

Type I calls are not given by infants. Young gibbons about two years of age first begin to learn to make this series of calls. Considerable improvement in calling may be made for six months or more after the first calls are given. "Lo" improved greatly while she was with me in camp. Naturally, also, as would be expected, the quality of the calling varies somewhat with age.

A marked characteristic of gibbon vocalizations is that calls stimulate similar calls in associated animals. This is true of most types of gibbon calls but it is especially true of Type II. When a group in a particular region has given a series of Type II calls, one nearby group then another and another will echo the sound until most of the groups of the region have called. This calling and copying of calling may continue for an hour on some mornings. Likewise, the calls of one individual stimulate another individual to call. It is relatively easy for a person roughly imitating the Type II calls to stimulate calling in captive gibbons. . . .

Restating descriptive generalizations which I gave in a previous monograph as to the functions of vocal signaling behavior, the following points may be made: 1. Vocalizations coordinate group activity by providing a single kind of dominating stimuli to which all individuals may respond, 2. A vocal pattern may predispose a number of individuals to make common responses to the same or to a variety of stimulus situations, 3. Vocalizations serve to synchronize in time the behavior of the individuals in a group. In addition it seems important to note that vocal responses and reciprocal stimulation may facilitate the overt aggressive behavior of associated animals by enhancing their general excitement. Furthermore, negative withdrawals are produced by some types of sounds and positive, affinitive responses by other types.

In summary, social coordination of behavior first involves actual contact control or manipulation, then through processes of learning similar to that of redintegration, gross expressive movements, i.e., gestures and series of sound patterns, come to have communicative functions. These make up a complex system of signs and signals which coordinate the behavior of individuals.

9. Language and Perception of the World

DOROTHY LEE

Perception of events, and the relation between events, is differently viewed in different cultures, according to modern linguistic theory. Dorothy Lee, using data collected by Bronislaw Malinowski, offers us a case in point. Trobriand language does not show development nor express causation by regular syntactical means and the Trobriand Islanders therefore tend to express things in terms of being. Since we must see Trobriand thought through our language, this is not easy to express. But the essay illustrates the importance of seeing different cultures in terms of their own viewpoint. More important, it shows how language is a force in shaping man's attitude toward his environment.

Dorothy Lee was for several years Professor of Anthropology at the Merrill-Palmer School in Detroit until she joined the staff at Harvard University in 1959. Born in Constantinople, she studied at Vassar and took her doctorate at the University of California, Berkeley. There she studied the Wintu Indians, a California tribe, whose mythology and language she analyzed. The essay from which this selection was taken is "Being and Value in Primitive Culture," *Journal of Philosophy*, Volume 46, No. 13, June, 1949, pp. 401–415, and is reprinted here by kind permission of the publisher of that journal and the author.

The Trobrianders are concerned with being, and being alone. Change and becoming are foreign to their thinking. An object or event is grasped and evaluated in terms of itself alone, that is, irrespective of other beings. The Trobriander can describe being for the benefit of the ethnographer; otherwise, he usually refers to it by a word, one word only. All being, to be significant, must be Trobriand being, and therefore experienced at the appropriate time as a matter of course by the members of each Trobriand community; to describe it would be redundant. Being is never defined, in our sense of the word. Definition presents an object in terms of *what it is like* and *what it is unlike,* that is, in terms of its distinguishing characteristics. The Trobriander is interested only in *what it is.* And each event or being is grasped timelessly; in our terms, it contains its past, present, and future, but these distinctions are nonexistent for the Trobriander. There is, however, one sense in which being is not self-contained. To be, it must be part of an ordained pattern; this aspect will be elaborated below.

Being is discrete and self-contained; it has no attributes outside of itself. Its qualities are identical with it and without them it is not itself. It has no predicate; it is itself. To say a word representing an object or act is to imply the existence of this, and all the qualities it incorporates. If I were to go with a Trobriander to a garden where the *taytu,* a species of yam, had just been harvested, I would come back and tell you: "There are good taytu there; just the right degree of ripeness, large and perfectly shaped; not a blight to be seen, not one rotten spot; nicely rounded at the tips, with no spiky points; all first-run harvesting, no second gleanings." The Trobriander would come back and say "Taytu"; and he would have said all that I did and more. Even the phrase "There are taytu" would represent a tautology, since existence is implied in being, is, in fact an ingredient of being to the Trobriander. And all the attributes, even if he could find words for them at hand in his own language, would have been tautological, since the concept of taytu contains them all. In fact, if one of these were absent, the object would not have been a taytu.

Such a tuber, if it is not at the proper harvesting ripeness, is not a taytu. If it is unripe, it is a *bwanawa;* if overripe, spent, it is not a spent taytu but something else, a *yowana.* If it is blighted it is a *nukunokuna.* If it has a rotten patch, it is a *taboula;* if misshapen, it is a *usasu;* if perfect in shape but small, it is a *yagogu.* If the tuber, whatever its shape or condition, is a post-harvest gleaning, it is an *ulumadala.* When the spent tuber, the yowana, sends its shoots underground, as we would put it, it is not a yowana with shoots, but a *silisata.* When new tubers have formed on these shoots, it is not a silisata but a *gadena.* An object cannot change an attribute and retain its identity. Some range of growth or modification within being is probably allowed, otherwise speech would be impossible; but I doubt whether they are conscious of it. As soon as such change, if we may introduce one of our concepts here, is officially recognized, the object ceases to be itself.

As being is identical with the object, there is no word for *to be;* as being is changeless, there is no word meaning *to become*. Becoming involves temporality, but Trobriand being has no reference to time. With us, change in time is a value, and place in a developmental sequence is necessary for evaluation. We can not respond with approval or disapproval, unless we know that a thing is getting bigger or better or surer. If I am told that Robert Smith is an instructor at $3000, I can not respond to this adequately, unless I know that he is just out of graduate school, or that he used to be a professor at the age of forty, but now, at sixty, he has been demoted to this position. Our language is full of terms such as the one I have just used—demotion—giving us tools for the evaluation of being in terms of place in a climactic historical sequence. By dint of constant vigilance, we can refrain from using these terms; but we have no choice when it comes to placing events in time. Our language codifies reality in such a way as to predispose us to view events in terms of temporality. Even if I decide to use such expressions as "it be" or "it flow," I have achieved nothing, since you who hear me automatically make these acceptable to yourself by translating them into "it is" and "it flows," merely putting me down as uneducated. Whenever I make an assertion, I have to give it temporal limits, in reference to past, present, or future, or at any rate I have to imply temporality. Trobriand verbs are timeless, making no temporal distinctions. A Trobriander can, if he chooses, refer to an act as completed, but that, it seems to me, is an aspect of the act, not a temporal reference. History and mythical reality are not "the past" to the Trobriander. They are forever present, participating in all current being, giving meaning to all his activities and all existence. A Trobriander will speak of the garden which his mother's brother planted, or the one which the mythical Tudava planted, in exactly the same terms with which he will refer to the garden which he himself is planting now; and it will give him satisfaction to do so. . . .

Now our own language makes it easy, though not imperative, to compare beings at every turn. It provides us with a large number of comparatives, through morphology and vocabulary. Our speech is studded with terms such as *better, bigger, inferior, average, compared to, normal, equal, in relation to*, etc., showing that we constantly are passing judgment according to a comparative standard. The Trobriander has no such means, unless we accept his rarely used words "it-sames" and "it-differents" as comparatives. The magic formulas given by Malinowski are full of similes, as only in this way can they be made comprehensible to his readers. But in Trobriand, these are all metaphors. Where Malinowski's translation reads, for example, "thy shoots are as quick as the eyes of the black ant," the Trobriand text reads, "no thine eye, thine eye black-ant." When Malinowski says, "I am your senior," the Trobriand text reads, "old man I."

We can see this emphasis on *being* alone when we analyze the Trobriand sentence. Here we find that the words are presented discretely, without elements to show the relation of one word to the other. A verb contains its subject, a noun contains its "predicate" as well as its other attributes. The few words which Malinowski translated as adjectives are either nouns—*a big-one,* or verbs—*it-goods.* The language does not even express an object-to-object relationship, as ours does, for example, when it relates grammatical subject to the object which is acted upon. In English, we express this relationship through word order; when we say, for example, "Mary ate the pie," or "John kicked Mary," we clearly distinguish the actor from the one acted upon, by order of precedence, and we can not avoid making the distinction. The Trobriander, on the other hand, merely expresses act and participants: "i-wo-ye tau" "it-beat-man" means either that the man is beating someone or that someone is beating the man. Such a phrase usually refers either to a known situation, which needs no elucidation, or is told within a context which makes its meaning clear. If, however, the Trobriander for some reason feels that he must specify, he can do so; but he does not do so as a matter of course, as we do, since his language does not predispose or constrain him to do so. . . .

The Trobriander has no word for history. When he wants to distinguish between different kinds of occasions, he will say, for example, "Molubabeba in-child-his," that is, "in the childhood of Molubabeba," not a previous phase of *this* time, but a different kind of time. For him, history is an unordered repository of anecdote; he is not interested in chronological sequence. For example, Malinowski recorded an account of a famine which was given with complete disregard to chronology; an effect which is achieved only deliberately by our sophisticated writers. If we rearrange the clusters of statements so that they represent for us a historical sequence, we have to give them in the following order: one, four, three, two, five.

For us, chronological sequence is of vital importance, largely because we are interested not so much in the event itself, but rather in its place within a *related* series of events; we look for its antecedents and its consequences. We are concerned with the causal or telic relationship between events or acts. To the Trobriander, events do not fall of themselves into a pattern of causal relationships, as they do for us. I am not here concerned with the question of whether causality is given, or is read into existence. Whichever may be the case, we in our culture automatically see and seek relationships, not essence, and express relationship mainly in terms of cause or purpose. The maddeningly persistent question of our young children is "why," because this is the question implicit in most of our ordinary statements and other behavior,* to be answered either in causal or telic terms, since cause and purpose are equally dynamic for us, and are identified in our use of "why." Esthetically, as well as practically, cause and purpose are both important to us; cause gives us a satisfying explanation and purpose ennobles or gives meaning to the act. We teach the importance of purposive action to infants, directly and indirectly by act and speech. We teach it in the schoolroom, in sports, in politics, in moral precept. The unreflective scientist takes causation for granted, the orthodox historian studies history to discover the causes for events. To the Trobriander, on the other hand, being or event remains discrete, sufficient unto itself, true and of value as itself, judged and motivated and understood in terms of itself alone. In the face of this apprehension of being, concepts such as causation and purpose appear irrelevant; I have introduced them here only because they are so basic to our thinking that we accept them as given in experience, and their presence is assumed by us in all cultures, as a matter of course. In the language of the Trobrianders, there are no terms such as *because, so as to, cause, reason, effect, purpose, to this end, so that, why*. This does not mean that the Trobrianders are incapable of explaining a sequence in terms of cause and effect, but rather that this relationship is of no significance. . . .

We ask here, how is influence or motivation or effect phrased among the Trobrianders? How is magical action understood, for example? The answer is, it is understood in exactly these terms, as action, not cause. The magician does not *cause* certain things to be; he *does* them. As the gardener with his material implements burns the brush, breaks the clods, etc., so the garden magician with his various formulas

* This does not mean that Trobriand parents are relieved from such questions; they are probably constantly asked "what." According to Margaret Mead this is what the Manus children are continually asking adults.

"awakens the sprout," "drives up the shoots overground," "throws the headgear of the taytu," "makes several branches," "pushes the taytu tubers into the soil," according to Trobriand account. This is not influence, nor the force of magic; rather it is "to magic." Malinowski, in presenting accounts of magic, uses purposive phraseology, since in this way only can his readers understand magic. But where he gives in translation: The *okwala* rite is made so that taytu might really grow, so that it might ripen, the Trobriand has actually said: okwala, it-grow truly, it-ripen; just a number of events. It so happens, in the example, that the sequence in the account corresponds to the actual order of fact; but quite often there is not even such correspondence. And in the acts themselves there is often not even the sequence into which we could at least read causality. For example, when the Trobriander wants to fell a tree he first exorcises the *tokway,* the tree-dwelling spirit, reciting a spell which gets the tokway down. After that he gives the tokway some food. If the food was offered first, on the ground, or at least promised, we could see this as a causal inducement. Actually, the tokway has no alternative and no freedom of choice at all; he is brought down by the spell. The offering of the food itself is merely part of the established procedure, and is not causally related to the exorcism.

It follows that the Trobriander performs acts because of the activity itself, not for its effects; that he values objects because they are good, not good for; in fact, objects and activities that are good for, are of no value to him. Take, for example, his yams and his yam gardening. To Malinowski, who spent many months with them, dependent upon them socially as well as materially, gardening meant yam gardening, and food meant yams. It was only after he had occupied himself with his Trobriander material for about fifteen years and written several books on the subject, that he realized that taro was an ancient and substantial item of food, much easier to grow than yams, less demanding of care and good soil, perhaps almost as important as yams from the point of view of sheer material nourishment. But taro is only good *for;* it is only good for food, or, less than that, for stopping hunger; and it is grown for such use. Therefore it was of no value or importance to the Trobriander, and escaped Malinowski's notice. Yams, on the other hand, incorporate the social good. They are good in themselves, and participate daily in good situations, as free, non-utile gifts.

A man gardens yams with the expenditure of much care and effort, with physical and magical skills, putting in long, hot hours of work. He gardens as many plots as he is capable of—not as many as his neighbors, or as many as he "needs." About half of these he sets aside as the *urigubu* plots. These he harvests with pride, exhibiting beautiful heaps of taytu. Then he sends this harvest, by festively arrayed youths and maidens, not to his yam house, but to the hamlet of his sister's husband. In this man's garden the taytu are heaped again, and it is this man now who exhibits them with pride as the gift. Finally, his yam house is put in order, and magic is performed in it. Ideally, the magic makes the taytu rot uneaten in the yam house; it fills the owners with nausea at the thought of eating the taytu; it gives them, instead, an urge to go to the bush and eat what grows there. This keeps the taytu free of purpose; ideally, they are not food. Taytu are constantly being given and received as gifts, in a system of free giving without what we call ulterior motives; not for altruism, not in barter or exchange for. Most of the gift taytu are usually eaten eventually, but only incidentally. In the urigubu gardens of the man who grew them, have remained all the tubers which are not taytu; the ones which are misshapen, or unduly small or blighted in some way. These go to the gardener's not-good yam house. They are merely to be eaten, and we do not hear of them again. The taytu, however, have an important place in the everyday, as well as the ceremonial, life of the people. Taytu are not, like the *taro* good *for*. Taytu have value, not use; value lies in *being*, not in relationship. . . .

Here another aspect of Trobriand being is involved. I have spoken of being as discrete, and apprehended as itself alone. I must now qualify this statement. Being has no independent existence. It is itself only as part of an established pattern. To members of our culture, being is defined by its attributes, relationships, and functions; temporally in terms of becoming, spatially in terms of its relationships. For the Trobrianders, being is defined by a fixed place in an established pattern.

It is perhaps too much to ask my readers to believe that one element in a pattern can be and is perceived only in terms of its specific position within the pattern itself, and without reference to any other element; that in fact a pattern is conceived as something other than a system of relationships. Nevertheless, I believe such to be the case among the Trobrianders. Being is not seen in terms of its relationships to a plurality of elements in the pattern, but rather as a fixed point in a single, changeless whole. Only in this place can being be itself; only as it fills its place is it desired or valued. Being is good and true in terms of pattern. Gift-giving, for example, is good only within a patterned Trobriand situation. It is neither virtuous nor altruistic; both these terms involve meaningless relational concepts. In Trobriand gift-giving, the

need of the recipient, or the effect upon him, is not involved. I doubt
whether the Trobrianders could be persuaded to send yams to the starving Bikinians; and even if they did send yams, their act would not have
value. The harvest gift to the sister's husband is not an act of altruism.
The giver is concerned only with fulfilling his rôle, his place in a specific
Trobriand pattern. If he gave taro to his sister's husband, the gift would
not have been good; if he gave the yams to his own brother, his act
would not have been good. What is good in this situation is the *urigubu*.
To be good, this gift must be urigubu; to be true, that is, to be urigubu,
it must be, (a) a gift of taytu; (b) from man to sister's husband; (c) at
harvest time. Both the good and the true are defined by place in pattern.
Taytu figure as gifts upon different occasions, between different individuals. In each case the gift is named and valued differently. When
taytu are given to a friend at the launching of a canoe, they follow a
different procedure, and are *kabigodoya;* when they are a harvest gift to
a specialist, they are a *karibudaboda.* Taytu, then, are urigubu, kabigodoya, karibudaboda, according to their place in different patterns; and
each gift derives different being, and different value in accordance to
the pattern in which it has place. I should explain here that in each case
the taytu remain taytu though they participate in different situations; it
is the gift which is different according to its place in a different pattern.

This conception of being and value gave the early pearl traders
much trouble. They found out soon that money or the things they
offered were no inducement to work. They noticed, however, that the
Trobrianders set great store by certain large blades made of stone. At
first, they had these imitated carelessly, but found that the natives did
not want them; then they had them made of slate in Europe, but these
also were rejected by the Trobrianders. Finally they had the native stone
quarried and sent to Parisian craftsmen; but these beautiful blades also
were rejected. These things, of course, could not be valued, since they
were not truly Trobriand, had not been made "as ordained of old"; but
more than that, they could not be an inducement, and could have no
meaning, since they were external to the pattern. When the Trobrianders
were finally persuaded to dive for pay, it was only the natives of those
villages which had always dived for oysters who were persuaded; those
of the other coastal villages, where diving had not been ordained of old,
would not dive. And the natives of the appropriate villages did so
grudgingly. To the disgust of the pearl traders, they would leave their
diving and go off fishing for the day, as soon as a number of baskets of
yams made their appearance on the beach, even though the traders

offered them twenty times as many yams. The natives would work for extraneous inducement as long as there was no good undertaking to indulge in; but when their gift-partners arrived with yams, they initiated a patterned situation which had meaning for the natives.

You will say, "But is not this an inducement or cause?" I think it is not. By themselves, the few baskets of yams on the beach are just a few baskets of yams. Offered by the trader they would have had no meaning. Brought from a different Trobriand village, they would have effected nothing; and when they come from the appropriate village, it is only the partners of the specific givers who go off fishing as a matter of course. Given from anyone to anyone, the taytu are of no value. I think the yams are not an inducement to action. The giving of them, however, starts a pattern; once the gift has taken place, the pattern becomes evident and the recipient is presented with a rôle which holds value for him; to get satisfaction from it, to be a good Trobriander, he must fill it. By us, the two acts, the receiving of the yams and the procuring of the fish, are seen in relationship; and this relationship is seen as dynamic; one act influences the other, or causes the other. To the Trobriander, what is dynamic is the validity and value derived from the pattern.

10. Language, Thought, and Reality

BENJAMIN L. WHORF

Benjamin Lee Whorf was an engineer who, when examining insurance cases, discovered that people were frequently fooled into making costly mistakes by the words they used. For example, a man threw a match into an "empty" barrel—which still had gasoline vapors in it. Thus, Whorf became interested in the semantics of language and the divergent ways that different languages have of expressing the world of reality. With Edward Sapir, he was responsible for developing the basic thesis that language is an instrument through which reality is perceived by its speakers. In the present essay he shows how language formulates our thoughts.

The essay was first published in the *Technological Review*, Volume 42, No. 6, April 1940, pp. 229–231; 247–248, and has been reproduced in a collection of his essays, *Language, Thought, and Reality; Selected Writings of Benjamin Lee Whorf* (John B. Carroll, ed.), Cambridge, Mass.: The Technology Press of Massachusetts Institute of Technology and John Wiley and Sons, New York, 1956. It is reprinted with the kind permission of both publishers.

Every normal person in the world, past infancy in years, can and does talk. By virtue of that fact, every person—civilized or uncivilized—carries through life certain naïve but deeply rooted ideas about talking and its relation to thinking. Because of their firm connection with speech habits that have become unconscious and automatic, these notions tend to be rather intolerant of opposition. They are by no means entirely personal and haphazard; their basis is definitely systematic, so that we are justified in calling them a system of natural logic—a term that seems to me preferable to the term common sense, often used for the same thing.

According to natural logic, the fact that every person has talked fluently since infancy makes every man his own authority on the process by which he formulates and communicates. He has merely to consult a common substratum of logic or reason which he and everyone else is supposed to possess. Natural logic says that talking is merely an incidental process concerned strictly with communication, not with formulation of ideas. Talking, or the use of language, is supposed only to "express" what is essentially already formulated nonlinguistically. Formulation is an independent process, called thought or thinking, and is supposed to be largely indifferent to the nature of particular languages. Languages have grammars, which are assumed to be merely norms of conventional and social correctness, but the use of language is supposed to be guided not so much by them as by correct, rational, or intelligent THINKING.

Thought, in this view, does not depend on grammar but on laws of logic or reason which are supposed to be the same for all observers of the universe—to represent a rationale in the universe that can be "found" independently by all intelligent observers, whether they speak Chinese or Choctaw. In our own culture, the formulations of mathematics and of formal logic have acquired the reputation of dealing with this order of things: i. e., with the realm and laws of pure thought. Natural logic holds that different languages are essentially parallel methods for expressing this one-and-the-same rationale of thought and, hence, differ really in but minor ways which may seem important only because they are seen at close range. It holds that mathematics, symbolic logic, philosophy, and so on are systems contrasted with language which deal directly with this realm of thought, not that they are themselves specialized extensions of language. . . .

When linguists became able to examine critically and scientifically a large number of languages of widely different patterns, their base of reference was expanded; they experienced an interruption of phenomena hitherto held universal, and a whole new order of significances came into their ken. It was found that the background linguistic system (in other words, the grammar) of each language is not merely a reproducing instrument for voicing ideas but rather is itself the shaper of ideas, the program and guide for the individual's mental activity, for his analysis of impressions, for his synthesis of his mental stock in trade. Formulation of ideas is not an independent process, strictly rational in the old sense, but is part of a particular grammar, and differs, from slightly to greatly, between different grammars. We dissect nature along lines laid down by our native languages. The categories and types that we isolate from the world of phenomena we do not find there because they stare every observer in the face; on the contrary, the world is presented in a kaleidoscopic flux of impressions which has to be organized by our minds— and this means largely by the linguistic systems in our minds. We cut nature up, organize it into concepts, and ascribe significances as we do, largely because we are parties to an agreement to organize it in this way—an agreement that holds throughout our speech community and is codified in the patterns of our language. The agreement is, of course, an implicit and unstated one, BUT ITS TERMS ARE ABSOLUTELY OBLIGATORY; we cannot talk at all except by subscribing to the organization and classification of data which the agreement decrees.

This fact is very significant for modern science, for it means that no individual is free to describe nature with absolute impartiality but is constrained to certain modes of interpretation even while he thinks himself most free. The person most nearly free in such respects would be a linguist familiar with many widely different linguistic systems. As yet no linguist is in any such position. We are thus introduced to a new principle of relativity, which holds that all observers are not led by the same physical evidence to the same picture of the universe, unless their linguistic backgrounds are similar, or can in some way be calibrated. . . .

When Semitic, Chinese, Tibetan, or African languages are contrasted with our own, the divergence in analysis of the world becomes more apparent; and, when we bring in the native languages of the

Americas, where speech communities for many millenniums have gone their ways independently of each other and of the Old World, the fact that languages dissect nature in many different ways becomes patent. The relativity of all conceptual systems, ours included, and their dependence upon language stand revealed. That American Indians speaking only their native tongues are never called upon to act as scientific observers is in no wise to the point. To exclude the evidence which their languages offer as to what the human mind can do is like expecting botanists to study nothing but food plants and hothouse roses and then tell us what the plant world is like!

Let us consider a few examples. In English we divide most of our words into two classes, which have different grammatical and logical properties. Class 1 we call nouns, e. g., 'house, man'; class 2, verbs, e. g., 'hit, run.' Many words of one class can act secondarily as of the other class, e.g., 'a hit, a run,' or 'to man (the boat),' but, on the primary level, the division between the classes is absolute. Our language thus gives us bipolar division of nature. But nature herself is not thus polarized. If it be said that 'strike, turn, run,' are verbs because they denote temporary or short-lasting events, i.e., actions, why then is 'fist' a noun? It also is a temporary event. Why are 'lightning, spark, wave, eddy, pulsation, flame, storm, phase, cycle, spasm, noise, emotion' nouns? They are temporary events. If 'man' and 'house' are nouns because they are long-lasting and stable events, i. e., things, what then are 'keep, adhere, extend, project, continue, persist, grow, dwell,' and so on doing among the verbs? If it be objected that 'possess, adhere' are verbs because they are stable relationships rather than stable precepts, why then should 'equilibrium, pressure, current, peace, group, nation, society, tribe, sister,' or any kinship term be among the nouns? It will be found that an "event" to US means "what our language classes as a verb" or something analogized therefrom. And it will be found that it is not possible to define 'event, thing, object, relationship,' and so on, from nature, but that to define them always involves a circuitous return to the grammatical categories of the definer's language.

In the Hopi language, 'lightning, wave, flame, meteor, puff of smoke, pulsation' are verbs—events of necessarily brief duration cannot be anything but verbs. 'Cloud' and 'storm' are at about the lower limit of duration for nouns. Hopi, you see, actually has a classification of events (or linguistic isolates) by duration type, something strange to our modes of thought. On the other hand, in Nootka, a language of Vancouver Island, all words seem to us to be verbs, but really there are no classes 1 and 2; we have, as it were, a monistic view of nature that gives us only one class of word for all kinds of events. 'A house occurs' or 'it houses' is the way of saying 'house,' exactly like 'a flame occurs' or 'it burns.' These terms seem to us like verbs because they are inflected for durational and temporal nuances, so that the suffixes of the word for house event make it mean long-lasting house, temporary house, future house, house that used to be, what started out to be a house, and so on. . . .

One significant contribution to science from the linguistic point of view may be the greater development of our sense of perspective. We shall no longer be able to see a few recent dialects of the Indo-European family, and the rationalizing techniques elaborated from their patterns, as the apex of the evolution of the human mind, nor their present wide spread as due to any survival from fitness or to anything but a few events of history—events that could be called fortunate only from the parochial point of view of the favored parties. They, and our own thought processes with them, can no longer be envisioned as spanning the gamut of reason and knowledge but only as one constellation in a galactic expanse. A fair realization of the incredible degree of diversity of linguistic system that ranges over the globe leaves one with an inescapable feeling that the human spirit is inconceivably old; that the few thousand years of history covered by our written records are no more than the thickness of a pencil mark on the scale that measures our past experience on this planet; that the events of these recent millenniums spell nothing in any evolutionary wise, that the race has taken no sudden spurt, achieved no commanding synthesis during recent millenniums, but has only played a little with a few of the linguistic formulations and views of nature bequeathed from an inexpressibly longer past. Yet neither this feeling nor the sense of precarious dependence of all we know upon linguistic tools which themselves are largely unknown need be discouraging to science but should, rather, foster that humility which accompanies the true scientific spirit, and thus forbid that arrogance of the mind which hinders real scientific curiosity and detachment.

11. Language, Time, and the Law

WALTON H. HAMILTON and **DOUGLAS ADAIR**

Millions of dollars can depend upon the meaning of a word. And the meaning can change. Walton Hamilton and Douglas Adair became interested in the word *commerce* when, in a famous legal case before the Supreme Court, the decision rested upon the meaning that the word commerce had for the justices. Though commerce now tends to have a more restricted meaning, it apparently had a broader meaning when the word was used in the Constitution of the United States—more like the words business and industry today. The example not only shows how words change, but shows the importance of that change for ordinary human events.

Walton Hamilton received his doctoral degree in economics from Michigan in 1913, taught at Michigan, Chicago, Amherst, Brookings Institute and Yale, was special assistant to the U.S. Attorney General (1938–1945) and was U.S. delegate to the International Labor Organization Conference in Geneva in 1935. He wrote widely on economics and law. Douglas Adair took his doctorate in History at Yale University and is a professor at Williams and Mary College, specializing in early American History and intellectual history of the eighteenth century.

The selection was excerpted from Chapters 1 and 3 of their *The Power To Govern: The Constitution—Then and Now*, New York: W. W. Norton, 1937, and is printed by kind permission of the publisher. Copyright 1937 by W. W. Norton & Company, Inc.

A fate of a public policy hangs on the validity of an act; an act awaits the judgment in a case; a case turns upon the boundaries of a word. This is the way of the law.

The caption of Carter v. Carter Coal Co.—save for the suspicion aroused by its patronymic beat—smacks in no way of the unusual. It is technically the first of a quartet of kindred suits which are Nos. 636, 649, 650, and 651, in the calendar of the United States Supreme Court for the October term of 1935. In reality it marks the most important judicial battle of recent years over the power of the Federal Government in the control of industry. The resulting decree has—for the time at least—placed bituminous coal outside the realm of national regulation; and the result was reached because the majority of the justices could not make the word "commerce" in the Constitution comprehend all that was included in the challenged statute. . . .

There is nothing unseemly in matters of public policy turning upon niceties of diction. Here a great issue waits upon an ordeal of words and invites an excursion into English, judicial, and economic usage. The Constitution is at once a document, a code of judge-made law, and a changing body of understandings. It may be that the document compels such an interpretation, as those who bless their opinions with the sanctions of venerable words would have us believe. It may be that changing occasions in the life of a people bring fresh meanings to abiding words and make ancient verbal symbols instruments of their purpose. Or it may be that "the gloss, not the text, is the thing," as an old Simeon proverb has it. But whatever the Constitution and the way of the mind with it, we are by judicial usage compelled to look at the words in the light of the utterances of the founders. If we are to probe the meaning of its clauses, we must call as a witness the age that produced it.

An utterance of the Court is the law; a quotation of a quotation has double authority. A statement by Mr. Justice Lamar is approvingly cited by Mr. Justice Sutherland, "No distinction is more popular to the common mind, or more clearly expressed in economic and political literature than that between manufacture and commerce." Set down this statement, make it a text, and add a question-mark. There emerges an issue of the dependence of a great public policy upon a simple verbal usage.

A century-and-a-half has elapsed since the event. It is hardly to be expected that we can now recapture with complete accuracy the character, particulars, and domain of the "commerce among the several states" the regulation of which was entrusted to the Congress by the Fathers in 1787. None of them left a canonical statement of what might come to be comprehended within a few simple words. An attempt to surprise their import by interpretation, piecing together bits of evidence, and arguing from contemporary circumstance is not without its hazards. An extraction of meaning from the conditions of the times, the exigencies to be met, and the disposition of the delegates yields something less than absolute truth. But to disregard available evidence is to ignore the events which called "the supreme law of the land" into being and to allow its provisions uncritically to be endowed with a meaning from today. Its character was—it had to be—shaped within the general circumstances which called it forth.

Words are the names of things. The "commerce" of the great document is not a legalistic category to be explored in the law reports, but the miscellany of economic activities which were everyday realities to the men of 1787. . . .

It is easier to read the words than to sense the meaning of the Constitution. The document is written in the idiom of the late Eighteenth Century; and verbal currency passes most uncertainly between the generations.

A language is the verbal expression of a culture. As the things, the activities, and the ideas which make it up change, the diction of a people makes its accommodation. Words quickly shed old meanings and take on fresh ones; verbal concepts get newly filled with the stuff of everyday life; and idioms old and new come to reflect novel twists in thought-ways among the folk. One is prone to assume that, when words abide, meanings remain; yet some fifteen decades of cultural change—and their restless impact upon the language—lie between us and the words of the Constitution. We are doomed, unless we make a heroic attempt to get back into a world which is gone, to read the classic document in the light of a later understanding. . . .

. . . For all their wisdom the Fathers could not anticipate the speech of the distant future; the judicial terms of a century and a half later were quite beyond their linguistic reach. In thought, in action, in resort to parchment their choice was limited to the words at hand and by prevailing usage in respect to those words.

To them business was a word out of reach. Its etymology makes its eighteenth-century meaning clear enough. It had—in days when spelling was less regimented than today—ceased to be spelled with a "y"; but its content was still "busy-ness." A poet might make his love for her an all-consuming business; a critic might make it his business to lash the faults of others; and a disciple of Christ might plead that he "must be about his Master's business." . . .

The word "industry" was hardly within closer reach. The term was there, to be sure. It described a quality of ant and bee which man might well emulate; it was one of the cardinal virtues of a rising industrial Puritanism. An idle brain was the devil's workshop; and the provident man was enjoined by parson, squire, and almanac towards thrift, industry, and sobriety. In the dictionaries it is repeatedly associated with diligence, painstaking, assiduity. It is "the constant application of the mind or exercise of the body." . . .

Nor had manufacture as yet attained verbal eminence. As "any sort of commodity made by the work of the hands of things that are naturally produced," it covered the processing of agricultural products for use. Wheat ground into flour, hides cured and worked into jackets and shoes, vegetable or animal fiber spun and woven at home, tobacco sun-cured and prepared for pipe or as snuff—all these were "manufactures." Thus farmers—as well as the "laboring poor" of the great cities —were manufacturers. The word was still a name, not for an activity apart but for an aspect of the art of husbandry. . . .

But the lack of the familiar term is not the want of a word. If the Eighteenth Century did not anticipate modern usage in the words "business," "industry," and "manufacture," it did have terms of its own with which to describe the seamless web of activities by which commodities are fashioned for use, men earn their livings, and nations acquire wealth. In 1787 three words of different stock—traffick, trade, and commerce—were at hand for this multiple verbal duty. Each was suited by shade and variation to its own distinctive usage; yet each in its own right was capable of a verbal coverage almost as comprehensive as the prevailing economic order.

Of the three, traffick was the oldest. It was of lowly origin, and had come to be vulgar in repute. As a verbal *émigré* from France, it had come into use early in the Sixteenth Century when the itinerant peddler was a fellow of low cunning and devious ways and exchange was tolerated only along the fringes of respectable society. One had traffick with mendicant, huckster, merchant, hussy, and evil spirit. Although during the Eighteenth Century the word came to mean "trade," large or small, "merchandising" and even "commerce," the ancient moral stigma still remained. And, as a verb, it meant "to trade meanly or mercenarily." . . .

The origin of trade is unknown. It seems to have come into England from the Hanseatic Towns in the Fourteenth Century. . . . Trade came to be the "Art of Getting, Preparing and Exchanging Things Commodious for Humane Necessities and Convenience." As, however, it came to denote the fashioning and vending of goods for other goods or money, it narrowed its coverage of employment. By 1755 it was no longer used for activities which required "constant exercise of the mind," and was especially applied to the "mechanical" pursuits in contradistinction to the "liberal arts and learned professions." The "master-manufacturer" and the great merchant, as well as the lowly artisan and small shopkeeper, were "in trade," for trade had come to encompass all those activities that were "manual or mercantile." . . .

The word "commerce" is of more exalted rank. It came into English, not by way of some vulgar tongue, but directly from the Latin. It is, in etymology, a "buying together," and from the beginning it signified a bartering of wares, an engagement in the general practice of merchandising, and all the arrangements appertaining thereto. . . . Its prestige, however, had carried it far from its original base. Almost all the dictionaries of the times set down as a secondary meaning such a miscellany of terms as "conversation," "society," and "intercourse." Between its original core of meaning and its periphery lies a vast territory.

Its sprawling domain and multiplicity of meaning are explored by all the reputable dictionaries of the period, popular and literary. The smaller and more popular of them are content to identify the word with trade or traffic; and to limit their definition to these naked words. The more pretentious tomes make excursions in various directions to find out the boundaries of the unknown domain. Dyche sets down "dealing," adds "conversation by word or letter," and reaches out to "correspondence of every kind." Barclay, with an eye to mundane matters, ventures more carefully from his verbal base. He sets it down that commerce is "the exchange of commodities," or "the buying and selling of merchandise both at home and abroad," and adds "in order to gain a profit or increase the conveniences of life." He makes the concern of both "trade" and "commerce" the "manufacture and vending of merchandise." . . .

. . . Usage is forever modifying its decrees; and the exuberant verbal growth during the century makes futile any final judgments in jurisdictional disputes. Trade, traffic, and commerce, in general identical in content, were usually distinguished only in ethical flaw or social prestige. Only lexicographers meticulous in their diction attempted to endow them with subtle shades of meaning. Samuel Johnson declares that "formerly trade was used of domestic and traffick of foreign commerce," and implies that the three words have no essential difference. Barclay insists that "trade" had not lost the color of "domestic" interchange of commodities, but "seems to imply the manufacturing and vending within ourselves." He feels that "commerce" and not "trade" should be called upon properly to denote "negociating with other countries." But no other dictionary seems to find this distinction necessary. As "trade" had moved forward from occupation or calling to exchange, so "commerce" had moved backward from market-place to manufacture for profit. It was all eminently logical, for in the economy of the time fabrication and sale were all but inseparable. It was the wideness of its domain which forbids a narrow definition of its content.

But as an aspect of the economy of the nation or as a province of government, "commerce" was pent within sharper limits. In a letter to her husband Abigail Adams, proud in the possession of a cow and a garden, writes, "but whortleberries and milk we are not obliged to commerce for." Such a distinction between that which was bought and that which was produced on the place permeates the literature of the period. The American might make his own shoes, grind his own grain, process his raw materials into articles for his own "farm hands"; but if he fashioned wares for the market, his efforts were directed towards commerce. The expression "in commerce" was habitually employed to designate shop, mill, factory, or foundry whose products were intended for sale. A grist-mill, a sawmill, an iron works, a shoe factory were in commerce; and such persons as sold their own services for hire were engaged in the commercial callings. The manufactures, whose wares went to market, and the staple crops of agriculture were "in commerce." The age knew only two ways of making a living, the direct application of labor to land, and the making and exchange of wares. In the world of the Fathers the agricultural economy of self-sufficiency and the commercial, or the moneyed, economy stood in sharp contrast. In their minds the boundaries of commerce extended to the frontiers of the domestic economy.

A rule of status has never been imposed upon the tongue of a people. An axiom of language holds that where activities are continuous, words tend to be contagious; and another has it that when things change, the old term obligingly goes along. As time passes, nouns, forgetful that they are the names of things, tend to grow up, or to drift off. To such a liberty, which allows words to roam and to come to rest and make language immune to the blueprint, the noblest word of trade was granted indulgence. Commerce—free from the moral taint that attached to traffic and blessed with the charm of elegance—was far along that respectable road. In 1787 all actions or dealings made with an eye to the market were "in commerce." . . .

. . . Commerce was then more than we imply now by business or industry. It was a name for the economic order, the domain of political economy, the realm of a comprehensive public policy. It is a word which makes trades, activities and interests an instrument in the culture of a people. If trust was to be reposed in parchment, it was the only word which could catch up into a single comprehensive term all activities directly affecting the wealth of the nation.

III.

TECHNOLOGY

Man's Special Power

If language is the human attribute that makes culture possible, technology is the characteristic of culture that makes it advantageous to man. For man's knowledge and his ability to make things have rendered this essentially weak and defenseless animal one of nature's most formidable and successful beings. Through technology, man has mastered almost every point on the earth's surface and a good deal of the seas and upper atmosphere as well. He has substituted an understanding of nature for such purely biological endowments as might have made him adaptable to one part of the world or another and by this means has supplied himself with the material necessities to survive in all—the damp jungle, the dry plains, the frozen Arctic, as well as in the more moderate climates that are his natural habitat. He has done this by learning to shape, combine, and transform the products of nature to his own purposes, to render inedible substances digestible, to clothe, warm, and protect himself. In the process of doing these things, he has accumulated a vast storehouse of technology. While man is not the only animal to make things or even to use tools, man is the only animal for which making things and using tools is basic to his whole way of life.

What is most important is this: man's manufactures are a product of his culture; they are learned skills; they are knowledge. As Kenneth Oakley points out in the first reading of this section, most animals who use tools and make things do so out of instinct, as exemplified by the weaverbird, who built a nest in exactly the same pattern as his great-great-great grandparents, though none of the intervening generations had seen a weaverbird's nest. It is quite the opposite with man.

The upright posture, which frees the forelimbs from the task of support and locomotion, is a fundamental element in the human capacity for technical development. As a result, the arm could be limber, the hand could develop into a refined grasping tool, and the whole assemblage serve a wide variety of uses. This ability to manipulate (to be able to throw, carry, shove, pick up, twist; to be able to handle heavy things and to make delicate adjustments) is more highly developed in man than in any other primate, and more highly developed in the order of primates than in any other order of animals. Presumably, we owe this invaluable endowment to our ancestry. It is safe to say that without it we would not have culture, for unless we could be tool-using, the cultural mode of life would not have an advantage over the instinctual.

Closely associated with this physical attribute is another: the eyes. Stereoscopic vision and accurate focusing devices, which enable us to perceive in the round and to estimate distance, the ability to focus clearly both at the distant horizon and close to the eye, and to make discrimination of color, are in varying degrees essential to the making and using of tools.

But these physical attributes clearly do not give us the full story of man's competence as a creator, however essential they may be. We must also recognize that other attributes enter into this talent for making things; attributes of the mind, of which we know all too little. Some of these we share with other animals; some apparently are either far more highly developed in man than in other beings or are entirely unique.

Among these mental attributes is, of course, learning, and behind learning the ability to make refined sensory discrimination and to remember. These man shares with other animals, though he seems to have developed them to a higher degree. Beyond this, there is the ability to perceive the unseen, to imagine events as they might take place—that is, to anticipate in the mind that which will be done. The psychologist Wolfgang Köhler firmly believed that the chimpanzees he was studying displayed a moment of insight in which they solved a problem; that they suddenly perceived in their mind a solution as to how to get the banana, which solution they then proceeded to execute. This quality is usually assumed to take place in man when he is creating something new.

The nature of the human intellect must ultimately be understood by the psychologists, who study perception, learning and the attributes of the brain. But we may note that there are in the human intellectual process elements which have a social component; something closely akin to what we discussed in the preceding section on language; namely, the capacity to symbolize. The human mental quirk which makes man abstract qualities and treat them as unities (which may also occur to a lesser degree in other animals) may be thought of as crucial to the human capacity to make things—for in order to do so, he must see general features, both in his raw materials and in his finished product.

There is another similarity between human technology and human languages; namely, man's ability to see the relationship between events. Just as grammar and syntax necessarily indicate a relationship between the "events" that are the subject of discourse; so, too, technology requires that the toolmaker perceive the relationships between events as they actually occur, for he must be able to predict the outcome of his actions. It is not necessary that man know the whole and true relations between all events in the universe—this, undoubtedly men will never know. It is only necessary that he perceive causal relations among the elements in the specific sphere of activity with which he is momentarily concerned, so that he can anticipate the consequences of his actions. Men in all cultures do this, just as they also—ourselves included—connect magical notions and superstitions for those consequences for which they have no rational explanation.

What we have been saying thus far is that man has the physical ability to make things, an ability which rests largely on his marvelous hands and his versatile stereoscopic eyes and the coodination between them and other attributes of the nervous system. We have also been saying that man has a combination of mental capacities that enables him to invent and manufacture. These capacities are his heightened ability to learn, his acute sensory perception and discrimination, his developed memory, his capacity for abstracting generalizations and symbolizing, his ability to see events in their interrelationships, and his insight into events which have not yet occurred. We do not know whether any of these are truly unique to man or whether it is only a heightened capacity, but clearly man's creative capacity is of a different order from that of other animals. And, clearly, men in all parts of the world, and since the beginning of humanity, have used these powers to alter their environment to their own interests—whether by inventing the use of fire or the fabrication of the humble but essential string.

One other attribute of man is particularly important to his technological achievements: namely, culture itself—that is, the processes of learned, shared behavior, passed on through generations and communicated through language. We will return to this point shortly.

In discussing language, we said that no language could be thought of as more primitive or more advanced than another; that each had an equal capacity to transmit the knowledge and understanding of its speakers. Manifestly, the same cannot be said for technology. Read an account of the technical apparatus of, say, the Bushmen of the Kalahari Desert in Africa and you will marvel that they can survive at all, but you will know how inferior their knowledge is to that of the modern world. Is this an indication that the intelligence or ability of such people is less than our own? Anthropologists believe not; and the point is so important that we must examine carefully their reasons for not thinking so.

To face this question, we must first examine the degree to which primitive man is a creative inventor. We know he must have been so, for the basic inventions—use and making of fire, manufacture of missiles, dressing of skins, spinning of fibers, taming of animals, and domestication of plants were all the discoveries or inventions of primitive man. We have no notion as to what peoples were responsible for the earlier of these developments, but certainly they were not modern Europeans. That primitive man of other than our own race was responsible for many inventions is clear from the case of America. Erland Nordenskiöld, in an essay that follows in this section, has demonstrated a number of inventions made by the American Indian—though those listed are by no means the total inventory. They must be credited to the American Indian because they were unknown to the Old World prior to the discovery of America.

Another example may be seen in the highly developed technologies of certain primitive peoples. Take those Bushmen to whom reference has been made, who have discovered that the pupae of one certain species of beetle contains a deadly poison that works on the central nervous system. This discovery they must have made themselves, for it is unique to them. Or consider the elaborate technology of the Eskimo, of which only a minute part is recorded in the selection from Edward M. Weyer, Jr. Clearly primitive man has the capacity to invent.

If, then, their technology is not a matter of competence, of native ability, how do anthropologists account for the unmistakable differences in knowledge between one people and another?

The answer to this question lies in a series of interrelated matters, of which the first and foremost is the way in which technology grows. Other pertinent facts are the accidents of geographical location, the nature of the environment and the materials it provides, the peculiarly intertwined character of the various facets of culture, and, finally, the cultural attitudes toward innovation and technical skill.

We must first make a distinction between the possession of knowledge, and the discovery or invention of something new. Once a technique or piece of knowledge is learned, it passes from one person to another and continues through the generations, so long as it remains useful. Such is the stuff of culture. What happens, therefore, is that when a technique is discovered it continues through time, and it also spreads out to neighboring peoples in a process that anthropologists call diffusion. Gradually, as inventions are made, they accumulate. The older ones spread widely; the newer ones and those limited by environmental conditions do not spread so far. Nothing is clearer from the archeological record than that there has been a gradual increase and improvement of man's technical knowledge through this process of accumulation. Because inventions themselves tend to breed inventions, the rate of increase is accelerated. In other words, those peoples with a more advanced technology are apt to get further ahead, because they have more to build on, and because their richer life and greater population (which increased technology makes possible) give them more time and personnel to work on new developments.

At the same time, we must recognize that certain discoveries are crucial, for on them can be built many others. The first such discovery, at the very dawn of humanity, must have been the use of fire. Some others are: the discovery of planting seed and maintaining gardens, the domestication of animals, the invention of pottery, metallurgy, the wheel, and writing. V. Gordon Childe speaks of revolutions, comparable to the industrial revolution, and discusses, in his essay in this section, the character of these changes. The first revolution he calls the neolithic revolution; it was brought about when man learned to keep gardens, to grow a portion of his food. The second he calls the urban revolution, and it was brought about through the coming together of farming, the use of domestic animals for draft, and the use of metals which, taken together in a fertile environment, made possible the first cities. (We may, of course, think of an earlier revolution, when man first began the use of tools at all; a revolution into humanity itself). With the invention of writing, which followed shortly, we have the basis for an increased tempo of technical florescence which led to the high civilizations of the Near East and Mediterranean world. North Europe has been heir to that civilization, which in fact did not make any further important technological breakthrough (except the Arabic concept of the zero in numeration) until the Renaissance. Thus, being placed in the stream of history, rather than somewhere in the back eddies, determines whether a people will have available to them the accumulated knowledge of millennia—though it does not determine what they will do with that knowledge. We cannot find a better expression of this phenomenon than in the following ironical statement by Ralph Linton:

> Our solid American citizen awakens in a bed built on a pattern which originated in the Near East but which was modified in Northern Europe before it was transmitted to America. He throws back covers made from cotton, domesticated in India, or linen, domesticated in the Near East, or wool from sheep, also domesticated in the Near East, or silk, the use of which was discovered in China. All of these materials have been spun and woven by processes invented in the Near East. He

slips into his moccasins, invented by the Indians of the Eastern wood-lands, and goes to the bathroom, whose fixtures are a mixture of Euro-pean and American inventions, both of recent date. He takes off his pajamas, a garment invented in India, and washes with soap invented by the ancient Gauls. He then shaves, a masochistic rite which seems to have been derived from either Sumer or ancient Egypt.

Returning to the bedroom, he removes his clothes from a chair of southern European type and proceeds to dress. He puts on garments whose form originally derived from the skin clothing of the nomads of the Asiatic steppes, puts on shoes made from skins tanned by a proc-ess invented in ancient Egypt and cut to a pattern derived from the classical civilizations of the Mediterranean, and ties around his neck a strip of bright-colored cloth which is a vestigial survival of the shoulder shawls worn by the seventeenth-century Croatians. Before going out for breakfast he glances through the window, made of glass invented in Egypt, and if it is raining puts on overshoes made of rubber discovered by the Central American Indians and takes an umbrella, invented in southeastern Asia. Upon his head he puts a hat made of felt, a material invented in the Asiatic steppes.

On his way to breakfast he stops to buy a paper, paying for it with coins, an ancient Lydian invention. At the restaurant a whole new series of borrowed elements confronts him. His plate is made of a form of pottery invented in China. His knife is of steel, an alloy first made in southern India, his fork a medieval Italian invention, and his spoon a derivative of a Roman original. He begins breakfast with an orange, from the eastern Mediterranean, a cantaloupe from Persia, or perhaps a piece of African watermelon.

With this he has coffee, an Abyssinian plant, with cream and sugar. Both the domestication of cows and the idea of milking them originated in the Near East, while sugar was first made in India. After his fruit and first coffee he goes on to waffles, cakes made by a Scan-dinavian technique from wheat domesticated in Asia Minor. Over these he pours maple syrup, invented by the Indians of the Eastern woodlands. As a side dish he may have the egg of a species of bird domesticated in Indo-China, or thin strips of the flesh of an animal domesticated in Eastern Asia which have been salted and smoked by a process developed in northern Europe.

When our friend has finished eating he settles back to smoke, an American Indian habit, consuming a plant domesticated in Brazil in either a pipe, derived from the Indians of Virginia, or a cigarette, derived from Mexico. If he is hardy enough he may even attempt a cigar, transmitted to us from the Antilles by way of Spain. While smok-ing he reads the news of the day, imprinted in characters invented by the ancient Semites upon a material invented in China by a process invented in Germany. As he absorbs the accounts of foreign troubles he will, if he is a good conservative citizen, thank a Hebrew deity in an Indo-European language that he is 100 per cent American.*

There is another aspect of this cumulative character of technology that we must appreciate. Each machine or device of the modern world is made up of numerous separate elements. Examine any process and you will see its ramifications, but we will use as an example that crucial invention of modern life: printing. We think of it merely as the invention of movable type, but it is much more. It required the metallurgist's art to make castings; it required paper (for parchment was far too dear) that would take and hold the ink; it required an ink of the right consistency; it required techniques for reasonably accurate measurement, as each matrix must be of exact depth and height; and it required presses which would push the paper firmly against the forms. Printing, in turn, is an element in the further complex of technical development; it is important to the growth of technology. This example shows that the processes of advancement necessitate the coming together of the right things at the right time; that the more technical knowledge a people has, the more likely it is to be able to advance yet further. Contrariwise, a people cut off from one element in a complex (as Europe was from the knowledge of cheap paper) may prevent the possibilities of the whole from developing. This accounts for the extremely slow beginning of technological evolution and its ever increasing tempo. It helps to account for the wide gulf between the more- and the less-advanced peoples.

Primitive people in the modern world stand in relation to the advancing front of technological development much as the Gauls and Germanic tribes and the Anglo-Saxons did in the time of Caesar who, we remember, viewed the inhabitants of the British Isles with affection but despaired of their ever being able to sustain civilization.

So the primitive peoples known to modern ethnography have technologies fundamentally like those of prehistoric times—not in detail, but in basic features and with various adaptations. Their technologies are poorer than ours not because they have inherited poorer or less creative brains, but because they did not inherit the cumulation of cultural

* From *The Study of Man,* pp. 326–27, by Ralph Linton. Copyright, 1936, D. Appleton-Century Co., Inc. Reprinted by permission of Appleton-Century-Crofts, Inc.

advancement which took place in those areas more favorably endowed by nature and more centrally located with respect to human populations.

While each culture differs in detail from each other with respect to its inventory of knowledge, it is nevertheless useful to classify cultures in terms of their economic level. Fundamentally, cultures can be divided into four basic economic orders: (1) hunters and food-gatherers, who do not plant their food or keep animals (except dogs); (2) horticulturists, who plant gardens using a hoe or simple digging stick, and frequently also keep pigs, fowl or other animals; (3) nomadic herders, who live off of flocks or herds (with little or no agricultural production) on the high plains, tundras or arid parts of the world; and (4) farmers or agriculturists, whose cultivation of the soil is advanced by the use of the plow and draft animals, by irrigation, fertilization, terracing, or some other device. Holding aside the category of herders and with other exceptions that need not detain us, the three basic forms correspond to the stages of human prehistory: the hunters and food-gatherers correspond to the period before the neolithic revolution—that is, to paleolithic times; the horticulturists to the stage between the neolithic and the urban revolutions—that is, to neolithic times; and the agriculturists to the stage after the urban revolution—that is, to the beginning of the metal ages. Some of the discoveries and inventions characteristic of each are outlined in the selection by Childe.

Herding represents a very special adaptation to dry lands. Evidently the keeping of animals in association with gardening (as the Trobriand Islanders keep pigs and many African peoples keep cows) is an old trait. But many archeologists believe that keeping large flocks of grass-eating animals, developed with the growing of small grains; that it did not appear until after the practice of true agriculture and the maintenance of the fields upon which grazing animals could flourish. They believe, therefore, that such nomadic herders as are found in the Near East and North Africa, whose life is almost totally dependent upon their animals, are a late development—are off-shoots of early farming in the Fertile Crescent. At any rate, it is a special adaptation to a particular type of environment—one in which water is too scarce to sustain farming, but where grasses that grow wild can be transformed by grazing animals into milk, blood and meat for human consumption.

The hunters and food gatherers utilize the wild fruits and berries, the shellfish along coasts, the seeds of grasses, and often almost every last thing that is edible—unless it is under a special tabu. Most of them who are known directly to modern times live in deserts, tundras or other harsh environments, for nearly all the better areas have long since been taken over by cultivators. A few, however, such as on the west coast of North America, had rich environments and could therefore sustain a richer life. There is considerable variation both in technology and in other aspects of culture. Some, like the Australians, had no weapons more advanced than the spearthrower, while the people of the island of Tasmania south of Australia did not even have that. Others had blow-guns, and bows and arrows of varying degrees of efficiency and com-plexity. Similarly, some had woodworking, stoneworking, elaborate weaving techniques, and the like, while others had only limited or poor development. To some extent, these differences reflect environmental characteristics, but they probably also reflect that great span of tech-nological advancement that took place within the paleolithic era, which comprises about 98 percent of man's history.

Horticulturists, using a hoe or sometimes merely a sharpened stick, grow a variety of plants. But since cultivated plants use up the nutrients in the soil and the horticulturists have no means of replenishing these nutrients, they must shift their gardens to new land every two or three years. Horticulture provides a steady and fairly reliable source of food, but it requires a great deal of energy to clear new plots; the yield is low, and the need for new lands makes it impossible for the horticulturists to remain permanently in one location. Thus there is neither the per-manence nor the surplus population to make cities possible (except under especially favorable conditions) and most horticulturists live a tribal kind of life.

By use of animal power and animal fertilizer, or by irrigation (which also carries soil onto the land) the yield increases in relation to the output of work. Furthermore, fertilizer and irrigation make it pos-sible to use the land year in and year out. Under such circumstances cities can be sustained, and then many men are freed from the daily routine of food production and can devote themselves to various crafts and other specialties. It is under such circumstances that the arts prosper and human technology can advance. By and large, true agri-culture is a necessary basis for what we often call civilization.

This discussion of the relation between the basic technical economy of a people and their life mode leads us to our final point. We cannot view technology as something apart from the rest of culture. In the first chapter we discussed at length the fact the every culture is a more or less highly integrated whole—a unity. Every aspect of culture is involved with every other; each element has some effect upon the character of every other. This applies to the technological aspects as well. Because food and shelter are basic animal requirements, the fulfillment of these needs is an important and basic element in every culture. Perhaps their importance is greater in primitive societies, which generally have less surplus foods available, than among ourselves.

But man does not live by bread alone, and what he feels and thinks, his religion and his tabus and his attitude toward the world, shape his feelings about food production, just as food production shapes his outlook toward the world. Childe believes, and there is much evidence to support him, that the manner in which a people get their food will have a profound influence on their religious beliefs and social attitudes.

We have included three brief essays to show the interaction between technology and other aspects of life. The first of these, by Lewis Mumford, describes the origin of the clock, which had its inception in the monasteries of medieval Europe. Keeping track of time is a universal human trait, but among primitive peoples the march of the seasons, the phases of the moon, and the movement of the sun are sufficient. The new outlook toward time that developed in the late Middle Ages ushered in a machine that we now take for granted. But consider the importance of that machine, without which our elaborate technology would not be possible. And, when we turn to a discussion of ethics, we will see how the precise measurement of time has come to have a very important meaning in our attitudes toward the world.

The other two essays deal with cultural improvements; one with a stone-age people of Australia, the other with a post-war American community. In both cases, the introduction of improvements was disruptive to the patterned behavior of the people; the change reached out and influenced not only the economic arrangements but the social system and religious values as well. Just because there is disruption of the normal course of events, these essays show how the technical aspects of the culture are interwoven with every other phase. They also demonstrate the difficulties that technical change brings about, explaining man's conservatism and the fact that the growth of technical culture has been slow. Finally, they demonstrate, with two contemporary examples, that the long road between the control of fire and the control of atomic energy has been fraught with myriad human difficulties.

It is, however, through these technical improvements, slowly accumulating through time, building one upon another, changing man's life habits, capacities, and attitudes, that man has achieved his current position as the most powerful creature in the world.

12. Skill as a Human Possession

KENNETH P. OAKLEY

Man is not the only animal that can make things, though he makes so many more things than any other that his operations are on an entirely different level from the most advanced of his fellow creatures. In this introductory section to the five volume *History of Technology*, Kenneth P. Oakley examines animal fabrications and points out some of man's unique creative qualities.

Oakley received his doctorate in the University College of London, is Vice-President of the Prehistoric Society in England, and has been visiting professor at the University of Chicago and a Viking Fund lecturer.

The essay is taken from *History of Technology*, Volume I (Charles Singer, E. J. Holmyard and A. R. Hall, eds.), Chapter 1, "Skill as a Human Possession," New York and London: Oxford University Press, 1954, and is published with the kind permission of The Clarendon Press, Oxford.

Some consideration must be given to the uniqueness of human skill. 'Man is a tool-making animal', said Benjamin Franklin (1778). To appreciate the significance of this and all that stems from it, it is useful to consider other animals which use tools but which, unlike man, do not make them.

Among animals without backbones (invertebrates), most striking is the occasional use of a pebble as a hammer by a North American solitary burrowing wasp (*Ammophila*). When the female is due to lay eggs she excavates an oblique tunnel in the soil, then seeks and paralyzes a caterpillar, places it in the burrow, lays an egg on it, and temporarily closes the nest with stones. As soon as another caterpillar is found, the nest is reopened and the process repeated. When the nest is fully stocked, she removes every sign that the earth has been disturbed. The manner of this camouflage varies somewhat with the individual. One wasp, after filling the neck of the burrow with earth, was seen to bring a quantity of sand-grains to the spot and, seizing a pebble in its mandibles, use it as a hammer in pounding them down, to make the spot as hard and firm as the surrounding surface. The process was repeated until all trace of the nest was obliterated. An individual of another species of the same genus has been known to use a pebble in the same way.

Is such action intelligent, that is, does it imply learning by experience? Most activities of insects clearly do not. They are instinctive, performed as part of an inherited pattern of behavior. Yet all animals have some power of learning by experience, for were this not so, the evolution of instincts would be incomprehensible. When an instinct is sufficiently strongly established, there appears to be little room for adaptation of behavior. Thus, if a caterpillar has constructed half its cocoon, and then that half is removed, it will continue unperturbed to build the second half. On the other hand, in fields of activity where instinct does not compel particular action, behavior is more flexible. . . .

Behavior which depends on learning by trial and error is influenced by the development of the individual in the company of its kind. In some species, innate behavior patterns are more firmly established than in other kinds. The South African weaverbird builds a complicated nest of sticks, with a knotted strand of horse-hair as foundation. A pair was isolated and bred for five generations under canaries, out of sight of their fellows and without their usual nest-building materials. In the sixth generation, still in captivity but with access to the right materials, they built a nest perfect even to the knot of horse-hair. However, in many other birds trial and error play an important part in acquiring skilled behavior in nest-building. . . .

The male satin-bird of Australia in the breeding season paints the stems of its bower with the bluish-brown pulp of certain deeply coloured fruits. Again, *Cactospiza,* one of Darwin's finches in the Galapagos Islands, which feeds on insects embedded in the branches or trunks of trees, uses a cactus spine or a twig held lengthwise in its beak to poke them out. As soon as an insect is extracted, the finch drops the spine and seizes its prize. In dry districts *Cactospiza* chooses the spine of a prickly pear, but in humid regions, where cactuses do not grow, it breaks off small twigs from trees. It will reject too short or too flexible a twig. . . .

Mammals exhibit a very wide range of intelligence, but some show less ability to learn by experience than birds. All mammals inherit instinctive tendencies to avoid pain, to obtain suitable food and drink, to mate, and even to explore—but in the higher mammals, at least, the means to attain these ends are in greater or less degree learnt by experience, including play and parental training. The hunting skill of a cat, for example, is largely developed through its play as a kitten. The remarkable achievements of the Canadian beaver, however, are generally ascribed to instinct. Young beavers on the river banks instinctively gnaw trunks of trees, and these may fall and produce dams, but full elaboration of the behavior characteristic of the species develops only within a large colony. Not only do these colonies construct island lodges in ponds of their own making, and control the level of the water in them, but they make canals along which they convey the felled timber, stockpiling it for the food which the bark provides. These feats of engineering must involve individual learning by trial and error. It has been reported that young beavers which do not readily work for the common good are driven out of the colony and, instead of making proper lodges, revert to living in simple burrows. When, as a result of protection, the rare European beavers in the Rhône valley increased in numbers, they began to build dams like the Canadian variety. . . .

Among mammals, the line of evolutionary advance that is most significant for our purpose is an increase of behaviour dependent on learning. The South African naturalist Eugéne Marias reared an otter-pup far from water, and a baboon-child far from its troop. He fed both on substances foreign to their normal way of life. When they were fully grown, he returned them to their native environment. The otter immediately began diving after fish, but the baboon was helpless, terrified by grubs and scorpions—the staple diet of its species—and began eating poisonous berries which no normal adult baboon would touch. Members of the primates, the order which includes monkeys, apes, and man, have instinctive tendencies or "drives" like other animals, but, proportionately, many more of their patterns of behavior are learned. It is broadly true of a species that the more slowly the offspring matures, the greater the intelligence of the adult. In the evolution of man there has clearly been a progressive delay in the onset of stultifying adult characteristics. . . .

. . . Brain-size is an unreliable criterion of humanity, and it is now recognized that a functional criterion, as for example, ability to make tools, is at least equally valid. We may consider some of the chief factors which led to man's becoming a tool-maker.

It has been said that "Man's place in nature is largely writ upon the hand" (Wood Jones). Any evidence bearing on the evolution of the human hand would be extremely interesting. Unfortunately the fossil evidence on this point is very meagre, but it is not probable that the origin of tool-making was related to any advancement in the functional anatomy of the hand. . . .

Man owes much of his skill to his visual powers, and yet apes and many monkeys have eyes capable of refined stereoscopic and color vision. Man is, however, psychologically distinguished by his capacity for close visual attention, and for prolonged co-ordination of eye and hand. These are reflections of cerebral rather than ocular functions. Convergence of the eyes upon hand-work is largely dependent on conscious concentration—in other words, it is under the control of the cortical motor areas, which act in response to co-ordinated impulses from the eyes. It has been reported that chimpanzees can learn to use their hands under the direction of their eyes for long enough to thread a needle, but in general the attention that an ape can give to manipulating an object is very fleeting. . . .

The mere use of tools is not confined to primates, but their planned manufacture requires mental activity of a different order. Systematic making of weapons and tools could not follow until the cortex of the brain had attained a sufficient complexity of organization. Even then it is unlikely to have become a regular practice until new habits of life were demanded by some drastic change of environment.

The qualitative difference between tool-using and tool-making is worth considering in some detail. Chimpanzees are the only apes reliably reported to make tools. Sultan, a male chimpanzee observed at the anthropoid station in Tenerife (1913-17), fitted a small bamboo cane into a larger one so as to make a stick long enough to secure a bunch of bananas which could not be reached with either rod singly. On one occasion he attained this result by fitting into a cane a piece of wood which he pointed for the purpose with his teeth. Apes can thus evidently make tools. It is, however, important to note that all the improvisations effected by Sultan were carried out with visible reward as incentive. There is no indication that apes can conceive the usefulness of shaping an object for use in an imagined eventuality. "The time in which the chimpanzee lives is limited in past and future. . . . It is in the extremely narrow limits in *this* direction that the chief difference is to be found between anthropoids and the most primitive human beings. The lack of an invaluable technical aid (speech) and a great limitation of those very important components of thought, so-called 'images', . . . prevent the chimpanzee from attaining even the smallest beginnings of cultural development" (W. Köhler). . . .

Certain observations illustrate yet more clearly the difference between the mental capacity of ape and man. When embarrassed by lack of a stick, a chimpanzee will pull a loose board from an old box and use it as a substitute. If the boards are nailed together so as to present an unbroken surface, the chimpanzee, though strong enough to break up the box, will not perceive a series of possible sticks in it—even if his need of one be urgent. Men, on the other hand, seeking to make a tool of a shape suited to a particular purpose, will visualize it in a formless lump of stone and chip it until that which was imagined is actualized. In other words, man is basically an artist in the sense of Aristotle's definition of art, which 'consists in the conception of the result to be produced before its realization in the material' (*De partibus animalium,* 640).

There is, of course, the possibility of gradation between these two extremes, perceptual thought in apes, conceptual thought in man. Nevertheless, it is well to stress the contrast, because there is a tendency to be so impressed by the occasional manufacture of tools by apes that the difference in level of mentality implied between these and the earliest efforts of man may be overlooked. Even the crudest Palaeolithic artifacts indicate considerable forethought. The range of types of tool in the earliest Stone Age industries shows that almost at the dawn of culture tools were being made to make other tools. Using a hammerstone to make a handaxe, and striking a stone flake to use in shaping a wooden spear, are activities which epitomize the mental characteristics of man—as most logically defined.

13. Primitive Man as Inventor

ERLAND NORDENSKIÖLD

The independent advance of human technology in the New World affords us our best evidence of the multiple development of civilization and the creative capacity of primitive man. Similar inventiveness in primitive parts of the Old World would undoubtedly be as impressive, but it is not so easy to show that it had not been a product of civilization that spread to these outlying parts of the world. Erland Nordenskiöld here lists some of the important contributions of the American Indian to modern civilization, but his list is far from complete. For instance, it does not even mention that the Mayan concept of zero and the place value of digits was discovered in the New World before it was known in the Old. The essay should give us a realization not only of the creative powers of primitive man, but should remind us of their capacity for rational, practical thought.

Nordenskiöld was Keeper of the Ethnological Section of the Gothenburg Museum in Sweden from 1913 until his death in 1932. His principle works dealt with the Indians of South America based upon first-hand field investigations. The material here was taken from "The American Indian as an Inventor," *Journal of the Royal Anthropological Institute,* Volume 59, 1929, pp. 273–309, and is printed by kind permission of the publisher.

I shall . . . begin by pointing out what must have been invented and discovered by the Indians themselves, for the simple reason that it was unknown in the Old World prior to the discovery of America. By this we shall obtain a very fair picture of the Indians' capacity as discoverers and inventors. After that, we may well ask ourselves whether it is not possible that the Indians, who have discovered and invented so many things that were unknown among the variegated cultures of the Old World, might have been capable of hitting upon something or other that also was known there. It is a question that to me, at any rate, appears in a high degree pertinent.

In the first place, then, we may consider the cultivation of all the purely American cultivated plants. These the Indians must have found in their wild state, and by degrees brought under cultivation. These plants, as we know, are very numerous, and I shall confine myself to mentioning only the most important ones. . . .

Of outstanding importance is maize. At the time when America was discovered this plant was being cultivated in a number of varieties all the way from Central Chile to 55° of northern latitude. A good many of the implements that were used in connection with the cultivation of maize, such as grinding-stones on three or four feet, graters, husking-pins, etc., must necessarily be Indian inventions. The different dishes prepared from maize must also be of Indian origin, as well as different methods of storing maize.

As I have already indicated, the cultivation of maize is of exceedingly wide range in America, and the Indians have found out how to adapt the method of cultivating this American plant according to the varying climatic conditions. Among other things, in Peru, and in southwestern North America, for example, there were in pre-Columbian times very large-scale irrigation constructions with an important canal system. As to whether the idea of these is native to America is a question that I for the present prefer to leave unanswered.

Next to maize, manioc [tapioca] is the most important of the cultivated plants of the New World. The Indians cultivate both a non-poisonous and a poisonous variety of manioc. In this case the Indians have made a very remarkable invention, in that they have discovered how to eliminate the deadly prussic acid from the manioc roots, and then use them for food. It thus follows that the Indians must have invented that most peculiar straining-bag of basketwork by means of which the poison is squeezed out, and also the various kinds of graters that are used for reducing the manioc to a pulp. Of the former there are two varieties, and of the latter many different types. . . .

Another very remarkable thing is also the Indian invention of utilizing the poison squeezed out of the manioc, for preserving meat against putrefaction in a tropical climate.

A plant very important to the Indians of the Andes in pre-Columbian time was—and still is—the potato. The Aymara Indians of Bolivia distinguish between no fewer than 240 different varieties of potato. The method of preserving potatoes by freezing and drying in the sun, for preparing so-called "chuño," must be an Indian invention.

Other important food plants that we have received from the Indians are our common beans, pea-nuts, Jerusalem artichoke, sunflower, as also cacao, quinua, tomatoes, etc. These and many others have been discovered by the Indians.

The tobacco plant is one of the most well-known Indian discoveries, as well as smoking, snuff-taking, and chewing. Thus we see that snuff, cigarettes, cigars, pronged cigar-holders, and tobacco-pipes are Indian inventions. If we study all the different kinds of Indian pipes in America we shall find that they vary most considerably as to shape, and that in this department the Indians have achieved quite a number of more or less ingenious inventions, as, for example, the use of a filter for draining off the tobacco juice. It is possible in America to note down the evolution of a number of pipe types from the simple tubular pipe.

The coca bush, from which we obtain cocaine, also hails from America. All of the very complicated cultivation of the coca bush must have been tried out by the Indians, just as they have discovered the remarkable qualities of the coca leaves. Coca is chewed together with ashes or lime, and in this we meet with a noteworthy parallel in betel-chewing. Therefore we are unable to declare, off-hand, that the idea of chewing coca together with lime was invented in America independently of influences from Oceania, among other things because the receptacles for the lime in America and Melanesia are so striking similar, and, in addition, they are even made from gourds (*Lagenaria*), i. e. one of the few cultivated plants that were common to the Old and the New Worlds in pre-Columbian times.

Cacao, too, is another of the important cultivated plants that we have originally obtained from the Indians. In pre-Columbian times the Indians drank cacao unsweetened, or sweetened with honey.

Among textile plants cultivated in America, cotton is the most important, and it was known to the Indians in pre-Columbian times. At that time the species of cotton that were cultivated in America were different from those that were cultivated in the Old World before the discovery. Hence we cannot, of course, know whether the spinning of yarn or the art of weaving cloth was independently invented by the Indians.

The Indians of America cultivate a spice plant, Spanish pepper (Cayenne pepper), which is of the greatest importance to them. They have discovered that by the burning of this pepper there is developed a sort of "poison gas" that proves effective in laying siege to villages fortified by palisades. . . .

There are many wild-growing plants that the Indians have put to use for different purposes, and in this direction they have made a number of important inventions. It is to Indians that credit is due for the discovery of rubber and its utilization in the form of rubber balls, enema syringes, waterproof fabric, elastic rings, etc. It is a matter of fact that in pre-Columbian times the Indians were acquainted with all the qualities that make rubber so valuable in modern industry. No corresponding discovery had ever been made in the Old World prior to the discovery of America, in spite of the fact that both in Asia and Africa there are found rubber trees of various kinds.

The Indians have discovered a number of poisons, among others the terrible curare poison which they produce from certain *Strychnos* varieties, including *Strychnos toxifera,* and principally used for their blowgun darts. A horrible cardiac poison is obtained by the Chocó Indians from a tree called pakurú-neará. These Indians also produce a very virulent arrow-poison from the secretions of a certain frog.

In addition to cultivated narcotic plants, the Indians know several wild-growing ones, as, for instance, parica (*Piptadenia*). They have invented curious tubes, which they used in snuffing up powdered parica seeds, whereby a strongly intoxicating effect is produced. They are also known to have used parica for intoxicating enema injections. Guaraná, peyote (a kind of cactus), and Paraguay tea (maté) have also been discovered by Indians.

The Indians possessed a considerable knowledge of medicinal plants. Among the most important discovered by them are quinine, balsam of copaiba, and ipecacuanha. It is probable that the Indians, before it was known in the Old World, understood the application of aseptics, seeing that certain tribes dress their wounds with boiled water, without having learned this from the whites.

The Indians have discovered how to make use of a number of wild-growing American plants for making cord, etc. Among these, caraguata (*Bromelia serra*) may be noted. A certain proportion of the tools they used in working up the fibre are undoubtedly also Indian inventions.

From the bark of certain trees the Indians manufacture bast cloth, but as a similar manufacture is also known from Oceania, it cannot definitely be asserted that in this case the Indians have made an entirely independent discovery. Similarity between the implements used both within and outside America in the preparation of bark-cloth even speaks against such a supposition.

From the above it will be seen that the Indians in a wonderful way have known how to utilize the plant world by which they were surrounded, and in this province the peoples of the Old World have learnt a very great deal indeed from the Indians. In fact, during the period exceeding 400 years that Europeans have been in America, they have achieved not one single important discovery in this department. Evidently the Indians have carried out tests and experiments with everything they found available.

Here I may add that the very idea of cultivation must, in America, be an Indian invention, for if it had been introduced from abroad it must have been imported in association with some alien cultivable plant. For we have no reason whatever for supposing that the plants first cultivated by the Indians were the sweet potato and the bottle-gourd (*Lagenaria*) —plants that in pre-Columbian time probably they had in common with Oceania—cultivation having instead been inaugurated with some purely American utility plant. It is in fact evident that the sweet potato is in America a plant whose cultivation began at a later date than, for example, maize. . . .

If we now pass on to domestic animals we shall find that not many are of purely American origin. For this we cannot blame the Indians, but the American fauna. They have domesticated the llama, alpaca, guinea-pig, musk-duck and the turkey. The dog's companionship with man is of such remote antiquity that it was possibly brought along when man first immigrated into the New World. It is, however, probable that the Indians have domesticated also one or more indigenous species of the Canis family. A couple of American bee species have also been adopted for cultivation by the Indians. That this was a perfectly independent development is quite obvious. The cultivation of the cochineal bug, for the production of red pigment, is also an Indian invention. The employment of the llama as a beast of burden must necessarily be an Indian invention, as also the pack-saddle pertaining to it.

Plants and domestic animals of the New and Old Worlds respectively with one or two exceptions differ from each other, hence we are able to ascertain that their discovery and utilization must have been independently made in the New World. This does not, however, apply in the case of metals, as the same metals are found both in the New World and the Old. It is nevertheless probable that it was the Indians who first discovered, at any rate, one metal which is found in the Old World as well as in the New, namely, platinum. In regard to the working of metals, the Inca Indians achieved an invention that we of the Old World only in recent times have succeeded in accomplishing—and then by a method quite different from that of the Indians—namely, the art of welding copper. Thus we have in the Gothenburg Museum a copper rattle from Peru, in which the different parts are not soldered together, but welded, as has been shown by one of Sweden's leading metallurgists, Mr. Hultgren.

If we turn to the subject of dwellings, clothing, ornaments, tools, weapons, and so on, we shall find that the Indians do not possess much that is not also found in the Old World and which may, off-hand, be stated as having been invented by them, but nevertheless it appears improbable that man would find it easier to subject a new plant to cultivation than to invent some new implement or process in order to benefit by it.

We shall see that the Indians have invented more than one thing that was not known to any of the innumerable peoples of widely variegated culture in the Old World—that is to say, that they have made certain inventions that cannot be explained by the fact that they alone possessed the raw material. I have already referred to those objects which they manufacture from rubber.

In the realm of ceramics the application of sponge spicules in the clay, for cohesion and durability, is an invention made in Amazonas, and, so far as I am aware, not known from any other part of the world.

The spicules, which act as do iron rods in reinforced concrete, impart great strength to the clay vessels. Of ceramic forms many exist in the New World that are not met with in the Old. Thus, for example, vessels with a hollow rim . . . probably represent a type that is of a purely American origin.

The hammock is an invention that we have received from the Indians. Its autochthonous occurrence in New Guinea may well be considered highly doubtful. It is, moreover, unquestionably established that this comfortable form of bed was unknown outside America prior to the discovery of that continent. The hammock is an essentially Amazonian cultural element.

The reduction of head-trophies, by removing the skull and shrinking the head to the size of a fist, whilst still retaining the shape of the facial features, as the Jivaro Indians do, is a strange custom which is not known outside America.

Among musical instruments in America there are many that do not occur in the Old World, such as a quaint wind-instrument from Guiana, a strange-looking flute in the shape of an axe, described by Bolinder, from the Motilones. Many forms of signalling gongs, too, are of purely Indian origin, as is also the "teponatzli," the well-known "Zungentrommel" of the Mexicans. . . .

Of weapons there is none of especially Indian type, but, on the other hand, the Indians have made certain minor inventions as to weapons that are not found in the Old World, such as several methods of affixing feathers to arrows: for example, Peruvian cemented feathering, sewed feathering, and others. Neither can it with certainty be maintained that any Indian method in hunting is entirely original. Nor—as regards fishing—can there be any method pointed to that only the Indians know. This latter is quite interesting to note in view of all we know of their important contribution as agriculturists to the progress of human culture. . . .

If we study the distribution of those discoveries and inventions which the Indians must have independently made, on account of their non-occurrence in the Old World, we shall find that a surprisingly great proportion of them fall within the Amazon region. The impression is also forced upon one that the independently made inventions belong more to the agricultural tribes than to those living by hunting and fishing. It is also evident that the Inca region was at least as important a culture center as Central America and Mexico. As the present paper principally deals with South America it is probable that I have overlooked some discoveries and inventions made by the Indians of North America.

It is mostly where the Indians have been prosperous that one meets with a large proportion of inventions and discoveries. I am afraid it is not always true that necessity is the mother of invention. If it were true, then inventions ought to have been made in places where the struggle for existence was very hard. But instead they are made where conditions of life are easy.

14. The Accumulation of Technological Knowledge

V. GORDON CHILDE

V. Gordon Childe's theories of cultural development were built on a long career of detailed archeological investigation and have received wide circulation through a number of popular works. The item printed here was excerpted from Chapters 4 to 6 of his *Man Makes Himself*. It shows the growth of culture from its near-animal beginnings to the advent of urban social existence in the Mediterranean area, and gives us a glimpse of the many creative acts necessary to bring man to this point in his development. Childe was particularly interested in the effect of food production and cultural development upon social life. He saw the shift from living off of the products of nature to producing food by farming as a revolution in man's history and the shift to true agriculture as a second ("urban") revolution—both comparable to the "industrial revolution" of more recent history.

Childe was Director of the Institute of Archeology of the University of London (1946–1956) and prior to that had been Professor of Prehistoric Archaeology at Edinburgh. He was trained at Oxford University in classics.

The selection is from *Man Makes Himself* by V. Gordon Childe. 1939. Reprinted by permission of Oxford University Press.

Man's emergence on the earth is indicated to the archaeologist by the tools he made. Man needs tools to supplement the deficiencies of his physiological equipment for securing food and shelter. He is enabled to make them by the delicate correlation of hand and eye rendered possible by the constitution of his brain and nervous system. The first tools would presumably be bits of wood, bone, or stone, very slightly sharpened or accommodated to the hand by breaking or chipping. In so far as they were made of wood, they will have perished. The earliest stone tools will normally be indistinguishable from the products of natural fracture (stone splintered by frost or heat or shattered by jostling in a river gravel). However, even from times prior to the first Ice Age, archaeologists have recognized pieces of flint that appear to be intelligently chipped, as if to adapt them to serve as knives, choppers, and scrapers. The human workmanship of such "eoliths" is indeed still disputed, but is admitted by the majority of authorities.

In quite early pleistocene times there were certainly "men" manufacturing unmistakable implements of stone and also controlling fire. Conclusive evidence has been obtained from the cave of Choukou-tien near Pekin (Pei-ping). There, together with the fossilized remains of "Pekin man" and of extinct animals, were found very crudely fashioned flakes of quartzite and other stones, and also bones that had indubitably been subjected to the action of fire. Superior tools have been found in geological deposits of the same age in East Anglia and elsewhere, but not definitely associated with "human" skeletons. Little is to be learned from tools of this sort; they reveal that some manlike creature was adapting stones to his rudimentary needs, but little more. . . .

The control of fire was presumably the first great step in man's emancipation from the bondage to his environment. Warmed by the embers, man could endure cold nights, and could thus penetrate into temperate and even arctic regions. The flames would give him light at night and allow him to explore the recesses of sheltering caves. Fire would scare away other wild beasts. By cooking, substances became edible that would be indigestible if eaten raw. Man is no longer restricted in his movements to a limited range of climates, and his activities need not be entirely determined by the sun's light.

But in mastery of fire man was controlling a mighty physical force and a conspicuous chemical change. For the first time in history a creature of Nature was directing one of the great forces of Nature. . . .

The discovery was one of first-class significance. Man could thereafter not only control but also initiate the puzzling process of burning, the mysterious power of heat. He became consciously a creator. The evocation of flame out of a pair of sticks or from flint, pyrites, and tinder looks very like making something out of nothing. When it was a less familiar event, it must have had a very exhilarating effect; you must have felt yourself a creator indeed. But of course man was a creator in shaping a piece of wood or stone into a tool. He was asserting a power over Nature and molding objects to his will.

Such are the only certain facts that emerge from a study of the remains actually left by early pleistocene and pre-pleistocene "men." What they lived on is unknown. It is assumed that the earliest men snared and hunted wild animals and birds, caught fishes and lizards, collected wild fruits, shellfish, and eggs, and dug for roots and grubs. It is also assumed, but with less confidence, that they made coats of skins. Some certainly took refuge in caves, others may have erected rude shelters of boughs. Success in hunting could only be attained by prolonged and accurate observation of the habits of game; the results must have been built up into a collective tradition of hunting lore. The distinction between nutritive and poisonous plants again had presumably to be learned by experience, and once more incorporated in a communal tradition.

Man must learn the right seasons for hunting the different species of game or collecting the several kinds of eggs and fruits. To do so successfully he must eventually decipher the calendar of the heavens; he must observe the phases of the moon and the risings of stars, and compare these observations with the botanical and zoological ones already mentioned. And, as noted, man had to discover by experiment the best stones for making tools and where such occurred. For even the earliest men success in life required a considerable body of astronomical, botanical, geological, and zoological knowledge. In acquiring and transmitting this our forerunners were laying the foundations of science.

It may equally well be inferred that men learned to cooperate and act together in getting their livelihood. A creature so weak and poorly endowed as man could not in isolation successfully hunt the large or fierce animals that quite early provided an important item in his diet. Some form of social organization beyond the simple family (in the modern European sense of that word) has to be postulated, but the precise form is unknown. . . .

First about 50,000 years ago does it become possible to add any significant details to the foregoing vague sketch. As the last Ice Age was approaching, groups of "men" who used to be termed Mousterians became prominent in Europe. As they habitually lived in caves to escape the intense cold, more details are known of their lives than of those of earlier groups. . . .

Economically the Mousterians were hunters and had specialized in trapping huge arctic mammals—the mammoth and the woolly rhinoceros, whose carcasses they would drag to the mouth of their cave and there cut up. Naturally such big beasts cannot have been pursued by individuals or small families; mammoth hunting is a trade for some larger social unit co-operating for economic ends.

Historically the most notable fact about the Mousterians is the care they devoted to the disposal of the dead. More than a dozen Neanderthal skeletons have been found in France, ritually buried in the caves where their group lived. . . .

A few millennia later the glacial climate of Europe improved slightly for a time. During this warmer interval men of our own species first appear positively in the archaeological record in Europe, North Africa, and Hither Asia. Neanderthal "man" abruptly disappears; his place is taken by modern men, whose bodies would hardly provoke comment in a mortuary today. . . .

All Upper Paleolithic groups are far better equipped for dealing with the environment than any previously encountered. They have learnt to make a variety of distinct tools adapted to particular uses; they even make tools for making tools. They work bone and ivory as skilfully as flint; they have even invented simple mechanical devices like the bow and the spear-thrower to supplement human muscular power in hurling weapons. And, of course, such an array of new tools indicates not only increased technical skill, but also greater accumulations of knowledge and wider applications of science. . . .

Favorable conditions prevailed in Central France. The limestone plateaus were steppes on which browsed mammoths, reindeer, bisons, musk oxen, horses, and other edible animals. Salmon ran every year in the waters of the Dordogne, the Vezère, and other rivers as abundantly as in British Columbia today. The walls of the valleys are honeycombed with caves offering convenient habitations. By exploiting this environment intelligently, the Aurignacians and their successors, the Magdalenians, multiplied and created a rich culture. They were no more homeless nomads than were the Kwakiutl of British Columbia who last century, despite a "paleolithic" economy, lived in substantial and even ornate wooden houses grouped in permanent villages. Such prosperity is a warning against underrating the possibilities of food-gathering as a livelihood.

The deep Upper Paleolithic deposits in the caves, the masses of tools that can be collected, suggest an increased population. The number of Upper Paleolithic skeletons found in France alone exceeds that of all earlier skeletons put together. Yet the period over which they must be distributed is not one-twentieth of that to which the latter belong. Nevertheless, the number of Upper Paleolithic skeletons is not one-hundredth of that attributed to the neolithic period in France, which did not last a fifth of the time assigned to the Aurignacian and Magdalenian phases. Intelligent exploitation of an eminently favorable environment enabled the Aurignacian hunters to multiply beyond all former inhabitants of Western Europe, but their numbers fell far short of those attained by their successors after the neolithic revolution.

With game so abundant as to ensure security and even leisure, the Aurignacians were enabled to build up on traditions inherited from unknown ancestors a varied cultural life. On the material side its most striking traits are the possession of engines—the spear-thrower and the bow. . . .

These peoples must have lived in communities large enough to hunt successfully big game like mammoth and bison. How they were organized is, of course, unknown. Economically each group was self-sufficient. But self-sufficiency does not spell isolation; shells brought from the Mediterranean have been found in the caves of Central France. Presumably they were brought thither by some rudimentary form of trade. Still, shells, though valued for supposed magical virtues, are luxuries, not necessities. The trade they denote played no essential part in the group's economy. That was based upon hunting and collecting and, at least by Magdalenian times, on fishing. No evidence for the production of food by the cultivation of plants and breeding of animals has yet come to light in France or anywhere else at this period. Steps for the conservation of game by the observance of close seasons may be inferred from the customs of contemporary savages. . . .

The most surprising and celebrated aspect of Upper Paleolithic cultures is the artistic activity of the hunters. They carved figures in the round in stone or ivory, modeled animals in clay, decorated weapons with representations and formal designs, executed bas-reliefs on the rock walls of cave shelters, and engraved or painted scenes on the ceilings of caverns. In many instances their products are in themselves of high artistic merit. . . .

Nevertheless it was not among the Magdalenians of Europe that the neolithic revolution was initiated and the new economy created. The Magdalenians owed their prosperity to a successful adjustment to a special environment. When, with the passing of the last Ice Age, forest invaded the former steppes and tundra and ousted the herds of mammoth, bison, horse, and reindeer from France, the culture, based upon the hunting of these animals, decayed. Other peoples, who have left no such brilliant memorials behind them, created the new food-producing economy. It is, in fact, conceivable that, even in the days of the Aurignacian and Magdalenian hunters of Europe, tribes in other continents had begun cultivating plants and breeding animals. . . .

. . . The first revolution that transformed human economy gave man control over his own food supply. Man began to plant, cultivate, and improve by selection edible grasses, roots, and trees. And he succeeded in taming and firmly attaching to his person certain species of animal in return for the fodder he was able to offer, the protection he could afford, and the forethought he could exercise. The two steps are closely related. . . .

Quite a large variety of plants are capable of providing a staple diet under cultivation. Rice, wheat, barley, millet, maize, yams, sweet potatoes, respectively support considerable populations even today. But in the civilizations which have contributed most directly and most generously to the building up of the cultural heritage we enjoy, wheat and barley lie at the foundations of the economy. These two cereals offer, in fact, exceptional advantages. The food they yield is highly nutritious, the grains can easily be stored, the return is relatively high, and, above all, the labor involved in cultivation is not too absorbing. The preparation of the fields and sowing certainly demand a considerable effort; some weeding and watching are requisite while the crop is ripening; harvest demands intensive exertion by the whole community. But these efforts are seasonal. Before and after sowing come intervals in which the fields need practically no attention. The grain grower enjoys substantial spells of leisure, during which he can devote himself to other occupations. The rice grower, on the other hand, enjoys no such respite. His toil need perhaps never be so intensive as that demanded by the grain harvest, but it is more continuous. . . .

As a revolution the introduction of a food-producing economy should affect the lives of all concerned, so as to be reflected in the population curve. Of course, no "vital statistics" have been recorded to prove that the expected increase of population did occur. But it is easy to see that it should. The community of food-gatherers had been restricted in size by the food supplies available—the actual number of game animals, fish, edible roots, and berries growing in its territory. No human effort could augment these supplies, whatever magicians might say. Indeed, improvements in the technique or intensification of hunting and collecting beyond a certain point would result in the progressive extermination of the game and an absolute diminution of supplies. And, in practice, hunting populations appear to be nicely adjusted to the resources at their disposal. Cultivation at once breaks down the limits thus imposed. To increase the food supply it is only necessary to sow more seed, to bring more land under tillage. If there are more mouths to feed, there will also be more hands to till the fields.

. . . Certain methods of cultivation impose a sort of nomadism upon their practitioners. To many peasants in Asia, Africa, and South America, even today, cultivation means simply clearing a patch of scrub or jungle, digging it up with a hoe or just a stick, sowing it, and then reaping the crop. The plot is not fallowed, still less manured, but just resown next year. Of course, under such conditions the yield declines conspicuously after a couple of seasons. Thereupon another plot is cleared, and the process repeated till that too is exhausted. Quite soon all the available land close to the settlement has been cropped to exhaustion. When that has happened, the people move away and start afresh elsewhere. Their household goods are simple enough to be easily transported. The houses themselves are flimsy hovels, probably grown foul by prolonged occupation, and can readily be replaced.

What has just been described is the most primitive form of cultivation, often termed hoe-culture or garden-culture. Nature soon posed a question to the first cultivators—the problem of soil exhaustion. The easiest way of dealing with the issue was to dodge it and move away. Actually that solution is perfectly satisfactory so long as there is plenty of cultivable land and the cultivator is content to do without such luxuries and refinements as impede migration. It was, of course, a nuisance to have to clear a new bit of forest every few years, but that was surely less trouble than thinking out a new solution. In any case this sort of cultivation prevailed throughout Europe north of the Alps in prehistoric times. It may have survived among some German tribes down to the beginning of our era; for the geographer Strabo remarks upon their readiness to shift their settlements. It is still practiced today, for example, among the rice-growing Nagas in Assam, among the Boro in the Amazon basin, and even by grain growers in the Sudan. Yet it is a wasteful method, and ultimately limits the population, since suitable land is nowhere unrestricted. . . .

In practically all the oldest food-producing settlements examined by archaeologists in Europe, Hither Asia, and North Africa, the basic industry is mixed farming; in addition to the cultivation of cereals, animals are bred for food. This economy is characteristic of the "neolithic" stage wherever such exist. The food animals kept were not very varied: horned cattle, sheep, goats, and swine. Comparatively few species—fowls are the most important—have been added to the farmyards in subsequent periods or other countries. . . .

Whatever its origin, stock-breeding gave man control over his own food supply in the same way as cultivation did. In mixed farming it becomes an equal partner in the food-producing economy. But just as the term "cultivation" covers many distinct modes of gaining a livelihood, so the single phrase "mixed farming" marks an equal disparity and diversity. The several different modes of cultivation may be combined in varying degrees with distinct attitudes to the livestock. The diversity of the permutations and combinations has just been suggested. The multiplicity of concrete applications of the food-producing economy must never be forgotten.

It must be remembered, too, that food-production does not at once supersede food-gathering. If today hunting is only a ritual sport and game is a luxury for the rich, fishing is still a great industry, contributing directly to everybody's diet. At first hunting, fowling, fishing, the collection of fruits, snails, and grubs continued to be essential activities in the food-quest of any food-producing group. Grain and milk began as mere supplements to a diet of game, fish, berries, nuts, and ants' eggs. Probably at first cultivation was an incidental activity of the women while their lords were engaged in the really serious business of the chase. Only slowly did it win the status of an independent and ultimately predominant industry. When the archaeological record first reveals neolithic communities in Egypt and Iran, survivals from the food-gathering régime clearly stand on an equal footing with grain-growing and stock-breeding. Only subsequently does their economic importance decline. . . .

Two other aspects of the simple food-producing economy deserve attention. In the first place, food-production, even in its simplest form, provides an opportunity and a motive for the accumulation of a surplus. A crop must not be consumed as soon as it is reaped. The grains must be conserved and eked out so as to last till the next harvest, for a whole year. And a proportion of every crop must be set aside for seed. The conservation is easy. But it means on the one hand forethought and thrift, on the other receptacles for storage. These are quite as essential as, and may actually be more elaborate than, dwellings. In the neolithic villages of the Fayum, perhaps the oldest of their kind, excavated silos, lined with straw basketry or matting, are the most substantial constructions that have survived.

Again, livestock that has been laboriously carried over the dry season must not be indiscriminately slaughtered and devoured. The young cows and ewes at least must be spared and reared to provide milk and to augment the herd or flock. Once these ideas have been driven home, the production and accumulation of a surplus are much easier for food-producers than for food gatherers. The yield of crops and of herds soon outstrips the immediate needs of the community. The storage of grain, the conservation of live meat "on the hoof" is much simpler, especially in a warm climate, than the preservation of stocks of slaughtered game. The surplus thus gathered will help to tide the community over bad seasons; it will form a reserve against droughts and crop failures. It will serve to support a growing population. Ultimately it may constitute a basis for rudimentary trade, and so pave the way to a second revolution.

Secondly, the economy is entirely self-sufficing. The simple food-producing community is not dependent for any necessity of life on imports obtained by barter or exchange from another group. It produces and collects all the food it needs. It relies on raw materials available in its immediate vicinity for the simple equipment it demands. Its constituent members or households manufacture the requisite implements, utensils, and weapons. . . .

In the later part of the Old Stone Age axe-like tools seem to have been unknown. The ground stone celt does not seem to derive directly from the "hand axe" of flaked stone or flint current earlier in the Old Stone Age. The essence of the neolithic tool is that its edge is sharpened by grinding. The new technique might be suggested by effects observed on stone rubbers used for grinding grains on other stones. Or perhaps for digging up the garden plots a split pebble was lashed on to the end of a stick to make a sort of hoe; then the end of the pebble might be rubbed sharp by friction with sandy soil. But, though neolithic celts are almost invariably found in the oldest settlements of simple food-producers, it is not certain that the implement is really a result of the new economy. . . .

Still, wherever it arose, the ground stone celt provided a tough implement and a resistant edge that would not be chipped or blunted by a few blows. It enabled man to hew and to shape timber. Carpentry could begin. Plows, wheels, plank-boats, wooden houses all require axes and adzes for their manufacture. The invention of the ground stone celt was an essential pre-condition for these later achievements.

The preparation and storage of cereal foods may be supposed to have put a premium upon vessels which would at once stand heat and hold liquids. A universal feature of neolithic communities seems to have been the manufacture of pots. . . .

The new industry has great significance for human thought and for the beginning of science. Pot-making is perhaps the earliest conscious utilization by man of a chemical change. . . .

To early man this change in the quality of the material must have seemed a sort of magic transubstantiation—the conversion of mud or dust into stone. It may have prompted some philosophical questions as to the meaning of substance and sameness. How is the plastic clay the same substance as the hard but brittle earthenware? The pot you put into the fire has much the same shape as what you draw out, but the color has changed and the texture is quite different. . . .

Among the remains of the earliest neolithic villages of Egypt and Hither Asia we find the first indications of a textile industry. Manufactured garments, woven out of linen, or later wool, begin to compete with dressed skins or skirts of leaves as protection against cold and sun. For this to be possible another complex of discoveries and inventions is requisite, a further body of scientific knowledge must be practically applied. In the first place, a suitable material was needed, a fibrous substance that would yield long threads. The neolithic villagers on the Fayum lake were already using flax. They must have selected this from all other plants and begun to cultivate it deliberately in addition to growing cereals. Another variety of flax may have been discovered and grown in Asia. A local European flax was cultivated and utilized in Switzerland in neolithic times.

Other materials must have been tried. Cotton was certainly being grown in the Indus valley soon after 3000 B.C. . . .

All the foregoing industries require for their exercise a technical skill that can only be acquired by training and practice. Yet all were household crafts. In our hypothetical neolithic stage there would be no specialization of labor—at most a division of work between the sexes. And that system can still be seen at work today. Among hoe-cultivators the women generally till the fields, build up and fire the pots, spin, and weave; men look after animals, hunt and fish, clear the plots for cultivation, and act as carpenters, preparing their own tools and weapons. But, of course, to such a generalization there are many exceptions: among the Yoruba, for instance, weaving is in the hands of men.

All the industries named, from garden culture to weaving, have been rendered possible only by the accumulation of experience and the application of deductions therefrom. Each and all repose on practical science. Moreover, the exercise of each craft is throughout regulated and directed by a constantly expanding body of practical science. The appropriate lore is handed on from parent to child for generation after generation. The cultivator, for instance, must know in practice what soil it is most profitable to till, when to break up the ground, how to distinguish young grain shoots from sprouting weeds, and a host of other details. The young potter must learn to find and choose proper clay, how to clean it, with what proportion of water and grit it should be mixed, and so on. . . .

The neolithic crafts have been presented as household industries. Yet the craft traditions are not individual, but collective traditions. The experience and wisdom of all the community's members are constantly being pooled. In a modern African village the housewife does not retire into seclusion in order to build up and fire her pots. All the women of the village work together, chatting and comparing notes; they even help one another. The occupation is public; its rules are the result of communal experience. And so in prehistoric times all the pots from a given neolithic village exhibit a monotonous uniformity. They bear the stamp of a strong collective tradition rather than of individuality.

And the neolithic economy as a whole cannot exist without co-operative effort. The heavier labor of clearing patches in a forest or draining a marsh must be a collective undertaking. The digging of drains, the defense of the settlement against wild beasts or floods, must again be communal responsibilities. The dwellings in neolithic villages both in Egypt and in Western Europe have been proved to be arranged in a regular order, not scattered about indiscriminately. All this implies some social organization to co-ordinate and control the communal activities. What that organization was we can never know exactly. . . .

The neolithic revolution, just described, was the climax of a long process. It has to be presented as a single event because archaeology can only recognize the result; the several steps leading up thereto are beyond the range of direct observation. A second revolution transformed some tiny villages of self-sufficing farmers into populous cities, nourished by secondary industries and foreign trade, and regularly organized as States.

Some of the episodes which ushered in this transformation can be discerned, if dimly, by prehistory. The scene of the drama lies in the belt of semi-arid countries between the Nile and the Ganges. Here epoch-making inventions seem to have followed one another with breathless speed, when we recall the slow pace of progress in the millennia before the first revolution or even in the four millennia between the second and the Industrial Revolution of modern times.

Between 6000 and 3000 B.C. man has learnt to harness the force of oxen and of winds, he invents the plow, the wheeled cart, and the sailboat, he discovers the chemical processes involved in smelting copper ores and the physical properties of metals, and he begins to work out an accurate solar calendar. He has thereby equipped himself for urban life, and prepares the way for a civilization which shall require writing, processes of reckoning, and standards of measurement.

15. Eskimo Ingenuity

EDWARD M. WEYER, JR.

The technical knowledge of primitive peoples is far more impressive than the poor circumstances of their daily life indicates. As they must do everything for themselves, they must have detailed knowledge of their environment—its animals, plants and other natural products, its dangers and potentialities. This knowledge they must store in their memories, for they have no books. It is fair to say that the average native must retain as much practical information in his head as the average American.

No technology of primitive people is so remarkable as that of the Eskimo—especially of those Eskimos living in the extreme north. Were we to make a compilation of all their practical knowledge, it would fill a large book; the following essay offers us a mere sample of their ingenuity. It is worth noting that Eskimos, who are in contact with modern ways, take readily to the mechanical arts and can fix cars and watches that seem to be hopelessly broken —for their mechanical aptitude is a deep-seated culture trait.

Edward M. Weyer took his doctorate in anthropology from Yale University and was for a long time editor of *Natural History Magazine*. He is widely known as an explorer and popularizer of science, he has been Curator of the Anthropology Museum of the University of California, Berkeley. The material here was taken from a book reporting his first expedition, to the Arctic: *The Eskimos, Their Environment and Folkways,* "Influence of Geographical Conditions on Modes of Life," (Chapter IV, pp. 70–74), New Haven: Yale University Press, 1932, and is printed by kind permission of the publisher and author.

The Eskimo shows remarkable ingenuity in making use of what simple resources his homeland offers, and, unlike the man with but one talent, makes the utmost of his scanty materials. His house of snow needs only to be mentioned in this connection. Knowing nothing of glass he fashions his window out of ice, or from the translucent intestinal membrane of a sea mammal, the gullet of the white whale or of birds, or the pericardium of the caribou. For thread he uses sinews, generally procured chiefly from the back and hind legs of the caribou but also from the white whale, and from the gullet, tail, back, and flippers of the seal. Whalebone serves as cord for lashing implements; and the thin fiber stripped from the surface of bird quills is used for finer lashing.

Only a small proportion of the Eskimos used metal before the coming of the white man. Two centers of metal working existed: one including the natives about Coronation Gulf, who are appropriately called the Copper Eskimos because of their utilization of native copper; the other in northwestern Greenland, where the Eskimos worked meteoric iron on a small scale.

In the absence of metal the Eskimos used stone, of course, for blades and weapon points. They also used stone, commonly soapstone, for lamps and cooking pots. The importance of soapstone along the lower reaches of the Great Fish River is evident from the fact that the tribal name there, Utkuhikhalingmiut, means "Dwellers in the land of soapstone." Iron pyrites, in addition, was of value in generating fire among practically all Eskimos. Everywhere, however, the Eskimos were familiar with the process of generating fire with a drill. Of course, they never employed such an intricate principle in kindling fire as that of a lens of ice.

Stone for implements and iron pyrites were in general available to all Eskimos, though in some cases they would have to travel to procure them.

In natural resources, particularly in wood, the Eskimos of the central and northernmost regions are most poorly supplied. Their own resourcefulness is correspondingly conspicuous as under these circumstances they make their sledges of bone or ivory. In Baffin Island if wood is scarce the natives make a strange shovel-shaped sledge by stitching together sheets of whalebone. The height of ingenuity is displayed in the building of a sledge of frozen hide. Pieces of walrus skin or musk-ox skin are soaked in water, folded into the desired forms, and allowed to freeze solid. Thus the Eskimo fights the inexorable North with its own weapons; the extreme cold that makes his homeland a woodless country he utilizes in improvising this frozen sledge. This method is most common in the region of the Magnetic Pole, but is also practiced among the Iglulik and Copper Eskimos. The frozen hide is used chiefly for runners, the crosspieces being commonly of bone. The Arvilingjuarmiut (Pelly Bay) would roll up raw meat or fish in the hide that was to be frozen for sledge runners. After thawing, the skins were fed to the dogs that had drawn the sledge, while the contents were eaten by their masters. Boas mentions sledges of frozen salmon. Klutschak depicts a sledge of ice from Simpson Strait, and Boas refers to the making of a sledge by freezing together slabs of ice. Eskimos of the central regions are even known to make harpoon shafts by freezing walrus hide. And the Arvilingjuarmiut "made long slender harpoon shafts of horn, the pieces being straightened out laboriously in warm water and joined length to length. Tent poles were fashioned in the same way." . . .

The foregoing examples taken from the industries and diet of the Eskimos show how they circumvent the privations of their ungenerous habitat. It is significant that in an environment affording a minimum of natural resources they catch and kill the largest animals in the world—whales. Groups having no metal for weapons and only enough wood for harpoon shafts, boat paddles, and the frame of the skin-covered umiak have waged successful battle against these monsters of the sea.

It is largely from the animals the Eskimo kills that he manufactures his hunting weapons. From the skin of the seal the Bering Strait native fashions a net with which to catch more seals. To attract fish to his hook the Diomede Islander attaches the bright orange flap from the corner of the beak of the crested auklet. From whalebone the Eskimo fashions "spring bait," one of the most ingenious of his hunting accessories. To make this he sharpens the ends of a strip of the baleen, doubles the springy material up under tension, and ties it in that position with sinew. He buries the mass in fat and allows it to freeze. When the wolf is enticed and swallows it, the warmth of his stomach and his digestive juices release the barbed baleen, which pierces the creature internally and kills it.

Some central groups smear a knife with blood, and bury it in the snow with only the blade protruding. A hungry wolf licks the keen edge and cuts his tongue. Excited by the taste and smell he gormandizes, literally whetting his own appetite. Finally, he dies, bled to death and gorged with his own lifeblood.

To catch birds an Eskimo sometimes builds a small snow hut with a hole in the roof around which he scatters bits of meat and blubber as bait. From inside he deftly snatches the feet of the attracted birds. East Greenlanders, having poured train oil on the water so that swans alighting cannot easily take off, approach in a kayak and harpoon them.

The Eskimo acknowledges no superior throughout the animal kingdom. Though sometimes dangerously challenged, he remains the master of his stern world. The largest animals, as has been pointed out, are his prey. Indeed, he outwits all forms from the whale down to the tiniest creature. He even tricks the lice which infest his body, by drawing a piece of bear fur on a string under his clothes and pulling it out filled with the vermin.

Occasionally the Eskimos show an equally astonishing lack of resourcefulness, as, for instance, when Jenness observed that the Copper Eskimos obtained all their water throughout the winter from snow, being ignorant apparently of the fact that ordinary sea ice loses its salinity with age, and that an old cake of the previous winter will yield perfectly fresh water.

But, in general, the Eskimo has achieved harmony with his habitat. Generations of cultural evolution have developed a mode of living that fits his life-conditions. By mode of living we refer chiefly to his self-maintenance mores; and by life-conditions we mean the actual, physical, concrete, perceptible circumstances of his life. But here ends, in a large measure, the perfection of his judgment. Aside from his physical environment, the Eskimo faces another set of life-conditions, his spirit world. As with all peoples, though perhaps to a greater degree than among most groups, his imagination fills the world with ghosts, demons, and deities, to him just as exacting in their requirements as the forces of the natural world. And in his responses to this supernatural environment, in contrast with his responses to the physical environment, he often displays what, on the surface at least, might seem to be inefficiency and lack of economy.

16. The Clock and Technological Development

LEWIS MUMFORD

Lewis Mumford's concern with the modern city is based upon his knowledge of the historic processes by which it developed. His works on the emergence of urban industrial life are classics. He is aware that there is a close relationship between the kind of civilization we have and its technical apparatus, and therefore looks to the historical relation in the development of these. Clocks are so much a part of our everyday world that we forget how important they are to our modern technology—and to the essential spirit of our technological civilization. This brief essay shows that importance.

Mumford has written widely on history, architecture and city planning. His more important works are *Technics and Civilization, The Culture of Cities* and *The Transformation of Man*. He was for some years Professor of Humanities at Stanford University and was co-chairman of the Wenner-Gren Foundation Conference of Man's Use of the Earth in 1955.

The essay is taken from the section "The Monastery and the Clock," in the first chapter of *Technics and Civilization* by Lewis Mumford, copyright, 1934, by Harcourt, Brace and Company, Inc., and is published here by kind permission of the publisher.

Where did the machine first take form in modern civilization? There was plainly more than one point of origin. Our mechanical civilization represents the convergence of numerous habits, ideas, and modes of living, as well as technical instruments; and some of these were, in the beginning, directly opposed to the civilization they helped to create. But the first manifestation of the new order took place in the general picture of the world: during the first seven centuries of the machine's existence the categories of time and space underwent an extraordinary change, and no aspect of life was left untouched by this transformation. The application of quantitative methods of thought to the study of nature had its first manifestation in the regular measurement of time; and the new mechanical conception of time arose in part out of the routine of the monastery. Alfred Whitehead has emphasized the importance of the scholastic belief in a universe ordered by God as one of the foundations of modern physics: but behind that belief was the presence or order in the institutions of the Church itself.

The technics of the ancient world were still carried on from Constantinople and Baghdad to Sicily and Cordova: hence the early lead taken by Salerno in the scientific and medical advances of the Middle Age. It was, however, in the monasteries of the West that the desire for order and power, other than that expressed in the military domination of weaker men, first manifested itself after the long uncertainty and bloody confusion that attended the breakdown of the Roman Empire. Within the walls of the monastery was sanctuary: under the rule of the order surprise and doubt and caprice and irregularity were put at bay. Opposed to the erratic fluctuations and pulsations of the worldly life was the iron discipline of the rule. Benedict added a seventh period to the devotions of the day, and in the seventh century, by a bull of Pope Sabinianus, it was decreed that the bells of the monastery be rung seven times in the twenty-four hours. These punctuation marks in the day were known as the canonical hours, and some means of keeping count of them and ensuring their regular repetition became necessary.

According to a now discredited legend, the first modern mechanical clock, worked by falling weights, was invented by the monk named Gerbert who afterwards became Pope Sylvester II near the close of the tenth century. This clock was probably only a water clock, one of those bequests of the ancient world either left over directly from the days of the Romans, like the water-wheel itself, or coming back again into the West through the Arabs. But the legend, as so often happens, is accurate in its implications if not in its facts. The monastery was the seat of a regular life, and an instrument for striking the hours at intervals or for reminding the bell-ringer that it was time to strike the bells, was an almost inevitable product of this life. If the mechanical clock did not appear until the cities of the thirteenth century demanded an orderly routine, the habit of order itself and the earnest regulation of time-sequences had become almost second nature in the monastery. Coulton agrees with Sombart in looking upon the Benedictines, the great working order, as perhaps the original founders of modern capitalism: their rule certainly took the curse off work and their vigorous engineering enterprises may even have robbed warfare of some of its glamor. So one is not straining the facts when one suggests that the monasteries—at one time there were 40,000 under the Benedictine rule—helped to give human enterprise the regular collective beat and rhythm of the machine;

for the clock is not merely a means of keeping track of the hours, but of synchronizing the actions of men.

Was it by reason of the collective Christian desire to provide for the welfare of souls in eternity by regular prayers and devotions that time-keeping and the habits of temporal order took hold of men's minds: habits that capitalist civilization presently turned to good account? One must perhaps accept the irony of this paradox. At all events, by the thirteenth century there are definite records of mechanical clocks, and by 1370 a well-designed "modern" clock had been built by Heinrich von Wyck at Paris. Meanwhile, bell towers had come into existence, and the new clocks, if they did not have, till the fourteenth century, a dial and a hand that translated the movement of time into a movement through space, at all events struck the hours. The clouds that could paralyze the sundial, the freezing that could stop the water clock on a winter night, were no longer obstacles to time-keeping: summer or winter, day or night, one was aware of the measured clank of the clock. The instrument presently spread outside the monastery; and the regular striking of the bells brought a new regularity into the life of the workman and the merchant. The bells of the clock tower almost defined urban existence. Time-keeping passed into time-serving and time-accounting and time-rationing. As this took place, Eternity ceased gradually to serve as the measure and focus of human actions.

The clock, not the steam-engine, is the key-machine of the modern industrial age. For every phase of its development the clock is both the outstanding fact and the typical symbol of the machine: even today no other machine is so ubiquitous. Here, at the very beginning of modern technics, appeared prophetically the accurate automatic machine which, only after centuries of further effort, was also to prove the final consummation of this technics in every department of industrial activity. There had been power-machines, such as the water-mill, before the clock; and there had also been various kinds of automata, to awaken the wonder of the populace in the temple, or to please the idle fancy of some Moslem caliph: machines one finds illustrated in Hero and Al-Jazari. But here was a new kind of power-machine, in which the source of power and the transmission were of such a nature as to ensure the even flow of energy throughout the works and to make possible regular production and a standardized product. In its relationship to determinable quantities of energy, to standardization, to automatic action, and finally to its own special product, accurate timing, the clock has been the foremost machine in modern technics: and at each period it has remained in the lead: it marks a perfection toward which other machines aspire. The clock, moreover, served as a model for many other kinds of mechanical works, and the analysis of motion that accompanied the perfection of the clock, with the various types of gearing and transmission that were elaborated, contributed to the success of quite different kinds of machines. Smiths could have hammered thousands of suits of armor or thousands of iron cannon, wheelwrights could have shaped thousands of great water-wheels or crude gears, without inventing any of the special types of movement developed in clockwork, and without any of the accuracy of measurement and fineness of articulation that finally produced the accurate eighteenth century chronometer.

The clock, moreover, is a piece of power-machinery whose "product" is seconds and minutes: by its essential nature it dissociated time from human events and helped create the belief in an independent world of mathematically measurable sequences: the special world of science. There is relatively little foundation for this belief in common human experience: throughout the year the days are of uneven duration, and not merely does the relation between day and night steadily change, but a slight journey from East to West alters astronomical time by a certain number of minutes. In terms of the human organism itself, mechanical time is even more foreign: while human life has regularities of its own, the beat of the pulse, the breathing of the lungs, these change from hour to hour with mood and action, and in the longer span of days, time is measured not by the calendar but by the events that occupy it. The shepherd measures from the time the ewes lambed; the farmer measures back to the day of sowing or forward to the harvest: if growth has its own duration and regularities, behind it are not simply matter and motion but the facts of development: in short, history. And while mechanical time is strung out in a succession of mathematically isolated instants, organic time—what Bergson calls duration—is cumulative in its effects. Though mechanical time can, in a sense, be speeded up or run backward, like the hands of a clock or the images of a moving picture, organic time moves in only one direction—through the cycle of birth, growth, development, decay, and death—and the past that is already dead remains present in the future that has still to be born.

Around 1345, according to Thorndike, the division of hours into sixty minutes and of minutes into sixty seconds became common: it was this abstract framework of divided time that became more and more the point of reference for both action and thought, and in the effort to arrive at accuracy in this department, the astronomical exploration of the sky focused attention further upon the regular, implacable movements of the heavenly bodies through space. Early in the sixteenth century a young Nuremberg mechanic, Peter Henlein, is supposed to have created "many-wheeled watches out of small bits of iron" and by the end of the century the small domestic clock had been introduced in England and Holland. As with the motor car and the airplane, the richer classes first took over the new mechanism and popularized it: partly because they alone could afford it, partly because the new bourgeoisie were the first to discover that, as Franklin later put it, "time is money." To become "as regular as clockwork" was the bourgeois ideal, and to own a watch was for long a definite symbol of success. The increasing tempo of civilization led to a demand for greater power: and in turn power quickened the tempo.

Now, the orderly punctual life that first took shape in the monasteries is not native to mankind, although by now Western peoples are so thoroughly regimented by the clock that it is "second nature" and they look upon its observance as a fact of nature. Many Eastern civilizations have flourished on a loose basis in time: the Hindus have in fact been so indifferent to time that they lack even an authentic chronology of the years. Only yesterday, in the midst of the industrialization of Soviet Russia, did a society come into existence to further the carrying of watches there and to propagandize the benefits of punctuality. The popularization of time-keeping, which followed the production of the cheap standardized watch, first in Geneva, then in America around the middle of the last century, was essential to a well-articulated system of transportation and production.

To keep time was once a peculiar attribute of music: it gave industrial value to the workshop song or the tattoo or the chantey of the sailors tugging at a rope. But the effect of the mechanical clock is more pervasive and strict: it presides over the day from the hour of rising to the hour of rest. When one thinks of the day as an abstract span of time, one does not go to bed with the chickens on a winter's night: one invents wicks, chimneys, lamps, gaslights, electric lamps, so as to use all the hours belonging to the day. When one thinks of time, not as a sequence of experiences, but as a collection of hours, minutes, and seconds, the habits of adding time and saving time come into existence. Time took on the character of an enclosed space: it could be divided, it could be filled up, it could even be expanded by the invention of labor-saving instruments.

Abstract time became the new medium of existence. Organic functions themselves were regulated by it: one ate, not upon feeling hungry, but when prompted by the clock: one slept, not when one was tired, but when the clock sanctioned it. A generalized time-consciousness accompanied the wider use of clocks: dissociating time from organic sequences, it became easier for the men of the Renascence to indulge the fantasy of reviving the classic past or of reliving the splendors of antique Roman civilization: the cult of history, appearing first in daily ritual, finally abstracted itself as a special discipline. In the seventeenth century journalism and periodic literature made their appearance: even in dress, following the lead of Venice as fashion-center, people altered styles every year rather than every generation.

The gain in mechanical efficiency through co-ordination and through the closer articulation of the day's events cannot be over-estimated: while this increase cannot be measured in mere horse-power, one has only to imagine its absence today to foresee the speedy disruption and eventual collapse of our entire society. The modern industrial regime could do without coal and iron and steam easier than it could do without the clock.

17. Technology and Social Institutions: Australia

LAURISTON SHARP

The interdependence of technology with other aspects of society is shown in this and the following essay. When things run smoothly, we do not see this involvement, but when change takes place, we can see the consequences that follow. In this example the introduction of steel axes, a considerable material improvement over the stone axes that the Australian aborigines formerly used, was a major disruptive factor in social relations and religious belief.

Lauriston Sharp, Professor of Anthropology at Cornell University, was leader of the North Queensland expedition to Australia in 1933–35, and has also done research among the American Indians, Africans and the Siamese. He received his Ph.D. from Harvard University. The selection was taken from "Steel Axes for Stone Age Australians," in *Human Problems in Technological Change* (Edward H. Spicer, ed.) New York: Russell Sage Foundation, 1952, and is reprinted by kind permission of the author and publisher.

Like other Australian aboriginals, the Yir Yoront group at the mouth of the Coleman River on the west coast of tropical Cape York Peninsula originally had no knowledge of metals. Technologically their culture was of the old stone age or paleolithic type; they supported themselves by hunting and fishing, obtaining vegetable foods and needed materials from the bush by simple gathering techniques. Their only domesticated animal was the dog, and they had no domesticated plants of any kind. Unlike some other aboriginal groups, however, the Yir Yoront did have polished stone axes hafted in short handles, and these implements were most important in their economy.

Toward the end of the nineteenth century metal tools and other European artifacts began to filter into the Yir Yoront territory. The flow increased with the gradual expansion of the white frontier outward from southern and eastern Queensland. Of all the items of western technology thus made available, none was more acceptable, none more highly valued by aboriginals of all conditions than the hatchet or short-handled steel axe.

In the mid-1930's an American anthropologist was able to live alone in the bush among the Yir Yoront for thirteen months without seeing another white man. They were thus still relatively isolated and they continued an essentially independent economic life, supporting themselves entirely by means of their old stone-age techniques. Yet their polished stone axes were fast disappearing and were being replaced by steel axes, which came to them in considerable numbers directly or indirectly from various European sources to the south.

What changes in the life of the Yir Yoront still living under aboriginal conditions in the Australian bush could be expected as a result of their increasing possession and use of the steel axe? . . .

If we concentrate our attention on Yir Yoront behavior centering about the original stone axe, rather than on the axe—the thing—we should get some conception of the role this implement played in aboriginal culture. This conception, in turn, should permit us to foresee with considerable accuracy some of the results of the displacement of stone axes by steel axes acquired directly or indirectly from Europeans by the Yir Yoront.

The production of a stone axe required a number of simple skills. With the idea of the axe in its various details well in mind, the adult men—and only the adult men—could set about producing it, a task not considered appropriate for women or children. First of all, a man had to know the location and properties of several natural resources found in his immediate environment: pliable wood, which could be doubled or bent over the axe head and bound tightly to form a handle; bark, which could be rolled into cord for the binding; and gum, with which the stone head could be firmly fixed in the haft. These materials had to be correctly gathered, stored, prepared, cut to size, and applied or manipulated. They were plentifully supplied by nature, and could be taken by a man from anyone's property without special permission. Postponing consideration of the stone head of the axe, we see that a simple knowledge of nature and of the technological skills involved, together with the possession of fire (for heating the gum) and a few simple cutting tools, which might be nothing more than the sharp shells of plentiful bivalves, all of which were available to everyone, were sufficient to enable any normal man to make a stone axe.

The use of the stone axe as a piece of capital equipment for the production of other goods indicates its very great importance in the subsistence economy of the aboriginal. Anyone—man, woman, or child —could use the axe; indeed, it was used more by women, for theirs was the onerous, daily task of obtaining sufficient wood to keep the campfire of each family burning all day for cooking or other purposes and all night against mosquitoes and cold (in July, winter temperature might drop below forty degrees). In a normal lifetime any woman would use the axe to cut or knock down literally tons of firewood. Men and women, and sometimes children, needed the axe to make other tools, or weapons, or a variety of material equipment required by the aboriginal in his daily life. The stone axe was essential in making the wet-season domed huts, which keep out some rain and some insects; or platforms, which provide dry storage; or shelters, which give shade when days are bright and hot. In hunting and fishing and in gathering vegetable or animal food the axe was also a necessary tool; and in this tropical culture without preservatives or other means of storage, the native spends more time obtaining food than in any other occupation except sleeping.

In only two instances was the use of the stone axe strictly limited to adult men: Wild honey, the most prized food known to the Yir Yoront, was gathered only by men who usually used the axe to get it; and only men could make the secret paraphernalia for ceremonies, an activity often requiring use of the axe. From this brief listing of some of the activities in which the axe was used, it is easy to understand why there was at least one stone axe in every camp, in every hunting or fighting party, in every group out on a "walk-about" in the bush.

While the stone axe helped relate men and women and often children to nature in technological behavior, in the transformation of natural into cultural equipment, it also was prominent in that aspect of behavior which may be called conduct, primarily directed toward persons. Yir Yoront men were dependent upon interpersonal relations for their stone axe heads, since the flat, geologically recent alluvial country over which they range, provides no stone from which axe heads can be made. The stone they used comes from known quarries four hundred miles to the south. It reached the Yir Yoront through long lines of male trading partners, some of these chains terminating with the Yir Yoront men, while others extended on farther north to other groups, having utilized Yir Yoront men as links. Almost every older adult man had one or more regular trading partners, some to the north and some to the south. His partner or partners in the south he provided with surplus spears, and particularly fighting spears tipped with the barbed spines of sting ray which snap into vicious fragments when they penetrate human flesh. . . . While many other objects may move along these chains of trading partners, they are still characterized by both bush and station aboriginals as lines along which spears move south and axes move north. Thus trading relations, which may extend the individual's personal relationships out beyond the boundaries of his own group, are associated with two of the most important items in a man's equipment, spears and axes, whether the latter are of stone or steel. Finally, most of the exchanges between partners take place during the dry season at times when the great aboriginal fiestas occur, which center about initiation rites or other totemic ceremonials that attract hundreds and are the occasion for much exciting activity besides trading.

Returning to the Yir Yoront, we find that not only was it adult men alone who obtained axe heads and produced finished axes, but it was adult males who retained the axes, keeping them with other parts of their equipment in camp, or carrying them at the back slipped through a human hair belt when traveling. Thus, every woman or child who wanted to use an axe—and this might be frequently during the day— must get one from some man, use it promptly, and return it to the man in good condition. While a man might speak of "my axe," a woman or child could not; for them it was always "your axe," addressing a male, or "his axe."

This necessary and constant borrowing of axes from older men by women and children was done according to regular patterns of kinship behavior. A woman on good terms with her husband would expect to use his axe unless he were using it; a husband on good terms with his wives would let any one of them use his axe without question. If a woman was unmarried or her husband was absent, she would go first to her older brother or to her father for an axe. Only in extraordinary circumstances would she seek a stone axe from a mother's brother or certain other male kin with whom she had to be most circumspect. A girl, a boy, or a young man would look to a father or an older brother to provide an axe for her or his use, but would never approach a mother's brother, who would be at the same time a potential father-in-law, with such a request. Older men, too, would follow similar rules if they had to borrow an axe.

It will be noted that these social relationships in which the stone axe had a place are all pair relationships and that the use of the axe helped define and maintain the character of the relationships and the roles of the two individual participants. Every active relationship among the Yir Yoront involved a definite and accepted status of superordination or subordination. A person could have no dealings with any other on exactly equal terms. Women and children were dependent on, or subordinate to, older males in every action in which the axe entered. Among the men, the younger was dependent on the older or on certain kinds of kin. The nearest approach to equality was between brothers, although the older was always superordinate to the younger. Since the exchange of goods in a trading relationship involved a mutual reciprocity, trading partners were usually a kind of brother to each other or stood in a brotherly type of relationship, although one was always classified as older than the other and would have some advantage in case of dispute. It can be seen that repeated and widespread conduct centering on the axe helped to generalize and standardize throughout the society these sex, age, and kinship roles, both in their normal benevolent and in exceptional malevolent aspects, and helped to build up expectancies regarding the conduct of others defined as having a particular status.

The status of any individual Yir Yoront was determined not only by sex, age, and extended kin relationships, but also by membership in one of two dozen patrilineal totemic clans into which the entire community was divided. A person's names, rights in particular areas of land, and, in the case of a man, his roles in the totemic ceremonies (from which women are excluded) were all a function of belonging to one clan rather than another. . . .

Among the many totems of the Sunlit Cloud Iguana clan, and important among them, was the stone axe. The names of many members of this clan referred to the axe itself, or to activities like trading or wild honey gathering in which the axe played a vital part, or to the clan's mythical ancestors with whom the axe was prominently associated. When it was necessary to represent the stone axe in totemic ceremonies, it was only men of this clan who exhibited it or pantomimed its use. In secular life the axe could be made by any man and used by all; but in the sacred realm of the totems it belonged exclusively to the Sunlit Cloud Iguana people.

Supporting those aspects of cultural behavior which we have called technology and conduct is a third area of culture, including ideas, sentiments, and values. These are most difficult to deal with, for they are latent and covert or even unconscious and must be deduced from overt actions and language or other communicating behavior. In this aspect of the culture lies the "meaning" of the stone axe, its significance to the Yir Yoront and to their cultural way of life. The ideal conception of the axe, the knowledge of how to produce it (apart from the purely muscular habits used in its production) are part of the Yir Yoront adult masculine role, just as ideas regarding its technical use are included in the feminine role. These technical ideas constitute a kind of "science" regarding the axe which may be more important in relation to behavioral change than are the neurophysiological patterns drilled into the body by years of practice. Similarly there are normative ideas regarding the part played by the axe in conduct which constitute a kind of "morality" of the axe, and which again may be more important than the overt habits of social interaction in determining the role of the axe in social relationships. More than ideas regarding technology, ideas regarding conduct are likely to be closely associated, or "charged," with sentiment or value. Ideas and sentiments help guide and inform overt behavior; in turn, overt behavior helps support and validate ideas and sentiments.

The stone axe was an important symbol of masculinity among the Yir Yoront (just as pants or pipes are among ourselves). By a complicated set of ideas which we would label "ownership" the axe was defined as "belonging" to males. . . .

The mythical sacred world of the ancestors with which time began turns out on investigation to be a detailed reproduction of the present aboriginal world of nature, man, and culture altered by phantasy. In short, the idea system expressed in the mythology regarding the ancestral epoch was directly derived from Yir Yoront behavior patterns—

normal and abnormal, actual and ideal, conscious and unconscious. The important thing to note, however, is that the native believed it was just the other way around, that the present world, as a natural and cultural environment, was and should be simply a detailed reproduction of the world of the ancestors. He believed that the entire universe "is now as it was in the beginning" when it was established and left by the ancestors. The ordinary cultural life of the ancestors became the daily life of the Yir Yoront camps, and the extraordinary life of the ancestors remained extant in the recurring symbolic pantomimes and paraphernalia found only in the most sacred atmosphere of the totemic rites.

Such beliefs, accordingly, opened up the way for ideas of what *should be* (because it supposedly *was*) to influence or help determine what actually *is*. . . .

The introduction of the steel axe indiscriminately and in large numbers into the Yir Yoront technology was only one of many changes occurring at the same time. It is therefore impossible to factor out all the results of this single innovation alone. Nevertheless, a number of specific effects of the change from stone axes to steel axes may be noted; and the steel axe may be used as an epitome of the European goods and implements received by the aboriginals in increasing quantity and of their general influence on the native culture. The use of the steel axe to illustrate such influences would seem to be justified, for it was one of the first European artifacts to be adopted for regular use by the Yir Yoront; and the axe, whether of stone or steel, was clearly one of the most important items of cultural equipment they possessed.

The shift from stone to steel axes provided no major technological difficulties. While the aboriginals themselves could not manufacture steel axe heads, a steady supply from outside continued; and broken wooden axe handles could easily be replaced from bush timbers with aboriginal tools. . . .

Having acquired an axe head through regular trading partners of whom he knew what to expect, a man wanting a stone axe was then dependent solely upon a known and an adequate nature and upon his own skills or easily acquired techniques. A man wanting a steel axe, however, was in no such self-reliant position. While he might acquire one through trade, he now had the new alternative of dispensing with technological behavior in relation with a predictable nature and conduct in relation with a predictable trading partner and of turning instead to conduct alone in relation with a highly erratic missionary. If he attended one of the mission festivals when steel axes were handed out as gifts, he might receive one simply by chance or if he had happened somehow to impress upon the mission staff that he was one of the "better" bush aboriginals (their definition of "better" being quite different from that of his bush fellows). Or he might—but again almost by pure chance— be given some brief job in connection with the mission which would enable him to earn a steel axe. In either case, for older men a preference for the steel axe helped create a situation of dependence in place of a situation of self-reliance and a behavior shift from situations in tech- nology or conduct which were well structured or defined to situations in conduct alone which were ill defined. It was particularly the older ones among the men, whose earlier experience or knowledge of the white man's harshness in any event made them suspicious, who would avoid having any relations with the mission at all, and who thus ex- cluded themselves from acquiring steel axes directly from that source.

The steel axe was the root of psychological stress among the Yir Yoront even more significantly in other aspects of social relations. This was the result of new factors which the missionary considered all to the good: the simple numerical increase in axes per capita as a result of mission distribution; and distribution from the mission directly to younger men, women, and even children. By winning the favor of the mission staff, a woman might be given a steel axe. This was clearly intended to be hers. The situation was quite different from that involved in borrowing an axe from a male relative, with the result that a woman called such an axe "my" steel axe, a possessive form she never used for a stone axe. . . .

The trading partner relationship was also affected by the new situ- ation. A Yir Yoront might have a trading partner in a tribe to the south whom he defined as a younger brother, and on whom as an older brother he would therefore have an edge. But if the partner were in contact with the mission or had other easier access to steel axes, his subordination to his bush colleague was obviously decreased. Indeed, under the new dispensation he might prefer to give his axe to a bush "sweetheart" in return for favors or otherwise dispose of it outside regu- lar trade channels, since many steel axes were so distributed between natives in new ways. Among other things, this took some of the excite- ment away from the fiesta-like tribal gatherings centering around initia- tions during the dry season. These had traditionally been the climactic annual occasions for exchanges between trading partners, when a man might seek to acquire a whole year's supply of stone axe heads. Now he might find himself prostituting his wife to almost total strangers in return for steel axes or other white men's goods. With trading partnerships weakened, there was less reason to attend the fiestas, and less fun for those who did. A decline in one of the important social activities which had symbolized these great gatherings created a lessening of interest in the other social aspects of these events.

Not only did an increase in steel axes and their distribution to women change the character of the relations between individual and individual, the paired relationships that have been noted, but a new type of relationship, hitherto practically unknown among the Yir Yoront, was created in their axe-acquiring conduct with whites. In the aboriginal society there were almost no occasions outside the immediate family when one individual would initiate action to several other people at once. For in any average group, while a person in accordance with the kinship system might be superordinate to several people to whom he could suggest or command action, at the same time he was also subordinate to several others, in relation with whom such behavior would be tabu. There was thus no over-all chieftainship or authoritarian leadership of any kind. Such complicated operations as grass-burning, animal drives, or totemic ceremonies could be carried out smoothly because each person knew his roles both in technology and conduct. . . .

The most disturbing effects of the steel axe, operating in conjunction with other elements also being introduced from the white man's several subcultures, developed in the realm of traditional ideas, sentiments, and values. These were undermined at a rapidly mounting rate, without new conceptions being defined to replace them. The result was a mental and moral void which foreshadowed the collapse and destruction of all Yir Yoront culture, if not, indeed, the extinction of the biological group itself.

From what has been said it should be clear how changes in overt behavior, in technology and conduct, weakened the values inherent in a reliance on nature, in androcentrism or the prestige of masculinity, in age prestige, and in the various kinship relations. A scene was set in which a wife or young son, his initiation perhaps not even yet completed, need no longer bow to the husband or father, who was left confused and insecure as he asked to borrow a steel axe from them. For the woman and boy the steel axe helped established a new degree of freedom which was accepted readily as an escape from the unconscious stress of the old patterns, but which left them also confused and insecure. Ownership became less well defined, so that stealing and trespass were introduced into technology and conduct. Some of the excitement surrounding the great ceremonies evaporated, so that the only fiestas the people had became less festive, less interesting. Indeed, life itself became less interesting, although this did not lead the Yir Yoront to invent suicide, a concept foreign to them.

18. Technology and Social Institutions: America

W. F. COTTRELL

An American community can be disrupted by technological change just as a native one can be. Here we see how a single shift—from steam to diesel trains—almost totally disrupts a thriving community.

This example is furnished by W. F. Cottrell, Professor of Sociology and Government at Miami University in Ohio. Cottrell, who took his Ph.D. at Stanford University, has specialized on the effects of technology upon society and has written *Energy and Society* (McGraw-Hill, 1955). The essay reproduced here is a brief excerpt from "Death by Dieselization: A Case Study in the Reaction to Technological Change," *American Sociological Review*, Volume 16, June, 1951, pp. 358–365, and is printed by kind permission of the author and publisher.

In the following instance it is proposed that we examine a community confronted with radical change in its basic economic institution and to trace the effects of this change throughout the social structure. . . .

The community chosen for examination has been disrupted by the dieselization of the railroads. Since the railroad is among the oldest of those industries organized around steam, and since therefore the social structure of railroad communities is a product of long-continued processes of adaptation to the technology of steam, the sharp contrast between the technological requirements of the steam engine and those of the diesel should clearly reveal the changes in social structure required. . . .

In a sense it is an "ideal type" railroad town, and hence not complicated by other extraneous economic factors. It lies in the desert and is here given the name "Caliente" which is the Spanish adjective for "hot." Caliente was built in a break in an eighty-mile canyon traversing the desert. Its reason for existence was to service the steam locomotive. There are few resources in the area to support it on any other basis, and such as they are they would contribute more to the growth and maintenance of other little settlements in the vicinity than to that of Caliente. So long as the steam locomotive was in use, Caliente was a necessity. With the adoption of the diesel it became obsolescent.

This stark fact was not, however, part of the expectations of the residents of Caliente. Based upon the "certainty" of the railroad's need for Caliente, men built their homes there, frequently of concrete and brick, at the cost, in many cases, of their life savings. The water system was laid in cast iron which will last for centuries. Business men erected substantial buildings which could be paid for only by profits gained through many years of business. Four churches evidence the faith of Caliente people in the future of their community. A twenty-seven-bed hospital serves the town. Those who built it thought that their investment was as well warranted as the fact of birth, sickness, accident and death. They believed in education. Their school buildings represent the investment of savings guaranteed by bonds and future taxes. There is a combined park and play field which, together with a recently modernized theatre, has been serving recreational needs. All these physical structures are material evidence of the expectations, morally and legally sanctioned and financially funded, of the people of Caliente. This is a normal and rational aspect of the culture of all "solid" and "sound" communities.

Similarly normal are the social organizations. These include Rotary, Chamber of Commerce, Masons, Odd Fellows, American Legion and the Veterans of Foreign Wars. There are the usual unions, churches, and myriad little clubs to which the women belong. In short, here is the average American community with normal social life, subscribing to normal American codes. Nothing its members had been taught would indicate that the whole pattern of this normal existence depended completely upon a few elements of technology which were themselves in flux. For them the continued use of the steam engine was as "natural" a phenomenon as any other element in their physical environment. Yet suddenly their life pattern was destroyed by the announcement that the railroad was moving its division point, and with it destroying the economic basis of Caliente's existence. . . .

In its demands for service the diesel engine differs almost completely from a steam locomotive. It requires infrequent, highly skilled service, carried on within very close limits, in contrast to the frequent, crude adjustments required by the steam locomotive. . . .

. . . The introduction of diesels ordinarily would have taken a good deal of time. The change-over would have been slowed by the high capital costs of retooling the locomotive works, the long period required to recapture the costs of existing steam locomotives, and the effective resistance of the workers. . . . The shift to diesels was greatly facilitated by the war. In consequence, every third and sometimes every second division point suddenly became technologically obsolescent.

Caliente, like all other towns in similar plight, is supposed to accept its fate in the name of "progress." The general public, as shippers and consumers of shipped goods, reaps the harvest in better, faster service and eventually perhaps in lower charges. . . . What are the losses, and who bears them?

The railroad company can figure its losses at Caliente fairly accurately. It owns 39 private dwellings, a modern clubhouse with 116 single rooms, and a twelve-room hotel with dining-room and lunch-counter facilities. These now become useless, as does much of the fixed physical equipment used for servicing trains. Some of the machinery can be used elsewhere. Some part of the round-house can be used to store unused locomotives and standby equipment. The rest will be torn down to save taxes. All of these costs can be entered as capital losses on the statement which the company draws up for its stockholders and for the government. Presumably they will be recovered by the use of the more efficient engines.

What are the losses that may not be entered on the company books? The total tax assessment in Caliente was $9,946.80 for the year 1948, of which $6,103.39 represented taxes assessed on the railroad. Thus the railroad valuation was about three-fifths that of the town. This does not take into account tax-free property belonging to the churches, the schools, the hospital, or the municipality itself which included all the public utilities. Some ideas of the losses sustained by the railroad in comparison with the losses of others can be surmised by reflecting on these figures for real estate alone. . . .

Probably the greatest losses are suffered by the older "non-operating" employees. Seniority among these men extends only within the local shop and craft. A man with twenty-five years' seniority at Caliente has no claim on the job of a similar craftsman at another point who has only twenty-five days' seniority. Moreover, some of the skills formerly valuable are no longer needed. . . .

Operating employees also pay. Their seniority extends over a division, which in this case includes three division points. The older members can move from Caliente and claim another job at another point, but in many cases they move leaving a good portion of their life savings behind. The younger men must abandon their stake in railroad employment. . . .

The local merchants pay. The boarded windows, half-empty shelves, and abandoned store buildings bear mute evidence of these costs. The older merchants stay, and pay; the younger ones, and those with no stake in the community will move; but the value of their property will in both cases largely be gone.

The bondholders will pay. They can't foreclose on a dead town. If the town were wiped out altogether, that which would remain for salvage would be too little to satisfy their claims. Should the town continue there is little hope that taxes adequate to carry the overhead of bonds and day-to-day expenses could be secured by taxing the diminished number of property owners or employed persons.

The church will pay. The smaller congregations cannot support services as in the past. As the church men leave, the buildings will be abandoned.

Homeowners will pay. A hundred and thirty-five men owned homes in Caliente. They must accept the available means of support or rent to those who do. In either case the income available will be far less than that on which the houses were built. The least desirable homes will stand unoccupied, their value completely lost. The others must be revalued at a figure far below that at which they were formerly held.

In a word, those pay who are, by traditional American standards, *most moral.* Those who have raised children see friendships broken and neighborhoods disintegrated. The childless more freely shake the dust of Caliente from their feet. Those who built their personalities into the structure of the community watch their work destroyed. Those too wise or too selfish to have entangled themselves in community affairs suffer no such qualms. The chain store can pull down its sign, move its equipment and charge the costs off against more profitable and better located units, and against taxes. The local owner has no such alternatives. In short, "good citizens" who assumed family and community responsibility are the greatest losers. Nomads suffer least.

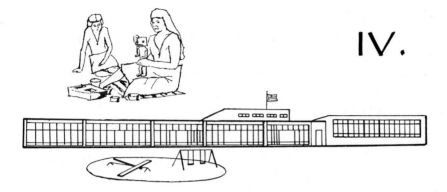

IV.

EDUCATION

The Continuity of Culture

Education is crucial to the cultural mode of life. This follows from the fact that culture is learned behavior; for if there is learning, there must be teaching. Education may be viewed as the means by which culture is passed from one person to another and, therefore, the way it continues through time.

By education we mean more than schooling. Schools are a part of our educational system, growing in importance with each succeeding year, and they are found in many other societies as well. But schools are not universal, and we shall see that for primitive man they are not necessary. What we include here under the term education is the total process by which the infant acquires the knowledge, understanding, attitudes, and orientation that are charactertistic of his culture.

For the infant taken naked from his mother's womb is naked of culture as well. And all of us, however primitive or civilized we may be, have entered our culture in precisely this way. From that moment forward, the baby is surrounded by the culture into which he is born and in the course of time he acquires the knowledge, understandings, attitudes and ways of doing things of the people among whom he lives and grows up. Nothing is more important in the whole realm of anthropology than to understand the processes by which the naked infant is clad in the uniform of his culture. Only a small part of this process takes place in the schools, even in our own stage of civilization.

Anthropologists call this process enculturation, sociologists call it socialization, and both are good and useful terms. Here we have used the older and more general term education, for we want to include formal training along with the subtler informal processes of acquiring cultural values and attitudes and the indoctrination into social life.

Two sets of distinctions will help us to understand the educational process. First, we must distinguish between skills, or explicit knowledge, (which were the subject of the preceding section) and the ideals, attitudes, and values (which will be discussed in several sections to follow). Next, we must distinguish the conscious, deliberate education of the young man from the unconscious, unwitting patterning of his behavior. By and large, skills are taught quite consciously, while values and attitudes tend to be transmitted less explicitly—though there are important exceptions.

The transmission of skills raises no particular problems. For most people of the world, skills are acquired on the job. Certainly the daily economic activity of the hunter and his wife and of the primitive farmer and her husband are acquired by the children through participating with their elders as part of their everyday life. The notion that schools should exist for the transmission of the ordinary skills—even of specialized crafts—is a quite recent innovation. One can still see in Germany the apprentice cabinetmaker traveling through the countryside in his special costume, seeking the experience that will establish his journeyman's status; in America such skills are frequently taught in schools.

In most primitive societies all adult males engage in essentially the same work; all adult females in "women's work," and every grown person knows how to do almost all of the things that everyone else of his sex knows. The child learns the skills necessary to his adult life through daily habituation. To be sure, there are some skills that not everyone shares in like degree—one man is handier at chipping flint into arrowheads and another at making traps, perhaps—and these differences in skill are recognized. The child is usually taught by a relative who is skilled. We can see this in a description of the way Yurok girls learn to make baskets:

> As a very little girl she watched the older weavers of the family. Usually she and her age mates attempted to duplicate the efforts of their elders with any kind of sticks and green grasses available. This was only playing; it resulted in nothing recognizable as a basket and no one paid any attention to it. But if the child persisted in working she was finally noticed by her elders. She could not be trusted to go on with a basket in process of construction, so her mother would start a root on discarded sticks for her. After a round or two of the child's weaving, the older woman took it from her to make a course, straightening the sticks where twining turns had been put in with uneven tension. The work alternated between them in this way until its abandonment as a diversion or its completion as a rough little bowl. . . .
>
> The child was six or seven years old when the first basket was started for her; it would be five years probably before she could begin her own baskets. In this interim she might make a dipper which is always plain, or possibly an acorn soup basket with simple grass overlay pattern, or a small trinket basket in which twining elements regularly progress over two sticks at a time. . . .
>
> Old weavers still laugh at memories of their first baskets. Some were so sharp at the bottom they could only be hung up, surfaces were fluted from the insertion of too many sticks, and dippers were so loosely woven that they could not be swollen sufficiently to hold water. Yet between a girl's first efforts and her results which had value for

use or exchange, a young weaver learned certain of the established requirements. She had gathered and dried materials for the old people of her family who could not get to the patches themselves, and was commended or criticized for quality; she helped "cook" and split tree roots for twining elements; she was taught to set an acorn basket on the ground during its making to watch its shape and proportions—features every beginner must know, and she did considerable ripping out of work in order to make the necessary corrections. . . .

Grown women will refer to their training with pride. If one's mother or aunt was a "good hand at baskets," presumably she taught the right methods which would never have to be relearned.*

Not all skills are acquired through direct teaching. People learn to use their muscles by unconscious imitation of those around them (just as they unconsciously imitate the use of the muscles of the mouth in speech) so that the people of a region will tend to have the same way of walking or use similar gestures. It has been noted that the American Indian uses a knife by drawing the blade toward him, while a person of European descent whittles away from the body. Though these patterns may reflect the differences between stone and steel blades, they nevertheless are unconscious patterns of behavior and usually represent an unconscious transmission of technique. Later in this volume, Miguel Covarrubias tells us that every Balinese child can carve, just as he can play in the gamelin orchestras. Though this may seem mysterious to us, the fact is that artistic activity is as much a part of the daily life of the Balinese as driving cars or writing is with us. Not every Balinese is equally adept, yet it is so much a part of the everyday environment that the skills are, one might say, subconsciously acquired.

Schooling as a separate aspect of life is a product of literacy—and the three R's still have a dominant part in our educational program. However, with the increased specialization of labor in modern society and with the increased need for skills on the job, specialized training plays an ever increasing part in the educational process. For centuries formal schooling, as distinct from apprentice craftsmanship, was limited to a small sector of our society and was primarily for the upper classes or for a separate learned class. Democratic institutions tended to spread literacy over the population, while the spread of literacy through the invention of printing was a factor which, in turn, furthered democratic

* Lila M. O'Neale, "Yurok-Karok Basket Weavers." *University of California Publications in American Archaeology and Ethnology,* Volume 32, No. 1, pp. 10-. 11. Berkeley: University of California Press, 1932.

institutions. The operation of our society depends upon widespread literacy (consider only its importance for driving a car in a modern city). But more than this, the elaborate technical apparatus of the modern economy requires a populace highly trained in thousands of different specialties. Schools are a necessary element in the skill-training of the citizen for life in today's society; they are necessary for maintaining a modern society.

Skills and the use of muscles are only a part of what every child learns. He learns also a wide range of tabus, rules, behavior patterns, myths, explanations of the world, rituals; he learns the values, attitudes and sentiments that characterize his culture. Some of these are carefully communicated to him, explicitly and directly, by his elders—frequently on ceremonial occasions. Thus, though a Hopi lad has heard many moral principles repeated, they are brought home to him at the time of his initiation through the formidable presence of spirit impersonators, the element of personal pain in whipping, and by the whole religious paraphernalia of an impressive ceremony in which he has an important role. Such ceremonial inductions into adult status are widespread, and are certainly an effective means of inculcating moral precepts.

But subtler influences are at work in communicating values and attitudes, and these are more important in the aggregate, though less dramatic than the initiatory rites. The child hears a person praised or condemned by his elders; he sees persons with prestige acting one way and those poorly thought of conducting themselves differently. In modern parlance, he finds models for behavior in his community. And in doing so, he acquires the fundamental set of his character; that is, he takes on the features approved by his culture. We can see this process at work in the essay on Plainville education.

Though universal and unconscious, the process is not automatic, and in no culture is everybody stamped precisely in one mold. Variations due to personal attributes and individual circumstances make for differences in response to such cultural forces. Yet the central tendencies are so clear that it is possible to see the characteristic temperaments not only of different tribes in different parts of the world but even between the peoples of modern nations, the members of social classes, or the populations of regions within large countries.

There are still subtler processes at work that tend to mold the character of the individual to the shape that his culture finds congenial, that make for the continuity of patterns of behavior and attitudes which the people themselves are unaware they exhibit. It is this kind of educational process that Margaret Mead is speaking of when she discusses the transmission of parental anxieties among modern middle-class Americans.

The processes here are not too well understood and are the subject of much debate. Most anthropologists interested in them have been to some extent influenced by Freudian psychology, which holds not only that the first five years of life establish the personality of the child, but also that the infant goes through a series of erotic stages (oral, anal, and genital), and that the character of his experiences at various times, and his relations with his immediate family (particularly his mother) determine the features of his personality and basic patterns of cultural attitudes. This theoretical orientation has led to an emphasis in the study of such aspects of child training as suckling, weaning, toilet training, and patterns of body contact.

There can be little doubt that the treatment of the infant and child during the first years of life is important to his subsequent behavior, whatever psychological orientation one has. We are reasonably certain that the dominant parental attitudes are unwittingly transmitted in much the same manner as are nuances of speech. If parents themselves have many fears or much suppressed hostility, if they are easygoing or phlegmatic, or if they are harsh and demand much of themselves, these feelings are communicated by the parents and taken over by the children though neither may be aware of the transmission. Indeed, where such attitudes exist as cultural norms, they are taken to be as natural to man as the need for food or sleep. In the section on Art, Alan Lomax tells us that these elements of intimate interpersonal family life are expressed in the folksongs of a people. He believes these attitudes tend to persist for centuries, so that the music that expresses the sentiments and feelings of a population dates back, in some parts of Italy, for instance, to pre-Roman and even pre-Etruscan times.

It is the subtle and pervasive kind of cultural learning that tends to make the people from a given tribe or culture behave in somewhat consistent fashion. These consistencies have led to the anthropological study of "national character," the general features of modern countries or regions. Anyone who has traveled through Europe will recognize certain pervasive qualities in different areas; qualities which distinguish one land from its neighbors.

No one believes all Frenchmen act alike; as we have said, the process is not like a stamp-machine, stamping out so many precise replicas. People vary, and in a broad set of European acquaintances one will usually know a volatile Englishman or a jolly Scot. For each person has his own individual set of educational experiences, and his own physiology as well. No population is homogeneous with respect to temperament, any more than with respect to any other trait. Yet, a Channel crossing will convince one that there is a sharp difference between the English and the French—in their bearing, in their interpersonal relationships, in the very way they eat or dress or make love. Older generations used to speak of these peoples as separate races and assumed that their characteristics were determined by inherited factors or by the climate. We now know they are differences in culture and that the different patterns of behavior are subtly learned in the process of growing up.

We must remember that the institutions by which a culture trains its children—from the mother cradling her child to the great universities teaching modern physics—are themselves all part of that culture. But they are also that part through which all parts of the culture are acquired by the oncoming generation; through which every aspect of the culture is inevitably filtered. It is this element of the teaching process that makes it so important for an understanding of culture itself. Since educational practices serve this filtering function, the manner of teaching is suited to the cultural needs.

Thus, for example, a recent analysis of the child-training practices among a variety of primitive societies showed that hunting and food-gathering peoples tend to train their children more for individualistic behavior, agriculturists and herders more for cooperative life. The authors point out that hunters need more autonomy of action and dependence upon individual initiative than do primitive farmers, who must more often operate in concert and suppress individualism.

This brings out a more general point. Some people, admiring the educational practices found in other cultures, have advocated their adoption by our own society. But a virtue in one situation is not necessarily good for another, and before the importation of other practices is undertaken, their consequences and cultural entanglements should be carefully examined. The same caution should be used when we endeavor to impose our practices on others. (This is true for all aspects of culture, but is perhaps more important in education than elsewhere.)

We do not mean to imply that each culture has an educational system perfectly and automatically adapted to its needs. In our own society there is a long-standing debate over the proper way of rearing and training children, and considerable variation from place to place and gradual shift through time. The patterns described for Plainville, for example, are quite different from those that most city children have undergone.

As a matter of fact, America is quite diverse with respect to cultural background; we have only begun to forge a common culture; and there is much variation in the manner in which we rear our children, though our formal education tends to be pretty much the same all over the United States. As Mead points out, certain uniformities in child-rearing are appearing in middle-class America—tendencies brought about by the strains of middle-class life, including a strain to conformity by people of diverse cultures.

Education, in sum, is the process by which both the obvious aspects of culture and its hidden minutiae are transmitted from one generation to another and thus passed on through time. It is partly a conscious and deliberate process, partly automatic or unconscious, both on the part of the teacher and the pupil. Education does not cause or create culture, for it is itself a part of culture: cultural patterns set the attitudes of education and training. Yet, insofar as each of us is a piece of our own culture, the educational process to which we have been subjected has created that part in us.

19. The Educational Process

CLYDE KLUCKHOHN

Clyde Kluckhohn has long been concerned with the manner in which culture is acquired by the child. Here he discusses the general educative processes, recognizing that part of education deals with the technical and obvious parts of culture while another part is the subtle, hidden transmission of values and attitudes.

Kluckhohn is Professor of Anthropology at Harvard University where he received his Ph.D. in 1936 after studying at Oxford and Vienna. He was Director of the Russian Research Center at Harvard (1947-1954) and developed a program of research on values in the Southwestern United States. He has written widely on the Navaho, and was co-editor of *Personality in Nature, Society and Culture*. The selection here was taken from his prize winning general work, included with permission of the publishers from *Mirror for Man* by Clyde Kluckhohn. Copyright, 1949, by the McGraw-Hill Book Company, Inc.

The characteristics of the human animal which make culture possible are the ability to learn, to communicate by a system of learned symbols, and to transmit learned behavior from generation to generation. But what is learned varies widely from society to society and even in different sectors of the same society. The manner of learning also shows patterned and characteristic forms. The emotional tone of the parents and of other agents for transmitting the culture has typical and culturally enjoined modes. The situations in which learning takes place are differently defined and phrased in different societies. The rewards for learning, the "squeezes" in learning situations, the sanctions for failing to learn take many different forms and emphases. This is true not only for the culture as a whole but also for various subcultures within it. The formation of the American child's personality is affected by the particular social, economic, and regional subgroup to which the parents belong. The patterns for physical growth and maturation are about the same for Café Society and Lower East Side children, but the child training practices, preferred life goals and manners, rewards, and punishments belong to quite different worlds.

All animals exhibit certain limitations, capacities, and requirements as organisms. These must never be forgotten in enthusiasm over the determining powers of culture. Margaret Mead's well-known book *Sex and Temperament in Three Primitive Societies* has given many readers an impression that she is arguing that the temperamental differences between men and women are completely produced by culture. The one-line book review by a fellow anthropologist is a sobering corrective: "Margaret, this is a very brilliant book. But do you really know any cultures in which the men have the babies?"

The pressures of child training bring their influences to bear upon different biological materials. Metabolic needs vary. Digestion does not require precisely the same time in every baby. The first cultural disciplines are directed toward three very basic organic responses: accepting, retaining, and releasing. Cultures vary widely in the extent to which they place positive or negative stress upon one or more of these reactions. A potent source of individual variation within a society rests in the fact that the reaction to cultural training is modified by the child's relative degree of neurological maturity. Even apart from babies known to be born prematurely, the nervous equipment of newborn infants shows a sizable range.

Nevertheless there is still considerable leeway among the organically defined possibilities. The requirements of human animals for survival and gratification can be attained in more than one way through the given capacities. Especially in the case of a symbol-using animal like man, these are significant questions: what is learned? who teaches it? how is it taught? There is a continuous and dynamic interrelationship between the patterns of a culture and the personalities of its individual members. Though certain needs are universal, they receive different emphases in different societies. A society perpetuates itself biologically by means that are well known. Less fully realized is the fact that societies are constantly perpetuating themselves socially by inculcating in each new generation time-tried ways of believing, feeling, thinking, and reacting.

Like rats learning to run a maze that has food at its exit, children gradually familiarize themselves with the well-trodden but often devious intricacies of the cultural network. They learn to take their cues for response not merely from their personal needs nor from the actualities of a situation but from subtle aspects of the situation as culturally defined. This cultural cue says: be suspicious and reserved. That says: relax; be sociable. In spite of the diversities of individual natures, the

Crow Indian learns to be habitually generous, the Yurok habitually stingy, the Kwakiutl chieftain habitually arrogant and ostentatious. Far from being always resentful at the walls of the cultural maze, most adults, and even children to some extent, derive pleasure from the performance of cultural routines. Human beings generally find it highly rewarding to behave like others who share the same culture. The sense of running the same maze also promotes social solidarity. . . .

Granted that personality is largely a product of learning and that much of the learning is culturally determined and controlled, it should be pointed out that there are two kinds of cultural learning: technical and regulatory. Learning the multiplication tables is technical, whereas the learning of manners (*e.g.,* in our society, not to spit indiscriminately) is regulatory. In neither case does the child have to learn everything for himself; he is given the answers. Both of these types of education are socially desirable and necessary to the individual, although he is certain to resist them to some extent. The one type is intended to make the individual productive, socially useful, to increase the group's wealth and strength. The other type of education is intended to reduce the nuisance value of the individual within the group as much as possible, to keep him from disturbing others, creating in-group disharmony, etc. In this connection it is noteworthy that common speech makes this distinction in the two connotations of the word "good" when used as an attribute for a person. A person is said to be "good" either in the sense of being morally and socially amenable, or he is "good" in the sense of being unusually skillful, accomplished, etc.

In our society, the school is traditionally appointed for the development of technological training, the home and church for regulatory training. However, there is considerable overlapping, the home teaching some skills and the school also teaching certain morals and manners.

There are certain limitations both as to how far and how rapidly technical and regulatory learning can proceed. The physical structure and organization of each human organism determines the limits; the physical maturity and the amount of prior learning determines the rate. For example, the child cannot acquire the skill of walking until the necessary connections between nerve tracts are completed. Instruction learning cannot occur to a very marked extent until language has developed. Each stage or age has its own special and characteristic tasks. Both the age limits and the task vary greatly in different cultures, but everywhere development is by steps, stages, degrees. One level of adjustment is attained only to be superseded by another and another. This is very explicit in many nonliterate societies, but the extent to which school grades and, in adult life, lodges and clubs carry out this same segmentation in our own society must not be overlooked. To some extent, this means that any adult personality is a succession of habit strata, even though the organizing principles of the personality probably achieve rather early a relative fixity which makes for continuity. Only in earliest infancy does a child appear to behave in a haphazard manner. Soon he seems to have a personality policy which, albeit in disguised forms, often supplies the directional trends for his whole life.

In other words, the adult personality is an architectural integration. There are integrating principles, but there are also various levels and areas that are more and less central to the structure as a whole. If we study a personality by levels, we see how characteristic responses of one degree of complexity supersede or disguise any direct manifestation of reactions that are typical at a different degree of complexity. The same personality responds to different situations with differences which are sometimes very dramatic. Every personality is capable of more than one mode of expression. The particular mode depends upon the total psychological field and upon cultural phrasings. If one reaches for an object, the movement of one's hand is steered by its perceived position in perceived surroundings. Likewise, personality manifestations are regulated, in part, by the person's perception of himself and others within the cultural setting.

It is descriptively convenient to speak of nuclear and peripheral regions of personality. Changes in the nuclear region, though sometimes trivial in themselves, always modify the personality policy and are necessarily of the either-or variety. Changes in the peripheral region may be purely quantitative and may occur without altering other personality traits. The major stages (oral, anal, genital) require nuclear changes, but together with these are those more superficial adaptations to status and role which every culture expects of persons of a given age, sex, and office. In most cases the periphery is where there is relative freedom to make adjustments. There is always the question of interrelationship, of what the peripheral adjustments mean to the less yielding nucleus. Cultures have precisely this same architectural property.

The sequence of development, or personality growth, is not wholly spontaneous or self-determined. Most stages or aspects of stages will persist just precisely so long as they work for the organism. There will be as much continuity in any individual's life as there is serviceability in his value system. The child goes on as long as his private variant of the cultural value system works. But when his environment demands change to obtain satisfaction he will change. Thus personality growth is rather a product of the continuous and often tempestuous interaction of the maturing child and his older, more powerful mentors upon whom falls the responsibility of transmitting the culture and who in so doing convert him into a particular kind of human being.

The fact that personality development must proceed in this way carries with it two important complications: It means that education must be a prolonged process, costly from the point of view of both time and effort. It predisposes the individual to regression, i.e., to a return to an earlier stage of adjustment if difficulty is encountered in a later stage. Since permitting an infant or child to make an adjustment on a lower level means that he becomes more or less "fixated" at this level and since this development by successive "fixations" predisposes him to the danger of regression, it might seem reasonable to try to circumvent both of these complications by not allowing any fixations to occur. Why should we not teach the child the ultimately correct type of behavior from the very outset, or, when this is patently impossible, allow him to learn nothing until he becomes capable of learning precisely what will be ultimately expected of him as an adult member of society?

No one has seriously advocated this sort of short-circuiting of the educational process in the technical sphere. Children have not been expected to do calculus without first having learned simple arithmetic. But in the realm of regulatory education, serious attempts have been made to make children conform from the very outset of their lives to the demands for renunciation which will ultimately be made of them as adults—in the spheres, notably, of sex, cleanliness, and respect for property. For reasons not yet fully understood, it appears that fewer maladjusted individuals will result if certain infantile impulses are allowed to run their course. Indulgence and reassurance during the period when the oral drive is strong seem to be the best guarantees that the individual will later be able to restrict the pleasures of the mouth willingly and without distortion. To attain basic security the infant needs to be safe both from the physical world (supported) and from the cultural world (excused). Certain forms of learning can be achieved with less injury after language has been acquired. Without speech, the infant has to learn by trial and error and by conditioning. With speech, he can profit from instruction. When one type of activity is forbidden, the child can be told how to achieve his goal by a different type of behavior.

Speech itself has to develop in the slow, primitive fashion, but, once it is acquired, other learning is greatly speeded.

The customary turns of phrase used to bring a child into line bear a relationship to the typical forms of adult character. Sometimes, as in our own society at present, the dominant tendency is for parents to assume full responsibility in the eyes of the child and to emphasize a sharp line between "right" and "wrong." "Do it because I say it is right." "Do it because I say so." "Do it because I am your father and children must obey their parents." "Don't do it because it is nasty." "Do it or I won't buy you any candy." "If you aren't a good little boy, mamma will be unhappy"—or even—"If you aren't a good little boy, mamma won't love you." While the threat of shaming ("If you wet your pants people will make fun of you") which is the primary instrument of socialization in many primitive societies is also used by Americans, most socialization after the verbal period is built around the threat of withdrawal of parental love and protection. This can give the child a sense of unworthiness with lifelong consequences. The fear of not measuring up is with many Americans a principal driving force. A persistent need is felt to show the parents that, after all, the child was capable of constructive achievements.

This tendency is reinforced by other cultural goals. Parents try to make their children "better" than they; they become "ambitious for their children," want their children to accomplish what they did not. Parents are under social pressure and are judged by their children. They compete with each other through their children, not having security enough themselves to resist this pressure. By pressing their children for renunciation and accomplishment they can ease their own anxieties. . . .

Even if the need for physical and moral sanctuary during childhood be recognized, the practical problems are not solved by a policy of leaving the child alone. During infancy the child will in any event be developing an "attitude toward life": confidence, resignation, optimism, pessimism. These attitudes will be largely determined by the kind and amount of "care" given. The connection between child care and personality has not been fully appreciated. But its importance is twofold: it is useful in helping the child develop basic skills which will be later useful when indulgence ends and the child has to venture out on its own; and it is especially useful to have positive attitudes toward parents and others when regulatory training starts.

For the emotional pattern toward parents or brothers and sisters often becomes the prototype of habitual reactions toward friends and associates, employers and employees, leaders and deities. In a society where the childhood experience is typically that of overstrong but unsatisfied dependency upon the father there is a fertile soil for the demagogue. On the other hand, a culture like that of the Zuñi Indians, where the child's attachments are spread among many relatives and where dependence is focused upon the group as a whole rather than upon particular individuals, is peculiarly resistant to leaders of the Hitler type. Where the mother is the true center of family life, divinities are apt to be portrayed in female form. . . .

In other societies methods for inhibiting the responses of children which may be either socially objectionable or personally dangerous give the parents more ways of avoiding personal responsibility. A greater number of persons, uncles, aunts, and other members of the extended family, share in the disciplinary actions so that there is a less intense emotional involvement between child and one or both parents. The mechanism of shaming makes possible some displacement beyond even the circle of the family. Dominant reliance upon this technique would seem to result in a quite different sort of conformity, characterized by "shame" ("I would feel very uncomfortable if anybody saw me doing this") rather than "guilt" ("I am bad because I am not living up to the standards of my parents"). Finally, the sanctions may be placed to greater or lesser extent outside the range of all living persons. Supernatural beings (including ghosts) may be the punishing and rewarding agents. The child is told that misconduct will be punished in accord with supernatural laws. Eventually, misfortune or accident overtakes the erring child, and his preceptors are careful to impress upon him the connection between his misdeeds and his suffering. Although this method has certain obvious advantages in promoting positive adjustments to other people, it also tends to keep the individual from coming to grips with the external world. If one is at the mercy of more powerful and perhaps capricious forces, if one can always blame supernatural agencies instead of oneself, one is much less likely to make the effort for realistic adjustments. . . .

In every culture, however, success, or reward, is essential to all learning. If a response is not rewarded, it will not be learned. Thus all responses which become habitual are "good" from the organism's point of view; they necessarily provide some form of satisfaction. The "badness" of habits is a judgment that is attached to them by other persons; *i.e.,* a habit is "bad" if it annoys another person or persons. The great problem of personal adjustment to a social environment is that of finding behavior that is satisfying to the individual and also either satisfying to other persons or at least acceptable to them. All men learn the responses that are to them motivation-reducing, problem-solving, but one of the factors which determines which responses are motivation-reducing is the given social tradition. Culture also largely determines, of course, which responses other persons will regard as "good" or as annoying. Learning, as related to motivation, deals either with a change in needs or a change in the means of their satisfaction.

The common assumption has been that habits are eliminated only by punishment, *i.e.,* by making them followed by more suffering than satisfaction. It is true that habits can be "broken" in this fashion, but this is costly in that the punishing person often earns the distrust of the child. There is, however, another mechanism utilized by cultural systems, namely the mechanism of extinction. Just as reward is essential to the establishment of a habit, so is it essential to its continued function. If the satisfaction that an organism usually obtained from a given habitual response can be withheld, this habit will eventually disappear. Aggression may occur as the first response to non-reward, but if this aggression is neither rewarded nor punished, it, too, will soon give way to a renewal of exploratory, variable behavior, from which a new habit or adjustment may evolve.

Although extinction is a valuable device for getting rid of objectionable habits, it also operates to eliminate those habits in an individual which others may like, or call "good," if these habits are not continually rewarding also to the individual. Thus good behavior, either in the child or in the adult, cannot be taken for granted; it must be satisfying to the individual as well as to the others. These considerations show the inadequacy of the old notion that repetition necessarily makes a habit stronger. We now know that habits can be either strengthened or weakened by repetition. It is not repetition as such but reward that is the crucial factor in determining whether a habit will grow or wane with repetition.

The next important fact about the learning process is that just as a correct response tends to become more and more strongly connected to the drive which it reduces, so does this response tend to become connected with any other stimuli which happen to be impinging upon the organism at the time the successful response occurs. For example, in many societies physical nearness to the mother soon becomes to the child a promise of reward. Therefore, any renunciation such as that involved in toilet training becomes learned much more easily when the mother is present. We are inclined to exaggerate the specificity of innate responses. We tend to think of nursing behavior, for example, as something automatic. But it isn't simply a chain of reflexes, as anyone who has seen the clumsy and inadequate behavior of a newborn infant realizes. Reflexes are involved, but so are other organic conditions and also learning. Thus if a newborn baby is hungry, pressure on its cheek will elicit the response of quick turning—which can bring the breast into view. But this response can be produced only with great difficulty from a baby who has just been fed.

A culture directs attention to one feature of the stimulus situation and gives it a value. In this way the responses to even very basic organic drives may be determined as much by cultural values and expectations as by internal pressures.

20. The Education of the Hopi Child

LAURA THOMPSON and ALICE JOSEPH

The study of Hopi child training and educational patterns is one of a series of similar studies on which the Committee on Human Development of the University of Chicago collaborated with the Indian Service. They were done so that the administration could better understand the problems of adjustment from the Indian point of view, but the studies have also given us better insight into the educational process. We include this essay to show how differently the subtle influences of child care can be handled from our own, and how these relate to the world view and the economic necessities of life.

Laura Thompson is Professor of Anthropology and Sociology at the College of the City of New York. She received her Ph.D. from the University of California, Berkeley, and has done research in Iceland, the Fiji Islands, Guam, and Hawaii, as well as on many of the cultures of the Southwest. Alice Joseph is a psychiatrist who has worked with the Papago and the Carolinians of Saipan. She has been staff psychiatrist for the Veterans Administration and Lecturer in Social Relations at Harvard University.

The essay here is taken from Chapter 2, "The Journey from Birth to Death," pp. 52–59 in *The Hopi Way*, originally printed at the Haskell Institute for the United States Indian Service in 1944 and reissued by The University of Chicago Press in 1947. It is printed by kind permission of the authors and The University of Chicago Press. Copyright 1947 by The University of Chicago.

Training in the basic disciplines and other types of self-control demanded by the Hopi Way, as well as initiation into the intricacies of the kinship system with its complex reciprocity patterns, is the responsibility of the household group, which continues to exercise a certain restraining influence on the individual throughout life. During childhood and youth for girls, and up to about the sixth year for boys, the learning process is chiefly in the hands of the mother and other females of the household, aided by the mother's brother when stricter discipline is needed, and also by the father and the maternal grandfather. All these relatives may scold the child on occasion or ridicule him for wrongdoing, the mother and the mother's brother spanking him if necessary. They are also aided by the gift-giving *kachinas,* who by rewarding children for good behavior, serve as important behavior motivators, and on rare occasions, by the cannibal *kachinas,* who appear at their door and threaten to eat or carry away bad little children.

The Hopi pattern of discipline, however, is in general an absorptive and permissive one, the child learning largely by imitating and experimenting and being treated as an important member of the group with individual rights and privileges as well as incipient duties and responsibilities. On the one hand he is given considerable freedom of mobility to explore his environment; on the other he is gently but firmly held within the limitations of physical safety and protected from supernatural dangers.

Some of these dangers, such as those connected with witches, evil spirits, drought, sickness and death, are very real from the Hopi point of view, but others, such as those connected with the *kachinas,* are feigned and dramatized realistically by the adults to reward or frighten the child into obedience without arousing his hostility toward themselves. These shocks have a particular aspect as they are not given from individual to individual, but from the external environment, natural or supernatural, to all children, so that the quality of the shock lacks the feeling of personal persecution and hostility against individuals. Such fear-provoking experiences, whether due to real or imaginary dangers, apparently condition the child at a very early age to the hazardous nature of the Hopi environment.

In this connection it is important to realize, however, that in the face of these threats to his existence, the child is never allowed to feel isolated or abandoned but always has whole groups of relatives to whom he may turn for comfort and reassurance. Outstanding among these, besides his father, are his father's clansfolk, especially his paternal aunts in whose households he is at all times welcome. The relationship between the paternal aunt and her nephew is particularly warm and may serve somewhat to counterbalance the exceedingly close bond between the females of the maternal household, especially mother and daughter.

Although most Hopi children learn the basic disciplines with little difficulty, thumb sucking, temper tantrums and even stealing begin to be manifest in a few individual boys in the third year, whereas no "behavior problems" have been reported for girls until the fifth year. These early signs of adjustment difficulties among the boys coincide with weaning and cleanliness training for both sexes, and also, in some cases, with the arrival of another sibling in the family and the removal of the child from his mother's bed to that of a female relative or his grandfather. Their early appearance among males only, is understandable, however, when we consider the differences between the position of the female and the male child in the household and the expectancies in regard to each sex.

As has been noted, the little girl is born into a household group in which she is expected to grow up, marry, and even in many cases to continue to live until she dies as a member of a closely knit and powerful group of females. On the other hand, the little boy is expected to break away from the group into which he has been born, beginning at the age of four or five years, for the less stable and more hazardous world of *kiva,* field and range, and to remain throughout life in a marginal position in regard to the household.

While the roles of both sexes require endurance, industry, and patience, that of the Hopi male, in contrast to the female, requires constant vigilance and a high degree of adaptability in order to cope with the natural, supernatural, and social forces of the less restricted and less secure masculine world. Hopi character delineations were built up in the past when a man had to be not only an expert dry farmer, rain maker, and stone age hunter, but also a warrior in the struggle for survival. But they still persist and are functional today, for as we have seen, in spite of the cessation of defensive warfare, the reduction of game and the increase in herding, the essential Hopi life problems have not changed intrinsically in modern times.

Apparently almost from birth the child begins to be aware of these sex-differentiated expectancies, which are constantly impressed on him in his interpersonal relations. The efforts of the little girl are encouraged by telling her that she will grow up to be a good cook and those of the boy that he will be a swift runner. Even the gift-giving *kachinas* aid in defining the sex roles by presenting the girls with *kachina* images which are fertility symbols designed primarily to be hung up in the house and not to be used as dolls, and the boys with arrows which, although used in play, are important symbolically and are highly valued. In fact, the whole training process is oriented toward these ends.

In view of these facts it is not surprising that the business of growing up presents more problems to the boy than to the girl, and that cases of men who assume the dress and perform the role of women occur among the Hopi, though rarely, whereas instances of women rejecting their role for that of the opposite sex are unknown.

Of course the girls also have adjustment difficulties, for the female role, aside from its procreative function (which is particularly hazardous in Hopiland, to judge from maternal mortality estimates and population statistics), offers less mobility and stimulation and fewer actively creative outlets than that of the male, which allows abundant, though stylized, self-expression in ceremonial art and craft work, as well as the intense excitement of the hunt and formerly of war.

The little Hopi girl apparently begins to feel the restrictions of the female role in the fifth year, at the age when her male agemate begins to break away from the women's household group, while she must remain at home, helping her mother with the household tasks or caring for the younger children. Now cases of maladjusted behavior such as temper tantrums, stealing, thumb sucking, and fighting—though less prevalent than among the boys—first appear among the girls.

That the adjustment problems of the little boy also increase in the fifth year is shown by the rise in behavior problems at this age, which includes fighting as well as all those manifested earlier. . . .

In spite of their early responsibilities, however, Hopi children have a great deal of time for fun and play. Duties come first and when they are finished, children are free to wander about the village and amuse themselves as they wish, so long as they do not interfere with the activities of the adults. At this age little boys and girls play freely together. They usually form two types of play groups, however, one comprising the older girls with their small charges and the other, uninitiated boys of four years or older. The little girls build houses with wet mud. They use sticks or bones as dolls to represent the individuals in the household. They also play at grinding and pottery making. The little boys play at farming and herding and practice shooting with bows and arrows. They also run races and play at horseback riding. Although most Hopi children have no toys except those which they receive from the *kachinas* or make themselves, they often keep small animals such as birds, rabbits and prairie dogs as pets and these they handle so roughly that the creatures frequently are mauled to death. A certain cruelty to animals is also noticeable in the behavior of adults.

Children begin at a very early age—when they can barely walk and talk—to practice dance steps, singing and drumming. And as young as four years they may begin to participate in certain ceremonials such as the Snake and Buffalo dances. Moreover, as part of some festivities, special children's events are planned such as the children's race day which may initiate a kickball contest.

But there is no well defined boundary in the learning process between work, play and ceremonial, the child spending his time in one or another of these activities, which to him are events in the "ever-becoming-later" duration which is Hopi childhood. And when this first phase of life ends with the *kachina* initiation between the ages of six and ten years, the child is expected to have mastered not only the basic disciplines, the fundamentals of the kinship system and the main tenets of the Hopi Way, but also to have become a useful member of society with social and economic duties, responsibilities and privileges, in accordance with his sex and age.

The ceremonial initiation of the child into the *kachina* cult marks the second great crisis in his life cycle, the transition from Childhood to Youth. This first initiation . . . takes place every four years in February as a part of the *Powamu* or "Bean Dance," which is designed especially to speed the early stages of development and is marked by the forced growth of beans and corn in the *kivas* and their distribution to the young children by masked *kachinas*. As the birth rites introduced the child to his father, the Sun, and inaugurated a series of life-long, mutual obligations and privileges between himself and his father's clanspeople, so the *kachina* initiation introduces him to his ancestors, the *kachinas,* and sets up a pattern of regular, correlative obligations by which the *kachinas* give rain and thus food and other essentials to human welfare in exchange for prescribed ritual behavior. It also marks his adoption into another clan, namely that of the man and his sister who become his godfather and godfather's sister and sponsor him in his ceremonial career. Henceforth the child is considered to be related to these ceremonial kin and their clansmen and phratry members, as he is related to his father's clan, and with similar reciprocal obligations and privileges. . . .

During the *kachina* initiation the child learns that the supernatural beings whom he has known from infancy as bringers of gifts and rain and also as dispensers of punishment, are really only people he knows dressed up to impersonate them, but he also learns of the *kachinas'* key role in the scheme of things and his own part in the cosmic exchange for the mutual welfare of all. His godfather gives him a new name and from now on he may participate in the *kachina* rites and gradually assume his share of responsibility for the great annual cycle of ceremonies which gives significance and zest to Hopi life. He has acquired a certain status in the tribe as a whole and may return to the Underworld when he dies.

Some time after his first initiation the boy is expected to join one or more secret societies usually those of his godfather, and the girl is expected to join those of her ceremonial aunt. . . . This means a gradual expansion of ties, responsibilities and creative activities especially for the boy since it opens the definitely male world of the kiva to him and a new field of esoteric knowledge. It also gives him a well defined place in the ceremonial organization of the village which tends to compensate for his position in the household group, to build up his self-confidence, and to steer him toward the adult male role.

At about the age of eight the boy is expected to kill his first game, usually a rabbit, according to the rules of the chase, and consequently to acquire a "hunt" father and to be formally initiated as a hunter. . . .

The economic responsibilities of the boy during these years increase gradually. Whereas formerly his chores consisted mainly of helping his female relatives with water and fuel hauling, now he frequently accompanies his male relatives, particularly his father and grandfather, to the fields and sheep camps where his work changes with his growing skill from guarding the orchards and fields to helping with planting, harvesting and herding, and finally, at about the age of 14, to being able to take charge of his own herd (if he has one) and his mother's fields. In the winter months, when farm work is slack and the men gather in the *kivas,* he also learns the Hopi men's crafts—carding, spinning, and finally weaving, moccasin making and other handwork—to the accompaniment of story and song. The learning of all these skills contributes to his understanding of the Hopi Way, which is systematically taught him in *kiva* and camp. During long, quiet days and nights away from the distractions of the household, he is expected to master the secrets of his clan and society rituals and to learn the tribal lore.

The initiated boys form their own play groups from which the uninitiated, as well as peers of the opposite sex, are usually excluded. These groups are spontaneous and unrestricted as to clan or other affiliations, as are all Hopi play groups. Most of the youths' play occurs in the late afternoon and evening after the day's work is done. Besides imported games such as basketball, which is very popular, the boys play a number of organized Hopi games, many of which are seasonal and competitive. An analysis of these reveals that rivalry is expressed between teams rather than individuals and in the form of running, throwing, shooting with arrows or darts, and striking or whipping balls or tops —activities which, according to Hopi ideology, have magical efficacy. Moreover, each activity occurs at the season of the year when it is part of the ceremonial pattern used as an aid in the fertilization and growth of crops. . . .

Besides providing a socially approved outlet for aggression, and the display of skill and initiative, the boys' games afford an opportunity for the expression of peer preferences. They also channelize sport into a pattern of give-and-take or reciprocity between two teams, neither of which can expect to win the goal easily even with a high degree of skill and teamwork. Moreover, the interest is centered not so much on winning as on the actual playing of the game for its own sake, and even in the case of imported games such as baseball, there is little or no interest in the score.

Compared with the boys, the girls have few organized games and these are mainly non-seasonal. The girls rarely compete through opposing teams except in races such as the ceremonial Basket Race, but seem rather to follow either the big-girl-little-girl set-up of the girls' play groups or the cooperative pattern of the women's household groups. The former is illustrated by the Pursuit Game and the latter by the Grinding Party. In the Pursuit Game the leader chases the other players along a complicated and twisted path marked in sand from the outside of the play area to the center, while any girl who steps off the path must drop out of the game. Here the guidance role of the mother and the difficult and centripetal life course of the Hopi girl are faithfully portrayed. On the other hand, at the Grinding Party, a group of girls grind together for several days, each girl working each day for a different relative who reciprocates by supplying her with corn. This takes place before the

Niman ceremony and serves also as a means of accomplishing necessary work in a pleasant manner. . . .

To the little boy the early school experience, beginning just at the time when he is allowed to accompany the men to the fields and range during the period of expansion of mobility and interest from the female to the male world, has the effect of curbing a newly developing freedom by drawing him into another restricted and largely female-dominated situation. On the other hand, for the little girl, who by the age of six is already carrying a considerable burden of work which limits her mobility and play time, the school, in freeing her from childcare and housework for part of the day and giving her time to associate with her peers, has a liberating effect. In spite of the fact that outside of school hours she is expected to continue her nursemaid duties and to start learning to grind, cook and tend the household fire, her work is still comparatively light, and the early school years are for her a period of greater freedom than she has had before or will have again for many years, if ever.

21. Childhood Education in Rural America

J A M E S   W E S T

Old-fashioned child-rearing practices continue in rural America today, and this example from the Ozarks gives us an insight into that pattern. Carl Withers (pseudonym: James West) studied the life and culture of Plainville in the same way that anthropologists have studied tribes all over the world. His study, like the Lynd's *Middletown*, has become a classic exposition of a segment of American culture.

Carl Withers is a native of the Ozark region, he studied at Harvard, has taught at Yale, and engaged in field work in Cuba and Guatemala, as well as in Plainville. He has also collected a volume of popular children's poems. He is currently serving the National Institutes of Health.

The material presented here comes from Chapter 5, "From Cradle to Grave," pp. 165–200 of *Plainville, U.S.A.*, New York: Columbia University Press, 1945, and is printed by kind permission of the publishers and the author.

About one hundred babies a year are born in Woodland County; "new lives" number about twice those of all ages who die. The arrival of a new baby is attributed—when people "bother to think about the matter"—to parental desire for a child, to "laziness," "pure carelessness," or an "accident," to "ignorance" of preventive methods, to "nature," or even to "God's will." Most married couples want children, as "heirs," playthings, companions, or as instruments toward attaining full family status in the community. People also say that they "like to watch young life grow," and that "children bless a home."

Not all want as many children as are born to them, however, and many would wish the intervals between births to be longer than they are. "Planned families," that is, families in which the number of children and their approximate arrival dates are planned, are less frequent in the lower class than in the upper class, where people feel strongly that parents should have no more children than they can "afford to take care of" properly. Families of six to twelve children, commonplace only forty to fifty years ago, are now rare, even among the lower class. Such large families are both ridiculed and condemned, and are attributed to selfishness, laziness, or carelessness on the part of the husband, or, in some very religious lower-class families, to an "old-fashioned" idea that children are the gift of God, whose will should not be interfered with. Only a few people are ignorant of simple commercial contraceptives. Contraception may apparently be practiced freely without compunction, although even men are abashed by discussion of the matter on any level except the ribald. "People here don't like to speak about that." Any "sexual" subject, including pregnancy, is "delicate" and embarrassing, unless discussion is confined to one's own sex group and, loosely speaking, to one's own age group, and is couched light-heartedly in a special and obscene "male" vocabulary.

Most pregnant women are embarrassed at being seen in public and they often blush when "spoken to" (greeted) on the street. Women are criticized for appearing publicly "in that condition." The only women who seem to feel that pregnancy is wholly "natural" are a very few "modern" and educated women and certain backwoods women who "don't seem to even understand" that pregnancy gives them grounds for embarrassment. The latter will even "offer the breast" to their babies publicly, without effort to conceal it from the gaze of bystanding men and children. Most women, when they become pregnant, keep the fact secret as long as possible from all except close adult relatives. . . .

Parents claim to love all children equally. None ever admits "favoring" one child over another, though many are accused of favoritism by neighbors and kinsmen, including their own children (usually in retrospect, after growing up). Actually the youngest child, or "baby" (so-called up to any age) in a household is very often favored. Occasionally an eldest child is favored, or a single child of one sex born into a household of children of the opposite sex. In the latter case, some favoritism, not only by the parents but also by the other children, seems to be approved and considered natural. When an eldest child is favored, it is because he or she assumed a partially parental and managerial role toward the younger children and special responsibilities in the family's economic life. Several factors conduce toward favoring a youngest child. First, the older children, as partial caretakers, filling an imperfectly defined mixed role as siblings and substitute disciplinarians, have a hand in "spoiling" them when they are very young. Second, younger children are in general much less strictly disciplined than older children. And third, the youngest child comes to be especially cherished by parents because he generally remains at home for some time after the older children have married off. The second point is a matter of agreement and frequent comment in Plainville. "They certainly don't make him mind the way I had to . . . People are always easiest on the younger children." Older children often express resentment, even long after they are grown, at the fact that "the younger ones" received less punishment in childhood than they themselves suffered. Married children are also frequently very watchful of the youngest child's spending habits and fearful that he may get into a favored situation regarding the parental property. As a matter of fact, property is almost always divided among children with rigid equality.

There is as much variation in routines for babies as there is in the rest of Plainville life and technology. Some babies are "raised by the book," others by old or hit-and-miss methods, others by every conceivable combination of granny lore and modern methods of child care. One informant said concerning her four children (now thirteen to nineteen years old) that she had raised them all in the "old way." She had in recent years read books on child care, and "always knew something (from magazines and hearsay) about book practices." Even when her own babies were small she "agreed with what the books said," but she raised them in the old way because it was easier.

Babies are breast-fed. According to the vocational agriculture teacher's wife, there had been only two or three bottle babies in the community since she moved there in 1937, except her own two (aged two and a half and three and three quarters in 1940), whom she was raising "scientifically" in every respect, under the guidance of a Large-town pediatrician. This was unique for Plainville. Her children were admired for their good looks, "cute ways," and healthy bodies, but they were rather pitied for having received too little "attention." Older women thought that the mother had needlessly deprived herself of numerous small pleasures natural to motherhood in having played with them and fed them "by the clock." It was thought especially strange that she owned no rocking chair, in which to "sit and rock her babies." An interesting fact in connection with "bottle babies" is that with the bottle comes the whole complex of modern child training: food formulas, heating of food to proper temperature, and regular times for feeding, play, sleep, and affection. The average baby is nursed whenever it wants food, sleeps in bed with its mother and father, and tugs at the mother's breast at will during the night. When it cries it is lifted up, cuddled, and carried in an effort to comfort and "quieten" it. It receives attention whenever it demands it, at any time of the day or night. . . .

The nursing period in general has been shortened to between twelve and twenty-four months, despite the fact that the old pressure has largely ended for weaning one child to make way for the next one. The few backwoods families who still produce "a baby a year, like animals," are greatly ridiculed. Actual weaning ordinarily follows a gradual introduction of other foods quite early, while the child is still being nursed. When the child is six or eight months old, the mother begins to offer it food from the table, where she sits holding the baby at meal times. She gives it sips of milk from a glass, and tastes of gravy, potatoes and other vegetables, and sometimes meat, from her plate. She sometimes pre-chews the harder foods before putting them into the baby's mouth. A man said, "The first thing we used to give our'n was som'p'n soft to chew on, that we knowed wouldn' hurt 'em, like a little fat side-meat." Meanwhile, to discourage the child's interest in the breast, various techniques are employed. The intervals between breast feedings are lengthened, and the feeding period is often shortened. It may be told, "You eat *real* food now, you don't want to suck any longer." Sometimes it is shamed severely each time it asks for the breast. Most children are allowed to suck at night later than in the daytime because they sleep with their parents. Finally they are taken from the breast entirely. An effort is usually made to end breast feeding gently and without shock, though some people initiate weaning, and others terminate the weaning problem of a persistent child, by methods intended to arouse revulsion toward the breast, such as painting it with black stove soot or with quinine. Sometimes (by an old and now rare practice) "sugar tits"— cloth teats filled with butter and sugar—are given to a weanling to "pacify" it, but the standard use of pacifiers is to assist infants in teething. . . .

Sphincter control is introduced, except by the most "modern" people, when the child can understand through language what is expected of it. . . . Many children are scolded severely for "making a mistake" after sphincter control is initiated, and some are spanked harshly. Mothers do not seem to believe that any special problems are ordinarily encountered in teaching sphincter control to their children, full control being usually established at about the age of two or two and a half years, but not often before. Urethral control meets apparently with more difficulties, since a considerable number of large children and grown people are known as bed-wetters. All of the known adult bed-wetters are males, and they suffer a great deal of shame from their "failing."

Differential treatment of children according to sex begins very young. Little boys, it is thought, are "just naturally different from little girls," and the supposed and expected differences are accented and encouraged "from the cradle on." (Cradles, by the way, are no longer used.) Boy babies, as "naturally stronger," are offered fingers to lift themselves up by earlier than girl babies; girl babies who lift themselves up young by older people's fingers are "strong as boys." Girl babies oftener than boy babies are admired as "pretty." Girl babies are "dolls." Boy babies are "little men." Girl babies are dressed "prettier" than boys. The same first clothing is worn by both sexes, because it was acquired before birth, but in all clothing made or bought for them after birth there is a tendency to distinguish between the sexes. More lace and ribbons are put on girl babies' clothing; boy babies' clothing is made plainer. Men like their sons, as soon as they can walk, to have at least one pair of blue-denim overalls patterned as closely as possible on the working garb of men.

This differential treatment . . . applies in every department of a child's life. It seems to be the purpose of the society to establish very early separate sets of behavior habits for boys and girls—habits which have to do with clothing, work, morality, and personality—especially with the development of aggressiveness and domination in boys, and with passivity and submissiveness in girls. Such patterns breed in boys feelings of their own superiority, and of contempt for the work, interests, and intelligence of girls and women, but of admiration for their physical attractiveness. Most girls subscribe, with the boys, to the superiority of being a boy. These mores hold, with few exceptions, for all classes. Boys and girls are treated "equally" however in one important respect. From both is "expected," though not always obtained, implicit obedience to the will of their parents. All children are supposed to "obey" without question, yet even here there is a difference: a boy is often spoken of as having a spirit like that of a colt, which must be broken to obedience as a colt is broken. Girls are "naturally more willing" to obey, and "give less trouble" in management and discipline.

In most families, children of opposite sex (and sometimes in prudish families, sisters also, but never brothers) are taught not to undress in front of each other after they are old enough to change their own clothes. It would be inconvenient for the mother to separate them earlier. As they begin learning to dress themselves under her supervision, she begins to teach them the principles of modesty, both by verbal instruction and by backing one out of sight of the other behind a stove, a chair, or some other piece of furniture, or off into another room. Children begin to try to undress and dress themselves at about two years of age, but they do not often become fully competent at the task before about age five. Yet with all this early stress on modesty, the mother frequently bathes children of the opposite sex together in the same tub until they are four or even five years old. Here, however, she is faced with a problem of efficiency, since water has to be carried in from the well and heated on the stove. She is more apt to bathe her children in turn, using the same water; if she follows this plan she is likely to bathe the larger children or the girls first, the smaller children or the boys last.

The strictures on modesty, especially concerning the exposure of sexual organs to the sight of others, are very rigid. Most married couples would consider it immodest to undress completely before each other in a lighted room; many married couples are said never to have seen each other undressed. Siblings must never see siblings of the opposite sex (except very small children) undressed, and children, as soon as they can bathe and dress themselves, begin to conceal themselves carefully from the eyes of parents. Boys of any age strip off freely in each others' presence in a room or at a swimming hole, and boys micturate before each other, but not before adult men, without turning their backs. Adult men ordinarily turn away from others when micturating. . . .

Techniques of securing obedience are whipping, spanking, slapping, shaming, teasing, scolding, nagging, threats, privations, rewards, encouragements, demonstrative verbal approvals, and physical affection. . . .

People differ in opinion about the amount of corporal punishment children should receive, and about how and by whom it should be administered. A "reasonable amount" of whipping is recommended and practiced by most parents, especially on boys, but children "should not be whipped till the blood comes, or every day like they used to be." The average boy gets perhaps a dozen or two actual "lickings" during his childhood. He is seldom whipped after the age of twelve or fourteen. The average girl gets less. Some children get "one a day" or "one a week"; some get none. The idea is not uncommon that a parent should not punish a child while angry; but few parents are credited with so much restraint. Parents, however, who "seem to enjoy whipping their children" are severely condemned, though serious physical injury would have to be done to the child before there would be legal or even neighborly interference. It is told satirically of some parents that "they never whale a child without saying, 'This hurts me more than it hurts you.' "

Teasing, kidding, and shaming, alone or in combination, are among the most effective means of molding a child to the patterns desired in the community. Of these three techniques, however, only shaming is recognized as of formal disciplinary and instructional value. ("I *shame* oftener than I *whip*. And I *reason* as often as I *shame,*" said one mother.) A child is ordinarily shamed on the grounds that it is not living up to the standard expected of its sex, its size, or its age. . . .

Common privations for disobedience (or other bad conduct) are keeping children indoors from play, or at home from play with neighboring children; or depriving them of an expected trip to town or elsewhere, or of some desirable foodstuff or "treat" (cake or pie at home; candy, gum, or an ice-cream cone in town). Threats of privation, however, are more frequent than the privations themselves. Parents often secure obedience by threatening a dilatory child, "If you *don't* do that you won't get . . . etc." Yet even when a child has been "bad" in the face of a definite threat of deprivation, the parent often "forgets" or the child secures the desired treat anyhow as a bribe to "stop whining and wheedling," especially if it takes advantage of a conversation between the parent and a friend in town to start "pleading." Plainville children are never "sent to bed without their suppers," or locked up in a dark closet for their ill deeds, but many are threatened with the "bugger-man" (bogey-man) who "lives outside in the dark" to punish or "git" bad children. The bugger-man is a great unseen ally of harassed mothers, and most children develop a fearful dread of the dark. . . .

There are some rather interesting differences in the relative disciplinary powers of mothers and fathers. A few mothers are reported to be more severe with children than their fathers are, but most children regard their mothers as some measure of protection against severe punishment from fathers. Children do not ordinarily mistake for more than a threat the mother's frequent threat, "If you don't obey me, I'll ask your father to punish you when he comes in from the field." They know that her patience will have to be frayed in the extreme (or the offense must be very grave) before she will substitute a "big trouble," involving the father, herself, and the child, and perhaps her other children too, for a "small trouble," which will quickly blow over even if she fails to solve it. The majority of mothers do their own punishing, and the father his own. A father generally gets quicker obedience from a child than its mother does because—though he actually has much less role than the mother in rearing and disciplining the child—punishment from him when it occurs is more sudden, sure, and severe. He is less apt to "threaten first," and he will stand less argument or "back-talk." That many mothers will plead, cajole, nag, urge, and threaten but not often actually punish a child above seven or eight years old is a fact so well understood by most children that as a form of sport they often deliberately arouse the whole process "just to see how far they can go." . . .

It can perhaps be said that while the father stands in the background as a final judge and power—and for boys an ideal of male competence and superiority which they are urged to imitate, the main tutelary and executive power for very small children is the mother. Her authority is in many ways a reflection of the father's position as "lord and master," but the early ideal for *moral* imitation is probably the mother. In her role as an "obedient and dutiful" wife, she inculcates in young children the ideals of goodness, obedience, and all good conduct. Most men will say, "I leave all this (that is, discipline and early instruction) up to my wife." The situation is altered greatly for boys, when they start "follering" the father about his work. It is altered also for both sexes when they start to school.

Not all of the whole "socialization" process, of course, is in the hands of mothers or even of parents. The school and even the Sunday school, but more especially play groups, brothers and sisters, other children of various ages but especially older children, and many adults outside the family all have a hand in "socializing" each child. A listing of what children "learn" and where they learn it would fill several books. The formulation of personality, especially the personality of boys, begins very early to pass away from the mother. A fact well worth mentioning in this connection is that rural children and small town children of both sexes, for all the "isolation" of rural life, know warmly more adults (though usually fewer children) than most urban children know. Through schools and parental interests, urban children are segregated much more rigidly than country children into very narrow age grades. Many learn to know intimately only two adults: their parents. This fact must be of enormous significance in the personality development of urban children and in their understanding of adult life in general. If the city child's parents are "peculiar," "neurotic," or badly adjusted to each other, then he must get a very strange idea of normal adult relationships. Country children, in observing rather intimately the patterns of domestic and economic life in other families, have innumerable opportunities to correct through comparison any misconceptions of "normal" family or other adult life which they receive in their own homes.

From brothers, neighbor boys, and other males, including adult males, the growing Plainville boy begins gradually to learn, as soon as he is old enough to toddle or be led away from "his mother's apron strings," a great number of things that boys (and usually only boys) are "supposed to know." Here, too, age grades are of great importance, because males (like females) are gathered informally through play, and formally through school, into a rising series of narrow age groups. Until he is fully "grown up," his own age group is a group of boys whose ages differ from his only by a year or two. . . .

. . . Girls' age groups, while formally and theoretically similar to those of boys, are less rigidly exclusive. The girls' "gangs" are only a weak imitation of boys' gangs. For a growing girl, the task of the society is to teach her how finally to pass from a situation under her mother to one resembling her mother's. All the techniques and ideals learned from her mother will apply in the new situation. She can, and often does, make the whole transition, from infancy to "a home of her own," without serious inner conflict. The growing male, however, must learn, as the Danish fairy tale writer phrased it, that "the world is not like what one's mother says, but what the neighbors say." In league to prevent his learning this are his mother and other women, the church, his schoolteachers, all "genteel" and "respectable" forms, stated ideals, and rituals in the community, and usually the "spoken word" of his father. In league to teach him, however, are the older boys and men, gossip, actual observation of trading practices and the like, and often the tacit connivance of his father. He must learn all that he is supposed to, "sow a few wild oats" without acquiring any fixed bad habits, and finally break away from the domination of his parents and settle down, into a new situation either "outside" or in his home community, where *he* is dominant in at least a matrimonial situation. To attain fully approved adult status he must finally subscribe anew, ostensibly at least, to the fictions of "respectability" which overlie the bringing up of the next generation.

The earliest work techniques are taught by the mother; little boys and girls first learn simple chores: putting their playthings away (from the middle of the floor), hanging their coats and caps up, fetching objects for mother, bringing in chips and cobs for kindling; later, carrying in wood, at first a stick at a time; still later, picking berries or fruit, gathering in the eggs, feeding and watering the chickens, working in the garden (hoeing, weed-pulling, and gathering the vegetables). . . .

By age six to nine, girls can dry the dishes; a little later they can wash them. Most boys also learn to dry and wash dishes, but "they don't like to." It is girls' and women's work, and boys don't want to be "caught doing it." Girls often begin to sew at about the same age; a little later to sweep and dust, to make the beds, to wash and iron and mend clothes, and sometimes to cook. Mistakes in cooking "ruin good food" and bring "complaints from the menfolks," however, and many girls do not learn to cook until much later. Some girls learn to do "fancy work": tatting, crocheting, embroidering, and sometimes fancy quilting. Gardening work begins for both sexes at age nine or ten.

Boys begin to milk at eight to ten. Girls sometimes do too, though milking is "men's work." At about the same age boys learn to split and chop wood, to keep the water bucket filled and the wood box full, to do "barn chores" like feeding, and they begin to work in the field. Few girls learn to do these men's tasks except for carrying water into the house. Yet girls do not scorn "men's tasks," as boys scorn dishwashing, sweeping, and bed-making, nor would they be ashamed to do them. Many girls envy boys their work, their greater mobility of action, and their future roles. No boy ever says, "I wish I was a girl." Fathers and brothers however are criticized for letting women and girls do "heavy work," especially for letting them "chop wood" or "work in the field."

Many girls are fully competent to "take care of a home" (including the "mothering" of smaller children) by the time they are eleven.

Most boys are fully competent to do all but the heaviest of field work at the same age. Boys learn first to drive a team, then in turn to harrow, plow ("break") ground, ride a rake, cultivate corn, ride a mower, etc. Hay-pitching and other tasks require greater strength. The order of learning is shifted somewhat on tractor-run farms, but the average boy knows from observation very early how tractors and cars are operated, and boys are often allowed to handle gasoline-run machinery as early as at age eleven. The father teaches all these skills; the boy "begs to learn" and is encouraged to learn. In learning to handle team-operated farm implements, he first follows the father. He then "takes the lines" (by which the team is controlled) himself. He next is allowed to harrow or plow a round by himself, watched or accompanied by the father. Finally, he is able to "make a full-time hand."

In the old days he would from this point on have made a full-time hand in the fields. Any schooling he got would have been got when he was not needed at home. Now, however, compulsory schooling interferes at age six with the full exploitation of children's work. Boys and girls alike must attend school, theoretically, until they are fourteen or until they have "passed the eighth grade." Almost all better-class children and many lower-class children now go on to attend the high school in Plainville. . . .

The school is the first important formal disciplinary institution which the child enters outside his own home. The teacher is a new "parent," often cherished as "younger" than the real parents, but often regarded through folkloristic devices which induce fear of teachers and dread of school as more unsympathetic and formidable in authority than parents themselves. A teacher can "love" a child, but she (or he) can also "whip," in all schools outside the consolidation, despite a state law against corporal punishment. In school, by processes bearing little resemblance to suggestions in the state syllabus, most children are somehow taught the rudiments of reading, writing, and figuring. In school also, the common moral sentiments on which all "nice people" agree are again reiterated, though "nothing is said in school" (outside the vocational agriculture classes) either to reinforce or weaken any "fanatical" moral strictures, or any superstitions or magical ideas which the child may have learned at home. The school "tries to serve the whole community" without offending anybody.

A more important aspect of schooling, however, is that here the child is drawn partially away from the mother's apron strings and begins long periods of contact with more children than he has been accustomed to. All the children in a neighborhood are gathered into a rural school; most of those from a wide area into the consolidated school. In either case, the children are thrown together by age, regardless of sex, for formal class work. Outside of classes, the boys play mostly with boys, the girls with girls. Until recently, most rural school grounds were divided into two areas, for mutually exclusive use by the sexes. . . .

But this is not the only important division or discrimination. An older boy is greatly superior to a younger one, in strength, skills, and valuable knowledge. The age lines between boys are very narrowly drawn. Younger boys desire acceptance by older boys; older boys admit younger boys to their society only when they are "useful," in games, for teasing, and as an audience for the ostentation of superior knowledge. Considerable cruelty is practiced by older boys on a younger boy: they attempt to shame, tease, or torture out of him any weakness, cowardice, or "babylike" quality he manifests. A boy becomes aligned most closely with the group of boys whose ages are within a year or two of his own. While such alignments are in many ways exclusive, they also overlap with similar alignments of younger boys and of older boys: an eight-year-old boy who is a leader and impressive "big shot" with the six-to eight-year-old group is at the same time often an underling among the eight-to ten-year olds. From these he collects, as a tolerated spectator or object of condescending enlightenment, habits, attitudes, and information and misinformation, which he passes on to the awestruck members of his younger group. The main process of male socialization takes place in this fashion. Male traits and "knowledge" are passed down and inculcated, from age-group to age-group. This is one of the main social functions of the boys' gangs and age-groups.

Something similar, but weaker, happens among girls. Among girls, however, the teasing patterns are negligibly evident. Girls are "taught to be nice" to younger girls; this fits in with the doll pattern, with the ultimate roles of girls as mothers, and with the single developmental line followed by female lives. . . .

Sex education for Plainville boys is largely left up to "nature" and, tacitly, to other boys. Sex is a subject which neither mothers nor fathers "feel they could discuss" with their sons. Parents teach small children no names for their sex organs (beyond perhaps the words "that" or "it"), and tell them no facts about childbirth. When a new baby is expected, the other children are generally bundled off to a neighbor's until after the birth. They may be told that mother is "not feeling well." They are supposed to be greatly surprised at seeing the new baby when they return home. About it they are told one of several customary myths:

the doctor fetched it in his satchel, a stork brought it through the sky, swinging in a big diaper, Mother came across it in the grass, or Daddy found it in the orchard.

Only very young children, however, subscribe to these myths. The average six-year-old child has frequently observed intercourse of animals (boys have especially—it is easier to protect girls from such sights), and most of them have seen the births of kittens, puppies, pigs, calves, or colts. They have asked questions, first of their parents, whose hush-hush dissemblings have indicated that these are no proper subjects for adult-child discussions. Later they have sought and learned from other children a body of information in the main correct, though some garbling naturally occurs as taboo knowledge is circulated downward through the age-groups. The average seven- or eight-year-old child has learned to integrate fairly well what he has seen with what he can learn from other children. Most children of that age "know where animals come from and where *they* come from," though they still know nothing of periods of gestation. A common early misconception regarding birth is that every act of coitus results in offspring, and that offspring follows coitus almost immediately. "Lots of girls used to believe that till they got married—if they knowed *any*thing."

The total lack of realism with which fathers face the problem of instructing their boys about sex is curious. Either they tell them nothing whatever, or, when the boy is fifteen or sixteen years old, they manage to transmit the popular notion that "self-abuse" will cause pimples, or general debility, or insanity. The boy, more likely than not, has already heard this story from other boys, as a discredited myth (but not sufficiently discredited to remove all fear) which adults either actually believe or wish youngsters to believe. At about the same time the father is likely to become less guarded with his son—he may tell a smutty story to him or in his presence, or relate sexual gossip, as a form of "treating him more like a man." Many fathers say, "Boys really ought to be told about things, but I wouldn't know how to start." Considerable constraint regarding discussion of sexual matters persists between most fathers and sons until after the son is married and has children of his own.

Mothers or older sisters, on the other hand, generally prepare girls to expect menstruation, and sometimes they tell girls "about men" before marriage. Sexual explanations arouse less embarrassment between mother and daughter than between father and son. At one time, however, according to several women, "Girls were told absolutely nothing. That was considered the duty of their husbands." Menstruation is a fearfully taboo subject. Even women do not like to say the word to each other; they prefer to refer to it by euphemisms like "that way," "not feeling well," "indisposed," or "in that sickly way."

What all this taboo on sex actually means is difficult to say. It is undoubtedly related to the fact that sexual relations between husband and wife are said to be usually unsatisfactory. . . .

I must at this point go back a number of years and suggest how a young man has attained enough knowledge of property and economic procedure to undertake the hazard of starting a new family.

By the time he was fifteen, at latest, the farm boy was equipped with all the skills and techniques for making a living, except the skill of "managing." When not in school he did a man's work. In fact, one of the first important blows to his self-esteem and happiness probably came about then with his discovery that through his own early eagerness to learn he had been jockeyed into doing a man's work, without gaining any voice in planning or helping to manage the family enterprise. "As soon as he learned to do things he got to do 'em, but nobody asked him what ought to be done next or how." His parents also very early taught him frugality, "the proper respect for money," by telling him how scarce and valuable money is, by doling out small sums of spending money to him painfully (as if "somebody was pullin' a tooth"), and by urging him, "Don't spend it. Save it." From other boys he learned the art of "swapping": pocket knives, marbles, toys, string, broken bits of farm machinery, anything he carried in his pockets. "Swapping," in the boys' world, is a duplicate of trading among men. Boys learn by swapping to be "smart traders" who make a profit, or "suckers" who get cheated, or the more average property owners who "keep what they have" without risking it on a gamble or a trade. Yet real money or property beyond small spending money—a nickel or dime at a time, begged often from his mother—were, like planning and managing, very probably outside his domain. A few girls are allowed to raise a setting of eggs, to sell as fryers; some boys are given a pig or calf to raise. The proceeds, in either case, usually go for clothes which they would get anyway, yet children seem very proud when allowed ownership and management even to this limited degree. People often comment on how "children love to own something." Most people agree that "they *should* own something," but few own anything.

Some are allowed to "claim" a calf or pig, until it is sold or eaten, but without voice in its disposal or any share of the money it brings.

Children are never paid for work they do at home. Boys, however, have the right to "work out," when not needed at home. They are paid about half of men's wages when they are, say, fifteen, and of average size and strength for that age; a year or two later, they get full wages ($1.00 to $1.50 a day in 1939–40) for the days they work. Boys and girls both have a right (though no exclusive right) to any salable wild products. For girls this means that they can gather and sell wild blackberries and wild gooseberries beyond family needs, if they can find anyone who wants to buy them. Boys can trap and hunt. Not all boys trap and hunt—prairie boys generally live too far from the timber to set a trap line. But many a boy, in good trapping years, earns all his spending money, clothes, and sometimes school supplies, by trapping, skinning, and selling the hides of skunks, muskrats, 'possums, and perhaps a few mink and raccoons. Until 1939 he also had a sale for rabbits (shipped away as meat), at ten to fifteen cents per carcass. (The upper-class contempt for "hunting and trapping" does not apply to boys; it applies only to adults who hunt and trap as an old-fashioned way of livelihood or a way to "escape honest work.") Two girls from the hills were rather admired for having earned the money for "high school clothes" by "trapping just like boys do," in 1937–38. Children are in general allowed to spend whatever they earn even though it may be well understood between them and their parents that they have to spend it all for necessities.

Before a youth gets married, then, he knows how to farm. He has earned some money and handled its expenditure. He may have some savings, or a head or two of livestock. He has been "outside," on shopping trips, hauling stock to market, or visits, perhaps on "work jobs." He is anxious to break away from his father's economic domination, a situation which is "all work and being bossed" without ever being consulted about "where should we plow today?" or "Which field should we plant to corn next year?" He "has no opportunity, working with his father."

22. Cultural Transmission of Parental Anxiety

MARGARET MEAD

Margaret Mead's studies of the learning process in a variety of different cultures are probably the most widely read anthropological documents in the world today. She has investigated the processes by which the individual grows up ∼nd adopts his culture in several tribes of Melanesia, in Samoa and in Bali. She has long used the insights of such investigation in the analysis of child-rearing in modern America. Her best known works on primitive peoples are *Coming of Age in Samoa, Growing up in New Guinea,* and *Sex and Temperament in Three Primitive Societies.*

Mead is Associate Curator of Ethnology at the American Museum of Natural History and Lecturer at Columbia University, where she took her doctorate in 1929 under Franz Boas.

The essay here discusses some of the subtler aspects of cultural transmission of feelings and attitudes that develop out of parent-child relationships and the modern anxieties that beset middle-class American parents. The essay was written during World War II, so that what Mead says relates to that period of time. As she writes, things change fast in American culture. The selection is from *And Keep Your Powder Dry,* by Margaret Mead, copyright 1942 by Margaret Mead, by permission of William Morrow and Company, Inc., and the author.

. . . When we ask how babies become Americans, we are asking how all the precipitates, in the American language, in American jokes and American songs, in American attitudes towards politics and the world and the universe, which were originally created by the attempt of many diverse peoples to assimilate themselves to a pattern which others would accept as identical with their own, have been re-created in the upbringing of the growing child.

The American baby is born into a family which is isolated from both paternal and maternal lines of kindred. His parents typically live in a house by themselves. If they do not, they seek to create some sort of social isolation to recompense themselves for the presence of relatives. The mother dreams in secret of the day when "John's mother won't have to live with us any more," and the father hopes that "One of Mary's brothers will be able to take Mary's mother before long." This attitude is conveyed to the baby. He learns that only his father and his mother are really relevant to his life, that grandparents should live at a distance if at all, and are not really necessary. . . .

In old societies when the extended family or the clan is still an important part of the way of life, the child moves easily among many relatives, many of whom bear his name, with some one of whom he can almost certainly find a community of interest and even a common physique. But in America, with the family whittled down to father and mother, a child may often feel he is like neither of them. The fact that two parents are all the anchors he has in a world which is otherwise vague and shifting, over-emphasizes the tie and brings it into question. . . .

From this curious structure of the American family, from the fact that two young people, often of quite diverse backgrounds, are sent out into the world together to make a way of life, with no oldsters by to help them, with no guides except the movies, the pulp magazines, and the fumbling experiences of those very little older than themselves, it follows also that each child's experience will be different from each other's. However much his mother may study the daily specials, may deck his baby carriage in the type of tailored cover in style this year, and dress him in the most approved sun suit or slacks, beneath the outward conformity there lies always the mother's sense of difference. How does her marriage compare with that of the other women who stroll beside her with their impeccably dressed babies? She doesn't know, she doesn't dare to ask, even if she had words in which to ask such a question. The questions themselves might betray her, might betray some peculiarity in her own make-up or some inadequacy in her husband. The endless query: "Am I happy?" can in part be translated into the question: "How close am I to what I should expect to be?" Back of her lies her single experience with family life—her view of her own parents. She lives in the only other experience she may ever have. She cannot know how her worried version of life compares with the average, with the normal, with those who are "really" happy. And her voice is sharp as she admonishes her child if he deviates from the public behavior which is common for all of the children of the block, if he fights when they don't or fails to fight when they do. The basis of her life, her membership in her new family, like her membership in her old one, is secret, and probably deviates in a thousand ways from that which others would respect and envy—if they knew. To compensate for this, she insists on conformity. Their house, their car, their clothes, their patterns of leisure time, shall be as much like other people's as possible. Her face cream, her powder, her lipstick, shall be publicly validated. But inside the walls of that home, there is no one to tell her, or to tell her husband, whether their expectations are too high or two low, no one to quote from the experience of other generations, no yardstick, no barometer.

Some of this desperate uncertainty is conveyed to the baby, as she dresses him to take him out, as she undresses him when she brings him in. Just as virtually no American family is completely certain of its social antecedents, or can produce a full complement of unblotted escutcheons, so also no American family is sure of its position on an unknown chart called "happiness." The mother anxiously searches her baby's face. Are his "looks" something which should make her happy, is his health something which shows she is a good mother, does he walk and talk early enough to be a credit to her, to prove to others and so prove to herself that she has a right to be what she wants to be—happy? From the day when self-conscious fathers stand outside the glass-walled hospital nursery and anxiously compare the shape of their own babies' heads with those of the other babies, the child is valued in comparative terms, not because he is of the blood and bone and "name" of his parents, but because of his place on some objective (but undefined) rating scale of looks and potential abilities. In his parents' every gesture, the child learns that although they want to love him very much, although they hope they will love him very much—for loving your children is one of the things that books say parents do—they are not quite sure that he will deserve it, that when they check him up against the baby book and the neighbors' baby he will come out A-1 and so worthy of complete blind love.

Each civilization conveys different things to its children. The Balinese mother mimicking a desperate fear as she calls the wandering child back to her side teaches him forever after to fear the unknown, to cling, he knows not why, to well-trodden paths. *"Aroh!"* she shrieks, "Wild cat!" or "Witch!" or "Snake!" or "Fire!", making no effort to adapt the scare word to the circumstance. If she screamed "Snake" when the child went into the grass, and "Scorpion" when he climbed the wood-pile, he might learn to look and find patches of grass without snakes and piles of wood without scorpions. But instead any scare word in any context will do; the child gets no chance to test reality out, he remains frightened of an unknown.

"He's so strong," says the Iatmul [New Guinea] mother. "He runs so fast. I can't catch him." "When I catch him I will hit him and kill him," she says, as she pretends to chase and fails to catch her erring two-year-old. She acts as if the child were as strong and fleeter of foot than she, and the terrified baby, pushed beyond his endurance into an assertive role for which he is not ready, learns that safety lies in stamping and shouting and pretending to be bigger and stronger and fiercer than one really is.

Not with a single phrase or a single gesture, not with one punishment alone, but in every tone of the voice, in each turn of the head, these nuances are conveyed to the child, and as the Balinese baby learns that the unknown is always to be avoided, and the Iatmul baby learns to play at being strong, the American baby learns that its parents' love—even if they are his parents and he isn't adopted—is conditional upon the way in which he compares with others. "He's such a poor eater. I don't know what to do with him. I just can't get him to eat like other children." His mother thinks he isn't listening, as he digs with his shovel under the park bench, but the "won't eat" and the deprecating tone in which she says it gets through to him—she is not worrying because her beloved child does not take the food which she has lovingly prepared for him, but because he is showing himself inferior at being a growing child. At his next meal he looks guiltily at his carrots. If he rejects them again that same depreciatory note will recur tomorrow in his mother's voice.

So while the child is learning that his whole place in the world, his name, his right to the respect of other children—everything—depends upon his parents and on what kind of a house they have been able to build or buy or rent, what kind of a car they are able to drive, what kind of toys they are able to buy him, he also learns that his own acceptance by these parents, who are his only support, is conditional upon his achievements, upon the way in which he shows up against other children and against their idea of other children. To the anxiety with which small boys in many if not all cultures of the world view grown men and wonder if they will ever be as tall and strong, is added in America, for both boys and girls, the anxiety as to whether they will be successful in keeping their parents' love as children. American girls of college age can be thrown into a near panic by the description of cultures in which parents do not love their children. Against the gnawing fear that their personal achievement has made them unworthy of love, they have placed a vague persistent belief in "mother love," a belief that somehow or other their parents won't be able to get out of loving them some—because they are parents, and theirs. Any evidence that destroys their faith in this "maternal instinct" is profoundly disturbing. . . .

Recently, students of comparative education, philosophers of improved family relationships, have made this point articulate and begun to scold American mothers because they do not love their children unconditionally. This has merely added to the confusion. It is only possible to love a child as part of oneself, unconditionally, if one loves oneself in a certain sense unconditionally. The unconditional mother must have once been an unconditionally loved child, taking into her own soul part of the approval which was showered upon her. The peculiarity of the American version of "To him that hath shall be given" lies in this, that the child who, because it was bright or strong or beautiful, did receive great approval from its parents, is in turn able to love friends and lovers and children as parts of its highly approved self. . . .

This whole emphasis upon achievement in order to deserve that parental love which is so essential, in a world where everything else is shifting, where one's home is a number of a street, where one may change schools every year and move always among half-familiar faces, is further sharpened by the parents' inability to applaud themselves in their children. In societies where the father rears his son to his own trade, it is possible for him to feel a fine thrill of identification and pride the first time the child manipulates the tools of the trade with a distinguished touch. "Ha, a chip off the old block!" says father. "My child shares my skill." But in America, with the rapid rate of change, most parents know that the child will not do what the parent did, but something different. A parent cannot think back to his own boyhood and simply make an inaccurate comparison. When he was a boy, it was his pride to ride a bicycle thirty miles a day, not drive a car four hundred miles a day, to tap out a few words on a home-built radio set, not to build a model aeroplane of beautiful accuracy and new design. He must applaud in his son something which he did not do himself, and something which he has no way of judging. If he knew more than his son about building model aeroplanes, then he could judge his son's model on its merits. As it is, he vacillates between fatuous attacks of paternal pride, for whose undiscriminating nature his son despises him, and anxious requests as to whether the model has won or will win a prize, and so give him the right to be proud. Any approval which he does give must be necessarily ill-informed and not of the sort to win his son's respect. Only from outside sources, from school grades, competitions, rises in salary, prizes, can he learn whether this son whom he has reared is really as good as he hopes that he is.

Yet the further the child goes from standards that his parents know, the greater is his need for success. He is leaving them, he is giving up every concrete thing which they did, he will neither eat like them, nor dress like them, nor have the same standards as to what is appropriate to say to a girl or how he should plan his life insurance or where he should take his vacation. In big things and in small, in all the habits of life through which they taught him what the world was like, he will leave them, he will in a sense betray them. All he can offer in return is success. As a high school principal said recently to the parents of the graduating class: "They lay their success, their achievement, before you, a thank-offering for all that you have done for them."

When we see this situation dramatized in the immigrant father, himself with no book learning and hardly an English word, pathetically delighted because his son has won some academic honor, we are touched with the pity of it, of the father who cannot, himself, realize the inwardness of what his son has done. We can sympathize with the young research chemist who is offered a job as the president of a small college— "President! Now that is something my father and mother would understand. They don't get this sort of thing I am doing at all. But a title, a limousine, to live in a big house called the President's house. They'd know I'd made good then." And he hesitates and goes back not quite happy to the research work which his fine mind is so perfectly fitted to do, not able to be gay in the rejection of the conspicuous role which would have made sense to his less schooled parents. These seem to us extreme cases, part of the drama of immigration, of the rapid rise from generations of peonage to a place in a free world. But they are only extreme cases of what happens to almost every American parent, no matter how successful his son. And we find a curious reflection of this dependence upon externals for the validation of success, in the anxiety of wives, or of the husbands of professional women, to be assured that the spouse is really good, really recognized by his or her colleagues. A husband who has regarded his wife's excursions into the academic world with kindly contempt will grow suddenly respectful when she is offered a fellowship. "They" have recognized her, she must have something in her after all.

This anomalous state in which American parents are forever looking for a right to be proud of, and a right to love, their children, and forever recognizing that the proofs of worthiness must come from a world which itself has already slipped beyond them, is dramatized also in the relationship between parents and teachers. The teacher, in the American school, is teaching the child something which the parents don't know. . . . The teacher symbolizes a gulf between parents and children which will grow year by year—not the inevitable gulf between old and young, for that, like the seasons, is a circumstance to which man can bow with dignity, but the more dishonorable gulf which results from the parents getting out of date. . . . It is small wonder that American parents retaliate by taking a savage interest in the teacher's character, by surveying her morals with a scrutiny accorded no one else except the minister's wife and the characters of political opponents. In a sense she is the enemy. They have given in, they have turned their children over to her to be made smarter than themselves and to learn a lot of things they, the parents, never needed to know. But just let them find her wanting in some way, failing to teach the children what the parents *do* know—that sacred symbol of the little bit of the Past which is worthy of respect, the Three R's—and they become merciless.

. . . In more static societies where there are schools, it is the duty of teachers merely to represent the parents, teaching what the parents would have the children learn. The teachers are the custodians of the past, the preservers of tradition. In America, the teacher is, in fact, never the representative of the parents . . . she is always the representative of the future into which the parents are anxious that their children should enter, and enter well prepared.

23. Educational Practices of the North American Indian

GEORGE A. PETTITT

The American Indians taught their children without formal schools. Most of the training was informal, but initiation rites and other special events were effective elements in this learning process. George A. Pettitt surveyed the existing literature and analyzed these teaching practices in the only systematic study of its kind every attempted. We present here only a section from his introduction and his general conclusions.

Pettitt is Lecturer in Anthropology at the University of California, Berkeley, where he took his Ph.D. in 1940. The selection here is taken from his Primitive Education in North America, *University of California Publications in American Archeology and Ethnology,* Volume 43, No. 1, Berkeley and Los Angeles, 1946, and is reproduced with the kind permission of the author and publisher.

It may seem a far cry from primitive education to the pedagogical problems of modern society. But modern pedagogy is not something entirely different from the primitive type. It is more complex, but the added complexities are largely superimpositions taken over by the schools. Cultural ideals have changed, but cultural goals fall into largely the same categories. In short, in primitive society, which had no school system, we find a fairly complete picture of what a people must do to insure the transmittal of its traditions, beliefs, ideals, and aspirations to the younger generation. Through study of such school-free efforts we may obtain a clearer conception of the manifold ramifications of the process of conditioning children and of safeguarding a culture pattern. With such a conception in mind we are then in a better position to judge whether schools and professional teachers, either in justice to themselves or to the public, should be expected to assume the whole responsibility at so much per month.

We cannot read deeply in ethnological literature without being struck by the fact that primitive education was a community project in which all reputable elders participated at the instigation of individual families. The result was not merely to focus community attention on the child, but also to make the child's education a constant challenge to the elders to review, analyze, dramatize, and defend their cultural heritage. Their own beliefs, understanding, and faith, their personal integration in the culture, and their collective unity, all were promoted by the necessity of assuming the role of educators of their children. Modern teachers are fond of stressing the chasm between the professional and amateur collector of knowledge with the aphorism that no man can really understand or appreciate a subject until he has tried to teach it. There is, perhaps, a broader truth in and wider application to this conclusion than those who use it have yet stressed. . . .

. . . Generalizations concerning primitive indulgence of children in North America, and concerning the almost complete absence of discipline, even of the physical type, are not universally applicable. The evidence presented indicates that the unquestioned high degree of child indulgence by parents is not, as seems often to be tacitly accepted, a result of a psychic difference between primitives and civilized peoples— of a specifically primitive attitude toward progeny in the abstract; that disciplinary practices are not an example of primitive culture weakness, but are in rather neat balance with the objectives of primitive society and with its other beliefs and practices. . . . The significant features of primitive disciplinary practices for this purpose are: the universal tendency to refer discipline or the authority for it to some individual or agency outside of the group, and the tendency to rely most practically on supernatural agencies as the ultimate reference.

Primitive education is usually treated as a process of culture transmission brought into play for the purpose of perpetuating an already established culture and the social group associated with it. Attention is called to the fact that culture transmission, or education, had to begin contemporaneously with social groups and cultures themselves; that it developed not as a late addition to culture, but as a fundamental and primordial part of a culture which laid down certain restrictions and provided certain stimuli to which the development of the culture had to respond. The psychology of the child presents the same social problem to all cultures, and so far as the complexity of the culture demands that it be met, and it is met, there is a ubiquitous factor tending to promote culture parallels and convergences, not to mention influencing culture diffusion. . . .

The major conclusions of this study [of educational practices in aboriginal America] are the following:

1. Corporal punishment is rare among primitives not because of an innate kindliness, but because it is antipathetic to the development of the type of individual personality set up as an ideal.

2. Aside from corporal punishment, there is no particular lack of discipline for children. Its apparent absence is often traceable to a failure to note that immediate relatives tend to refer discipline to outsiders, to the mother's brother or father's sister, to other individuals, to societies, to the social group and its effective coercive weapon, ridicule, and perhaps most important of all, to the supernaturals and their impersonators.

3. Contrary to popular opinion, spontaneous imitation is not the basic motive for the learning process in primitive children. The fundamental stimuli are ridicule, praise, and reward.

4. Personal names play an effective role as stimuli to learning and to accepted social behavior, through the use of trivial or ridiculous names for those who have not achieved, through prestige names as a reward for achievement, and through the social fiction of transferring personality and power with a name.

5. Economic activities are not slighted in favor of religious training in the primitive curriculum, but the application of praise and reward

for economic achievement, through first-fruits rites, is one of the basic and probably oldest expressions of pedagogical concern.

6. The vision quest and the acquisition of guardian spirits are not psychic experiences of such complexity that they can be fully participated in only by abnormal individuals. They are expressions of a desire to achieve an inner conviction of social and economic competency and spiritual security. The vision quest has educational applications aside from those connoted by its religious aspects, which can be equated in some degree with practices in areas where the vision quest is more rarely found.

7. Myths and folk tales are not merely instruments of adult satisfaction and entertainment providing only content to the curriculum and used casually for educational purposes. Rather, they show internal evidence, in their etiologic episodes, and in their *utilization of juveniles as leading characters,* of having been influenced in their development by educational requirements. Collections of myths and folk tales are not representative of the whole of primitive oral literature. Genre literature, particularly episodic biographies and autobiographies, are of as great if not greater importance in primitive education.

V.

THE FAMILY

Incubator for Culture

The processes of procreation being universal, people everywhere are surrounded by kin. Everywhere, also, people regard their kin in special ways, distinguishing relatives from nonrelatives; making distinctions between the various classes of kin, and reserving special sentiments for the ties of kinship. And because the child first relates to his culture and the world as a whole through his close relatives—because the family has so important a role in education—the patterns of family life play a particularly important role in culture. We may say that the basic elements (and particularly the subtle orientations) of every culture are first transmitted to each normal member of a community by his family.

In modern America we recognize the normal family as made up of an adult male, an adult female, and a number of preadults of either sex. Sometimes one or the other adult is missing, but then we speak of it as a "broken" home—a partial family. Sometimes there are no children, but this, too, is viewed as something less than a family. And occasionally there are outsiders in the household—a spinster aunt or a grandfather, a servant or resident nephew—but they are not quite the same as the immediate family—the nuclear family.

We also recognize another kind of family, an ever widening spread of kinfolk, extending through cousins and uncles and nephews and in-laws. In America, this family is vague and variable and plays a lesser role in our lives. Yet each of us has such a network of kindred and all of us feel a bond to those who make up this network simply because they are recognized as kin.

Now every society known to anthropology recognizes family relationships of both these kinds; every society has some kind of nuclear family and every society recognizes a broader set of kindred. Each recognizes that kinship creates special bonds and kinship ties evoke special sentiments. No people are indifferent to the fact that there are mothers and sons, fathers and daughters, brothers, sisters and the whole panoply of kinship; but rather, they fix upon these facts of relatedness in formulating the ties between men.

But each society places its own stress on which kin are important, what the particular relationship between kin should be, how one treats and feels about kin who are connected in this particular way or that. Indeed, the very make-up of the nuclear family, as well as the characteristic behavior patterns within it, differs from one culture to another. Let us discuss first this nuclear family and then the broader group of kindred.

The nuclear family exists as a child-rearing institution in every society, whatever other functions it performs. The long period of infant maturation requires that the children be nurtured. This places a clear domestic burden on the mother which she can hardly escape. But the exigencies of life require the aid of the father as well—though not with the same degree of insistence. The nuclear family therefore is an almost universal institution, its members sharing economic resources and collaborating in mutual aid. How the tasks will be apportioned among them, who dominates, how closely their lives are intertwined with one another, the sentiments and feelings that go into their relationships, all these vary widely.

Marriage rules affect the nuclear family. In some cultures a man may have several wives, in other (much rarer) a woman may have several husbands, and in a very few cases, a group of men and women form a family unit, each man having sexual relations with each woman. These variant marriage patterns influence the nature of the nuclear family. Households in most societies are built on monogamous unions, and in almost every case where multiple wives exist, each wife has her own household with, as it were, a part-time husband. So the pattern of man and wife (we should perhaps say woman and husband) together with the children before maturity, serves as the basis of nuclear family life. Furthermore, the children generally remain together, so that the relation between siblings is strong and enduring—though not necessarily free of tensions.

It used to be popular to speak of matriarchal and patriarchal societies—societies where women or men dominated—but these terms are not very meaningful. To be sure, the rights and duties of men and women and their relative freedom and power vary from one society to another. Among the Hopi of the Southwest, for instance, a woman may simply put her husband's things outside the door—it is her house—to divorce him, and the same is true among the Iroquois of New York. In other societies, only the men can initiate a divorce. In some societies, the husband spends a good deal of his time with other men, sleeping and working in the men's house, hunting or fighting. Though in such cases the degree of involvement between husband and wife seems much less than among ourselves, yet the husband has, and fulfills, a responsibility to his wife and children. In final analysis, marriage and child-rearing always depend upon a certain degree of mutual confidence, always involve an interplay between individuals.

This nuclear family operates within a broader set of kindred.

Among ourselves, this is a loosely defined and vague group, but in many societies large strong groups with important social functions are formed through kin ties. We will return to a discussion of kin-based social groups in the next section, but must examine them briefly here, in order to appreciate the nature of this extended family life. Such broader kinship groups are defined by rules of descent and residence. In our society we take our surname from our fathers, and to that extent we are patrilineal. But inheritance does not necessarily proceed from father to son, and we generally feel as much kindred with our mother's side as with our father's. We really have a bilateral system. Because we treat both sides almost equally, the boundaries of our kindred are vague. Many primitive societies place greater emphasis on one side of the family, practically considering the opposite side as all but unrelated. Some emphasize the father's side and we call them patrilineal, others the mother's and we call them matrilineal. The selection on Trobriand family organization by Bronislaw Malinowski that appears in this section is an example of a matrilineal society, and we see that a man inherits his position and receives his discipline and training from his mother's brother, rather than his father. This is not an infrequent arrangement in primitive societies. The Chinese, described by Yang, are patrilineal.

Where there is a firm rule of descent—that is, where a person's "real" (in the social, not biological sense) kin are reckoned only from one side—there is often a very clear feeling that this larger kindred are a social group. In such a case, it is generally considered wrong for a person to marry into his own group. Where this rule of exogamy or marrying-out exists, its breach is viewed—and treated—as incest, even though the marriage is between persons of no traceable biological connection. We will call such units clans (anthropologists have various words for refined distinction of type), which in formal terms can be defined as large, named, unilateral, exogamous social groups whose members feel themselves a kindred, even though they may not be able to trace their kinship to one another. The Tlingit Indians of the northwest coast of North America had such clans, and a person's clan affiliation was the most important thing in his life, as we will see in the next section.

In most societies there are also quite clear rules as to where a couple shall live after marriage. We have such rules ourselves. We consider it highly desirable (though not absolutely mandatory) for a young couple to establish an independent household as soon as they are married. It is not thought quite proper for them to live with either set of parents, however convenient or economical this might be. Anthropologists call it the rule of neolocal residence, and it is sometimes found among primitive people. But in many tribes, a couple is expected to move into the house or join the camp or village of the husband's family; in many others, that of the wife's. These we call patrilocal and matrilocal marriages. The Iroquois Indians, for example, are matrilocal, and the husband is an outsider to the house of his wife and his sons. (There are many other arrangements such as a period of matrilocal residence followed by patrilocal, residence with the mother's brother, and the like.)

These rules of descent and residence place the nuclear family within the larger group of kindred. The whole pattern of family independence in America which de Tocqueville noted nearly a century and a half ago and which is geared so closely both to our pioneer pattern of life and modern urban existence is expressed in the independence of the new couple's household and the absence of coercive broader family ties. But where there are unilinear rules of descent forming larger kin groups, and where there are strict rules of residence, the nuclear family becomes firmly embedded in the larger unit. A whole village or a large sector of it is often such a kin group. The Kwakiutl and Tlingit Indians of the northwest coast of North America and the Iroquois of New York have large houses divided into apartments. Each separate apartment houses a nuclear family, but these nuclear families are all related to one another. Among the Tlingit, most of the men are the nephews (sisters' sons) of the head of the household, or the nephew of these nephews. Among the Iroquois, the women are daughters and granddaughters to the woman who is head.

These matters are of importance to the life ways of the people themselves. We can see this in terms of a particular contrast: the Chinese peasant family and the American middle-class family. These two family patterns are described in detail in the selection in this chapter taken from Martin Yang and from Seeley, Sim, and Loosley, respectively. It will pay us to examine some of the structural features in advance.

The Chinese peasants of Taitou (we speak of the time before the Sino-Japanese war), like peasants everywhere, live close to the land. They have barely enough to live on at best, and they hunger for more land and husband what they have with great care. To have land makes one a member of the community; not to have it makes one a nobody. Since there is very little of it and since all livelihood comes from farming, this concern with land is not surprising. Nor is it surprising that concern with land affects family life, as apparently it does.

The Taitou family clusters around the land, the sons helping their father with its management and their sons helping them in turn. A strong sense of family solidarity, a spirit of cooperation and unity among them, is greatly desired and highly valued. Of course, as time goes on there is a tendency to split apart; sometimes the land is divided among brothers, sometimes one son takes it all. But the emphasis is upon continuity. As a result, the family consists of three or more generations living together and working under the old father's direction, the women keeping house and helping in the fields at planting and harvest times. In the Taitou peasant's view, family and land are one, continuing through the generations, the sons holding to their heritage of land and revering the father from whom it is obtained.

Thus, the Chinese peasant family forms a patrilineal, patrilocal lineage. In such a household, a marriage is viewed more as the acquisition of a daughter-in-law than as the taking of a bride. The nuclear family formed by this marriage is held firmly in the framework of the larger unit; its members are subordinated to it, and work is under the direction of the senior man and wife. The young married man quite clearly owes his first allegiance to his father and mother, not to his wife. This pattern makes for continuity, and the Chinese family is one continuous organization through the generations—using the same house with the same furniture, working the same land with the same tools. Its main axis is through the vertical line connecting father to son to grandson, indefinitely.

Contrast this to the suburban family of Crestwood Heights (or with your own). Here the head of the family normally works for a salary, and as each son grows up he obtains a job—usually not at his father's occupation nor with the same organization—and is entirely independent of the father. Each nuclear family is separate; there are never three, let alone four, generations living under the same roof. For both bride and groom, a marriage is a leaving of the parental home and the launching of a new, independent family unit, and the cycle will repeat indefinitely. The emphasis here is clearly on the marital couple, whose love is considered the mainstay and support of family solidarity. A man owes his first loyalty to his wife, not to his parents. When that union breaks, through death or divorce, the family as a group effectively comes to an end.

There are advantages and strengths in each system, as there are problems and weaknesses. The lineal system of the Chinese gives support both to the young and to the aged; it makes for security in social relations and for stability. The American system offers youth more freedom, gives priority to the ties of marriage over the filial bond, allows for change and therefore makes it easier to achieve progress. The Chinese system has the disadvantage of subordinating the young people; an examination of the position of the bride and daughter-in-law (entirely subject to the dictates of her mother-in-law) will demonstrate this disadvantage. The American system is particularly hard on the old people, who tend to find themselves entirely alone after the children have left to establish their families.

But this matter of virtue and fault is not our major concern. What is important is, first, that we understand that family structure can vary widely, and second, that the family structure relates to other aspects of the society; it generally fits in with the mode of economic life and the ethical system of the people.

Let us stop to examine this point for a moment. Where families like the Chinese or clans like the Tlingit exist, they usually share some important economic activity. Clans are found widely among the primitive peoples of the world, and are usually mutual-aid groups. A person who has food is expected to share it with clan members; the more fortunate are expected to help their less fortunate clan brothers. Repeatedly, when such a system comes into contact with Western culture, it starts to disintegrate. Why? Because European dominance changes the economic life, substituting wage labor for the old patterns of food producing. That is, now each man works for himself, rather than contributing to a cooperative enterprise. This makes sharing and mutual aid difficult and old clan loyalties weaken or disappear.

Before closing this discussion on family life, we must return to the point made at the outset, namely, that it is within the family that the child first acquires his culture. To put the matter differently, the educational function, and particularly that subtle, unconscious part of education that we discussed in the preceding section, is very largely carried out within the family setting. The child normally learns his culture from the family outward; his first contacts are with his nuclear family, beyond that with his broader range of kin, and so to the whole community.

It follows, therefore, that the pattern of attitudes within the family setting is projected outward. If the intrafamilial setting is warm and comforting, the child will come to regard people as essentially friendly; if it is bristling with hostility and ill will, he will tend to view the world as made up of dangerous persons, and so on. Some anthropologists have pointed out that even attitudes toward monogamy and polygamy are acquired not merely as a matter of custom, but in terms of orientation to the world: if a man is nurtured by many mothers, he finds it easy to relate to many women; if he differentiates sharply between his own mother and other women, he is oriented toward seeking the satisfaction of his affectional needs from a single source. Of course, factors other than the relation between a child and his mother are at work and this is carrying the point further than the data of anthropology can yet support. Yet it is clear that our adult attitudes are set in the constellation of family life.

Perhaps we can see some of this patterning of attitudes in terms of certain changes that have been taking place in America and to which we have already made reference in an earlier section. In nineteenth-century America, the father was expected to be remote and stern; he was the provider and the disciplinarian. No child would question his father's authority, and to flout it often led to a permanent disruption between father and son. In those days, too, all dominant male figures stood above junior or subordinate ones in this way. The boss, the minister, the male teacher, the banker, and the judge were stern, remote, and authoritative. From the child's point of view, he projected his image of his father onto these other men and related to them in the same general way.

This pattern has slowly changed. Nowadays a good father is expected to be a buddy to his son, to play with him, to understand him, to counsel him, but to guide him more with a warm friendliness than with a firm hand. We need not here examine why this change has taken place, but it is interesting to note that it has simultaneously occurred in these other relationships as well: Ministers counsel their congregations in a very different vein than did their grandparents; schoolteachers are enjoined from punishing their pupils; the banks advertise their friendly atmosphere (and have even changed their architecture to fit), while modern industrial relations experts counsel the bosses of today on how to make their employees happy and satisfied.

Family organization varies from one people to another. There is a relationship between the form of family organization and the nature of its basic food-getting techniques. Because each individual is reared within the setting of a family system, because he first sees his culture through that pattern of family life, the organization of family institutions has a pervasive influence on the character of the culture and on the attitudes and values of its members.

24. The Essentials of Family Life

RALPH LINTON

Ralph Linton was a pioneer in applying sociological concepts to anthropological data. His *The Study of Man* is a classic synthesis and one of the more widely read books in anthropology. In this selection he discusses very broadly the unity and variety of family life and gives us an overview of the different ways in which mankind has organized the business of procreation and the nurturing of its young.

Linton also pioneered in the collaboration between anthropology and psychology, particularly in his work with the psychoanalyst Abram Kardiner. Linton received his Ph.D. from Harvard University in 1925; taught at the University of Wisconsin and Columbia University before being appointed Sterling Professor of Anthropology at Yale, a post he held until his death in 1953.

The selection below is taken from the chapter on "The Family," from *The Study of Man*, by Ralph Linton. Copyright, 1936, D. Appleton-Century Co., Inc. Reprinted by permission of Appleton-Century-Crofts, Inc.

All societies recognize the existence of certain close-knit, internally organized cooperative units intermediate between the individual and the total society of which he is a part. Theoretically, every person is assigned to one or another of these units on the basis of biological relationships established through mating or common ancestry. Actually, membership may also be ascribed on the basis of recognized substitutes for such relationships, such as presumptive paternity and adoption. Such units always have specific functions with relation both to their members and to the total society. Membership in the unit entails upon the individual specific rights and duties with regard to other members and also a series of rather clearly defined attitudes. The unit is expected to be the primary focus of its members' interests and loyalties. Those who belong to it are in duty bound to cooperate with and assist each other and to place each other's interests above those of outsiders. The interaction of the personalities within the unit is close and continuous, and their mutual adjustment is expected to be correspondingly complete. Ideally, the members of a family are bound together by ties of affection as well as by those of common interest, and quarrels between them are considered more reprehensible than quarrels between members and outsiders.

There can be little doubt that all such units are derivatives of the primitive, biologically determined grouping of mates and offspring. However, they are widely variable in both form and content. The most constant feature in connection with them seems to be the general attitudes enjoined upon their members. Both their personnel and their functions differ so much in various societies that we are forced to conclude that these features are now determined by cultural factors. In other words, the family, although it began as a biological phenomenon, a primate reproductive unit, has evolved into a social phenomenon, something more nearly comparable to such units as a monastic order or a craft guild than to its own remote ancestor. . . .

. . . To the student of society and culture the functions of these units are vastly more important than their personnel. Their social significance lies in what they do for their members and the total group rather than in what they are. If we can get a fairly clear picture of these functions, we will be in a better position to understand why the membership of such units can be so variable.

Every society has assigned certain functions to its family units. In nearly all cases some of these derive from the biologically determined functions of the ancestral mating group, but such derived functions cannot be considered a part of the family pattern unless they are given social recognition and approval. Even the most intimate physiological aspects of the mate relationship are often controlled by culturally established patterns. Practically all societies have taboos on sexual intercourse between socially recognized spouses under certain circumstances. . . .

There is even one society which has completely excluded the satisfaction of sexual needs from the functions of its family units. The people, the Nayar, provide no place for husbands or fathers in their social system. Their women marry, in accordance with Hindu law, but the marriage is contracted with a stranger and is terminated at the end of three days by a formal divorce. The husband does not enter the picture again. The satisfaction of sexual needs and the perpetuation of the group are provided for by a series of informal love affairs which, although socially recognized, establish no permanent bond between the parties or between the man and his offspring. If the lovers are compatible the relationship may continue for years, but it can always be broken without notice. The woman is in complete control of the situation and can dismiss her lover by simply returning his last gift. She is free to have several lovers simultaneously, and no greater degree of faithfulness is required of the man. The real family unit in this society consists of a woman and her sons and daughters. The children continue their association after the mother's death, and the son regards his sister's house as home and takes much the same interest in her children that a father would take in his own children in our society. The rationalization which the Nayar give for this system is that since they are a warrior caste, making their living mainly as mercenaries, it is better for their men not to set up households or assume the duties of paternity. Freedom from such responsibilities makes it possble for them to take the field at a moment's notice and without regret.

Nayar society shows that it is possible to eliminate from the functions of the social family the very items which brought the biological family into existence. No better proof could be asked for the extreme mutability both of men and of their social institutions. At the same time there is another function which has its roots in the biological family which is still characteristic of all family units. This is the care and rearing of children. It seems that among the sub-human primates the care of the young is left almost entirely to the female. At the human level the assistance of some adult male is vitally necessary. This aid is of less importance on the economic side than it is on that of the proper training of children for participation in adult society. A woman can conceivably provide for the physical needs of her children without male assistance, but she cannot train her sons in the special male attitudes and activities necessary to their success as men. We recognize that even in our own society boys brought up by their mothers are at a serious disadvantage.

There is a tendency in nearly all societies for certain aspects of child training to be taken over by agencies outside the family, such as schools and initiation groups. However, the physical dependence of the young child on its mother sets an age limit below which these agencies cannot operate. Conditioning to social life begins so early that much of the groundwork of the personality is laid before such extra-family agencies can be brought into play. . . .

In addition to these functions which derive directly from conditions present in the original biological family, each society has selected and ascribed to its family units a series of other functions. These are culturally determined and in no society do they exhaust the unit's potentialities for function. Thus in our own society the family is not used as a basis for a religious cult. In China it is utilized for this purpose, the family's worship of its ancestors taking precedence over all other forms of religious devotion. Again, our families do not, as units, assume responsibility for the conduct of their adult members. An American business man can transfer his assets to his wife and then, after an interval, "fail" with impunity. Many other societies do make the family responsible, thus assigning to the unit highly important functions in relation to social control.

Among these socially ascribed functions of the family unit the most important seem to be those connected with economic production. Our own culture is witnessing a rapid diminution in the importance of these, but our own situation is quite atypical for mankind as a whole. In all societies the family is normally the smallest organized unit for both production and consumption and tends to be self-sufficient as far as its members' ordinary needs are concerned. The labor involved in satisfying these needs is apportioned among its members in such a way that the activities of each individual supplement those of the rest and all share in the benefits. The male members do certain things and the female members other things, and the specialization is usually so complete that persons of each sex have only a vague general knowledge of the techniques employed by the opposite one. The difficulties of the average American husband when called upon to cook and look after the children in his wife's absence are familiar to most of us. This specialization and the organization which is its necessary accompaniment are of tremendous importance in ensuring the continuity of the family. Neither a man nor a woman can provide for all wants when alone, and when marriage is utilized as the core of the family unit realization of the discomforts inevitably resulting from separation make for tolerance of a partner's foibles. Similarly, when the unit rests on some other type of relationship the loss of a member means the disorganization of its cooperative system and will be prevented whenever possible.

The care of aged and infirm members is also an almost universal function of the family. There is no society in which the individual's connection with his family group is severed as soon as his usefulness to it is passed. Having given service, the old are entitled to receive service in return. There are certain societies which lighten the family's burden in this respect by killing the old, but such acts are usually rationalized in terms of the best interests of the old themselves. It is said that in ancient Fiji it was the duty of a good son to watch his father and to kill him when he showed signs of approaching senility or extreme decrepitude. Since the condition of the soul in the next world corresponded to that of the individual at the time of his death, it would be cruel to do otherwise.

In any case the family has an obligation to provide its aged members with good funerals and to look after their well-being in the next world.

Another universal function of the family is that of protecting its members' interests against outsiders. This function varies rather in degree than in kind. There are societies in which the individual can feel sure of his family's support no matter what the nature of his trouble with outsiders may be, where the fault lies, or what the cost to his relatives. In certain Madagascar tribes the possession of land was vitally necessary to the family's survival, yet it would be sold to ransom a relative who had been captured and enslaved. The family honor required that he be redeemed even though the act entailed hardship for generations to come. Again, in some tribes which have the pattern of vendetta a murderer's relatives must shield him at all costs and fight for him even when they know that to do so means almost certain destruction for the family. More commonly, there are socially defined limits to the demands which the individual may make upon his family. . . . For example, we ourselves have no patterns governing assistance to relatives as distant even as first cousins. There is a feeling that we should help them, but the kind and degree of assistance always depend upon personal factors. . . .

If we take the universal functions of the family, we find that there are only two absolute prerequisites for their successful performance. The family unit must include able-bodied adults of both sexes, and the association between these adults must be close enough and prolonged enough to permit of their training and their organization into an effective cooperative unit. Unless they live and work together for some time, they will not be able to reach satisfactory personality adjustments or to reduce their complementary activities to matters of habit. It is obvious that until such adjustments have been made and cooperation has become more or less automatic the family unit cannot perform its socially ascribed duties with any high degree of efficiency.

Such prolonged associations between individuals of opposite sex can be assured in either of two ways. A society may capitalize the sexual attraction between adults and do all it can to give permanence to mated relationships, or it may capitalize the associations formed on an asexual basis during childhood, reinforcing them and continuing them into adult life. Such asexual associations are most readily established between individuals brought up in the same functional family unit, i. e., real or socially designated brothers and sisters. In other words, the association of adults which is the necessary nucleus of any family as a functional unit may be based on either a conjugal or a consanguine relationship. Our own society has stressed the conjugal relationship as the foundation of its functional family unit to such a degree that we tend to think of marriage and the family as inseparably linked, but many other societies draw a clear distinction between the two.

In societies organized upon the conjugal basis we can picture the authentic functional family as consisting of a nucleus of spouses and their offspring surrounded by a fringe of relatives. In those organized on the consanguine basis we can picture the authentic family as a nucleus of blood relatives surrounded by a fringe of spouses. Under the first system it is the fringes of relatives which interlock and connect family with family. Under the second it is the marriages which, by their interlocking, link family to family. Under the first system the blood relatives of the spouses are of only incidental importance to the functioning of the family unit. Under the second, the spouses are of only incidental importance. . . .

Families organized upon a consanguine basis can . . . perform all the functions possible to those organized upon a conjugal basis, with the exception of the satisfaction of sexual needs and the production of children. These functions are ruled out by the universal human pattern prohibiting incest. The consanguine groups can even perform most of the family functions more successfully. Nevertheless, the Nayar appear to be the only group who have taken consanguine relationship as the exclusive basis for their family organization. This is presumably because the factors which brought the conjugal family into existence at the sub-human level are still operative. Social systems have changed and evolved, but the innate qualities of human beings have remained very much the same. The consanguine family may be a more efficient functional unit as far as society is concerned, but it is less emotionally satisfying to the individual than is the conjugal unit. Man shares with other primates sexual jealousy and a desire for the exclusive possession of a mate. These tendencies can be inhibited by training, but they remain strong enough to ensure the continued existence of conjugal units side by side with consanguine ones in practically all societies.

Although nearly all societies recognize both conjugal and consanguine groupings, most societies tend to put their emphasis on one or the other, making it the basis for the authentic, functional family as far as their own social system is concerned. On the basis of shifting emphasis, it might be possible to arrange societies in a graded series with such devotees of conjugal organization as ourselves and the Eskimo at one end of the scale and the exclusively consanguine Nayar at the other.

Most societies would fall between these two extremes but with a recognizable leaning toward one grouping or the other as the focus both for family functions and individual loyalties.

25. A Woman-centered Family System

BRONISLAW MALINOWSKI

Bronislaw Malinowski's studies on the Trobriand Islanders have been extensive, thoughtful, and extremely influential on anthropological theory. Malinowski took his doctorate in mathematics but was drawn into anthropology under the influence of the psychologist Wilhelm Wundt and, he says, by reading Sir James Frazer's *The Golden Bough*. He began field work in Melanesia, received a D.Sc. in anthropology from the University of London in 1916 where he became Professor of Anthropology in 1927. He received an honorary degree from Harvard in 1936 and was Bishop Museum Visiting Professor of Anthropology at Yale University at the time of his death in 1942. Malinowski was particularly interested in the interrelationships between one part of a culture and all others, and the method by which culture was organized to satisfy human needs. His studies of Trobriand sexual life and family organization are of particular interest.

The present essay is taken from Chapter I of his *The Sexual Life of Savages in North-Western Melanesia* (London: Routledge and Kegan Paul, Ltd., 1929) and is printed here with the kind permission of the publisher. This essay gives us a glimpse into an entirely different kind of family situation—one where descent is calculated through the mother's line; where the father's relation to the children is very much like that of an uncle in our society, whereas the mother's brother has the responsibility of training the children and seeing to it that they become proper and productive adults.

We find in the Trobriands a matrilineal society, in which descent, kinship, and every social relationship are legally reckoned through the mother only, and in which women have a considerable share in tribal life, even to the taking of a leading part in economic, ceremonial, and magical activities—a fact which very deeply influences all the customs of erotic life as well as the institution of marriage. It will be well, therefore, first to consider the sexual relation in its widest aspect, beginning with some account of those features of custom and tribal law which underlie the institution of mother-right, and the various views and conceptions which throw light upon it; after this, a short sketch of each of the chief domains of tribal life—domestic, economic, legal, ceremonial, and magical—will combine to show the respective spheres of male and female activity among these natives.

The idea that it is solely and exclusively the mother who builds up the child's body, the man in no way contributing to its formation, is the most important factor in the legal system of the Trobrianders. Their views on the process of procreation, coupled with certain mythological and animistic beliefs, affirm, without doubt or reserve, that the child is of the same substance as its mother, and that between the father and the child there is no bond of physical union whatsoever.

That the mother contributes everything to the new being to be born of her is taken for granted by the natives, and forcibly expressed by them. "The mother feeds the infant in her body. Then, when it comes out, she feeds it with her milk." "The mother makes the child out of her blood." "Brothers and sisters are of the same flesh, because they come of the same mother." These and similar expressions describe their attitude towards this, their fundamental principle of kinship.

This attitude is also to be found embodied, in an even more telling manner, in the rules governing descent, inheritance, succession in rank, chieftainship, hereditary offices, and magic—in every regulation, in fact, concerning transmission by kinship. Social position is handed on in the mother-line from a man to his sister's children, and this exclusively matrilineal conception of kinship is of paramount importance in the restrictions and regulations of marriage, and in the taboos on sexual intercourse. The working of these ideas of kinship can be observed, breaking out with a dramatic intensity, at death. For the social rules underlying burial, lamentation, and mourning, together with certain very elaborate ceremonies of food distribution, are based on the principle that people joined by the tie of maternal kinship form a closely knit group, bound by an identity of feelings, of interests, and of flesh. And from this group, even those united to it by marriage and by the father-to-child relation are sharply excluded, as having no natural share in the bereavement.

These natives have a well-established institution of marriage, and yet are quite ignorant of the man's share in the begetting of children. At the same time, the term "father" has, for the Trobriander, a clear, though exclusively social, definition: it signifies the man married to the mother, who lives in the same house with her, and forms part of the household. The father, in all discussions about relationship, was pointedly described to me as *tomakava,* a "stranger," or even more correctly, an "outsider." This expression would also frequently be used by natives in conversation, when they were arguing some point of inheritance or trying to justify some line of behavior, or again when the position of the father was to be belittled in some quarrel.

It will be clear to the reader, therefore, that the term "father," as I use it here, must be taken, not as having the various legal, moral, and biological implications that it holds for us, but in a sense entirely specific to the society with which we are dealing. It might have seemed better, in order to avoid any chance of such misconception, not to have used our word "father" at all, but rather the native one *tama,* and to have spoken of the *"tama* relationship" instead of "fatherhood"; but, in practice, this would have proved too unwieldy. The reader, therefore, when he meets the word "father" in these pages, should never forget that it must be defined, not as in the English dictionary, but in accordance with the facts of native life. I may add that this rule applies to all terms which carry special sociological implication, that is to all terms of relationship, and such words as "marriage," "divorce," "betrothal," "love," "courtship," and the like.

What does the word *tama* (father) express to the native? "Husband of my mother" would be the answer first given by an intelligent informant. He would go on to say that his *tama* is the man in whose loving and protecting company he has grown up. For, since marriage is patrilocal in the Trobriands, since the woman, that is to say, moves to her husband's village community and lives in his house, the father is a close companion to his children; he takes an active part in the cares which are lavished upon them, invariably feels and shows a deep affection for them, and later has a share in their education. The word *tama* (father) condenses, therefore, in its emotional meaning, a host of experiences of early childhood, and expresses the typical sentiment existing between a boy or girl and a mature affectionate man of the same household; while socially it denotes the male person who stands in an intimate relation to the mother, and who is master of the household.

So far *tama* does not differ essentially from "father" in our sense. But as soon as the child begins to grow up and take an interest in things outside the affairs of the household and its own immediate needs, certain complications arise, and change the meaning of *tama* for him. He learns that he is not of the same clan as his *tama,* that his totemic appellation is different, and that it is identical with that of his mother. At the same time he learns that all sorts of duties, restrictions, and concerns for personal pride unite him to his mother and separate him from his father. Another man appears on the horizon, and is called by the child *kadagu* ("my mother's brother"). This man may live in the same locality, but he is just as likely to reside in another village. The child also learns that the place where his *kada* (mother's brother) resides is also his, the child's, "own village"; that there he has his property and his other rights of citizenship; that there his future career awaits him; that there his natural allies and associates are to be found. He may even be taunted in the village of his birth with being an "outsider" (*tomakava*), while in the village he has to call "his own," in which his mother's brother lives, his father is a stranger and he a natural citizen. He also sees, as he grows up, that the mother's brother assumes a gradually increasing authority over him, requiring his services, helping him in some things, granting or withholding his permission to carry out certain actions; while the father's authority and counsel become less and less important.

Thus the life of a Trobriander runs under a two-fold influence—a duality which must not be imagined as a mere surface play of custom. It enters deeply into the existence of every individual, it produces strange complications of usage, it creates frequent tensions and difficulties, and not seldom gives rise to violent breaks in the continuity of tribal life. For this dual influence of paternal love and the matrilineal principle, which penetrates so far into the framework of institutions and into the social ideas and sentiments of the native, is not, as a matter of fact, quite well adjusted in its working. . . .

In entering the village we had to pass across the street between the two concentric rows of houses. This is the normal setting of the every-day life of the community, and thither we must return in order to make a closer survey of the groups of people sitting in front of their dwellings. As a rule we find that each group consists of one family only—man, wife, and children—taking their leisure, or engaged in some domestic activity which varies with the time of day. On a fine morning we would see them hastily eating a scanty breakfast, and then the man and woman preparing the implements for the day's work, with the help of the bigger children, while the baby is laid out of the way on a mat. Afterwards, during the cool hours of the forenoon, each family would probably set off to their work, leaving the village almost deserted. The man, in company with others, may be fishing or hunting or building a canoe or looking for timber. The woman may have gone collecting shell-fish or wild fruits. Or else both may be working in the gardens, or paying a visit. The man often does harder work than the woman, but when they return in the hot hours of the afternoon he will rest, while the woman busies herself with household affairs. Towards evening, when the descending sun casts longer, cooler shadows, the social life of the village begins. At this time we would see our family group in front of their hut, the wife preparing food, the children playing, the husband, perhaps, seated amusing the smallest baby. This is the time when neighbors call on one another, and conversation may be exchanged from group to group.

The frank and friendly tone of intercourse, the obvious feeling of equality, the father's domestic helpfulness, especially with the children, would at once strike any observant visitor. The wife joins freely in the jokes and conversation; she does her work independently, not with the air of a slave or a servant, but as one who manages her own department. She will order the husband about if she needs his help. Close observation, day after day, confirms this first impression. The typical Trobriand household is founded on the principles of equality and independence of function: the man is considered to be the master, for he is in his own village and the house belongs to him, but the woman has, in other respects, a considerable influence; she and her family have a great deal to do with the food supply of the household; she is the owner of separate possessions in the house; and she is—next to her brother—the legal head of her family.

The division of functions within the household is, in certain matters, quite definite. The woman has to cook the food, which is simple, and does not require much preparation. The main meal is taken at sunset, and consists of yams, taro, or other tubers, roasted in the open fire—or, less frequently, boiled in a small pot, or baked in the ground—with the occasional addition of fish or meat. Next morning the remains are eaten cold, and sometimes, though not regularly, fruit, shell-fish, or some other light snack may be taken at mid-day.

In some circumstances, men can and do prepare and cook the food: on journeys, oversea voyages, fishing or hunting expeditions, when they are without their women folk. Also, on certain occasions, when taro or sago dumplings are cooked in the large clay pots, men are required by tradition to assist their wives. But within the village and in normal daily life the man never cooks. It would be considered shameful for him to do so. "You are a he-cook" would be said tauntingly. The fear of deserving such an epithet, or being laughed at or shamed, is extreme. It arises from the characteristic dread and shame, found among savages, of not doing the proper thing, or, worse still, of doing something which is intrinsically the attribute of another sex or social class.

There are a number of occupations strictly assigned by tribal custom to one sex only. The manner of carrying loads is a very noteworthy example. Women have to carry the special feminine receptacle, the bell-shaped basket, or any other kind of load upon their heads; men must carry only on the shoulder. It would be with a real shudder, and a profound feeling of shame, that an individual would regard carrying anything in the manner proper to the opposite sex and nothing would induce a man to put any load on his head, even in fun.

An exclusively feminine department is the water supply. The woman has the water bottles of the household in her charge. These are made out of the woody shell of a mature coconut, with a stopper of twisted palm-leaf. In the morning or near sunset she goes, sometimes a full half-mile, to fill them at the water-hole: here the women foregather, resting and chatting, while one after the other fills her water-vessels, cleans them, arranges them in baskets or on large wooden platters, and, just before leaving, gives the cluster a final sprinkling of water to cover it with a suggestive gloss of freshness. The water-hole is the woman's club and centre of gossip, and as such is important, for there is a distinct woman's public opinion and point of view in a Trobriand village, and they have their secrets from the male, just as the male has from the female.

We have already seen that the husband fully shares in the care of the children. He will fondle and carry a baby, clean and wash it, and give it the mashed vegetable food which it receives in addition to the mother's milk almost from birth. In fact, nursing the baby in the arms or holding it on the knees, which is described by the native word *kopo'i,* is the special role and duty of the father (*tama*). It is said of the children of unmarried women who, according to the native expression, are "without a *tama"* (that is, it must be remembered, without a husband to their mother), that they are "unfortunate" or "bad" because "there is no one to nurse and hug them." Again, if anyone inquires why children should have duties toward their father, who is a "stranger" to them, the answer is invariably: "because of the nursing, because his hands have been soiled with the child's excrement and urine."

The father performs his duties with genuine natural fondness: he will carry an infant about for hours, looking at it with eyes full of such love and pride as are seldom seen in those of a European father. Any praise of the baby goes directly to his heart, and he will never tire of talking about and exhibiting the virtues and achievements of his wife's offspring. Indeed, watching a native family at home or meeting them on the road, one receives a strong impression of close union and intimacy between its members. Nor, as we have seen, does this mutual affection abate in later years. Thus, in the intimacy of domestic life, we discover another aspect of the interesting and complicated struggle between social and emotional paternity, on the one hand, and the explicitly acknowledged legal mother-right on the other.

It will be noticed that we have not yet penetrated into the interior of a house, for in fine weather the scene of family life is always laid in front of the dwelling. Only when it is cold and raining, at night, or for intimate uses, do the natives retire into the interior. On a wet or windy evening in the cooler season we would find the village streets deserted, dim lights flickering through small interstices in the hut walls, and voices sounding from within in animated conversation. Inside, in a small space heavy with dense smoke and human exhalation, the people sit on the floor round the fire or recline on bedsteads covered with mats.

26. The Chinese Family Pattern

MARTIN YANG

The Chinese family contrasts sharply with the family organization that we know in America. In China the lineal descendants from father to son to grandson are the backbone of the family organization, and the family continues on through time as a permanent social entity. These men, of course, marry, but a marriage is considered to be more the acquisition of a daughter-in-law than the taking of a wife. In this essay we follow some of the implications of this type of family organization; see some of its strength and some of the problems that derive from such a "lineal" family organization.

Martin Yang's study of Taitou, a village of 720 persons in north China, is one of the best descriptions of the Chinese community we have. It refers to a time before the Chinese were engulfed by the Japanese and communism and, apparently, is the community of Yang's origin. The selection that follows is taken from Chapter 6, "Intrafamilial Relationships" of *A Chinese Village: Taitou, Shantung Province*, New York: Columbia University Press, 1945, and is printed by kind permission of the publisher and author.

The real core of family life lies in the behavior of the individual members toward one another. Marriage and descent are its foundations and determine its most important interrelationships. Within the family circle the individual develops his personal attitudes, a self-evaluation and interpretation of his place in the larger society, and a sense of the significance of his relations with people outside the family.

Since marriage in an old-fashioned Chinese family is arranged by the parents, and since the two young people do not know each other before the wedding, the problem of adjustment for the newly married couple is a difficult one. They do not have their own home, but live with the husband's family. Although the couple often achieve a genuine affection for each other after a brief period of living together, they must not let their love be apparent and the husband, if he is to be considered a filial son and a good brother, must maintain closer relations with his family than with his wife. A young husband must not mention his wife too often; he must not praise her in family gatherings or to the villagers; if she passes by when he is with other persons, he must not speak to her unless either one or the other has an urgent message. When a husband returns from a trip he must greet his parents and his brothers and his sisters before he greets his wife. Only after several hours have elapsed may he excuse himself and join his wife in their room, and that only on the pretext that he must clean up and change his clothes. Although he may be most anxious to be with his beloved one, and his family (especially his mother and sisters) understand this perfectly, he must nonetheless affect indifference.

A young wife must also keep from showing that she loves her husband. The general attitude is that a decent wife should love her husband, but must not let her love spoil his career or make him neglect his duty to his family. A good wife stays at her work with her mother-in-law or sisters-in-law during the day, and at night she must wait until all the family members have retired before she can go to her room and be with her husband. She should avoid sitting with her husband at social gatherings and should act as if she does not know him. She, too, must avoid referring frequently to him, or when it is necessary for her to do so, she should not use his name nor say "my husband," but instead use the pronoun "he." In speaking to her younger brother-in-law, or younger sister-in-law, she may refer to her husband as "your No. x brother." When her husband returns home from a prolonged trip, she does not greet him. Instead she prepares hot water and a meal for him, according to her mother-in-law's order. However, every member in the family knows that, after his mother, she is the one who is happiest at his return. The younger sister-in-law may tease her and this she will secretly enjoy.

A newly married wife cannot but feel lonesome and strange, because she is really in a strange home with strange people. The sudden separation from her mother, the stern face of her mother-in-law, the pretended dignity of the father-in-law, and above all, her sudden introduction to the continuous housework, all make her feel that she is completely at the mercy of these people. Since she cannot go back to her mother, the only one from whom she can seek protection is her husband. She will generally respond with great warmth and gratitude if she is well received by him. It is true that the husband has been hardened by the heavy work, by the rude country life, and in many cases by his never-joking father. But, on the other hand, he is just a fully grown adolescent who has not been permitted to be alone with any grown-up girl before. Now he has a wife to whom he can express his romantic ideals and reveal his love. For these reasons the young people usually become much attached to one another.

The partners of an unsuccessful marriage are in an unhappy plight. Divorce is out of the question: they must make the best of it. Outwardly they may seem no different from any other couple. They will not quarrel openly; the husband will not beat his wife; she does her work dutifully. However, it is easy to note that the loved wife is active, cheerful, and energetic, while the unhappy wife is listless and slow in her work. Although a newly married couple must put on a show of indifference in the presence of others, a keen observer can soon discern whether the indifference is pretended, as in the case of a happy couple, or real. The indifference of the ill-mated pair continues even in the privacy of their room. The husband goes to bed with a great sigh; the wife can only weep in secret and swallow her tears into her stomach. The husband will not approach her unless driven to do so, and she will be merely permissive. The two live together and have children, but their marriage is a gloomy one.

However, if an initially unhappy marriage survives at all, if the hopelessness and sorrow and burden of work do not break down the unhappy wife, the relationship between the couple improves with time. A woman who survives these hardships without committing suicide or breaking down becomes a heroine in the eyes of her relatives. She has proved that she has patience, far-sightedness, and unusual wisdom and kindness. As the couple grow older and their children reach maturity, their feelings toward each other mellow. Husband and wife can now sit together and talk more freely at family gatherings; they can walk together in public. The husband can joke at the expense of his wife in the presence of other people, even before the father-in-law, and the wife can also offer some humorous counterattack. In referring to each other in conversation, they no longer use the pronouns "he" and "she," but say "child's father" or "child's mother." If the name of their first child, for example, is Lien-pao, then the wife would say to her mother-in-law: "Lien-pao's Daddy said that."

In privacy, romantic love decreases, while the feeling of companionship grows stronger. In their bedroom the wife will tell her husband what has happened in the household during the day and what she thinks about their problems. She will also talk to him about their children. The husband tells her about the crops in the field, the work of his brothers and the hired laborers, and so on. Because of his consciousness of being a man, a filial son, a good brother, and a dignified husband, he is supposed not to listen to, or at least not to believe, his wife's complaints about other household members. In spite of this he frequently accepts her statements, and secretly acts on her suggestions and advice on other matters.

As the husband and wife mature, they come to have their own home and undivided authority over their children. The companionship ripens and is no longer kept secret but becomes the foundation of the newly independent family. The wife now becomes the undisputed head of the home. Arranging the children's marriages falls to her. The husband oversees the farm and deals with all matters pertaining to it, but since there is no clear-cut demarcation between domestic and farm affairs, and since cooperation and mutual advice between husband and wife is well-established in practice, this division occasions no real separation. According to a Confucian idea, the husband and wife relationship in this period is "Husband leads and wife follows." But in practice the wife may play the leading part while the husband follows, depending upon which is the more capable in this matter or that. The wife may become more eager to take on responsibility, but this does not mean that her respect for her husband diminishes, or that she does not acknowledge him as head of the family.

When a couple reaches the age of fifty or sixty, the wife generally becomes the dominant person in the household. She is now the mother-in-law of one, two, or even four daughters-in-law. She is the grandmother of a long line of children and is also the overseer of a large household. The middle-aged sons have almost invariably developed strong attachment to their mother but not to their father. The father's authority in the fields, now that he does not work there, is considerably lessened. He has lost his role in business transactions because he is too old to take the farm products to the market town and deal directly with the dealers. To a certain extent, his importance in relations with the neighbors is diminished, because people find that he is no longer the real authority and that his position as family head is more nominal than real, although he is still respected by all the household. His wife must see to it that he is well fed, well clothed, and well cared for. He preserves also the privilege of venting his anger upon any member of the family, except his daughters-in-law. Nevertheless, he sometimes recognizes his real position, and this may make him envy his wife. He may show this in quarrels which will elicit soothing words and apologies from her, but the real situation will remain unchanged.

After the sons and their families have departed to establish independent homes, relations between the old couple may undergo still another change. The wife now loses all her authority and is on equal terms with the husband. They may have a common feeling of neglect, and a need to look to each other for real sympathy and understanding. They thus reestablish the earlier companionship, except that where it was positive, creative, and had the achievement of a prosperous household as a mutual concern, it is now self-pitying and negative.

The relationship between father and child has none of the warmth and freedom existing between mother and child. The father's attitude is dignified, even remote; his authority is unquestioned and he expects submissiveness from his sons. Although in a farm family some informalities are permitted—as, joking in the presence of one's parents, taking a place of equal importance to that occupied by one's father, not rising when the father approaches—yet the father and son relationship is far from free or intimate. When the son is an infant, the father may on rare occasions play with him or take him out. When the boy is old enough to help in the fields, father and son walk together and work together quite often. But by the time the boy reaches the age of fifteen, the father assumes a more dignified attitude toward him and is frequently severe. The son feels uncomfortable with his father and prefers to work with other men in the fields. When father and son do work together, they have nothing to say, and even at home they speak only when there is business to discuss. At street gatherings or in places of amusement, they mutually avoid each other.

The relationship between mother and son, on the other hand, is comparatively close. Although a boy who reaches the age of ten is dependent entirely upon his father's authority and teaching, this does not interfere with his intimacy with his mother. Because of the lack of female companions and the meager possibilities for recreation, a young man spends much time talking to his mother during his formative years. After supper, when the father is absent and she is busy with the household chores, he talks with her freely of the things which concern him. . . . At this time the son may also complain of his father's harshness or confide that he would like to learn some trade other than farming, or that he would like to continue study. In her turn, the mother may tell him what she and his father think of him. A son at this time has no one, except his mother, to whom he can tell his thoughts freely, and this provides an unshakable foundation for the long-lasting mother-son relationship. . . .

Legally, the son is the head of the household after his father is dead, and the mother is under his authority. A woman's position is defined in a local saying, "At her parents' home she obeys her father; after marriage, her husband; when he dies, her son." When land or a house is sold, it is done in the name of the first son, the mother only being asked to vouch for it. . . .

When a girl is born, she is cared for by her mother in much the same way a boy is. The father maintains his usual attitude of indifference. When the next baby is born, the three- or four-year-old girl has a place of her own or is temporarily taken care of by her grandmother rather than sharing her father's side of the bed as a boy does. When she is six or older, she gradually starts helping her mother to look after the younger sister or brother. By the time she is thirteen, she begins to learn to sew, cook, spin, and many other things. By fifteen, she is indispensable to her mother. Mother and daughter develop an intimate relation, and the father and daughter become more distant. He may have genuine affection for his daughter, especially if the latter conforms to the prevailing standard of a good girl, but the affection between them must be restrained. His knowledge of his daughter is gleaned indirectly through her mother. . . .

Relations between mother-in-law and daughter-in-law are sometimes strained, sometimes harmonious, but always less intimate than those of a daughter and her own mother. A daughter-in-law's obligations to her mother-in-law and to her husband are similar, but there are many points of friction inherent in the situation between the two women. The son's transference of affection from his mother to his wife, creates tensions between the women. The wife now takes care of mending and sewing his personal garments; to everybody else these changes seem natural, but to the mother, it is a great blow. She feels that she has been deserted by her son, that she has lost her greatest treasure. For this she cannot blame him, because she loves him so well, yet needing somebody to blame, she naturally turns to his new wife. At first, she may say that her daughter-in-law should not be so appealing to her son as to make him neglect his parents, brothers, and family duties. Later she may come to believe that the young woman purposely defames her to her son, and a bitter resentment may grow up in her mind. Also, as a result perhaps of the traditional expectations or of the loneliness and feeling of insecurity occasioned by the new environment, a daughter-in-law is always ready to feel that she is being ill-treated by her mother-in-law. Thus suspicion and self-pity on both sides create fertile ground for the sowing of conflicts, and minor incidents assume undue importance. . . .

The relationship between a man and his father's brother is almost the same as that between him and his parents when the large family is still together under one roof. The nephew is required to listen to his father's brother, and if the uncle is not married, he has as much authority over his nephew as the boy's father has. He may punish the boy without interference. After the uncle is married and has his own children, he must refrain from exercising his authority. If his nephew defies him, he should ask the boy's own father or mother to correct him. If he scolds the boy, his scolding should not be as severe as the boy's parents would administer. . . .

The adjustments necessary between the members of a large family are delicate ones and it is only when they can be made with a minimum of friction that a large household can hold together. Jealousies and disagreements between certain members will throw the entire organization out of balance, and, if no immediate remedy is found for the situation, the household may break up. It is the most important duty of the head of a household to keep these relationships functioning smoothly. The task would be impossible, even for a family head of great tact and skill, were it not that so many traditions, rituals, and social sanctions operate as controls in the situation.

There are two basic relationships: that between parents and children (with the emphasis, of course, upon the sons), and that between a son and his wife. Theoretically, these two should be complementary. In practice, however, they are antagonistic to one another. It is true that when parents find a wife for their son they hope that the couple will be compatible and are pleased on the wedding day to receive such congratulations as "Harmony in one hundred years"; "A heavenly sanctioned union"; "Sincerity and love between husband and wife." However, the parents are displeased when the young couple are too devoted to each other, for this menaces the relationship between parents and son, especially that between mother and son. We have previously seen how a mother becomes bitter if her son loves his wife or his wife loves him too much. We also pointed out how a father's instruction may be neglected, rejected, or misinterpreted if his son listens too attentively to his wife's words. In case he is not satisfied with his wife, he must, if he wants to be a filial son, not quarrel too much with her lest his parents' consciences be hurt, nor must he complain too much. That is why, as we have seen, a young husband is required to assume an attitude of indifference while his parents or other family members are present, and why such mottos as, "Listening to wife's words and turning one's back to one's bone and flesh relations is not the behavior of a righteous man," are highly praised by all Chinese parents. Marriage is not primarily for the happiness of the husband and wife alone, but also for the parents— to help in their work, to wait upon them, to satisfy their desire for grandchildren while they are living, and to continue their "incense and fire" when they die.

27. The Suburban Family Pattern

JOHN R. SEELEY, R. ALEXANDER SIM,
and ELIZABETH W. LOOSLEY

Suburban family life stands in marked contrast to that of the Chinese village. Here we see the well-to-do modern city dweller in his fine home, separated from his neighbors by a parklike lawn. The suburban family does not continue through time but is created anew with each marriage and disappears after a generation. The authors show us the characteristic relationships between the various members of the family in suburbia, and through them we see the advantages and disadvantages of this type of organization.

John R. Seeley was Executive Director of Community Surveys in Minneapolis and is now Director of Research of the Alcoholism Research Foundation of Toronto, Canada. He was born in England and trained at the University of Chicago where he has also taught. R. Alexander Sim was former Assistant Director of the UNESCO International Seminar on Adult Education at Salzburg and is now with the Canadian Department of Citizenship and Immigration. Elizabeth W. Loosley did graduate work at the University of Chicago and the University of London and is editor of *Food For Thought*, the official journal of the Canadian Association for Adult Education.

The essay below is adapted from Chapter 7, "The Family: Primary Socialization," in *Crestwood Heights, A Study of the Culture of Suburban Life,* 1956, and is printed by kind permission of the publishers, Basic Books, Inc., New York, the University of Toronto Press, Toronto, Constable and Company, Limited, London, and of the authors.

The upper middle class family is particularly well known, in its external features at least, through the happy, prosperous families portrayed by Hollywood, by innumerable radio and television programs, and by novels. "Ozzie and Harriet," "Father Knows Best," J. P. Marquand's less eccentric New England characters (where the middle-class dream sometimes rubs a little thin), Spencer Tracy's "Father of the Bride"— all have become as familiar as neighbors in the next street. These are the comfortable, delightful, middle-class families of fantasy. The Crestwood Heights family is not like these—and not unlike. How much like and unlike this chapter attempts to sketch.

Origin and Context

The family of Crestwood Heights approximates these fictitious representations at least in that it consists of father, mother, and two (rarely more) children. The children are healthy, physically well developed, attractively dressed, and poised as to outward behavior. The mother, assured in manner, is as like an illustration from *Vogue* or *Harper's Bazaar* as financial means and physical appearance will allow. The father, well tailored, more or less successful in radiating an impression of prosperity and power, rounds out the family group.

This small family is both lone and love-based. It is, more often than not, formed by the marriage of two persons from unrelated and often unacquainted families; persons perhaps differing in temperament and background, who are assumed to have chosen each other because they are "in love." Other reasons for the choice (perpetuation of property within one family, the linking of business or professional interests, an unadorned urge to upward social mobility and so on), even if influential, could not reputably be admitted as grounds for marriage.

This family unit is not embedded in any extended kinship system. The newly formed family is frequently isolated geographically and often socially from the parental families. It is expected that the bride and groom will maintain a separate dwelling removed by varying degrees of distance from that of each set of parents—a physical separation which is often equalled psychologically by an upward movement in society of the younger couple, or by mutually antagonistic patterns of social behavior, resulting from differences in age or history between the generations. In a period of rapid social change, parents and children may no longer share beliefs or attitudes. The isolation of each family acts to decrease the ability of the family to transmit traditional patterns of behavior, which might otherwise be absorbed from close contact with, for instance, grandparents. The absence of kinship bonds also tends to concentrate the emotional life of the family upon a few individuals; institutions are now emerging expressly to supply the support once given by kinship ties. Where relationships with kin do, however, exist, neither set of relatives has marked precedence, although the existence of the time-honored mother-in-law jokes, related chiefly by men, may be indicative of a slightly deeper, if culturally unsanctioned, bond between the wife and her relatives. There are also other reasons for the existence of this tie: in Crestwood Heights it is the wife who performs the functions symbolic of family solidarity: letter-writing, sending gifts and cards, and keeping in touch by telephone.

. . . The larger kinship group in Crestwood Heights . . . usually meets only on ritual occasions. Otherwise, the relationship between the family unit and kin resembles friendship, in which individual preference rather than ties of blood determines association. Conversely, friends may take on functions resembling those of kin, as in the common instance of the unrelated "aunt." . . .

Functions

The Crestwood Heights family, although it varies in organization, composition, and orientation from families in other cultures and from the family of other periods in the history of Western civilization, regulates, as the family always has, sexual and affectional expression in the patterns approved by the society. The life-long relationship between one man and one woman for the procreation of children is the basis of the family in Crestwood Heights. Given the highly mobile nature of the population, the relative lack of secondary institutions capable of absorbing unmarried individuals, and the absence of kin, the tie between husband and wife indeed becomes pre-eminently important, providing, as it does, the one enduring human relationship in the society. Even child-rearing, central as it is in Crestwood, is not so lasting a commitment, since, given the lengthened life-span of the individual, it now occupies relatively few years.

Child-rearing is still considered as essentially the responsibility of the family, and it is the father and mother who must legally assume the child's economic support. And no matter to what degree one parent or both may rely upon institutions and people outside the immediate family for guidance in the child-rearing process itself, it is the parents alone who must decide whether to accept or to reject the proffered services. Strong pressures will, of course, be brought to bear to ensure that they make the "right" decision, but technically it is they who decide.

The family, too, remains the primary social unit in which individuals ideally relate to each other, first of all as human beings, free to express feelings of love and affection, anger or hostility. It is the family which ideally gives emotional security, enabling the individuals comprising it to play their cultural roles in the larger societies, and which provides, if they are provided, the models for identification without which the psycho-sexual development of the child cannot be assured. Thus the family is both the biological and psychological nexus of the society.

Most Crestwooders value highly the privilege of functioning individually in the institutions of the culture. It is the economic and social status of the family which allows them so to function. Economic and social status is closely tied in with the ownership of property. The house, then, as has been already pointed out, in addition to being a powerful symbol of material prosperity, stands for family solidarity and strength; from this base of home and male career, which are almost inseparable, the family can articulate with the community. The family, together with the male career, provides the rationale and the validation of the man's role; and the family provides the chief content of the woman's role.

Finally, the family in Crestwood Heights, since it is ultimately responsible for child-rearing, must, in some sense, "transmit the culture." This transmission of the culture (or, rather, the cultures), as in the case of another important institution, the school, is no longer to any great degree a process of passing on fixed items of tradition; where the family is concerned, the process seems rather to result in the freeing to a considerable extent of individual members to create new cultural and family patterns, independent of those of the family of orientation, and often radically different. Parents and children alike must learn continually to accept forms of social behavior unlike those previously known and practised. . . .

The Crestwood family . . . is definitely oriented to the future, which, apart from its likely disparity with the past, is felt as unknown and unpredictable. The past tends otherwise to be obliterated from the collective thinking of the family. Consciously, the future is optimistically viewed; and the task of the family is to equip the child as effectively as possible in the present with all available means for his later solitary climb to better and more prosperous worlds lying far ahead in time. This passionate optimism tends to be of an essentially catastrophic type— useless as belief and motive force unless *all* its conditions are realized. That the chances for a total realization are slight indeed, is a fact which many Crestwooders cannot easily accept. But the future nevertheless beckons with sufficient force that the parental generation, if it seriously hinders the child's "upward" progress, must be virtually abandoned; this is well understood by both parents and children. Only the promise of continuous upward social mobility (or, at the very least, continually validated status at the present level) can nerve the Crestwood Heights family to its obligations; and for its members to feel the full poignancy of the separation to which it, as a family, is dedicated, might well wreck the whole precarious structure. Such a family is peculiarly vulnerable to outside circumstance. A severe economic depression, for example, would have immediate and serious repercussions which the Crestwood family, given the primary functions outlined, has, it would seem, but few inner resources to meet. . . .

Ideals of Family Life

. . . "Good" parents . . . are emotionally secure, free from hyper-anxiety, and from covert or overt conflict with persons in their immediate environment. Sexual relations should be confined to the marriage partnership, free from tension and "anti-social tendencies." Serious marital disagreement or conflict which may lead to dissolution of the marriage, while seen (perhaps strangely) as less serious than "disturbed behavior" involving extra-marital sex relations, is nevertheless viewed as damaging to the whole family constellation.

The good mother must not be over-solicitous or over-protective. She must be undisturbed by worries about the future, confident in her status and in her acceptance by the community, and sure of her adequacy in the fulfilment of her maternal role. She should not find it necessary to translate any anxieties she may have into specific worries about the child's health, safety, or ability to measure up to academic or social expectations, particularly in the school setting. The ideal mother is not "over-dominant"—an attitude manifested in nagging or "bossing" the child. She is neither over-permissive nor inconsistent in discipline; nor does she cater to the child's every whim.

The good father also exhibits these characteristics (although most discussion of parental behavior seems to refer to mothers). But in avoiding the Scylla of "authoritarianism," the good father must not run against the Charybdis of "indulgence." The Victorian father, patriarchal head of the family and owner of wife and progeny, is as frowned upon as the "over-dominant" and nagging mother. Severe discipline, a primary *differentium* of the authoritarian father, is defined—and disapproved of—as the "expectation of instant obedience, modelled on the military pattern." The good father should not leave complete or almost complete responsibility for the child's upbringing to the mother (even though he provides for the child's material needs) no matter how pressing are his business or professional duties.

Both father and mother are expected to feel a high degree of love for the child. Outright rejection of the child is, of course, a cardinal sin; and behavior which might *possibly* be interpreted by the child as a rejection (preoccupation with adult concerns, for example) is similarly condemned. "Unconditional" parental affection and acceptance, where the child is concerned, has now become the central ideal.

Conflict between mother and son, mother and daughter, father and son, father and daughter, is regarded as a symptom of family malfunction. Adolescent rebellion, likewise labelled as contributing to family disharmony, is a phase of family life with which the good parent must cope without allowing any open breaks in family solidarity to occur. On the other hand, family relationships must not become too binding, lest they shackle the child in his progress towards autonomy.

The relations between brothers and sisters must also be harmonious; this harmony is expected as a direct result of the soundness of the husband-wife relationship. Jealousy, rivalry, or open conflict between siblings, usually attributed to faulty parental attitudes (favoritism, for instance) is not to be tolerated.

Finally, this ideal Crestwood family operates as a *separate* unit— it must not share living quarters or dependencies with other families; even the apartment building with its many divisions is not considered the proper material environment for family life. The detached house, which the family owns and inhabits in its entirety, is the only fully approved physical basis for a healthy, happy family. To share this house with kin is considered undesirable and, in many cases, a genuine hardship, since the presence of grandparents or other close relatives is viewed as inimical to smooth family functioning. . . .

Roles Within the Family

When the Crestwood family is viewed as a unit composed of a certain number of individuals related to each other and to the outside world, a complex pattern of behavior (or perhaps, behaviors) becomes apparent.

Even though the patriarchal powers once associated with his role are largely dissipated, the father still stands as the symbolic head of the family. Under the new dispensation, he is expected to share his authority among all members of the family, in varying degrees; and, indeed, because of his frequent absence, his power to deal with situations and with persons within the family may largely pass to the woman. But, even more difficult, the man is at the same time now required to "participate" in the whole child-rearing process, and sometimes in the actual household routine as well. The Crestwood doctor who frequently puts his children to bed, staying at home for the evening while his wife goes out with friends or for a game of bridge, has few if any counterparts in Europe. Yet the man's role in Crestwood Heights is more clearly defined than that of the woman, for whatever the cultural additions to it by way of demands for "companionship" and shared activities on a basis of equality with wife and children, he is viewed predominantly as the earner of the income upon which rests the whole structure of family life in Crestwood Heights. And, in return, the family, by its activities, often divorced entirely from those of the father, contributes indirectly to his career.

The father now seems to have more responsibility within the home, but without commensurate authority. Conversely, his position in the occupational world, *vis-à-vis* the family, is different from what it was in previous decades, when, for the urban dweller, occupation and home were more rigidly separated. There are now greater pressures in the pursuit of occupational success, and the man is held ultimately and personally responsible if, in this more hectic chase, the family, or any of its members, should "fail." If his wife cannot discharge the social obligations which facilitate his business or profession, it is he who is considered to have shown poor judgment in his choice, an error which is generalized with a potentially disastrous effect upon his career. If it is his child who cannot measure up to cultural expectations, the fault is attributable either to him or to his wife. If the fault is his, then he is held directly accountable; if it is his wife's, the man is still to blame, for he made the marital mistake in the first place. But since such a great part of his life is lived outside the home, the man has not the means, such as are available to him in his office, to supervise this particular department of his career. . . .

Thus the family, for the man, represents a vital element in his occupational success, as well as the only approved source of emotional security. Difficulties in combining the two functions are often evident. One may predominate over the other, as in the case of the business man who said that when he shut the door of his home behind him in the morning he felt as if he "were going out into the jungle." Other men, who also primarily wanted home as an emotionally safe refuge, for this very reason refused to become deeply involved with the members of their families. They needed protection against disturbance, and so chose a life of non-involvement. This was especially noticeable in some professional men, who spend their working hours in situations harassing psychologically.

Nevertheless, though the man's individual emotional security largely depends on his roles as husband and father, these must necessarily become secondary to his primary role of breadwinner. And the occupational role differs widely from the roles of husband and father, in terms of ends, obligations, involvement, and emotional content. The man's life experience, primarily oriented as it is to the competitive world of business or profession, therefore does not prepare him to meet the new secondary cultural demands upon him as husband and father. Many men try to solve this conflict by carrying over into family life the standards and attitudes useful in building the career. Needless to say, these are in direct opposition to the woman's values, and therefore a potent source of strain within the family. Indeed, many Crestwood Heights women express resentment at being regarded merely as decorative or useful adjuncts to their husbands' careers.

The woman's role is again, like that of the man's, divided. She must not devote herself *wholly* to husband and children; yet they are still to be her first and most important responsibility—the woman must remain both for husband and for children the emotional hub of the family. . . . As a mother, the Crestwood Heights woman is expected to provide an atmosphere of warmth, security, and unconditional love for her children. The education and pre-marital life experience of the Crestwood woman, however, have not usually prepared her particularly well to make this provision. Educationally, it is rare for a Crestwood woman, in her younger years, to have devoted much attention to the learning of housewifely skills or child care. And, psychologically, she herself, in all probability, has not had, as a child, the kind of gratification which would allow her to fulfil at all easily the cultural demands for unconditional love where her children are concerned. Her upbringing tends to drive her early to concentrate on those arts of glamor and physical attractiveness which will ultimately win and keep a husband able to maintain her in the style of Crestwood Heights. Then suddenly, after the excitement of romance and marriage, she may find herself alone in a Crestwood Heights home, well equipped mechanically, but intermittently empty of life until the arrival of her first baby. Moreover, while there is temporary relief for mothers of small children, none of the available resources provides the Crestwood woman with continuous companionship in her task, or relieves her in any way of the responsibility. . . .

The child's time, particularly as he grows older, is also divided between home—where he or she is simultaneously son or daughter to the parents and also a brother or a sister—and peer group activities. The latter come to occupy more and more of his day, as he leaves the home for school and other institutions. Within the family circle, the child is the promise of the future, the family's main ostensible justification for existence, and the target of the whole elaborate socialization process of Crestwood Heights—which, in the end, as we have learned, will gradually dissolve all close ties between him and his parents, and often between him and his brothers and sisters as well. . . .

Within the family, the child must establish relationships with brothers and sisters, older or younger than himself. Here again, although the ideals of individuality and equality may seem more easily attainable, each child cannot share identically in privileges and favors. A small child, to quote only one example, must submit or agree to an earlier bed-time than his older brother or sister, no matter what his own ideas on the subject may be. To determine and to put into practice these necessary limitations to the child's freedom—without recourse to "authoritarian" measures—may tax parental ingenuity to the limit. Sex differences between siblings may also open up possibilities of strain within the family, since a girl cannot be treated in exactly the same manner as a boy by even the most permissive of parents. Indeed, extreme impartiality in this regard may make it difficult for the child to learn the approved sex role.

While the child is undergoing an intensive and strenuous socialization process in relation to father, mother, and siblings within the home itself, he is also required to learn adjustments to peers and to other adults outside the family altogether. In much the same way as the Crestwood man is divided between occupation and family, the child, particularly during adolescence, may be torn between the home and peer group, in which he spends more and more of his time as he grows older. . . .

The family in Crestwood Heights is located, as it were, at but a *point* in time; it is a constellation of human beings, related to one another for a relatively short period by strong emotional bonds, which will again dissolve after the task of child-rearing is completed. Within this nexus, the psychosexual development of the child occurs; if successfully completed, it culminates in marriage and the founding of a new family unit. Also from the family, supplemented by increasing contacts with the personnel of outside institutions, the child acquires the patterns of social behavior which permit him to function in his society. As he grows older, the child returns less and less frequently to the island of emotional security which the Crestwood family represents; and finally he installs himself upon a similar psychological refuge, almost entirely isolated from the original base which launched him on his solitary voyage.

Family Activities

What occurs within the family during its relatively brief span of intense activity as a unit? What are its day-to-day concerns and what its major goals? How do its members co-operate to reach these ends, and how do they balance responsibility to the family with obligations to the world outside this circle? . . .

Economic Activities. The Crestwood family, as has been said earlier, is essentially a consumption unit. Unlike, for instance, the Irish peasant family, which is focused on production, the Crestwood Heights woman and her children do not usually contribute directly through their work to the economic enterprise of the family. The relatively few Crestwood Heights children who work and live at home while still unmarried, are not required to contribute to the family income; or, should the rare exception occur, the contribution is nominal, a token only, for the sake of the child's "independence." The earning sphere is thus clear-cut, dominated by the male; the area of spending (which may, or may not, be male-dominated to some degree) is almost always shared with other members of the family. The most general pattern appears to be one in which the man decides, after consultation, on such major expenditures as a car or life insurance, and the woman decides, sometimes after discussion with her husband, upon the much larger aggregate of small things. . . .

The cash income is all-important to the solidarity of the Crestwood Heights family, since upon it depends the social status of the family, which, in turn, determines the sense of belonging to the community— indeed the very possibility of staying in it. The self-image of each family member depends largely on the income, as we have had occasion to conclude before. Unlike the upper-class English family, which may preserve its feeling of worth almost intact in the face of dwindling wealth, the self-estimate of the Crestwood upper middle class family tends to rise and fall with income. In view of the central position which money occupies in the family, the preoccupation with teaching children to handle finances is completely understandable. . . .

Household Duties. Despite the reduced volume of work within the home itself, traditional divisions of labor are still discernible. The general administration of the household, the feeding and clothing of the children, are regarded as the wife's responsibility, although the woman who derives her maximum satisfaction in life from such activities is becoming increasingly rare, and the role of housewife tends to be devalued in the culture. Some Crestwood wives discharge their duties by supervising either full or part-time domestics; and many, by directing the services which enter the home from outside. But performance varies, and the Crestwood woman may do as much or as little of the housework herself as her inclination and means permit—provided only that the required neat and unlived-in appearance of the house is maintained.

Over and against this reduction, however, is an incredible increase in what must be done if the Crestwood home is to be a proper exhibition of status and thus an aid to the male career. No longer can the house be decorated once and for all time, or the furniture be placed finally, for the period of one's married life. Every month brings a wealth of opulently illustrated magazines which show the Crestwood woman new styles, materials, furniture, and arrangements for the home beautiful, the home efficient, the home livable, and, indeed, the home reputable. The woman must keep abreast of these constant changes for one of two reasons: so that she may defend her former arrangements successfully—even if only to herself—or be encouraged to sweep these aside in favor of new. She can accomplish neither defense nor attack unless she carefully follows the argument laid down in the decorating magazines, nor can she feel safe unless she is in a position to reject or to accept their dictates. As one woman informant commented: "I'm not as bad as X., I went right ahead and switched the whole living room over to modern. *She* actually kept a room in her house empty for two years before she could make up her mind what to put into it!"

The Crestwood man is ritually responsible for those tasks requiring physical strength—gardening, window-cleaning, putting on storm windows, and so on. In practice, however, these duties are often delegated to commercial services. . . . Although the home is defined as the woman's world, Crestwood Heights husbands and children do "pitch in" to help the mother, particularly in emergencies. Where the man does share the woman's tasks, it is on a voluntary and flexible basis, seldom rising —without raising doubts about maleness—to the level of a regular and expected contribution. . . . Through such participation in the woman's mainly routine and instrumental tasks, the husband's assistance may take on particular emotional significance for the wife, since she cannot reciprocate by equivalent participation in the man's work. Many Crestwood wives try by all possible means to involve their husbands in responsibilities around the house. One woman whose husband's contribution consisted merely in *paying* the gardener, not in doing the task himself, stated with some satisfaction that she thus "had secured her husband's participation in the household routine." . . .

Child care and control. While these economic and domestic activities are important in Crestwood Heights, neither is seen as a sufficient reason for the family's existence. Both father and mother, within and without the home, perform their various roles largely, as we are now aware, "for the sake of the children." With only rare exceptions, Crestwood parents pretty well take for granted their responsibility for the physical care and social training of their children. But beyond their fundamental and obvious legal responsibility, Crestwood Heights parents often wonder "what to do next" with their children, since they are given no support by traditionally sanctioned methods of child-rearing. There is great variation in the patterns of child care and control, and considerable parental uncertainty.

Nor are father and mother commonly agreed even in uncertainty as to how this function is to be discharged. Background for this division of opinion may be found in the career. It does not usually occur to the Crestwood Heights male to inquire deeply, if at all, into the emotional reactions of the subordinates who assist him in his occupation. Human beings, in this setting, exist to facilitate the flow of goods or services from which money is made. True, the Crestwood man may be well informed about personnel practices, but he usually views such innovations as "good for business" and only indirectly as good for people. If the experts in industrial relations can prove with figures that production is increased through their ministrations, the Crestwood Heights male will accept their advice, although he may still feel "diametrically opposed to the whole philosophy."

For such a man, the child-rearing theories which his wife espouses may seem arrant nonsense; and the male experts from whom she derives her information frequently appear to him, unless they are doctors, as inadequate men who have not been able to make the grade in the *really* masculine world. In the office, whatever his private reservations, the Crestwood man is prepared to go quite a distance along the personnel-directed path for the sake of production and industrial peace. At home, he is under no obligation to moderate his views; in the family he can give vent to his true feelings unopposed. Out of love for wife and children, he may, in time, be persuaded to take an interest in the new-fangled notions; rarely, however, he will come wholeheartedly to endorse the democratic and permissive norms now seeping into the family. A father who does not pretend to understand the underlying psychological reasons for a child's failure to achieve in school is, nevertheless, deeply concerned over the immediate situation of the child's inability to meet the required standards. In such circumstances he often inclines first towards old-fashioned disciplinary measures as a remedy, only reluctantly and sometimes after exhausting all other possibilities accepting the methods of school, experts, and wife. Another type of father, as indicated below, moves in a rather uneasy but would-be helpful manner at the edge of the enterprise, feeling the uncertain willingness of the novice rather than the unwillingness of an opponent. . . .

At certain points in the history of the family, however, the father becomes automatically involved. The mother's power to discipline children decreases sharply after they enter their teens, particularly where boys are concerned. Certain privileges, such as access to the family car, are customarily controlled by the father. The son may sometimes be felt acutely as a potential rival by the father; but, in general, disputes are avoided, and father and son tacitly by-pass any situations which call for direct paternal intervention and which might openly disrupt the cultural ideal of the "pal" relationship between father and son. The Crestwood Heights concept of time makes aging and the looming prospect of the termination of the career a very real threat to the man; the prospect can be softened by playing down the actual gap in years between father and son. Greater age, connoting superior wisdom, is not a disciplinary weapon as readily available to the Crestwood Heights father as to his Victorian predecessor. As the son grows older, the father's last control over the son's behavior is likely to be only an economic one. . . .

The whole area of child care and control is at present in a state of considerable flux in Crestwood Heights. Fathers may differ from mothers at almost every point in the complex socialization process. Families are divided between permissive and authoritarian ways of handling children, and so are individuals at different times or—worse—the same time. Despite the general, over-all preoccupation with individual development and preparation for a future independent of the family of orientation, the Crestwood Heights child does not receive in the family the same consistent direction where discipline is concerned that he experiences in learning to earn and to spend money.

Social Activities. "Social activities" involve the Crestwood Heights family more with individuals and institutions outside the home circle than with those inside it. The Crestwooder, when he thinks of such activities, does not envisage his family group gathered round the dining-room table playing games, or grouped in a sing-song near the living-room piano. Should he associate such activities with home at all, he would naturally think of the children entertaining their own "gang" in the recreation room, while he and his wife watched television in the living-room above or played a game of bridge with friends who might have crossed Big City in order to join them. "Social activities" in Crestwood Heights mean leisure spent with persons outside the family, sometimes including kin, mostly not. These activities are considered highly important for all members of the Crestwood Heights family. They may be pleasurable in themselves, but many use them (consciously or unconsciously) primarily as important means of maintaining or enhancing social status in the community. . . .

In view of the importance of social activities for family status and for the man's career, it is perhaps somewhat surprising to find that the Crestwood Heights woman is usually the initiator of social activities. A busy doctor, for instance, when asked to dinner by a friend during office hours, referred the latter to his wife, remarking "Give A. a call—she handles all that." Social activities, no matter how institutionalized, or rationalized, or career-relevant, are still considered in Crestwood Heights to be primarily related to expression and emotion, which may account for their relegation to the woman's sphere. Whatever the reason, social activities, both within and without the family, are nearly always thought up, planned, decided upon, and carried out by the wife.

In Crestwood Heights the amount of time which the family spends together is very restricted. Breakfast and lunch are almost universally eaten separately or in small groups at the convenience of the individual members. Dinner is frequently a family occasion. Some families tend to keep the evening meal a purely social affair, with only light talk exchanged. Others make this meal a time for family discussions and decisions. In a few, the presence of all members opens up so many conflicts that it may be felt more convenient to have them eat separately. . . .

When the child participates in social activities within the home, there is no clear-cut distinction between his status as a child and that of the adults around him. The old edict that a child should be seen and not heard, of course, no longer holds in Crestwood Heights. Young children join in the conversation of their elders at the dinner table and remain in the living-room, frequently interrupting the talk of the grown-ups, demanding attention for their play. More rarely, the child may be formally included in the social activity, perhaps helping to serve at a tea or cocktail party. A European boy of four who, when invited with his parents to afternoon tea, took the toys he had brought with him to a corner, and played quietly by himself without approaching the adults, was noteworthy to Crestwood Heights. There children are not led to believe that there are certain adult privileges which children cannot share. This constant inclusion of the children in adult concerns may deprive them of valuable help in the growing-up process, since they now are not required to listen in silence while the adults carry on a discussion of their own affairs, from which children might learn a great deal about adult behavior, ideas, and ideals.

As the child approaches his teens, participation in the family's social activities grows less and he joins more and more in the peer group fun, until finally his social life may be carried on in almost entire separation from that of his parents.

28. American Individualism in Historical Perspective

ALEXIS de TOCQUEVILLE

Alexis de Tocqueville described American culture after his extensive travels in the United States in 1831. He was particularly interested in the character of society under a democracy and was concerned with understanding the social merits and relative advantages of a democratic social system as opposed to the monarchical patterns of Europe. His analysis of America is insightful and remains one of the best descriptions of this country ever made by a foreigner. Surprisingly, much that he observed appears still to be largely true today.

We print this brief excerpt, which deals more with individualistic tendencies in America than it does with the family as such, because we feel that his analysis throws light on the character and pattern of family life in the modern world. The selection is taken from the second volume of his *Democracy in America*. This book has had many editions; it is available as a Vintage Book (1954). It is reprinted from *Democracy in America* by Alexis de Tocqueville, by permission of Alfred A. Knopf, Inc., New York. Copyright 1945 by Alfred A. Knopf, Inc.

I have shown how it is that in ages of equality every man seeks for his opinions within himself; I am now to show how it is that in the same ages all his feelings are turned towards himself alone. *Individualism* is a novel expression, to which a novel idea has given birth. Our fathers were only acquainted with *égoïsme* (selfishness). Selfishness is a passionate and exaggerated love of self, which leads a man to connect everything with himself and to prefer himself to everything in the world. Individualism is a mature and calm feeling, which disposes each member of the community to sever himself from the mass of his fellows and to draw apart with his family and his friends, so that after he has thus formed a little circle of his own, he willingly leaves society at large to itself. Selfishness originates in blind instinct; individualism proceeds from erroneous judgment more than from depraved feelings; it originates as much in deficiencies of mind as in perversity of heart.

Selfishness blights the germ of all virtue; individualism, at first, only saps the virtues of public life; but in the long run it attacks and destroys all others and is at length absorbed in downright selfishness. Selfishness is a vice as old as the world, which does not belong to one form of society more than to another; individualism is of democratic origin, and it threatens to spread in the same ratio as the equality of condition.

Among aristocratic nations, as families remain for centuries in the same condition, often on the same spot, all generations become, as it were, contemporaneous. A man almost always knows his forefathers and respects them; he thinks he already sees his remote descendants and he loves them. He willingly imposes duties on himself towards the former and the latter, and he will frequently sacrifice his personal gratifications to those who went before and to those who will come after him. Aristocratic institutions, moreover, have the effect of closely binding every man to several of his fellow citizens. As the classes of an aristocratic people are strongly marked and permanent, each of them is regarded by its own members as a sort of lesser country, more tangible and more cherished than the country at large. As in aristocratic communities all the citizens occupy fixed positions, one above another, the result is that each of them always sees a man above himself whose patronage is necessary to him, and below himself another man whose co-operation he may claim. Men living in aristocratic ages are therefore almost always closely attached to something placed out of their own sphere, and they are often disposed to forget themselves. It is true that in these ages the notion of human fellowship is faint and that men seldom think of sacrificing themselves for mankind; but they often sacrifice themselves for other men. In democratic times, on the contrary, when the duties of each individual to the race are much more clear, devoted service to any one man becomes more rare; the bond of human affection is extended, but it is relaxed.

Among democratic nations new families are constantly springing up, others are constantly falling away, and all that remain change their condition; the woof of time is every instant broken and the track of generations effaced. Those who went before are soon forgotten; of those who will come after, no one has any idea: the interest of man is confined to those in close propinquity to himself. As each class gradually approaches others and mingles with them, its members become undifferentiated and lose their class identity for each other. Aristocracy had made a chain of all the members of the community, from the peasant to the king; democracy breaks that chain and severs every link of it.

As social conditions become more equal, the number of persons increases who, although they are neither rich nor powerful enough to exercise any great influence over their fellows, have nevertheless acquired or retained sufficient education and fortune to satisfy their own wants. They owe nothing to any man, they expect nothing from any man; they acquire the habit of always considering themselves as standing alone, and they are apt to imagine that their whole destiny is in their own hands.

Thus not only does democracy make every man forget his ancestors, but it hides his descendants and separates his contemporaries from him; it throws him back forever upon himself alone and threatens in the end to confine him entirely within the solitude of his own heart.

VI.

GROUPS

The Commitment to Social Life

Culture is shared behavior. Those who share a culture form a society. It follows, therefore, that we must examine the nature of societies if we are to understand human behavior.

Human beings, by their very nature, live in aggregates. The long period of maturation and the fact that the human must learn how to gain his livelihood, make this association necessary. Psychologically, too, humans seem to feel the necessity of association. At any rate, they always live in social aggregates. Such social aggregates are societies, which is to say that they have an internal structure.

There is an additional, obvious, reason for the organization of men into societies: they make possible greater human accomplishment, they protect their members and, through cooperation, enable them to obtain more of the material things necessary for survival.

The structure of a society involves two things: first, there is a division into smaller social units, which we call groups; and second, there are recognized social positions (statuses) and appropriate behavior patterns to such positions (roles). In this section we will deal with the former of these two organizational elements, in the following section we deal with the latter.

Society itself may be viewed as a group—the group that contains within it all other groups. All people feel that they belong to a body of people; they recognize a distinction between their society and outsiders. Such a society may be constituted of millions of people—as are modern nations—or may be made up of a few dozen. But whatever its size, there is a sense of unity among its members (which is not, quite emphatically, to say that they are in complete harmony) and a distinction between fellow members and outsiders. The boundary may be quite clearly demarcated, so that a map of its territory can easily be drawn. It may, however, be quite shifting or vague. It may in actuality be only in the minds of the people themselves, and thus be quite difficult for an outsider to comprehend. But everywhere we find that people make a distinction between their own group and other peoples, whom they regard as outsiders.

It is the society which shares a culture, or, to put the matter another way, people with identical language and customs tend to constitute a society.

But if humans live together because they are enriched through cooperative effort, it follows that the population must be organized. Persons must learn not only to do their own part, but must be able to anticipate that others will do theirs. Unless there is organization, and reasonably clear definition of who does what, when, and how, the advantages of group life are rapidly lost.

There is every reason to believe that some kind of organization is necessary, aside from the need to cooperate. If there were no rules of behavior, no patterns of action and expectation, very soon everybody would be in everybody else's way, conflict would be endemic and interaction impossible. Social organization may be defined as the regularization of interpersonal relations.

Though organization is universal to societies, the mode of organization varies greatly. The manner in which a society is organized is established through tradition; that is, social organization may be considered a part of culture. Thus we must recognize that though the fact of social existence requires that there be organization in society, the manner in which the society is organized, even to the definition of what constitutes a particular society, is set by tradition.

How a society is organized depends to some extent on other aspects of the culture. For instance, we do not get elaborate political systems among hunting and food-gathering societies where the economy can sustain only a few people per square mile, nor can a modern industrial order be built solely on the ties of kinship. Some of the requirements appropriate to the various levels of cultural development will emerge in the discussion in succeeding sections.

The division of a society into groups is, as we have said, one aspect of social organization. The first and universal basis for group formation rests on the sentiments of kinship; that is, on various forms of the family. We have already discussed the family, and are aware of some of the ways that family organization can differ. We have also seen the internal structure of the family, and have shown how it tends to shape the outlook of the individual.

The family is a primary group. Charles H. Cooley coined this apt phrase for those groups which are in intimate daily contact, for he rightly believed that much of a person's attitudes and feelings are acquired through primary group association. He spoke of them as primary because they have a first order of importance, and also because they are usually the first groups to which a person belongs. Sociologists also speak of secondary groups; that is, larger, less intimate groups which have significant but less important bearing upon their members. Obviously, there is no hard and fast line between these categories, but the distinction is a useful one.

In this section we have included one essay which, in a sense, does not deal with groups at all, yet just because it discusses the absence of group affiliation it tells us a great deal about the importance of group ties. This essay by Harvey Zorbaugh consists chiefly of the autobiographical account of an unmarried woman, as obtained by a sociological interviewer. She is one of many such men and women who dwell in the single-room districts in modern cities, lacking any close social ties. We see that in the absence of such ties the normal restraints on behavior are weakened; that the girl could do things that she herself considers wrong, although she is aware that there is no person who can condemn her. It is not that she is unaware of propriety; obviously she was reared in a stern and moral tradition, and she carries these attitudes with her. She was once part of a group. The group not only communicates culture to the individual, it also constantly reenforces expected behavior. Such an absence of any sense of affiliation is not possible in primitive society; it is a product of urban life, where the individual can remain entirely anonymous to all his associates, becoming an item on the payroll to an employer, a tenant in an upstairs room to a landlady, and a face in the crowd to everybody else.

The strength of group affiliation can vary widely. It may be no more than the casual joining of an association that offers a single shared interest, or it may be totally absorbing. Under some circumstances, the individual is so closely identified with his group that whatever affects his group affects him in like degree, and whatever happens to him reflects upon his group. The Tlingit Indians offer us an example, for their whole legal system is built upon the individual's complete identification with his clan. This clan is a family organization; that is, it is built upon ties of kinship—a matter we have already anticipated in the preceding section. A person is born into the clan of his mother and remains in that clan throughout his life. Indeed, since the spirits continue their affiliations after death, he remains a member of that clan forever. Nothing he can do will change this affiliation, if he is to remain in the society.

Under such circumstances, the sense of identity between the individual and his clan can become very great. If he wrongs a person of another clan, every man of his clan is responsible in like degree. If he does an honorable deed, the whole clan gains in prestige. If the clan must sacrifice a member to right a wrong—for the law here requires the death of an equivalent person in compensation for a murder—an individual must be willing to sacrifice himself, even though the original fault was not his.

Though we have no groups to which we normally feel this level of responsibility, it is not entirely incomprehensible to us, for there are certain situations where we behave in a similar fashion. Many parents would sacrifice themselves for their children. Modern military annals demonstrate that individual soldiers frequently sacrifice themselves for their buddies in the field. And, on a broader and more generally recognized level, we expect each man to be willing to lay down his life for the nation as a whole. This last example is the only truly comparable one, for it involves social expectation rather than personal predilection, and is built upon the same general concept of group responsibility that influences the Tlingit Indian.

This matter of military behavior brings forth the importance of group affiliation to the individual, and the importance of groups in the workings of society. Edward Shils and Morris Janowitz analyzed the factors which made for loyalty in the German army and discovered that the basic element was the strong identification of the individual soldier with his group. Colonel S. L. A. Marshall, in a book on military morale and problems of command, has made a similar observation with respect to the importance of group relationships in our own army:

> Individual stragglers had almost no combat value when inducted into a strange organization. The majority of them were unwilling to join any such solid unit which was still facing the enemy. The minority, after being given food and a little rest, took their place in line. But the moment the new unit came under enemy pressure, these individuals quit their ground and ran rearward, or sought cover somewhere behind the combat line.
>
> On the other hand, that was not true of gun crews, squad groups, or platoons which had been routed from their original ground and separated from their parent unit, but had managed in some way to hold together during the fall-back. Upon being inducted into a strange company, they tended to fight as vigorously as any element in the command which they had newly joined, and would frequently set an example of initiative and courageous action beyond what had been asked of them.*

This points up the fact that group relationships are not only a matter of concern to the anthropologists and sociologists who are analyzing social behavior, but that they have a direct bearing on the practical aspects of life. This is true not only in military operations but in everyday civilian life as well. For the world's work is done by groups in cooperation.

* S. L. A. Marshall, *Men Under Fire, The Problem of Battle Command in Future War.* New York: William Morrow and Co., 1947, p. 151.

The full importance of this fact has not always been appreciated. We recognize, of course, that work groups like that in Dahomey described by Melville Herskovits exist in one form or another in most societies. We know, too, that our business corporations, our unions, and many other units in our society are work groups. In one sense, so are our families which share the task of rearing children. But sociological studies have recently discovered how important informal work groups can be in the morale and output of modern industrial enterprises. The first study to show this was the now classic investigation of F. J. Roethlisberger and William J. Dickson in their researches at the Hawthorne plant of Western Electric Company. The relation of the individual to his group and the sense of involvement with his work group have an influence on such things as take-home pay and worker output, even though the workman himself may not be aware that these factors exist. Many subsequent studies have re-affirmed the importance of the group to the individual worker's output and work satisfactions.

These studies also demonstrate another thing about social groups; namely, that they have a structure. Like society as a whole, the groups, that make up society are organized; they have recognized leadership and allocation of rights and responsibilities. Such organization may be formally established, as it tends to be in clubs and the more formal groups of a society. It may be barely at the level of awareness. In a subsequent section, we will show how authority is recognized within informal groups by analysis of a street-corner gang. Here each gang has a hierarchy which all its members recognize, even though there are no formal offices. Similar informal structure, often characterizes groups among primitive peoples, though there is usually some established basis—age, kinship, or other—for positions in the group.

Groups may be viewed as subdivisions of society, when we take the broader point of view. But from the point of view of the individual, groups afford the context for normal everyday action. Thus, the individual relates to his fellow man through common group affiliations, he learns the expectations of his culture and of his particular place in that culture through the groups in which he operates (of which the family is, obviously, of first importance). It is in the context of groups that the individual obtains a measure of himself and the satisfaction of personal acceptance to others, of affectional ties, and a feeling of adequacy and importance. For these reasons, an appreciation of the nature and function of groups is essential to the understanding of society, the nature of culture, and the behavior of the individual.

29. Groups in Human Society

WALTER GOLDSCHMIDT

Groups are the building blocks of society. This essay deals with the kinds of social groups and their functions and points out that the way a society is divided into groups will depend, among other things, on the level of economic life achieved. The essay defines groups as one of the imperative elements in the organization of every society and discusses both their universality and variety.

Walter Goldschmidt is Professor of Anthropology and Sociology at the University of California, Los Angeles, having taken his graduate degree from the University of California, Berkeley. He has made studies of American Indian tribes, of an African tribe and of modern American communities. The selection printed below is taken from *Man's Way: A Preface to the Understanding of Human Society,* World Publishing Company, Cleveland, and Henry Holt and Company, New York, 1959, and appears here with the kind permission of the publishers.

The Nature of Groups

The universal existence of groups is perhaps the most evident of all the components of a social system. It is necessary, however, to appreciate the meaning of groups in the conduct of human affairs and to examine their nature and variety.

All human beings normally enter their first group—the family—at the moment of birth, and in the course of a lifetime become part of many such social entities. Their size may vary from the dual relationship of a childless family to a loose and massive social system such as a modern political party. It is proper to consider society as a whole to be a group—the largest group containing within it all the other groups.

What does "groupness" consist in? First, members of a group sense their unity and commonality. There is a felt distinction between the personnel of the group and the outsider, a kind of psychological membrane which marks those within from those outside. This barrier may be virtually impenetrable, as the castes of India or the clans of many primitive tribes. It may be relatively open, as the membership of the American Anthropological Association, which requires no more than the payment of a small fee and the expression of interest.

Second, each group must have a focus of interest. This may be no more than the collection of strange customs of exotic peoples, but it could be as important as the maintenance of power and authority over a large territory. With such common interest come certain common activities, which again may be far-reaching or slight, depending upon the circumstances. People do not form a group merely by being together but rather by sharing interests and engaging in activity to further the interests of the group. Indeed, in our modern system of communication often the members of a group are not physically together and, in fact, the same can be said of primitive clans, as we shall see.

Finally, groups are organized. There is an internal structure, a distinction of statuses and roles, lines of communication, and foci of authority. This is obviously true of the larger groups in modern American society, but it is equally true of the simple and informal groups that we call cliques. William F. Whyte clearly demonstrated the existence of a firm structure in the apparently transitory gangs of Boston slum youths; and in his novel, *The Ox-Bow Incident,* Walter Van Tilburg Clark took pains to show that the mob that did the lynching was closely organized, with a leader and a couple of lieutenants organizing even so short-lived a group.

When we examine groups from a variety of social systems, we can recognize three separate, general bases for group formation. The first form is the *familistic,* where the central unity and the basis of membership depends upon ties of kinship. Which ties are considered important, how large such groups become, and what their functions are differ from one society to another, but all social systems have familistic groups. The second general type is *spatial.* Spatial groups are based upon persons having a common dwelling place or area. Our towns, counties, states, and nations may be viewed as territorial groups, and our membership rests fundamentally on residence, though other criteria may be brought into consideration. Third, groups may be formed merely on the basis of some special interest or activity irrespective of space or kinship. A group unified for purposes of some common recreation, such as a society for ham radio operators; a group brought together for some kind of economic activity, such as a union; or a group brought together for certain kinds of prestigeful activities, such as the secret societies found in Melanesia and on the American plains or in a modern college are all examples of this last type. Most, but not all, societies have such social units. In some primitive societies, it is possible to get the world's work done in the context of familistic and spatial grouping.

One important attribute of groups is the manner in which membership is attained. Sociologists usually make distinctions between those groups in which membership is foreordained by some circumstance beyond the control of the person himself, and those in which the individual can freely choose to select or reject affiliation. The former have sometimes been called groups of common origin and the latter, groups of common interest; but the terminology is unfortunate because all groups have a common interest. We shall distinguish them as *ascribed groups* and *volitional groups*. Since no one has the power to choose his parents, the family into which he is born is always an ascribed group. In the modern world, nationality is usually ascribed; in American society, the social involvements of racial affiliation are ascribed. Some primitive societies have volitional groups, but some appear not to have. The evolution of society from the simple to the complex appears to bring with it a shift in emphasis from ascribed to volitional groups.

The choice of membership in a volitional group is not entirely free. An individual may be rejected from membership or there may be very strong pressures on him to join. The former is readily illustrated by exclusive clubs, the latter by such occupational association as the American Medical Association, for its influence on medical services and facilities makes it almost mandatory for a doctor to maintain his membership if he wishes to practice.

This matter of volition has some important implications for the character of the group. Where a group is foreordained—and there are societies in which a person is a group member from before his birth until the last memory of him disappears—it can maintain an assumption of unity that is not available to a group whose members are free to move in and out. It is not that the unity is greater but that the individual members are more completely caught in group demands, which are inescapable and therefore potentially more autocratic.

Groups perform functions in society, and each group normally has a manifest function. The manifest function of the family is procreation and the maintenance of the physical and economic satisfactions of its component members; the function of a union is the protection and furtherance of mutual interest; a social club functions to provide recreation for its members. It is within the context of group life that the world's work is done. But the group also frequently performs one or more of a second set of functions, latent functions, which relate to the needs of its individual members.

One of these is that the group functions as a body through which the cultural attitudes or special social demands and expectations are communicated to the individual. The child acquires his culture first through his family; the scholar acquires a knowledge of professional ethics, special terminology, and the construct of ideas, through the organization of academicians with which he associates. The fraternity brother learns the secret signs and symbols, and the express values of his group. A second function is that the group gives the individual strength; it supports him in his behavior and assures him of the propriety of his actions and attitudes. This can be particularly seen with such deviant groups as nudists, who as individuals would be acting immorally as well as illegally, but who as members of the group are engaged in activities which are both morally sanctioned and legally admissible. Indeed, some state laws have distinguished the psychopath from the religious cult leader arbitrarily by the size of the group of followers he can claim. Finally, the group provides a social matrix in which people get personal responses of affection, prestige, and status; it is within the context of the group that they satisfy these needs.

Other animals live in social aggregates but it is doubtful if any other animal has something that can be called "social groups" except the total herd or flock, and even these probably may not have the psychological characteristics that are part of the human group. Separation of this kind is found among the social insects, but the basis of distinction is so thoroughly biological that it is quite improper to make analogies with mammalian social systems.

Human societies are everywhere made up of numerous groups and it is important to give some consideration to the relationships that may exist between the different groupings in a social system. Groups may be distinguished as between those which are *mutually exclusive* and those which are *overlapping*. In the former case, membership in one group precludes membership in another, as for example the castes of India. Where clan systems prevail, if a person belongs to one clan, he usually cannot be a member of another. Many societies are made up of a mosaic of separate but comparable groups. These groups may be coequal with one another in power or prestige, or they may be hierarchical. Clans are generally coequal, castes hierarchical.

By overlapping groups we mean groups in which the membership of one includes or may include members from another. These in turn can be divided into two kinds. If all members of one group are included within the broader group, this relationship is referred to as *inclusive*. Thus, for instance all the persons in any one state are also members of the United States. In primitive societies there frequently exist lineages, the members of which are also members of a larger and more inclusive clan made up of several lineages, and these in turn may be included in a yet larger group. The other kind of overlapping is called *noninclusive*. Under these conditions, membership in one neither establishes nor precludes membership in another, so that normally there are persons in one group who do and others who do not have membership in a second. Our system of clubs and associations is generally of this kind.

Membership in a group involves a measure of commitment, and group loyalties tend to organize sentiment in the society. In many social systems, as in clan-organized societies, the loyalty to special groups overrides the loyalty to the society, and the social system may even rest upon a balance of power between mutually exclusive coequal groups standing in opposition to one another. Where mutually exclusive groups are ordered hierarchically, prestige is a matter of group affiliation, and power usually goes with prestige. Where overlapping groups are inclusive, the sentiments of the larger are not generally in conflict with the smaller units but broadly subsume the more specific and more intimate ties. But where overlapping groups are noninclusive, where some members of one group belong to another and other members of the first do not, then group loyalties may truly come into conflict. Thus in modern society, where ties to neighborhood, church, occupation group, and fraternity are each individually contracted, the sentiments invoked by each may differ, and the group loyalties may draw the individuals apart rather than serve to reinforce one another and strengthen the sense of commitment.

Evolutionary Change in Groups

Among the most primitive peoples in the world we usually find only two spatial groupings, the band and the tribe, and these tend to have considerable uniformity in their character. The *band* is a group which shares a common territory and exploits it as a unit. Its members defend it against trespass to protect their resources. Normally they spend most of the year together, wandering through their territory in search of food and using their knowledge of the variant possibilities and difficulties as the seasons progress. When they split up into small units, they do so out of economic necessity, and they come together again when conditions permit. The fate of the members is closely tied to the group. Furthermore, an individual normally lives his full life within the group, except that persons from different groups may marry, a fact which requires one partner to move into the territory of the other. Usually it is the wife who comes to her husband's band. This setup is called *patrilocal,* or more properly, *virilocal residence.* This places an emphasis upon the paternal line, which may be further emphasized by a rule that all men must marry outside their band. Under such circumstances the band forms a kind of lineage and may be considered familistic in the sense that the band members consider themselves to be somewhat of a kin group. Fundamentally, however, it is a residence group, for normally the wives represent a wide source of alternate bands.

Everywhere under these primitive circumstances there is a larger social entity which is generally called a *tribe.* It is normally made up of a number of bands; it usually has a name; it has a clearly delimited territory; and usually its members feel that they share certain distinctive features of culture and language. But under the most primitive circumstances, the tribe is not an action unit; it is, so to speak, only a sentiment. The members of the tribe do not get together, for instance; they have no means of organizing for common action; they have no common governance. An Andaman Islander will say that he belongs to a certain band which is part of a certain tribe, and he can give you the boundaries of each. But you may also discover that his band is at war with another belonging to the same tribe and in this fight is allied with a third band that belongs to an alien tribe. Yet the Andamanese tribal sentiment exists.

These two spatial groupings persist throughout much of human history and in pretty much the same way. Under more advanced conditions, the band turns into a village, or perhaps even a town; but these villages tend to be autonomous. The Indians of central California were organized into autonomous villages, sometimes called *tribelets,* which recognized themselves as part of a large group having a common culture and dialect. Because they were more closely spaced, several would sometimes come together under a common leader, but again not as a tribe, not with that consciousness of nationhood which we assume in modern life. The same may be said for the still richer peoples farther north on the coasts of Canada and Alaska, and for most of the peoples whose economy is based upon horticulture. At this level other groupings tend to provide a means for unifying action and giving a greater degree of social cohesion to the tribe as a whole. Yet the tribe rarely takes on a truly political character.

Some horticultural peoples hold a wide area together through weakly established political ties. This is particularly true in parts of Africa and Middle America, even where farming techniques are not advanced. With the development of agriculture the possibility of nationhood is increased, and larger political entities are held together through the concentration of power. The village entity continues, and most peasants retain their ties to the local community. Under such circumstances intermediate levels of spatial groupings—counties or regions—may emerge. Where cities exist, wards or neighborhoods may appear and serve those who live in close proximity with mutual ties.

In broad outline, spatial groups have tended to spread outward; yet the core of a local group sharing a territory remains constant through most of human history. This core has been somewhat undermined by modern means of transportation, particularly the automobile. Larger unified geographical units that capture some of man's loyalties, and which we call states, were a relatively late development, impeded perhaps by a generic xenophobia—which is the reverse side of ties to the familiar.

At the most primitive level, family groups tend to be small units, comprising a man and wife and their unmarried children. Polygyny is generally allowed but rarely prevalent. This family unit shares a common hearth, and its adult members have their appointed tasks by means of which each contributes to the common welfare. This household—if it can be so called in the absence of houses—is the regular commensal group; it is in a sense independent of all other groups, yet it is closely tied through the band to other co-ordinate groups. At this level there is rarely any extension of such family unity, except where, as noted, the band takes on a kind of familistic quality. Among certain Australians, elaborate ties of kinship set up a series of kin groupings, though the kind and degree of their unity of action is far from clear. Clans are occasionally found.

It is with further technological development that the clan begins to assume a place of importance in the group life of primitive peoples, often dominating it at the expense of spatial unity. The clan builds its loyalty on the sentiment of kinship, drawing its members widely from within the tribe, and creating a unity by arbitrary rules of descent. A true clan is exogamous, so that it inevitably splits the family (or hearth group); each spouse is a member of a different clan and the children are all members of one or the other, according to the rule of descent that prevails.

The role of clans in the system of authority will appear later. Here, however, we must note that among many peoples the clan sentiments dominate every action. The clan becomes a kind of corporation—or corporate group, as it is called in current anthropological literature— continuing as an entity through time, holding land and other privileges, and having an internal structure providing for unity of action. The spiritual unity of each member with his clan is so great that the clan is responsible for the acts of the individual, and the individual is responsible for the acts of the clan.

In such more developed systems, the family or hearth group generally continues. The process of procreation involves two persons, and each child must be nurtured close to the woman at least. Often, however, clan loyalties are so strong that a child must live with his clan rather than with his parents, and in matrilineal societies he may therefore go to live with his mother's brother (to whose clan he belongs) rather than with his father.

Where clans dominate the organizational machinery of society, there may be groupings of clans into larger entities (which are called *phratries*) and subdivisions of them into *lineages,* or localized units within the clan. The variations on the theme are legion, so that scholars argue over definitions, inclusions, and borderline cases. But the central notion of a large group based on the arbitrary and artificial extension of kin sentiments, having economic and social functions, and unified by common ceremonies and by common religious and other symbols, is widely recurrent in that middle range of social systems which lies between the hunters and food-gatherers on one hand, and the developed political states on the other.

Where statehood enters, the clan withers, for reasons that will emerge later. Clans may continue to exist and demand loyalties, as in the relatively impotent social entities that continued in China, until recent years at least. They may take on new functions, as they had tended to in the kingdom of Buganda before European penetration. Or they may be transformed into wards or *barrios,* as some Aztec scholars believe happened to the calpulli, the twenty patrilineal geographical divisions.

Nor do we find industrial society maintaining the extended kinship ties for the organization of social life, though in modern Japan old feudal patterns retain some force and are woven into the modern industrial system. Under these conditions the family of parents and children regain importance, though the emphasis may be either on the line of descent (as is usually the case among peasants), or on the marital couple and their immature children, as it is with us.

The general evolutionary trend of kin-based group life involves the generic difference between the immediate family or hearth group and those special groups built outward into larger social units. The former are always present. They are more important under both the most primitive conditions of life and the most advanced, tending to be submerged only in the middle range of social development. The latter are absent or relatively unimportant at the primitive level, rise to frequent dominance in the middle range, decline in importance under primitive political states, and disappear entirely under conditions of industrial production.

Special-interest groups are rare at the most primitive levels of social existence. Occasionally a group of initiated men will be distinguished and form a kind of secret association, which cuts across both kin and geographical ties. Some Australian tribes have totemic groups, made up of people whose spirits come from the same body of mythical ancestors (not a matter of paternity or maternity, but dependent upon a determination of what spirit entered the womb to bring about conception). Such units are rare.

In the middle range non-kin groups are increasingly important. Among the Indians of central California, there was a relatively weak secret society of men; on the Northwest Coast it was stronger, and such special associations were widely present in the horticultural communities of Melanesia, Africa, and North America. There is always a magico-religious aspect to such groups. They are characterized by ritual induction or initiations, by secret rites and ceremonies, and by a system of mythological justification. Often they also have a power function, uniting the senior men, the adults, or some specially selected group as against the women and children or all outsiders. Occasionally there are countervailing women's organizations. Such specially segregated sexual groups appear at the most primitive levels, but they seem to be more virulent at the more advanced, and it would be worth examining the degree to which they are associated with increased feminine power resulting from the predominantly female economic functions that develop under horticultural circumstances.

Special-interest groups continue through the remainder of social evolution, increasing in importance as the specialization of labor differentiates the life activities of various segments of the society. State systems generally have some form of guilds for each major occupation. There is almost always a special priesthood and often a ruling group. Under such economic conditions, those with the highest status are frequently a group apart, a point to which we shall turn when we discuss the subject of status.

The evolution of special-interest groups involves a gradual increase from virtual absence at the most primitive level to a great proliferation in industrial society. The earlier groupings are based largely on religious belief and separate out a body of males. At the advanced end of the scale, groups are concerned chiefly with occupation and with social and economic cooperation.

30. The Primary Group

CHARLES HORTON COOLEY

Charles H. Cooley focused sociological attention on the primary group. One of the founders of sociology, he recognized that the individual acquires his values and attitudes in the process of socialization. The family and other small groups within which the individual operates, transmit these cultural elements to the individual. In focusing on the primary group, Cooley was therefore not only pointing out an aspect of social organization, but was also developing a basic thesis about the way culture is transmitted and the individual is adapted to his culture.

Reprinted with the permission of Charles Scribner's Sons from *Social Organization* by Charles Horton Cooley, copyright 1909 Charles Scribner's Sons; renewal copyright 1937 Elsie Jones Cooley.

By primary groups I mean those characterized by intimate face-to-face association and cooperation. They are primary in several senses, but chiefly in that they are fundamental in forming the social nature and ideals of the individual. The result of intimate association, psychologically, is a certain fusion of individualities in a common whole, so that one's very self, for many purposes at least, is the common life and purpose of the group. Perhaps the simplest way of describing this wholeness is by saying that it is a "we"; it involves the sort of sympathy and mutual identification for which "we" is the natural expression. One lives in the feeling of the whole and finds the chief aims of his will in that feeling.

It is not to be supposed that the unity of the primary group is one of mere harmony and love. It is always a differentiated and usually a competitive unity, admitting of self-assertion and various appropriative passions; but these passions are socialized by sympathy, and come, or tend to come, under the discipline of a common spirit. The individual will be ambitious, but the chief object of his ambition will be some desired place in the thought of the others, and he will feel allegiance to common standards of service and fair play. So the boy will dispute with his fellows a place on the team, but above such disputes will place the common glory of his class and school.

The most important spheres of this intimate association and cooperation—though by no means the only ones—are the family, the playgroup of children, and the neighborhood or community group of elders. These are practically universal, belonging to all times and all stages of development; and are accordingly a chief basis of what is universal in human nature and human ideals. The best comparative studies of the family, such as those of Westermarck or Howard, show it to us as not only a universal institution, but as more alike the world over than the exaggeration of exceptional customs by an earlier school had led us to suppose. Nor can any one doubt the general prevalence of play-groups among children or of informal assemblies of various kinds among their elders. Such association is clearly the nursery of human nature in the world about us, and there is no apparent reason to suppose that the case has anywhere or at any time been essentially different.

As regards play, I might, were it not a matter of common observation, multiply illustrations of the universality and spontaneity of the group discussion and cooperation to which it gives rise. The general fact is that children, especially boys after about their twelfth year, live in fellowships in which their sympathy, ambition and honor are engaged even more, often, than they are in the family. Most of us can recall examples of the endurance by boys of injustice and even cruelty, rather than appeal from their fellows to parents or teachers—as, for instance, in the hazing so prevalent at schools, and so difficult, for this very reason, to repress. And how elaborate the discussion, how cogent the public opinion, how hot the ambitions in these fellowships. . . .

Of the neighborhood group it may be said, in general, that from the time men formed permanent settlements upon the land, down, at least, to the rise of modern industrial cities, it has played a main part in the primary, heart-to-heart life of the people. Among our Teutonic forefathers the village community was apparently the chief sphere of sympathy and mutual aid for the commons all through the "dark" and middle ages, and for many purposes it remains so in rural districts at the present day. In some countries we still find it with all its ancient vitality, notably in Russia, where the mir, or self-governing village group, is the main theatre of life, along with the family, for perhaps fifty millions of peasants.

In our own life the intimacy of the neighborhood has been broken up by the growth of an intricate mesh of wider contacts which leaves us strangers to people who live in the same house. And even in the country the same principle is at work, though less obviously, diminishing our economic and spiritual community with our neighbors. How far this change is a healthy development, and how far a disease, is perhaps still uncertain.

Besides these almost universal kinds of primary association, there are many others whose form depends upon the particular state of civilization; the only essential thing, as I have said, being a certain intimacy and fusion of personalities. In our own society, being little bound by place, people easily form clubs, fraternal societies and the like, based on congeniality, which may give rise to real intimacy. . . .

But the fact that the family and neighborhood groups are ascendant in the open and plastic time of childhood makes them even now incomparably more influential than all the rest.

Primary groups are primary in the sense that they give the individual his earliest and completest experience of social unity, and also in the sense that they do not change in the same degree as more elaborate relations, but form a comparatively permanent source out of which the latter are ever springing. Of course they are not independent of the larger society, but to some extent reflect its spirit; as the German family and the German school bear somewhat distinctly the print of German militarism. But this, after all, is like the tide setting back into creeks, and does not commonly go very far. Among the German, and still more among the Russian, peasantry are found habits of free cooperation and discussion almost uninfluenced by the character of the state; and it is a familiar and well-supported view that the village commune, self-governing as regards local affairs and habituated to discussion, is a very widespread institution in settled communities, and the continuator of a similar autonomy previously existing in the clan. "It is man who makes monarchies and establishes republics, but the commune seems to come directly from the hand of God." [de Tocqueville]

In our own cities the crowded tenements and the general economic and social confusion have sorely wounded the family and the neighborhood, but it is remarkable, in view of these conditions, what vitality they show; and there is nothing upon which the conscience of the time is more determined than upon restoring them to health.

These groups, then, are springs of life, not only for the individual but for social institutions. They are only in part moulded by special traditions, and, in larger degree, express a universal nature. The religion or government of other civilizations may seem alien to us, but the children or the family group wear the common life, and with them we can always make ourselves at home.

31. The Absence of Group Affiliations

HARVEY W. ZORBAUGH

The importance of group membership to human behavior can most forcefully be demonstrated by examples of the absence of group ties, such as the one printed here. This essay is largely devoted to the account of a young girl who went to the big city, was cut off entirely from home and never succeeded in developing social relationships in Chicago. The consequences of this failure to identify with any social groups are clearly set forth. The essay is part of one of the earlier efforts to survey urban life in terms of sociological theory. It appeared in *The Gold Coast and the Slum, A Sociological Study of Chicago's Near North Side,* Chicago: The University of Chicago Press, 1929, in a chapter entitled "The World of the Furnished Room."

Harvey W. Zorbaugh is now in the executive office of the Communication Arts Group of New York University. The essay is printed here with the kind permission of the author.

Back of the ostentatious apartments, hotels, and homes of the Lake Shore Drive, and the quiet, shady streets of the Gold Coast lies an area of streets that have a painful sameness, with their old, soot-begrimed stone houses, their none-too-clean alleys, their shabby air of respectability. In the window of house after house along these streets one sees a black and white card with the words "Rooms To Rent." For this is the world of furnished rooms, a world of strangely unconventional customs and people, one of the most characteristic of the worlds that go to make up the life of the great city.

This nondescript world, like every rooming-house district, has a long and checkered history. . . .

An analysis of the *Illinois Lodging House Register* reveals the fact that there are 1,139 rooming- and lodging-houses on the Near North Side, and that in these houses 23,007 people are living in furnished rooms of one kind and another. Ninety blocks in the better rooming area north of Chicago Avenue were studied intensively, by means of a house-to-house census. This study revealed the additional facts that 71 per cent of all the houses in this district keep roomers; and that of the people who live in these rooms, 52 per cent are single men, 10 per cent are single women, and 38 per cent are couples, "married," supposedly with "benefit of clergy." The rooming-house area is a childless area. Yet most of its population is in the productive ages of life, between twenty and thirty-five.

The rooming-house is typically a large, old-fashioned residence, though many apartments are converted into rooming-houses as well. And the population living in these rooming-houses is typically what the labor leader refers to as the "white collar" group—men and women filling various clerical positions—accountants, stenographers, and the like, office workers of various sorts. There are also students from the many music schools of the Near North Side. Most of them are living on a narrow margin, and here they can live cheaply, near enough to the Loop to walk to and from their work if they wish.

The constant comings and goings of its inhabitants is the most striking and significant characteristic of this world of furnished rooms. This whole population turns over every four months. There are always cards in the windows, advertising the fact that rooms are vacant, but these cards rarely have to stay up over a day, as people are constantly walking the streets looking for rooms. The keepers of the rooming-houses change almost as rapidly as the roomers themselves. At least half of the keepers of these houses have been at their present addresses six months or less. . . .

The rooming-house which has replaced the boarding-house is a very different sort of place to live. It has no dining-room, no parlor, no common meeting place. Few acquaintanceships spring up in a rooming-house. . . .

Such complete anonymity could be found nowhere but in the city of today, and nowhere in the city save in the rooming-house.

The peculiar social relationships of the world of furnished rooms are reflected in the behavior of the people who live in this world. Nothing could bring this out more clearly and significantly than the story which follows, the life-story of a "charity girl."

Emporia, Kansas, was my home until I was twenty-two. My father had a small business there. He was an upright, God-fearing man. . . . He taught us to obey the Ten Commandments, to go to church on Sunday, to do all the things the "respectable" do in a small, gossiping place.

We were a large family but father managed to save enough to send me, the oldest, to a small college in the state. And from the time I was a little girl I had music lessons. It is about these music lessons that the story of my life revolves.

I was always looked upon as something of a prodigy about the town. At ten I played at Chopin and Bach. I played my little pieces at church recitals, at firemen's benefits, when mother entertained the Ladies' Aid Society, and at our high school graduating exercises. I was told that I had talent, "wonderful feeling for the soul of the masters," that I ought to go to New York, or abroad, where I could have competent instruction; that some day I would be a concert star.

Through my fours years of college this ambition slumbered, but never died. And the day I got my diploma I wrote home that instead of going back to Emporia to marry a "Babbitt" and live on "Main Street," I was going to Chicago to study music. I went home for a stormy week. Father was amazed that I should suggest living alone in Chicago, and sternly forbade my going, saying that if I did he would send me no money—indeed, he had little to send. Mother said little, but when I left she put into my hand fifty dollars which she had been saving for a new dress. All told, when my ticket was bought, I had less than one hundred dollars on which to begin the conquest of a career.

Never shall I forget the time of the night that I arrived at the Northwestern Station, my purse clutched tightly in one hand, and my bag in the other, shaking my head at redcaps, confused and dazzled by the glare of the lights—but my heart singing, my ambition aflame; it was the gate to the promised land. I went to the Travelers' Aid Bureau and inquired how to get to the Y.W.C.A. I walked uptown, carrying my bag, too excited to be tired. I still remember the romantic appeal the sluggish blackness of the river made, gleaming in the lights of the great electric signs. How differently it was to look two short years later!

The first few weeks went by like magic. It was all so strange and maddeningly stimulating to my small-town soul. The "Y" was a pleasant enough place to live—not at all the institutional sort of place I had expected it to be. But even in these first weeks I began to know what loneliness is. Most of my evenings were spent sitting in corners of the sitting-room, watching the old girls playing the piano and victrola, or entertaining their beaux. I got acquainted with a few other newcomers —a girl from Indiana who came to study, like myself, a girl who came from Alabama to get work as stenographer, and four or five others, from small towns in Illinois. All but myself seemed to have acquaintances or connections of some sort in Chicago. And sometimes, when I felt too unbearably lonely, I would go back to the big station in the evening, at the time when the train I came on would be coming in, and watch the faces in the crowd for a face from Emporia.

It was at the "Y" that I had my first acquaintance with that most pitiable figure of the rooming-house world—the old and unmarried woman who works. They were conspicuous in either the cafeteria or the upstairs sitting-room, because of their loneliness—eating lunch at a solitary table, sitting by themselves knitting, with shabby and unbecoming clothes, care-worn faces, and toil-worn hands. I was to learn later some of the tragedies their mute lips harbored.

After six weeks at the "Y" I moved to the Near North Side, to be nearer my music school. And during the next few months I lived at a dozen rooming-houses and homes for girls. The boarding-homes were more comfortable and pleasant, but I was working all day and taking lessons at night. I was out late, and this conflicted with their rules. I soon found a rooming-house was the only place I could live. But it was hard to find a rooming-house where I wanted to live. The rooms I could afford were in gloomy old houses on La Salle Street, bleak and bare, and so large that usually I had to share them with one or two other girls. The beds were hard, and often vermin-infested. The landladies were queer-looking and dowdy, tight-lipped and suspicious of eye, ignorant and coarse. They rarely took any other interest in you than to see that you paid your week in advance. The men and women living in the house were mostly a tough lot. There were goings on that shocked me then—though I would pay scant attention to them now.

My first year is a nightmare as I look back upon it. In order to keep clothes on my back and to pay for my lessons I had to work seven days in the week. My college education had fitted me for nothing. I tried one thing after another—salesgirl at Marshall Field's, milliner's helper, running a simple machine in a garment factory, ushering at a movie, and finally waiting at a "white tile" restaurant. Somehow I never held any of the positions very long.

The days were long and exhausting—up at six, a bath, a cup of coffee on a "sterno" stove, tidy my room a bit, and in the Loop by seven-thirty or eight. Then a long steady grind until five; a mile walk out to my rooming-house; supper in a nearby restaurant—and a plain supper at that; the evening devoted to my lesson or practicing; back to my room at ten-thirty or eleven, often too tired to undress until I had slept an hour or so.

I had come to the city in June. By Christmas my loneliness amounted almost to desperation. I had made no friends—a girl brought up on the Commandments doesn't make friends in rooming-houses or as a waitress very readily. I didn't talk the same language as the girls I worked with. At the theater or the restaurant men often came up to me and said things in a way that made me blush, though often I had no idea what they meant, unsophisticated little fool that I was. Mother was ill, and letters from home came less and less frequently. Shortly after Christmas she died, and the last tie that bound me to Emporia was gone. I was "on my own," and very nearly "on my uppers" as well. But I still had my ambition—I would some day be a great *artiste,* and all this loneliness and hardship would be forgotten. . . .

In February, I think it was, I met a girl from Tennessee at the music school, with whom I became quite friendly. Within a few weeks we decided to get a room together, and we moved over to a house on Dearborn, just north of Division. The house consists of several large old residences thrown together. It has perhaps forty rooms, and there have been as many as seventy roomers in it at one time. It is cleaner than the run of rooming-houses, and quieter, and the man and the woman who run it are decent enough. But you would never mistake it for anything else than a rooming-house. Somehow, one gets to loathe that card in the window—"Rooms"! And the life and people were not much different from those on La Salle Street.

One gets to know few people in a rooming-house, for there are constant comings and goings, and there is little chance to get acquainted if one wished. But one doesn't wish. . . . There were occasional little dramas—as when a baby was found in the alley, and when the woman in "the third floor back" took poison after a quarrel with her husband, or when police came to arrest a man who had eloped from Pittsburg with his wife's sister, and a new trio of roomers robbed most of the "guests" on the second floor; there were these occasional little dramas when the halls and bathrooms were the scenes of a few minutes' hurried and curious gossip. But the next day these same people would hurry past each other on the stairs without speaking.

As the months went by, my lessons cost more and more; I had to work shorter hours to get in my practice; our room was costing more; and I found myself always a week or so behind. It was a humiliating experience to have to cajole the landlady into giving me credit— humiliating to a girl who had been brought up to believe it wrong to have debts. But I got so that I could invent a reason for putting it off as brazenly as the "gold digger" in the next room.

[A year of this had gone by, when one day her music teacher told her there was no hope of her ever realizing her ambitions.] I turned dazedly from the piano . . . I scarcely heard him. I picked up my music and tossed it into a waste-basket in the corner; and then I walked out of the room.

It was late afternoon, and I walked the streets, neither noticing nor caring where, until late that night I ended up along the embankment in Lincoln Park, and sat down exhausted, on the stone wall by the lake. My head was a bit clearer by now, and I began to take stock of myself. . . .

The ambition for which I had sacrificed, which had kept me alive and going, was dead. There was nothing to hold me to home and family. Mother was dead. No one ever wrote. And my oldest brother, in Chicago a few months before, had told me that father never allowed my name to be mentioned about the house, save to use me as a horrible example of the wilful daughter gone wrong—he once referred to me as a street-walker. Those words kept repeating themselves in my mind —"street-walker, street-walker!" And a great bitterness burned in my heart, turning to ashes every love, every tie, every ideal that had held me at home.

Then I began to look at my life in Chicago. What was there in it, after all? My music was gone. I had neither family nor friends. In Emporia there would at least have been neighborhood clubs or the church. But here there was neither. Oh, for someone or something to belong to!

My room-mate had been going to Sunday night services at the Fourth Presbyterian Church, over on the Lake Shore Drive. She told them about me, and one day some pastor's assistant's assistant came to call on me. I went one night after that. I was greeted with ostentatious and half-hearted civility. It was all so impersonal. . . . I never went back; and no other church ever took an interest in me. The only other group I had had anything to do with, outside of my work, had been a social agency from which I had tried to get a little help in the spring. They treated me as impersonally as though I had been a rag doll. There was ringing of buzzers, long documents with endless questionings to be filled out—and not a human touch in it all.

The city is like that. In all my work there had been the same lack of any personal touch. In all this city of three million souls I knew no one, cared for no one, was cared for by no one. In a popular science story in the evening newspaper a few days before I had read how the universe is composed of millions of stars whirling about. I looked up at the sky. I was just like that—an atom whirled about with three million other atoms, day after day, month after month, year after year.

What *did* I have? I had no clothes, no shows, no leisure—none of the things all girls are supposed to love. My health was breaking under the strain. I was in debt. The answer was, Nothing—absolutely nothing! And there stretched ahead of me long years of nothing, until I married an honest but poor clerk or salesman and tried to make ends meet for a brood of hungry mouths, or until I became one of those broken-down, old working women that I had patronizingly pitied that first week at the Y.W.C.A.

Of course, there were two ways out: I might slip into the lake, there, and end it all. But somehow I didn't think seriously of that. Or I might do as some of the girls in the house, become a "gold digger," play life for what there was in it, pay with what there was in me. The idea half-sickened me, yet I played with it for a while—for so long that I drew up startled at the unknown possibilities that lurked within me, cold at the thought that there was neither person nor thing to hold me back.

I never went back to music school. I had been working as a waitress of late, . . . and I kept on with it. But the days and nights were empty now—and at last I knew to the full what loneliness could be. One night a nice boy came into the restaurant—it was one of the larger downtown restaurants—and sat down at my table. He talked to me, as they all did; told me he was from a small town in Oklahoma, that he'd made money, and had come to see the big city. He was friendly, and ended by asking me to a show. I accepted, and we went to a cabaret afterward. In a spirit of reckless bravado, to show the small-town boy I was a city-wise woman, I smoked my first cigarette and took my first drink.

There's no use in making a story of it. He had an engaging smile, and was in search of adventure. I was unutterably lonely—and tired. He said that he loved me, and I was willing not to question too closely. I left the rooming-house, and we took a little flat out near Rogers Park. For a month I played at being respectable, got acquainted with young wives in other apartments, had lovely clothes, lazy hours, ate at the best restaurants, saw the best shows, shopped in smart shops, drove my own car. Then, one day, B. came home and told me he was going back to Oklahoma, and that I wasn't going with him. I said little; I had known it must come, of course, though I had hoped it wouldn't come so soon. There was a generous check. And I moved back into the rooming-house.

No, I felt no remorse. Life had cheated me. There was no one to care. Why slave and work when I might have the things I wanted? And not the least of these was the intimate touch and glance of a man —even if it were half make-believe. Someone to talk intimately with, someone to come home to, someone to ask where you've been—these, too, are things one can't live without.

32. Group Solidarity among the Tlingit

KALERVO OBERG

The group demands loyalty in return for providing support, as well as being the means of socializing the individual. Where a man's group is based on kinship, is heavily sanctioned by religious beliefs, and shares its economic circumstances, its demands upon him may be absolute. This essay deals with such groups—the clans among the Tlingit Indians. Group responsibility not only demanded that a person endanger his life for the welfare of the clan, but that he actually sacrifice his life in order to maintain its position in society. This essay treats with Tlingit law in general, and only one small aspect of clan life (it will be well to look back at this selection when reading the section on Authority), but it does demonstrate the degree to which they view the clan as a legal entity—very much as our law treats the corporation as an individual.

Kalervo Oberg took his Ph.D. degree from the University of Chicago in 1937, having studied the Tlingit Indians for his doctoral dissertation. He has subsequently done research in Brazil, where he long resided as an American civil servant before moving to Surinam. The selection is taken from "Crime and Punishment in Tlingit Society," *American Anthropologist*, Volume 36, No. 2, 1934, and is printed here by the kind permission of the editor and the author.

Every Tlingit is born into one of three matrilineal phratries. He is either a Tlaienedi, a Shinkukedi, or a Nekadi. If he is a Tlaienedi, he calls himself a Raven; if a Shinkukedi, a Wolf, if a Nekadi, an Eagle. The Nekadi, however, are so few in number that they may be neglected, and we may speak of the Tlingit as Ravens and Wolves, each person referring to a member of the other phratry as his opposite. The members of a phratry consider themselves blood relatives and prohibit marriage within the group. A phratry possesses no territory, has no property, no political unity, no chiefs. While members of a phratry perform certain types of labor and ceremonies for their opposites, it is not the phratry that acts as a unit.

What is more important to a Tlingit is the fact that he is born a member of a clan. This clan has a name denoting its place of origin, a story of its genesis, a history of its migrations. The crests of the phratries have become securely established through a tradition reaching back to the mythical beginnings of the Tlingit people. The crests of the clans, on the other hand, are not on so secure a foundation. A clan possesses a number of these crests or emblems which it has gained in numerous ways throughout its history and the right to them is often questioned by other clans of the same phratry. These crests, along with songs, dances, legends, and face paintings, are jealously guarded by the clans. But the clan as a whole has no property.

The local division of the clan, however, possesses definite territories for hunting and fishing, houses in the village, and has a chief or ceremonial leader. While labor, ceremonies and potlatches are performed by members of one phratry for the members of the other, it is the clan that forms the active nucleus. In practice it is a wife's clan that builds a man's house or buries him. It is a clan that invites clans of the opposite side to a potlatch. It is a clan that carries on feuds and sees that customary law is enforced.

From what has been said it would seem that the clan was a group of great solidarity, and theoretically this is true. In practice, however, this solidarity is weakened by individual status. Within the clan every person has his or her rank which is definitely known. The people of higher status, the anyeti, wield considerable power through their position and wealth, and are able to decide legal issues to their own advantage at the expense of their less important kinsmen.

In the matter of crime and punishment, the relation of the individual and the clan comes out clearly. Theoretically, crime against an individual did not exist. The loss of an individual by murder, the loss of property by theft, or shame brought to a member of a clan, were clan losses and the clan demanded an equivalent in revenge. That is to say, if a man of low rank killed a man of high rank in another clan, the murderer often went free while one of his more important kinsmen suffered death in his stead. Slight differences in status could be overcome by payments of property, but the general demand in case of murder was the life of a man of equal rank. In some instances the offending clan was of lower status and therefore none of its members could compensate for a crime committed against an important clan. It was therefore necessary to select a clan of the offender's phratry that could show some relationship to the offending clan; but in this case war usually followed, as this procedure was not legally established. In general, it made no difference whether the opposing clans were in the same phratry or in opposite phratries. Some of the bitterest feuds were between the Ganaktedi and Tluknakadi, both of the same phratry.

Thus a clan appears to be the group of greatest unity, solidarity, and integration. There was no penalty within the clan for murder, adultery, or theft. A clan punished its members by death only when shame was brought to its honor. Crimes of this nature were incest, witchcraft, marriage with a slave, and prostitution.

Murder among the Tlingit was punishable by death when committed outside the clan. The number of murders, however, was not excessive until the advent of liquor. In the old days rivalry over women and disputes about individual privileges during potlatches sometimes led to murder. Murder was generally committed in the heat of argument, and if clansmen of both sides were present, a general fight was prevented by a chief of high rank stepping between the angry clansmen with an important crest in his hand. It was considered a desecration of the emblem or crest if fighting occurred under these circumstances.

Immediately after a murder was committed spokesmen from both clans met to decide who was to die in compensation for the murder. If the murdered man happened to be of low rank and of poor reputation, a payment of goods could satisfy the injured clan. But if the murdered man was of high rank, a man of equal standing was demanded from the murderer's clan. There was generally much haggling over the rank of the murdered man and the rank of the one who was to die in compensation. These disputes always appeared in the peace dance which followed the complete settlement of the crime. The man selected as compensation prepared to die willingly. He was given much time to prepare himself through fasting and praying. The execution took place before his house.

On the day set for the execution, the man put on all his ceremonial robes and displayed all his crests and emblems. He came out of his house, stood at the doorway, and related his history, stressing the deeds that he and his ancestors had performed. All the villagers were gathered around for this solemn occasion. He then looked across to the clan whom his death was to satisfy to observe the man who had been selected to kill him. If this man was great and honorable he would step forth gladly; but if the man was of low rank he would return to the house and wait until a man of his own rank or higher was selected to kill him. When this was done he stepped forth boldly with his spear in his hand, singing a girl's puberty song. He feigned attack but permitted himself to be killed. To die thus for the honor of one's clan was considered an act of great bravery and the body was laid out in state as that of a great warrior. His soul went to Kiwa-Kawaw, "highest heaven."

The actual murderer, if a man of great rank and wealth, often went free, but if the man was of low rank and came from a poor house he went as a slave to that house in his clan which had given up a man in compensation for the murder. If property was passed as partial payment to the murdered man's clan, the actual murderer could be handed over as a slave. Even if the murderer was not forced into slavery, his position was an uncomfortable one. There was a feeling of very close unity among clansmen and when one had brought shame to his own clan, he felt the matter keenly and for a time led a miserable life. . . .

Theoretically, stealing did not exist within the clan. Natural resources were held in common and food was but loosely guarded by the various house groups within the clan. If a man took a tool or a weapon that belonged to a member of his own clan, he was forced to return it. If a man of low rank was caught stealing from another clan, the injured clan could kill him. If he was of high rank, his own clan would make reparation by a payment of goods. If, by some chance, a man of very high rank was caught stealing, he was said to be bewitched. Then a shamanistic performance was held over him to discover the sorcerer who had forced him to steal in order to injure his social position. The sorcerer when discovered was killed and the crime thus compensated.

If anyone beside the clansmen or those invited were caught taking fish from clan territories, or if they were caught hunting there, they could be killed. This was also true if anyone trespassed on clan domain or used their trade routes. Sometimes when a powerful party came to fish on another clan's territory, the owning clan would invite the transgressors to a feast, treat them well, and give them presents. This they did to shame the aggressors, who generally withdrew after such treatment. If a man was hungry he could shoot an animal in someone else's territory, but he was forced to give the hide or pelt to the owning clan.

Adopting the crest of another clan was considered stealing, but the aggressor always claimed the right to the crest through some event in the past. Conflict over the use of crests led to war between the clans or was settled by the opinion of the phratry or the transfer of property. . . .

If a man was injured or accidentally killed while out hunting with the members of another clan, this clan would have to compensate the dead or injured man's clan by a payment of goods. If the man killed was of very high rank and his death could be shown to be due to the carelessness of his hosts, then the dead man's clan could demand that a man of the hosts' clan be killed.

If a person was injured by a dog belonging to another clan, the owner of the dog would compensate for the injury by a payment of goods to the injured man. Harm coming to pass through another clan's property had very wide ramifications and was always settled by a payment of goods. Falling twice before a man's house would entitle the one who fell to ask for a payment of goods. Catching a chill in another man's house, injuring one's self with another man's tools, or becoming angry or irritable due to contact with others, would give a right to a small payment of goods, provided these injuries were caused by members of another clan.

Another example of this appears in the case of suicide. If it could be shown that a man had committed suicide because his wife had treated him badly, then a man of his wife's clan could be selected and killed. Therefore a Tlingit woman was very careful how she treated her husband. This punishment was also meted out to others who caused a man to commit suicide.

Many articles, such as canoes, tools, traps, weapons, and such lesser ceremonial gear as masks and dancing shirts, were owned by individuals. Other individuals, either within the clan or outside, could borrow these, provided they brought them back or replaced them at some later date. If the borrower failed to return the article within a reasonable time, the lender could disseminate stories of ridicule about him. These stories were somewhat in the nature of the paddle songs of the Tsimshian, but not so highly stylized, and like the paddle songs they heaped ridicule upon the debtor until he came to terms. These stories were used only when it was well known that the debtor was able to pay but refused for selfish reasons. If these stories did not have the desired effect, the creditor could discuss the matter with members of his own clan. If the debtor belonged to the same clan and was in a position to pay, the social pressure of the clan was sufficient to bring him to terms. If, however, he was unable to pay and there was little likelihood of his ever being able to pay, the clan would permit the creditor to take the debtor as a debt slave. . . .

If the debtor belonged to another clan, a different procedure took place after ridicule ceased to have effect. The creditor would have a crest of the debtor's clan made which he placed on the front of his own house or on a totem pole. Among the Tlingit clan crests were jealously guarded, and the fact that another clan had taken one brought great shame to the clan to which it belonged. All the people in the village would at once notice it and the story come out. The debtor's clan was now dishonored and would make considerable efforts to pay the debt. Usually a wealthy house group paid the debt and took the debtor as a debt slave, thus saving the honor of the clan.

The taking of an important clan crest was always resorted to in the case of a prestige potlatch. If a clan refused to give a return potlatch to another clan of the opposite phratry, the creditor clan could take a crest and keep it until payment was made.

Names could be used in place of crests for debt exactions. Names, like crests, were clan property and were not supposed to go outside the clan. An interesting case of name adoption occurred at Klukwan. It happened that a Chilcat Indian was engaged by Lieutenant Schwatka as a guide when he made his famous trip into the interior. Schwatka had promised the Indian a certain sum of money which, it is said, he did not pay. The Indian promptly took Schwatka's name, which is still in use among the people of Klukwan. The name is now pronounced Swatki and is of great importance in the Daklawedi clan of Klukwan. During wars between clans, names and even crests were taken in payment to bring about the equality which is a prerequisite of peace. Names sometimes remained permanently in a foreign clan, but crests were sooner or later brought back.

The above is a brief summary of the main types of Tlingit crimes and their punishment. From this summary certain social characteristics stand out prominently. The first of these is the importance of a clan as a sovereign group. The second is the importance of individual status.

33. Primary Group Loyalty in Military Action

EDWARD A. SHILS and MORRIS JANOWITZ

Group loyalty is as important to the modern soldier as it is to the primitive warrior. The practical importance of group identification has increasingly been realized by the military, both in America and Europe. This essay demonstrates that a primary factor in morale (as evidenced by a low rate of surrender and desertion) is the solidarity with and loyalty to a group. It demonstrates how the group operates to serve the psychological needs of the individual; even the transitory primary group of a military unit calls for strong loyalties and sentiments.

Edward A. Shils took his doctorate in political science from the University of Pennsylvania in 1940. He is widely known for his contributions to sociological theory, and has taught both in America and in England. Morris Janowitz took his Ph.D. from the University of Chicago in sociology and is at present Professor of Sociology at the University of Michigan. He has been a consultant to the President's Committee on Civil Rights, the Committee on Human Resources, the Resources and Development Board of the National Military Establishment, and for the United States Department of the Army. He is co-author of *Dynamics of Prejudice*, co-editor of *A Reader in Public Opinion and Communication*, and the author of *The Community Press in an Urban Setting*.

The material below is taken from their "Cohesion and Disintegration in the Wehrmacht in World War II," which was published in *Public Opinion Quarterly*, Volume 12, 1948, and is printed here by kind permission of the publisher of that journal and the authors.

This study is an attempt to analyze the relative influence of primary and secondary group situations on the high degree of stability of the German Army in World War II. . . .

Although distinctly outnumbered and in a strategic sense quantitatively inferior in equipment, the German Army, on all fronts, maintained a high degree of organizational integrity and fighting effectiveness through a series of almost unbroken retreats over a period of several years. In the final phase, the German armies were broken into unconnected segments, and the remnants were overrun as the major lines of communication and command were broken. Nevertheless, resistance which was more than token resistance on the part of most divisions continued until they were overpowered or overrun in a way which, by breaking communication lines, prevented individual battalions and companies from operating in a coherent fashion. Disintegration through desertion was insignificant, while active surrender, individually or in groups, remained extremely limited throughout the entire Western campaign.

In one sense the German High Command effected as complete a defense of the "European Fortress" as its own leadership qualities and the technical means at its disposal permitted. Official military analyses, including General Eisenhower's report, have shown that lack of manpower, equipment, and transportation, as well as certain strategical errors, were the limiting factors. There was neither complete collapse nor internally organized effort to terminate hostilities, such as signalized the end of the first world war.

This extraordinary tenacity of the German Army has frequently been attributed to the strong National Socialist political convictions of the German soldiers. It is the main hypothesis of this paper, however, that the unity of the German Army was in fact sustained only to a very slight extent by the National Socialist political convictions of its members, and that more important in the motivation of the determined resistance of the German soldier was the steady satisfaction of certain *primary* personality demands afforded by the social organization of the army.

This basic hypothesis may be elaborated in the following terms.

1. It appears that a soldier's ability to resist is a function of the capacity of his immediate primary group (his squad or section) to avoid social disintegration. When the individual's immediate group, and its supporting formations, met his basic organic needs, offered him affection and esteem from both officers and comrades, supplied him with a sense of power and adequately regulated his relations with authority, the element of self-concern in battle, which would lead to disruption of the effective functioning of his primary group, was minimized.

2. The capacity of the primary group to resist disintegration was dependent on the acceptance of political, ideological, and cultural symbols (all secondary symbols) only to the extent that these secondary symbols became directly associated with primary gratifications.

3. Once disruption of primary group life resulted through separation, breaks in communications, loss of leadership, depletion of personnel, or major and prolonged breaks in the supply of food and medical

care, such an ascendancy of preoccupation with physical survival developed that there was very little "last-ditch" resistance.

4. Finally, as long as the primary group structure of the component units of the Wehrmacht persisted, attempts by the Allies to cause disaffection by the invocation of secondary and political symbols (e.g., about the ethical wrongfulness of the National Socialist system) were mainly unsuccessful. By contrast, where Allied propaganda dealt with primary and personal values, particularly physical survival, it was more likely to be effective. . . .

> The company is the only truly existent community. This community allows neither time nor rest for a personal life. It forces us into its circle, for life is at stake. Obviously compromises must be made and claims be surrendered. . . . Therefore the idea of fighting, living, and dying for the fatherland, for the cultural possessions of the fatherland, is but a relatively distant thought. At least it does not play a great role in the practical motivations of the individual.

Thus wrote an idealistic German student in the first world war. A German sergeant, captured toward the end of the second world war, was asked by his interrogators about the political opinions of his men. In reply, he laughed and said, "When you ask such a question, I realize well that you have no idea of what makes a soldier fight. The soldiers lie in their holes and are happy if they live through the next day. If we think at all, it's about the end of the war and then home."

The fighting effectiveness of the vast majority of soldiers in combat depends only to a small extent on their preoccupation with the major political values which might be affected by the outcome of the war and which are the object of concern to statesmen and publicists. There are of course soldiers in whom such motivations are important. Volunteer armies recruited on the basis of ethical or political loyalties, such as the International Brigade in the Spanish Civil War, are affected by their degree of orientation toward major political goals. In the German Army, the "hard core" of National Socialists were similarly motivated.

But in a conscript army, the criterion of recruitment is much less specialized and the army is more representative of the total population liable to conscription. Therefore the values involved in political and social systems or ethical schemes do not have much impact on the determination of a soldier to fight to the best of his ability and to hold out as long as possible. For the ordinary German soldier the decisive fact was that he was a member of a squad or section which maintained its structural integrity and which coincided roughly with the *social* unit which satisfied some of his major primary needs. He was likely to go on fighting, provided he had the necessary weapons, as long as the group possessed leadership with which he could identify himself, and as long as he gave affection to and received affection from the other members of his squad and platoon. In other words, as long as he felt himself to be a member of his primary group and therefore bound by the expectations and demands of its other members, his soldierly achievement was likely to be good.

Modern social research has shown that the primary group is not merely the chief source of affection and accordingly the major factor in personality formation in infancy and childhood. The primary group continues to be the major source of social and psychological sustenance through adulthood. In the army, when isolated from civilian primary groups, the individual soldier comes to depend more and more on his military primary group. His spontaneous loyalties are to its immediate members whom he sees daily and with whom he develops a high degree of intimacy. For the German soldier in particular, the demands of his group, reinforced by officially prescribed rules, had the effect of an external authority. It held his aggressiveness in check; it provided discipline, protection, and freedom from autonomous decision.

Army units with a high degree of primary group integrity suffered little from desertions or from individually contrived surrenders. In the Wehrmacht, desertions and surrenders were most frequent in groups of heterogeneous ethnic composition in which Austrians, Czechs, and Poles were randomly intermixed with each other. In such groups the difficulties of linguistic communication, the large amount of individual resentment and aggressiveness about coercion into German service, the weakened support of leadership due to their inability to identify with German officers—all these factors hampered the formation of cohesive groups. . . .

Among German deserters, who remained few until the close of the war, the failure to assimilate into the primary group life of the Wehrmacht was the most important factor, more important indeed than political dissidence. Deserters were on the whole men who had difficulty in personal adjustment, e.g., in the acceptance of affection or in the giving of affection. They were men who had shown these same difficulties in civilian life, having had difficulties with friends, work associates, and their own families, or having had criminal records. Political dissidents on the other hand, when captured, justified their failure to desert by invoking their sense of solidarity with their comrades and expressed the feeling that had they deserted when given a post of responsibility their comrades would have interpreted it as a breach of solidarity. For the political dissident, the verbal expression of political dissent was as much anti-authoritarianism as he could afford, and submission to his group was the price which he had to pay for it.

The persistent strength of primary group controls was manifested even in the last month of the war, when many deserters felt that they would not have been able to have taken the initial step in their desertion unless they had discussed the matter with their comrades and received some kind of legitimation for the action, such as a statement of approval. And, on the other hand, the same ongoing efficacy of primary group sentiment was evident in the statements of would-be deserters who declared they had never been able to cross the threshold because they had been told by their officers that the comrades who remained behind (i.e., the comrades of the men who had deserted) would be shot. Hence, one of the chief forms of disintegration which occurred in the last stages of the war took the form of group surrender in which, after ample discussion within the unit, the authorization of the leading personalities and often of the NCO's had been granted for the offering of token resistance to facilitate capture, or even for outright group surrender. . . .

The factors which affect group solidarity in general were on the whole carefully manipulated by the German general staff. Although during the war Germany was more permeated by foreigners than it had ever been before in its history, the army was to a great extent carefully protected from disintegrating influences of heterogeneity of ethnic and national origin, at least in crucial military situations. German officers saw that solidarity is fostered by the recollection of jointly experienced gratifications and that accordingly the groups who had gone through a victory together should not be dissolved but should be maintained as units to the greatest degree possible.

The replacement system of the Wehrmacht operated to the same end. The entire personnel of a division would be withdrawn from the front simultaneously and refitted as a unit with replacements. Since new members were added to the division while it was out of line they were thereby given the opportunity to assimilate themselves into the group; then the group as a whole was sent forward. This system continued until close to the end of the war and helped to explain the durability of the German Army in the face of the overwhelming numerical and material superiority of the Allied forces.

Deterioration of group solidarity in the Wehrmacht which began to appear toward the very end of the war was most frequently found in hastily fabricated units. These were made up of new recruits, dragooned stragglers, air force men who had been forced into the infantry (and who felt a loss of status in the change), men transferred from the navy into the infantry to meet the emergency of manpower shortage, older factory workers, concentration camp inmates, and older married men who had been kept in reserve throughout the war and who had remained with the familial primary group until the last moment. The latter, who were the "catch" of the last "total mobilization" carried with them the resentment and bitterness which the "total mobilization" produced and which prevented the flow of affection necessary for group formation. It was clear that groups so diverse in age composition and background, and especially so mixed in their reactions to becoming infantrymen, could not very quickly become effective fighting units. They had no time to become used to one another and to develop the type of friendliness which is possible only when loyalties to outside groups have been renounced—or at least put into the background. . . .

The disintegration of a primary group depends in part on the physical and spatial variables which isolate it from the continuous pressure of face-to-face contact. The factor of spatial proximity in the maintenance of group solidarity in military situations must not be underestimated. In February and March of 1945, isolated remnants of platoons and companies were surrendering in groups with increasing frequency. The tactical situation of defensive fighting under heavy American artillery bombardment and the deployment of rear outposts forced soldiers to take refuge in cellars, trenches, and other underground shelters in small groups of three and four. This prolonged isolation from the nucleus of the primary group for several days worked to reinforce the fear of destruction of the self, and thus had a disintegrative influence on primary group relations. A soldier who was isolated in a cellar or in a concrete bunker for several days and whose anxieties about physical survival were aggravated by the tactical hopelessness of his situation, was a much more easily separable member of his group than one who, though fearing physical destruction, was still bound by the continuous and vital ties of working, eating, sleeping, and being at leisure together with his fellow soldiers.

34. The Work Group in Dahomey

MELVILLE J. HERSKOVITS

Group activity is an everyday affair the world over. It is through group activity that most of the world's work gets done. In many primitive cultures work is eased through the cooperative effort in formal or informal groups. Among the Dahomey, most heavy work is done in organized groups, as indicated in the brief account of the Dókpwê organization. Note that group activity is organized and that group membership and group solidarity is important.

Melville J. Herskovits, from whose book this essay is taken, is Professor of Anthropology and Director of the Program for African Studies at Northwestern University. He received his doctorate from Columbia University in 1923 and has made anthropological investigation in Dutch Guiana, Dahomey, Haiti, Trinidad, and Brazil. The New World studies were all devoted to Negro populations. Herskovits has been editor of the *American Anthropologist* and president of the African Studies Association. The discussion of the Dókpwê is taken from *Dahomey, An Ancient West African Kingdom*, Volume I, Chapter 4, "The Cooperative Element in Dahomeyan Life," New York: J. J. Augustin, 1938, and is printed by kind permission of the author.

The Dahomean love of organization is perhaps best exemplified in the numerous associations for mutual self-help which characterize all phases of life. These include such diverse types of societies as those for cooperative farming, for the production of tools and weapons, and for subsidizing the cost of funerals, marriages, and other ceremonies which exact large expenditures from the individual. The basic, and most widely-spread of these cooperative groups is known as the *dókpwê*. On cursory examination, this institution might be thought an organization of young men, as, indeed, is indicated by the answer that most Dahomeans give when casual queries regarding the nature of the *dókpwê* are asked. To a certain extent this is true, for as far as active membership in these societies is concerned, the young men undoubtedly predominate, since the work they perform is of a kind which elderly men are not capable of doing. When one sees a *dókpwê* at work, however, it soon becomes evident that it includes more than just the young men, for the elderly members of a village can usually be found helping the younger robust fellows by doing such tasks as their strength permits.

One of the most striking aspects of this cooperative organization is the attitude of the Dahomean toward it. It makes little difference whether one speaks of the *dókpwê* to chief or commoner, the immediate response is characteristically one of pleasure. For one thing, to be a member of a *dókpwê* means that a man is a full-fledged Dahomean, and his expression of pride in his membership is an expression of pride in being a Dahomean. Again, the work of the *dókpwê* is regarded not as arduous labor but rather as recreation, and discussions of the *dókpwê* by natives are always interwoven with accounts of the singing, the feasting and the competition, that make the work to be done so pleasurable. The reaction of the Dahomean to the *dókpwê* was phrased as follows by a chief, when he discussed the institution: "It is for everyone; whether you are a chief or a common man, the *dókpwê* will help you. If you need a house, it will build one for you; if you have a field to cultivate, it will break your ground. When you are sick, it helps you; when you die, it buries you. Every man must show respect for the head of the *dókpwê;* when he comes here, I take off my chief's cap to him." Its universal appeal was further explained, when at the same time it was stated that should a chief and a poor man both need the help of the *dókpwê,* it would be given only in the order of asking, so that had the poor man asked first for it, the chief, coming later, would have to wait his turn.

The *dókpwê* aids in the three principal tasks a man must assume —the three . . . every man must master—making a farm, roofing a house, and building a wall. These all are of a type that may best be performed by group labor, and the relative ease with which they are done cannot but impress an observer who sees a *dókpwê* at work. To witness the speed with which forty or fifty men break the ground for a field, each man hoeing his own row, the hoes striking the ground in unison, the strokes timed by the rhythm of the song of those who, for the moment, have been relieved from work, makes the efficiency of this group attack at once apparent. To see between seventy-five and one hundred men thatching a roof, some sitting in the shade preparing the thatch, some stripping the poles, some erecting a frame for the thatch on the walls, all to the accompaniment of genial chatter, gives an immediate sense of the feeling of enjoyment which the men get from this cooperative toil. The building of a wall offers another demonstration of this attitude, particularly when the most difficult work, that of digging up the earth out of which the wall is to be made, is witnessed. Here the hoes come into play in the deep pit from which the clay is taken, where there is room for only a few men to work at one time. The other members of the *dókpwê* stand on the edge of the embankment, and to the accompaniment of gongs and rattles, aid their comrades working in the pit below by singing their *dókpwê* songs, which comprise the most rhythmic, the most melodious and the most stirring of all types of Dahomean music.

Each *dókpwê* is headed by its chief, the *dokpwégâ,* whose office is hereditary. The *dokpwégâ* is a person of considerable importance, not only because he is the head of the men of his village, commanding their unquestioning obedience in all non-political phases of life, but because the *dokpwégâ* also has charge of the burial ceremonies for every member of his village. . . .

Under each *dokpwégâ* are three officials, who assist him in the execution of his duties. The first of these is the *asúfagâ,* who acts as a general supervisor and is his principal assistant. Next comes the *lègèdè,* an official who observes the course of events in the village, makes arrangements for communal work and funerals, sees that all are present when they have been called, and is the functionary who looks after most matters of detail. The third official, the *agutagâ,* functions only at funerals, but there he plays an important rôle, for he is the crier who makes all announcements for the *dokpwégâ.* These officials are chosen from the young men of the village by the *dokpwégâ* with the advice and consent of the village chief. There is no ceremonial when these minor officials are installed, and they hold their offices for life unless remiss in the performance of their duties.

The *dokpwégâ* is the chief of the young men of the village; to the Dahomean, however, this means that he commands all the men of his village, since, to quote one informant, "What man will admit he is no longer young?" Indeed, to call a young man *dókpwê* means that he is recognized as an adult, for this term may not be applied to a young man until he is old enough to take his position in the community. The rule of the *dokpwégâ* over the young men is absolute, obedience to his word being strictly exacted and unquestioningly given. Thus, if a party of more than four are about to undertake a common task, they must obtain permission from the *dokpwégâ* of their village, for five men constitute a "little *dókpwê,*" and such a gathering of any number from five upwards is regarded as falling under the control of the *dokpwégâ.* No man would without serious cause refuse to obey the call of the *dokp-*

wégậ. Should he do so without permission, he would be ostracized by his fellow-villagers, his wives would leave him, and his family, punished because of his offense, would become poor. Neither he nor any of his relatives could obtain burial, and if when forced to see his error he wished to make amends, he would have to humble himself before the *dokpwégậ* whose word he had ignored, and pay a heavy fine. . . .

The functions of the *dókpwê* during funerals will be considered in the later chapters dealing with death, and only its economic aspects will be treated here. First of all, it may be summoned to render mutual aid to its members. The case of a villager who is ill, or who is too old to do the hard work of preparing his field for planting and has no one to call on to aid him, may be considered. In such an instance the *dókpwê* is assembled by the *dokpwégậ* to break the ground for the one who is incapacitated, so that planting may be done and the man will not lack food that year. If the owner of such a field is poor, neither the nominal fee for the *dokpwégậ* nor food for the *dókpwê* is exacted. He will, of course, have participated in the work of the *dókpwê* during the earlier years of his life, or, if he happened to be a young man and ill, he would expect to continue this cooperation. In this sense, therefore, the *dókpwê* is to be regarded as an organization which insures to each member the cultivation of his fields, even though he himself may be incapacitated.

A second type of cooperative activity engaged in by the *dókpwê* is exemplified in the case of a man whose fields are too extensive to permit them to be hoed by his own labor and the labor of those whose service he has at his disposal. Such a man may summon the *dókpwê* to help clear his fields, but for him the work is not done altogether free of cost, though the amount the owner of the fields must expend is small in comparison with the labor involved. When such a man wishes to call the *dókpwê,* he goes to the *dokpwégậ* with a bottle of spirits, four yards of cloth, and two francs fifty centimes, which is divided between the *dokpwégậ* and his sub-chiefs. The *lègèdè* is then instructed to notify the members of the *dókpwê* that at the time agreed upon, they are to gather at the appointed place to do this work. It is incumbent upon the owner of the field, however, to provide a feast, and for this he slaughters a goat or a pig, and provides as rich and varied fare as he can afford. This meal is the only recompense the individual member of the *dókpwê* receives.

A *dókpwê* is also called upon to aid men fulfil the duties they owe the parents of their wives. The system, known as *asitoglê,* renders it mandatory for a son-in-law to perform a major piece of work once every year or two for his father-in-law, and to keep the house of his wife's mother in good repair. To neglect these duties entails a serious breach, and should a son-in-law fail without good cause to discharge these obligations, his tardiness will first be called to his attention by his father-in-law, while if he persists in ignoring these duties over a period of years, his wife will be taken away to the home of her parents and will eventually be divorced from him. It is not usual for such tasks to be neglected, however, and for the man with numerous wives, whose total amount of work owed his various parents-in-law is far beyond the power of any one individual, the institution of the *dókpwê* makes it possible for the *asitoglê* system to exist. When a son-in-law has arranged for a *dókpwê* to do work of this category, he requests of his father-in-law to be allowed to perform some task for him. This request is couched in terms which reflect the code of understatement that the relationship of inferior to superior in Dahomey demands, for he says to the older man, "May I be permitted to do some slight piece of work for you in three or four days?" When the wife's father asks for details, the reply is, "I have ordered some thirty or forty men to come and work in your fields," or "I have arranged for thirty or forty men to build the wall you have been wanting built," or "I have asked sixty men to come to thatch the roof of your new house." It is evident, therefore, why it is said "A man who has many daughters is a rich man."

Yet the inference must not be drawn that a man does not desire sons as well as daughters, nor that sons do not help increase the patrimony, for a son works for his father until the age of twenty or twenty-five. Before a man establishes his own household, however, he does have his own fields, and this establishes a fourth category where the *dókpwê* functions. A son who has his own fields, but who must still serve his father, will request the *dokpwégą̂* to summon the *dókpwê* to do his required work for him. If he has sufficient means, he will pay; if not, the villagers will do this work for him under the direction of their chief without any cost to him, except his obligation to do the same for them when he is summoned by the *dokpwégą̂*. Even when a man has passed the age when he is under the direct control of his father, he does not necessarily put aside these earlier obligations, but as a courtesy to his parent may send a "little *dókpwê*" of perhaps fifteen or twenty men to work his father's fields.

Once a date is settled upon with the *dokpwégą̂*, the members of a *dókpwê* who are to perform a given task assemble at the place named by the *lɛ̀gɛ̀dɛ̀*, and set out together for the field where the hoeing is to be done, or for the compound where the wall is to be erected or the house to be thatched. They are led by a flutist whose shrill notes they can easily follow, for the distance is often great and perhaps not known to some of them. They have drums, gongs, and rattles, and use these to accompany the songs they sing. If the one who has summoned them is a man of large means, they may find upon arriving at their destination that other *dókpwê* are at work. This gives added zest to the occasion, for it allows competition in the work. If a field is to be hoed, each *dókpwê* strives against the others to see which can first finish its allotted portion. If the task is to thatch a roof, each *dókpwê,* if there are two, takes a side and, in each stage of construction tries to be first to reach the ridge-pole. The reward for those who are quickest is the privilege of singing songs of derision against the opposing *dókpwê* until the laggards have caught up with the winners. This desire for competitive struggle goes so far that if only one *dókpwê* is present, it will be divided, one-half of the members competing against the other half. What is accomplished by a *dókpwê* bulks large, but the labor of any one individual is not arduous. The work may involve the expenditure of much muscular energy, it is true, but what a man does as *dókpwê* is performed to the accompaniment of the rhythms of the *dókpwê* work-songs, while the fact that his fellows are watching him is a never-failing drive. Then, too, no one individual works for too long a stretch, for one man relieves the next who, while he rests, joins in the singing before he again takes his place. To climax the occasion is the feast, where quantities of relished food, which the day's sponsor of the work provides as plentifully as he is able, are spread before the workers. For no small measure of social prestige accrues to him who gives with an open hand, gaining as he does the reputation of having the means with which to provide bountifully.

35. The Work Group in a Modern Factory

F. J. ROETHLISBERGER and
WILLIAM J. DICKSON

The sociology of modern industry and industrial workers had its inception with the classic study of the Hawthorne plant of Western Electric, from which this essay has been taken. Here we see the formation of groups on an informal basis within the context of modern industrial production. These informal groups run contrary to the official organization of the plant, yet work is done collaboratively in these units. The essay also shows the mechanisms of group identification and the patterns of status seeking within the group, and makes it clear that the social aspects of the work situation are as important to the workers' motivations as the economic factors.

F. J. Roethlisberger is Donham Professor of Human Relations at the Graduate School of Business Administration, Harvard, and has written several books on the social aspect of labor and the problems of industrial morale.

The data presented below are taken from Chapters 21 and 22, reprinted by permission of the publishers from Fritz Jules Roethlisberger and William John Dickson, *Management and the Worker*, Cambridge, Mass.: Harvard University Press, copyright, 1939, 1946, by The President and Fellows of Harvard College.

On the basis of [our studies] some conclusion can be drawn as to the informal organization of this group of workmen. In the first place, it is quite apparent that these people were not integrated on the basis of occupation; they did not form occupational cliques. In the second place, it is equally apparent that there did exist certain configurations of relations in this group. With one exception, every record examined seemed to be telling something about these configurations. Whether the investigators looked at games, job trading, quarrels over the windows, or friendships and antagonisms, two groups seemed to stand out. One of these groups was located toward the front of the room, the other toward the back. "The group in front" and "the group in back" were common terms of designation among the workmen themselves. The first of these groups will be referred to as clique A, the second, the group toward the rear of the room, as clique B.

What was the membership of these two cliques? This question can be answered only approximately. Clique A included W_1, W_3, W_4, S_1, and I_1, and clique B included W_7, W_8, W_9, and S_4. W_5, S_2, and I_3 were outside either clique. With W_2 and W_6, however, the situation was not so clear. W_2 participated in the games of clique A, but beyond this the similarity of his behavior to theirs ceased. He entered very little into their conversations and tended to isolate himself from them. Much of his behavior suggested that he did not feel his position in the group to be secure. He was the only wireman in soldering unit A who traded jobs with S_4, the solderman in clique B, and he traded jobs with his own solderman more than anyone else did. In so far as the social function of job trading was to differentiate wiremen from soldermen, this could be interpreted as meaning that W_2 felt rather keenly the necessity of constantly emphasizing his position by subordinating the soldermen. Taking all the evidence into consideration, then, it may be concluded that W_2 was not a bona fide member of clique A. W_6 tended to participate in clique B. He was continually "horsing around" with the selector wiremen and had relatively little to do with the members of clique A. That

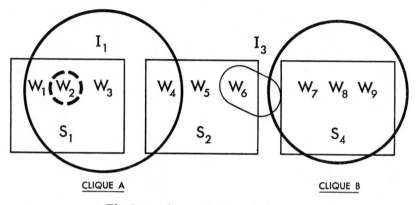

CLIQUE A   CLIQUE B

The internal organization of the group

he was not entirely accepted in clique B was shown in many ways, chief of which was the way in which clique B co-operated in resisting his attempts to dominate anyone in their group. Yet he participated in clique B much more than W_2 did in clique A. It may be concluded that although W_6 tended to participate in clique B, he was still in many ways an outsider.

As a means of summarizing the results of this inquiry, the accompanying figure has been prepared to represent diagrammatically the internal organization of the observation group. . . .

In considering the output of the members of the group it is necessary, first of all, to recall their general attitude toward output. It has been shown that the official "bogey" [standard] meant nothing to the operators. In its stead they had an informal standard of a day's work which functioned for the group as a norm of conduct, as a social code. They felt that it was wrong to exceed this standard.

W_3 and W_6 in refraining from reporting all the work they produced were expressing their adherence to this code. Both of these men were good workers and both of them liked to work. Occasionally they produced too much, but instead of reporting all their output, which would have affected their standing in the group, they refrained from doing so. The fact that they claimed less daywork than they could have is explainable in the same terms. If they had claimed the daywork they were entitled to, they would have raised their reported average hourly output too high. Their adherence to the group standard also accounts for their remarkably constant output rate. Both of these men kept their reported output rate almost exactly on the line representing the day's work.

But here an apparent contradiction arises. Why, it might be asked, if these two men were so mindful of the group's sentiments regarding output, did they not occupy the same position in the group? W_3 was a member of clique A and was the best-liked person in the group, whereas W_6 was excluded from clique A and tended to associate with clique B. Unlike W_3, W_6 was subjected to sarcasm and ridicule and given such nicknames as "Runt" and "Shrimp." This was in spite of the fact that he conformed to the output standards of the group and helped more people than anyone else in the group. What, then, accounts for this apparent contradiction? The answer is that output, like occupational status, was not the only determinant of position in the group. One of the things which made W_6 objectionable to clique A was his irrepressible tendency to "horse around." Moreover, he had no compunctions about telling another person what he thought of him. Of still more importance, however, was his striving for leadership of the group. This was an honor no one was willing to confer upon him; yet he persisted in attempting to achieve it. The result was that he became a constant source of irritation. W_6, in other words, conformed to the group's sentiments attaching to output but violated those attaching to personal conduct. This was reflected in the position assigned him in the group, which was by no means an unfavorable one. He got along with everyone fairly well. It is quite likely that his adherence to the group's rules of output served to sustain him in the eyes of his associates. The sentiments he violated were much weaker than those attaching to output.

Let us next examine the relation between W_2's position in the group and his output. W_2, as interviews with him indicated, was not the type of person to conform to another's wishes. He was hard, enigmatic, self-reliant, and entered very little into relations with other people. In the observation room he tended to isolate himself, and his attitude toward his associates was one of mild contempt. This found expression in his output. By keeping his output high, he was expressing his disregard for the sentiments of the group. He knew he was doing something the others disliked and commented on it in his interviews. "They don't like me to turn out so much," he said, "but I turn it out anyway." He seemed to get a certain satisfaction from doing so. W_2's high output, then, which was consistently above the group's standard, was a means by which he expressed his antagonism toward his associates. They reciprocated by excluding him from clique A. Social isolation was the only measure at their command for bringing pressure to bear upon a member of the wiring group. But, unfortunately for them, it did not work as they wished it to in the case of W_2.

The above explanation accounts not only for W_2's high output but also for the fact that, unlike W_3 or W_6, he reported more output than he produced and claimed a good deal of daywork. The net effect of this was to boost his reported output even higher than it should have been, thus doing even more violence to the group's standard.

Let us next examine the wiremen in clique B to see if their output was related to the position they held in the group's informal organization. Clique B was looked down upon by clique A. The actual average hourly output rates of the members . . . were lower than the output rate of any other operator. W_7 and W_9 ranked unusually low. For this group, therefore, there was a direct correspondence between rate of output and informal standing in the group. . . .

There was a clear-cut relation between their social standing and their output. But, it may be asked, did their low output determine their position in the group, or did their position in the group determine their output? The answer is that the relation worked both ways; position in the group influenced output, and output influenced position in the group. In other words, these two factors were in a relation of mutual dependence. Let us attempt to show more clearly just how this was so.

The selector wiremen, being differentiated from the connector wiremen, banded together and achieved a certain amount of solidarity among themselves. This internal solidarity resulted in increased opposition to those people who were not members of their group. Some such process usually occurs when a group becomes unified. The very process of unification entails a drawing away from those who are not members of the group. The entity retains or increases its unity by opposing other entities. In the case of the selector wiremen, opposition was expressed toward those occupational groups who stood in a relation of superordination to them; to those groups, in other words, in comparison with whom they were subordinated. These were the inspection group, represented in their case by I_3, and the connector wiremen. Their inspector, I_3, experienced the most forceful and the most personal expression of their opposition, and he eventually had to be removed from the room. The medium through which they expressed opposition to the inspector was daywork allowance claims, but with respect to the connector wire-men there was no such medium at their disposal. However, they could express their opposition to connector wiremen indirectly through output, and that is what they did. By keeping their output low, they not only lowered the earnings of the connector wiremen but at the same time they themselves managed to draw a wage quite out of proportion to their own contributions. They were, to use one of their own expressions, "chiseling" the other wiremen. This was, of course, resented particularly by W_2, W_5, and W_6. The bona fide members of clique A may have been equally annoyed, but they said nothing about it. W_2, W_5, and W_6, however, time and again tried to get clique B to raise their output. For the most part, their tactics were indirect. Frequently they traded jobs with S_4 and while in that position heckled the wiremen. They bragged that they could solder for a dozen men like W_9. Sometimes they finished their soldering very quickly and then made elaborate gestures of en-forced idleness. At other times they subjected the members of clique B to direct personal criticism. The interesting thing about these tactics was that they served to subordinate clique B still further and as a result to strengthen their internal solidarity still more. So, instead of increasing their output, the members of clique B kept it low, thus "getting back" at those who were displaying their superiority. . . .

From the foregoing analysis it is apparent that this group of oper-ators held certain definite ideas as to the way in which an individual should conduct himself. These sentiments, which were connected chiefly with occupation, output, and supervision, may be summarized as follows:

1. You should not turn out too much work. If you do, you are a "rate-buster."
2. You should not turn out too little work. If you do, you are a "chiseler."
3. You should not tell a supervisor anything that will react to the detriment of an associate. If you do, you are a "squealer."
4. You should not attempt to maintain social distance or act officious. If you are an inspector, for example, you should not act like one.

It may be concluded that the individual's position in the group was in large part determined by the extent to which his behavior was in accord with these sentiments. The members of clique A, the people who held the most favored position in the group, conformed to the group's rules of behavior in all respects. Members of clique B conformed to rules 1, 3, and 4. Indeed, they attached more importance to these rules than anyone else. This is easily understood because the higher the output of their associates, the more unfavorable their own output appeared. "Squealing" was more objectionable to them than to the others because more of their actions were wrong from the standpoint of management. Finally, they resented any show of superiority more than the others did because they were in the most subordinate position.

The social organization of the bank wiremen performed a twofold function: (1) to protect the group from internal indiscretions, and (2) to protect it from outside interference. The same mechanism sometimes served to fulfill both functions.

The mechanisms by which internal control was exercised were varied. Perhaps the most important were sarcasm, "binging," and ridicule. Through such devices pressure was brought to bear upon those individuals who deviated too much from the group's norm of acceptable conduct. From this point of view, it will be seen that the great variety of activities ordinarily labeled "restriction of output" represent attempts at social control and discipline and as such are important integrating processes. In addition to overt methods, clique membership itself may be looked upon as an instrument of control. Those persons whose behavior was most reprehensible to clique A were excluded from it. They were, in a sense, socially ostracized. This is one of the universal social processes by means of which a group chastises and brings pressure to bear upon those who transgress its codes. . . .

It can be seen, therefore, that nearly all the activities of this group may be looked upon as methods of controlling the behavior of its members. The men had elaborated, spontaneously and quite unconsciously, an intricate social organization around their collective beliefs and sentiments. . . .

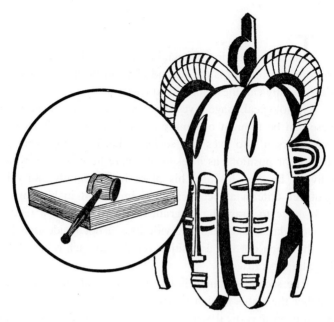

VII.

STATUS AND ROLE

The Relationships Among Men

The differentiation of social positions and the regulation of behavior appropriate to them is the second element in the organization of society. We generally call these status and role.

Sociological usage gives the word status two meanings. The first of these can be thought of simply as position, which is its Latin meaning. Every person who lives in a society (that is to say, every person) has a position or positions as a result of where he was born, what he does for a living, his sex, his age, his place in the family and other groups— whatever criteria are conceived as important in his particular culture. If we were to draw the diagram of a society with a rectangle showing the boundaries and each individual as a dot inside that box, we could say that each dot has a position relative to each other. This would be a diagram of statuses.

The second meaning is like the first, only more limited. It fixes on whether the status is high or low; it concerns itself with only the relative position on a vertical scale. This is the more common use of the term, and because this vertical status, or relative prestige, is of primary importance, we shall emphasize this aspect of status. But we must not overlook the fact that statuses may be different even though one is not higher than another.

Another way to view status, is to think of each status as an office or a rank. The office is there irrespective of who fills it; it may exist when no one holds it at all. This is true of status as well; in fact, an office is a particular kind of status. If we think of an army as a system of offices, we recognize immediately that there are differences in rank, corresponding to vertical status. But we also recognize that the mess sergeant and the supply sergeant, though each has the same rank, have different statuses. That is, their relation to other personnel is different.

There is another point about status that we must not overlook, and that is that one person may have several statuses. He may be father, lawyer, church elder, and club president at the same time. These variant statuses relate him to different social groups, so that he may be said to have one status in each group. When we speak of his general status, we are summarizing the influence of his various particular statuses as they place him in the society as a whole.

The importance in seeing society in terms of statuses emerges when we examine the concept of role. For every social position carries with it an appropriate mode of behavior. A role may be thought of as the blueprint for the behavior that is considered suitable to a particular social position; it is not the behavior itself, but the rules and expectations—what should be done when a particular office is held.

What we want to point out most clearly is that every society has social positions and appropriate behavior for each position. Persons relate to one another in accordance with these statuses and act in terms that the role sets forth, whether it be between lover and sweetheart, husband and wife, employer and employee, salesman and customer, doctor and patient, valet and master, fraternity member and pledge—indeed any recognized social position in the society. We must note that not all status relations are found in all societies. (The employer-employee relationship so important to us is rare among primitive peoples.) We must also note that the same statuses may have different role expectations in different societies. Finally, we must emphasize that the role is a generalized set of expected behavior, not behavior itself. Many special factors may intervene. The employer may have prejudices that keep him from fulfilling his role to an employee, or may have a favorite—perhaps because of other status relationships such as kinship or friendship with the employee's parents. Or, again, an individual may not have the requisite personality to perform the expected role, as when a meek person tries to exert the necessary authority over subordinates. Let us examine some of these points in terms of one universal status.

We have already discussed in other contexts the status of father, which exists in all societies and is held by most adult men. While no two fathers behave exactly alike, we do expect certain things of a father in our culture. He is responsible for his child's health and welfare; he is expected to love, advise, and admonish his children, to mete out punishment where necessary, and to do all he can to launch the child on his career. In the section on the family, we discussed how the role expectations of the father have changed over the past half-century, so that they are now different from what they once were. In that same section we learned from Malinowski that the role of the father in the Trobriand Islands is more like the one we expect of a kindly uncle, while the mother's brother acts very much as we expect a father to behave. From these examples we learn that the role expectations are set by the culture, and that from one culture to another, or from one time to another, they may vary widely, though expectations may be quite explicit in a given time and place.

In sum, every society has a set of social positions or statuses, a set relationship among its personnel, and every culture defines the behavior assigned to that status. A similar status in two different cultures may require quite dissimilar roles. To understand the organization of any society therefore requires that we see what positions are recognized, how these positions relate to one another, and the proper behavior for each set of relationships. But remember that the individual has status within each of the groups he belongs to, and that each group may be analyzed in terms of its statuses and their appropriate roles. Sometimes it is also useful to analyze the status of the group itself, relative to other groups.

We must emphasize again that role is not the behavior itself, but the blueprint for behavior. There are two points here. The first is that each individual interprets the blueprint according to his own lights; he fills the roles according to his own capacities and in terms of his own personality. The term role is taken from the theater, and we may say that the individual, like the actor, interprets the role as he understands it.

The second point is that not only does the person himself fulfill the role appropriate to his status, but those around him anticipate that he will act according to the traditional pattern of the role. A moment's reflection will make one aware how important this is to social life. If the teacher could not assume that the students of his class were going to fulfill their roles, his classroom would be chaos; it is enough disruption when one among them does not act according to expectation. And if the students could not anticipate that the professor would, as a regular thing, act like a professor while in the classroom, they could not themselves act like students in any meaningful sense. (Of course, the professor and student may have a different relationship in another context and would behave differently, but not normally in a way that would run contrary to the teacher-student relation.) Every social situation has the same requirement, and it is the normal fulfillment of expected roles and the anticipation that all carry into the situation that make for normal social intercourse. The more important the situation, the greater is the requirement; hence the careful concern over protocol among the heads of state. Disruptions do occur, but they are seen as disruptions, not as the normal course of events.

In the essays that follow in this section, we have chosen to illustrate the concept of role with cases in which there has been disruption. We have done this because a disruption of normal events discloses the importance of the normal, which otherwise seems only to be the humdrum of everyday activity. We made the point in the section on technology, when we showed the interrelationship among social institutions by examining cases where newly introduced techniques disturbed the orderly procession of events.

Consider first the divergent roles of Moochie—his rather pathetic figure as a civilian and his brilliant leadership role in the special society of prison inmates. His personal qualities were such that he filled not a normal, but a much needed role in the prison camp, and acquired a status of great prestige. It is not a role that has a place in everyday civilian life, and as the shift was made his status fell from him as clearly as if he had removed his coat. Since it was a high status, it was natural that he regret its loss—so much so that he wished himself back under the strains of prison life. We are not surprised that he undertook to recover his sense of well-being through boxing.

The case of the Soga chiefs offers us an example of a status system based largely upon kinship. The importance of kinship among these peoples was so great that there was a tendency to create fictitious bonds of kinship where a role relationship between two persons existed that was normally (among them) handled in a kinship idiom. This is a frequent (one may almost say usual) thing among people living at the tribal level, and perhaps the unusual part of it is only that the Soga had developed a large measure of political centralization using the bonds of kinship. Still, feudal societies generally pattern authority along some kind of real or imputed kin relationship, and even modern industrial Japan sometimes uses fictitious kinship in places where we would use unpersonalized employer–employee relationships.

We must digress on the matter of kinship. In the section on the family we discussed the universality of kin ties and in the section on groups we pointed out that kin-based social groupings were found in all societies and were the dominant institution in many. Kinship may be expected to play a large part in the establishment of individual status and role. In some societies, notably those of the Australian aborigines, everybody is considered kin in one way or another to everybody else. (We need not here discuss the techniques by which the relation to a previously unknown person from a distant part of the tribe is determined.) In such societies a kin status between two persons establishes the appropriate behavior of each toward the other. For instance, a man must assiduously avoid any relationship whatsoever with his mother-in-law—he may not even look at her. He treats every woman who is related to him in this way, whether or not he is actually married to her daughter. One may say that kinship provides a kind of grammar of behavior, offering a set number of ways to relate to others. Such a system is possible only when the tribe is relatively small, numbering perhaps a few hundred. Yet kinship can, through such classificatory devices as clans, serve as a guide to action for most people even in a relatively large and complex society.

Kinship is only one element in Soga role relationships, but it does tend to set the pattern for what Fallers calls their bureaucratic system. But it is quite out of keeping with our notion of fair play in government, for we have rules against nepotism, which we consider a false basis for appointing officers. Under the impact of Western role expectation with respect to the fulfillment of the office of chieftain, it is no wonder that the Soga has difficulty. But our concern here is to show how each culture defines the appropriate behavior for a particular role.

The problem is not unknown to our own society. Surely most people have experienced situations where they did not know what role was expected of them, or where persons around them have not behaved according to expectation, based upon unformulated but clearly felt assumptions about role definition. The case of the union leader described by Gouldner is a conflict of roles that occurs as a result of different definitions of the job and divergent and (in a sense) mutually exclusive demands. The "progressive" union leader sees himself as a reformer, a person with a "calling," and expects to sacrifice himself to a cause. Above all, he associates himself with labor: the "blue collar" man. Yet there are many subtle forces at work which press him into acting like white collar workers and managers. He sits at the bargain table with salaried men, and often at lunch in the best hotels. Such factors of his daily life tend to force him into the role patterns of white collar status. More than anything else, his domestic roles as husband and father tend to force the issue.

As we indicated earlier, status has the dual meaning of position in general and position in a vertical scale with respect to the social order. Though this second sense may not be relevant to the social relation between two statuses—say, that of cousins—each person does inevitably have status in a hierarchy and in all societies the individual is normally concerned with this hierarchical position.

In all societies some people are recognized as having more prestige, more honor, more authority than others. People normally seek such status, according to the manner in which it is meted out in their culture and by the means that the culture provides.

Vertical status can only be fully understood in terms of the values of the culture, and to this subject we will turn in a later section. Here we need only to point out that there are qualities in every culture which are desired—kinds of behavior, social circumstances, personality attributes or possessions. Having these gives a person status, in this vertical sense. As Ralph Linton points out in the essay which follows, in some societies the status of the individual is virtually determined at birth, and there is little or nothing that he can do about it. In others it is relatively open, and he can make of himself what his abilities, interests and ambitions allow. The former is called ascribed status, the latter achieved. No society is purely one or the other—even Indian castes show evidence of some measure of self-determination, while in our own society, which emphasizes individual achievement, some persons are at an advantage and others at a disadvantage by reason of birth or other arbitrary criteria. Yet the distinction is useful and important.

Since status is a public thing, it follows that there must be some way of giving it public expression. That is, there are symbols of status. These symbols vary from one culture to another and from one time to another. Though they often appear the sheerest nonsense to an outsider, they are of consummate interest to the active participant in the culture. The Arunta of Australia indulge in a series of initiations which are severe physical ordeals, and the ultimate symbol of this achievement is the privilege of seeing certain sacred stones in which the spirits dwell; the Yurok Indians of California work and struggle to accumulate the skins of albino deer and other paraphernalia which are used in their religious rituals, because the possession of such goods marks a man of prestige and is necessary for leadership; the Kwakiutl and Tlingit Indians of the northwest coast of North America borrow and save in order to accumulate masses of food, bundles of blankets, and beaten copper shields which they then give away to rivals in an elaborate potlatch. Such behavior must be seen in the total context of their culture—and some we have already examined—in order that they may be fully understood. Thus seen, they are not sheer nonsense. For the individual is operating within the symbol system of his culture, and is using recognized symbols to demonstrate that he has the qualities that are valued by his fellow man.

Sometimes, however, the symbol seems to become so excessive—. like the horns of the Irish elk—that the people themselves become aware of it. The case of the pieces of cloth among the New Guinea natives that H. G. Barnett describes exemplifies this point. These symbols marked the owner as a man of power, just as power was necessary for their acquisition. Yet they were in themselves of no intrinsic worth, and the hectic pursuit led to difficulties. Whether this situation might have broken of its own accord is difficult to say. European administrators among some head-hunting tribes have asserted that when they offered honorable substitutes for head-hunting, this was met with a general feeling of relief. Hunting heads is also a symbol of prestige, and no tribal member could call a halt without impugning his own honor. The situation in New Guinea is reminiscent of the tulip mania in Holland, where, in the 1630's, the speculation in bulbs created an entirely fictitious evaluation, so that bulbs which cost $50 a pound were sold for over $1400—until the bubble broke.

There are many symbols of status in modern America, and occasionally these grow out of hand, too. Most of our symbols have a utilitarian purpose, yet nobody really believes the money spent on clothes is merely for purposes of modesty and comfort (frequently they serve neither purpose well), nor that cars are merely efficient modes of transportation. The automobile industry is well aware of the status meaning of cars, and sociologists have discovered that different cars tend to have special status meanings, connected with certain social roles. Advertisements have tried both to create and to capitalize on these implications. As with the New Guinea natives' cloths, the automobile seems to be losing its force as a status symbol—as ornate mansions did nearly a generation ago. John Fischer's article treats with the status symbol in an ironic but not inaccurate vein in his brief essay. He points out, incidentally, that the symbol is not only sought after by those who are concerned with status, but is created by the tastes and attitudes of those whose status is established and secure. This circularity has probably always characterized status symbols, though societies which are more stable and tradition-oriented than our own probably do not change them so frequently (mass production tends rapidly to deteriorate the differentiating value of an object). Through such symbols the individual can quietly but publicly proclaim his position.

Social intercourse is made possible through the establishment of position based upon criteria that the society considers relevant. Interaction takes place in terms of behavior appropriate to status which, in turn, makes it possible to anticipate how, in a general way, others will act.

36. The Nature of Status and Role

RALPH LINTON

The concepts of status and role have long been a part of general sociological theory, but Ralph Linton was the first to offer a cogent presentation and to use the ideas in relation to the study of primitive people. This essay offers his formulation and gives us a basic understanding of the meaning of the terms and their usefulness for the analysis of human societies.

The essay is taken from Chapter 8, "Status and Role," of *The Study of Man*, by Ralph Linton. Copyright, 1936, D. Appleton-Century Co., Inc. Reprinted by permission of Appleton-Century-Crofts, Inc.

. . . The functioning of societies depends upon the presence of patterns for reciprocal behavior between individuals or groups of individuals. The polar positions in such patterns of reciprocal behavior are technically known as *statuses*. The term *status*, like the term *culture*, has come to be used with a double significance. *A status*, in the abstract, is a position in a particular pattern. It is thus quite correct to speak of each individual as having many statuses, since each individual participates in the expression of a number of patterns. However, unless the term is qualified in some way, *the status* of any individual means the sum total of all the statuses which he occupies. It represents his position with relation to the total society. Thus the status of Mr. Jones as a member of his community derives from a combination of all the statuses which he holds as a citizen, as an attorney, as a Mason, as a Methodist, as Mrs. Jones's husband, and so on.

A status, as distinct from the individual who may occupy it, is simply a collection of rights and duties. Since these rights and duties can find expression only through the medium of individuals, it is extremely hard for us to maintain a distinction in our thinking between statuses and the people who hold them and exercise the rights and duties which constitute them. The relation between any individual and any status he holds is somewhat like that between the driver of an automobile and the driver's place in the machine. The driver's seat with its steering wheel, accelerator, and other controls is a constant with ever-present potentialities for action and control, while the driver may be any member of the family and may exercise these potentialities very well or very badly.

A *role* represents the dynamic aspect of a status. The individual is socially assigned to a status and occupies it with relation to other statuses. When he puts the rights and duties which constitute the status into effect, he is performing a role. Role and status are quite inseparable, and the distinction between them is of only academic interest. There are no roles without statuses or statuses without roles. Just as in the case of *status,* the term *role* is used with a double significance. Every individual has a series of roles deriving from the various patterns in which he participates and at the same time *a role,* general, which represents the sum total of these roles and determines what he does for his society and what he can expect from it.

Although all statuses and roles derive from social patterns and are integral parts of patterns, they have an independent function with relation to the individuals who occupy particular statuses and exercise their roles. To such individuals the combined status and role represent the minimum of attitudes and behavior which he must assume if he is to participate in the overt expression of the pattern. Status and role serve to reduce the ideal patterns for social life to individual terms. They become models for organizing the attitudes and behavior of the individual so that these will be congruous with those of the other individuals participating in the expression of the pattern. Thus, if we are studying football teams in the abstract, the position of quarter-back is meaningless except in relation to the other positions. From the point of view of the quarter-back himself it is a distinct and important entity. It determines where he shall take his place in the line-up and what he shall do in various plays. His assignment to this position at once limits and defines his activities and establishes a minimum of things which he must learn. Similarly, in a social pattern such as that for the employer-employee relationship the statuses of employer and employee define what each has to know and do to put the pattern into operation. The employer does not need to know the techniques involved in the employee's labor, and the employee does not need to know the techniques for marketing or accounting.

It is obvious that, as long as there is no interference from external sources, the more perfectly the members of any society are adjusted to their statuses and roles the more smoothly the society will function. In its attempts to bring about such adjustments every society finds itself caught on the horns of a dilemma. The individual's formation of habits and attitudes begins at birth, and, other things being equal, the earlier his training for a status can begin the more successful it is likely to be. At the same time, no two individuals are alike, and a status which will be congenial to one may be quite uncongenial to another. Also, there are in all social systems certain roles which require more than training for their successful performance. Perfect technique does not make a great violinist, nor a thorough book knowledge of tactics an efficient general. The utilization of the special gifts of individuals may be highly important to society, as in the case of the general, yet these gifts usually show themselves rather late; and to wait upon their manifestation for the assignment of statuses would be to forfeit the advantages to be derived from commencing training early.

Fortunately, human beings are so mutable that almost any normal individual can be trained to the adequate performance of almost any role. Most of the business of living can be conducted on a basis of habit, with little need for intelligence and none for special gifts. Societies have met the dilemma by developing two types of statuses, the *ascribed* and the *achieved*. *Ascribed* statuses are those which are assigned to individuals without reference to their innate differences or abilities. They can be predicted and trained for from the moment of birth. The *achieved* statuses are, as a minimum, those requiring special qualities, although they are not necessarily limited to these. They are not assigned to individuals from birth but are left open to be filled through competition and individual effort. The majority of the statuses in all social systems are of the ascribed type and those which take care of the ordinary day-to-day business of living are practically always of this type.

In all societies certain things are selected as reference points for the ascription of status. The things chosen for this purpose are always of such a nature that they are ascertainable at birth, making it possible to begin the training of the individual for his potential statuses and roles at once. The simplest and most universally used of these reference points is sex. Age is used with nearly equal frequency, since all individuals pass through the same cycle of growth, maturity, and decline, and the statuses whose occupation will be determined by age can be forecast and trained for with accuracy. Family relationships, the simplest and most obvious being that of the child to its mother, are also used in all societies as reference points for the establishment of a whole series of statuses. Lastly, there is the matter of birth into a particular socially established group, such as a class or caste. The use of this type of reference is common but not universal. In all societies the actual ascription of statuses to the individual is controlled by a series of these reference points which together serve to delimit the field of his future participation in the life of the group.

The division and ascription of statuses with relation to sex seems to be basic in all social systems. All societies prescribe different attitudes and activities to men and to women. Most of them try to rationalize these prescriptions in terms of the physiological differences between the sexes or their different roles in reproduction. However, a comparative study of the statuses ascribed to women and men in different cultures seems to show that while such factors may have served as a starting point for the development of a division the actual ascriptions are almost entirely determined by culture. Even the psychological characteristics ascribed to men and women in different societies vary so much that they can have little physiological basis. Our own idea of women as ministering angels contrasts sharply with the ingenuity of women as torturers among the Iroquois and the sadistic delight they took in the process. Even the last two generations have seen a sharp change in the psychological patterns for women in our own society. The delicate, fainting lady of the middle eighteen-hundreds is as extinct as the dodo.

When it comes to the ascription of occupations, which is after all an integral part of status, we find the differences in various societies even more marked. Arapesh women regularly carry heavier loads than men "because their heads are so much harder and stronger." In some societies women do most of the manual labor; in others, as in the Marquesas, even cooking, housekeeping, and baby-tending are proper male occupations, and women spend most of their time primping. Even the general rule that women's handicap through pregnancy and nursing indicates the more active occupations as male and the less active ones as female has many exceptions. Thus among the Tasmanians seal-hunting was women's work. They swam out to the seal rocks, stalked the animals, and clubbed them. Tasmanian women also hunted opossums, which required the climbing of large trees.

Although the actual ascription of occupations along sex lines is highly variable, the pattern of sex division is constant. There are very few societies in which every important activity has not been definitely assigned to men or to women. Even when the two sexes cooperate in a particular occupation, the field of each is usually clearly delimited. Thus in Madagascar rice culture the men make the seed beds and terraces and prepare the fields for transplanting. The women do the work of transplanting, which is hard and back-breaking. The women weed the crop, but the men harvest it. The women then carry it to the threshing floors, where the men thresh it while the women winnow it. Lastly, the women pound the grain in mortars and cook it.

When a society takes over a new industry, there is often a period of uncertainty during which the work may be done by either sex, but it soon falls into the province of one or the other. In Madagascar, pottery is made by men in some tribes and by women in others. The only tribe in which it is made by both men and women is one into which the art has been introduced within the last sixty years. I was told that during the fifteen years preceding my visit there had been a marked decrease in the number of male potters, many men who had once practised the art having given it up. The factor of lowered wages, usually advanced as the reason for men leaving one of our own occupations when women enter it in force, certainly was not operative here. The field was not over-crowded, and the prices for men's and women's products were the same. Most of the men who had given up the trade were vague as to their reasons, but a few said frankly that they did not like to compete with women. Apparently the entry of women into the occupation had robbed it of a certain amount of prestige. It was no longer quite the thing for a man to be a potter, even though he was a very good one.

The use of age as a reference point for establishing status is as universal as the use of sex. All societies recognize three age groupings as a minimum: child, adult, and old. Certain societies have emphasized age as a basis for assigning status and have greatly amplified the divisions. Thus in certain African tribes the whole male population is divided into units composed of those born in the same years or within two- or three-year intervals. However, such extreme attention to age is unusual, and we need not discuss it here. . . .

In the case of age, as in that of sex, the biological factors involved appear to be secondary to the cultural ones in determining the content of status. There are certain activities which cannot be ascribed to children because children either lack the necessary strength or have not had time to acquire the necessary technical skills. However, the attitudes between parent and child and the importance given to the child in the family structure vary enormously from one culture to another. The status of the child among our Puritan ancestors, where he was seen and not heard and ate at the second table, represents one extreme. At the other might be placed the status of the eldest son of a Polynesian chief. All the *mana* (supernatural power) of the royal line converged upon such a child. He was socially superior to his own father and mother, and any attempt to discipline him would have been little short of sacrilege. I once visited the hereditary chief of a Marquesan tribe and found the whole family camping uncomfortably in their own front yard, although they had a good house built on European lines. Their eldest son, aged nine, had had a dispute with his father a few days before and had tabooed the house by naming it after his head. The family had thus been compelled to move out and could not use it again until he relented and lifted the taboo. As he could use the house himself and eat anywhere in the village, he was getting along quite well and seemed to enjoy the situation thoroughly.

The statuses ascribed to the old in various societies vary even more than those ascribed to children. In some cases they are relieved of all heavy labor and can settle back comfortably to live off their children. In others they perform most of the hard and monotonous tasks which do not require great physical strength, such as the gathering of firewood. In many societies the old women, in particular, take over most of the care of the younger children, leaving the younger women free to enjoy themselves. In some places the old are treated with consideration and respect; in others they are considered a useless incumbrance and removed as soon as they are incapable of heavy labor. In most societies their advice is sought even when little attention is paid to their wishes. This custom has a sound practical basis, for the individual who contrives to live to old age in an uncivilized group has usually been a person of ability and his memory constitutes a sort of reference library to which one can turn for help under all sorts of circumstances. . . .

Not only do the statuses assigned by different societies to persons standing in the same blood relationships vary markedly, but there is also a high degree of variation in the sorts of blood relationship which are recognized and used as reference points for the assignment of status. Some societies, like our own, tend to recognize only close relatives and to be vague as to the reciprocal rights and duties of any relationship more remote than first cousin. Others select the line of the mother or the father and utilize relationships in this line to remote degrees while ignoring all but the closest relationships in the other line. In a very few cases, relationship in both lines is recognized to remote degrees, with a consequent assignment of status. Where this is the case the statuses based on relationship may actually include a whole tribe and determine the mutual rights and duties of all its members. Thus in certain Australian groups recognized blood relationships are extended to include not only the whole tribe but numerous individuals in other tribes as well.

It is said that when a stranger visits such a tribe the old men investigate his genealogy until they find some point in common with one of the genealogies within their own group. When such a point of contact has been established, they can determine the relationship of the newcomer to all the various members of their own group and assign him a series of statuses which immediately fit him into the social body. If they are unable to find such a common point of relationship, they usually kill the stranger simply because they do not know what else to do with him. They have no reference points other than blood relationships by which statuses might be assigned to him.

There is another type of biologically conditioned relationship which is recognized in practically all societies. This is the relationship arising from the more or less continuous sexual association of individuals, i.e., marriage. The real importance of such associations lies in their continuity, in social recognition, and in the new series of blood relationships to which they give rise through the offspring which they produce. Casual or temporary sexual associations usually receive only a negative recognition from society, being ignored when not actually reprehended. Patterns may be developed to govern the behavior of individuals in such casual associations, but these patterns are usually extremely limited in their scope. They only affect the individuals who are directly involved and do not establish new statuses for the members of the families to which the contracting parties belong. Marriage, on the other hand, always establishes a series of such statuses. Thus the parents of a man and his mistress do not become parties to any reciprocal pattern of rights and duties, while the parents of a man and his wife always do become parties to such a pattern. . . .

Feudal Europe offers an excellent example of the ascription of statuses on the basis of social class. A man born into the noble class could look forward to being a bachelor, in the technical sense of a boy beginning his training for knighthood, a squire, and lastly a knight and lord of a manor. The performance of the roles connected with the final status required a long and arduous training both in the use of arms and in administration. The woman born into the same class could also look forward to being lady of a manor, a task which entailed special knowledge and administrative ability fully on a par with that of her husband. A man born into the peasant class could look forward only to becoming a tiller of the soil. He would pass through no statuses corresponding to those of bachelor or squire, and although he might be trained to the use of weapons, these would be different weapons from those used by the knight. The woman born in this class could only look forward to becoming a simple housewife, and her necessary training for this status was limited to a knowledge of housekeeping and baby-tending. The third class in medieval society, the burghers, also had its own series of statuses, the boy looking forward to becoming first an apprentice and then a master training apprentices in turn. All these divergent, class-determined statuses were mutually interdependent, and all contributed to the successful functioning of medieval society. The noble provided protection and direction, the peasant provided food, and the burgher took care of trade and manufactures. . . .

Most societies make only a grudging admission of the fact that a limited number of statuses do require special gifts for their successful performance. Since such gifts rarely manifest themselves in early childhood, these statuses are, of necessity, thrown open to competition. At the same time, the pattern of ascribing all vital statuses is so strong that all societies limit this competition with reference to sex, age, and social affiliations. Even in our own society, where the field open to individual achievement is theoretically unlimited, it is strictly limited in fact. No woman can become President of the United States. Neither could a Negro nor an Indian, although there is no formal rule on this point, while a Jew or even a Catholic entering the presidential race would be very seriously handicapped from the outset. Even with regard to achievable statuses which are of much less social importance and which, perhaps, require more specific gifts, the same sort of limited competition is evident. It would be nearly if not quite impossible for either a woman or a Negro to become conductor of our best symphony orchestra, even if better able to perform the duties involved than any one else in America. At the same time, no man could become president of the D. A. R. . . .

As social systems achieve adjustment to their settings, the social value of individual thought and initiative decreases. Thorough training of the component individuals becomes more necessary to the survival and successful functioning of society than the free expression of their individual abilities. Even leadership, which calls for marked ability under conditions of change, becomes largely a matter of routine activities. To ensure successful training, more and more statuses are transferred from the achieved to the ascribed group, and the competition for those which remain is more and more rigidly delimited. To put the same thing in different terms, individual opportunities decrease. There is not an absolute correlation between the degree of adjustment of a social system to its setting and the limitation of individual opportunity. Thus if the group attaches a high value to individual initiative and individual rights, certain statuses may be left open to competition, when their ascription would result in greater social efficiency. However, well-adjusted societies are, in general, characterized by a high preponderance of ascribed over achieved statuses, and increasing perfection of adjustment usually goes hand in hand with increasing rigidity of the social system.

Americans have been trained to attach such high values to individual initiative and achievement that they tend to look down upon societies which are rigidly organized and to pity the persons who live in them. However, the members of a society whose statuses are mainly prescribed are no less happy than ourselves and considerably more at peace. It would never occur to an orthodox Hindu that he was to be pitied because he could not change his caste. His whole life is arranged and oriented in terms of caste, and if he ever envies the members of other castes the emotion is on a par with our own envy of some animal's obvious comfort or satisfaction. His religion provides him with rationalizations of the whole system and with an explanation of his presence in the caste as a result of his soul's evolutionary status. It also holds out the hope of a better position in his next incarnation if his work in this is properly done. As a caste member his social and even emotional needs are amply provided for. There are even a small series of achievable statuses open to him if he is ambitious. He may become a member of the caste's governing body or the best goldsmith in a group of goldsmiths, admired by those whose admiration is based on a thorough knowledge of the work. In any struggle for advancement he knows exactly who his competitors are and what it is he wants to attain. He is much less likely to be disappointed than a man living under our own system, where every other man may be a rival and where the limits for ambition are not socially defined.

In India the idea of ceremonial pollution makes social intercourse between the castes difficult; but in societies which have strong class lines, without this idea, the presence of classes actually makes for ease of social intercourse. Here also, classes serve to delimit fields of competition. Where there can be no rivalry in vital matters and no social climbing, snubbing becomes unnecessary and indeed meaningless. Social status is something fixed and understood by both parties, so it can be ignored under circumstances where it has no direct bearing. Members of different classes can form friendships which are the stronger because their interests can never clash and they can evaluate each other as human beings with a clarity unclouded by fear of rivalry. Membership in a rigidly organized society may deprive the individual of opportunities to exercise his particular gifts, but it gives him an emotional security which is almost unknown among ourselves. Which of these is best or which makes for the greatest happiness to the greatest number the reader must decide for himself.

37. Situational Aspects of Social Role

WALDEMAR A. NIELSON

Does the situation make the man? This description of the behavior of a group of soldiers immediately after their release from a Japanese prison camp at the close of World War II analyzes for us the behavior of a young man who had no status in the outside world, but was acknowledged leader of the war prisoners. It shows how, with a turn of the conversation, the mantle of leadership fell from him, and therefore is a poignant example of the way that situational and personality factors make for leadership and social position.

The essay by Waldemar A. Nielson was first printed in *The New Yorker*, February 1, 1947, under the title *Moochie, The Magnificent*. Copyright © 1947 The New Yorker Magazine, Inc. Reprinted by permission of the author.

There may be a flicker of greatness in all men, and perhaps the only trouble is that most of us never find ourselves in a situation where our particular brand has a chance to show itself. One morning recently, as I was walking to work, I saw in a store window a poster announcing a wrestling show. The semifinal bout was between Moochie the Magnificent and someone whose name meant nothing to me. Under Moochie's name, in small letters, were the words "Marine Hero of Jap Prison Camp." His picture was on the poster, and I recognized him. In September of 1945, soon after the surrender of Japan, I had heard a lot about him in Osaka, and I had ridden with him on a train from Osaka to Yokohama. Moochie had a lower directly across the aisle from me. The train was filled with American, British, and the Australian former prisoners of war, the last of some forty-three hundred men who had been rounded up in the vicinity of Osaka. Many of the Americans had been taken at the very start of the war, on Guam and in the Philippines, and had been in prison camps for more than three years. Most of the British and Australians had been taken to China or Burma. For all of them, the trip to Yokohama was the first leg of the journey home. I happened to be along because the Navy had sent me to Osaka to write publicity stories about any of the ex-prisoners who had been sailors or Marines.

The train was one of the few sleepers operating on Japanese railroads at that time. The arrangement of berths was similar to that of Pullmans, and, except that they were somewhat shorter than those on American trains, they were no more inconvenient.

Moochie had come from a small town in upstate New York. He had quit high school to work in a garage and had spent his spare time in poolrooms or playing baseball for the town team. In 1940, he had joined the Marines just for the hell of it, had been sent to Guam, and three days after Pearl Harbor was captured there, together with all the others in his outfit.

They were moved by the Japanese from one island to another, and finally to Japan. Some of the camps were all right, but most of them were bad. The prisoners did all kinds of labor—unloading ships, digging drydocks, and building barracks. In May of 1943, ninety prisoners were taken to a camp near Osaka, and from then until the end of the war they worked as coolies on the railroad docks. The work was hard, and the food was bad. The men lost weight steadily, and a number of them fell sick. They often had long discussions about food—descriptions of meals they had once eaten, the kinds of food they liked best, the smells of food, the tastes, the colors, Army food, Navy food, Marine food. They had food dreams at night and some of them talked in their sleep about food. Constant hunger blotted out thoughts of home, of women, and of everything except food for long periods of time.

But even worse than the trouble about food was their continuous sense of insecurity. In the narrow world of the prison camp, which consisted of a circle of bare earth and a few wooden barracks surrounded by barbed wire and armed guards, death was a constant possibility. The prisoners were under the protection of neither civil nor military law. The comfort of physical strength was gone. They were ninety foreigners in a hostile country, and they were helpless. Except for a daily trip to the railroad docks, they were confined to their little compound. As the months dragged on, rumor, suspicion, and anxiety wore away at the men's spirits. Then, gradually, and without design, Moochie became the leader of the prison camp. He was reckless and fearless, and he had always been big—on Guam, before he was taken, he had weighed two hundred and thirty-five pounds. He was friendly and cheerful by nature and he laughed easily. In the prison camp, these commonplace civilian virtues, which in ordinary life had brought him very little reward, became respected and admired. He made jokes at the expense of the guards and took his punishment without flinching. He devised a system by which the prisoners regularly looted the cargoes they unloaded of quantities of sugar and fish. When the men fell sick, his laughter was their only medicine.

Moochie's final elevation to a minor form of greatness came almost accidentally, as such things usually do. In February and March of 1945, American air raids and strafing attacks were added to the prisoners' complement of sorrows. Twice they were burned out of their camp, and once they were machine-gunned. In retaliation for the raids, the Japanese in charge of the camp became even more ruthless in their treatment of the prisoners. For the slightest infraction of the rules, men were beaten until they couldn't move, and a rumor spread through the camp that if more raids came, they were all to be killed.

One evening, when the prisoners were leaving the railroad docks, a guard discovered several pouches of stolen sugar strapped to the body and legs of one of them. Moochie met the danger of that much-feared moment head on. He felled the guard with a single blow, and then knocked another down. A free-for-all began, in which some of the Japanese coolies on the dock took part on the side of the prisoners. When the fight was over, eighteen of the guards were laid out unconscious on the tracks.

For his leadership in this uprising, Moochie was thrown into solitary confinement, and the other prisoners were locked in the compound. All of them expected to be killed. Moochie was compelled to stand at attention sixteen hours a day for nineteen days; then he was released and sent back to work. He had lost thirty pounds during his ordeal. His release was a genuine victory. It was taken to mean that in the eyes of the Japanese the prisoners had a little value and could therefore count on some small measure of clemency. The men knew that, whereas Japanese coolies drew wages, P.W.s were free labor for the shipping companies, and they considered it likely that to save ninety pay envelopes a week someone had picked up a telephone and made a practical plea for lenience.

Whatever the source of their protection or the identity of their protector, the memory of Moochie's victory provided for the last few months of the war the thread by which hung their common faith that they might, after all, come out of it alive.

I watched Moochie with interest that night on the train. He was wearing only an undershirt above his trousers, and I could see the well-separated muscles of his great shoulders and arms. He had a mane of black hair, a long jaw, and a big pleasant face.

For several hours after we pulled out of Osaka, the men who had lived through so much with him kept lurching down the aisle to his berth and paying awkward tribute to his leadership. Some of them sat on the edge of his berth beside him, others stood up in the aisle. There was a great quantity of Japanese beer aboard and almost unlimited amounts of American Army food. With their belt knives, the men opened bottles of beer and punched open cans of K-ration cheese and biscuits. They passed around opened cans of tomatoes. Someone brought out a gasoline stove and set it in the middle of the aisle, and they made a large tin can of hot coffee.

As the men ate, they talked about the camp, and about happenings on the docks, and told jokes on one another. Moochie ruled over the group with easy, kingly grace. He was the magnetic center toward which the others pointed their conversation, and in little ways they deferred to him and showed their regard. When, now and then, a man left to go to his berth, he generally gave Moochie a friendly punch on the arm or tousled his hair.

And then, along about one o'clock in the morning, Moochie's crown was lifted from him. Quietly and rather suddenly, it just disappeared. The conversation had slowed down from time to time before that, and the silent gaps between stories had begun to grow longer and longer. Finally, everyone stopped talking. There was a long pause. A sailor who had been taken in the Philippines and who had spent a couple of years with Moochie in camp said, "Listen, goddam it, let's stop talking about it. It's over now and I'm ready to forget it. From now on, I'm concentrating on getting home."

"Right!" someone added quickly. "I'm ready to knock it off. Let's change the subject to something pleasant, something natural."

Just that suddenly, the conversation turned a corner. The talk from then on concerned home, wives, and Stateside things, and camp world passed into memory, and Moochie moved from the center to the periphery of the group. At first, neither he nor the others seemed to be aware of the change that had taken place. The next time I glanced across at him, Moochie was looking out of the train window at the dark, and the bull session was gradually breaking up. When I went to sleep, Moochie was still staring out of the window.

In the morning, I got up late, expecting that we would already have arrived in Yokohama, but the train had been delayed somewhere during the night and we still had a couple of hours to run. As I went down the car to the dirty washroom at one end, men were dressing and eating breakfast. The gasoline heater had been used to brew breakfast coffee, and food was strewn about. When I came back, Moochie's berth had been made up and he was sitting by himself. I said hello, and began to dress. He didn't reply.

The sun shone brightly that morning, and the men opened the windows and stood in the open entrances at the ends of each car. They waved and shouted at Japanese standing along the tracks and in the fields near the right-of-way. As the train moved through the outskirts of Yokohama, they began tossing cans of food out of the windows. At first, the flying objects from the train caused people to throw up their hands and run off in fright, but after the first few practice tosses the men learned to adjust their aim to the speed of the train, so that the cans dropped safely to the ground and skidded along until they reached the feet of the bystanders.

This brought grateful shouts and gestures of thanks. Moochie threw no food. After a time, he took a couple of cans and walked into the next car, where most of the Englishmen were riding. I followed him there.

In that car, there was considerable less excitement and exhilaration. The English were somewhat down at the mouth; unlike the Americans, they hadn't been told when or how they were to be sent home or what was to happen to them in Yokohama.

Moochie got into a conversation with an Englishman he knew whose name was Haines. He was a dour old seaman from Gorlestone, Great Yarmouth. "I don't know what the hell is wrong with me," Moochie told him, "but I just can't get very excited about getting to Yokohama."

"Ah, you're just blue, boy, because the old gang's breaking up," Haines said.

"No, it isn't that," Moochie said. "I don't know what it is."

"Throw your damned food out of the window, you crazy Yankee, and you'll feel better," Haines assured him. "You've got to keep your spirits up. You fellows have a big day ahead of you."

"Maybe my biggest days are in back of me," Moochie remarked.

"That's surely no way for you to be talking, Mooch. They'll be looking to you to lead the way."

"No, no more, Haines," Moochie said. "From here on in, I'm just a guy who used to work in a gas station." He looked down the aisle of the train and smiled. "Well, it was fun while it lasted." Then he laughed and shook his head. "Can you imagine talking like that about the camp?"

"I can imagine it," Haines said.

38. Role Conflict of the African Chief

LLOYD A. FALLERS

Role expectations can best be seen under circumstances where they are no longer clear. Any major social change will inevitably involve a redefinition of certain social roles. In aboriginal African political systems, positions of authority and social relationships were overwhelmingly defined in kinship terms; the total state organization rested fundamentally on a kinship basis. What was considered normal to these Bantu political leaders is viewed as nepotism and condemned by modern Western administrations. The conflict in social role that results (as well as the disruption of political affairs) is clearly set forth in the essay printed here.

Lloyd A. Fallers is Associate Professor of Anthropology at the University of California, Berkeley. He obtained his doctorate from the University of Chicago in 1953. He studied the Soga of Uganda under a Fulbright grant and was subsequently Director of the East African Institute of Social Research in Kampala, Uganda. He is author of *Bantu Bureaucracy* and other works dealing with African culture in the present day. The essay printed below is extracted from "The Predicament of the Modern African Chief: An Instance from Uganda," *American Anthropologist*, Volume 57, No. 2, 1955, and is printed by the kind permission of the editor and the author.

The role of the modern African chief poses difficult problems of analysis because it is a role which is played out in a matrix of diverse and often conflicting institutions. Perhaps it would be better to say that the chief occupies many roles. On the one hand, he has a series of roles in the indigenous institutions of African society. On the other hand, he occupies roles in the imported institutions of colonial government. Of course, in various parts of Africa institutions of African and European origin have met under widely varying circumstances and have inter-penetrated in varying degrees, but nearly everywhere the effect is con-fusing and bizarre. In Uganda, for example, if we were to visit a chief we might find him attending a committee meeting, helping to work out a budget for the coming fiscal year. If we ask for an appointment, we will be received in a modern office equipped with typewriters, telephones, filing cases, and the other apparatus of modern bureaucracy. If by chance we had called on another day, our chief would have been unavailable. He would have been meeting with his clan mates in the thatched hut of his paternal uncle, and the talk would have been of genealogical refinements and the wishes of the ancestors. If we are in-vited to have tea at the chief's house in the evening, we will be intro-duced to his several wives, and this may surprise us because we have heard that he is a pillar of the local Anglican parish and a patron of the Boy Scout troop. I have chosen a rather extreme, though not unreal, example. Reading the literature on the various areas of modern Africa, one is impressed by the patchwork character of the chief's social milieu. It appears to be a collection of bits and pieces taken at random from widely different social systems. Modern African society as a whole fre-quently gives this impression, but in the case of the chief the effect is heightened because his role is so often the meeting point, the point of articulation, between the various elements of the patchwork. . . .

Something of what I have in mind may be illustrated by the situa-tion of the chief today in the Busoga District of Uganda, where I have been engaged in field research. . . . Conditions in Busoga, and, indeed, in Uganda as a whole, have provided perhaps the optimum situation for the harmonious mutual adjustment of African and European social sys-tems. The absence of extensive European settlement has meant that there has been little or no competition for land. The successful importa-tion and cultivation on small peasant holdings of cotton, coffee, and groundnuts have provided a cash crop economy upon which a rising standard of living could be built without detriment to food crop culti-vation. Administrative policy has stressed the recognition and gradual remolding of indigenous political institutions without sharp breaks with the past. In this situation, European and African institutions have, indeed, merged to a striking degree, but the result remains a social system containing major elements of disharmony and conflict. In large measure, the role of the chief is the focus of this conflict.

Busoga was "discovered" by Europeans in 1862 and came under British administration in 1892; . . . The inhabitants of the area, the Basoga, appear to have numbered some half-million. They were sedentary subsistence cultivators and livestock breeders, relying for staple foods mainly upon their permanent plaintain gardens and plots of millet, sweet potatoes, and maize. The country is described by early travelers as being extremely fertile and closely settled, particularly in the south along the Lake Victoria shore.

Politically, Busoga was divided among some fifteen small kingdom-states, which varied widely in size but which shared a fundamental similarity in structure. The elements of this common political structure may be seen in three key institutions: *patrilineal kinship, rulership,* and *clientship.*

In its fundamentals, Soga kinship followed a pattern common in East Africa. Descent was traced in the patrilineal line, and kinsmen sharing common patrilineal descent formed corporate groups which were important units in the social structure. . . .

Units other than the lineage were also formed upon the basis of patrilineal kinship. The individual homestead was located in space by the practice of patrilocal residence, and where extended family homesteads were formed, these took the form of a small lineage group composed of a man and his sons together with their wives and children. Beyond the lineage, groups of lineages which were known to be related patrilineally but which were unable to trace the precise genealogical links among themselves formed clans which were unified by a common clan name, common totemic avoidances, and the rule of exogamy. Patrilineal kinship thus defined a large sector of the individual's life; it controlled inheritance and succession, structured marriage, gave form to religion, and strongly influenced the spatial distribution of homesteads.

. . . Through the institution of rulership, members of many patrilineal groups were bound together to form kingdom-states in which membership was defined, not in terms of kinship, but in terms of territorial boundaries and common allegiance to the ruler. In each of the kingdom-states there was a royal clan or lineage (in the case of the royal group, clan and lineage tended to be coterminous because royal genealogies were better remembered), which was set above commoner groups as having higher rank and an inborn fitness to rule. The ruler's position was hereditary within the royal clan. He was the active head of the kingdom and the overlord of all other holders of authority. He was also the chief priest for, as the ancestors of commoner lineages were thought to both assist and control the behavior of their descendants, so the royal ancestors were in a sense *national* ancestors who took a similar interest in the affairs of the nation as a whole. The ruler, being their descendant, was supported and controlled by them in his conduct of national affairs and was the intermediary through whom they might be approached on behalf of the nation. Inherited regalia and a courtly style of living centering around an impressively constructed capital symbolized and enhanced the ruler's political power.

To complete this outline of traditional Soga political structure requires the addition of the third of the institutions noted above—that of clientship. The administrative staff through which the ruler in each of the kingdoms governed was recruited neither through patrilineal kinship in commoner lineages nor through membership in the royal group. The ruler's leading lieutenants—the prime minister and the chiefs of territorial divisions—were commoners bound to the ruler by personal loyalty. Often they were chosen from the many servant boys, sons of ordinary peasants, who were sent to serve in the palace and to seek social advancement. This mode of recruitment to positions of subordinate power was a partial solution to a problem which apparently afflicted most Bantu kingdoms in the Great Lakes region. All members of the royal group shared in some measure the inborn fitness to rule, but within the royal group there was no clear-cut rule of seniority. Throughout the kingdom there were princes—junior members of the royal group —in control of villages or groups of villages, and these persons were a potential threat to the paramount authority of the ruler. When the problem of succession arose, any member of the royal group who could command a measure of support might assert a claim to rulership and fighting not uncommonly broke out. The institution of clientship, through which commoners of administrative and military ability were raised by the ruler to positions of authority and thus were bound to him as personal followers, provided an administrative staff which could be trusted with power. Not sharing the inherited rank of the princes, they were not potential usurpers. At times of succession, the major clients under the previous ruler participated along with members of the royal clan in choosing a new ruler and thus exercised a disinterested and stabilizing influence upon the ambitious princes. They also acted as a check upon the ruler's power, since if he failed to govern within the limits set by custom they might combine in support of a rival prince and drive him from his position.

Traditional Soga society thus took the form of a hierarchy. At the top was the hereditary ruler—the paramount holder of authority and the central symbol of the kingdom's unity. At intermediate levels were the princes administering villages or clusters of villages and, counterbalancing them, the ruler's administrative staff of client-chiefs administering other villages or village clusters in the name of the ruler. Forming the broad base of the society were the communities of commoner agriculturalists organized into corporate patrilineal groups. Commoner and royal, kinsman and kinsman, patron and client, were bound together by highly personal rights and obligations. Subordinates owed superiors economic support through the payment of tribute, military support in war, the recognition of judicial and administrative authority, and personal loyalty. Subordinates in turn received paternalistic protection and aid.

The sixty years which have passed since the establishment of the British Protectorate in Uganda have seen the radical reconstruction of this political system, to a great extent as a consequence of explicit planning by the administration. Innovations were introduced gradually, however, and under circumstances which contributed greatly to the willingness of the Basoga to accept them. During the early years, little was changed in the formal structure of Soga political institutions, though their day-to-day functioning was substantially altered. Initially, the aims of the administration were limited to the establishment of "law and order," which meant an end to warfare, and the creation of a system of revenue and trade. In the pursuit of these limited aims, the indigenous political structure was simply taken over intact, given new tasks, and allowed to continue functioning under the supervision of administrative officers. The rulers of the various kingdoms continued to hold hereditary office and to recruit their administrative staffs through personal clientship. The judicial and administrative powers of rulers and chiefs were recognized, and even enhanced, by Protectorate legislation which made them statutory judges and gave them the authority to issue administrative orders having the force of law. They continued to be supported by tribute paid by the commoner population. In recognition of the authority of the colonial government, they were required to collect taxes, to assist in public works, and to submit their judicial decisions to review by administrative officers. The one major structural innovation was the setting up of a District Council composed of the rulers of the several kingdoms.

Even during this initial period of limited aims, however, important developments were taking place within Soga society. Though the additional functions which were imposed upon the indigenous political structure were minimal, they involved one important change. This was the introduction of literacy. Tax collection involved bookkeeping and administrative supervision over the courts required the keeping of written records of litigation. Every chief or ruler now either had to be literate or required the services of a literate clerk. This development was made possible by, and in turn stimulated, the development of mission education. Soon the sons of important rulers and chiefs, and ultimately the rulers and chiefs themselves, were mission-educated and largely Christian.

The loss of political independence and the innovations which accompanied it were made much more palatable to the rulers and chiefs by the support which they received from the administration and by newly developed sources of wealth. As I have noted above, the position of the ruler or chief in traditional Soga society was not particularly secure. Warfare was more or less endemic and the threat of revolt served as a constant check upon the ruler's exercise of power. Now, not only were the traditional authorities backed by the superior power of the British administration, but they were also able to enhance their economic position. . . .

. . . The initial period, characterized by limited administrative aims and by the building up of the traditional authorities, came to an end in the nineteen-twenties and -thirties. The new policy of the administration came to be one of remolding the traditional political system in the direction of European-style civil service bureaucracy and electoral democracy. In a series of stages between 1926 and 1936, tribute was abolished and the chiefs and rulers began to be paid fixed salaries from a native administration treasury. The loss of tribute was painful to the chiefs and rulers, not only because it meant a reduction in monetary income, but also because tribute was in itself an important symbol of their power and prestige. Nevertheless, . . . the change was accepted. A further fundamental change was introduced which concerned the basis of recruitment to office. Over a period of years, the administration came to insist more and more upon the recruitment of chiefs upon the basis of objective competence, and during the nineteen-forties it became established that not only chiefs but also the rulers themselves, who had previously been hereditary, would be chosen upon this basis.

Since, at first, rulers' and chiefs' sons tended to monopolize the mission schools, "recruitment on the basis of competence" meant, essentially, recruitment of the most competent from this group. With more widespread education, the group from which chiefs were recruited became wider. Again, no serious opposition was encountered. What had previously been a hierarchy of hereditary rulers, princes, and client-chiefs thus became in a strict sense a hierarchy of civil service bureaucrats, recruited upon the basis of competence, increasingly as indicated by formal education; paid fixed salaries out of revenue from general taxation; subject to bureaucratic transfer and promotion; and pensioned upon retirement.

Within recent years, this bureaucracy has tended to proliferate, as the Uganda Government has pushed forward its policy of devolving more and more responsibility upon the native administration, now known as the African Local Government. The hierarchy of civil servant chiefs which replaced the traditional hierarchy of rulers and client-chiefs has been supplemented by specialist officials concerned with taking over from Protectorate Government departments responsibility for matters such as finance, public works, agriculture and forestry, public health, and law enforcement. Concerned that this bureaucracy not become an irresponsible monolith, the Government has also encouraged the growth of elected councils, leading up to a District Council which is responsible for advising the bureaucracy, framing legislation, and preparing an annual budget. The strength of this trend toward devolution of responsibility upon the African Local Government may be seen in the fact that the share of direct taxation allocated to the African Local Government treasury is now four times that collected for the Protectorate Government. In 1952, the African Local Government Budget called for the receipt and expenditure of more than a quarter of a million pounds.

During the period of British administration, Soga political structure has been radically altered by the introduction of new institutional forms, which have achieved widespread acceptance by the Basoga. The new civil servant chiefs are granted great respect and are popularly regarded as legitimate heirs to the former authority of the traditional rulers and client-chiefs. Appointment to the civil service is regarded as a highly desirable goal for the ambitious young man. The acceptance of new institutions does not mean, however, that a harmoniously integrated social system has resulted. In many cases traditional institutions which are in large measure incompatible with the new ones have survived. The result is a social system which shows major deviations from harmonious integration in its value system, in its system of communication and belief, and in the social personalities of its members.

Traditional Soga political institutions emphasized the value of particular personal rights and obligations . . . One owed particular loyalty to *one's own* kinsman, to *one's own* patron or client, or to one's ruler *as a person*. . . . Kinsmen . . . were expected to stand together as total persons and to take a legitimate interest in the most intimate aspects of each other's lives. A patron was similarly related to his client, as is indicated by the difficulty of distinguishing a political subordinate from a personal servant and by the common practice of linking client to patron through affinal ties. The basic virtue was personal loyalty between particular individuals.

The value system associated with bureaucratic organization is in most respects in opposition to this pattern. . . . As a civil servant, one ought to treat everyone alike without regard to particular status considerations. One applies general rules and procedures. One's competence is severely limited to what are called "official matters" and one is enjoined not to become involved in, nor even to know about, the personal lives of those with whom one has relations *as a civil servant*. . . .

In Busoga, these two value systems today exist side by side, and both are represented in major institutions. The patrilineal kinship system is very much a going concern, in large part because its stronghold, the traditional system of landholding, has remained intact. Corporate lineage groups continue to exercise jurisdiction over inheritance and succession and this keeps the ties of kinship alive and strong. The strength of kinship ties is, however, a constant threat to the civil service norm of disinterestedness. The wide extension of kinship bonds means that a chief is frequently put into position of having to choose between his obligation to favor particular kinsmen and his official duty to act disinterestedly. He may, for example, be asked to favor a kinsman in a legal case or to exempt him from taxation. Again, the institution of clientship survives and leads a *sub rosa* existence within the civil service. Although formally civil servants are chosen for their objective competence, in fact opportunities may arise for building up personal followings of clients. Senior members of the African Local Government, through their influence with the administration, are able to exercise substantial influence over the appointment and promotion of subordinates and are thus able to build up personal political machines. I want to emphasize that *both* these value systems are institutionalized in Soga society and that both are accepted by most Basoga as, in a sense, legitimate.

The system of belief and communication is also a focus of disharmony within the social system. Relatively widespread primary education and exposure to mass communications media have produced a situation in which at least two sets of symbols and two views of the nature of the world are current in the society. Again, as in the system of values, it is not so much that different individuals interpret events differently as that the same individuals are trying to work with two sets of symbols at the same time. A chief may, for example, read a newspaper and have a good working knowledge of world politics, but he may still not be quite certain that Europeans are not cannibals or that witchcraft does not really work. Again, these disharmonies in the system of belief and communication center upon the chief because it is he who is most simultaneously involved in the two systems through his relations with European officers on the one side and with peasants on the other.

Discontinuities in the systems of value and belief are reflected in inconsistencies in the social personalities of persons playing roles in the system. Since both the civil service norm of disinterestedness and the personal ties of kinship and clientship are institutionalized, both are also internalized in the personalities of individuals. It appears to be the case, though it is somewhat difficult to think about, that chiefs and most other Basoga hold both value systems and both systems of belief at the same time. This results in frequent conflict, both between persons and within persons. In social interaction, an individual is likely to uphold the value or belief which seems advantageous to him in a given situation. The kinsman of a chief is likely to expect preferential treatment in court and to bring the pressure of the lineage group to bear upon the chief if such preferential treatment is not granted. The same individual is outraged, however, if someone else does the same thing. Similarly, a chief is likely to exercise "pull" through a highly placed patron, if he can, in order to secure promotion, but complains bitterly about such behavior on the part of others. A chief who is requested to exercise favoritism on behalf of a kinsman or a friend is put into a literally impossible position. Both his internalized values and the sanctions impinging upon him from society pull him in opposite directions. Whichever way he jumps, he will be punished, both by his own remorse at having contravened values which are part of his personality, and by sanctions applied by others.

One of the consequences of these conflicts and discontinuities is a high casualty rate among chiefs. Where conflicting demands pull him in opposite directions, it becomes very difficult for the chief to avoid falling afoul of sanctions. The administration, of course, strongly upholds the civil service norm. If a chief is caught engaging in nepotism or embezzlement, he is dismissed. But he may also be dismissed for upholding the civil service norm. If he offends a prominent superior by refusing to grant particularistic demands, he may find that charges of corruption have been "framed" against him, and he may be dismissed for the very thing which he has refused on principle to do. The poor communication prevailing between the Basoga and the administration and the consequent dependence of the latter upon senior chiefs for information make it unlikely that such fabrications will be exposed. . . .

I have described the Soga political system only in outline as an example of the sort of disharmonious situation which I think we must be prepared to study if we are to reach greater understanding of the present-day role of the African chief. The situation is of course much more complex than I have been able to indicate. If there were more time, I should like to say something about what appear to be some of the consequences of the kind of institutional dilemma I have described for the personalities of chiefs. There are indications that for chiefs who do contrive to avoid falling afoul of sanctions, and who remain in office, this success is achieved at considerable psychic cost.

39. Role Conflict among Union Leaders

ALVIN W. GOULDNER

Domestic roles and work roles are demonstrated in this second example of conflict. The "progressive" union leader has entered his activity out of a strong sense of loyalty to a labor movement. His work situation, however, puts him in contact with well-to-do businessmen, and it demands of him the appropriate comportment for such social relationships. His wife and family, likewise, exert pressures toward middle-class status and role. In this conflict, we get further insight into the way in which status concern and role expectations define for the individual his appropriate behavior.

Alvin W. Gouldner is Professor of Sociology at Washington University in St. Louis and Chairman of the Department of Sociology and Anthropology. He received his doctorate in sociology from Columbia and has taught at Antioch

College and the University of Illinois. He has published two books on industrial relations, *Wildcat Strike*, and *Patterns of Industrial Bureaucracy* and edited *Studies in Leadership*. The present essay is taken from "Attitudes of 'Progressive' Trade-Union Leaders," *American Journal of Sociology*, Volume 52, No. 5, 1947, and is printed here by permission of the author and the University of Chicago Press. Copyright 1947 by The University of Chicago.

In a study of trade-union leaders in New York City we gathered data . . . concerned with the way in which external elements—in the social and cultural structures—play a role in modifying the leader's attitudes and values.

From the point of view of the way in which they regard their offices—and it is only this aspect of the union leader's value-system which we shall discuss—two polar types of trade-union leaders have been discerned. One of these, sometimes called the "business unionist," sees himself as the middleman involved in the sale of the union member's labor power to the employer. As such, he is very much subject to the same motivations as any other entrepreneur. He conceives of his office principally in terms of the pecuniary rewards, the security, and the prestige it affords him. Like other "captains of industry" he feels impelled to seek out and capture his own "main chance."

We have called the antithesis of this type the "progressive" leader. For about a year we studied the latter type in a single trade-union in New York City. . . .

Briefly, we found that the progressive union leader's attitudes toward his office are distinguished by the following concepts:

a. *The trade-union office as a "calling."* The union is viewed as that institution through which the progressive leader works for his "principles" and for "humanity." The progressive leader believes that his own goals are qualitatively different from those of the ordinary worker's in that they are superpersonal.

b. *Leader's responsibility.* The progressive leader places the greatest importance upon the fulfilment of those obligations which he has voluntarily undertaken or which inhere in his office. "Responsible" is the verbal status symbol used to commend behavior which manifests such an attitude.

c. *Inner union leadership.* The progressive leader believes that the offices in his union should be occupied by people who have ascended from the rank and file. Moreover, it is believed best that the leader possess the same objective characteristics, for example, ethnic origin, religion, and class origin, found among the union subgroup which he leads. "Pigeons can't lead ducks," say some leaders—but this is more practice than a rule.

d. *Diffidence and indifference to personal importance.* "Modesty," "humility," and other forms of self-effacement are deemed necessary virtues to be manifested by the progressive leader during the daily conduct of interpersonal relations. A "bad" leader is sometimes one who "thinks he's God." A desire to "get ahead" or to be a "big shot" or any open manifestation of a wish to use the union office as a means of climbing in the union hierarchy is frowned upon by the progressive leader.

To some extent these norms are at variance with those which are dominant in our society. To work for one's "ideals" or to work for "others," to belittle personal success and ascendancy—all these union norms implicitly contradict one of the basic elements in our culture, which, as Robert S. Lynd states, "stresses individual competitive aggressiveness as the basis of individual and collective security." As a consequence, the system into which these interrelated norms are integrated is subjected to an unrelenting pressure which, because it is often exercised through the most innocent and commonplace channels, is all the more effective.

The union is not isolated from the larger society in which it finds itself. The union leader was born into this larger society and matured in a family, neighborhood, and school, all of which accepted the premises of this society. The progressive leader cannot, of course, wish out of existence the norms he learned to accept in youth simply because they are now inconsistent with those prevailing in the union. Thus, the norms of the larger society become more or less repressed, in a sense "encysted," within the personality of the union leader. They can be and are, however, reactivated under certain conditions which are neither accidental nor idiosyncratic. . . .

The standards the progressive leader implicitly uses in assaying his own "job satisfaction" are a corollary of the general conception he has of his office. As such, they do not permit him to evaluate his position as the ordinary worker does, emphasizing wages and hours. But these, nevertheless, are precisely the criteria thrust upon him in his role as husband and father.

The typical developments are as follows:

a. Strains are induced in the leader's family life. This is partially verified by the plethora of rumors among union leaders about the many marriages which have been taxed and severed due to the conflicting demands of union and family life. As one union leader declared, "At one time wives wouldn't allow their husbands to go to work on the union staff, it was so hard. I know. Even today, I have a great many difficulties with my wife because of the hours I put into my union work." Not only are the hours of work long, but the leader's activity is concentrated in the evening hours, when members come to the union building for their meetings. The discontent thus engendered can be alleviated either by relinquishing or by redefining the family roles or the union official's role.

b.   Once having become a mother, and often before then, the union leader's wife tends to enact that role in the culturally approved way. This implies that she can no longer work but must, instead, keep house for her husband. Meeting her neighbors while sunning the baby or shopping reinforces within her the approved definition of her rights as a wife. She commences to wonder why her husband (who, after all, is such an important man, being an official) does not "come home at the hours that other men do."

c.   His wife increasingly expects him to provide for his family in a middle-class fashion. She herself no longer works and contributes to the upkeep of their household. Thus it is that the union leader may be impelled to re-evaluate his attitudes toward two key factors—wages and hours; and, as these are part of his entire pattern of attitudes toward his office, the whole scheme may have to be basically reorganized.

Most union leaders are, to some extent, aware of the changes which have been wrought in their conception of their office by their assumption of new roles. "The standards of leadership have changed," said one of them; "It once meant having to give your whole life to the union. Today, most of us do not."

40. Status Symbols and Status Roles in America

JOHN FISCHER

Symbols of status exist in every culture. Such symbols are the material aspects of the value system, and we shall confront them again in the section on values. Status symbols are the titles, possessions, and overt patterns of behavior which mark off a person of high rank, and therefore become valued objects to the population as a whole. They mark the high ranking persons in the societies; it is also true that what the high ranking people have and do make the status symbols. Cars, clothes, houses, and leisure-time activities have long been important markers of status in our own society. There is considerable evidence that the long period of postwar prosperity is bringing about a change in our attitude toward these symbols and undermining the importance of some.

John Fischer is here discussing these changes. If there is irony in his discussion, he is nevertheless saying something of great importance about status in our society, how its symbols operate and where our elite may be found. Fischer is editor of *Harper's* Magazine. He regularly publishes the "Editor's Easy Chair," from which column the following item is taken. It appeared under the caption *Recipe for a Fast Million* and was printed in the July, 1958, issue of *Harper's* Magazine. Copyright © 1958, by Harper & Brothers. Reprinted from *Harper's* Magazine by permission of the author.

Take your last look," Elmer said, "at the poor but earnest scholar. Next time you see me I will be a millionaire."

I looked. Twelve years of teaching Social Psychology at a fashionable woman's college is enough to unhinge even as sturdy a man as Dr. Elmer Hammacker; but so far as I could tell he was sane enough.

"In six months," he said, "Detroit and Hollywood will be stuffing checks under my office door. Every account executive on Madison Avenue will make pilgrimages to beg a word from The New Oracle. No, I don't mean Dr. Dichter. I mean me. I've got a deal that makes motivational research look primitive. It's big, son, real big."

So is Elmer, who once played tackle for Iowa State. He never had fitted comfortably into his cubicle on the third floor of the Agnes R. Appleton Memorial Hall for Behavioral Science, and now that he was pacing around the room—all aglow with avarice and enthusiasm—he looked a good deal like an excited bull in a box stall.

"The name alone is worth a million," he said. "I'm going to call it the Hammacker Institute for Status Symbol Prediction. Dignified but irresistible. What this country is bleeding for is a scientific way to predict coming changes in its status symbols. And I'm the man who can do it.

"Why is the automobile industry in such terrible shape? Simply because the symbols it is trying to sell have gone out of fashion. Everybody knows, of course, that for the last thirty years every automobile has been sold primarily as a badge of rank. As mere transportation, one car wasn't much different from another; but as marks of status in the social hierarchy there were enormous and subtle differences. This pecking order, as it existed till quite recently, was best codified by that distinguished social scientist, William H. Whyte, Jr.; he explained why one make of car was suitable for a rising young executive, another for his boss, and yet others for physicians, band leaders, and college boys.

"The Cadillac, obviously, stood at the top. A man bought one, when he could, because it made him feel superior to all those creeps who drove Chevrolets. It served, roughly, the same purpose as a knighthood in England—to inform the world that he had arrived. And he bought a new one every year, if possible, to demonstrate that only the latest and best was good enough for him.

"Then all of a sudden the symbolism changed. Lots of people began to discover that nobody they really wanted to impress was much impressed by *any* automobile, no matter how big and shiny.

"Detroit spends king-size money on market research—but this disastrous shift took the industry entirely by surprise. Some of the big wheels out there won't believe it yet. My Institute could have told them what was coming at least five years in advance.

"In part Detroit can blame itself. It blurred its own symbols.

"Twenty years ago any school boy could identify most makes at a glance. But now that *all* of them have become over-sized, over-powered, over-priced, and over-decorated, so that you can scarcely see the car for the chrome, there isn't much point in trying to inch up the status ladder from a Ford to a Buick to a Cadillac. The caste marks got to looking too much alike.

"But it probably would have happened anyway."

By this time Elmer was so wrapped up in his dream of glory that he was lapsing into the lecture-room manner which had intimidated so many generations of undergraduates.

"You must remember," he said, "that this country has always changed its status symbols at fairly regular intervals—simply because ours is the kind of mobile society which refuses to put up with any permanent certificates of class standing. The process always works about the same.

"The cultural elite—the people whom Russell Lynes has called The Tastemakers—adopt a certain insignia to set themselves apart from the common herd. It can be almost anything—an article of clothing, a residential address, a favored group of restaurants, a holiday resort, a hobby, a habit of speech, or a combination of several such items.

"Pretty soon, however, the common herd catches on. Usually, in fact, it is tipped off by the advertising men, who point out that anybody who aspires to real class had better drink Olde Doghair, vacation in Miami Beach, and buy himself an Ivy League suit. Since the herd in America is not inhibited by anything like the British tradition and the elaborate mechanism of The Establishment, which keep most Englishmen neatly fixed in the niches where God placed them, our common man—with his ineradicable instinct for social climbing—begins to latch onto the symbols which he hopes will make him a member of the elite.

"They don't, of course. As soon as the herd moves in, the elite moves out. It promptly abandons its old status symbols, and begins the mysterious process of manufacturing an entirely different set.

"For example, by the time that mobsters, movie stars, Texas millionaires, and other crass types were riding in Cadillacs, the people who create new styles of living had decided that they wouldn't be caught dead in one. They moved on to Jaguars—or, more often, to the Volkswagen. The VW is, in effect, a device for thumbing a lofty nose at the whole idea of the auto as a measure of status. It is also, I suspect, the Tastemaker's gesture of hostility toward the men who run the automobile industry. He feels that they have never been properly respectful of his role (and his power) in our society; and now he is demonstrating that Detroit's designers and advertising men, for all their millions, can't do a thing about public taste without his help. Detroit is finding the lesson both painful and expensive.

"My institute," he said, "is designed to prevent this sort of corporate blindness. What we will do—for a suitable fee—is to inform businessmen when one set of caste marks is wearing out, and to predict the new ones which will take their place. My clients rarely will be able to do anything to prevent the change-over, but they will be able to get ready for it well in advance.

"Take the hotel men. I could have predicted two years ago that some of them were bound to lose their shirts on those rhinestone Taj Mahals they have been building in such profusion along Miami Beach. By 1956 the place already was being over-run by plumbers and used-car salesmen—and the people who set the trend in these matters were vacationing elsewhere.

"My charts indicate that a winter tan will remain an okay status symbol for at least another decade; but the elite groups will no longer get it anywhere near Miami. At the moment they are going to Phoenix and the Antilles; Bermuda is still all right if you have a cottage, but not if you stay at a hotel; even a hotel is permissible, however, at Tobago and Caneel Bay. Their next wintering place will be the Greek islands, and within eight years I forecast a strong migration to the South Coast of Turkey—perhaps the finest unspoiled riviera left anywhere in the world.

"Real-estate operators, obviously, will be among my leading clients, since they can be ruined by just one failure to foresee a trend. Zeckendorf ought to pay me handsomely for predicting just when the Upper East Side of New York is likely to lose its *cachet,* as Riverside Drive did about a quarter of a century ago; and he might even like to know why I expect a replica of Greenwich Village to develop near the Bowery.

"The entertainment industry needs me even more. Why, it seems like only yesterday when any man with pretensions to sophistication made a point of being seen in the right night clubs with the right blonde at least once a week. Now the head waiters are getting snow blind from looking at their empty tables. For the Institute it would be mere routine to predict when that particular form of ostentation—or any other—is about to go out of fashion.

"My method, like all strokes of genius, is basically simple," Elmer said. "I plan to place the American taste-making groups, for the first time in history, under continuous scientific observation.

"The techniques are well established; anthropologists have been using them for years on Papuans, Eskimos, Manu Islanders, and a few American towns such as Muncie and Newburyport. My staff—headed, I hope, by Margaret Mead—will simply apply the same detailed scrutiny to a few key segments of our own society. It will report the first symptoms of change in their habits, costumes, pastimes, and snobberies. We can then be sure, on the basis of past experience, that the herd will follow their lead about five years later—though in some cases this crucial time interval may be a trifle more or less.

"The only hard part is to decide what groups to watch; and I think I've already got that licked.

"I shall set up three Field Observation Teams. The first will be assigned to the Ivy League universities. Their potency as style-setters is pretty obvious; what they did for the Brooks Brothers suit, the motoring cap, and chino slacks is already history. Perhaps it is less well known generally that they also incubated the sports-car fad and the skiing boom. Today the dirty-white buck shoe—until recently the private badge of a rather small in-group at Yale—is spreading fast across the country. When it reaches the West Coast, about three months from now, its day will be over. Trends in taste don't originate in Hollywood; they go there to die.

"The reason why so many trends get started on the Ivy League campuses is now being explored by one of my graduate students. Her tentative findings indicate that a significant number of the men at Princeton, Harvard, Yale, Amherst, Dartmouth, and a few other colleges share four key characteristics: (1) enough money to indulge their whims; (2) enough self-assurance to liberate them from the usual undergraduate fear of appearing different; (3) at least the rudiments of taste; (4) enough snob-status to insure that their behavior will be widely imitated in the hinterland. Elsewhere this combination is rare.

"My second team of observers—I will thank you not to refer to them as snoops—will be stationed in Fairfield County, Connecticut. This area has a unique concentration of people in the communications industries: writers, TV executives, advertising men, publishers, and the like. A lot of them exhibit the same syndrome we discovered in the Ivy League universities—where, in fact, many of them were graduated, or expelled. In addition they are fearsomely articulate, and have ready access to channels for publicizing their own tastes throughout the country.

"Finally, they have a low boredom threshold; they change wives, hobbies, breeds of pets, and jobs more frequently than anybody else. An ideal culture medium, in short, for the rapid growth of status symbol mutations.

"The third research team will have a different kind of assignment. Its job will be to keep tabs on a carefully selected panel of fifty persons, chosen from all sections of the country, who have proven ability to create new behavioral trends. Our tentative list includes at least two of the Rockefeller brothers; Mrs. William Paley; Charles Eames, the designer; Walter Paepcke, the collector of paintings, ghost towns, and intellectuals; William Shawn of the *New Yorker;* David Riesman; Alfred Barr of the Museum of Modern Art; Just Lunning, the impresario of Scandinavian taste; Lincoln Kirstein; Mrs. Edison Dick; Arthur A. Houghton, Jr., of Steuben Glass; Mrs. Ronald Tree; and a representative selection of artists, novelists, and poets. These last are indispensable, because they are traditional bellwethers in matters of taste. As Cleveland Amory pointed out in *The Last Resorts,* most of the fashionable playgrounds— from Bar Harbor and Provincetown to Taos—were first settled by intellectuals, who were followed in due course by the social climbers. A good many other movements—in art, drinks, city residential areas, furniture, and social attitudes—get started the same way.

"Wealth, you understand, does not by itself qualify anybody for inclusion on my panel. A good many of the members do have money, but they all have things that are more important—a sense of style, for instance, confidence (verging on arrogance) about their own tastes, and an instinct for non-conformity. These are traits which you might not, at first glance, associate with the Rockefeller family; but they are all there, concealed beneath that sedate Baptist veneer. The family's influence on American taste, by way of Williamsburg, the Museum of Modern Art, and similar ventures has been incalculable; and Nelson Rockefeller right now may be establishing a new prestige symbol of enormous importance. He is making public service a prestigious activity for the rich.

"Any ordinary millionaire can display a yacht or a flock of chorus girls, but only a *very* wealthy man can afford to maintain a private staff of scholars for research into public issues, and in addition spend years of his own time on such chores as heading a commission to rewrite the New York state constitution. If you want to put it in Veblen's terms—which probably are over-cynical—you might say that this kind of disinterested public service is the ultimate form of conspicuous consumption.

"By way of contrast, look at the late Robert R. Young, a man who had practically no influence on the country's behavior patterns. He had money, but he lacked the leader's temperament. In fact, he not only was a natural-born follower, but one who followed fashions a whole generation out of date. He tried to be a tycoon when the Age of Tycoons was long past, and he was the only man of his time who thought it important to have big houses in both Newport and Palm Beach. He even curried the favor of dukes, a method of social escalation which had been abandoned by everybody else about 1917. Soon after he finally discovered that he was an anachronism whom nobody took seriously, he shot himself.

"It is of course unscientific for me to anticipate the reports of my Field Observation Teams, but I think I can already guess at a few of their findings—some trivial, others reasonably significant. For example:

"America's No. 1 status symbol—a place long held by the automobile—will again be the home, as it was fifty years ago. It will betoken the owner's social standing, not by any measure so crude as price alone, but by a whole set of more subtle indicators—the quality of its architecture, the layout of its garden, the pictures on the walls, the nature of its library and record collection. This phenomenon is of course closely related to the turning inward, the domestication—the withdrawal from gregarious activities, including night-clubbing and political movements—which are such pronounced characteristics of our younger generation.

"Incidentally, the automobile industry eventually will get over its present state of shock, and will start selling transportation instead of glamor. The company which will prosper will be the one that gets to the market first with a simple, sturdy, comfortable, economical, and unobtrusively good-looking car, which you can depend on not to get obsolescent for at least ten years—something like the Mercedes-Benz. As a matter of fact, the Rambler seems to be prospering on this formula already.

"Gentlemen farmers will raise Black Angus cattle rather than race horses. This will be a natural step in the trend away from gaudy ostentation, which started shortly after World War II. We have already seen its effect on men's clothes, office decoration, haircuts, domestic architecture, and the disappearance of such loud displays as the debutante ball. Today nobody, however wealthy, would dream of building a palace like Hearst's San Simeon. Instead of conferring prestige, it would make him look silly.

"Amateur painting will become increasingly respectable. Once rather suspect, it has now been sanctified by the two great war leaders, Churchill and Eisenhower. It will lead, in turn, to a steadily growing market for professional artists. Already more canvases—most of them bad—are being sold at higher prices to more people than at any time since the Medicis made painters into gentlemen and painting a lucrative profession.

"In Texas there are now only three approved ways for a rich man to spend his money. He can buy a ranch—a big one; a little bitty ranch won't do—he can finance a reactionary politician, or he can endow a Texas university. I predict that within the next ten years the opinion leaders in Texas will discover the rest of the United States, and that the most venturesome among them will make their first tentative contacts with the world overseas, and all the delightful possibilities it offers for spending money in unheard-of ways.

"But that's enough of this idle speculation. I have to go phone Margaret Mead. If I don't get the Institute under way pretty fast, those Bureau of Applied Social Research boys at Columbia might beat me to it."

Elmer went charging down the hall to borrow the dean's telephone; the college had never felt it could afford to give him one for his own office. It occurred to me that he hadn't said a word about the kind of status symbols which might be needed to keep ambitious men in the teaching profession.

41. Status Symbols and Power Roles in New Guinea

H. G. BARNETT

Status symbols can change in primitive societies as well as in modern, though we have fewer examples. The following essay illustrates the way in which certain imported cloths took on a symbolic meaning out of all relation to any intrinsic worth or esthetic value and came to dominate the attitudes, feelings, and social relations of a group of New Guinea tribesmen. The sudden change in their evaluation illustrates the essentially cultural definition of the symbols and also shows that the elite make the symbols rather than the other way about.

Homer G. Barnett is Professor of Anthropology at the University of Oregon, having taken his doctoral degree from the University of California, Berkeley, in 1938. Barnett has been anthropologist for the Smithsonian Institution, adviser for the Netherlands New Guinea Government and a Senior Fellow of the National Science Foundation. He was staff anthropologist for the Trust Territory, Pacific Islands, a member of the West Coast Advisory Committee of the Pacific Science Board, on the Research Council of the South Pacific Commission, and chairman of a Social Science Research Council Summer Seminar. He has done ethnographic research in North America, Micronesia, and New Guinea. He is the author, among other works, of *Innovation* and of *Anthropology and Administration*. The essay was first presented to the meeting of the Southwestern Anthropological Association in April, 1959, and subsequently printed under the title "Peace and Progress in New Guinea," in the *American Anthropologist*, Volume 61, No. 6, 1959. It is reproduced by kind permission of the author and editor.

Administratively the Dutch designate a large sector of the Vogelkopt in western New Guinea as the Ajamaroe District. The same term is applied to the inhabitants of the area, though they are divided into many small groups by linguistic differences and have no common name for themselves. Very little is known about any of them except those whom the government has induced to take up part-time residence in about 50 hamlets clustered about a chain of shallow, muddy lakes in the mid-interior. . . . In this district, as in other parts of the interior, the Dutch government has moved very slowly in extending its authority over the natives, mostly because of a lack of manpower and resources.

In Ajamaroe, regular patrols enforcing some semblance of justice do not get much beyond a day's march from the lakes. Even this control is recent and in many respects is superficial. . . .

The area was first penetrated by a small contingent of the Dutch Army in 1935. One of its objectives was to suppress the petty but incessant warfare that made life and property insecure and kept the Ajamaroe in constant turmoil. Their ideal man was belligerent and vengeful, and those with outstanding records as killers were their head men or chiefs. They were called in Malay *kapala parang*—literally "head knives." They were products of a mass anxiety characterized by suspicion, vindictiveness, deceit, and avarice. According to Ajamaroe belief, no death was natural unless it came at the end of a long life, and perhaps not then. Furthermore, every unnatural death demanded revenge, though a life could be paid for if the murder was such by inference or through negligence. Payment was possible, for example, to atone for the death of guests. A host was always under suspicion if his visitors fell ill, and he had to pay their relatives if they died. On the same theory a man paid for the death of his wife if she died on his clan land, and her relatives paid for his death if he died on theirs. Suicides by married women were fairly common—consciously directed acts of aggression, for they called for a payment by the husband, who was assumed to be the cause.

All of this meant that unless a man could buy his way out of an accusation he was marked for death, and so had one of two courses open to him. Either he killed again and again in self-defense or in retaliation, and so began a career leading to the status of a kapala parang, or he placed himself under the protection and command of such a person. Ambition, envy, and vanity also played their part in aggravating aggression and in the building of a reputation based on its undisciplined exercise.

Kapala parang were important not only because of their reputation as killers. They were also rich men. Indeed, they need not be physically formidable at all if they had the wealth to buy men who were. In their capacity as rich men they were known as *bobots*—"possessors of many things"—and they gained and maintained their influence through the servile obedience of men and their wives who were indebted to them for past favors or hoped to benefit from their future patronage. Their wealth consisted of food, but also of trade goods that trickled into the area from the coast. An indispensable asset was a stock of cloths, known as *kain timor,* which were traded into the area from Ceram or Timor.

These cloths were of many kinds and sizes, their respective values known only to Ajamaroe connoisseurs, but there were two main categories pertinent to this account. In one were the ancient and sacred pieces transmitted from a man to his heirs, usually his sons. They were identified with the ancestral spirits of the family and were conceived to have supernatural power. They were kept away from the direct light of day, wrapped in moldy parcels the opening of which was an awesome ritual that gave health and success to their guardians. Their protective power, through associations with the dead, safeguarded the spiritual well-being of family and clan. In the other category were the many varieties of secular cloths that were kept in constant movement, passing from hand to hand out of family and clan lines. These goods were essential to the functioning of the Ajamaroe social system, for they were required as bride price, were the only acceptable payment for a life, and were the foundation for a system of property exchanges between parents-in-law and brothers-in-law.

The transactions involving the wife's relatives and the husband's were complicated and their details need not be described. Their outstanding feature was that they kept a husband heavily obligated to his wife's relatives. In addition to paying for his bride, he had to transfer more goods to them when she became pregnant, when she bore a child, when she died, and when their children were initiated into a secret society or into adult status. An even more burdensome obligation resulted from the exercise of the wife's relatives' privilege of making loans to the husband's relatives, loans which had to be repaid on call and with an increment. In order to meet these demands the husband loaned what he received to others, expecting them to return more than they received. As the result of an emphasis on keeping the kain timor in constant circulation, everybody, including the rich, lived mostly on credit.

Bobots financed the marriages of those who lacked the means and thus set in motion a series of property exchanges between the two parties to the marriage contract that continued for life. Consequently, unless a dependent person could work his way to solvency—which was not likely—he remained forever in bondage to his benefactor, who simply acted in his place, assuming his debts and accepting what was due him. When a young man without means or parental backing wished to get married, he approached one of these financiers—normally one with an already existing exchange relationship with the agent of the bride-to-be —and obligated himself for service in partial compensation for the payment of his bride price. . . . There was a great deal of bickering and bargaining for position in the marital negotiations, and the principals had little to say about the outcome.

A groom in service did manual labor for his benefactor, clearing and fencing his fields, building his houses and carrying his goods. He also supplied him with food and acted as servant, errand boy, and henchman. In return for this active loyalty, his benefactor took full responsibility for his actions under an employer liability concept known as *isti*. In accordance with this custom a kapala parang might order his dependent to do anything, including murder or theft, if he was prepared to meet the consequences by force or by financial restitution.

Kapala parang also trafficked in hostages and slaves. They kidnapped the children of delinquent debtors and either kept them until they were redeemed or traded them to other bobots for kain timor. Sometimes the victims were held as reserve capital to be used to pay an obligation when not enough kain timor were available. As long as they remained in captive status they were treated virtually as slaves, working for their masters and receiving little personal attention. Many passed from one owner to another until they fell into the hands of coastal traders. . . .

In their initial attempts to break this system of warrior capitalism, the Dutch resorted to cajolery and bribery. They offered beads, metal ornaments, knives, axes, fish hooks, and other European goods to the kapala parang as an inducement to declare a general amnesty and draw their people together in villages where they could be educated and given medical care. These inducements were met with suspicion and aloofness. They were not enough to establish permanent settlements. The hamlets that they created were little more than transient abodes, like the old ceremonial houses. But with repeated efforts and a strategic display of force, the authorities were able to break the power of the warriors in the lake area. At present every effort is made to ferret out breaches of the peace, and no reported crime goes unpunished.

The peace was secured; but imperceptibly something almost as disturbing to the government developed. This was an intensification and proliferation of bobotism. Not only did the kapala parang become more powerful in laying aside their knives; new bobots emerged in the vacuum of creeping pacifism. Then, robbed of their natural right to murder and mayhem, they turned their attention to the rapacious pursuit of kain timor with all its possibilities for gain and aggression. More men had more time to become involved in complicated financial deals that left no one solvent and made everyone a high-pressure bill collector. The multiplication of petty capitalists was made possible not only because they no longer had to be gunmen; they did not have to pay for protection, and the obligation of isti no longer held. Furthermore, their field of operations was greatly expanded because former enemies could be drawn into the game of financing the careers of dependents who no longer lived with them but were just as effectively tied to them and their ambitions.

In short, warfare was replaced by the manipulation of the people through the control of essential goods; and by 1954 everyone was so entangled and pressured by debtors that the police and other officials spent much of their time settling disputes, punishing assaulters, and investigating suicides resulting from quarrels about kain timor. The price of a bride went up, along with everything else. The marriage rate went down, and the marriage age went up. Few people got married before they were twenty-five. Domestic quarrels intensified. Odd marriages, some incestuous by clan rules, were negotiated to suit the convenience of financial backers.

Repeatedly the District Officer inveighed against the nuisance and tried to get the people to turn their attention to economic production, to more food and cash crops, to health standards, and to education. Finally, one day in March of 1954 at an open meeting called to investigate a row over kain timor debts, he lost his patience and exclaimed "Why don't you get rid of these useless things!" He expected no answer, but he got one immediately. A man in the group—a bobot—apparently sensing that the moment had arrived, spoke up and said, "All right, we will." There was no opposition. On the contrary, the crowd murmured its approval. It was a spontaneous and popular decision triggered by the District Officer's outburst. Realizing that he might have evoked expression of a widespread sentiment he paid visits to other hamlets, related what had happened at the first, and made a plea for the general abandonment of kain timor. The suggestion was so well received that he called a meeting of all the important men in the area, along with the Indonesian schoolteachers and pastors and a priest. Because it was crucial to everything else, his specific question was: What is to be done about the marriage payment? The first person to speak was the richest and most powerful man in the district, who argued for the abolition of kain timor. The District Officer suggested that cotton yardage and guilders in limited amounts be substituted. There was no dissent and everyone agreed to have all kain timor out of circulation in six months.

In August the District Officer made another patrol of the area to settle on a means of disposing of the troublesome cloths. At the first hamlet he suggested that the secular pieces be burned or deposited with him and that the sacred ones be registered with him and returned to their owners. Someone shouted that those in the first category should be burned, and then and there they were thrown on a bonfire. Word of this action spread rapidly, and when the officer arrived at the next hamlet a fire was already going and people began to throw their cloths on it as he approached. They were in a jubilant mood and suggested that they plant a tree on the spot to commemorate the event. With varying degrees of enthusiasm and spontaneity other communities elected either to destroy their treasures or to relinquish them to government officials.

The consequences of the sudden decision to renounce the traffic in kain timor were no less surprising than the decision itself. They began to develop immediately and were so apparent that even the Ajamaroe remarked about them. First, hamlets increased in size; people began leaving their gardens and taking up residence near the schoolhouses that the government had built. Second, more children came to school, the increase in the number of girls being especially marked. Third, the number of marriages increased, their age level dropped, and more children were born or were on the way. Fourth, there was a stir of excitement about economic development. Men began to talk about their need for money and trade goods, and finally the whole district committed itself to the building of a road to the coast. This was to serve not only as a communication link to the newly enchanting world outside but as the foundation for an import-export business, the Ajamaroe contribution to which was as yet unspecified. Native spokesmen began to ask officials when the jeeps and trucks were to arrive, as if a bargain had been made and they expected the government to fulfill its promise.

In trying to find an explanation for this combination of events, the District Officer suggested that rejection of kain timor was crucial to acceptance of all the other things that he and other officials had been advocating in the name of improvement or progress. Whatever the explanation, he was disturbed, for the government was not prepared for the revolution, which raised almost as many problems as it solved.

Structurally, the impact of peace and progress on Ajamaroe society was extensive. Bobots ceased to exist, and with them all the attendant bonds and groupings of relatives and nonrelatives that their operations created, physically and psychologically. Men and women began to live and work together for whatever purposes and for whatever individuals their personal interests dictated. Residence patterns changed with the movement from farm to hamlet. A new marriage market, the school, took the place of the dance houses annually constructed for the purpose of bringing young men and women together for premarital dalliance. Leadership qualifications changed without a change in top personnel, for the revolution came from above. New forms of wealth loomed as a basic requirement for chieftainship; but collaboration with the government became a recommendation for its formal acceptance. The number of headmen dropped sharply and a marked tendency toward individualism emerged. . . .

Men in high places often have less to lose in renouncing the supports for their position than appears on the surface. So it was with the leader of this revolution. In explanation on his advocacy of the new order, he says that he has become a Christian and as such he sympathizes with the poor people who were in perpetual bondage under the old system. When pressed further, he confides that he was unhappy even before his conversion, the reason being that there was too much quarreling and killing. Coming from a bobot of considerable distinction, this admission is likely to strike an outsider as hypocritical until he discovers that in this instance the aversion to homicide has an acutely personal reference. Back of it lies a murderous sequence of events that had not yet run their full course according to Ajamaroe logic. Their beginning is uncertain, but they came to a climax just prior to World War II when this man instigated the slaying of five others, two of them bobots. He took this action in his capacity as a kapala parang in revenge for the deaths of two of his brothers. In retaliation, the kinsmen of two of his victims killed his father. He issued orders for their execution and at the same time prepared to defend himself and his supporters from attacks by the clansmen of the other three.

At this point the feuding was interrupted by the Japanese invasion and detention of its key figure, along with other headmen, in a concentration camp. It was apparently during this period of enforced restraint that he found wisdom and perhaps personal advantage in supporting and being supported by a powerful foreign authority. In any event, with the return of the Dutch he abandoned his plans for revenge and cooperated with the police in their efforts to suppress violence. Whether or not he was inspired by fear for his life, this decision entailed no loss of influence or prestige. He now bears the title of Radja, an honor that the Dutch bestow on influential headmen in this region who support the

VIII.

AUTHORITY

The Power to Govern

Every society finds it necessary to reach decisions which are binding on the whole or some segment of the whole. Every society finds it necessary to provide for the resolution of internal dissent. Every society finds it necessary to reenforce its rules by punishing those who disobey them. These are the three elements of any system of authority. And every society also finds it necessary on occasion to back decisions with force. But, as in all things pertaining to culture, the mode of reaching and supporting decisions varies from culture to culture.

We must not confuse authority with authoritarianism. The rendering of decisions does not mean that they are harsh, unfair, arrived at without common consent, or in any way inimical to the welfare of the whole group. However, it does mean that people, by virtue of living in society, necessarily give up a measure of their independence of action. Indeed, the fact that each person is inducted into a culture and inculcated with its precepts means that true autonomy of action is neither possible for him nor desirable to him. Yet man everywhere has chafed at the restraints that demands of social life inevitably place upon him, and every society known to man has recorded examples of persons who ran counter to one or another of the regulations that his society has imposed. The allocation of the power to an individual or group to make decisions which are binding on others may be viewed as a kind of status and an aspect of role. But it is of such special importance to the organization of social life that it deserves separate treatment.

As MacIver points out, authority, like charity, begins in the home. The child is inevitably subordinated to the adults and, whether gently or harshly, whether by quiet insinuation or by stern disciplinary action, is brought into conformity with the expectations of his culture. So, too, there must in every family be persons with the responsibility of inculcating these patterns of behavior. It may be either father or mother or both, and not infrequently other relatives are involved as well; responsibility may be shared or each may take separate spheres. But the household is regularized in some fashion, and under normal circumstances within any one society, these patterns of authority are consistent. (Our own changing society is more variable in this regard than most, for we have in America a wide diversity of cultural backgrounds and economic activities, yet even here there is a clear central tendency in behavior.)

Governance among primitive peoples is frequently built upon kinship, and authority is a kind of extension of kinship roles and familial decision-making processes. (We use the term governance to emphasize the *process* of decision making; the more common term government suggests a set of political institutions, separate and distinct from other elements in the society, and such separate institutions are not always found.) We have already seen two examples of kin-based governmental procedure. The clans among the Tlingit are family groups, and it is through them that Tlingit decisions are reached: within the clan by established kinship roles; between clans by the principle of equivalence backed, where necessary, by fighting. The structure of government among the Soga also rests upon kinship. The hierarchical structure of authority which forges a kind of national unity operates through role relationships based largely upon kin ties. The former system is widespread among primitive peoples who have no special governmental institutions, vesting authority on elders of the band or tribe or placing it in the hands of the leaders of autonomous extended families or clans. Many African societies, like the Soga, unified a territory by recognition of a royal or chiefly lineage, within which power rested and in which the subdivisions were articulated through the kin relationships between the division chiefs and the higher levels on up to the king.

Another use of kinship for maintaining order is exemplified by the Iroquois, which is discussed in this section by the pioneer American anthropologist, Lewis Henry Morgan. The Iroquois league was a combination of several separate tribes, but the men who held the power in that organization were representatives of lineages or extended households who had the recognized prerogative of appointing these Sachems, as they were called, and these in turn represented the several separate clans. Thus the kin groups that extended across tribal boundaries served to link the separate tribes into a strong unity.

Not all authority in primitive society is based upon the sentiments of kinship. When the Plains Indians obtained horses brought by the Spanish and moved out on the plains to exploit the great herds of buffalo, they required adjustments in their social institutions to meet the new situations in which they found themselves. Some tribes, such as the Cheyenne, developed special police societies which maintained order and enforced the rules. They even formulated new regulations. Secret societies perform similar functions in other parts of the world.

This reminds us that authority is not limited to formal situations, but occurs in all groups. A study made by William F. Whyte of gangs in the Boston area, from which the essay in this section was taken, showed that these informal cliques of boys and young men were clearly structured, normally with a leader and a couple of lieutenants. Leadership was generally won the hard way—by fighting for predominance—but once it was attained it was generally recognized, and proper deference was shown, as we shall see.

We must distinguish between authority and government, a point to which we alluded earlier. Though all societies recognize authoritative roles, not all societies have political institutions which can properly be called government. We speak of government when we have a state; namely, a large and populous area under common administration. Government may be defined as a system of control where a kind of monopoly on the legitimate use of force is held by the rulers. It is a concentration of power recognized and accepted by the population over which it is exercised.

In this sense, primitive tribes frequently have no government, though there is governance—that is, institutions which permit of authoritative control over a sector of the population. They fail to have true government not only because authoritative roles relate to limited spheres of activity, but also because control only extends over small areas and few people. The first limitation applies to the Iroquois, for the elaborate structure which Morgan describes had very limited functions: it merely established peace and initiated war with neighboring peoples. It did not itself even conduct these wars, which were entirely in the hands of private war leaders with their personal following. It collected no taxes, maintained no public works, rendered no judgments over individuals, nor administered any of the many things we consider a normal part of government. The Tlingit legal material covers the second point. In a sense, each clan was a power unto itself, living interspersed with other clans, each with equal internal powers. None recognized the supremacy of another (as was the case among the Soga), but was jealous of its prerogatives and protected its members against any threat from members of other clans, though they might live in the house next door. The close interrelationship between clans, their mutual interdependence and intermarriage, and above all the fact that they shared the same culture, made it possible for them to live in relative peace and harmony. While conflict was frequent, it could be resolved by peaceable means, of which the most important was the potlatch (a custom they shared with the Kwakiutl, among other tribes, and which was discussed by Ruth Benedict in the section on Culture).

From what has already been said, it is clear that it is not necessary to have government in order to have laws. Indeed, though governmental institutions are often wanting, every tribe has law, in the anthropological sense. By law, we mean generally recognized rules of conduct, established tabus, expectations and limitations on conduct, together with recognized sanctions against the breach of such regulations. Such rules are not written down by peoples who have no writing, yet they are always present and are often quite explicit and detailed. The Yurok Indians of California, whom we will discuss in the section on Ethics, had specific fines and compensations for a wide variety of acts; similar details can be found among many other peoples, though the rules of primitive peoples are not often so sharply defined. Nevertheless, rules exist.

One may wonder how regulations can be enforced without government. The answer is that they are enforced by direct conflict between the person who is alleged to have committed an act and the person who feels himself wronged. Each may call upon his group (usually kindred or fellow villagers) to back him up. If the disputants cannot find a solution to their quarrel, they resort to bloodshed. This is, of course, the absence of government, for in this situation nobody has a monopoly on the use of force. But it is not anarchy, for the community has a recognized stake in the restoration of peace. Furthermore it provides rules according to which the disputants must conduct themselves, techniques for getting them together to work out a compromise, and criteria by which the claims of the two parties can be measured. The decision often rests on a duel. Among the Eskimos, the disputants may have either a wrestling or a song duel. In the latter case, each improvises words to a kind of chant with which he mocks the other, and the one whose verbal blows are the cleverer wins by popular acclaim. Among Australian aborigines, the person injured will throw spears at the culprit, endeavoring to harm him in proportion to his own loss.

These techniques may not seem like adjudication to us, but rather like the behavior of school boys. However, this is not the case. For factors are at work which lend these methods some elements of judicial process, though admittedly in a primitive form. In the first instance, they are carried on in front of the whole community, which has an interest in the equitable settlement of the dispute. It therefore lends the procedure legitimacy by supervising the duel, seeing to it, for instance, that the Australian who has done the proper amount of damage does not go too far and that his assailant does not try to retaliate. In the dueling situation, they give psychological support to the person whose cause seems most just; and where the duel is a song contest, they express their opinion quite directly. We do not mean that justice is always served—no court system ever devised has been able to make this assurance—but merely that the process does provide elements of adjudication.

The direct application of force operates on a more highly developed level in many primitive societies. This is exemplified by the Tlingit material, presented by Oberg. While feud still resolves force, the process brings together not merely the two individuals, but the two groups to which they belong. Here there is an elaborate procedure for negotiating the dispute in which both groups participate. Yet it is fundamentally the same pattern, for if these negotiations break down, the two sides enter into a fight. Thus, the force that sanctions law remains in the hands of the two parties to the dispute.

In many such instances, the difficulty is resolved by the payment of property—just as we pay fines for minor violations, or recognize financial compensation in civil-law suits. In some societies, such as the Yurok of northwestern California, there is a clearly established fine or compensation for every legal infraction, from a minor insult to murder. The payment of wergild, as the compensation to a murdered family is called, is a widespread practice among peoples who have money but no true courts, and was an element in old Germanic law. The basic principle of this practice continues, in effect, in compensation for damages recognized in our courts.

Our law, to be sure, differs in that the decision is rendered by a judge; that is, by a person who has been accorded a role in society which empowers him to render decisions binding upon both parties to the dispute. The recognition of a special adjudicative role is found among primitive people, but seems to be limited to those who have a more advanced form of economy and society. Some societies recognize both the use of feud and adjudication through courts. The Ba-Ila of Northern Rhodesia are an example: where a man may press a claim either directly himself, through his clan, or through a court presided over by the chief.

Where there are political states there must be courts of law; that is, the state must have the power to render decisions in disputes among its citizenry and these decisions must be recognized as binding upon the parties involved. In a sense, this is part of the definition of a state, for the state must have a monopoly on the legitimate use of force, and therefore cannot allow for legitimate feuds to take place. Throughout much of sub-Saharan Africa the state system provides courts with most of the elements of our own: testimony under oath, hearing of witnesses, rules of evidence and procedure, use of advocates or lawyers, appeals to precedent, right to appeal to higher tribunals, and the rendering of judgment as to guilt and the assessment of penalties. Citizen juries do not exist, but there is often a group of elders who advise the chief, who acts as judge.

Life in society, as we have said, involves surrendering to that society a measure of personal autonomy. Most of us, most of the time, take this as a matter of course, for we grow into customary behavior and would indeed be lost if we did not have social directives for behavior. We may sometimes feel that customary procedures hamper our freedom (must we really wear a necktie in summer?) but we are embarrassed when we don't know the customs that govern a situation. At any rate, the advantages of group life make it a worthwhile bargain to submit to the demands of custom and conformity.

In the course of human history, with the growth of human technological knowledge, societies have grown larger. With each advance in size, every local group and every other social entity gives up a measure of its autonomy for the preservation of the larger unity. An Andaman Island band of thirty or forty hunting and food-gathering Negritos is autonomous, recognizing no higher authority. But they cannot muster a large contingent to engage in a common enterprise. The Tlingit clans maintain a measure of autonomy, but recognize a general pattern of rules within which they operate. A Cheyenne tribe brings together several bands which recognize the authority of the soldier societies. The Iroquois welded together their separate tribes into a League covering a wide area. A glance at the history of Egypt in the fifth millennium B.C. or at England from the Saxon period to the Victorian era, displays a similar evolution of gradual increase in the size of social unit brought under a single-authority system.

Those who formulated the American constitution were aware of the problems inherent in size and its potential effect on autonomy, and the document they framed was a compromise between the advantages of unity and the dangers they saw in the concentration of power. The problem remains with us, but the rapid advance of technology has been a major force in furthering federal unity as against states' rights. Their conscious concern with the need for and dangers of authority in society is testified to by many documents, including the Constitution itself. The best known discussion of these problems is in the Federalist Papers, one of which is reproduced in this section.

It seems useful to analyze two kinds of law, which we may designate internal law and external law. Internal law is found where a role of authority is recognized as applying to the whole group. External law is where no such role is recognized, but where, nevertheless, the people do have common customs and common procedures for adjudication— that is, where they respect the same laws but have no adjudicative agent, no person or group with over-all authority. Each Andamanese band is independently governed by internal law; several may be bound together by external law. Each Tlingit clan is organized in terms of an internal law, the relation among them is regulated by external law. Beyond the range of external law lies an area where no law exists—that is, where no common set of practices are mutually agreed upon, through which disputes may be settled and justice maintained. The growth of modern nations may be seen as an expansion of internal law. And as these have grown, the pattern of external law has expanded beyond their borders, so that warfare and peace-making between modern nations is governed by external law. The difficulty is that when the procedures for external law break down, war breaks out; just as when two Eskimos could not work out their grievance, there would be a duel, or when two Tlingit clans could not resolve their conflict, there would be a feud.

Authority is universal, but the scope of that authority varies widely. The system of governance may be limited to a few nuclear families or may be spread across a continent. But, because society requires unity of action among men, there must be some focal point for the direction of action, there must be some allocation of decision making.

Furthermore, conflicts of interest within a society will inevitably occur. When they do occur, there must be techniques by which such conflicts can be resolved without endangering either the society itself or the cultural assumptions under which it operates.

42. The Essentials of Law and Order

ROBERT M. MacIVER

Robert M. MacIver demonstrates that law begins in the home. In this essay he shows the universal necessity of systems of authority and the network of authority that characterizes any social system. He offers us an understanding of the general problems of governments.

MacIver was born in Scotland and took his Ph.D. from the University of Edinburgh (1915) which awarded him an honorary degree in 1953. He has also been honored with special degrees from Columbia, Harvard, and Princeton. He was Lieber Professor of Political Philosophy and Sociology at Columbia University from 1929 to 1950. He has written widely on political theory from a sociological point of view including *Democracy and Economic Challenge, Academic Freedom in Our Time,* and *The Pursuit of Happiness.* The present essay comes from his *The Web of Government,* New York: The Macmillan Company, 1947, and is printed with the kind permission of the publisher and the author.

. . . Regulation is a universal aspect of society. Society means a system of ordered relations. The system may be informal, folk-sustained, uncentralized, and without specific agencies, or it may be highly organized. But social regulation is always present, for no society can exist without some control over the native impulses of human beings. Political government appears when social regulation is taken over or begins to be presided over by a central social agency. At first the business of regulation is mainly a family concern, broadly protected by the custom of the inclusive group. To ascribe the beginnings of government to force or to contract or to some particular conjuncture is to ignore the fact that already in the family, the primary social unit, there are always present the curbs and controls that constitute the essence of government. Government is not something that is invented by the cunning or the strong and imposed on the rest. Government, however much exploitation of the weak by the strong it may historically exhibit, is much more fundamental than these explanations imply. It is the continuation by the more inclusive society of a process of regulation that is already highly developed within the family.

373

The family is bound up with all the great crises and transitions of life. It is the focus of the most intimate relationships, those in which the personality of man and of woman is most profoundly expressed and most thoroughly tested. It is the primary agent in the molding of the life-habits and the life-attitudes of human beings. It is the center of the most impressive celebrations and rituals, those associated with marriage, with death, and with the initiation of the child into the beliefs and ways of the community. It is the hearth, the home, the place where the generations are brought continuously together, where old and young must learn to make ever changing adjustments to their ever changing roles in the life-cycle.

The same necessities that create the family create also regulation. The imperative of sex has for human beings no pre-established harmony with longer-range imperatives, with the upbringing of the young and the maintenance and enhancement through the generations of the mode of life that the group, on whatever level, has acquired. The long dependence of the human young necessitates the establishment of some kind of control of sexual relations. There must be rules, and against so powerful an appetite, against the recklessness and the caprice of desire, these rules must be guarded by powerful sanctions. They must have back of them the authority of the community, bulwarked by such myths as the prevailing culture can devise against so formidable a danger.

Here is government in miniature and already government of a quite elaborate character. For sex is so closely inwrought with other concerns, and particularly with those of possession and inheritance, that its control carries with it a whole social code. The existence of the family requires the regulation of sex, the regulation of property, and the regulation of youth. If we briefly examine what is involved in these three types of regulation we shall see why the family is everywhere the matrix of government.

Let us consider the regulation of sex. It has a number of aspects. First there are mating rules, determining who may enter with whom into the kind of sexual union that contemplates the establishment of family life. Mating is hedged about by restrictions and conditions. . . .

Then there are rules restricting sexual relations outside of mating. The main function of these is again to preserve the integrity of the family. Foremost among them is the practically universal incest taboo. If there is one rule that is common to all the endlessly divergent human societies that the earth knows or has known, it is this. . . .

. . . The family is itself a way of living, and the way of living is always governed by a code.

We select from this pervasive code the regulation of property. . . .

Furthermore, the economy of the simple community is a family economy. What is produced is shared within the family; what each provides is his or her contribution to the common stock. So much is true in degree of the family everywhere, but in the simpler community the family is a joint producer, not merely a beneficiary of the joint product. The family is, particularly in the agricultural economy, the functioning microcosm; within it there is division of labor, beyond it there is generally little. The primal division of labor, between the child-bearing female and the sustaining male, is developed and elaborated in the processes of family life. The routines of work and the customs of the economic scheme of things are learned, directed, and administered under the aegis of the family. . . .

With society, as always, goes regulation. . . . The home is the world of the child, and it is a governed world. Regulation is operative from the first, in the sequences of feeding and cleaning. Presently the child is disciplined in the exercise of his bodily functions. He is, so to speak, "house-broken." He is taught that this is right and that is wrong. As he learns the speech of the folk he learns the values that are conveyed by words. This is good and that is bad; this is honorable and that is shameful. So the long process of indoctrination and habituation begins. The child is governed in its going out and in its coming in, in its rising and in its lying down, in its learning and in its playing, in its doing and in its thinking, in its hoping and in its fearing.

The child knows no other world, no other values. In the circle of the home, affection and authority are combined, whatever the proportions may be. They are not likely to be wholly reconciled, for authority represses native inclinations. But the authority is final, as authority. There is no alternative, and there is no appeal. It may be disobeyed, but that is evasion. It may be defied, but that is rebellion. Here the authority is absolute. No other is even conceivable. Other authorities may rule outside, but to the child the outside is another world. The world of the child is a closed world of absolute authority, mitigated by affection. . . .

So far as the child is concerned the imperium of the home is always absolute at the first, and only the length of time through which it holds undisputed sway differentiates in this respect one form of culture from another. For the child the magic of the law begins as soon as it becomes aware of others and of its relation to others. What is right and what is wrong, the things it must not do and the things it must do, are delivered to it from on high, as the law was delivered to Moses. It is so ordained, it is the eternal way of things. It is incorporated in the rites and religious observances of the community. Beyond it there is no other law.

It is easy then to see how "the habits pertaining to government" are bred in childhood, and how the family itself is always, for the child at least, a miniature political realm. . . .

Before we proceed to show how government grew up from its cradle in the family we shall pause over a matter of definition. We have been speaking about "government," but the word "state" has crept into the argument. What is the difference? When we speak of the state we mean the organization of which government is the administrative organ. Every social organization must have a focus of administration, an agency by which its policies are given specific character and translated into action. But the organization is greater than the organ. In this sense the state is greater and more inclusive than government. A state has a constitution, a code of laws, a way of setting up its government, a body of citizens. When we think of this whole structure we think of the state. . . . the political structure itself, with its usages and traditions, with its framework of institutional relationships between the rulers and the ruled, should not be identified with its organ of government.

Under certain social conditions, particularly in the simpler societies, it is not appropriate to speak of a state. The political structure may be embryonic or rudimentary. Similarly there may be no structure properly called a church, even though a religion prevails and there are special officers of religion, priests or prophets. The terms "state" and "church" apply to specific associational forms that emerge at a later stage, and characterize more complex societies.

First comes the function, carried on by the undifferentiated community with little assistance from officials or special agencies within the community. There is religion without a priest. There is customary law, group-enforced, before there are judges or courts of law—such, for instance, is the situation among some Melanesian peoples. The function is signalized by particular ceremonies, often quite elaborate ones, which seem to be sufficiently directed and controlled by the tradition of the folk. But some members of the group are always at least the informal and occasional leaders at the performance of social functions, the knowing ones, the elders, the heads of families. We may presume that beginning in this way leadership becomes institutionalized. The medicine man becomes an institution, the priest is designated, the chief and the council of elders emerge. The communal functions now receive specialized direction. The organs of communal government are elaborated. But we are still some way from anything corresponding to a state in the proper sense. The process must advance much further before the political organization, with its seat of government, its continuity of office, its code of laws, and all the rest becomes sufficiently differentiated to have its own unity, its own being, and to be called a state. We may observe in passing that while social regulation can be carried on in the household or in the simple custom-ruled community without the necessity of the state-form it is quite otherwise under the conditions of a complex society. There the conduct of government requires the presence of the full-grown state. . . .

. . . Some peoples are warlike and make slaves of their captured enemies: among such the institutions of government often, though by no means always, become more rigid and hierarchical. Other peoples, whether because of natural conditions or because of disposition and the prevalence of different myths, have been peaceful in their ways, and among such the institutions of government tended to be less centralized and less authoritarian.

War and conquest have played their role not only in the extension of the area of government but also in the consolidation of political power. War makes urgent demands and exacts a discipline, a subordination to leadership, more rigorous than the discipline of peace. It intrudes with violence on the self-containedness of the kin-group, the local commune. The threat of a powerful enemy often persuades smaller groups to unite. On the other hand the victor in war extends his dominion over the vanquished. The most spectacular instance of this process in all history was the way in which the little tribes centered in Rome brought first Latium, and then gradually all Italy, and finally the whole Western world, together with the Near East, under the sway of their imperial city.

In appraising the role of war in the building up of greater political systems it should not, however, be forgotten that war is also a potent divider. Nothing separates human groups so much as the fear each entertains of the other, and perhaps nothing stimulates that fear so much as the threat or the danger of war. Every group tends to cherish its separate existence, is convinced of its own superior worth, regards its own ways as preferable to the ways of others, its own myths as exclusive deliverances from on high, and generally is suspicious, not infrequently contemptuous, of the outsider. But the arts of peace subtly increase the need for wider relationships, and culture permeates beyond any artificial boundaries, and trade proves profitable to both sides, and every advance of technology not only spreads from group to group but, unless the insulation of warlike attitudes stays its influence, at length knits the various groups in the necessities of interdependence. Thus we are at liberty to conjecture that in the absence of war the range of society and the aegis of common government might have extended from group to group, though no doubt in a very different manner from that which was actually exhibited.

There was another consequence of warfare that is not open to question. The conduct of war sharpens authority and creates a clean-cut system of subordination, rank above rank. Even the local raids and excursions that in many instances constituted tribal war imposed graded relations of command and obedience that differed greatly from the normal routine of peace. If the warfare led to the taking of captives they often became the serfs or slaves of the victors. If it led to the subjection of a neighboring tribe they often became tributary to the victors and sometimes were turned into an exploited colony or a class or caste of inferiors, hewers of wood and drawers of water. Finally, war sometimes meant a forcible transfer of economic resources, and its spoils, distributed in proportion to rank, established new disparities of wealth among the conquering people. On all these counts war proved a great agency in the creation of social inequalities, of a hierarchical class system.

We have much evidence that in very simple societies there is little or no organized subordination of group to group or class to class, no defined superiority and inferiority of social rank, rarely anything corresponding to slavery. Always there are of course differences of prestige, always there is leadership; there are those who because of prowess or personal distinction have greater influence, and there is the status attaching to age, sex, marital condition, and familial position. But these differences lie easy on the people; they seem to be in the nature of things and they are sustained by custom. All men are neighbors and share a common lot. There is little disparity of poverty or wealth. There is little division of labor outside the family. For the most part it is only when the community extends and grows more complex that the specific assignment of men and groups to higher and lower orders comes into effect.

It is only then that ruling and subject classes appear. It is only then that government becomes formalized, and, for the reasons already offered the practice of war gave a strong impetus toward this transformation. . . .

The passage from the simple kin-bound society to the differentiated hierarchical society was not possible without a corresponding transformation of the social myth. No custom or institution can subsist merely as a mode of behaving or as a set of external responses sanctioned by usage alone. Custom, said Herodotus, is the king of men, but custom to be king must be hallowed and sanctioned by myth. If the myth is rejected the custom collapses, and if the grand myth of authority is overthrown there is revolution. The social myth congenial to the kin-bound society conceives the whole universe in familial terms. The Gods too form a family and there is a patriarch God who is the father of all, the paterfamilias of the universe.

Without law there is no order, and without order men are lost, not knowing where they go, not knowing what they do. A system of ordered relationships is a primary condition of human life at every level. More than anything else it is what society means. Even an outlaw group, a pirate ship, a robber gang, a band of brigands, has its own code of law, without which it could not exist. The picture of the "lawless savage," running wild in the woods, is wholly fictitious. The "savage" is never lawless, he clings to his own laws more tenaciously, more blindly, than does the civilized man. Only the completely *déraciné,* the man torn from his social environment, or the extreme sophisticate, or the tyrant who emerges in a time of confusion, can be described approximately as lawless. The law of the "savage" is not our law, and there is no law between him and the outsider—a situation that still exists, in times of war, for civilized peoples. The world has been, and up to the present has remained, a collocation of areas of lawfulness, communities with no law binding the one to the other. . . .

. . . Thomas Hobbes was right when he explained that law in human society is not like the law that rules the communities of ants or of bees. It is not in that sense "natural," not biologically determined but socially constructed, a folk-creation. . . . Occasionally, at a more advanced stage, the heroic figure of a "law-maker" appears, like Lycurgus or Solon or Hammurabi or Moses. But the Great Legislator is usually represented as being either a codifier of the laws or a prophet who receives them from God. . . .

In a modern society we distinguish between custom and law, and recognize that custom and other non-legal principles control a great sector of human behavior. In simple societies there is no clear-cut distinction between custom and law. The specific legal code, with its specific machinery of enforcement, has not yet developed. Consequently such government as existed was not regarded as making rules for the community, but only as administering its affairs, settling disputes, and guarding the folkways against the dangerous violator. Where, however, communities expanded in population and resources, where they extended their boundaries, through war or otherwise, and took under their dominion other groups or communities, where by reason of such conditions the tempo of social change was accelerated, and especially where serious conflicts and maladjustments arose between the more demarcated economic categories or social classes of the larger society, there the old-established folkways no longer gave the needed guidance. Government took on the job of *legislation*. . . .

Every society, at every stage of civilization, rests on a firmament of law that is vastly greater and much more intricate than any ever devised by any government, one that is too great and too intricate to be completely overturned even by the most revolutionary of governments. We must recognize this elementary fact if we are to understand the nature of government and the authority of government. This firmament of law is composed of various interfused elements, the composition varying with the kind of society. There are societies in which it is almost wholly folk-sustained customary law, with practically no element of legal law, that is, of law interpreted and enforced by courts or judges. There are others in which the social firmament has a considerable element of common law, law accepted and enforced by courts but not enacted by governments. Then as we pass to more complex societies we find an increasing amount of statute law, law made expressly by governments, combined with the element of common law, while this more precise framework is filled in its myriad interstices with the pervasive element of custom. . . .

. . . The law of the land is far more secure where it does not clash with the customs, beliefs, or traditions of any important sector of the people. The question whether it is the *duty* of the citizen always to obey the law has generally arisen where the individual or the group has been confronted with two conflicting claims on loyalty, where Antigone has to choose between the command of her king and the sacred custom of the kin, where Orestes has to choose between the respect due to his mother and the obligation to avenge his father, where the persecuted religious sect has to choose between the law of the temporal power and the ordinance of God, where the pacifist has to choose between the order to take up arms and the dictate of his conscience or his faith. Whether we accept the position of those who concede to the state the prior authority in all situations or of those who in answer point out that a man's primary obligation is the loyalty and the course of action that for him is most compelling or most sacred, we must in any event agree that the law has no sure foundations when it denies or over-rides these other claims. Only where the various loyalties of men can live together, inter-adjusted within the same framework of legal law, can the firmament of order be sustained.

43. Iroquois Governance

LEWIS HENRY MORGAN

Lewis Henry Morgan was a pioneer American anthropologist. He is chiefly known for three major works. The first, *Systems of Consanguinity and Affinity in Human Society*, introduced to anthropology the study of kinship systems and their characteristics in primitive society. The second was his influential *Ancient Society* which delineated an evolutionary theory of culture. The third was his *League of the Ho-de'-no-sau-nee or Iroquois*, and was a comprehensive analysis of Iroquois political organization and culture. It was first published in 1851.

The Iroquois had one of the most highly developed political systems in what is now the United States. The League as a political instrument unified a broad area but left the separate tribes as independent sovereign political entities. It is an excellent example of the manner in which kinship is utilized to formulate and firm up a political system. The League cannot actually be called a state. It was concerned only with the maintenance of peace and solidarity; it maintained no control over civil affairs, had no courts, taxes, or public works. Nevertheless, it exemplified a high degree of political organization on what is essentially a tribal level. The material below is excerpted from Morgan's *League of the Ho-de'-no-sau-nee or Iroquois* (New York: Mead, 1901) and is printed with kind permission of Dodd, Mead & Company, Inc.

Among the Indian nations whose ancient seats were within the limits of our republic, the Iroquois have long continued to occupy the most conspicuous position. They achieved for themselves a more remarkable civil organization, and acquired a higher degree of influence, than any other race of Indian lineage, except those of Mexico and Peru. In the drama of European colonization, they stood, for nearly two centuries, with an unshaken front, against the devastations of war, the blighting influence of foreign intercourse, and the still more fatal encroachments of a restless and advancing border population. Under their federal system, the Iroquois flourished in independence, and capable of self-protection, long after the New England and Virginia races had surrendered their jurisdictions, and fallen into the condition of dependent nations; and they now stand forth in our Indian history, prominent alike for the wisdom of their civil institutions, their sagacity in the administration of the League, and their courage in its defence. . . .

The project of a League originated with the Onondagas, among whom it was first suggested, as a means to enable them more effectually to resist the pressure of contiguous nations. The epoch of its establishment cannot now be decisively ascertained; although the circumstances attending its formation are still preserved by tradition with great minuteness. These traditions all refer to the northern shore of the Onondaga lake, as the place where the Iroquois chiefs assembled in general council, to agree upon the terms and principles of the compact, by which their future destinies were to be linked together. It is evident from their traditionary history, which is entitled to considerable credit, that they had long occupied the country before their necessities or increase of numbers made the League a feasible or desirable consummation. . . .

After the formation of the League, the Iroquois rose rapidly in power and influence. It gave them additional strength by concentration of effort; a constant increase of numbers by the unity of the race; and a firmer establishment, through their more ample means for self-protection and foreign conquest. One of the first results of their federal system was a universal spirit of aggression; a thirst for military glory and political aggrandizement, which made the old forests of America resound with human conflicts from New England to the Mississippi, and from the northern confines of the great lakes to the Tennessee and the hills of Carolina. . . .

The period of their greatest prosperity, and of their highest numbers, was evidently about the year 1650, shortly after the commencement of their intercourse with Europeans. At that time, their total population may be safely placed at twenty-five thousand.

In their own account of the origin of the League, the Iroquois invariably go back to a remote and uncertain period, when the compact between the Five Nations was formed, its details and provisions were settled, and those laws and institutions were established, under which, without essential change, they afterwards continued to flourish. If we may trust their testimony, the system under which they confederated was not of gradual construction, under the suggestions of necessity; but was the result of one protracted effort of legislation. The nations were, at the time, separate and hostile bands, although of generic origin, and were drawn together in council to deliberate upon the plan of a League, which a wise man of the Onondaga nation had projected, and under which, he undertook to assure them, the united nations could elevate themselves to a general supremacy. Tradition has preserved the name of *Da-gä-no-we'-dä* as the founder of the League, and the first lawgiver of the *Ho-de'-no-sau-nee.* It likewise points to the northern shore of the *Gä-nun'-ta-ah,* or Onondaga lake, as the place where the first council-fire was kindled, around which the chiefs and wise men of the several nations were gathered, and where, after a debate of many days, its establishment was effected.

Their traditions further inform us, that the confederacy, as framed by this council, with its laws, rules, inter-relationships of the people and mode of administration, has come down through many generations to the present age, with scarcely a change; except the addition of an inferior class of rulers, called chiefs, in contradistinction to the sachems, and a modification of the law in relation to marriage. . . .

The central government was organized and administered upon the same principles which regulated that of each nation, in its separate capacity; the nations sustaining nearly the same relation to the League, that the American states bear to the Union. In the former, several oligarchies were contained within one, in the same manner as in the latter, several republics are embraced within one republic. . . .

The [official] titles or names were hereditary in the several tribes of which each nation was composed. When an individual was made a sachem, upon the death or deposition of one of the fifty, his name was "taken away," and the name of the sachemship held by his predecessor was conferred upon him. Thus, upon the demise of the Seneca sachem who held the title *Gä-ne-o-di'-yo,* a successor would be raised up from the Turtle tribe, in which the sachemship was hereditary, and after the ceremony of investiture, the person would be known among the Iroquois only under the name of *Gä-ne-o-di'-yo.* These fifty titles, excepting two, have been held by as many sachems, in succession, as generations have passed away since the formation of the League.

The Onondaga nation, being situated in a central position, were made the keepers both of the Council Brand, and of the Wampum, in which the structure and principles of their government, and their laws and treaties were recorded. At stated periods, usually in the autumn of each year, the sachems of the League assembled in council at Onondaga, which was in effect the seat of government, to legislate for the common welfare. Exigencies of a public or domestic character often led to the summoning of this council at extraordinary seasons, but the place was not confined to Onondaga. It could be appointed in the territory of either of the nations, under established usages. Originally the object of the general council was to raise up sachems to fill vacancies. In the course of time, as their intercourse with foreign nations became more important, it assumed the charge of all matters which concerned the League. It declared war and made peace, sent and received embassies, entered into treaties of alliance, regulated the affairs of subjugated nations, received new members into the League, extended its protection over feeble tribes, in a word, took all needful measures to promote their prosperity, and enlarge their dominion.

Notwithstanding the equality of rights, privileges and powers between the members of this body of sachems, there were certain discriminations between them which rendered some more dignified than others. The strongest illustration is found in the Onondaga sachem, *To-do-dä'-ho,* who has always been regarded as the most noble sachem of the League. As an acknowledgment of his eminence, two of the Onondaga sachems were assigned to him as hereditary counsellors. The great respect and deference paid by the Iroquois to this title, has led to the vulgar error, that *To-do-dä'-ho* was the king or civil head of the confederacy. He possessed, in fact, no unusual or executive powers, no authority which was not equally enjoyed by his compeers; and when the light of tradition is introduced, to clear up the apparent anomaly, it will be seen that the reverence of the people was rather for the title itself than for the person who held it, as it was one of their illustrious names. At the establishment of the League, an Onondaga by the name of *To-do-dä'-ho* had rendered himself a potent ruler, by the force of his military achievements. Tradition says that he had conquered the Cayugas and the Senecas. . . .

To several other of these officers or names, particular duties were affixed at the institution of the League. For example: the Senecas were made the door-keepers of the Long House; and having imposed upon *Do-ne-ho-gä'-weh,* the eighth sachem, the duty of watching the door, they gave to him a sub-sachem, or assistant, to enable him to execute this trust. . . .

The several sachems, in whom, when united in general council, resided the supreme powers of the League, formed, when apart in their own territories, the ruling bodies of their respective nations. When assembled as the Council of the League, the power of each sachem became co-extensive with the government, and direct relations were created between all the people and each individual ruler; but when the sachems of a nation were convened in council, all its internal affairs fell under their immediate cognizance. For all purposes of a local and domestic, and many of a political character, the nations were entirely independent of each other. The nine Mohawk sachems administered the affairs of that nation with joint authority, precisely in the same manner as they did, in connection with their colleagues, the affairs of the League at large. . . .

As the sachems of each nation stood upon a perfect equality, in authority and privileges, the measure of influence was determined entirely by the talents and address of the individual. In the councils of the nation, which were of frequent occurrence, all business of national concernment was transacted; and, although the questions moved on such occasions would be finally settled by the opinions of the sachems, yet such was the spirit of the Iroquois system of government, that the influence of the inferior chiefs, the warriors, and even of the women would make itself felt, whenever the subject itself aroused a general public interest. . . .

Next to the sachems, in position, stood the Chiefs, an inferior class of rulers, the very existence of whose office was an anomaly in the oligarchy of the Iroquois. Many years after the establishment of the League, even subsequent to the commencement of their intercourse with the whites, there arose a necessity for raising up this class. It was an innovation upon the original framework of the confederacy, but it was demanded by circumstances which could not be resisted. The office of chief, *Hä-seh-no-wä'-neh,* which is rendered "an elevated name," was made elective, and the reward of merit; but without any power of descent, the title terminating with the individual. No limit to the number was established. . . . At first their powers were extremely limited, and confined to a participation in the local affairs of their own nation, in the management of which they acted as the counsellors and assistants of the sachems, rather than in the capacity of rulers. But they continued to increase in influence, with their multiplication in numbers, and to encroach upon the powers of the sachems . . . After their election, they were raised up by a council of the nation; but a ratification, by the general council of the sachems, was necessary to complete the investiture. . . .

The powers and duties of the sachems and chiefs were entirely of a civil character, and confined, by their organic laws, to the affairs of peace. No sachem could go out to war in his official capacity, as a civil ruler. If disposed to take the war-path, he laid aside his civil office, for the time being, and became a common warrior. It becomes an important inquiry, therefore, to ascertain in whom the military power, was vested. The Iroquois had no distinct class of war-chiefs, raised up and set apart to command in time of war; neither do the sachems or chiefs appear to have possessed the power of appointing such persons as they considered suitable to the post of command. All military operations were left entirely to private enterprise, and to the system of voluntary service, the sachems seeking rather to repress and restrain, than to encourage the martial ardor of the people. Their principal war-captains were to be found among the class called chiefs, many of whom were elected to this office in reward for their military achievements. . . . Their whole civil policy was averse to the concentration of power in the hands of any single individual, but inclined to the opposite principle of division among a number of equals; and this policy they carried into their military as well as through their civil organization. Small bands were, in the first instance, organized by individual leaders, each of which, if they were afterwards united upon the same enterprise, continued under its own captain, and the whole force, as well as the conduct of the expedition, was under their joint management. They appointed no one of their number to absolute command, but the general direction was left open to the strongest will, or the most persuasive voice.

As they were at war with all nations not in their actual alliance, it was lawful for any warrior to organize a party, and seek adventures wherever he pleased to direct his steps. Perhaps some chief, filled with martial ardor, planned an inroad upon the Cherokees of the south; and, having given a war-dance, and thus enlisted all who wished to share the glory of the adventure, took the war-path at once, upon his distant and perilous enterprise. In such ways as this, many expeditions originated; and it is believed that a great part of the warlike transactions of the Iroquois were nothing more than personal adventures, or the daring deeds of inconsiderable war-parties. Under such a state of things, a favorite leader, possessed of the confidence of the people from his war-like achievements, would be in no want of followers, in the midst of a general war; nor would the League be in any danger of losing the services of its most capable military commanders. To obviate the dangerous consequences of disagreement, when the several nations were prosecuting a common war, and their forces were united into one body, an expedient was resorted to for securing unanimity in their plans, in the establishment of two supreme military chieftaincies. The two chieftains who held these offices were designed rather to take the general supervision of the affairs of war, than the actual command in the field, although they were not debarred from assuming it, if they were disposed to do so. These war-chiefships were made hereditary, like the sachemships, and vacancies were filled in the same manner. . . .

To the officers above enumerated, the administration of the League was intrusted. The congress of sachems took the charge of all those matters which pertained to the public welfare. With them resided the executive, legislative and judicial authority, so far as they were not possessed by the people; although their powers in many things appear to have been rather advisory than executive. The chiefs, from counsellors and intermediaries between the sachems and the people, increased in influence, until they became rulers with the sachems themselves, thus widening and liberalizing the oligarchy. In all matters of war, the power appears to have resided chiefly with the people, and its prosecution to have been left to private adventure. If several bands united, they had as many generals as bands, who governed their proceedings by a council, in which, as in civil affairs, unanimity was a fundamental law. The two high military chieftains had rather the planning and general management of the campaign, than the actual conduct of the forces. Running through their whole system of administration, was a public sentiment, which gave its own tendency to affairs, and illustrated to a remarkable degree, that the government rested upon the popular will, and not upon the arbitrary sway of chiefs. . . .

With a mere confederacy of Indian nations, the constant tendency would be to a rupture, from remoteness of position and interest, and from the inherent weakness of such a compact. In the case under consideration, something more lasting was aimed at, than a simple union of the five nations, in the nature of an alliance. A blending of the national sovereignties into one government was sought for and achieved by these forest statesmen. The League made the *Ho-de'-no-sau-nee* one people, with one government, one system of institutions, one executive will. Yet the powers of the government were not so entirely centralized that the national independencies disappeared. This was very far from the fact. The crowning feature of the League, as a political structure, was the perfect independence and individuality of the national sovereignties, in the midst of a central and embracing government, which presented such a cemented exterior that its subdivisions would scarcely have been discovered in the general transactions of the League. . . .

The government sat lightly upon the people, who, in effect, were governed but little. It secured to each that individual independence, which the *Ho-de'-no-sau-nee* knew how to prize as well as the Saxon race; and which, amid all their political changes, they have continued to preserve. . . .

The founders of the Iroquois Confederacy did not seek to suspend the tribal divisions of the people, to introduce a different social organization; but on the contrary, they rested the League itself upon the tribes, and through them, sought to interweave the race into one political family. A careful exploration of those tribal relationships which characterize the political system of the Iroquois, becomes, therefore, of importance. Without such knowledge as this will afford, their government itself is wholly unmeaning and inexplicable.

In each nation there were eight tribes [clans, as they would now be called], which were arranged in two divisions, and named as follows:—

Wolf,	Bear,	Beaver,	Turtle.
Deer,	Snipe,	Heron,	Hawk. . . .

The division of the people of each nation into eight tribes, whether pre-existing, or perfected at the establishment of the Confederacy, did not terminate in its objects with the nation itself. It became the means of effecting the most perfect union of separate nations "ever devised by the wit of man." In effect, the Wolf tribe was divided into five parts, and one fifth of it placed in each of the five nations. The remaining tribes were subjected to the same division and distribution. Between those of the same name—or in other words, between the separated parts of each tribe—there existed a tie of brotherhood, which linked the nations together with indissoluble bonds. The Mohawk of the Wolf tribe recognized the Seneca of the Wolf tribe as his brother, and they were bound to each other by the ties of consanguinity. In like manner the Oneida of the Turtle or other tribe received the Cayuga or Onondaga of the same tribe, as a brother, and with a fraternal welcome. This relationship was not ideal, but was founded upon actual consanguinity. In the eyes of an Iroquois, every member of his own tribe, in whatever nation, was as much his brother or his sister as if children of the same mother. This cross-relationship between the tribes of the same name, and which was stronger, if possible, than the chain of brotherhood between the several tribes of the same nation, is still preserved in all its original strength. It doubtless furnishes the chief reason of the tenacity with which the fragments of the League still cling together. If either of the five nations had wished to cast off the alliance, it must also have broken this bond of brotherhood. Had the nations fallen into collision, it would have turned Hawk tribe against Hawk tribe, Heron against Heron, brother against brother. . . .

With the progress of the inquiry, it becomes more apparent that the Confederacy was in effect a League of Tribes. With the ties of kindred as its principle of union, the whole race was interwoven into one great family, composed of tribes in its first subdivision (for the nations were counterparts of each other); and the tribes themselves, in their subdivisions, composed of parts of many households. Without these close inter-relations, resting, as many of them do, upon the strong impulses of nature, a mere alliance between the Iroquois nations would have been feeble and transitory. . . .

The succession of the rulers of the League is one of the most intricate subjects to be met with in the political system of the Iroquois. It has been so difficult to procure a satisfactory exposition of the enactments by which the mode of succession was regulated, that the sachemships have sometimes been considered elective, at others as hereditary. Many of the obstacles which beset the inquiry are removed by the single fact, that the title of sachem was absolutely hereditary in the tribe to which it was orginally assigned, and could never pass out of it but with its extinction. How far these titles were hereditary in that part of the family of the sachem who were of the same tribe with himself, becomes the true question to consider. The sachem's brothers, and the sons of his sisters were of his tribe, and, consequently, in the line of succession. Between a brother and a nephew of the deceased, there was no law which established a preference; neither between several brothers, on the one hand, and sons of several sisters on the other, was there any law of primogeniture; nor, finally, was there any positive law, that the choice should be confined to the brothers of the deceased ruler, and the descendants of his sisters in the female line, until all these should fail, before a selection could be made from the tribe at large. Hence, it appears, so far as positive enactments were concerned, that the office of sachem was hereditary in the particular tribe in which it ran; while it was elective, as between the male members of the tribe itself.

In the absence of laws, designating with certainty the individual upon whom the inheritance should fall, custom would come in and assume the force of law, in directing the manner of choice, from among a number equally eligible. Upon the decease of a sachem, a tribal council assembled to determine upon his successor. The choice usually fell upon a son of one of the deceased ruler's sisters, or upon one of his brothers—in the absence of physical and moral objections; and this preference of one of his near relatives would be suggested by feelings of respect for his memory. Infancy was no obstacle, it involving only the necessity of setting over the infant a guardian, to discharge the duties of a sachem until he attained a suitable age. It sometimes occurred that all the relatives of the deceased were set aside, and a selection was made from the tribe generally; but it seldom thus happened, unless from the great unfitness of the near relatives of the deceased.

When the individual was finally determined, the nation summoned a council, in the name of the deceased, of all the sachems of the League; and the new sachem was raised up by such council, and invested with his office.

In connection with the power of the tribes to designate the sachems, should be noticed the equal power of deposition. If, by misconduct, a sachem lost the confidence and respect of his tribe, and became unworthy of authority, a tribal council at once deposed him; and, having selected a successor, summoned a council of the League to perform the ceremony of his investiture. . . .

Each tribe in the nation thus formed a species of separate community. The members were all of consanguinity, and their relationships easily traced. In like manner those of the same tribe in each of the other nations were their consanguinii, and their relationships, near and remote, were also traceable. As two tribes were necessarily joined in each family, there was a perfect diffusion of tribes throughout the nation, and throughout the League. In this manner the race of the Iroquois, although consisting of different nations, was blended into one people. The League was in effect established, and rested for its stability, upon the natural faith of kindred.

44. Emergence of Law on the Plains

K. N. LLEWELLYN and E. ADAMSON HOEBEL

Law in the Plains was in transition at the time Europeans came to know those tribes. The use of the horse and gun and the devotion to buffalo hunting altered the pattern of life and made new elements of social organization necessary. One institution that flowered was the military societies which assured that no one would spoil the hunt. These societies among the Cheyenne acquired a great deal of authority and helped to formulate the law.

One of the classic studies of primitive law is *The Cheyenne Way* by Karl N. Llewellyn and E. Adamson Hoebel. Llewellyn was Betts Professor of Jurisprudence at Columbia University until 1951, when he joined the faculty of the University of Chicago Law School. He received his LL.B. (1918) and his J.D. (1920) from Yale University. E. Adamson Hoebel is chairman of the Department and Professor of Anthropology at the University of Minnesota. In addition to his Cheyenne study he has studied the law ways of the Comanche and some of the Pueblo Indian groups, and has recently written *The Law of Primitive Man*. The present essay is taken from Chapter 5, "The Military Societies," of *The Cheyenne Way*, by Karl N. Llewellyn and E. Adamson Hoebel, published by the University of Oklahoma Press, 1941, and is printed by permission of the authors and the publisher.

There were six military societies among the Cheyenne Indians— the Fox Soldiers, Elk Soldiers, Shield Soldiers, Bowstring Soldiers, Dog Men, and Northern Crazy Dogs. These were free associations in which membership was voluntary and at the discretion of the individual. Open to all men of all ages, they were of the ungraded type. . . . The functioning of these societies in matters of intra- and intergroup control is the subject of special attention here. . . .

The coercive authority of the military leaders bordered on the dictatorial in the hands of some of the fighting leaders. . . . There is evidence which indicates that any order of a military society chief had to be obeyed if the order had been issued. The authority of the office was supreme. Nevertheless, one sees the Cheyennes always struggling to keep officialdom within bounds, because the dictatorial tendency of egotistic officials was dangerous to Cheyenne principles of freedom. Yet an authoritative officialdom was needed and sought by the Cheyennes to hold in check the impetuous individualism which Cheyenne military practice nourished and which the Cheyenne sense of order feared. The discrimination which western medieval Europe found so difficult to work into clarity, that between the office and its occupant, the Cheyenne legal genius felt and marked throughout. Their method, however, was not the modern American method of limiting the powers of the office. It was, instead, one of developing machinery for anticipatory pressure on the officer.

Thus the Dog Soldiers in 1863 forbade Bull Bear, their chief, to accompany Elbridge Gerry, emissary of the United States Commissioner of Indian Affairs, to attend a treaty council with the American Commissioners. Bull Bear had expressed a willingness to go with Gerry, but of his followers Grinnell wrote, "it is apparent that they did not trust their chiefs and thought that they had been bribed or cajoled into signing the treaty of 1861. They said that the treaty of 1861 was a swindle." . . .

Indicators that the military societies of the Plains had actually penetrated many phases of tribal life beyond the food-getting emergency of the buffalo hunt were indeed already at hand. Lowie's report on the Hidatsa had recorded that the pipe-bearers of the Blackmouth Society, the policing unit of this tribe, functioned to adjust quarrels and preserve the peace, to restrain cherry-pickers from going out if enemies were reported to be near, and to restrain war parties from setting forth if for any reason the sortie was considered inauspicious. And on the basis of the shreds of data which are scattered throughout the several monographs on the Plains military societies in the American Museum of Natural History volume, Lowie himself had once written of Plains Indian justice in general, "The police society also restrained men from inopportune raids, preserved order on the march or on ceremonial occasions, and in general exercised authority when the success of collective undertakings was at stake." Doctors Provinse and MacLeod, working quite independently with such materials as are already available in the literature, have both felt constrained to go beyond what may be called the "classic" judgment. Provinse concludes, "Though the policing of the buffalo hunt has been frequently remarked by Lowie, Wissler, and others as the primary duty of the police officers, their duties as keepers of the public peace during tribal gatherings appear as important as regulation of the hunt. In fact, if one can judge the relative importance of the police functions by the number of references to each kind found in the reports, police duties in connection with settling disputes, punishing offenders, and maintaining order in the camp generally would seem to surpass in importance the police duties at the communal hunt." . . .

The reach of the soldier societies was wide, and widening, as the reach of active governing officials tends always to be. Not only in such matters of direct public concern, not only in the initiation and execution of needed charities, but also in matters relating to personal property, they could and did serve as law agents. Furthermore, in this field as in those previously discussed, they made law and enforced it.

. . . The history of Wolf Lies Down, owner of horses [illustrates this point].

While Wolf Lies Down was away, a friend took one of his horses to ride to war. This man had brought his bow and arrow and left them in the lodge of the horse's owner. When Wolf Lies Down returned, he knew by this token security who had his horse, so he said nothing.

A year passed without the horse's return, and then Wolf Lies Down invited the Elk Soldier chiefs to his lodge, because he was in their society. "There is this thing," he told them. "My friend borrowed my horse, leaving his bow and arrow; there they are yet. Now I want to know what to do. I want you to tell me the right thing. Will you go over and ask him his intentions?"

The borrower was in another camp well distant, yet the chiefs agreed. "We'll send a man to bring him in, get his word, or receive his presents," they promised.

The camp moved while the messenger was gone, but he knew of course where it would be on his return. The soldier returned with the borrower, who was leading two horses, "one spotted, one ear-tipped." He called for the four Elk chiefs on his arrival. The chiefs laid before him the story told by Wolf Lies Down.

"That is true," the man assented. "My friend is right. I left my bow and arrow here. I intended to return his horse, but I was gone longer than I expected. I have had good luck with that horse, though. I have treated it better than my own. However, when I got back to camp I found my folks there. Our camps were far apart and I just could not get away. I was waiting for his camp and mine to come together. Now, I always intended to do the right thing. I have brought two good horses with me. My friend can have his choice. In addition I give his own horse back, and further, I am leaving my bow and arrow."

Then up spoke Wolf Lies Down, "I am glad to hear my friend say these things. Now I feel better. I shall take one of those horses, but I am giving him that one he borrowed to keep. From now on we shall be bosom friends."

The chiefs declare, "Now we have settled this thing. Our man is a bosom friend of this man. Let it be that way among all of us. Our society and his shall be comrades. Whenever one of us has a present to give, we shall give it to a member of his soldier society.

"Now we shall make a new rule. There shall be no more borrowing of horses without asking. If any man takes another's goods without asking, we will go over and get them back for him. More than that, if the taker tries to keep them, we will give him a whipping."

Thus was a situation fraught with possible friction brought to an amicable close through the good offices of the chiefs of the society of an aggrieved member.

Far more important, however, was the crystallization of a new social policy, the formulation of a law making it a crime henceforth to borrow an owner's horse without his expressed permission. The old custom of free utilization of another's goods, providing one left an identifying "security," was apparently creating friction as it came to be applied to horses. What between good friends could develop into a tense situation—as evidenced here by the resort to soldier chiefs as spokesmen of inquiry—could become immediately and actively disruptive if the concept "friend" were loosely interpreted by a borrower, or the horse not cared for, or if the unnotified borrowing broke in upon the owner's plans, or one owner became the recipient of too many such evidences of friendship. Pawnee's case of horse "borrowing" and its punishment . . . shows the degree of social irresponsibility which the older practice, left unguarded, could engender. Black Wolf stated that the soldiers, and even the tribal chiefs, had been for some time talking about means of putting a stop to the practice. The Elk Soldier chiefs on this occasion took the opportunity to make the step. After declaring the case at hand settled, they moved into general policy. They did not mix the two. Note also, as a soldier society moves into the very unfamiliar matter of legislation, their sound technical attention to what they shall do, if. . . .

Wolf Lies Down died a half century ago, an old man of over eighty years. By rough interpolation this ruling must have been made a bit less than one hundred years ago. This means, of course, that the circumstances as recounted do not make first-hand evidence. But that the story is so clearly told after three generations is indicative of the importance of the step in the minds of the people. Such distinctive legislation was uncommon. . . .

. . . It becomes increasingly clear that for the Cheyennes the military societies had truly become an ever-ready arm of a state "towering immeasurably above single individuals," not only on the particular occasion of the communal hunt, but in internal private and civic affairs as well. Though, in general, subordinate to the tribal Council in policy-making, the military functioned importantly in meeting individual situations of tribal concern.

When a company on duty handled a violation of the law, it rolled police, judiciary, and correctional activities into one breathless action. Their law was anything but dilatory. What is more, it was usually effective in restraining a people not used by custom to restraint.

45. Leadership and Authority in Informal Groups

WILLIAM FOOTE WHYTE

Authority is present in every group situation and structures the course of events. It may be official and formal, or it may be unofficial and informal. The analysis of gang organization in an Italian slum community is an example of the latter case. A casual observer might think that the leader is such because he is the best fighter or sportsman, but this is not the case. For the leader is apt to win the fights and the games because he is the leader; that is, because the gang recognizes his social position and defers to his authority. It has an interest in his winning which gives legitimacy to the informal power that they have accorded him.

William Foote Whyte's *Street Corner Society* is a classic monograph in sociology. Whyte spent several years with this group and others, analyzing the social organizations of these gangs, and not only shows their internal structure, but the relation of these groups to urban political organization. After study at Swarthmore and Harvard, Whyte took his doctorate from the University of Chicago (1943). He is Professor of Sociology of the New York State School of Industrial Relations at Cornell University, Director of the Social Science Research Center and Editor of the journal *Human Organization*.

The essay from *Street Corner Society: The Social Structure of an Italian Slum* is reproduced here with the kind permission of the author and the University of Chicago Press. Copyright 1943, 1955, by The University of Chicago.

The Nortons were Doc's gang. The group was brought together primarily by Doc, and it was built around Doc. When Doc was growing up, there was a kids' gang on Norton Street for every significant difference in age. There was a gang that averaged about three years older than Doc; there was Doc's gang, which included Nutsy, Danny, and a number of others; there was a group about three years younger which included Joe Dodge and Frank Bonelli; and there was a still younger group, to which Carl and Tommy belonged. . . .

Doc was born on Norton Street in 1908. His mother and father, who came from the province of Abruzzi, were the first non-Genoese Italians to settle on the street. In a large family, Doc was the youngest child and his mother's favorite. His father died when he was a small boy. When he was three years old, infantile paralysis shriveled his left arm so that it could never again be normal, but by constant exercise he managed to develop it until he was able to use it for all but heavy work.

Doc spoke of his early years in this way:

> When I was a little boy, I used to dress very neatly. I always used to have a clean suit on, and when I sat down on the doorstep my mother told me always to sit on a newspaper. . . . Other mothers would tell their sons, "Look at the way Dicky dresses. Why can't you be like Dicky?" It's only natural that they didn't like me—until I showed them they'd have to respect me. . . .
>
> I was about twelve when I had my first fight. I had a brother two years older than me. He got in an argument with a kid my size. He said to me, "He's too small for me, you fight him." At first I didn't want to, but finally I fought him. And I beat him up. . . . After that I began to think maybe I was pretty good.
>
> Nutsy was the head of our gang once. I was his lieutenant. He was bigger than me, and he had walloped me different times before I finally walloped him. When he walloped me, there weren't many people around, so I didn't mind, but the one time he broke his promise that he wouldn't hit me, there was a big crowd around. I was a proud kid. I couldn't let him get away with that. . . . You see, I was wrestling him, and I had him down. I said, "If I let you up, will you promise not to hit me?" He promised, but when I let him up and turned away, he cracked me on the nose, and I got a bloody nose. I went after him, and I was beating him up when the big fellows stopped us. . . . Next day I saw him leaning up against the wall. I went up to him and said, "I'll kill you," and I let him have one. He didn't fight back. He knew I was his master. And that got around. So after that I was the leader, and

he was my lieutenant. . . . That was when I was thirteen or fourteen. . . . Nutsy was a cocky kid before I beat him up. . . . After that, he seemed to lose his pride. I would talk to him and try to get him to buck up.

After I walloped him, I told the boys what to do. They listened to me. If they didn't, I walloped them. I walloped every kid in my gang at some time. . . .

Doc's most serious challenge came from Tony Fontana. As he told me:

Tony was in my gang when we were kids together. He was a good fighter. When he entered the ring as an amateur, he started off winning three fights by knockouts. When he turned pro, he was still knocking them out. . . . At that time I was the leader of the gang. I was the tough guy. But he began to get fresh with me. One night he began pushing me around and talking big. I listened to him. I thought, "He must be tough. All those knockouts have got to mean something." So after a while I said, "I'm going up to bed." I got undressed and went to bed, but I couldn't sleep. I put on my clothes and came down again. I said, "Say that to me again!" He did and I let him have it—pow! . . . But he wouldn't fight me. Why? Prestige, I suppose. Later we had it out with gloves on the playground. He was too good for me, Bill. I stayed with him, but he was too tough. . . . Could he hit! . . .

When Doc's kids' gang broke up, Nutsy was the only member who continued to spend all his spare time on Norton Street. Since he took up with the younger boys, Doc and Danny called him "the King of the Kids." Frank Bonelli became particularly attached to Nutsy. Joe Marco, known as Joe Dodge, was a good friend of both men. Carl and Tommy, who had belonged to a still younger group, now accepted Nutsy's leadership. Alec had gone to school with a younger brother of Joe Dodge, and he first took to hanging on Norton Street in order to be with Joe. . . .

Close friendship ties already existed between certain of the men, but the Nortons, as an organization, did not begin to function until the early spring of 1937. It was at that time that Doc returned to the corner. Nutsy, Frank, Joe, Alec, Carl, and Tommy had a great respect for Doc and gathered around him. Angelo, Fred, and Lou followed Doc in making the corner their headquarters. Danny and Mike were drawn to Norton Street by their friendship for Doc and by the location of their crap game, right next to "the corner." Long John followed Danny and Mike.

The men became accustomed to acting together. They were also tied to one another by mutual obligations. In their experiences together there were innumerable occasions when one man would feel called upon to help another, and the man who was aided would want to return the favor. Strong group loyalties were supported by these reciprocal activities.

There were distinctions in rank among the Nortons. Doc, Danny, and Mike held the top positions. They were older than any others except Nutsy. They possessed a greater capacity for social movement. While the followers were restricted to the narrow sphere of one corner, Doc, Danny, and Mike had friends in many other groups and were well known and respected throughout a large part of Cornerville. It was one of their functions to accompany the follower when he had to move outside of his customary social sphere and needed such support. The leadership three were also respected for their intelligence and powers of self-expression. Doc in particular was noted for his skill in argument. On the infrequent occasions when he did become involved, he was usually able to outmaneuver his opponent without humiliating him. I never saw the leadership three exert their authority through physical force, but their past fighting reputations tended to support their positions.

Doc was the leader of the gang. The Nortons had been Doc's gang when they had been boys, and, although the membership had changed, they were still thought to be Doc's gang. The crap game and its social obligations prevented Danny and Mike from spending as much time with the Nortons as did Doc. They were not so intimate with the followers, and they expected him to lead.

Long John was in an anomalous position. Though he was five years younger than Doc, his friendship with the three top men gave him a superior standing. As Doc explained:

> It's because we've always catered to Long John. When we go somewhere, we ask Long John to go with us. We come up to him and slap him on the back. We give him so much attention that the rest of the fellows have to respect him. . . .

One evening in October, 1937, Doc scheduled a bowling match against the Italian Community Club, which was composed largely of college men who held their meetings every two weeks in the Norton Street Settlement House. The club was designed to be an organization of well-educated and superior men, although Doc was a member, and

Angelo, Lou, and Fred of the Nortons had been voted in upon his recommendation. The other Nortons felt that the club was "high-toned," and around the corner it was known as the "Boys' Junior League." They were a little flattered that members of their group could mix with such a club, but their opinion was formed largely from the personalities of Chick Morelli, the president, and Tony Cardio, another prominent member, both of whom they considered snobbish and conceited. Consequently, the Nortons took this match very seriously. . . .

Feeling ran high. The Nortons shouted at the club bowlers and made all sorts of noises to upset their concentration. The club members were in high spirits when they gained an early lead but had little to say as the Nortons pulled ahead to win by a wide margin. . . .

The Community Club match served to arouse enthusiasm for bowling among the Nortons. Previously the boys had bowled sporadically and often in other groups, but now for the first time bowling became a regular part of their social routine. Long John, Alec, Joe Dodge, and Frank Bonelli bowled several nights a week throughout the winter. Others bowled on frequent occasions, and all the bowlers appeared at the alleys at least one night a week.

A high score at candlepins requires several spares or strikes. Since a strike rarely occurs except when the first ball hits the kingpin properly within a fraction of an inch, and none of the boys had such precise aim, strikes were considered matters of luck, although a good bowler was expected to score them more often than a poor one. A bowler was judged according to his ability to get spares, to "pick" the pins that remained on the alley after his first ball.

There are many mental hazards connected with bowling. In any sport there are critical moments when a player needs the steadiest nerves if he is to "come through"; but, in those that involve team play and fairly continuous action, the player can sometimes lose himself in the heat of the contest and get by the critical points before he has a chance to "tighten up." If he is competing on a five-man team, the bowler must wait a long time for his turn at the alleys, and he has plenty of time to brood over his mistakes. When a man is facing ten pins, he can throw the ball quite casually. But when only one pin remains standing, and his opponents are shouting, "He can't pick it," the pressure is on, and there is a tendency to "tighten up" and lose control.

When a bowler is confident that he can make a difficult shot, the chances are that he will make it or come exceedingly close. When he is not confident, he will miss. A bowler is confident because he has made similar shots in the past and is accustomed to making good scores. But that is not all. He is also confident because his fellows, whether for him or against him, believe that he can make the shot. If they do not believe in him, the bowler has their adverse opinion as well as his own uncertainty to fight against. When that is said, it becomes necessary to consider a man's relation to his fellows in examining his bowling record.

In the winter and spring of 1937–38 bowling was the most significant social activity for the Nortons. Saturday night's intra-clique and individual matches became the climax of the week's events. During the week the boys discussed what had happened the previous Saturday night and what would happen on the coming Saturday night. A man's performance was subject to continual evaluation and criticism. There was, therefore, a close connection between a man's bowling and his position in the group.

The team used against the Community Club had consisted of two men (Doc and Long John) who ranked high and three men (Joe Dodge, Frank Bonelli, and Tommy) who had a low standing. When bowling became a fixed group activity, the Nortons' team evolved along different lines. Danny joined the Saturday-night crowd and rapidly made a place for himself. He performed very well and picked Doc as his favorite opponent. There was a good-natured rivalry between them. In individual competition Danny usually won, although his average in the group matches was no better than that of Doc's. After the Community Club match, when Doc selected a team to represent the Nortons against other corner gangs and clubs, he chose Danny, Long John, and himself, leaving two vacancies on the five-man team. At this time, Mike, who had never been a good bowler, was just beginning to bowl regularly and had not established his reputation. Significantly enough, the vacancies were not filled from the ranks of the clique. On Saturday nights the boys had been bowling with Chris Teludo, Nutsy's older cousin, and Mark Ciampa, a man who associated with them only at the bowling alleys. Both men were popular and were first-class bowlers. They were chosen by Doc, with the agreement of Danny and Long John, to bowl for the Nortons. It was only when a member of the regular team was absent that one of the followers in the clique was called in, and on such occasions he never distinguished himself.

The followers were not content with being substitutes. They claimed that they had not been given an opportunity to prove their ability. One Saturday night in February, 1938, Mike organized an intraclique match. His team was made up of Chris Teludo, Doc, Long John, himself, and me. Danny was sick at the time, and I was put in to substitute for him. Frank, Alec, Joe, Lou, and Tommy made up the other team. Interest in this match was more intense than in the ordinary "choose-up" matches, but the followers bowled poorly and never had a chance.

After this one encounter the followers were recognized as the second team and never again challenged the team.

On his athletic ability alone, Frank should have been an excellent bowler. His ball-playing had won him positions on semiprofessional teams and a promise—though unfulfilled—of a job on a minor-league team. And it was not lack of practice that held him back, for, along with Alec and Joe Dodge, he bowled more frequently than Doc, Danny, or Mike. During the winter of 1937–38 Frank occupied a particularly subordinate position in the group. He spent his time with Alec in the pastry shop owned by Alec's uncle, and, since he had little employment throughout the winter, he became dependent upon Alec for a large part of the expenses of his participation in group activities. Frank fell to the bottom of the group. His financial dependence preyed upon his mind. While he sometimes bowled well, he was never a serious threat to break into the first team.

Some events of June, 1937, cast additional light upon Frank's position. Mike organized a baseball team of some of the Nortons to play against a younger group of Norton Street corner boys. On the basis of his record, Frank was considered the best player on either team, yet he made a miserable showing. He said to me: "I can't seem to play ball when I'm playing with fellows I know, like that bunch. I do much better when I'm playing for the Stanley A.C. against some team in Dexter, Westland, or out of town." Accustomed to filling an inferior position, Frank was unable to star even in his favorite sport when he was competing against members of his own group.

One evening I heard Alec boasting to Long John that the way he was bowling he could take on every man on the first team and lick them all. Long John dismissed the challenge with these words: "You think you could beat us, but, under pressure, you die!"

Alec objected vehemently, yet he recognized the prevailing group opinion of his bowling. He made the highest single score of the season, and he frequently excelled during the week when he bowled with Frank, Long John, Joe Dodge, and me, but on Saturday nights, when the group was assembled, his performance was quite different. Shortly after this conversation Alec had several chances to prove himself, but each time it was "an off night," and he failed.

Carl, Joe, Lou, and Fred were never good enough to gain any recognition. Tommy was recognized as a first-class bowler, but he did most of his bowling with a younger group.

One of the best guides to the bowling standing of the members was furnished by a match held toward the end of April, 1938. Doc had an idea that we should climax the season with an individual competition among the members of the clique. He persuaded the owners of the alleys to contribute ten dollars in prize money to be divided among the three highest scorers. It was decided that only those who had bowled regularly should be eligible, and on this basis Lou, Fred, and Tommy were eliminated.

Interest in this contest ran high. The probable performances of the various bowlers were widely discussed. Doc, Danny, and Long John each listed his predictions. They were unanimous in conceding the first five places to themselves, Mark Ciampa, and Chris Teludo, although they differed in predicting the order among the first five. The next two positions were generally conceded to Mike and to me. All the ratings gave Joe Dodge last position, and Alec, Frank, and Carl were ranked close to the bottom.

The followers made no such lists, but Alec let it be known that he intended to show the boys something. Joe Dodge was annoyed to discover that he was the unanimous choice to finish last and argued that he was going to win.

When Chris Teludo did not appear for the match, the field was narrowed to ten. After the first four boxes, Alec was leading by several pins. He turned to Doc and said, "I'm out to get you boys tonight." But then he began to miss, and, as mistake followed mistake, he stopped trying. Between turns, he went out for drinks, so that he became flushed and unsteady on his feet. He threw the ball carelessly, pretending that he was not interested in the competition. His collapse was sudden and complete; in the space of a few boxes he dropped from first to last place.

The bowlers finished in the following order:

1.	Whyte	6.	Joe
2.	Danny	7.	Mark
3.	Doc	8.	Carl
4.	Long John	9.	Frank
5.	Mike	10.	Alec

There were only two upsets in the contest, according to the predictions made by Doc, Danny, and Long John: Mark bowled very poorly and

I won. However, it is important to note that neither Mark nor I fitted neatly into either part of the clique. Mark associated with the boys only at the bowling alleys and had no recognized status in the group. Although I was on good terms with all the boys, I was closer to the leaders than to the followers, since Doc was my particular friend. If Mark and I are left out of consideration, the performances were almost exactly what the leaders expected and the followers feared they would be. Danny, Doc, Long John, and Mike were bunched together at the top. Joe Dodge did better than was expected of him, but even he could not break through the solid ranks of the leadership.

Several days later Doc and Long John discussed the match with me.

> Long John: I only wanted to be sure that Alec or Joe Dodge didn't win. That wouldn't have been right.
>
> Doc: That's right. We didn't want to make it tough for you, because we all liked you, and the other fellows did too. If somebody had tried to make it tough for you, we would have protected you. . . . If Joe Dodge or Alec had been out in front, it would have been different. We would have talked them out of it. We would have made plenty of noise. We would have been really vicious. . . .

I asked Doc what would have happened if Alec or Joe had won.

> They wouldn't have known how to take it. That's why we were out to beat them. If they had won, there would have been a lot of noise. Plenty of arguments. We would have called it lucky—things like that. We would have tried to get them in another match and then ruin them. We would have to put them in their places.

Every corner boy expects to be heckled as he bowls, but the heckling can take various forms. While I had moved ahead as early as the end of the second string, I was subjected only to good-natured kidding. The leaders watched me with mingled surprise and amusement; in a very real sense, I was permitted to win.

Even so, my victory required certain adjustments. I was hailed jocularly as "the Champ" or even as "the Cheese Champ." Rather than accept this designation, I pressed my claim for recognition. Doc arranged to have me bowl a match against Long John. If I won, I should have the right to challenge Doc or Danny. The four of us went to the alleys together. Urged on by Doc and Danny, Long John won a decisive victory. I made no further challenge.

Alec was only temporarily crushed by his defeat. For a few days he was not seen on the corner, but then he returned and sought to re-establish himself. When the boys went bowling, he challenged Long John to an individual match and defeated him. Alec began to talk once more. Again he challenged Long John to a match, and again he defeated him. When bowling was resumed in the fall, Long John became Alec's favorite opponent, and for some time Alec nearly always came out ahead. He gloated. Long John explained: "He seems to have the Indian sign on me." And that is the way these incidents were interpreted by others—simply as a queer quirk of the game.

It is significant that, in making his challenge, Alec selected Long John instead of Doc, Danny, or Mike. It was not that Long John's bowling ability was uncertain. His average was about the same as that of Doc or Danny and better than that of Mike. As a member of the top group but not a leader in his own right, it was his social position that was vulnerable. . . .

The leader is the focal point for the organization of his group. In his absence, the members of the gang are divided into a number of small groups. There is no common activity or general conversation. When the leader appears, the situation changes strikingly. The small units form into one large group. The conversation becomes general, and unified action frequently follows. The leader becomes the central point in the discussion. A follower starts to say something, pauses when he notices that the leader is not listening, and begins again when he has the leader's attention. When the leader leaves the group, unity gives way to the divisions that existed before his appearance.

The members do not feel that the gang is really gathered until the leader appears. They recognize an obligation to wait for him before beginning any group activity, and when he is present they expect him to make their decisions. One night when the Nortons had a bowling match, Long John had no money to put up as his side bet, and he agreed that Chick Morelli should bowl in his place. After the match Danny said to Doc, "You should never have put Chick in there."

Doc replied with some annoyance, "Listen, Danny, you yourself suggested that Chick should bowl instead of Long John."

Danny said, "I know, but you shouldn't have let it go."

The leader is the man who acts when the situation requires action. He is more resourceful than his followers. Past events have shown that his ideas were right. In this sense "right" simply means satisfactory to the members. He is the most independent in judgment. While his followers are undecided as to a course of action or upon the character of a newcomer, the leader makes up his mind.

When he gives his word to one of his boys, he keeps it. The followers look to him for advice and encouragement, and he receives more of their confidences than any other man. Consequently, he knows more about what is going on in the group than anyone else. Whenever there is a quarrel among the boys, he hears of it almost as soon as it happens. Each party to the quarrel may appeal to him to work out a solution; and, even when the men do not want to compose their differences, each one takes his side of the story to the leader at the first opportunity. A man's standing depends partly upon the leader's belief that he has been conducting himself properly.

The leader is respected for his fair-mindedness. Whereas there may be hard feelings among some of the followers, the leader cannot bear a grudge against any man in the group. He has close friends (men who stand next to him in position), and he is indifferent to some of the members; but, if he is to retain his reputation for impartiality, he cannot allow personal animus to override his judgment.

The leader need not be the best baseball player, bowler, or fighter, but he must have some skill in whatever pursuits are of particular interest to the group. It is natural for him to promote activities in which he excels and to discourage those in which he is not skilful; and, in so far as he is thus able to influence the group, his competent performance is a natural consequence of his position. At the same time his performance supports his position.

The leader is better known and more respected outside his group than are any of his followers. His capacity for social movement is greater. One of the most important functions he performs is that of relating his group to other groups in the district. Whether the relationship is one of conflict, competition, or cooperation, he is expected to represent the interests of his fellows. The politician and the racketeer must deal with the leader in order to win the support of his followers. The leader's reputation outside the group tends to support his standing within the group, and his position in the group supports his reputation among outsiders.

The leader does not deal with his followers as an undifferentiated group. Doc explained:

On any corner you would find not only a leader but probably a couple of lieutenants. They could be leaders themselves, but they let the man lead them. You would say, "They let him lead because they like the way he does things." Sure, but he leans upon them for his authority. Many times you find fellows on a corner that stay in the background until some situation comes up, and then they will take over and call the shots. Things like that can change fast sometimes.

The leader mobilizes the group by dealing first with his lieutenants. It was customary for the Millers to go bowling every Saturday night. One Saturday Sam had no money, so he set out to persuade the boys to do something else. Later he explained to me how he had been able to change the established social routine of the group. He said:

> I had to show the boys that it would be in their own interests to come with me—that each one of them would benefit. But I knew I only had to convince two of the fellows. If they start to do something, the other boys will say to themselves, "If Joe does it—or if Chichi does it—it must be a good thing for us too." I told Joe and Chichi what the idea was, and I got them to come with me. I didn't pay no attention to the others. When Joe and Chichi came, all the other boys came along too.

Another example from the Millers indicates what happens when the leader and his lieutenant disagree upon group policy. This is Sam talking again:

> One time we had a raffle to raise money to build a camp on Lake Blank [on property lent them by a local businessman]. We had collected $54, and Joe and I were holding the money. That week I knew Joe was playing pool, and he lost three or four dollars gambling. When Saturday came, I says to the boys, "Come on, we go out to Lake Blank. We're gonna build that camp on the hill."
>
> Right away, Joe said, "If yuz are gonna build the camp on the hill, I don't come. I want it on the other side."
>
> All the time I knew he had lost the money, and he was only making up excuses so he wouldn't have to let anybody know. Now the hill was really the place to build that camp. On the other side, the ground was swampy. That would have been a stupid place. But I knew that if I tried to make them go through with it now, the group would split up into two cliques. Some would come with me, and some would go with Joe. So I let the whole thing drop for a while. After, I got Joe alone, and I says to him, "Joe, I know you lost some of that

money, but that's all right. You can pay up when you have it and
nobody will say nothin'. But, Joe, you know we shouldn't have the
camp on the other side of the hill because the land is not good there.
We should build it on the hill."

So he said, "All right," and we got all the boys together, and we
went out to build the camp.

Disagreements are not always worked out so amicably. I once asked
Doc and Sam to tell me who was the leader of a corner gang that was
familiar to both of them. Sam commented:

Doc picked out Carmen. He picked out the wrong man. I told him
why he was wrong—that Dominic was the leader. But that very same
night, there was almost a fight between the two of them, Dominic and
Carmen. And now the group is split up into two gangs.

Doc said:

Sometimes you can't pick out one leader. The leadership may be
in doubt. Maybe there are a couple of boys vying for the honors. But
you can find that out.

The leadership is changed not through an uprising of the bottom
men but by a shift in the relations between men at the top of the structure. When a gang breaks into two parts, the explanation is to be
found in a conflict between the leader and one of his former lieutenants.

This discussion should not give the impression that the leader is
the only man who proposes a course of action. Other men frequently
have ideas, but their suggestions must go through the proper channels
if they are to go into effect. . . .

The actions of the leader can be characterized in terms of the
origination of action in pair and set events. A pair event is one which
takes place between two people. A set event is one in which one man
originates action for two or more others. The leader frequently originates
action for the group without waiting for the suggestions of his followers.
A follower may originate action for the leader in a pair event, but he
does not originate action for the leader and other followers at the same
time—that is, he does not originate action in a set event which includes
the leader. Of course, when the leader is not present, parts of the group
are mobilized when men lower in the structure originate action in set
events. It is through observation of such set events when the top men

are not present that it is possible to determine the relative positions of the men who are neither leaders nor lieutenants.

Each member of the corner gang has his own position in the gang structure. Although the positions may remain unchanged over long periods of time, they should not be conceived in static terms. To have a position means that the individual has a customary way of interacting with other members of the group. When the pattern of interactions changes, the positions change. The positions of the members are interdependent, and one position cannot change without causing some adjustments in the other positions. Since the group is organized around the men with the top positions, some of the men with low standing may change positions or drop out without upsetting the balance of the group. For example, when Lou Danaro and Fred Mackey stopped participating in the activities of the Nortons, those activities continued to be organized in much the same manner as before, but when Doc and Danny dropped out, the Nortons disintegrated, and the patterns of interaction had to be reorganized along different lines.

46. The Problem of Authority in Formulating the American Constitution

ALEXANDER HAMILTON

The problems inherent in recognizing authority were given quite clear recognition by those who drafted the American Constitution. They were aware of the necessity of government but experienced in the problems of tyranny. They sought the experience of other societies in framing a constitution that would provide the former without bringing on the latter. Among those who participated in the discussion were Alexander Hamilton, James Madison and John Jay who, writing under the pen name Publius, discussed some of the problems and solutions inherent in establishing our government. We produce here one of these papers *(The Federalist No. 15)* which deals with the necessity of allocating authority and the problems this entails.

To the People of the State of New York:

In the course of the preceding papers, I have endeavored, my fellow-citizens, to place before you, in a clear and convincing light, the

importance of Union to your political safety and happiness. I have un-
folded to you a complication of dangers to which you would be exposed,
should you permit that sacred knot which binds the people of America
together to be severed or dissolved by ambition or by avarice, by jealousy or by misrepresentation. In the sequel of the inquiry through which
I propose to accompany you, the truths intended to be inculcated will
receive further confirmation from facts and arguments hitherto un-
noticed. If the road over which you will still have to pass should in
some places appear to you tedious or irksome, you will recollect that
you are in quest of information on a subject the most momentous which
can engage the attention of a free people, that the field through which
you have to travel is in itself spacious, and that the difficulties of the
journey have been unnecessarily increased by the mazes with which
sophistry has beset the way. It will be my aim to remove the obstacles
to your progress in as compendious a manner as it can be done, without
sacrificing utility to dispatch.

In pursuance of the plan which I have laid down for the discussion
of the subject, the point next in order to be examined is the "insuffi-
ciency of the present Confederation to the preservation of the Union."
It may perhaps be asked what need there is of reasoning or proof to
illustrate a position which is not either controverted or doubted, to which
the understandings and feelings of all classes of men assent, and which
in substance is admitted by the opponents as well as by the friends of
the new Constitution? It must in truth be acknowledged that, however
these may differ in other respects, they in general appear to harmonize
in this sentiment, at least, that there are material imperfections in our
national system and that something is necessary to be done to rescue us
from impending anarchy. The facts that support this opinion are no
longer objects of speculation. They have forced themselves upon the
sensibility of the people at large and have at length extorted from those,
whose mistaken policy has had the principal share in precipitating the
extremity at which we are arrived, a reluctant confession of the reality
of those defects in the scheme of our federal government, which have
been long pointed out and regretted by the intelligent friends of the
Union.

We may indeed with propriety be said to have reached almost the
last stage of national humiliation. There is scarcely anything that can
wound the pride or degrade the character of an independent nation
which we do not experience. Are there engagements to the performance
of which we are held by every tie respectable among men? These are

the subjects of constant and unblushing violation. Do we owe debts to foreigners and to our own citizens contracted in a time of imminent peril for the preservation of our political existence? These remain without any proper or satisfactory provision for their discharge. Have we valuable territories and important posts in the possession of a foreign power which, by express stipulations, ought long since to have been surrendered? These are still retained, to the prejudice of our interests not less than of our rights. Are we in a condition to resent or to repel the aggression? We have neither troops, nor treasury, nor government. Are we even in a condition to remonstrate with dignity? The just imputations on our own faith, in respect to the same treaty, ought first to be removed. Are we entitled by nature and compact to a free participation in the navigation of the Mississippi? Spain excludes us from it. Is public credit an indispensable resource in time of public danger? We seem to have abandoned its cause as desperate and irretrievable. Is commerce of importance to national wealth? Ours is at the lowest point of declension. Is respectability in the eyes of foreign powers a safeguard against foreign encroachments? The imbecility of our government even forbids them to treat with us. Our ambassadors abroad are the mere pageants of mimic sovereignty. Is a violent and unnatural decrease in the value of land a symptom of national distress? The price of improved land in most parts of the country is much lower than can be accounted for by the quantity of waste land at market, and can only be fully explained by that want of private and public confidence, which are so alarmingly prevalent among all ranks, and which have a direct tendency to depreciate property of every kind. Is private credit the friend and patron of industry? That most useful kind which relates to borrowing and lending is reduced within the narrowest limits, and this still more from an opinion of insecurity than from the scarcity of money. To shorten an enumeration of particulars which can afford neither pleasure nor instruction, it may in general be demanded, what indication is there of national disorder, poverty, and insignificance that could befall a community so peculiarly blessed with natural advantages as we are, which does not form a part of the dark catalogue of our public misfortunes?

This is the melancholy situation to which we have been brought by those very maxims and councils which would now deter us from adopting the proposed Constitution; and which, not content with having conducted us to the brink of a precipice, seem resolved to plunge us into the abyss that awaits us below. Here, my countrymen, impelled by every motive that ought to influence an enlightened people, let us make a firm stand for our safety, our tranquility, our dignity, our reputation. Let us at last break the fatal charm which has too long seduced us from the paths of felicity and prosperity.

It is true, as has been before observed, that facts, too stubborn to be resisted, have produced a species of general assent to the abstract proposition that there exist material defects in our national system; but the usefulness of the concession, on the part of the old adversaries of federal measures, is destroyed by a strenuous opposition to a remedy, upon the only principles that can give it a chance of success. While they admit that the government of the United States is destitute of energy, they contend against conferring upon it those powers which are requisite to supply that energy. They seem still to aim at things repugnant and irreconcilable; at an augmentation of federal authority, without diminution of state authority; at sovereignty in the Union, and complete independence in the members. They still, in fine, seem to cherish with blind devotion the political monster of an *imperium in imperio*. This renders a full display of the principal defects of the Confederation necessary, in order to show that the evils we experience do not proceed from minute or partial imperfections but from fundamental errors in the structure of the building which cannot be amended otherwise than by an alteration in the first principles and main pillars of the fabric.

The great and radical vice in the construction of the existing Confederation is in the principle of LEGISLATION for STATES or GOVERNMENTS, in their CORPORATE or COLLECTIVE CAPACITIES, and as contradistinguished from the INDIVIDUALS of which they consist. Though this principle does not run through all the powers delegated to the Union, yet it pervades and governs those on which the efficacy of the rest depends. Except as to the rule of apportionment, the United States has an indefinite discretion to make requisitions for men and money; but they have no authority to raise either, by regulations extending to the individual citizens of America. The consequence of this is that, though in theory their resolutions concerning those objects are laws, constitutionally binding on the members of the Union, yet in practice they are mere recommendations which the states observe or disregard at their option.

It is a singular instance of the capriciousness of the human mind that, after all the admonitions we have had from experience on this head, there should still be found men who object to the new Constitution, for deviating from a principle which has been found the bane of the old, and which is in itself evidently incompatible with the idea of GOVERN-

MENT; a principle, in short, which, if it is to be executed at all, must substitute the violent and sanguinary agency of the sword to the mild influence of the magistracy.

There is nothing absurd or impracticable in the idea of a league or alliance between independent nations for certain defined purposes precisely stated in a treaty regulating all the details of time, place, circumstance, and quantity; leaving nothing to future discretion; and depending for its execution on the good faith of the parties. Compacts of this kind exist among all civilized nations, subject to the usual vicissitudes of peace and war, of observance and nonobservance, as the interests or passions of the contrasting powers dictate. In the early part of the present century there was an epidemical rage in Europe for this species of compacts, from which the politicians of the times fondly hoped for benefits which were never realized. With a view to establishing the equilibrium of power and the peace of that part of the world, all the resources of negotiations were exhausted, and triple and quadruple alliances were formed; but they were scarcely formed before they were broken, giving an instructive but afflicting lesson to mankind, how little dependence is to be placed on treaties which have no other sanction than the obligations of good faith, and which oppose general considerations of peace and justice to the impulse of any immediate interest or passion.

If the particular states in this country are disposed to stand in a similar relation to each other, and to drop the project of a general DISCRETIONARY SUPERINTENDENCE, the scheme would indeed be pernicious, and would entail upon us all the mischiefs which have been enumerated under the first head; but it would have the merit of being, at least, consistent and practicable. Abandoning all views toward a confederate government, this would bring us to a simple alliance offensive and defensive and would place us in a situation to be alternately friends and enemies of each other, as our mutual jealousies and rivalships, nourished by the intrigues of foreign nations, should prescribe to us.

But if we are unwilling to be placed in this perilous situation, if we still will adhere to the design of a national government, or, which is the same thing, of a superintending power, under the direction of a common council, we must resolve to incorporate into our plan those ingredients which may be considered as forming the characteristic difference between a league and a government; we must extend the authority of the Union to the persons of the citizens—the only proper objects of government.

Government implies the power of making laws. It is essential to the idea of a law that it be attended with a sanction, or, in other words, a penalty or punishment for disobedience. If there be no penalty annexed to disobedience, the resolutions or commands which pretend to be laws will, in fact, amount to nothing more than advice or recommendation. This penalty, whatever it may be, can only be inflicted in two ways: by the agency of the courts and ministers of justice, or by military force; by the COERCION of the magistracy, or by the COERCION of arms. The first kind can evidently apply only to men, the last kind must, of necessity, be employed against bodies politic, or communities, or states. It is evident that there is no process of a court by which the observance of the laws can, in the last resort, be enforced. Sentences may be denounced against them for violations of their duty, but these sentences can only be carried into execution by the sword. In an association where the general authority is confined to the collective bodies of the communities that compose it, every breach of the laws must involve a state of war, and military execution must become the only instrument of civil obedience. Such a state of things can certainly not deserve the name of government, nor would any prudent man choose to commit his happiness to it.

There was a time when we were told that breaches, by the states, of the regulations of the federal authority were not to be expected; that a sense of common interest would preside over the conduct of the respective members and would beget a full compliance with all the constitutional requisitions of the Union. This language, at the present day, would appear as wild as a great part of what we now hear from the same quarter will be thought, when we shall have received further lessons from that best oracle of wisdom, experience. It at all times betrayed an ignorance of the true springs by which human conduct is actuated, and belied the original inducements to the establishment of civil power. Why has government been instituted at all? Because the passions of men will not conform to the dictates of reason and justice without constraint. Has it been found that bodies of men act with more rectitude or greater disinterestedness than individuals? The contrary of this has been inferred by all accurate observers of the conduct of mankind; and the inference is founded upon obvious reasons. Regard to reputation has a less active influence, when the infamy of a bad action is to be divided among a number, than when it is to fall singly upon one. A spirit of faction, which is apt to mingle its poison in the deliberations of all bodies of men, will often hurry the persons of whom they are composed into improprieties and excesses, for which they would blush in a private capacity.

In addition to all this, there is, in the nature of sovereign power, an impatience of control that disposes those who are invested with the exercise of it to look with an evil eye upon all external attempts to restrain or direct its operations. From this spirit it happens that, in every political association which is formed upon the principle of uniting in a common interest a number of lesser sovereignties, there will be found a kind of eccentric tendency in the subordinate or inferior orbs, by the operation of which there will be a perpetual effort in each to fly off from the common center. This tendency is not difficult to be accounted for. It has its origin in the love of power. Power controlled or abridged is almost always the rival and enemy of that power by which it is controlled or abridged. This simple proposition will teach us how little reason there is to expect that the persons intrusted with the administration of the affairs of the particular members of a confederacy will at all times be ready, with perfect good humor, and an unbiased regard to the public weal, to execute the resolutions or decrees of the general authority. The reverse of this results from the constitution of human nature.

If, therefore, the measures of the Confederacy cannot be executed without the intervention of the particular administrations, there will be little prospect of their being executed at all. The rulers of the respective members, whether they have a constitutional right to do it or not, will undertake to judge of the propriety of the measures themselves. They will consider the conformity of the thing proposed or required to their immediate interests or aims; the momentary conveniences or inconveniences that would attend its adoption. All this will be done; and in a spirit of interested and suspicious scrutiny, without that knowledge of national circumstances and reasons of state which is essential to a right judgment, and with that strong predilection in favor of local objects which can hardly fail to mislead the decision. The same process must be repeated in every member of which the body is constituted; and the execution of the plans, framed by the councils of the whole, will always fluctuate on the discretion of the ill-informed and prejudiced opinion of every part. Those who have been conversant in the proceedings of popular assemblies; who have seen how difficult it often is, where there is no exterior pressure of circumstances, to bring them to harmonious resolutions on important points, will readily conceive how impossible it must be to induce a number of such assemblies, deliberating at a distance from each other, at different times, and under different impressions, long to co-operate in the same views and pursuits.

In our case, the concurrence of thirteen distinct sovereign wills is requisite, under the Confederation, to the complete execution of every important measure that proceeds from the Union. It has happened as was to have been foreseen. The measures of the Union have not been executed; the delinquencies of the states have, step by step, matured themselves to an extreme which has, at length, arrested all the wheels of the national government and brought them to an awful stand. Congress at this time scarcely possesses the means of keeping up the forms of administration, till the states can have time to agree upon a more substantial substitute for the present shadow of a federal government. Things did not come to this desperate extremity at once. The causes which have been specified produced at first only unequal and disproportionate degrees of compliance with the requisitions of the Union. The greater deficiencies of some states furnished the pretext of example and the temptation of interest to the complying, or to the least delinquent states. Why should we do more in proportion than those who are embarked with us in the same political voyage? Why should we consent to bear more than our proper share of the common burden? These were suggestions which human selfishness could not withstand, and which even speculative men, who looked forward to remote consequences, could not, without hesitation, combat. Each state, yielding to the persuasive voice of immediate interest or convenience, has successively withdrawn its support, till the frail and tottering edifice seems ready to fall upon our heads and to crush us beneath its ruins.

PUBLIUS

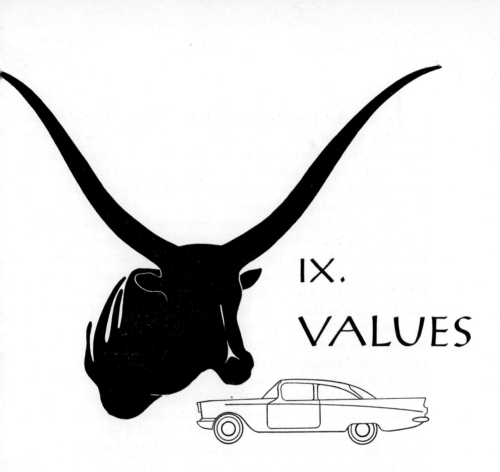

IX.
VALUES

Culturally Established Standards

In all societies people seem to desire acceptance by their fellow men; they want to be looked upon as the right kind, to be esteemed: acceptance, recognition, and prestige are universally sought after. In order for a person to gain this sense of acceptance and recognition, his behavior must conform to expectations—that is, it is measured in terms of the culturally established values.

If a society is to recognize some persons as having high status and others as low, it must have some scale by which it measures these individuals. The scale used, the criteria for judgment, we call values. We may define values as those personal characteristics and patterns of behavior upon which a people look favorably; those aspects of the individual which give him prestige or win for him the esteem of his fellows.

The scientific study of values is a rather recent development. Indeed, some would not admit that values are a proper subject for scientific study, but regard the subject as appropriate only for the philosopher. It is to this question that A. L. Kroeber addresses himself in the first essay in this section. While nobody questions that values are an appropriate subject for the moralist and the philosopher, the study of their manifestation among different peoples is also a proper subject of inquiry for sociologists and anthropologists. It is, in fact, quite impossible to understand the behavior of a people without knowing their own value assumptions. But the scientific study of values must remain a study of them; it is not concerned with evaluating these values—which is the philosophers' or moralists' task.

There is also some diversity in thinking as to just what is meant by the concept of values. To some it involves the general orientations of a culture; to some it places emphasis upon choice between alternatives, while to others its refers to the desirable rather than the desired. These definitions have more in common than they have in conflict, and the differences need not detain us here. They all carry the notion that every culture makes implicit assumptions regarding propriety of action which every normal and proper person accepts, and in terms of which he organizes his behavior, even when he doesn't act in accordance with these prescriptions.

Let us pause for a moment on this last point. In our culture, to be slender is considered valuable; excessive fat is viewed as vulgar. Not all cultures share this attitude, for in certain West African tribes young girls of social standing are carefully fattened to make them more desirable. There is an element of esthetic taste here, but the value also relates to the fact that we believe an individual should have sufficient self-restraint to curb his appetite; that is, there is a moral element, an element of behavioral values, as well. Obviously, not all persons achieve this value in like degree, and many find that their hunger—for whatever physiological or psychological reason—is a greater force than their desire to fulfill the cultural dictates. The same can be said of other and more important values.

Thus far in discussing values, we have placed emphasis on behavior, but more than behavior is involved. For values relate both to something deeper than mere behavior and to something more superficial. The deeper element relates to the character of the individual. Take our example of eating: it relates not only to the behavior of gluttony versus moderation, but also to the basic characterological feature of self-control which plays so important a role in our Judeo-Christian morality. We may have physiological, psychoanalytic, or religious explanations as to what causes these character attributes, but we are nevertheless concerned with them. Values therefore relate directly to the quality of the individual as he is conceived to be.

On the other hand, values relate to more superficial aspects of the individual; namely, the external expressions of behavior and character: value symbols are found in every culture. To understand this, we must make a slight digression.

In those primitive societies where there are only a few people in a band or village, all persons are necessarily in close interaction. Under such circumstances each is known intimately to all. If a man is energetic, a good hunter, even-tempered, wise, or whatever, these attributes are apt to be quite clearly known to his fellows. But when the community gets so large that people do not all know one another, they must then make their judgments on limited criteria. It is under such circumstances that the use of symbols becomes important. Such symbols may be expressed in dress, in mode of speech, in one's bearing as he goes through the streets, in the possessions and services he may command. These are the symbols of status which John Fischer discussed in a preceding section. They are not the criteria by which we as individuals judge the worth of those we know well, but they are the criteria which anonymous society uses to judge the individual—to place him in a status hierarchy.

Such symbols may seem quite arbitrary to the outsider, as was noted in our discussion on status in an earlier section. But they are not as unrelated as they seem. As is pointed out in the discussion of *areté* (p. 429), the value symbols do relate to the kind of accomplishments that are particularly valued in the community, and these accomplishments are related to the basic economic structure of that society. To be sure, there is a certain arbitrariness in every symbol, which, being a symbol, comes to mean much more than is explicitly there. Despite this arbitrary quality, the symbol is expressive of the kind of behavior required for its mode of attainment. Thus the ownership of horses and the extravagant display of bravery express the two important attributes of men in Plains Indian life: hunting and warfare. The importance of the former is obvious; the latter was required because of the fluidity of tribal boundaries during the short period when these Indians had the horse. The pomp and circumstance of princes in old feudal societies or primitive states expresses the inherited status in a class society. In the modern world of Europe and America, the possession of things reflects the business acumen of the owners in an essentially commercial society.

Of course, an individual may have or may acquire the symbols of a status out of keeping with the abilities or character elements which those symbols are presumed to represent. People have faked their genealogies (in societies where family line is important) long before credit buying was invented. In many societies there are sumptuary regulations; that is, laws which limit the enjoyment of certain privileged goods to those with a "legitimate" claim to their use, in order to protect these symbols from such abuse. They usually are found in those societies where the values are inherited (that is, where status is ascribed rather than achieved, to use Linton's phrasing).

We must remember that man does not make a sharp distinction between symbol and "reality." It is in the very nature of symbols that they are taken for the qualities they represent, whether it be a tabooed word, the cross, or a Cadillac. Therefore, in everyday action we treat persons in terms of their symbolic representation and only in reflective moments question the assumption that they are reality.

If values represent prestigeful behavior, then it follows that they have reference to a group—for prestige must be conferred by a population. Normally, this population is the society as a whole. But in large complex societies like our own, very few individuals are known to the society at large—a few political figures, writers, artists, actors, athletes, and perhaps some scientists are recognized by a wide range of Americans. But, as we have already seen, all of us operate in terms of more limited groups, which confer acceptance and prestige. Such groups may have divergent values, so that the behavior necessary for prestige will vary significantly. Something of this idea is expressed in the phrase "honor among thieves," for sociologists have long known that there is an elaborate and clear code of values in the underworld—though it is not in accord with the balance of society. This sense of values in different groups adds to the complexity of understanding values in society at large. But even in complex and culturally divergent America, a common core of values cuts across the more particular and the diverse values. We share certain general notions of both the qualities that are desirable and the symbols expressive of them. Most of us would agree that the impressive list of American values Williams presents are widely recognized and adhered to.

It is useful to look at values from the cultural, the social, and the individual points of view. From the cultural standpoint, the values of any society are a part of its cultural heritage. The individual is inculcated with the values of the community in the process of growing up. Some of these are given direct, overt expression, often in connection with religious ritual. Some are expressed more obliquely or transmitted without awareness on the part either of the child or the adult; they are the unspoken assumptions upon which judgments are made. Thus the cultural values are passed from generation to generation and are part of the cultural heritage. They tend to be conservative; that is, they tend to endure over long periods. The very manner in which they are transferred accounts for their tendency to continue. Furthermore, those who possess these values to the greater degree are by that very fact more influential in the community, and they also have a natural interest in preserving the values they themselves possess.

Nevertheless, values do change. We know this both from shifts that take place in primitive societies as a result of Western influence, and from our own history. Since values relate to the ongoing economic structure, we would expect them to be influenced by economic change, and there is evidence that this is the case. Many scholars, notably Max Weber, who is quoted in a subsequent section, and R. H. Tawney, have considered that there was a direct relationship between the new individualistic value orientation which is a part of Protestantism and the growth of an industrial type of economy. Pioneer life in America placed a great emphasis upon self-reliance and individual initiative and by its very nature, made inherited status of little account. The continuing importance of these "Protestant" values in America is not unrelated to this historical fact. Some moral philosophers believe values are changing because of our increasing involvement with large-scale organization, the reduction of opportunity for individual initiative, and increased dependence upon stable employment. In primitive societies, values in group cooperativeness and family loyalty often are destroyed by the Western emphasis upon individual initiative and the shift to wage work.

From the social point of view, values serve to increase the cohesiveness in a group. It is through the recognition of common values that a society senses its unity. Furthermore, the adherence to common values and the desire for recognition in terms of them makes it possible for society to reward and punish the individual.

From the individual point of view, values act as a directive for action, a kind of lodestar to individual conduct. They channel ambition and orient the person's action. So, as a child grows up, those around him tend to guide him toward that behavior which the culture deems proper. They do this in the varied ways that we discussed in the section on education: he is given verbal instruction, is rewarded for valued behavior and punished for disvalued conduct; he sees deference shown to those whose activities conform to the values of the culture and disrespect to those who run counter to these standards. He comes not only to accept the values of his culture, but to associate the symbols of prestige with them—whether they be the cordiality of a Nyakyusa villager, the esthetic taste of an Athenian gentleman, or the ownership of cattle among the Ruanda overlords.

In complex societies his situation is more difficult. Where there are sharply divided social classes, valued patterns of life may be available only to those born to certain classes, while members of lower classes are debarred from prestigeful position. Such clearly was the case for the people of Ruanda, and the whole pattern of the behavior of the Wahutu is different from that of Watutsi. It was also true in ancient Greece, for the values we know were those of the literate free class, not of the slaves. Yet within each class there are values to which the individual may aspire, and which relate him to other members of his own class.

A further difficulty in complex societies lies in a certain internal inconsistency in the value system, which keeps the individual from getting a coherent set of values. In America, for instance, there has always been a conflict over the status of education; there has always been a strong and important place for higher learning and scholarly activity, but throughout our history scholars have also been condemned and derided. It is an area in which we are quite uncertain of our values, though the increasing importance of knowledge has had some effect on the increased prestige of education.

Another problem that is more likely to stand in the way of getting a coherent set of values in complex society lies in what Ruth Benedict has called "discontinuities" in cultural patterning. She points out that in many ways we express one set of values to children but reward other patterns of behavior in adults. She writes:

> The major discontinuity in the life cycle is of course that the child who is at one point a son must be a father. These roles in our society are strongly differentiated; a good son is tractable, and does not assume adult responsibilities; a good father provides for his children and should not allow his authority to be flouted. In addition, the child must be sexless so far as his family is concerned, whereas the father's sexual role is primary in the family. The individual in one role must revise his behavior from almost all points of view when he assumes the second role.*

The failure of individuals to make the cultural values a part of their orientation to life frequently leads to distress both for them and for the society. Since they cannot achieve acceptance and prestige, they are frustrated in their own life activities, and it is out of such situations that anti-social behavior is apt to emerge. Delinquency can often be ascribed to the failure adequately to inculcate values acceptable to society, either because parents do not themselves adhere to these values, because they cannot communicate them, or because the child is frustrated in his efforts to fulfill valued expectations.

When we first examine the standards held by different peoples, we are apt to think that most of them are universal. Such values as industriousness, honesty and thrift seem natural. Yet we can find cases in which each of them is not valued at all. Our own South did not place a high value on work during the slave period, and even today industriousness is not valued in the South so much as is the pursuit of leisure and the capacity to relax. Cultures have been described in which honesty is not a virtue, unless specifically under oath, for a person should be told what he wants to hear. One look at Northwest Coast Indian potlatch will convince you that thrift cannot be considered very virtuous

* Ruth Fulton Benedict, "Continuities and Discontinuities in Cultural Conditioning," *Psychiatry,* Volume I, p. 162, William Alanson White Psychiatric Foundation, 1938.

there. Though many values occur in many different places, they are not natural, nor necessarily universal.

Are any values universal? Are some human qualities, some kinds of action found in all cultures? No research on this problem in sufficient detail has been made to answer that question, but we do know that many we would assume to be universal are not. A review of the few examples in this selection already makes this clear. It is perhaps true that all peoples recognize that one should not kill or harm one's fellows, but there is such a wide variation in what constitutes one's fellows (from a handful of coresidents to a large nation), that the rule is hardly uniform and the value rather vague. It is no more than the recognition that all people have community feeling with some sector of humanity.

Finally, can we say that some values are better than others? It has already been pointed out that this question is not appropriate to scientific analysis, but belongs to the realm of moral philosophy. The question can best be posed in terms of the likely consequences of various values. For instance, a high evaluation of personal and material success tends to create an energetic and inventive population. Such a value is particularly useful for the conquest of new land, for pioneering of the nineteenth-century kind. It is also useful for the development of science and technology. It is difficult to see how a peasant population, rooted in the land and lacking opportunity, could develop such values, and one can question whether they would serve the needs of such a population. On the other hand, such a value emphasis seems to take its toll in neurotic symptoms, putting the individual under psychological strain. Contrariwise, the reflective mode of Hindu and Buddhist philosophy seems suitable to an agrarian, caste-oriented and stable society, but it does not provide the orientation which leads to efforts to conquer poverty and disease. The congeniality of Nyakyusa hospitality makes for pleasant social relationships among men (their wives seem to suffer from this somewhat), but is not conducive to the accumulation of capital by which large-scale enterprises can be developed.

Some would see the solution as lying in a kind of moderation, a balancing off of values. Thus Ruth Tuck, in describing Mexican-Americans in Southern California, speaks of the more adjusted members of the community trying to take the best of the two worlds— American efficiency and Spanish repose. But this is more simply said than accomplished. For the two orientations make different kinds of demands upon the individual, and rather than achieving a compromise, he may find himself a battleground for two warring factions within him.

To discuss the consequences of different value systems for other elements in the cultural life of a people can not establish the relative value of these standards. For we will still judge these consequences in terms of our own values. To some extent they can be measured in terms of the needs of society at a given time and place. Certainly Moochie, whom Nielson has described in the section on Status and Role, had characteristics which were of highest usefulness to life in prison, though they certainly were not esteemed outside that situation. Similarly, Hopi emphasis upon cooperation and individual subordination is useful to life worked out in their harsh desert environment, while bravery in hunting and warfare was a necessary element among the Plains Indians, surrounded by other warlike tribes.

We come back, therefore, to a point made earlier: the value patterns of a society relate to the life circumstances in which the society exists and these appropriate values are inculcated in its growing youth, symbolized by elements that relate to the values of the culture itself.

47. The Scientific Study of Values

ALFRED L. KROEBER

Whether values may be viewed as objects of scientific inquiry has been a matter of some debate. In this brief statement, Alfred L. Kroeber points up the fact that inasmuch as values are a part of culture, they can be subjected to the same kind of analytic treatment as other elements in the culture.

This paper was originally read before the National Academy of Sciences and published in its Proceedings (Volume 35, 1949). It appears in Kroeber's collection of essays, *The Nature of Culture* (Chapter 15), Chicago: The University of Chicago Press, 1952. The article is published by the kind permission of both the National Science Foundation and the University of Chicago Press and by special permission of the author.

This essay maintains the proposition that the study of values is a proper and necessary part of the study of culture, viewed as an existing part of nature. This is said not merely as proposal or program, but as a descriptive fact holding for much of actually existing practice in anthropology and the study of culture.

Whenever a cultural fact has significance or historical reference, it also contains a value. Significance must be distinguished from cause— from that which made a cultural phenomenon happen or come to be. Significance must also be distinguished from the end or purpose served; and from organic needs, which in their turn can be resolved either into causes or into ends of culture phenomena.

That needs—also called drives, press, imperatives, and such—exist, and that they underlie and precondition culture, is indubitable. It is also obvious that culture cannot be explained or derived from needs except very partially. Hunger has to be satisfied; but *how* it is satisfied by human beings can never be derived from their being hungry, nor from their specific bodily construction. Overwhelmingly the *how* can be understood only with reference to the remainder of the culture adhered to, present and past; modified somewhat—or preconditioned—by interaction with the opportunities afforded by natural environment. Moreover, large segments of culture begin to operate, to come into being, only after the primal needs have been satisfied, have had their tensions reduced or alleviated. Such are art, religion, science. Hence these segments cannot be explained at all from physiological needs.

The essential characteristic things about a culture are its forms and patterns, the interrelations of these into an organization, and the way these parts, and the whole, work or function as a group of human beings lives under them. A culture is a way of habitual acting, feeling, and thinking channeled by a society out of an infinite number and variety of potential ways of living. The particular channeling adopted is heavily preconditioned by antecedent ways and organizations or systems of culture; though it is not predetermined thereby except within certain limits. Every such system of channeling is accompanied by or contains a system of affects, which vary from place to place of their appearance, and from time to time, but some of which are usually powerful and persistent. Interconnected with these affects is a system of ideas and ideals, explicit and implicit. The combined affect-idea system of a culture at once reflects the habitual ways of action of members of the society, validates these ways to themselves, and to an extent controls and modifies the ways. It is in this affect-laden idea system that, in a certain sense, the core of a culture is usually considered to reside: in it lodge its values, norms, and standards—its ethos and its eidos.

When we speak of the significance of a cultural trait or item or complex of traits, what is meant is the degree to which the trait is meshed, affectively as well as structurally and functionally, into the remainder of the total system or organization that constitutes the culture. Low degree of integration normally indicates that the trait has relatively low significance for the culture as a functional unit—though it may still have considerable significance as an index of historical relationship with other cultures.

It follows that if we refuse to deal with values, we are refusing to deal with what has most meaning in particular cultures as well as in human culture seen as a whole.

What we have left on elimination of values is an arid roster of cultural traits or cultural events which we are constantly tempted to animate by reintroducing the values we have banned, or else by back-handedly introducing values from our own culture. Or it is possible to attempt to explain the value-rid phenomena of the culture and their changes in terms of some causality—or possibly by a teleology.

As a matter of fact, it is and long has been prevailing practice in the description of cultures by anthropologists, or of civilizational phases by historians, to formulate the values of these cultures. Thereby the description becomes a physiognomic characterization of the culture. Such a characterization has internal import as regards both its own coherence and consistency, and its external import through implicit or explicit comparison with other characterized cultures. This type of presentation, with clear-cut value designations, comprises all the most successful characterizations or resynthesized analyses of cultures, . . . as far back as the Germania of Tacitus.

Reference in this matter is to values as they exist in human societies at given times and places; to values as they make their appearance in the history of our species; in short, to values as natural phenomena occurring in nature—much like the characteristic forms, qualities, and abilities of animals as defined in comparative zoology. There is no reference to any absolute standard or scale of values, nor to judgments of values as better or worse—which would imply such a standard.

48. The Comparative Study of Values

WALTER GOLDSCHMIDT

The comparative analysis of values developed by Walter Goldschmidt takes for granted that values are a proper subject of scientific inquiry. Here, using the Greek word *areté,* he points out that each culture has its own definition of areté but all cultures have some idea of what constitutes areté for them. Furthermore, he shows that though the values in a culture are not directly economic, they nevertheless relate to those qualities in individuals which have usefulness in terms of the mode of life in a particular culture. It should be noted that Goldschmidt is here using values in a somewhat different sense than Kroeber does, for he is including in the value system the material elements and circumstances by which individual qualities are made public.

The essay was first published in the *American Sociological Review,* Volume 18, 1953, under the title "Values and the Field of Comparative Sociology" and is published by kind permission of the editor of that journal.

The term values has been so variantly and broadly used in the past few years that there is a temptation to introduce a new word for the precise concept needed—particularly since a perfect term exists in the language from which neologisms are properly derived. The Greek word *areté* carries the meaning of those qualities of person, circumstance, and position that distinguish an individual of honor from the run of the mill, and hence those qualities which are the desiderata, the goals, the hopes and expectations of every proper person within a culture. The words values and areté are used interchangeably here, and in either case they have this more particular sense, narrower than that of Parsons and Kluckhohn, of Lundberg, or of Florence Kluckhohn.

This phenomenon of areté may be a universal characteristic of society—a necessary aspect of social organization if a population is to be more than an aggregate of individuals. This is an assertion of the universality of elites, but it is also more. It is an argument that culture must provide a form of conduct which its members consider ideal; must provide with a special status those that fulfill this behavioral pattern, and must symbolize this ideal quality with honors, possessions or special privileges. Areté then has three components: status, role, and symbolic representation. These three are always packed as a unit, so that a person within the culture regularly reads from one to another. Indeed, one may question whether it is proper to refer to the symbol of areté, since these symbols are the tangible and actual goals of conduct. At any rate, the participants regularly associate these components, regularly assume that a person possessed of the symbols has the qualities, and that persons with proper attributes are filling the statuses of the elite. When they know better they rationalize away the lack of concordance, just as failure in magic is rationalized away. We must then think of the status, the role, and the symbolic representation as parts of a single whole, for that is the logic of cultural behavior.

Perhaps an illustration will make the point more clearly. Within the business culture of modern America, the business man is supposed to be honest, aggressive, industrious, and assiduously concerned with his own interest. Such conduct appropriately followed leads to wealth, which offers a means for the public proclamation of the social position that gives him respect in the community. In the case of the academic man, we have a different, but equally well-defined appropriate conduct, by means of which we attain status in the academic community, and which is symbolized by various honors, degrees, a publication record, membership in learned societies and appearances in symposia.

It is suggested then that all social systems must have a definition of areté, though the particular qualities and the nature of the symbolic representations may show infinite variety. It is further suggested that the determination of the valued qualities or elements is the first and most crucial task in the understanding of the social organization of any community. For the value system relates not only to matters of prestige, but also defines status and the nature of social class, acts as a basis for leadership and power within the society, and sets the tone of behavior that dominates the culture.

The value system in any culture continues through the mechanism of the self-fulfilling prophecy. That is to say, the close association between value symbols, desired status, power and prestige, and forms of behavior will be mutually supportive. The youth in the society will see that those persons who have prestige and power also have the symbolic elements in areté, so that they will in turn direct their attention to these value symbols as means to achieve similar social goals. Indeed, the association between personal position and the cultural definition of areté is offered as a condition of life, rather than as a matter of choice, much as we take the need to work as a necessary condition of life.

Insofar as societies are characterized by achieved status, the conduct will be inculcated as a means of achievement—the high status and their symbolic representations will be held out as goals or rewards for "good conduct." Where, on the other hand, the elite is preordained by birth, the conduct is inculcated as behavior appropriate to the established position; a natural and necessary attribute of the elite. Insofar as societies may be distinguished in terms of achieved versus ascribed status, the association between behavior and goals is altered but the closeness of that association is not impaired.

It is not possible to prove that areté is in fact an imperative element to social systems, but only to demonstrate its existence in a variety of cultures. For instance, it is shown in that classic of anthropology, *The Arunta,* that the opportunity for an Arunta to see his own Churinga and those of his totem ancestors represents a value symbol which is internalized by the male members of Arunta society. The description by Spencer and Gillen of the fulfillment of this privilege leaves no doubt on this score. It is important to appreciate, however, that this opportunity to see one's Churinga is made available only after the individual has demonstrated his capacity for proper conduct according to the Arunta code of behavior. Spencer and Gillen make explicit that the privilege is determined by the old men, who already have this privilege and who delay the appropriate initiation ceremonies until they are sure of the neophyte's maturity, as modern psychologists would say. But having gained this privilege—having viewed their Churinga—they now are among the Arunta elite, demonstrating the nature of Arunta areté to the lesser members of their community. It seems appropriate to say that the Arunta male internalizes this privilege as a goal, and that this goal orientation makes him willing to conform to the cultural directives of his community; that the requisite compliance leads him to a position of prestige and power in the community as defined by the Arunta.

The Plains Indians offer another classic example. In the proto-historic period, the chief activities of the men were warfare and the hunt, which require agility, endurance, and bravery. The areté of a Plains man involved a strict self-discipline, a religiously inspired and supported endurance of pain and hardship, and a bravery verging on the suicidal. These values were expressed by the vision quest, by stealing horses and counting coup. The successful development of these attributes led to an important place of honor in the affairs of the tribe, either directly or through the acquisition of wealth with which such honors could be purchased. An alternate value orientation for males in Plains society allowed them to engage in women's work, but this in no way impairs the theoretical position. We must merely note that among primitive people as among ourselves, there may be alternative value patterns for significant subdivisions of the total community; "substitute profiles," to use Florence Kluckhohn's phrase. Where the value pattern is as delimited and as harsh as that of the Plains, it might very well be necessary for alternative patterns to be institutionalized to prevent organized resistance against the dominant values.

The Indians of Northwest California held certain ceremonial objects (particularly white deerskins and flint blades) to be their wealth, and the acquisition of such goods was internalized as the prime goal of all members of these societies. These goals functioned as directives to behavior, and the acquisition of such wealth was evidence of the quality of the person, and could, in theory at least, only be accumulated through appropriate deportment. The ownership of such goods enabled a person to perform prestigeful acts, such as organizing religious dances, and was an important determinant of his power and influence.

The Indians of the Northwest Coast offer the most obvious example of culturally established value orientations. Here the symbols are a series of crests, certain goods such as "coppers" and blankets, and above all the giving of a potlatch. These goods are directly associated with certain honored positions and indeed the potlatch (which has dramatically and erroneously been charged with leaving a man destitute) is a public claim to such position, and to the control of property which goes with that position. The dictates to behavior, that is, the personal qualities that go into the making up of areté, are equally sharp—aggressive, hostile, proud, quick to take resentment, and zealous in maintaining "face."

But what of the Pueblos—for Benedict has directed our thoughts to this contrast? The values are different. The personal qualities, the symbols, the positions are not like those of the Northwest Coast or the Plains, but they are nevertheless differentiating. Note, for instance, what Ruth Bunzel says: "In Zuni a poor man has no special knowledge or position in the ceremonial system. A valuable man has knowledge and prestige." And An-Che Li points out that it is easy for us to assume that leadership is not sought by those quiet subdued people, but notes that there are in fact many public functionaries with well-guarded prerogatives. Areté consists of ceremonial position, knowledge of dances and religious lore, and behavior characterized by a careful muting of personal ambition by religious zeal and by indirection. The Zuni and their Pueblo neighbors do not provide a negative case. They show rather a clear but different pattern of values which act as goals, and they show that the nature of these goals is functionally related to a particular type of personality.

Melanesia offers several different value systems centered in secret society positions, head-hunting success, or yam harvest. The importance of yams among the Trobriand Islanders, for example, directs our attention to the relation between values and economic ends. The fact that the size of his yam crop largely establishes the status of the gardener has led some to an assumption of naive economic determinism. This idea is abandoned when we learn that the gardener does not benefit from his own work and that, indeed, yams are allowed to rot in elaborate public display.

Yet economic forces are not altogether to be gainsaid. Farming is an important capacity. Though self-interest is not directly at work, it is nevertheless true that the symbol of abundant yams gives ideological support to the most crucial form of economic activity; that it therefore sanctions a mode of behavior of high economical utility—the skillful and assiduous gardener. And in Melanesia, areté is explained in terms of religious belief: to have a good yam harvest, a man must have *mana*. To have mana, one must make excellent harvest. The concept of mana generalizes that which is virtue and power in the individual and the social symbol is the verification of that quality, not only to the public but to the individual himself.

The Trobriand Islands example raises the question of the economic implications of the value systems. Repeatedly we see a relationship between such symbolic representations of status and elementary economic activity: the cattle of Africa, the horses of the Plains Indians, land in peasant communities. But on closer examination, our notions of direct economic importance are often wide of the mark—cattle are perhaps not important as food; the land, perhaps valued in relation to its antiquity rather than to its productivity; horses become a burden and the wealth of the Northwest Coast Indians is lavishly destroyed in ritualized conspicuous waste. Such a direct connection is erroneous because it implies our own cultural assumptions about work, productivity, wealth and power—in Weber's terms "economic rationalism." This is no place to enter into the comparative sociology of rationality; the intention is to note that there is a means-end relationship between, say, a muted personality and the acquisition of ceremonial position among the Zuni. Economic calculus is replaced by another kind, which we may call status calculus. And economic calculus emerges as but a special case of status calculus.

Though the relation between value orientations and the economic order is not simple economic determinism, their repeated association is not fortuitous. It is here tentatively suggested that the personal attributes that define the elite are in fact those very attributes which make for economic usefulness; that, further, the value objects themselves tend to symbolize economic virtues. Thus, horses represent valor and agility, useful equally to the warrior and the hunter of the plains, while the harsh desert life of the Hopi and Zuni requires cooperation appropriately symbolized by the ceremonial unity of action. It is at this level that a connection between values and the economy must be seen rather than on the direct level.

49. Athenian Values

EDITH HAMILTON

Edith Hamilton is an outstanding scholar of Greek culture. She graduated from Bryn Mawr in 1894 and did graduate work in Munich, Germany. She has written widely on the culture of ancient Greece. The present essay may be found in *The Greek Way to Western Civilization,* originally published by W. W. Norton in 1930 and available as a Mentor Book, published by the New American Library for Literature, Inc. It is here reprinted from *The Greek Way* by Edith Hamilton. By permission of W. W. Norton & Company, Inc. Copyright 1930, 1942 by W. W. Norton & Company, Inc.

In a very few pages, Edith Hamilton captures the special values that characterize the Greek upper class. The pattern seems strange to us because it succeeds in combining values which we ourselves hold very closely with other qualities which we do not hold in high regard. From it, we begin to see how each culture has a special quality by combining elements in a unique way.

Once upon a time—the exact date cannot be given but it was not far from 450 B.C.—an Athenian fleet cast anchor near an island in the Ægean as the sun was setting. Athens was making herself mistress of the sea and the attack on the island was to be begun the next morning. That evening the commander-in-chief, no less a one, the story goes, than Pericles himself, sent an invitation to his second in command to sup with him on the flag-ship. So there you may see them sitting on the ship's high poop, a canopy over their heads to keep off the dew. One of the attendants is a beautiful boy and as he fills the cups Pericles bethinks him of the poets and quotes a line about the "purple light" upon a fair young cheek. The younger general is critical: it had never seemed to him that the color-adjective was well chosen. He preferred another poet's use of rosy to describe the bloom of youth. Pericles on his side objects: that very poet had elsewhere used purple in the same way when speaking of the radiance of young loveliness. So the conversation went on, each man capping the other's quotation with one as apt. The entire talk at the supper table turned on delicate and fanciful points of literary criticism. But, nonetheless, when the battle began the next morning, these same men, fighting fiercely and directing wisely, carried the attack on the island.

The literal truth of the charming anecdote I cannot vouch for, but it is to be noted that no such story has come down to us about the generals of any other country except Greece. No flight of fancy has ever conceived of a discussion on color-adjectives between Caesar and the trusty Labienus on the eve of crossing the Rhine, nor, we may feel reasonably assured, will any soaring imagination in the future depict General Grant thus diverting himself with General Sherman. That higher truth which Aristotle claimed for poetry over history is here perfectly exemplified. The little story, however apocryphal, gives a picture true to life of what the Athenians of the great age of Athens were like. Two cultivated gentlemen are shown to us, of a great fastidiousness, the poets their familiar companions, able the evening before a battle to absorb themselves in the lesser niceties of literary criticism, but, with all this, mighty men of action, soldiers, sailors, generals, statesmen, any age would be hard put to it to excel. The combination is rarely found in the annals of history. It is to be completely civilized without having lost in the process anything of value.

Civilization, a much abused word, stands for a high matter quite apart from telephones and electric lights. It is a matter of imponderables, of delight in the things of the mind, of love of beauty, of honor, grace, courtesy, delicate feeling. Where imponderables are the things of first importance, there is the height of civilization, and if, at the same time, the power to act exists unimpaired, human life has reached a level seldom attained and very seldom surpassed. Few individuals are capable of the achievement; periods of history which have produced such men in sufficient numbers to stamp their age are rare indeed.

Pericles, according to Thucydides, held the Athens of his day to be one of them. The most famous of his sayings gives, in brief but to perfection, the height of civilization attained with undiminished power to act. The Athenians, he says, are "lovers of beauty without having lost the taste for simplicity, and lovers of wisdom without loss of manly vigor."

We need no proof that the Greeks of the fifth century B.C. had not lost their manly vigor. Marathon, Thermopylae, Salamis, are names that will forever be immortal for valor matched against overwhelming numbers, and the grandsons of those same great warriors whom Pericles was addressing were themselves engaged in a stern and bitter war. But it is difficult for us today to realize how important the imponderables were in Greece. The poet Sophocles, so the story is told, in his extreme old age was brought into court by his son who charged him with being incompetent to manage his own affairs. The aged tragedian's sole defense was to recite to the jurors passages from a play he had recently written. Those great words did not fall on deaf ears. Judge a man who could write such poetry not competent in any way? Who that called himself Greek could do this? Nay: dismiss the case; fine the complainant; let the defendant depart honored and triumphant.

Again when Athens had fallen and her Spartan conquerors held high festival on the eve of destroying the city altogether, razing to the ground the buildings, not a pillar to be left standing on the Acropolis, one of the men charged with the poetical part of the entertainment— even Spartans must have poetry at their banquet—gave a recitation from Euripides, and the banqueters, stern soldiers in the great moment of their hard-won triumph, listening to the beautiful, poignant words, forgot victory and vengeance, and declared as one man that the city such a poet had sprung from should never be destroyed. So important were imponderables to the Greeks. Poetry, all the arts, were matters of high seriousness, which it appeared perfectly reasonable that the freedom of a man and a city's life might hang upon.

It is clear that in Greece the values were different from our own today. Indeed we are not able really to bring into one consistent whole their outlook upon life; from our point of view it seems to involve a self-contradiction. People so devoted to poetry as to make it a matter of practical importance must have been, we feel, deficient in the sense for what is practically important, dreamers, not alive to life's hard facts. Nothing could be further from the truth. The Greeks were pre-eminently realists. The temper of mind that made them carve their statues and paint their pictures from the living human beings around them, that kept their poetry within the sober limits of the possible, made them hard-headed men in the world of everyday affairs. They were not tempted to evade facts. It is we ourselves who are the sentimentalists. We, to whom poetry, all art, is only a superficial decoration of life, make a refuge from a world that is too hard for us to face by senti-mentalizing it. The Greeks looked straight at it. They were completely unsentimental. It was a Roman who said it was sweet to die for one's country. The Greeks never said it was sweet to die for anything. They had no vital lies.

The great funeral oration of Pericles, delivered over those fallen in the war, stands out as unlike all other commemoration speeches ever spoken. There is not a trace of exaltation in it, not a word of heroic declamation. It is a piece of clear thinking and straight talking. The orator tells his audience to pray that they never have to die in battle as these did. He does not suggest or imply to the mourning parents before him that they are to be accounted happy because their sons died for Athens. He knows they are not and it does not occur to him to say anything but the truth. His words to them are:

> Some of you are of an age at which they may hope to have other children, and they ought to bear their sorrow better. To those of you who have passed their prime, I say: Congratulate yourselves that you have been happy during the greater part of your days; remember that your life of sorrow will not last long, and take comfort in the glory of those who are gone.

Cold comfort, we say. Yes, but people so stricken cannot be comforted, and Pericles knew his audience. They had faced the facts as well as he had. To read the quiet, grave, matter-of-fact words is to be reminded by the force of opposites of all the speeches everywhere over the tombs of the Unknown Soldier.

Completely in line with this spirit is the often quoted epitaph on the Lacedemonians who fell at Thermopylae. Every one of them fell, as they knew beforehand they would. They fought their battle to the death with no hope to help them and by so dying they saved Greece, but all the great poet who wrote their epitaph found it fitting to say for them was:

> O passer-by, tell the Lacedemonians that we lie here in obedience to their laws.

We rebel; something more than that, we feel, is due such heroism. But the Greeks did not. Facts were facts and deeds spoke for themselves. They did not need ornament.

Often we are repelled by words that seem to us wanting in common human sympathy. When Œdipus appears for the last time before his exile and speaks his misery, all that his friends say is:

> These things were even as thou sayest.

And to his wish that he had died in infancy they answer:

> I also would have had it thus.

The attitude seems hard but it is always to be borne in mind that the Greeks did not only face facts, they had not even a desire to escape from them. When Iphigenia says that Orestes must die but Pylades may go free, he refuses to take his life on such terms, but he refuses like a Greek and not a modern. It is not love of his friend alone that constrains him but also fear of what people would say, and he knows it and speaks it straight: "Men will whisper how I left my friend to die. Nay—I love you and I dread men's scorn." That is honest but we cannot any more be honest like that. It shocks us. The combination that resulted in the Athenian is baffling to us, lovers of beauty who held poetry and music and art to be of first importance—in their schools the two principal subjects the boys learned were music and mathematics—and at the same time, lovers of fact, who held fast to reality. Pindar prays: "With God's help may I still love what is beautiful and strive for what is attainable." "What I aspire to be and am not, comforts me," would never have appealed to a Greek.

The society these men made up whose sense of values is so strange to us, can be in some sort reconstructed, an idea of what their ways and their manner of life was like is to be had, even though the historical records, as usual, say nothing about the things we most want to know. Stories like those given above were not told of the Greeks because one man or two, a Pericles, a Socrates, had such notions. The golden deeds of a nation, however mythical, throw a clear light upon its standards and ideals. They are the revelation that cannot be mistaken for the people's conscience, of what they think men should be like. Their stories and their plays tell more about them than all their histories. To understand the mid-Victorians one must go not to the history writers but to Dickens and Anthony Trollope. For the Athenians of the great age we turn not to Thucydides, the historian, interested in Athens rather than her citizens, but to two writers unlike in every respect but one, their power to understand and depict the men they lived with: to Aristophanes, who made fun of them and scolded them and abused them and held them up for themselves to see in every play he wrote, and to Plato, who, for all that his business lay with lofty speculations on the nature of the ideal, was a student and lover of human nature too, and has left us in the personages of his dialogues characters so admirably drawn, they still live in his pages.

Many of the men met there are known to us from other writers. Some of the most famous persons of the day take part in the discussions. Whether all of them were real people or not there is no means of knowing, but there can be no doubt that they all are true to life, and that they seemed to Plato's hearers perfectly natural men, such as any upper-class Athenian was used to. Nothing else is credible. To suppose that Plato's idealism extended to his dramatis personæ, and that he put his doctrines in the mouths of personages who would appear unreal and absurd to his pupils, is to insult their intelligence and his. It is true that he does not give a cross-section of Athens, any more than Trollope does of England. A few people "not in society" make their appearance—a man who earns his living by giving recitations from Homer; a soothsayer, to Plato on the same social level as a clergyman to Sir Roger de Coverley —but the people he really knows are the gentlemen of Athens and he knows them as Trollope knows his parsons and his M.P.'s.

This society he introduces us to is eminently civilized, of men delighting to use their minds, loving beauty and elegance, as Pericles says in the funeral oration, keenly alive to all the amenities of life, and, above all, ever ready for a talk on no matter how abstract and abstruse a subject: "When we entered the house"—the speaker is Socrates—"we found Protagoras walking in the cloister; a train of listeners accompanied him; he, like Orpheus, attracting them by his voice and they were following. Then, as Homer says, 'I lifted up my eyes and saw' Hippias the Elean sitting in the opposite cloister and many seated on benches around him. They were putting to him many questions on physics and astronomy and he was discoursing of them. Also Prodicus the Cean was there, still in bed—the day, be it noted, was just dawning —and beside him on the couches near, a number of young men. His fine deep voice re-echoed through the room." Socrates begs Protagoras to talk to them of his teaching and when the great man agrees, "As I suspected that he would like a little display and glorification in the presence of Prodicus and Hippias, I said, 'But why should we not summon the rest to hear?' 'Suppose,' said Callias, the host, 'we hold a council in which you may sit and discuss?' This was agreed upon and great delight was felt at the prospect of hearing wise men talk." And so they all settle down happily to argue about the identity of virtue and knowledge and whether virtue can be taught.

It is, one perceives, a leisured society. Socrates speaks to young Theaetetus of "the ease which free men can always command. They can have their talk out in peace, wandering at will from one subject to another, their only aim to attain the truth." But the direct witness is hardly needed; an atmosphere of perfect leisure is the setting of all the dialogues and to immerse oneself in them is to be carried into a world where no one is ever hurried and where there is always time and to spare. "I went down yesterday to the Piraeus with Glaucon," so the *Republic* begins, "to offer up my prayers to the goddess and also to see how they would celebrate the festival. When we had finished and were turned toward the city, Polemarchus appeared and several others who had been at the procession. 'You are on your way to the city?' he said. 'But do you see how many we are? And are you stronger than all these? If not, you will have to stay.' 'But,' said I, 'may there not be an alternative? May we not persuade you to let us go?' 'Can you, if we refuse to listen? And you may be sure we shall. Stay and see the torch race on horseback this evening. And there will be a gathering of young men and we will have a good talk.' "

After some such fashion nearly every dialogue begins. The most charmingly leisured of them is, perhaps, the *Phaedrus*. "Where are you bound?" Socrates asks Phaedrus, to which the young man answers that he is going for a walk outside the wall to refresh himself after a morning spent in talk with a great rhetorician: "You shall hear about it if you can spare time to accompany me." Well, Socrates says, he so longs to hear it that he would go all the way to Megara and back rather than miss it. With this, Phaedrus begins to be doubtful if he can do justice to the great man: "Believe me, Socrates, I did not learn his very words—oh, no. Still, I have a general notion of what he said and can give you a summary." "Yes, dear lad," replies Socrates, "but you must first of all show what you have under your cloak—for that roll I suspect is the actual discourse, and much as I love you, I am not going to have you exercise your memory at my expense." Phaedrus gives in—he will read the whole essay; but where shall they sit? Oh, yes, under "that tallest plane-tree, where there is shade and gentle breezes and grass on which to sit or lie." "Yes," Socrates answers, "a fair resting place, full of summer sounds and scents, the stream deliciously cool to the feet, and the grass like a pillow gently sloping to the head. I shall lie down and do you choose the position you can best read in. Begin." A number of hours are spent under that plane-tree, discussing "the nature of the soul —though her true form be ever a theme of large and more than mortal discourse"; and "beauty shining in company with celestial forms"; and "the soul of the lover that follows the beloved in modesty and holy fear"; and "the heavenly blessings of friendship"; and "all the great arts, which require high speculation about the truths of nature"; and men who "are worthy of a proud name befitting their serious pursuit of life. Wise, I may not call them, for that is a great name which belongs to God alone—lovers of wisdom is their fitting title." That is the way two gentlemen would while away a summer morning in the Athens of Plato.

It is a society marked also by an exquisite urbanity, of men gently bred, easy, suave, polished. The most famous dinner-party that was ever given was held at the house of Agathon the Elegant, who declared to his guests as they took their places that he never gave orders to his servants on such occasions: "I say to them: Imagine that you are our hosts and I and the company your guests; treat us well and we shall commend you." Into this atmosphere of ease and the informality past masters in the social art permit themselves, an acquaintance is introduced by mistake who had not been invited, a mishap with awkward possibilities for people less skilled in the amenities than our banqueters. Instantly he is made to feel at home, greeted in the most charming fashion: "Oh, welcome, Aristodemus," said Agathon, "you are just in time to sup with us. If you come on any other matter put it off and make one of us. I was looking for you yesterday to invite you if I could have found you."

Socrates is late. It appears that he has fallen into a meditation under a portico on the way. When he enters, "Agathon begged that he would take the place next to him 'that I may touch you and have the benefit of that wise thought which came into your mind in the portico.' 'How I wish,' said Socrates, taking his place as he was desired, 'that wisdom could be infused by touch. If that were so how greatly should I value the privilege of reclining at your side, for you would fill me with a stream of wisdom plenteous and fair, whereas my own is of a very questionable sort.' " An argument is started and Agathon gives way: "I cannot refute you, Socrates." "Ah, no," is the answer. "Say rather, dear Agathon, that you cannot refute the truth, for Socrates is easily refuted." It is social intercourse at its perfection, to be accounted for only by a process of long training. Good breeding of that stamp was never evolved in one generation nor two, and yet these men were the grandsons of those that fought at Marathon and Salamis. Heroic daring and the imponderables of high civilization were the inheritance they were born to.

Through the dialogues moves the figure of Socrates, a unique philosopher, unlike all philosophers that ever were outside of Greece. They are, these others, very generally strange and taciturn beings, or so we conceive them, aloof, remote, absorbed in abstruse speculations, only partly human. The complete embodiment of our idea of a philosopher is Kant, the little stoop-shouldered, absent-minded man, who moved only between his house and the university, and by whom all the housewives in Königsberg set their clocks when they saw him pass on his way to the lecture-room of a morning. Such was not Socrates. He could not be, being a Greek. A great many different things were expected of him and he had to be able to meet a great many different situations. We ourselves belong to an age of specialists, the result, really, of our belonging to an age that loves comfort. It is obvious that one man doing only one thing can work faster, and the reasonable conclusion in a world that wants a great many things, is to arrange to have him do it. Twenty men making each a minute bit of a shoe, turn out far more than twenty times the number of shoes that one cobbler working alone did, and in consequence no one must go barefoot. We have our reward in an ever-increasing multiplication of the things everyone needs but we pay our price in the limit set to the possibilities of development for each individual worker.

In Greece it was just the other way about. The things they needed were by comparison few, but every man had to act in a number of different capacities. An Athenian citizen in his time played many parts. Æschylus was not only a writer of plays; he was an entire theatrical staff, actor, scenic artist, costumer, designer, mechanician, producer. He was also a soldier who fought in the ranks, and had probably held a civic office; most Athenians did. No doubt if we knew more about his life we should find that he had still other avocations. His brother-dramatist, Sophocles, was a general and a diplomat and a priest as well; a practical man of the theatre too, who made at least one important innovation. There was no artist class in Greece, withdrawn from active life, no literary class, no learned class. Their soldiers and their sailors and their politicians and their men of affairs wrote their poetry and carved their statues and thought out their philosophy. "To sum up"—the speaker is Pericles—"I say that Athens is the school of Greece and that the individual Athenian in his own person seems to have the power of adapting himself to the most varied forms of action with the utmost versatility and grace"—that last word a touch so peculiarly Greek. . . .

In a sense, therefore, extraordinary man though he was, Socrates yet holds up the mirror to his own age. A civilized age, where the really important matters were not those touched, tasted, or handled, an age whose leaders were marked by a devotion to learning and finding out the truth, and an age able to do and dare and endure, still capable of an approach to the heroic deeds of a past only a few years distant.

Mind and spirit in equal balance was the peculiar characteristic of Greek art. Intellectuality and exquisite taste balanced by an immense vitality was the distinctive mark of the people—as Plato saw them.

50. Ruanda Values

J. J. MAQUET

An aristocratic tradition in a primitive society is illustrated by the essay on the Ruanda. These people are divided into three social strata and have a kind of feudal system built on cattle herding. At the top are the Watutsi who governed, engaged in military activity, and maintained large herds of beautiful longhorn cattle. In the middle are the Wahutu, who were peasant farmers subordinate to their Watutsi overloads. At the bottom is a small class of people, engaged mainly in hunting, the Batwa. These three classes are physically dissimilar, and there still is a strong feeling against intermarriage. Value patterns in the three classes are distinctly different.

Jacques J. Maquet took his doctoral degree from the University of London in 1952. He has published *Le System Fédération Social dans la Ruanda Ancienne* (Institute Royale Congo Belge, 1954). He was chief anthropologist for the Institute de Recherche Scientifique de l'Afrique Sud at Astrida, Ruanda-Urundi, and is now Professeur à l'Université Officielle du Congo Belge et du Ruanda-Urundi in Elizabethville.

Maquet's essay appeared in *African Worlds: Studies in the Cosmological Ideas and Social Values of African Peoples* (Daryll Forde, ed.) published under the auspices of the International African Institute by the Oxford University Press, London, 1954. It appears here with the kind permission of the author, the publisher, and the International African Institute.

Human action is determined partly by cultural values, partly by the socially recognized means of attaining them. By cultural values we mean the final or intermediate aims that are considered the proper purposes of human activity in a particular society.

In a stratified society, such as that of Ruanda, each layer is likely to have its own set of values, although some of those originating in one group may extend to others. Let us begin with the Batutsi. When a Mututsi informant is asked what the people of his group wish for above all, the answer comes immediately: "children and cattle." A further question, "why?", discloses that these are not ultimate values sought for themselves, but intermediate ones, means to reach more abstract ends. The latter are power (*amaboko*) and reputation (*ugukomera*).

Power is understood here in connection with persons (power over somebody) rather than with things (power to do something). It is, to paraphrase Lasswell's definition, the ability that a person, engaged in a human relationship with another, has to oblige the latter to do or not to do something (on pain of suffering severe privation). Power is essentially the capacity to exert a significant pressure on somebody. In Ruanda, to be powerful is to be able to exact from others tribute in labor or in kind, or support for one's claims to some advantage to be obtained from the king. In the latter case pressure may remain undefined and indirect: for instance, a threat to withhold backing which may later be necessary to the person who is now asked to support a request. We desire to have cattle, say our informants, because by giving one or two beasts to a Muhutu, he becomes our client (*mugaragu*) and then has to do, to a large extent, what we ask of him. We also like to have cattle in order to get as vassal another Mututsi who lacks them. The services expected from a vassal are not manual, but he will increase the influence of his lord by his family connections and will be useful through his diplomatic shrewdness in dealing with his lord's intrigues. Finally, we desire to become ourselves the vassals of great chiefs, or even of the king, because we are then under the protection of somebody very important, we get more cows and that allows us to have more clients. . . .

A Mututsi also greatly desires to be regarded as having *ubugabo*. This means the quality of being a man (*mugabo*); it includes trustworthiness in keeping promises, generosity in treating one's friends well, liberality towards the poor, moral courage in accepting one's responsibilities. In a society where relations of inferiority and superiority are predominantly personal, in the sense that authority is rarely abstract (a law, a principle) but generally identified with a person (chief, king, lord, etc.), emphasis is laid on fidelity in any personal relationship.

Another quality that the Batutsi are extremely proud to have is *itonde*. This may be translated as "self-mastery." To lose one's temper, to manifest violent emotion by crying is really shameful. Anger, in particular, should not be violently expressed. The demeanor of a Mututsi should always be dignified, polite, amiable, if a little supercilious. Batutsi manners have often been called hypocritical. This would be true if such behavior were displayed in an extrovert culture where it is considered unethical not to express to a person exactly what one thinks about him.

But in Ruanda it is taken for granted that only vulgar persons reveal all their attitudes and emotions. . . .

To sum up, the ultimate values for the aristocracy are power and reputation. Children and cattle are their main intermediate values in the sense that they are the almost indispensable means for achieving these ends. The originality of Ruanda culture does not lie in its high valuation of power and fame. These are recognized ends in many cultures. What is distinctive is the paucity and the indispensability of the means provided in that society for effecting these purposes.

An ordinary Muhutu could never hope to achieve a position of power over other men comparable to that which a Mututsi could attain without difficulty. A well-to-do Muhutu could acquire a few servants either by ensuring the subsistence of other Bahutu poorer than himself or, like a Mututsi, by the gift of cattle. But this is not common. Ambition for power is proper to people who do not have to worry about fundamental human needs such as food, shelter, etc. The ultimate value for Bahutu is security, for this means protection from the things our informants say they fear above all: accusations of witchcraft, starvation, and the arbitrary actions of the powerful. There are no direct methods of protecting oneself against the first of these threats. All that can be done preventively is to be a good neighbor, not to be envied by anybody, not to have enemies. . . . But there are ways of reducing the other two dangers and these are the intermediate values which the Bahutu earnestly seek: work, children, and patronage. . . .

Although he is not indifferent to his reputation, the Muhutu does not seem to stress its importance as much as does the Mututsi. The reputation he desires reflects the values of his caste. He likes to be considered a *mugabo* (a rich man) and a *mukungu*—a very rich man possessing a few cows, many fields, goats, and bee-hives. He enjoys the recognition of his fidelity to his master and his qualities as a laborer.

The Batwa never had the stability of peasants. They were hunters, potters, dancers, buffoons, and were regarded by their neighbors as being on the margin of society. They did not possess anything that others could envy. Consequently security from exactions was not such an important value for them. As people who lived a hazardous and unsettled existence, they greatly appreciated momentary and immediate satisfactions, and among these, food, especially during periods of scarcity, was the object of their activity. . . .

These values, ultimate and intermediate, were eagerly sought by

Banyarwanda but, as in any society, some means for realizing them were prohibited under certain circumstances. Stealing is rarely, if ever, culturally accepted as an ordinary practice for getting rich. Socially defined values are to be reached by socially approved means. We do not suggest that, in a particular society, the rules of action appear as merely social imperatives, or that the only basis for these rules is social. We would point out that some rules of action, whatever their origin and their philosophical foundation, are part of the collective heritage in any society. In Ruanda, as elsewhere, there are such rules of action. Murdering somebody who is not an enemy of one's family is prohibited. Women are forbidden to commit adultery and, among Batutsi and Bahutu, unmarried girls may not have sexual intercourse. When an order is issued by somebody in authority it has to be obeyed.

Does submission to the rules appear only as the rational behavior of one who wishes to avoid an external punishment or is it moral conduct? Does a prospective offender refrain from wrong-doing simply in order to avoid very probable and unpleasant consequences, or is it his conscience which tells him that he should not follow his desire?

Of course this is not an either-or problem, but the question of degree or relative stress is important. Even in cultures which lay most stress on the moral motivation to action, external social sanctions are useful deterrents from prohibited behavior. In Ruanda these external sanctions exist. Those who steal cattle, or set fire to huts, or commit adultery are punished by the political or family authorities. Social sanctions are not only physically enforced penalties, such as corporal punishment and compensations, but also the unorganized reactions of the people who know the delinquent: kin, neighbors, clients, and lord. For the Batutsi, for whom reputation stands high in the scale of values, this is extremely important. According to our informants, the fear of being considered a man without loyalty or without dignity, the dread of being despised by one's family, prevent many breaches of rules. To use Kluckhohn's terminology, we may say that Ruanda's is a shame-culture. But it is also a guilt-culture. When a Munyarwanda has trangressed some rule so secretly that there is not the slightest chance of his being found out and incurring punishment and shame, he nevertheless feels guilty and knows, our informants told us, that his action is bad. When a child has disobeyed his father without the latter's knowledge, he thinks not only of the unpleasant consequences that the discovery of his misbehavior might produce but also (and some informants say "mainly") of the wickedness of the act itself. The Ruanda word for conscience, *kamera,* means something that is internally felt. It is situated in the heart.

That the Banyarwanda have a "conscience" will not be rated as a great discovery by some. But since some recent studies, such as Kluck-hohn's on the Navaho, have stressed the fact that, in some cultures, submission to rules seems to be realized almost entirely through a rational concern to avoid punishment or shame, it does not seem super-fluous to consider how far observance of rules is, or is not, linked to ethical principles and feelings of guilt.

Let us now attempt to indicate more precisely how moral wrong is conceived in the Ruanda culture. As has been already mentioned, *Imana* is not the guardian of the moral order. Sometimes he seems to be regarded as its author in the sense that he might have decided that men should not steal; but it is clear that when a man steals another man's cows, *Imana* is not personally offended. . . .

The other agencies of the supernatural world have even slighter relations with ethical values. . . . Nor was there any punishment after death. For those who believe that there are two kinds of life after death —happy or unhappy—the qualification for the happy one is not to live a blameless life on earth, but to undergo initiation into the *Ryangombe* cult.

Thus the ethics of the Banyarwanda are not integrated on a reli-gious basis such as the will of God. What is the principle of integration, or rather, we should first ask, are their ethical conceptions integrated? On the surface they consist, like any moral code, of a multiplicity of prohibitions, orders, and exhortations. Have they achieved a synthesis of these separate elements by reducing the multiplicity to one or a few principles? Or, what amounts to the same thing, could they give a defi-nition of good and evil?

In Ruanda a great number of particular rules are subsumed under general principles such as: do not do what is harmful to people of your group or of your country; do what people related to you would like; submit to your superiors. Principles such as these are already on a higher level of abstraction than the particular rules. When informants are asked to account for a given rule or principle they give as the final justification: "It has always been done that way in Ruanda." We may perhaps express the Ruanda definition of good and evil in these terms: That is good (or evil) which tradition has defined as good (or evil). . . .

But it would be misleading to picture the Banyarwanda as follow-ing blindly the moral rules framed in a remote past without having any idea of their purpose. Some old men have a clear understanding of the social significance of certain rules. They explained, for example, that the duality of the rules concerning adultery committed by the husband or by the wife was accounted for by the importance of the wife's function in procreation. She has thus a greater responsibility than the husband for maintaining the integrity of the family. . . .

Two principles dominate the field of human relations in Ruanda: inequality of men and indefinite reciprocity.

For the Banyarwanda all men have indeed a common nature; they are ultimately the descendants of the same ancestor. But this notion does not seem to be very significant, for Banyarwanda are much more impressed by the differences displayed by the various castes. The characteristics of these castes are stereotyped and repeated in many folktales. Batutsi are intelligent (in the sense of astute in political intrigues), apt to command, refined, courageous, and cruel. Bahutu are hardworking, not very clever, extrovert, irascible, unmannerly, obedient, physically strong. Batwa are gluttonous, loyal to their Batutsi masters, lazy, courageous when hunting, lacking in restraint. These characteristics, with differences in stress and shading, are generally recognized by all Banyarwanda. As they reflect the Mututsi point of view, it appears that the superior caste has been able to make other people see themselves in important respects as Batutsi see them. Moreover, those qualities are considered to be innate, not acquired. A Mututsi is born clever and a Muhutu impulsive. Some tales, more widely known than those concerning the creation of man, relate how the first Batutsi came to Ruanda from the heavenly world. According to some versions of this tale, they came with their servant, Mutwa, who mated with a forest ape. From that union all Batwa are descended. Such tales clearly reveal the fundamental differences which the Banyarwanda see among their castes.

When such a picture of "natural" differences, so significant from the point of view of power, is accepted, the inevitable consequence is that some men are born chiefs and others laborers. Inferiority and superiority are due not to personal qualities but to membership of certain groups. By belonging to different castes, people have fundamentally unequal rights. If an ordinary Mututsi kills a Muhutu, one kinsman of the murderer could eventually be killed in retaliation if the king authorized it. If the murderer was a Muhutu and the victim a Mututsi, two lives were taken.

The principle of the fundamental inequality between social groups thus established in Ruanda has spread from the original inter-caste relations to intra-caste situations. A man superior to another member of his class because of his functions or his wealth, or even his ability, tends to assume towards his inferior an attitude similar to that of a Mututsi *vis-à-vis* a Muhutu. Of course the conception of inequality between superiors and inferiors of the same class is not so rigid as that between the castes, but it permeates all hierarchical situations in Ruanda.

The theme of inequality was embodied in the indigenous political organization, so that political relations clearly express the attitudes socially expected from superiors and inferiors. They are quite understandable if one bears in mind that they originate from an inter-caste situation. Authority as such is all-embracing. According to Western conceptions, any authority is defined not only as regards the people who are subject to it, but also in respect of the matters falling within its competence. A man who gives orders to another because they are on different levels in a hierarchical scale may be considered his equal in other relations. In Ruanda, there is almost no sphere of life in which an inferior is free from the interference of his superior. Because Batutsi are considered fundamentally superior to the Bahutu, there is no field in which they can feel equal. This attitude has been transferred to any hierarchical situation. The complementary attitude of dependence is, of course, expected from the inferior. Inferiority is the relative situation of a person who has to submit to another in a clearly defined field; dependence is inferiority in the totality of life. The dependent person has to submit to his master in any question. There is no domain where he is free even to express a contrary opinion. . . .

Everywhere men in authority enjoy advantages denied to those whom they command, but it is often felt that justification is needed for these privileges. In Ruanda such rationalizations do not seem to be required. It is taken for granted by everybody, the subjects included, that superiors as such should derive profits from their position. The very high standard of living of Europeans is accepted without any criticism by "traditional" Banyarwanda not yet imbued with egalitarian principles.

The conception of authority as all-embracing, unlimited, protective, profitable, and of inferiority as dependent, devoid of rights, fundamentally weak, and generally exploited, is exactly suited to a structure of castes composed of human beings who are thought to be fundamentally different and unequal. On these inter-caste relations all hierarchical relations have been modelled. This means that the conceptions and attitudes which have just been sketched pervade most human relations in Ruanda. Indeed, very many human interactions involve persons who, in Ruanda, are placed on a hierarchical scale: man and woman, husband and wife, mother and child, father and son, old and young, craftsman and apprentice, etc., and when there is also a superiority-inferiority situation, even though confined to one aspect of the relation, the whole of that relation is impregnated with inequality.

51. Nyakyusa Values

MONICA WILSON

Nyakyusa values offer a sharp contrast to those of their fellow Africans just discussed. The Nyakyusa have a tribal society in Southern Tanganyika. Their emphasis on equality, friendliness, and sociability stands in sharp contrast to the aristocratic tradition of the Ruanda upper class. Their social distinctions are built more on the basis of age than on class or property.

Monica Wilson studied the Nyakyusa in cooperation with her late husband, Godfrey Wilson, after earlier field studies among the Pondo of South Africa. She is Professor of Social Anthropology at Rhodes University College, Grahamstown, Union of South Africa. The essay on values was taken from her book, *Good Company: A Study of Nyakyusa Age Villages*, published under the auspices of the International African Institute by the Oxford University Press, London, 1951. It is printed here with the kind permission of the publisher, the International African Institute and the author.

One of the values most constantly stressed by the Nyakyusa is that of *ukwangala* which, in its primary sense, means "the enjoyment of good company" and, by extension, the mutual aid and sympathy which spring from personal friendship. It implies urbane manners and a friendliness which expresses itself in eating and drinking together; not only merry conversation, but also discussion between equals, which the Nyakyusa regard as the principal form of education. "It is by conversing with our friends," said one of our witnesses, "that we gain wisdom (*amahala*); it is bad to sit quite still in men's company. A man who does this is a fool; he learns no wisdom, he has only his own thoughts. . . . It is bad to live alone far from other people, such a man learns nothing: he never learns to express himself well, to converse wittily with friends, or to argue a case with eloquence. It is better to live with other people."

"To live with other people," says our informant, but he implies "to live with contemporaries." For *ukwangala,* in the sense of discussion and easy give-and-take, can never occur between men and women, and is made difficult between men of different generations by the respect required of sons for their fathers. Since men are held to acquire manners, eloquence, and wisdom only in company it is necessary, the Nyakyusa argue, that they should build in villages, rather than in scattered homesteads, and since *ukwangala* is only possible between contemporaries they must build with contemporaries. The value set on *ukwangala* is thus related to the age-village; male contemporaries build together, and the company of, and good fellowship with, his age-mates is what creates a man of wisdom and character. Such is the Nyakyusa view of society.

For conversation to flow merrily and discussion to be profound there must be *ifyakwangalela*—"the wherewithal for good fellowship," that is, food and drink—and very great stress is laid on sharing these. Men and boys are expected to eat regularly with age-mates. Traditionally, fathers and sons never ate or drank together—to do so was held to be incompatible with the respect due from son to father—and men sought the company of equals at meals. From the time a small boy begins to herd he is encouraged to bring home two or three friends to eat with him, and in turn he visits each of them. Since boys have no fields of their own until they marry, but cooperate in cultivation with their parents, it is to their own mothers they go for food, and parents are proud of a son bringing many friends. "Perhaps," said Angombwike, "a son will come with his friends and cut a huge bunch of bananas, and take thick milk and eat with them. When the father comes back his wives will tell him: 'Your son has eaten all the thick milk and cut a banana bunch!' Then he will ask: 'How many men were with my son?' 'Six.' 'Ah, he's a chief!' the old man will say, smiling proudly." "And formerly if a young man came home often alone to eat, his father would beat him, or even take a spear and wound him, and when people asked why he would say: 'This great fool comes *alone* to my place, again and again.' It is good to eat with friends, for boys to go round in groups of four or five."

After marriage each man is cooked for by his own wife, but he continues to eat with his friends, bringing them to his home or going to theirs. The first wife to come to a young men's village is said to have a hard life. "She has to draw water and cook for all the young men of the village—they come to drink, and to wash, and they beat her with a stick if she refuses them. No, the husband will not be angry; if he were, he would be mocked at: 'Did not your father provide marriage-cattle for this woman for you that she might be the wife (*unkasi*) of us all?' Sometimes, when the woman is cooking, her husband's friends come and take food out of the pot before she has finished cooking. When she protests, saying it is not yet cooked, the men say: 'It is your work to cook, ours to eat.' Then when her husband comes she tells him that so and so, and so and so, have eaten the food and there is only water left in the pot. . . . But when her husband's friends begin to get married they say to their wives: 'That woman is really our wife! Listen to her!' And she has honor among the other women, and when they go to fetch firewood she walks with nothing, another carries her axe and head-pad." . . .

Apart from eating regularly with certain close friends, well-to-do pagan men are expected to entertain generously, inviting fellow villagers to drink beer, or to a "dinner party"—an ample meal with delicious dishes, very carefully served—from time to time, and providing meat feasts at funerals and at the initiation and marriage of daughters.

As it is proper for men to eat with their equals it is improper for them to eat with their juniors, or with women. . . .

It is admitted that women also enjoy company and profit from it, and it is considered good that they should get on with their fellows, but there is no suggestion that it is a woman's duty to cultivate her mind by conversation, or to eat regularly in company. . . .

The Christians' code of hospitality differs somewhat from that of the pagans: the latter stress feeding *neighbors,* whether it be in the daily eating together, or at informal beer and dinner parties, or at ceremonies, while the Christians stress feeding strangers, quoting the text "I was a stranger and ye took me in" and the parable of the Good Samaritan. The pagans jibe at the Christians for being inhospitable because (as the Christians themselves admit) they entertain their neighbors less than pagans do; the Christians point to their wider obligations, and the fact that they do feed and house visitors from a distance, especially fellow Christians gathering for Church festivals. The Christians are very conscious also of the difficulties of hospitality in a monogamous household, for a wife must not only do all the cooking for visitors (and many Nyakyusa dishes require considerable labor to prepare), but she must also help to grow the food. The pagan who can afford to entertain much has several wives who share the work between them, whereas a Christian, no matter how rich, cannot have more than one wife and remain a member of his Church—unless it be one of the two small independent African churches which countenance polygyny. The difficulty is partially overcome in some well-to-do Christian families by hiring labor to work in their fields and to fetch water and wood, and by offering visitors coffee or tea, which are easily prepared, in place of home-brewed beer; nevertheless the conflict between the value of hospitality (to which pagan and Christian alike subscribe, though they define it rather differently) and the value of monogamy, is often acute. . . .

Though the Nyakyusa lay so much stress on geniality, and praise a man for being "a good mixer," yet they greatly admire dignity (*ubusisya*). To be *nsisya* (dignified, impressive) is one of the attributes of chiefs and village headmen, sought . . . through medicines; but ordinary men may also aspire to it in their persons and homesteads. Indeed, *ubusisysa bwa nkaja,* the dignity of the homestead, is one of the legitimate channels of ambition to a Nyakyusa, and is something achieved largely through hard work.

. . . For a homestead to be dignified the huts must be built of good bamboos, and the space between them packed with oval-shaped mud bricks, carefully worked in patterns. Special pains are taken with the ends of long huts (*ifibaga*) to get a good curve on the roof pole, and a pleasing design of bricks and criss-cross binding on the gable. Inside, the walls are plastered smooth, and house-proud women mold a pattern in the mud with their fingers, which runs round the wall like a frieze. A long hut, showing that the owner has many cattle and young wives to house, adds dignity, but the homestead of a relatively poor man may be *nsisya* if the huts are well built, the open space between them weeded and swept, and the bananas pruned and heavy with fruit; while a shabby long hut and a dirty court are never dignified, no matter how rich the owner. The insistence on cleanliness both within the huts and in the court is very marked; men themselves weed and sweep regularly around their homesteads, and their young sons must help them. The Nyakyusa jibe at their neighbors for being dirty in person, in cooking, and in their homesteads: indeed the dirty habits of the women is given as a main reason for not inter-marrying with the Kinga or Poroto; and a Christian confided in us that it was a great effort to her to accept food from the Poroto when she went on preaching tours, because their huts and pots were so dirty.

Trees are felt to add to the dignity of a homestead as well as throwing a grateful shade; the beautiful *umwali* trees have long been valued for this purpose, and today exotics are much sought after. For example, the old chief Mwaipopo, noticing a fine cypress when he visited us at Isumba (a cottage that had once been a German mission hospital) inquired whether there were not some seedlings under the tree. He himself carefully dug up one and took it away to plant in his "capital." . . . It is said that jacarandas planted out in an avenue at Tukuyu disappeared within a very short time.

The attributes of dignity in the homestead are changing perceptibly. Well-built huts in the old style, a long *ikibaga,* a well-swept court, fruitful bananas, and fine *umwali* trees are mentioned by the old men; but many of the younger ones prefer hip-roofed houses (a style introduced by Europeans and known, appropriately enough, as "the partridge") with windows and door of European pattern, beds of flowers, roses, fine coffee and exotic trees. Yet they keep the court well swept; for lawns have not become fashionable.

A fine presence, a well-kept homestead rich in cattle and bananas and shaded with stately trees, are in themselves impressive, but the possessor of them only reaches his full dignity when he acts as host, and uses his fine food and fine home for lavish hospitality. Wealth and an impressive manner, without urbanity and hospitality, may well lead to accusations of witchcraft.

Feasts provide opportunity for swaggering parades and dances in which the Nyakyusa delight to display themselves and their possessions; they are the great occasions for *ukumoga,* that is, display in approved forms. Dancing, exhibiting a beautiful body with only a narrow barkcloth belt to hide it, showing off physical strength and the aggressiveness of a warrior, parading ornaments and fine clothes, or a splendid herd of cattle—all these are forms of *ukumoga.*

Traditionally Nyakyusa women wore only a bark-cloth belt tied around the waist and drawn between the legs to fall in streamers in front, and the pagan women cling to this dress, maintaining that it is only "Swahili women with dirty diseases" who have to wear clothes to cover their sores, and if a pagan woman has a cloth she will probably wave it like a flag or hang it over one shoulder, when she dances. Except for the Christians, few Nyakyusa women regularly wear clothes.

The Christians like a brightly colored cloth tied under the armpits, and hanging to the knees. Women make their own bark-cloths with great care, and decorate them with geometrical patterns in red and black, the red dye being imported from the Livingstone mountains; they mix this same dye with a fatty ointment made from the seeds of the *unsyun-guti* tree, and rub it all over themselves. The most prized ornament (worn by both sexes) are body rings of coiled brass or copper wire. In the past men went naked except for these body rings but, unlike the women, they have taken enthusiastically to clothes, and swagger around in brilliant loin-cloths or flowing white togas; or, if rather more sophisticated, in freshly pressed shorts and shirts, or lounge suits and topees. . . .

[The] admiration of truculence, as shown in the funeral dance, reveals a contradiction in Nyakyusa values. On the one hand urbanity and good temper are praised—they are intrinsic to *ukwangala*—on the other truculence. Is the opposition one between old and new values, or is the contradiction itself traditional? It is obvious that a readiness to fight was a quality valuable to the village in the days of inter-village warfare, and the Nyakyusa tell of murderers and even thieves being reprieved just because they were so useful in war. "We did not drive away violent men (*abagasi*) in the old days; we said: 'They will fight along with us in the future' "; whereas since the pacification of the country, quarrelsome men have become nothing but a liability, likely to get their fellows and their chief into trouble with the Administration. The Christian emphasis, also, is all on the virtue of peaceableness. There has probably been some change in values with the disappearance of war from the villages, but we think that a certain contradiction always existed: swaggering young men were admired, and children were warned not to be quarrelsome (*nkali*) towards their fellows, lest they be accused of practising witchcraft, or rouse the anger of a witch. The contradiction is not, of course, peculiar to Nyakyusa society, and it may be resolved by defining the groups within which fighting is excluded, and those in which it is approved. Most Nyakyusa would hold that in the old days quarrelsomeness within the village was bad, that towards members of another village of the same chiefdom it was allowable, and towards members of another chiefdom it was good. In the wider society of today the same distinctions are apparent: the war dance at funerals is limited lest it lead to fighting between villages but admiring audiences watch their friends in the detachment of the King's African Rifles at bayonet drill in Masoko.

Display is felt to be particularly appropriate to young people, and bachelors were held to be the fiercest warriors, but neither dancing nor fighting was confined to young men. The chief Mwaipopo was famous as a skilful and ardent dancer when over seventy, and the leader in war was the senior headman of the country, who, if not already married when he took office, had to marry almost immediately, since his wife shared in the ritual of establishing his house. Furthermore the villages of married men of the ruling generation fought, as well as the villages of their bachelor brothers and sons. . . .

Cattle, whether they be spoils of war or inherited wealth, are displayed. Not only does a long byre add to the dignity of a homestead, but, when there is some ceremony at the home of a rich man, he shows off his herd by driving it round and round the homestead. At other times his sons gallop it along the village street, the iron bells with which the animals are adorned ringing merrily. Nyakyusa smiths make cow-bells in sets, to chime in harmony, and the aim of a rich man is to own a set of bells which ring a full chime, and a herd large enough to carry them. Nowadays those who own bicycles display them in the same sort of way, riding round and round the homestead at a ceremony, and ringing the bells madly.

Unlike the enjoyment of good company (*ukwangala*), display (*ukumoga*) is not confined to the company of contemporaries of the same sex. Indeed the liveliest dancing is before members of the opposite sex, and is often the preliminary to love-making; but full opportunity for display is thought to depend upon living in a village, rather than in scattered homesteads. Some Nyakyusa are colonists, cultivating and building out in unoccupied bush country five or six miles from a settled area; but living out in the bush is disliked by most people and is done, we were told, only for gain. Cattle are said to increase very much more quickly out in bush, where grazing is plentiful, than they do on the village pastures, and the yield of virgin fields made in the bush is high. Hence the Nyakyusa dictum: "People live in the villages for display, in the bush for gain." And individuals commonly display themselves as members of a group—a group of contemporaries of the same sex, that is, of village-mates.

The basis of Nyakyusa sexual morality is the separation of the sexual activities of successive generations, more particularly the separation of the sexual activities of mothers and sons, and the complete segregation of fathers-in-law and daughters-in-law.

Nyakyusa informants hold that boys are sent out of their parents' village to build apart so that their parents may have privacy. Mwaisumo explained: "If a boy over ten years old stays at home to sleep, he is laughed at by his friends, and his own parents send him away. They say, 'If he sleeps at home he will hear what his parents talk about at night'; the night is always full of lewd talk; and he may even see them undressing. He will grow up a fool, with little wisdom! You see at the boys' village," he went on to say, "the older boys tell all sorts of stories, especially about women, they discuss love-making and women, and tell tales of their own conquests. The younger ones listen to these things and that's all right in the boys' village, that is how we learn, but we compare in our minds and think that if a boy stays at home it is as if he listened to all this from his parents, and people always do talk lewdly at night; and that is very bad, that is foolishness. But in the boys' village it is good for the young ones to listen, that is how children grow up.". . .

It is in conversation and play with village contemporaries that some knowledge of sex is acquired. Girls learn about sex from their immediate seniors, and they get some sex experience, along with formal instruction on morals, at the puberty rituals of their seniors in the age-village and at their own initiation. Boys learn from the conversation of their older fellows at night, in the boys' village. Any suggestion that sex education should be given by parents or middle-aged teachers shocks the Nyakyusa profoundly, for they hold that discussion of sex is totally incompatible with the respect due from children to parents. The taboo on sex talk between members of different generations appears to be absolute among men, but is less emphasized among women, for formal instruction on morals is given to a girl by her mother's fellows during the initiation ritual, and a young wife of her father, or of her father's neighbor, may whisper advice on sex matters even though she is classed as a "mother."

. . . there are profound differences between pagans and Christians in their sex code. The Christian dogma that sex relations should only take place between adult married persons excludes the freedom of girls to have external sex relations before betrothal, or in the "bride's" hut; it excludes girls visiting their betrothed husbands before puberty; and it excludes homosexuality, which is regarded as a mortal sin. Segregation of successive generations is not a part of the Christian tradition, hence the modifications in the rules of avoidance among Nyakyusa Christians, and the tendency for fathers and sons to build fairly close to one another.

The forms of display approved among Christians are also changing

with the change in the sex code. The nakedness of the Nyakyusa shocked
the missionaries, and it is insisted that Christian women, as well as men,
should wear at least one cloth; also many of the traditional dances and
songs are felt by the Nyakyusa converts themselves to be incompatible
with the profession of Christianity, consequently at funerals and weddings there is often a group of Christians dancing quite separately from
the pagans, and singing their own song, which, more often than not, is
a hymn. A wedding dance to a hymn does not appear incongruous to
Nyakyusa, as it does to European observers.

There is a very close connection between the values we have cited,
and all save one are coherent with one another. The enjoyment of good
company implies observance of the rules of decency; *ukwangala* is between equals, not between parents and children; it merges into neigh-
borliness, for one who does not help, or seek help from, a neighbor
is unfriendly (*atikwangala kanunu*); and it is dependent upon that generous hospitality which is one of the manifestations of dignity (*ubusisya*).

The one value which is not wholly coherent with the others is the
value of display (*ukumoga*). Certain forms of display are compatible
with urbanity and friendliness between neighbors, but the swaggering
truculence of the warrior is not—it is liable to breed quarrels between
fellow villagers, as well as with outsiders; . . .

The all-embracing virtue to the Nyakyusa is wisdom (*amahala*).
It includes the enjoyment of company and the practice of hospitality,
for no man is wise who is surly, or aloof, or stingy; it includes neighborly behavior, dignity, and respect for law and convention, but it
does not include display. The wise may dance, but they do not need to
dance in order to be wise, and those who commit adultery, or are boast-
ful or quarrelsome show foolishness (*ubukonyofu*) and sinful pride
(*amatingo*), the opposite of wisdom. Wisdom is expressed in all relationships, not only in village relationships, but it is learned in the village;
pagan Nyakyusa insist that "it is by conversing with our friends that we
gain wisdom."

52. Generic American Values

R O B I N   M .   W I L L I A M S ,   J R .

American values are complex and varied. The diverse cultural streams that have made modern America and the rapidly changing basis of life as our land has been progressively farmed and industrialized, are both responsible for the variegated quality of American culture in general and of our cultural values in particular. Robin M. Williams, Jr., has drawn together what he believes to be the major value orientations of American culture, based upon wide reading in sociology, history, anthropology and literature—and, of course, his own observations.

Williams is Professor of Sociology at Cornell University, where he has taught since 1946. He studied at Cornell and received his doctorate from Harvard. He was director of the Social Science Research Center from 1949 to 1954. He has served as statistician for the U.S. War Department and taught in North Carolina and Kentucky. He is co-author of *The American Soldier* and author of *The Reduction of Inter-Group Tensions*.

The present essay is reprinted from *American Society, a Sociological Interpretation* by Robin M. Williams, Jr., by permission of the author and Alfred A. Knopf, Inc., New York. Copyright 1951 by Alfred A. Knopf, Inc.

First, American culture is marked by a central stress upon personal achievement, especially secular occupational achievement. The "success story" and the respect accorded to the self-made man are distinctly American, if anything is. Our society has been highly competitive—a society in which ascribed status in the form of fixed, hereditary social stratification has been minimized. It has endorsed Horatio Alger and has glorified the rail splitter who becomes president. . . .

Emphasis upon achievement must be distinguished from the broader valuation of personal excellence. All societies have standards of character and proficiency, and accord rewards to those best meeting whatever standards are most highly appraised, whether of military prowess, ritual knowledge, asceticism, piety, or what not. The comparatively striking feature of American culture is its tendency to identify standards of personal excellence with competitive occupational achievement. In the pure type, the value attached to achievement does not comprehend the person as a whole, but only his accomplishments, emphasizing the objective results of his activity. Because of the preoccupation with business, the most conspicuous achievements have been those centered in business enterprise. We can say, with Laski and many others, that the "values of the business man" dominate and permeate national life. Yet achievement has never been completely identified with sheer business success; for example, such an assumption does not account for the respect and prestige accorded to the professions. Seen in the context of other major value themes, business success seems to be a dominant focus, but not the dominant value-pattern, in American society. . . .

In the United States is to be found what is almost the ideal type of a culture that stresses activity; it is no accident that the business so characteristic of the culture can also be spelled "busy-ness." Although one might quibble over Laski's flat statement that few Americans "find it easy to be happy unless they are doing something," we know that a notable series of observers have overwhelmingly agreed that America is the land of haste and bustle, of strenuous competition, of "ceaseless activity and agitation." . . .

Directed and disciplined activity in a regular occupation is a particular form of this basic orientation. If Justice Holmes could say that the purpose of life "is to function," the resonance his words aroused in the culture applied particularly to *work* in a full time vocation. This high evaluation of work has been called typical of the culture by many students of the American scene.

A strong cultural emphasis upon disciplined productive activity was to be expected in America during the first two centuries in which value systems were being generalized out of experience. Work was required for *group* survival along the moving frontier from the first settlements until the continent had been won. The rule "he who does not work shall not eat" expressed the deadly struggles of the early settlement period. To this compulsion was added the dawning sense of the rich rewards to be had in a land of relatively unappropriated resources. . . .

A third major value-configuration relates to a particular type of ethical quality in the total cultural orientation. Authoritative observers from de Tocqueville, through Bryce, Siegfried and others, down to such recent studies as those of Vernon L. Parrington, Margaret Mead, Gunnar Myrdal, and Harold Laski, have agreed on at least one point: Americans tend to "see the world in moral terms." They do not mean mere conformity to the detailed prescriptions of a particular moral code, but rather to a systematic moral orientation by which conduct is *judged*. It is asserted that the quasi-mythical figure, the "typical American," thinks in terms of right or wrong, good or bad, ethical or unethical. This attitude goes beyond questions of expediency or immediate utility—and beyond purely traditional or customary criteria of behavior—to test conduct against some systematic ethical principles. For example, Mead cites the query of a student who asked whether we *ought* to have a conscience. And Myrdal says explicitly: "The conflict in the American concept of law and order is only one side of the 'moral overstrain' of the nation. America believes in and aspires to something much higher than its plane of actual life." . . .

We shall use the term "humanitarianism" to refer to another important value cluster in American society, meaning by it, emphasis upon any type of disinterested concern and helpfulness, including personal kindliness, aid and comfort, spontaneous aid in mass disasters, as well as the more impersonal patterns of organized philanthropy. . . .

. . . Of course, it is only in a wide comparative perspective that the importance of the humanitarian mores can clearly be seen, making probable such hypotheses as "Americans are especially likely to identify with the 'underdog' rather than the 'bully.' " This identification is indicated in a quick, impulsive sympathy for people who are in distress "by no fault of their own"; in anger at the overbearing individual, group, or nation; in pride in America as a haven for the downtrodden and oppressed. The proverbial generosity of American people toward other societies facing mass disaster—for example, earthquakes, floods, fire, famine—has elements of exaggeration and myth; but it does index a real and persistent theme broadly based on religious or quasi-religious ideas of brotherhood, even though it has often been overridden by dividing interests and competing values. The enormous range of relatively disinterested humanitarian activities in America—the commonplace Community Chest, the "service club" activities, the public welfare agencies, the numerous private philanthropies, and so on—stands in striking contrast to the treatment meted out to "the poor" and the "sturdy beggars" in many other parts of Western society within the past two centuries. . . .

American emphasis upon *efficiency* has consistently impressed outside observers. The Germans even coined the term *Fordismus* to refer to the standardization, mass production, and "streamlined" efficiency of American industrialism personified on the Continent by the name of Ford. "Efficient" is a word of high praise in a society that has long emphasized adaptability, technological innovation, economic expansion, up-to-dateness, practicality, expediency, "getting things done." The mere listing of these words and phrases serves to bring out the multiple extensions of efficiency as a standard against which activity is judged. Such a standard is premised in the first place upon that active orientation to the world of the here and now, so characteristic of our culture. . . .

Emphasis upon efficiency is obviously related to the high place accorded science (especially as translated into technology) and to the overweening importance attributed to practicality. One of the blackest public curse-words we have is "impractical"—in the culture at large, the practical man is the good man, an embodiment of a major value. Although we could trace this interrelated set of attitudes back to the frontier tradition, there are more immediate influences in the contemporary culture contributing to its survival. "Practical" (pragmatic) orientation is basically short-range adjustment to immediate situations. The practical man concentrates upon goals attainable in the given situation and solves immediate problems as they arise, leaving to others the more abstract and long-range problems. Thus it seems clear that practicality as a positive value involves very important presuppositions as to other values. For instance, it typically assumes the worth of the basic social order within which action occurs. It characteristically rests on a whole set of implicit premises, among which are the stress on *activity* and *rationality* already mentioned above. . . .

From the society's earliest formation there has been a diffuse constellation of beliefs and attitudes that may be called the cult of progress. This broad theme has no unitary value such as would tangibly regulate specific individual behavior, but is rather a certain "set" toward life that has permeated a wide range of behavior patterns. Various aspects of this complex are those allegedly typical American traits discussed earlier—"optimism," an emphasis upon the future rather than the past or present, "boosterism," receptivity to change, faith in the perfectibility of the common man. At least in the enterprising middle classes, progress has been a prime article of faith. Our rich vocabulary of epithets ("backward," "outmoded," "old-fashioned," "stagnant," and the like) can be understood *as epithets* only against the unquestioning assumption that the new is the better—that "forward" is better than "backward."

From de Tocqueville to Laski, inquiring foreign observers have been impressed with the faith in progress and the high evaluation of the future in the United States as contrasted with Europe. Americans have felt their present to be better than their past and have felt adequate to deal with a future that will be still better. . . .

The fact that material comfort undoubtedly is highly approved and sought after in the culture tells us very little in itself about what specific values are involved; the "American standard of living" has its undertones and overtones of meanings—from nationalistic identification, to symbol of success, competence, and power and from a token of moral excellence to something very close to a terminal "value" at the level of hedonistic gratification. . . .

The gratification motif appears in modern mass entertainment with all the clarity of a caricature. For motion pictures, Dorothy Jones's analysis of a hundred films appearing in 1941–2 showed a predominance of the "happy ending"—at the end of the picture, about 60 per cent of all major characters were indulged with respect to all of their wants; about 10 per cent were deprived as to all of their wants; about 14 per cent were indulged as to some wants and deprived as to others. . . .

The avowal of "equality," and often its practice as well, has been a persistent theme through most of American history. Even modern economic organization, which in many ways epitomizes inequality, has stressed "equality of opportunity." Yet few other value complexes are more subject to strain in modern times.

The United States began its independent political existence as a congeries of societies, which in the main had broken sharply with the traditions of social deference and with the hierarchical social structures that still characterized Britain and Europe. . . .

. . . It will suffice here to see that this society in its formative periods was one that could, and wished to, break with its hierarchical tradition and that this result was favored by fundamental objective and ideological conditions. Thus, until the late nineteenth century America was able to develop without having to face widespread conflict between the principle of equality and the principles of achievement or freedom. In this remarkable historical experience, through generation after generation the values of equality were crystallized and elaborated. People saw the disappearance of primogeniture, the abolition of indentured servitude, of imprisonment for debt, of slavery, of property qualifications for voting and public office; there was provision for the common man to acquire a stake in the land and to secure a free public education; women gained one legal right after another; and even discriminations against minorities were sharply challenged time after time.

However, as de Tocqueville saw more than a century ago, America had to face sooner or later a conflict of values that he described as a contradiction between the principle of freedom and the principle of equality. . . .

At the level of explicit doctrine, intrinsic equality is widespread in American culture, both in the form of a specifically religious conception (the equality of souls before God, the divine nature within every person, and so on), and in the more secularized formulations that attribute an irreducible quantum of value to every person: "a man's a man for all that," "after all they are human beings," or the categorical imperative to "treat others as ends rather than means." At the level of overt interpersonal relations, adherence to a sense of intrinsic human value is discernible in a wide variety of specific behaviors—perhaps most obviously in "democratic manners." America has always impressed observers from more rigid and hierarchical societies as being marked by an extraordinary informality, directness, and lack of status consciousness in person-to-person contacts. This general openness of social relations can only be maintained in a culture in which intrinsic personal value is a widespread and effective assumption.

In more concrete terms, equality is exhibited in the way individuals actually *relate* to others in ordinary interpersonal activities. Are individuals in American culture typically related to others by superordination and subordination, or are interpersonal relations typically horizontal? The answer to so sweeping a question can be built up only by induction from the enormous variety of social rules actually existing in our society; a definitive analysis must wait upon a great amount of further systematic research. However, much of the evidence in the preceding chapters on the major institutions is relevant here: we have seen, for example, how the central family-type emphasizes equality of in-law families, and how the relations of husband-wife, parent-child, and sibling-sibling tend to be nonauthoritarian and nonhierarchical modes. In examining educational organization, it was suggested that, in spite of definite hierarchical emphases, the teacher-student relation in America is less rigid, formal, and authoritarian than in analogous European situations. On the other hand, we have seen much evidence of strongly hierarchical and authoritarian emphases, especially in large-scale economic and political organizations. And, running through the whole society, is the salient thread of nonequalitarian beliefs and practices concerning interpersonal relations with persons of a different racial or ethnic grouping. Nevertheless, in our provisional appraisal equality rather than hierarchy seems on the whole characteristic of concrete social relations—although perhaps more clearly at the level of the *goals and standards* of conduct than in the uneven compromises of going practice. . . .

A second major type of equality consists of specific formal rights and obligations. In the United States the strain toward equality of legal rights for all citizens or even residents has been strong and continuing. Formally equal civil rights—from military service to voting, from public education to taxation—represent not only freedom but also equality. In the sense of freedom these rights may be said to guarantee the individual a certain openness in his life-space; in the sense of equality, they nominally establish a minimum life-space for every one. It is in this equality of specified rights that the second major theme of American equality has developed, rather than in doctrines of equal individual potentialities, achievements, or rewards.

The third type of equality is substantive equality of social and, above all, economic rewards. Here it seems quite clear that the principles of economic freedom and individual achievement have strongly dominated principles of equality. The reigning conception has been that of *equality of opportunity* rather than *equality of condition*. Concessions toward substantive equality of condition—for example, the income tax in so far as it is graduated—have not leveled differences in wealth, and the upper and middle classes of the society continually have insisted upon a moral claim to the existing differentials. It is quite striking that one of the earliest and most widespread reactions to Marxism, as popularly understood, was to select precisely the idea of "equal distribution of wealth" as the target of censure and moral outrage. . . .

We need no research to tell us that the verbal affirmation of the value of freedom is widespread and persistent. The widespread positive reaction to the symbolic value of the word is illustrated in many ways. For example, a Gallup poll released in August, 1946, showed that freedom in general, or in some specific application, such as freedom of the press or of worship, is most often mentioned as the greatest advantage of the American form of government. . . .

American conceptions of freedom mainly stem from an orientation that characterized European thought for several centuries: freedom is compatible with causality and determinism; it does not mean uncaused behavior, but rather behavior that is not subject to restraints that are in some sense external and arbitrary. In this view, although behavior is always determined—that is, influenced, caused, or conditioned—it is nevertheless possible to give a definite meaning to the statement that it may also be "free." All life in society involves the limitation of behavior not only by the physical world, including the limitations of the human body and mind, but also by reciprocal rights and obligations among persons; every social group furthermore must cope with problems of authority and power. . . .

The underlying psychological constellation in traditional American attitudes toward freedom seems to be a posture of self-confidence and expansiveness, coupled with a tendency to reject all absolute claims to personal authority. This syndrome permeates relations of parents and children, men and women, employers and employees, the citizen and *Monsieur le Bureau*.

Viewed in these terms, the theme of freedom is far broader than any particular institutional sector of the society. It rests in the last analysis upon an even more basic conception of the individual as an integral agent, relatively autonomous and morally responsible. . . .

Even as early as the 1830's de Tocqueville commented on the necessity of safeguards against a possible "tyranny of the majority" in America and thought that public compulsion had already penetrated into private affairs in a censorious way not usual in the France of his day. Nearly a century later Siegfried, another and more critical Frenchman, visualized America as a land of vast uniformity in speech, manners, housing, dress, recreation, and politically expressed ideas. In 1948, Laski pointed to an "amazing uniformity" of values, thought that "business *mores*" had permeated the culture, and tried to show that "the American spirit required that the limits of uniformity be drawn with a certain tautness." Many Europeans in the period prior to World War II had thought American conformity-behavior to have a certain harried, compulsive quality, and have referred to standardization, "flatness," and lack of individuality in comparison with the Continent. In the period between 1920 and World War II European observers seem to have been especially (and overly) impressed with conformity themes in America. . . .

These appraisals—which in fact have often been biased and exaggerated—come as something of a shock to a people that has made much of individual initiative, the rights of the individual, personal independence, "rugged individualism." Yet it should be no surprise that an intensely active, democratic society should define tolerance of individual nonconformity largely in terms of sanctioning technological and economic innovation. In the field of so-called personal morals, the culture is one that still bears the impress of theology; there is a tendency to legislate conformity—a tendency acted out again and again from the early "blue laws" to Prohibition and the Hays Office. In the field of intellectual heterodoxy, although the United States has produced its Thoreau, its Henry George, its free thinkers and dissenters, a considered judgment would be that really radical nonconformity in speculative thought has not been outstanding, at least in comparison with other countries of Western culture. American "individualism," taken in broadest terms, has consisted mainly of a rejection of the state and impatience with restraints upon economic activity; it has not tended to set the autonomous individual up in rebellion against his social group. In a nation of joiners, individualism tends to be a matter of "group individualism," of the particularized behavior of subcultures. . . .

Some preoccupation with external conformity is to be expected in a society in which upward social mobility is highly prized and frequently achieved. The competitive striving of an upwardly mobile group in a society organized around the economic enterprise requires stringent discipline over the expression of sexual and aggressive impulses, over patterns of consumption, over the uses of time and resources. In this aspect, conformity is derivative from equality of opportunity in conjunction with success-striving. Furthermore, an emphasis upon external conformity easily develops out of the premise of basic human equality: if all are equal, then all have an equal right to judge their fellows and to regulate their conduct accordingly to commonly accepted standards; some such cultural equation has been widely accepted in the broad middle classes of American society. . . .

Interestingly enough, the very heterogeneity of American culture tends to produce a stress upon external conformity. Given the varied cultural backgrounds of the population and the desire that the various groups should continue to live together in the same society, conformity in externals becomes a sort of "social currency" making it possible to continue the society in spite of many clashes of interests and basic values. If it is gradually learned that the exhibition of cultural differences—whether they be of dress, or language, or religious faith, or political philosophy—seems to lead to friction in interpersonal relationships or even to public disturbances, a whole series of complex adjustments are set in motion. Among the possible responses to such a situation is the practice of withdrawing tension-producing items from general social circulation: for example, one finds popular maxims such as "never argue about religion or politics." . . .

It has become a commonplace observation that the application of science and related secular rational approaches have transformed the external conditions of American culture—along with many other major cultures of the world. Applied science is highly esteemed as a tool for controlling nature. Significant here is the interest in order, control, and calculability—the passion of an engineering civilization. This interest is congruent with the externalized orientation that we have already met in several previous guises; historically it is linked also to the fundamental assumption of an ordered universe in which rational human beings can continually improve their situation and themselves. . . .

Very broadly, emphasis upon science in America has reflected the values of the rationalistic-individualistic tradition. Science is disciplined, rational, functional, active; it requires systematic diligence and honesty; it is congruent with the "means" emphasis of the culture—the focus of interest upon pragmatism and efficiency and the tendency to minimize absolutes and ultimates. The applications of science profusely reward the strivings for self-externalizing mastery of the environment. We think it fair to say that science is at root fully compatible with a culture orientation that attempts to deny frustration and refuses to accept the idea of a fundamentally unreasonable and capricious world. . . .

In every society we find men participating in certain groups to which they feel they owe loyalty and with which they identify themselves—and we find other groups identified as outgroups toward which the individual feels estrangement, sense of difference, or enmity. This distinction, in small, localistic nonliterate societies, is often so sharp that others are not considered "men." . . .

Nationalism in the modern sense is, of course, a relatively recent development in Western history. In the case of American nationalism, it is clear that the early colonists for a long time thought of themselves as Englishmen (or Germans, Swiss, etc.) rather than "Americans." Even after the establishment of the new nation it was not uncommon to find that "my country" might as well mean Dinwiddie county, Virginia, or the state of Vermont, as the nation taken as a whole. It took the Civil War and a whole series of subsequent developments to really displace provincial patriotism in favor of national feeling.

An important component of American nationalistic values is that a generalized sense of fulfilment and confident hope has been built into the culture for over two centuries, and even the shocks of recent depressions, wars, and other deep crises have not dissipated the widespread satisfaction of a people who feel that the country "has been good to them." . . .

. . . American nationalism, like the religions that have contributed so heavily to the culture, involves the idea that the American way of life is so obviously morally superior that it should be widely adopted elsewhere. This secular counterpart of the missionary spirit is both an index of the strength of nationalistic feeling and a potent source of understanding and resentment in international affairs. . . .

Like freedom or progress, democracy in American culture is a highly complex and derivative theme. The nation that fought a great war under the slogan of making the world safe for democracy lives under a Constitution that contains no direct reference to democracy. . . .

Along with majority rule, representative institutions, and the rejection of the monarchical and aristocratic principles under which the society began, early American democracy stressed the reservation of certain "inalienable rights" as unalterable by majority rule. Basically this sort of democracy rested upon the implicit belief in natural law as opposed to personal rule, and in the moral autonomy of the individual. The actual shape of the democratic credo was a synthesis of clashing ideologies; but it was the insistence of the average citizen upon equality of political rights that actually forced the Bill of Rights into the Constitution. Major themes in the gradual crystallization of the main democratic creed thus included equality of certain formal rights and formal equality of opportunity, a faith in the rule of impersonal law, optimistic rationalism, and ethical individualism. . . .

Writing in 1897 Émile Durkheim incisively described a pattern of value in Western civilization that he called the cult of individual personality. Basically this cult sets a high value on the development of individual personality and is correspondingly averse to invasion of individual integrity; to be a person is to be independent, responsible, and self-respecting, and thereby to be worthy of concern and respect in one's own right. To be a person, in this sense, is to be an autonomous and responsible agent, not merely a reflection of external pressures, and to have an internal center of gravity, a set of standards and a conviction of personal worth. . . .

The reality of the value of individualism in our culture is observed not only in derivative forms such as manifest ideology, law, and formalized behavior patterns but also at the level of implicit assumptions and unconscious practices. For example, it is typical of the culture that the question as to whether there is actually such an entity as "the individual," "self," or "ego" is usually not even thought of, and, if raised, is greeted with surprise or shock. *Of course* individuals exist, of course they have separate individual needs and rights. As Dorothy Lee says:

> The value of individualism is axiomatically assumed. . . . A newborn infant must become individuated, must be taught physical and emotional self-dependence; we assume, in fact, that he has a separate identity which he must be helped to recognize. . . . The need for privacy is an imperative one in our society, recognized by official bodies such as state welfare groups and the Department of Labor. And it is part of a system which stems from and expresses our basic values.

The commitment of large segments of American society to doctrines stressing the value and dignity of the individual has been real, deep, and widespread. The same can be said of the principles of equality, of humanitarian values, of political freedoms—and so on through the list of "publicly dominant" value patterns already listed. Once full weight has been given to all these "rational-humane" values in the received traditions of the society, it must be recognized at the same time that the values of the Creed have continually struggled against pervasive and powerful counter-currents of valuation. One of the chief conflicts, and in many ways the most important conflict, has centered around those diverse patterns which have as their common element *the ascription of value and privilege to individuals on the basis of race or particularistic group membership* according to birth in a particular ethnic group, social class, or related social category.

Racialistic doctrines were first given widespread currency and intellectual elaboration in the slavery controversy during the decades immediately prior to the Civil War. The value anomalies into which the pro-slavery position led, in a culture so strongly stressing an individualistic religion and a democratic political system, gradually produced an explicit system of thought which relied upon assumptions of biological superiority to buttress the existing system of power and privilege. . . .

This rather lengthy and schematic review has not done justice to any one theme, but perhaps it has at least placed before us a range of important value-positions current in our society, and hinted at their complex interrelations. Our descriptive scheme that necessitated separate isolation and labeling of themes must not be allowed to leave the impression that values are disembodied elements which somehow function apart from concrete social relations and personalities. Everything described in this chapter must be capable of observation, in some sense, in the behavior of real personalities and in actual social structures, or else we have mistaken fancy for fact.

Running through these patterns of interests and values are certain still more general "dimensions" or "orientations" that are not explicit but must be identified by highly abstract evidence.

1. American culture is organized around the attempt at *active mastery* rather than *passive acceptance.* Into this dimension falls the low tolerance of frustration; the refusal to accept ascetic renunciation; the positive encouragement of desire; the stress on power; the approval of ego-assertion, and so on.

2. It tends to be interested in the *external world* of things and events, of the palpable and immediate, rather than in the inner experience of meaning and affect. Its genius is manipulative rather than contemplative.

3. Its world-view tends to be *open* rather than closed: it emphasizes change, flux, movement; its central personality types are adaptive, accessible, outgoing and assimilative.

4. In wide historical and comparative perspective, the culture places its primary faith in *rationalism* as opposed to *traditionalism;* it de-emphasizes the past, orients strongly to the future, does not accept things just because they have been done before.

5. Closely related to the above, is the dimension of *orderliness* rather than unsystematic *ad hoc* acceptance of transitory experience.

6. With conspicuous deviations, a main theme is a *universalistic* rather than a *particularistic* ethic.

7. In interpersonal relations, the weight of the value system is on the side of "horizontal" rather than "vertical" emphases: peer-relations, not superordinate-subordinate relations; equality rather than hierarchy.

8. Subject to increased strains and modifications, the received culture emphasizes *individual personality* rather than group identity and responsibility.

X.

RELIGION

Man's Relation to the Unknown

Man is a creator. He makes the tools and instruments by means of which he sustains himself. He manipulates the events in his environment, and sees the relationship between events. This is all-important to his special status as a cultured being. It inheres in the very nature of his language. It involves him in assumptions of cause and effect; of forces at work in the world, of a concept of the universe. Much of what he sees and learns he understands. But many of his experiences he cannot understand. Yet these, too, are important to his everyday life, and he tries to understand their meaning and to manipulate them.

The gaps in pragmatic knowledge man fills with explanations, and these we can call his religion. The efforts to influence the course of events which he cannot manipulate by practical means are religious acts. Man everywhere has filled such gaps in direct knowledge and has tried to foresee and to influence future events. Man everywhere has religion.

It is sometimes useful to recognize a distinction between the sacred and profane aspects of life. In all cultures certain things are viewed as holy, are circumscribed with ritual and treated with awe and respect, while other things are given no such special psychological and emotional import. The cross and the flag have a sacred quality in our society. So does the institution of matrimony. The totem animal is sacred to the Australian totem group members. We treat with ritual respect the dead body of a human being, which among some African tribes is set out for the hyenas. While the distinction is useful and seems to be universal, it is not so sharp as these examples imply; there are borderline cases. Some things can be viewed as more sacred than others. Things can be sacred in one situation and not in another.

You will see that in this discussion and the readings that follow, we take an extremely broad view of religion, treating our own behavior as nearly as possible as an anthropologist newly arrived from Mars might do. That is, we treat behavior in our own society in the same manner that anthropologists treat the behavior of the unlettered peoples they study. Our society differs from that of the latter in that we are heir to two of the great religious traditions—Christianity and Judaism. In the brief compass of this discussion we cannot deal with these large and complex historical developments with which, at any rate, we are all more or less familiar. It would be helpful if we had different terms to separate these great "revealed" religions from religion in this broader anthropological meaning, but we do not. We should, however, see our particular religious orientations in the context of this more general character of religion, and should recognize religious behavior beyond that connected with our formal faith.

Many observers speak of our culture as being religious only on the Sabbath. We do tend to compartmentalize our life, and to think of religion as one phase of our activity, art another, economic life another, and so on. But this is true only of the organized aspect of religion, just as it is true only of the capital A sort of art, as we will point out in a subsequent section. The fact is that religious orientation—in that broad anthropological sense—suffuses our life, just as it does among primitive people. It expresses itself in the superstitious practices of everyday life (and who among us can claim truly to be entirely free of superstition?), in our recognition of sacred emblems and sacred responsibilities, in our food and other taboos, in our oaths of office and in the courts, and in our tendency to sanctify all public ceremonial occasions even though they are primarily secular. Contrariwise, our secular life has increasingly invaded our religious activities, as our churches take on many social functions. This tendency in our culture is somewhat restrained by the fact that we have many different religious traditions and that officially we endeavor not only to give recognition to both Christianity and Judaism, but to take into account the official religious convictions of such beliefs as those of Quakers and Mennonites. Nevertheless, we suffuse our daily lives in varying degrees with what, from the anthropological viewpoint, must be considered as religious behavior.

This leads to a consideration of the relation between science and religion; between logical and what was once called prelogical behavior. Malinowski, in an essay which follows, has something to say on this point. He notes that all peoples treat some things with the logic of the scientist, and that one cannot distinguish peoples on the grounds of their being given entirely to magical or entirely to logical thinking. What we can say is that the growth of human experience and the accumulation of knowledge has steadily reduced the areas which are treated magically and increased those to which scientific understanding has been applied. This has been a particularly clear development in the past few centuries, when man has had the advantages of writing and printing, which can store and disseminate knowledge. But our knowledge is still far from complete, and basic questions of the nature of matter and of life have not been amenable to scientific explanation.

There are two fundamental aspects to religion: the societal and the individual. Efforts to explain religion and to discover its origin have sometimes placed emphasis upon the one, sometimes upon the other. You can see these divergent orientations as they are influential on the various theories of the origin and nature of religion as summarized by Bronislaw Malinowski in the essay that opens this section. Students like Tylor, who were more concerned with forms of animism and belief in the soul, placed stress on the personal side of religious life. Those who were concerned with group life, notably Émile Durkheim and his school, saw religion as a social phenomenon.

It is profitable to examine both facets and wise to realize that man's religious behavior must be understood both in terms of the individual needs and psychological characteristics of the individual, and in relation to group life and the functions and requirements of social cohesion. Nor is there any necessary conflict between these two functions of religious experience, for man's individual needs are always met in social terms. We will first look at religious behavior from a social, and then from an individual point of view.

Though primitive man has no church, in our sense of the word, he does have religious rituals. These take many forms, but they always invoke sacred sentiments. Religious rituals generally involve dancing and singing and normally bring together some group—the clan, the village, the totem group, or whatever. The Australians, for instance, have totem group rituals. The ostensible purpose of these rites, which involve dance, song and the recounting of myths of the totemic ancestors, is to increase the numbers of the totemic plants and animals. We must not think of this as simply a fertility rite to increase the food supply of the group—for the totemic animal may not be eaten by the members (though it may be eaten freely by members of other totem groups). These plants and animals (and occasionally other natural phenomena such as lightning) are regarded as spiritual kin to the humans who bear their names, so that the ritual is one of strengthening the group as a social entity, not merely aiding its food supply. Such rituals are called rites of intensification, because they reenforce the group ties of the participants. The ancient myths give justification for the group's existence and their recounting reminds its members of the basis for their unity. Joining in song and dance gives physical expression to that unity. Above all, the entire ritual serves to tie the individual tribesman not only to his group, but to the spirit world from which he has come, to the past, and to that segment of nature to which he belongs through totemic affiliation.

Unification through religious ties is by no means limited to the

Australian. Clan rituals among such people as the Tlingit reenforce clan loyalties. In the villages of Europe, the cathedral was, and to a large extent remains, the focus of community life, while its ties to the mother church provide a wider sense of community. The Mohammedan in his daily prayers, bowing toward Mecca, likewise senses his unity with all Islam. Religious sentiments can thus reenforce unity against the limitations imposed by space and time.

Kluckhohn and Leighton show that the religious rituals of the Navaho serve a similar intensification purpose. They note particularly that the curing chants have the effect of reintegrating the individual who feels himself alienated from his group—by the rather direct means of having the group spend time and money in providing the curative ritual.

That which can integrate can also be divisive. The sense of clan unity among the Tlingit may be furthered through the potlatch and other ritual events, but it must also serve to create greater chasms between the several clans. In the same way, the village church which once was a focus for community loyalty has lost this power under the impact of multiple denominations. In the essay on Religious Participation and Social Position, it is shown that in the town of Wasco the several churches tend, as one of the ministers said, to represent the different elements in the community. This is not to say that the churches have created the social schisms of that town, but rather that the existing divisions are expressed through the separation of religious participation and divergence of religious belief. At the same time, each denomination reenforces the individual's sense of belonging to a particular stratum.

Ritual serves other functions also. One important and apparently universal aspect of religious ritual is to signify changes in the status of the individual as he moves through the cycle of life. Such rituals are called rites of passage, because they are ritual doors from one status to another. Among the more usual ones are: birth, which signifies a transformance from the world of the spirit to the world of the living (and for the mother, her new or renewed status of motherhood); puberty, which transforms the child into an adult; marriage, which proclaims the creation of a new nuclear family; and death, which marks the return to the world of the spirit. The timing, importance and character of these several transformations can vary widely. Some primitive people, for example, take little ritual cognizance at the birth of a child but do so after they feel he is safely past the dangers of early infancy; others take little cognizance of marriage, considering the birth of a first child as the truly transforming event (for before that, marriages are easily broken). In some societies, notably Australian ones, there is a long series of initiations with several recognized statuses for the men, separating, for instance, childhood from youth in a prepuberty ritual, and elders from adult status by a late and final rite.

Modern religions also have rites of passage in baptism, confirmation, marriage, and funeral services. Graduation exercises are a kind of rite of passage, and while they are largely secular in character, they are regularly solemnized by an invocation, and are also suffused with considerable moralization about the new privileges and responsibilities of the "initiates."

This brings up two very important points about rites of passage. First, they proclaim to the public that a particular individual has a new position, will fill a new role in his society. In primitive societies without written records, such ritual proclamations may be very important. One function of the Tlingit potlatch was to make public the knowledge as to just which nephew would take over control of the property upon the death of the incumbent.

The second point is that rites of passage make the individual undergoing the ritual aware of his new status. Initiation rituals at puberty are particularly important in this respect. They are of frequent occurrence among primitive people and almost always offer an opportunity for indoctrinating the initiate with his duties and responsibilities. Among the Hopi Indians, for example, youths are initiated by masked katchina spirits, who whip the boys as a kind of ordeal; during this time they are told much about the sacred elements of Hopi life. Physical suffering is frequently found; many Australian and African tribes circumcise boys at puberty rituals which initiate the youths into the status of manhood. There seems little doubt that the combination of pain, ritual, and moralization serves to implant the requisite attitudes firmly in the minds of the person undergoing such a rite of passage.

A third social function of religion is to give a rationale for existing social behavior. Though the person in a society does not and perhaps cannot view his religion in this way, it is clear that the idea system and world view provided by the religion of a people tend to offer a justification for the way the society operates. Among the phenomena that every people must try to understand are, so to speak, the manifestations of their own behavior. Religious belief gives a rationale for that behavior.

Perhaps this can most easily be observed in the emergence of political states. Nearly everywhere that political organization is found—

particularly under primitive or early historical conditions—the state is supported by special religious ideologies. A recurrent theme—found in the New World among the Incas and Aztecs, among such ancient peoples as the Egyptians, and among most of those African peoples who have state organization—is the notion that the ruler has a divine source of power. He may be a god or demigod, he may be descended directly from God, or he may have some other special relation to divinity. It is not surprising, therefore, that we generally find a priesthood associated with state systems. The kings of Baganda, for example, were supported by a state religion centering on the person of the king who was a descendant of Kintu, the first man—though the rank and file also maintained their clan religion and clan priests along with this official religion. The notion of divine right to rule played an important role in our own history and was gradually superseded only as the state became increasingly, though never entirely, secularized.

In this connection, the development of Protestantism is particularly important. In the next section, an essay by Max Weber discusses the relationship between what he calls the Protestant ethic and the development of the capitalist social order. Weber and others have shown that the kind of society built upon capital investments and industrial enterprise required a different moral justification from the society built upon land resources with an aristocracy of land owners. Consider only one point: the attitude of the medieval church toward interest charges (usury) and the consequent deterrent to risk capital, so necessary for industrial enterprise. The rise of a new class of entrepreneurs, whose social dominance could not be justified on the grounds of inherited social position, required a new set of moral attitudes, while at the same time this new merchant or middle class required ideological support in its challenge of the powers of the old aristocracy. Capitalism required a religious philosophy that justified a person's position in terms of his own accomplishments and gave divine sanction to social striving. No better example of the manner in which religion justifies the social order can be found in the annals of history and anthropology.

Religion also has an individual aspect, for religion provides the individual with a sense of the meaningfulness of his own acts. Each of us must come to terms with the social order, must accept our role in it, and must throughout preserve our sense of identity. Religious conviction may support the sentiment that the individual's identity should be submerged in a larger group; that his place in the social system is established by a natural or divine order, as is implicit in class and caste systems, or that his position is dependent upon his own acts, as is explicit in Calvinist theology and, as we shall see, among the Yurok Indians as well.

Primitive peoples frequently have special concepts which provide an explanation for the individual's position and power in society. The concept of mana, which Malinowski mentions, is the idea that a measure of spiritual power inheres in all things and persons, but not in like degree. It is a widespread concept. Other peoples—notably many American Indian tribes—believe that each person has a guardian spirit, whose strength determines his power. There are, in short, many modes of religious explanations for the position that the individual holds in his own society.

This is not the only way individual needs are met by religion. Each person must also face death and disease, fears and anxieties. Religion does not always allay these problems in human existence—the Navaho example shows that belief may further them. But it does provide a rationale and, through ritual and magical practices, through incantations and gestures, a kind of catharsis which helps the individual to survive moments of stress. The need to act, and to believe in the efficacy of the act, appears to be a universal human characteristic. As Miner points out with deft irony, we are ourselves not freed from such magical behavior.

Each religion has its own way of dealing with the recurrent problems of human existence, but some general items are universal, or nearly so. Chief among these are: the belief that each person has a soul which continues after death; the belief in other supernatural beings who influence human action for good or evil; a recognition of spiritual qualities inhering in nonhuman things; a recognition that certain individuals can influence the behavior of the spirit world, and in so doing can help or harm others and increase the fertility of plants, animals, or man. All people believe that certain acts are inherently bad out of religious conviction. Such negative rules are called taboos. All religions also make mandatory certain acts. Not all people believe in a single supreme being, but many do. Many peoples do not believe in any kind of post-mortem punishment for evil, though a large number believe experiences during a person's life will affect his situation after death: The Aztec warrior who dies in battle and his women who die in childbirth enjoy the most noble afterlife, as does a Tlingit who dies for the honor of his clan.

How spirits are conceived, what happens to the soul upon death, how spiritual phenomena are influenced, and how spirits influence human affairs are variable expressions of the basic recurrent themes. What acts are tabooed and what made mandatory will also vary widely—though some, such as incest taboos and taboos against menstrual blood are very nearly universal.

Religious attitudes and ritual behavior reflect some of the pressures of everyday life in the group. Where life is dangerous there will be protective magic; where droughts are recurrent, there will be rain magic; where crops are crucial, there will be fertility rites. This principle applies also to stresses in social life. Studies have shown, for instance, that witchcraft beliefs are stronger where there are anxieties and stresses in social life, and that the pattern of witchcraft belief and practice relate to the specific source of these anxieties. We are shown how this works with the Navaho. From this standpoint, religious beliefs and behavior afford an outlet for the psychological needs of the people.

There is also evidence that religious conceptions vary with the economic life of a people. Thus, most peoples who live by hunting and food-gathering seem to emphasize shamanism. A shaman is a person who has special power to influence spirits, and this influence seems to be chiefly concerned with curing or causing sickness. It may involve a conception of illness based upon intrusive spirits, which the shaman must remove by magical means. In Australia, among the California Indians, and elsewhere, the shaman sucks a wormlike object out of the body of the patient, but among the Eskimo the shaman recaptures a soul that has strayed from the body. Navaho medical practices are closely allied. Shamans may also have public functions (such as detecting or warding off an enemy raid), but they do not form a true priesthood.

Peoples engaged in farming generally have elaborate fertility rituals —fertility both for the crops and for people, frequently with an identity between the two. At this level they are also more likely to have some kind of totem group with its cult aspects, though these may also be found among the hunters and food gatherers. Priests—that is, persons responsible for group ritual—may exist but are relatively unimportant.

Where society takes on a settled character and where political institutions are developed, some form of national religious system is usually found. This involves an elaborate priestcraft and often centers about the person of the ruler, as we have already noted.

Everywhere religion deals with the mysteries of birth and death, with the problem of sickness, with the vagaries of fortune, with such universal but inexplicable aspects of life as dreams and mental aberrations. Everywhere also it is involved with man's relation both to nature and to his fellow man. It endeavors to make these things explicable and predictable. Nor must we fail to appreciate the importance that belief has for human behavior. The psychological force of conviction has an important effect upon the individual; the role of attitude in sickness and health is clearly recognized by modern medicine, if only poorly understood. The potency of such effects must not be overlooked when we examine the medical practices of the shaman, for his successes are sufficient to justify belief in his efficacy—and there is always an explanation for his failures. It is one of the important features of human psychology that the conviction men have that something is true can make that thing true; it is an equally important feature of culture that the conviction in the propriety of an act will make that act proper. Thus conviction justifies belief.

It is in the context of this relation between conviction and events that we must understand the religions of peoples. The faith men have supports the society as they know it and gives the individual the strength to meet the vicissitude inherent in his everyday life, whether they be imposed upon him by nature or by his own culture.

53. Primitive Man and His Religion

BRONISLAW MALINOWSKI

The varieties of religious expression are summarized by Bronislaw Malinowski in this brief selection from his essay, "Magic, Science and Religion." The essay first appeared in *Science, Religion and Reality* (James Needham, ed.) published originally by Macmillan and now available through George Braziller, Inc., in this country and the Society for the Propagation of Christian Knowledge in England. The essay also appears in a collection of Malinowski's works, *Magic, Science and Religion,* the Beacon Press, Boston, and the Free Press, Glencoe, Ill. The essay is printed with the kind permission of the Society for the Propagation of Christian Knowledge and George Braziller, Inc.

In this selection Malinowski does two things: he sets forth the various aspects of religious experience as they occur in primitive societies, and he summarizes briefly the major contributions to an anthropological theory of religion.

There are no peoples however primitive without religion and magic. Nor are there, it must be added at once, any savage races lacking either in the scientific attitude or in science, though this lack has been frequently attributed to them. In every primitive community, studied by trustworthy and competent observers, there have been found two clearly distinguishable domains, the Sacred and the Profane; in other words, the domain of Magic and Religion and that of Science.

On the one hand there are the traditional acts and observances, regarded by the natives as sacred, carried out with reverence and awe, hedged around with prohibitions and special rules of behavior. Such acts and observances are always associated with beliefs in supernatural forces, especially those of magic, or with ideas about beings, spirits, ghosts, dead ancestors, or gods. On the other hand, a moment's reflection is sufficient to show that no art or craft however primitive could have been invented or maintained, no organized form of hunting, fishing, tilling, or search for food could be carried out without the careful observation of natural process and a firm belief in its regularity, without the power of reasoning and without confidence in the power of reason; that is, without the rudiments of science.

The credit of having laid the foundations of an anthropological study of religion belongs to Edward B. Tylor. In his well-known theory he maintains that the essence of primitive religion is animism, the belief in spiritual beings, and he shows how this belief has originated in a mistaken but consistent interpretation of dreams, visions, hallucinations, cataleptic states, and similar phenomena. Reflecting on these, the savage philosopher or theologian was led to distinguish the human soul from the body. Now the soul obviously continues to lead an existence after death, for it appears in dreams, haunts the survivors in memories and in visions and apparently influences human destinies. Thus originated the belief in ghosts and the spirits of the dead, in immortality and in a nether world. But man in general, and primitive man in particular, has a tendency to imagine the outer world in his own image. And since animals, plants, and objects move, act, behave, help man or hinder him, they must also be endowed with souls or spirits. Thus animism, the philosophy and the religion of primitive man, has been built up from observations and by inferences, mistaken but comprehensible in a crude and untutored mind.

Tylor's view of primitive religion, important as it was, was based on too narrow a range of facts, and it made early man too contemplative and rational. Recent fieldwork, done by specialists, shows us the savage interested rather in his fishing and gardens, in tribal events and festivities than brooding over dreams and visions, or explaining "doubles" and cataleptic fits, and it reveals also a great many aspects of early religion which cannot be possibly placed in Tylor's scheme of animism.

The extended and deepened outlook of modern anthropology finds its most adequate expression in the learned and inspiring writings of Sir James Frazer. In these he has set forth the three main problems of primitive religion with which present-day anthropology is busy: magic and its relation to religion and science; totemism and the sociological aspect of early faith; the cults of fertility and vegetation. It will be best to discuss these subjects in turn.

Frazer's "Golden Bough," the great codex of primitive magic, shows clearly that animism is not the only, nor even the dominating belief in primitive culture. Early man seeks above all to control the course of nature for practical ends, and he does it directly, by rite and spell, compelling wind and weather, animals and crops to obey his will. Only much later, finding the limitations of his magical might, does he in fear or hope, in supplication or defiance, appeal to higher beings; that is, to demons, ancestor-spirits or gods. It is in this distinction between direct control on the one hand and propitiation of superior powers on the other that Sir James Frazer sees the difference between religion and magic. Magic, based on man's confidence that he can dominate nature directly, if only he knows the laws which govern it magically, is in this akin to science. Religion, the confession of human impotence in certain matters, lifts man above the magical level, and later on maintains its independence side by side with science, to which magic has to succumb.

. . . While science is based on the conception of natural forces, magic springs from the idea of a certain mystic, impersonal power, which is believed in by most primitive peoples. This power, called *mana* by some Melanesians, *arungquiltha* by certain Australian tribes, *wakan, orenda, manitu* by various American Indians, and nameless elsewhere, is stated to be a well-nigh universal idea found wherever magic flourishes. According to the writers just mentioned we can find among the most primitive peoples and throughout the lower savagery a belief in a supernatural, impersonal force, moving all those agencies which are relevant to the savage and causing all the really important events in the domain of the sacred. Thus *mana,* not animism, is the essence of "pre-animistic religion," and it is also the essence of magic, which is thus radically different from science. . . .

Totemism, to quote Frazer's classical definition, "is an intimate relation which is supposed to exist between a group of kindred people on the one side and a species of natural or artificial objects on the other side, which objects are called the totems of the human group." Totemism thus has two sides: it is a mode of social grouping and a religious system of beliefs and practices. As religion, it expresses primitive man's interest in his surroundings, the desire to claim an affinity and to control the most important objects: above all, animal or vegetable species, more rarely useful inanimate objects, very seldom man-made things. As a rule species of animals and plants used for staple food or at any rate edible or useful or ornamental animals are held in a special form of "totemic reverence" and are tabooed to the members of the clan which is associated with the species and which sometimes performs rites and ceremonies for its multiplication. The social aspect of totemism consists in the subdivision of the tribe into minor units, called in anthropology *clans, gentes, sibs,* or *phratries.*

In totemism we see therefore not the result of early man's speculations about mysterious phenomena, but a blend of a utilitarian anxiety about the most necessary objects of his surroundings, with some preoccupation in those which strike his imagination and attract his attention, such as beautiful birds, reptiles and dangerous animals. With our knowledge of what could be called the totemic attitude of mind, primitive religion is seen to be nearer to reality and to the immediate practical life interests of the savage, than it appeared in its "animistic" aspect emphasized by Tylor and the earlier anthropologists.

By its apparently strange association with a problematic form of social division, I mean the clan system, totemism has taught anthropology yet another lesson: it has revealed the importance of the sociological aspect in all the early forms of cult. The savage depends upon the group with whom he is in direct contact both for practical co-operation and mental solidarity to a far larger extent than does civilized man. Since—as can be seen in totemism, magic, and many other practices—early cult and ritual are closely associated with practical concerns as well as with mental needs, there must exist an intimate connection between social organization and religious belief. This was understood already by that pioneer of religious anthropology, Robertson Smith, whose principle that primitive religion "was essentially an affair of the community rather than of individuals" has become a *Leitmotiv* of modern research. According to Professor Durkheim, who has put these views most forcibly, "the religious" is identical with "the social." For "in a general way . . . a society has all that is necessary to arouse the sensation of the Divine in minds, merely by the power that it has over them; for to its members it is what a God is to its worshippers." Professor Durkheim arrives at this conclusion by the study of totemism, which he believes to be the most primitive form of religion. In this the "totemic principle" which is identical with *mana* and with "the God of the clan . . . can be nothing else than the clan itself." . . .

The third great subject introduced into the Science of Religion by Sir James Frazer is that of the cults of vegetation and fertility. In "The Golden Bough," starting from the awful and mysterious ritual of the wood divinities at Nemi, we are led through an amazing variety of magical and religious cults, devised by man to stimulate and control the fertilizing work of skies and earth and of sun and rain, and we are left with the impression that early religion is teeming with the forces of savage life, with its young beauty and crudity, with its exuberance and strength so violent that it leads now and again to suicidal acts of self-immolation. The study of "The Golden Bough" shows us that for primitive man death has meaning mainly as a step to resurrection, decay as a stage of re-birth, the plenty of autumn and the decline of winter as preludes to the revival of spring. . . .

There are two important contributions to the theory of primitive religion which I mention here only, for they have somehow remained outside the main current of anthropological interest. They treat of the primitive idea of one God and of the place of morals in primitive religion respectively. It is remarkable that they have been and still are neglected, for are not these two questions first and foremost in the mind of anyone who studies religion, however crude and rudimentary it may be? Perhaps the explanation is in the preconceived idea that "origins" must be very crude and simple and different from the "developed forms," or else in the notion that the "savage" or "primitive" is really savage and primitive!

The late Andrew Lang indicated the existence among some Australian natives of the belief in a tribal All-Father, and the Rev. Pater Wilhelm Schmidt has adduced much evidence proving that this belief is universal among all the people of the simplest cultures and that it cannot be discarded as an irrelevant fragment of mythology, still less as an echo of missionary teaching. It looks, according to Pater Schmidt, very much like an indication of a simple and pure form of early monotheism.

The problem of morals as an early religious function was also left on one side, until it received an exhaustive treatment, not only in the writings of Pater Schmidt but also and notably in two works of outstanding importance: the "Origin and Development of Moral Ideas" of Professor E. Westermarck, and "Morals in Evolution" of Professor L. T. Hobhouse. . . .

One achievement of modern anthropology we shall not question: the recognition that magic and religion are not merely a doctrine or a philosophy, not merely an intellectual body of opinion, but a special mode of behavior, a pragmatic attitude built up of reason, feeling, and will alike. It is a mode of action as well as a system of belief, and a sociological phenomenon as well as a personal experience. But with all this, the exact relation between the social and the individual contributions to religion is not clear, as we have seen from the exaggerations committed on either side. Nor is it clear what are the respective shares of emotion and reason.

54. Religion of the Australian Aborigines

A. P. ELKIN

Australian religion is highly developed despite the material poverty of the Australian aborigines. To the Australian, man, society, and all nature are one; the past, the present, and the future are intertwined. The Australian religion includes animism, totemism, and shamanism in a highly developed form. Its elaborate rituals unify the significant social groups, and its rites of passage mark the stages in the growth of the individual.

A. P. Elkin has been Professor of Anthropology at the University of Sydney since 1934 and has written extensively on the Australian aborigines. He has had a wide variety of field experience among the rapidly disappearing tribes of that continent. The present essay is reprinted from a contribution to *Ancient Religions* (Virgilius Ferm, ed.), New York: The Philosophical Library, 1950, and is reprinted by kind permission of the publisher.

. . . The Aborigines have worked out a ritual adjustment to nature. This ritual expresses the food-gatherers' dependence on nature—on the coming of rain and the increase of animals and plants in due season. But further, through it, they maintain continuity with the past, with the cult-heroes and ancestors; and by participation in it strengthen and revivify those social and moral sentiments, on which social unity depends. Behind this is a philosophy of life—of man and nature—which may be summed up as totemistic, animistic and historical.

The basic fact or premise is the Aborigines' complete unaided parasitical dependence on nature—a dependence which is not made indirect in any way—such as by gardening, clothing, flooring or any form of housing (except occasionally in some parts). On this basis they have developed a dogma that man and nature share a common life and belong to one moral order. Geographical and economic exigencies have caused human beings to be organized into groups; but it is obvious that the natural species and phenomena on which the former depend and with which they are ever associated, are also organized in groups—namely, species and related phenomena. In accordance with the same principles of segmentation (or group organization), mutual dependence and reciprocity which operate in social and economic life, specific segments of nature, that is species and objects belonging to the tribal environment are linked with specific human segments. Thus, one human group is linked to a particular species, say, the plains kangaroo, and possibly also to several other natural species and objects. The next human group may be linked with the emu and some other species and objects; and so on. Such species are the totems of the groups concerned.

This link, it must be remembered, is not a hook which can be unfastened; it cannot be "melted" or "cut off," nor can a new one be "forged." The segment of nature to which any individual is linked was determined by this conception on birth, that is, by his membership of a related human segment. It is not a matter of choice, but of "determinism," of history, of dogma. This being so, we are not surprised to learn that the link is more than nominal: it is one of life, not merely of name. . . .

The important aspect of totemism is its function. This is of two main types. The first is social: the group of human beings who say that a certain species is their totem or "flesh," regard it as the symbol of that common inheritance of flesh and blood which they have received through their mothers, mothers' mothers', and so on back to one matrilineal source. They, therefore, respect their totem as the flesh of their own mother, sister, brother, and mother's "uncle." They neither kill nor eat it, unless on occasions of dire distress, and then with prescribed ritual. On the other hand, the natural species acts as guardian of the totemites, warning them of danger by appearing in the flesh or in dreams, and strengthening them in illness. In addition, so real is this symbolism of common flesh that persons possessing the same social totem do not marry, never mind how distantly related they may be. Indeed in some tribes, a man does not even marry a woman whose father's social totem was the same as his own. It is "too close in religion." But there are, as far as we know, no ceremonies designed to increase the matrilineal social totems, and no sacred places connected with them, though there are myths explaining "historically" how the human groups came to be so named. Social totemism is confined to south- and central-east Australia.

This symbolic function of totemism is associated with the doctrine of pre-existence of spirits, and with a corollary that the father contributes nothing physiologically to the child, although the latter is socially and spiritually his. According to the most widely accepted doctrine, the "child-spirits" sojourn in known spirit-homes, where they were left by totemic cult-heroes or by the sky-hero in the period when these heroes walked on earth. In some regions the sky-being still creates them and puts them in the spirit-places ready for incarnation. From such places the spirits issue and directly, or sometimes indirectly in a particular vegetable or flesh food, enter the womb of the selected mother. The husband usually learns through a dream or a vision what is about to happen, or has happened. The spirit-child becomes flesh through its mother, the father contributing to this process, or "growing it up," by providing the mother with food. When born, the child belongs to its father's local group and country, and will share his ritual and mythological heritage.

Incidentally, the location in his "country" of the spirit-home from which he came, and to which he will return after death, binds a person indissolubly to his "country." The bond is spiritual; it is one of life.

The other fundamental function of totemism is to group men, according to various rules of birth, conception and locality, into "lodges" or "societies," for the observance of specific cults, each with a totemic aspect. The members of such a "lodge" will say that their totem is kangaroo, iguana, rain, emu, *etc.,* but this totem is not their "flesh" or "meat"; it is their "Dreaming." If we ask a man for his Dreaming, he might say kangaroo or iguana, or give the name of a hero; or he might commence the recital of a long myth, and even suggest organizing a rite to represent it. If he does not do so, a question about the travels, deeds and (sacred) place of the kangaroo or hero will bring reference to the myth. For cult-totemism is concerned with ritual myths which record the doings of heroes and ancestors, with sanctuaries (mostly rocks) associated with these, and with totemic groups or lodges. The heroes are (and were) human beings of heightened powers, thought of as having totems, and referred to by animal or bird names; in some cases they were great animals or birds.

The period in which these heroic beings traveled and hunted and made natural phenomena (the hills, valleys and rivers) is called the Dream-Time, while the hero or his totemic symbol is "Dreaming." The Dream-Time partakes of the nature of a dream in that the limitations of time are transcended. It is not merely past; it is present, and even the future becomes real in the present. It is a condition or state as well as a period. It includes both continuity with a creative past time, and participation in a present creative power. And man is a channel and a sacramental expression of, not merely a link with, the "Eternal Dream" in both its aspects—of time present and of present power.

The significance of the Dreaming is manifold. It explains through the myths how things came to be as they are. It enshrines sanctions for social rules in the examples and incidents "recorded" in the myths, and sets the patterns for the rites on which faith, hope and charity (social cohesion) depend. If through disintegration, following on the advance of white settlement, individuals have no Dreaming, they become aimless, like corks bobbing about in a ruffled stream. "He who has no Dreaming is lost."

This form of totemism, which is fundamentally an heroic cult, is found with some variations over most of Australia. . . .

Birth and descent bestow eligibility, and that only. Knowledge of the secrets, of the mystery, is imparted and gained only through initiation—a ritual death and a "rising" or re-birth, which all males must undergo. The general pattern of the initiation is the same all over the continent, but the symbol of killing varies from the knocking out of a tooth or cicatrisation, or simply the pulling out of facial and pubic hair in the east and south-west, to circumcision in the center and north-west, where some of the former operations are also practised. The new life which is gained is symbolized in the east by quartz, a substance closely associated with the sky-hero and with the rainbow, by being "painted" with red-ochre or human blood, especially in the western two-thirds of the continent, and by the gift of a pearl-shell pendant in the north-west in particular—pearl-shell, the symbol of the rainbow-serpent.

However, the chief objects revealed everywhere are the bull-roarer, the symbol and voice of the sky-hero or of the totemic Dream-Time heroes, and other sacred symbols, usually of stone; these are often transformed parts of the heroes. In addition, knowledge of myths, rites, and dogmas is imparted though only gradually and as the individual grows in strength—that is, in fitness to be the custodian of the esoteric, to be a channel of the Dreaming.

The rites revealed are of two chief kinds. In the desert and near-desert region of the continent, the most important series of rites is connected with centers associated with the totemic cult-heroes. At these places certain natural objects, mostly of rock, are said to be transformed bodies or parts of heroes or of totemic species which appear in the cult-myths. Myths in chant-form are sung, actors represent the heroic scenes, and as a rule, human blood (or else red ochre) is applied to the stone symbol. As a result the natural species increases, pre-existent "spirits" of the species going forth to be reincarnated. In some regions these "spirits" are thought of as emanations from a totemic hero or from the ancestral spirit of the species which are to be "incarnated." . . .

In the desert regions the performance of increase-rites is a very stern and serious business in which the whole tribe is concerned, for existence depends on the efficacy of the ritual. Cult-societies perform the rites, "commanded" and watched in each case by prescribed "associate-members" of the particular cult-society concerned. The preparations for the rites, the circumspection surrounding them, the concentration of thought, the expenditure of energy, and the use of human blood, express the importance attached to the rites. And what is very striking is that in most cases the members of the totemic group do not eat, except once and sacramentally, the species which has increased as a result of the rites. Members of other totems do so. In this way reciprocity operates in ritual and in the results which are believed to ensue. Each group denies itself one food, and depends on the other groups for the ritual increase of the foods it does eat.

There is a second series of totemic rites, including myth-chants, action and symbols. These are usually performed at temporary sacred places, and not at sanctuaries set apart by Dream-Time heroes. Moreover, they are seldom believed to result in the increase of the species which is symbolized in the totem or in parts of the rites. These ceremonies are historical, being a re-enactment of the revered creative past and of the heroic type-life, from which all must learn. In them, singers and onlookers become carried away. They often cut themselves and they dance with all their vigor in time-ordained style, as they realize the presence of the Dreaming and, indeed, are envelopd by it, even as they are by the dust which is raised by the stamp of feet and by beating the time with sticks on the ground. The energy expended and the abandon must be seen to be realized. But an important effect is the maintenance of continuity with the past, the enhancing of the feeling of social unity in the present, and the renewal of the social sentiments, ideals and sanctions on which faith, hope and social cohesion depend. . . .

While all men are initiated into the secret life of myths, ritual, and symbol, a few selected or gifted ones proceed further, entering the mysteries of the sky-world, and become through a "Second ritual death" endowed with psychic power. These "men of high degree," or "medicine-men" as they are generally called, practise meditation, telepathy and hypnotism, claim to know what is happening at a distance, and act as coroners and seers. They also heal the sick by physical and psychological means. In south-eastern Australia they played the leading part in initiation ceremonies, for there the latter introduced the novice to the sky-hero and his world, the special province of the "men of high degree." But everywhere they were and are the tribes' link and medium with the unseen world of spirits of the dead and of other types. They deal with the apparently contingent and unexpected, especially in the sphere of sickness and death, the causes of which are deemed animistic and personal. They protect revenge-parties from the magical dangers of the way, as these go forth to exact retribution for sorcery. They are the preservers of the tribes' psychological health, and perform at least part of the rôle of the priest. . . .

Doctrines differ regarding the fate of the soul. But extinction is seldom suggested. For the soul which pre-existed independently of human flesh before its incarnation, does not necessarily cease to exist after the instrument of its temporary embodiment is of no more use— or as the Aborigines would say, after the soul, the "shade," has finally left the body, not merely temporarily as in a dream or in a severe illness.

Thus, the child comes from the sacred Dreaming and spirit-world, and if a male, after a few years on the "outside" in the profane world, he is re-admitted through initiation to that same sacred world of the Dreaming or of the Sky, or at least to a knowledge of it in myth, rite and symbol. Finally, through the transition-rite of burial, he enters again the spirit-world—perhaps after being tested, to remain in a state of "plenty," or according to the doctrine of many tribes, to return to his spirit-home on earth, and eventually to be reincarnated. A female, however, does not travel the middle part of this path or cycle, though she does learn something of the fundamental doctrines and myths, especially as she grows old. And, of course, she is the means through which the pre-existing spirits are incarnated. She is not altogether profane, and her lot, in the other world or through reincarnation, is similar to that of the male.

55. Religious Participation and Social Position

WALTER GOLDSCHMIDT

Though America has a dominant religious tradition, divergent expressions of this religious philosophy have separated Americans into a variety of denominations. The expressions of our religious philosophy relate to our life circumstances, and in this essay Walter Goldschmidt shows how the religious values of the different churches in the community of Wasco, California, express the different social positions and economic standing of the citizens. Denominationalism does not create a division in Wasco society, but it reinforces that division and tends to rationalize each person's position in the social sphere.

The present essay is taken from *As You Sow*, a sociological study of the community made in 1940–41. It is published by the kind permission of the Free Press, Glencoe, Ill.

The churches in Wasco tend," according to the minister in its leading church, "to represent the different elements in the San Joaquin Valley." Such a statement leads us naturally to a closer scrutiny of the position of the church in the social hierarchy. The church—at least the Protestant church—is as much a social institution as it is a religious one. When a resident decides to belong to a church, and when he selects the denomination to which he will adhere, he makes a fundamental social choice which will affect his associates and his social behavior for the duration of his residence. And his choice is as much influenced by social considerations as by religious ones. Because the church plays an important social role—one of the most important of any institution in community life—it must be subjected to careful analysis. The value judgments made with respect to these institutions are evaluations of their social position and do not reflect upon their religious tenets, which are outside the province of this study. Nor is there any implication that congregations elsewhere have the same relative social position that they display in Wasco.

There are ten Christian churches for whites alone in the community, not counting a small Mormon group and the one or two unorganized religious groups which meet in private homes. Besides these, there are three Negro organizations and there was at one time a Mexican Pentecostal group. Before examining the nature of social separation of these denominations, it will be well to acquaint ourselves with the variation in religious content of some of the more important Protestant sects serving the whites of the community.

The first church in the community has a moderately elaborate structure surrounded by shrubs and lawns, with a special recreation room, and an air of middle-class well-being. It is the congregation of the elite. Its leading patrons are select, even among this elite. Its services are quiet and orderly; its sermons innocuous admonitions to moral conduct, or intellectualized explanations of the workings of God with man. It is said that an earlier minister left at the behest of one of the leading contributors because he preached the doctrine of equal rights, co-operative activity, and sharing of wealth. The sermon is preceded by a fixed ritual, including music by a vested choir, organ accompaniment, and the funereal hush of the carpeted and insulated edifice. Lay participation is hardly more than in the Catholic ritual, two or three hymns and the reading of the responses constituting the whole. To this service the congregation takes its obligation lightly; rarely are there more than two or three dozen well-clad substantial citizens present. Communion with God may be had or left, as the spirit moves, so long as the appearances of membership are maintained.

Coming down but half a step, we may place two or three congregations on a social level, the differences between them not being those of social status. Comfortable, unelaborate structures, completely adequate in size to meet the requirements of the congregation, house the religious services. The sermons are more fervid, the spirit is less subdued, and the lay participation is more spontaneous. Correlatively the congregation is more active, the pews are more nearly filled each week, revivalistic meetings are undertaken, and the emotional appeal of Protestantism more manifest. . . .

Stepping down once more in the social scale, we arrive at the level of the revivalistic churches. The buildings compare favorably with the preceding churches; they are newer, but not quite so nicely designed, so carefully finished, so well appointed, nor so centrally located, lying rather in the poorer sections of the community. The preachers are graduates of religious colleges but not graduates of general schools of higher learning. Informality may be considered the keynote of the services; for want of better clothes the congregation is modestly clad, the services are filled with colloquial expressions and homely illustrations, the participation of the congregation is easy and unself-conscious.

The emphasis on personal salvation and the intellectual-emotional appeal to the personal experience, following the pattern described in the Bible for the night of Pentecost, are not the annual or biennial expression of an itinerant evangelist, but the week-by-week fare of the Sunday services, heightened by the temporary elaboration of the revival meeting. The nature of the appeal of these sects and the spirit of their meetings can perhaps be caught in a sermon, and for that reason one is reproduced here very nearly as it was presented. For background, it may be added that this sermon was accompanied by the "Amens!" of the audience, as well as the presence of twisting and crying children and the informality of persons entering and leaving the congregation.

> You know, folks, the other day, I was visiting some friends of mine on a farm back East. I took a couple of days off and had a visit with some people. The farmer asked me if I had ever seen a mechanical corn-picker, and I said I'd like very much to see one, for I never had. Well, he got out his tractor and rigged up the corn-picker. It had some boards to the side, set together about an inch or two apart, and the stalk went between these and they just lifted the corn off the stalk and a belt took it back and put it in a wagon that followed. That was fine, but I still wasn't convinced, and I asked my friend what they did about stalks that were blown down, and he laughed, and said that they had taken care of that. They have experimented and bred for years and they have gotten a pure bred corn that will stand up. It sends its roots way down in the soil, and the wind can blow and the rains can come, but that corn stalk stands right up. The farmer pays twice as much for that corn, because it is pure bred, and will stand up no matter how hard the wind blows.
>
> What we need is more people that will stand up. We need to have people who are firmly rooted in their faith, and when the winds of adversity blow they stand right up to their God. We need real blue bloods. You know, a lot of people think that blue bloods all live in Kentucky, but the real blue bloods are those who are firm in their faith. You know there are plenty of blue bloods in the church, for in heaven everybody is a blue blood—no matter how poor you are.
>
> Well, I just got off on this story. The collection is taken, and so you won't have to pay an extra dime for it.
>
> [After a reading from the Bible] So no man can know when Judgment Day will come. There will be nothing different in the air, there will be no signs to show that Judgment is coming, one hour or one day or one week or one month before Judgment Day.

[The story of the flood was presented] Nobody paid any attention to the warning, for they were all living a life of sin. They ate, they drank, they married and gave in marriage, the night before Judgment. There was no difference between the night before Judgment and the night before, or the week before or the month before.

Abraham was willing to leave Egypt when God told him to. He didn't say he was too old to be moving. He didn't say, "You can't teach an old dog new tricks," and refuse to go. He went out to the promised land. Abraham later left, and went to Egypt. He said that the grass is greener over there. But he should have stayed and prayed the rain down from heaven, and made the grass green where he was. The same is true of the people in the church. They should go to their own church to pray, and not go to another one because it is doing better.

Abraham divided the land with Lot, saying there is enough for all of us in this wide world. And Lot went into the valley, and Abraham into the mountains. It is good to go into the mountains once in a while, and be alone, and pray, where the filth of man does not keep God away.

And three spirits came to Abraham, and he ran out to meet them, for he recognized them, and he welcomed them into his house. He didn't have to go to Sarah and tell her to put these cards away, and to hide that bottle, and to get rid of those *True Story* magazines. They may be true stories, but if they are, I'd pray to God that I could forget it and that He would forgive me. Amen, brother, amen.

The Lord decided to tell Abraham what He had planned, and He stayed behind after the others left. He decided to tell Abraham, because he managed well his household. Note that, he managed his household WELL. His daughter didn't manage his household, his son didn't, but Abraham managed his household. The son didn't come home at 2 A.M. and then when his father said, "Get up, go to Sunday school," he didn't answer, "No, I don't want to." He probably took them behind the woodshed. The woodshed is a fine place to learn things—more is learned there than at any college. Maybe the methods of impressing aren't the same, but you learn there. I remember the lessons that I learned behind the woodshed—and they didn't hurt me any. I don't seem so bad off.

About two years ago I visited in the home of a deacon, I won't say where, but it wasn't in California. The son came in and said, "Give me the keys. I want to use the car this afternoon." The deacon handed over the keys, and said, "Where are you going?" The son said, "I'm going to the movies with some friends. By the way, give me some money." "Well," said the father, handing over some money, "come back early for I want you to go to the young people's meeting." Why, that boy shouldn't pollute the church with his presence, after going to the movies on Sunday afternoon. Before I'd let that boy go to church, I'd scrub him good and clean with soap and a scalding bath, and I'd have him pray for about two hours, to get that filth off of him. And I'd take that deacon, that would let his children act that way, behind the woodshed. And I'd take his deaconship away from him.

Abraham tried to get the Lord not to bring destruction upon Sodom and Gomorrah. He asked the Lord if He would leave the city if he found fifty righteous men. Then he asked forty-five, then forty, and so on. He jewed the Lord down till He was willing to have ten good men in the city. He must have been counting—there's Lot and his family, and there are almost ten, right there.

The Lord went to Sodom and called on Lot. Lot wouldn't let the Lord sleep in the streets, for he knew the corruption of the people in the city. He made Him come into the house. The Lord told him what He planned, and Lot went to his sons-in-law, and to the people. They just laughed at him. They said, why Lot has been out to visit that crazy uncle Abraham out in the mountains, and he has been talking again. They ought to lock him up. And the people tried to get the angels, but the angels brought Lot out and with his wife and daughters. They led them out of the city. And as they walked away from Sodom, Lot's wife said, "I have to look back. All my friends back there, that I will never see again." "The Lord said that we must never look back." "But our friends are back there. We used to play a few innocent hands of bridge, and have such good times together." And she looked back and was turned into a pillar of salt. But Lot did not look back.

You have it better than Lot's wife, for you have a chance to repent. She would have been happy to repent a million times over, but the Lord didn't give her a chance to repent, nor did He give the fallen angels a chance to repent. But, you, my friends, can repent now, before it is too late.

And the day before Judgment was no different from any other day. They were not able to notice any difference between the day before Judgment and the day before that, nor the week before that, nor any other time.

The son of Nebuchadnezzar was drinking wine, and he ordered that the great chalices of some temple be brought in, filled with wine, and they all drank from that. God saw this, and He sent a warning—just the handwriting on the wall, no arms, body, or anything else. They were all afraid, as all wicked people are of supernatural things. They called in the fortune-tellers, and all the people who thought they might be able to read the handwriting of God, but none of them could. Finally, the king's wife said that she knew a man of God who might be able to read, and they brought David out from the dungeon. God always has somebody in the gap, so that the people had a warning. David wasn't afraid to tell the king that his kingdom would perish and that it would be divided between the Meads and the Persians—he wasn't afraid to tell them, though he had been brought in from the dungeon. And the next day one in every two was taken away.

And the last night before Judgment was like all the rest. It was no different from the day before, nor the week before, but was like all the rest.

After the sermon was over and the prayer offered, while the choir sang "Almost Believing," the evangelist came through the audience, and spoke to each man separately. Meanwhile most of the congregation went forward to the altar and were kneeling and praying, each aloud and for himself. The evangelist put his hand on each man's back, drew each to him insinuatingly, and asked them in a lowered voice, "Have you been saved? Don't you want to be saved today? It would be terrible to have to face Judgment Day without being saved, wouldn't it? Why wait, why not come up now?"

This sermon may be taken as a typical, though somewhat highly organized, example of the appeal that the churches on this level make to their audience. The major theme presents clearly the familiar fear psychology appeal for adherents based upon the threat of eternal retribution, plus the salesmanship technique of "act quickly, limited offer." If we examine some of the asides we glean still more of the special aspects of the appeal the institution has for its followers. Note first the homely quality of the illustrations, the corn-picker, the references to bridge, to the woodshed, to those familiar items of family quarrels, car keys, and the movies. Above all, we have here just an aside, a reference to the dominance in the hierarchy of values in the putative society of the Kingdom of God: "The real blue bloods are those who are firm in their faith." "In heaven everybody is a blue blood—no matter how poor you are."

This revivalistic religion has direct emotional appeal for salvation; it is presented in the homely fashion of the layman, and individual participation is heightened not only by Amens and much singing but also by shouted prayers, each person to himself. Still, as we shall see shortly, it is far more subdued than the schismatic churches. Its appeals are not pure release; there is a direct call to the reason. The individual does not merely shout his woes publicly; he is exhorted to make a rational choice, within the frame of reference that has been set.

Here, then, is a homier atmosphere for the people who have been accustomed to attending church "where you're just raised up among folks" and "you could go [dressed] any old way," and it has drawn many from the established churches. The special appeals of the homier atmosphere and the lay participation draw heavily on that part of the population whose ties are with the churches which in Wasco are serving the dominant class. In their social aspects, rather than in the special sectarian tenets, lies their particular attraction to this group. This has been forceful enough, not merely to catch a few strays, but to create a major shift in church participation.

As between one and another of the denominations which are on this same level, there is little to choose, and consequently no major shift has been observed. As between the belief in the ability to talk in tongues and the rejection of that belief, little in itself can affect the ordinary layman to whom the refinements of Biblical interpretations and theological philosophy are of minor concern. The ministers of these churches themselves treat lightly the existence of the different sects, comparing the situation to that found with commercial services, where personal whim leads to one or another grocer, and where space limitations require multiple gasoline stations. In part, this negation of sectarian differences is an attempt to create the illusion of unity with the churches on a higher social plane. The seminary ministers are quite conscious of the social distinctions between congregations; they minimize the agricultural labor adherents on the one hand, and the sectarian differences on the other.

The schismatic Pentecostal church represents a still lower level on the scale of formality, a higher one on the scale of emotional appeal. The small frame building housing this group stands in an outlying section of town. Inside there is ample evidence that "people living in tents would not feel uncomfortable." The pews are unfinished benches, embellished with the carved names of the bored unimpressed. Behind the altar the choir is seated on similar furniture and on the wall behind them are religious pictures, an electric sign advertising the young people's association and another proclaiming "Jesus Saves." A flag, a calendar, and other embellishments further relieve the dirty blue walls.

The services are conducted by a "brother" who "swamps" on a potato truck during the week. On one Sunday there were not over twenty persons, mostly women above forty, but some men and younger women. Several had children in their arms, while one young man sat in the rear, aloof to the whole proceedings. Young people sometimes go to these meetings, they say, merely for their entertainment value. They are more numerous in the evening services, when in the rear of the church flirtations and courtships are carried on, another aspect of the social appeal of the church. But these young people are not left unaffected by the services, even when their attention appears to be directed to other things. The description of part of a Sunday service from field notes will indicate the nature of this religious observance.

At the time I entered, a woman in the choir was giving testimonial and asking prayer for a young couple who had just come from Oklahoma. "And you just pray that those two children will get work. They came out here without a cent, and they have gone North now, but they will need work." This is to the accompaniment of "Hallelujahs" and "Amens" by the preacher and a few in the congregation. Immediately as she sat down another woman arose and asked prayer for her daughter and son-in-law, "I just asked that boy (and I know he's a good boy at heart) if he had ever been in church and had the Lord grip him, and he said that one time he did, and he had often wondered about that. I think he can be saved, and I just hope that you will pray for those two and help them." A third arose and asked that we pray for her neighbor. "Her husband was in the insane asylum and she came to church and almost got religion, but just then her husband got well and came back. Now he is sick again. She told me that if she hadn't backslid she believes her husband would never have suffered so. I think we should pray for her, and get her back into the church."

After these testimonials, everyone kneeled, bowed his head upon the bench and prayed aloud. At first only the voice of one or two individuals could be heard in agonized prayer, then more and more voices were raised out of the indeterminate murmur, shouting indistinguishable words. As each person finished he sat on the bench and waited till the rest were through, finally, only one shrill voice remained.

A hymn was started, the last praying woman arose and composed herself. After the song, there was a standing prayer led by the preacher, who walked up and down the platform, frequently turning his back on the congregation and looking upward stretched his arms over his head and shouted, "Jesus, Jesus, Jesus." The sermon followed.

At the outset the preacher explained that the Lord gave him his sermon, and that he considered this better than the usual method of asking blessings of a sermon already rendered. The sermon itself quite lacked coherent structure, it also lacked modulation. It was alternately a passage from the Bible and a few shouted comments regarding the content such as "the Lord says that if you are dirty you should wash, but He isn't speaking of the dirt of the earth, but the dirt of sin." In closing, he struck the salesmanship note, "Satan is working hard in the world today, because he knows his time is short. I can see that Jesus is getting ready to make His appearance soon, that the earthly kingdoms are destroying themselves. It is good to know we have the thing in hand for Jesus."

At the close there was a second standing prayer, then a duet in the inimitable flat nasal voice so typical of the singing in these churches, and the service was closed. Each person shook the hand of the others and said, "God bless you."

Personal participation, emotional release, informality, equality are all fulfilled in these services, three times each week for the fervent. We can hear their own expression of social anxieties and tensions in excerpts from their testimonials and prayers. The feeling of belonging was expressed in the Sunday evening testimonials. One said, "We should all pray for one another, pray for young and old alike. . . . We should pray for brotherly love. . . . There is no wrong in our acting like one big family, for that's what we are." A release from the personal sufferings is expressed in the following: "I've got a son in Oklahoma who's in trouble. Sometimes it takes trouble to make us appreciate the Lord. . . . It's wonderful to have someone to count on, but it's best to be in the arms of the Lord." But the greatest suffering of all, the common suffering of the selected group, is the economic worry and the feeling of inferiority engendered by the social system. For this reason a putative society is created by their wishful-thinking philosophy, a society in which they claim equality but in which they really feel themselves superior, for they are the saved. This is the society of the Kingdom of the Lord, and they "are all as precious in the eyes of the Lord." One called out in testimonial, "I've been broke, but you feel good if you know the Lord is watching you." Another professed that "I believe the less a person has of the world, the more they appreciate the Lord because they have to call on Him more." Again, "Sometimes I think I am worth nothing to the Lord or to anybody else, but when I realize what I am in His eyes, it makes me want to pray all the more."

Thus publicly proclaimed before their fellows and their God is their status in the commonly held dream world and the public negation of the real world of sin and disorder. There is little wonder that the depressed are drawn to this church, and that the more satisfied are repelled by it.

There is another aspect to the appeals of the several churches—that of belonging to a group of kindred spirits. This is a potent factor in the selection of members on a class basis. People like to "be with their own kind" when being with others means remaining always on the peripheries of participation. Yet people do not want to associate with people who are "beneath them." These social aspects have led to class segregation and such segregation is a specific denial of the basic tenets of the Christian philosophy. The church members deny any policy of exclusion, and can document their denial with examples. Yet the exclusion is of such an insidious nature that it is felt at both ends, and there is a tacit recognition that certain churches are for certain people, and this is sometimes given overt expression.

The first exclusion is on a racial basis. No Negro and white person attend the same church, even though their religious convictions coincide. This exclusion is specifically denied to be mandatory, yet it is without exception maintained. A leading minister toyed with the problem that would arise if a Negro would ask to join his congregation. His statement in this regard suggests, however, the reality of the unformalized type of exclusion.

> I would take it up before the Board of Deacons and recommend highly that he be admitted. There would have to be some reason, for instance he might be a teacher who had gone through our schools. I believe they would pass it. I would then let the church vote on the matter, and if there were dissenters, I would try to make the action unanimous. After that it would be a closed matter. If anyone objected, I would point out that this is a democratic organization and that the rule of the majority must be accepted. I think he would be taken in. I think he would have to—it would be all over town one way or the other.

A member of one of the poorer churches maintained, on the other hand, that her group has encouraged the Negroes to join, "but they just don't join. I don't know why unless it is because back East they don't mix with whites, and they don't feel free to." . . .

The Mexicans stand in an apparently different relationship, with regard to the church, for they are almost all members of the Catholic congregation. But the segregation is nearly as great, for though they attend Mass together, they remain apart socially. This distinction was pointed out by the priest, who said:

There is a large Mexican colony but there are also many Germans. There used to be one service in Spanish for them, but we have discontinued that. We make no distinctions between the two groups. Once a year we have a Spanish Mission for the Mexicans, which lasts a week.

The Mexicans are children of nature, and do not take their religion very seriously. They have a kind of inferiority complex and feel that they are looked down on. Many of the Mexicans have devotions in their own homes—they have little altars. They like the trimmings better than the essentials; it is better that way than if they had nothing.

We have card parties and socials to raise money. The Mexicans do not come to these. They would rather be with their kind. Every once in a while, usually in the spring, they have a fiesta. They have a good time. Some of the others come—it is open to everyone.

Here we have the internal segregation of the Mexicans. Since they are traditionally Catholic, we would expect very few among the Protestant churches, and in actuality there is but a single case. . . .

Perhaps the most telling documentation of status differentiation among the religious bodies of Wasco may be gained from an understanding of the changes of status that the different churches as wholes have undergone. The leading churches—the four which make up the substance of Wasco—have not just recently attained their places, though their relative status may have undergone some modifications with the building of new edifices. But in the lower brackets, those called by the dominant population the "Holy Roller" churches, the evidences of status change are manifest. One person recognized this change when he said, "I used to live across from one of those Holy Roller churches. My, but they were a noisy lot. They seem to have quieted down since then, though. They have built a new church and I suppose they have to live up to their new respectability." Such an observation might be written off to a development of understanding or acclimatization, but we have the following testimony from one of the ministers:

The first two ministers here were just farmer-preachers who had had no education. They attracted most of the transient migratory workers. Many of the transient migratory type were attracted by his type of leadership, but my predecessor and I have kind of—now I don't want to put it so you misunderstand, but our special appeal is to the middle class. Poor people get a sensual or physical thrill and in that there is an attraction. I have had a frank Pentecostal preacher tell me that many of his congregation come to church for just that thrill. That is shallow thinking. Those poor folks get no other thrill out of life. But you can't build a church on that kind of element. My predecessor and I have appealed to a more sturdy and consistent type of people. We are appealing to the professional type of person. We are giving a sane intelligent presentation of the Gospel Truths.

This church, according to one of its own historians, grew out of the holiness movement of the latter half of the nineteenth century, which was the result of dissatisfactions in the Protestant churches and a desire for salvation through personal experience. It was established only in 1908. The church in Wasco is but a decade old, yet it has grown from meetings in a private home through a tent and two small buildings to its present plant, valued at $20,000 [1940 evaluation]. This new and elaborate plant has, itself, furthered the growth along the lines of conservatism, for "the work has taken on an impetus with the building of the modern church." Another cause for this growth "is the intensely sacrificial nature of our people. Our class is the middle to upper-lower class, and those are the most sacrificial. [There are] a half dozen field laborers, but the biggest part is middle class."

Another church of similar status is affiliated to the Assemblies of God. Like the preceding, it was organized in Wasco under a lay minister. Though the original congregation was largely made up of small farmers (this pastor also made a general disclaimer for any large labor membership), actually many agricultural laborers are included in the congregation. But the evidence for social advancement, at least in the relative scale, in the Wasco social hierarchy (for this church preceded the extensive growth of the white outsider group) can be seen in the nature of the schism that has taken place within the Pentecostal movement. The Pentecostal movement itself was away from "modernism" and "higher criticism" and toward a "return to the old truth," namely, "infillment of the spirit" and the "second personal crisis." The movement was also imbued with a spirit of democracy, and even an active participation, intellectual and emotional, by the laity.

But the processes of status advance by the church, with the acquisition of property and a history, and perhaps a vested interest in its own permanence as an established institution, have taken their toll from the original tenets, and in the past ten years there has been a schism on a nation-wide basis. The older church is the one discussed above, and the schismatic faction is represented by a Pentecostal group, a religious body of field hands, poorest in equipment and with the poorest membership of all the churches of the community. Of this split perhaps the statement of a former (lay) minister of the schismatic group is most telling:

> There is no difference between our church and the other Pente-costal church except that we believe that the spirit has the right of way. The Council has tightened down and become formalized. Back East they are free, but here (especially in Southern California) many of the churches have tightened down. Educated ministers and college students who are stiff shirts came in and some of the people fell for it.

This inhibition of the spirit which has resulted from the formaliza-tion was given expression by a classic statement of a person whose affiliation was with the older Pentecostal church back home. She did not like their congregation in Wasco because "they set you down," that is, "they won't let you get up and shout when you get the spirit, and that isn't right."

The church with lay participation, especially the emotional par-ticipation through the religious experience as exemplified by the shout-ing, talking in tongues, rolling, etc., of the revivalistic churches, is the special province of the underprivileged. They are manifested in the Negro churches, in the revivalistic cults of the Indians of North America, and other primitive groups in contact with western civilization, as well as in the white community that is our particular subject of study. But in this last, where the underprivileged persons succeed in advancing some-what in the social scale, there are pressures upon the institution itself toward social advancement. An emotional church appealing to the "sensual" draws in a group, and a building is erected on a "faith basis." It grows under the impetus of lay participation, its coffers increase, and its building, outgrown or outmoded, is replaced with a more impos-ing structure. It becomes unseemly for the now relatively affluent church to have an uneducated minister, who, it is argued, cannot devote his full time to the congregation, so a preacher is hired from one of the seminaries of the parent church. Education, however, vests *de facto* authority in the minister's hands, inhibiting the congregation by pre-cept, if not by direct effort on his part. "The sane intelligent presenta-tion of the gospel" results in the "setting down" of the fervent adherents. The appeal goes out to the "stabler elements" who tend to take over the church. But this stabler element is made up of those who have made peace with their milieu, most frequently in terms of a fair amount of economic security; there still remain those distressed individuals whose emotional needs are not met by the intellectualized gospel of the seminary students. It is their turn for the new schism, the establishment of the new church where the "spirit has the right of way." And so the cycle is repeated.

Just as the poorer persons require the psychological reinforcement of the emotional religion and the negation of worldly goods, so do those better off find such a statement of the ethical situation at variance with their psychological needs. And as, first, the church exists in an environment in which prestige is expressed by evidences of economic worth, and, second, the congregation is exhorted to support the church to its fullest glory, there is a bourgeoisization of the church, to coin a phrase, that parallels the development of individual interest in worldly goods. The dilemma of the ethical system of the Protestant faith, which exhorts its followers on the one hand to reject the things of the world as unsuited to the servants of God, and on the other hand to the great virtues of industry, thrift and frugality, has not gone unheeded. Max Weber in his *Protestant Ethic* points out that "the whole history of monasticism is in a sense the history of a continual struggle with the problem of secularizing influence of wealth," and that "the same is true on a grand scale of the worldly asceticism of Puritanism."

As a matter of fact, John Wesley himself recognized this very problem which he expressed in the following:

> I fear, wherever riches have increased, the essence of religion has decreased in the same proportion. Therefore I do not see how it is possible in the nature of things, for any revival of true religion to continue long. For religion must necessarily produce both industry and frugality, and these cannot but produce riches. But as riches increase, so will pride, anger, and love of the world in all its branches. How then is it possible that Methodism, that is, a religion of the heart, though it flourishes now as a green bay tree, should continue in this state? For the Methodists in every place grow diligent and frugal, consequently they increase in goods. Hence they proportionally increase in pride, in anger, in the desires of the flesh, the desire of the eyes, and the pride of life. So, although the form of the religion remains, the spirit is swiftly vanishing away.

This frequently quoted passage from the Methodist leader implies what is clearly true, that the philosophy of emotional salvation for prestige in a putative society and of the negation of worldly systems of value appeals to the poor, and this for obvious reasons. That it applies to the church as a whole, as well as to the individual, is demonstrated in the data at Wasco.

56. The Religious World of the Navaho

CLYDE KLUCKHOHN and
DOROTHEA LEIGHTON

Navaho religion suffuses all of Navaho life. Kluckhohn and Leighton note that in a sense to speak of Navaho religion does violence to the viewpoint of Navaho, who have no word or phrase in their language that could possibly be translated as religion. Yet the religious view that the Navaho have of the world organizes their life, their interpersonal relations, and their attitudes toward nature. In comparing Navaho religion with that of the Australian, we can see some common elements in religious belief as well as variation.

The essay is reprinted by permission of the publishers from Clyde Kluckhohn and Dorothea Cross Leighton *The Navaho*, Cambridge, Mass.: Harvard University Press, copyright, 1939, 1946, by the President and Fellows of Harvard College.

When one first studies Navaho religious belief and practice, he thinks more than once that the Eskimos' description of their religion— "We do not believe; we fear"—would be appropriate for the Navahos as well. As one grows more familiar with The People's ways of thinking and feeling, however, he realizes that, although their religion points out that the world is indeed a dangerous place, religious activity is also a source of positive joys and confidence in life. Navahos working away from their kinfolk find it necessary to go home partly for a renewal of the sense of security that the Sings and the great chants bring. In this chapter we shall try to see how The People deal with their dangerous world, what things Navahos do in order to ward off danger and to place themselves in harmony with the beings and powers which are the source of danger and also of possible aid and benefit. Some of this knowledge and some techniques are a part of the daily life of all The People. Some of them are esoteric, that is, known only to those who have had special training. . . .

A very high proportion of all the acts which arise out of convictions about beings and powers are negative in character. Thus lightning-struck trees must be avoided. Coyotes, bears, snakes, and some kinds of birds must never be killed. The eating of fish and of most water birds and animals is forbidden, and raw meat is taboo. Navahos will never cut a melon with the point of a knife. They never comb their hair at night. No matter how crowded a hogan may be with sleeping figures, no Navaho may step over the recumbent body of another. Mother-in-law and son-in-law must never look into each other's eyes. Any kind of sexual contact (even walking down the street or dancing together) with members of the opposite sex of one's own or one's father's clan is prohibited. Most technical processes are hedged about with restrictions: the tanner dare not leave the pole on which he scrapes hide standing upright; the potter and the basket-maker work in isolation, observing a bewildering variety of taboos; the weaver shares one of these, the dread of final completion, so that a "spirit outlet" must always be left in the design. Let these few common examples stand as representative of the literally thousands of doings and sayings which are *báhádzid,* or tabooed. . . .

Navahos are brought up to fear many forces in the supernatural world, but they are also taught ways of coping with them. In most cases, there are ways to effect a cure after the threat has struck.

Every adult Navaho has "gall medicine," a preparation of the galls of various animals, which he takes as an emetic if he fears that he has absorbed a witch's "corpse poison." Everyone is particularly careful to carry a little sack of gall medicine on his person when he goes into large gatherings of strangers. In the hogan will be kept plants and other protectives against and remedies for witchcraft. In buckskin pouches in every dwelling will be found herbs, pollen, bits of turquoise and shell, tiny carved images of sheep and horses.

The use of the pollen of corn and other plants is very important in maintaining the proper relationship to the Holy People. In old-fashioned households the day still begins with the sprinkling of pollen from one of the little bags and a brief murmured prayer. After the evening meal the members of the family rub their limbs and say, "May I be lively. May I be healthy." More pollen may be offered and a Blessing Way song sung.

The spectacular ceremonials so capture the imagination that it is easy to forget that, for all their drama, they are quantitatively but a small part of the ritual life of The People. The daily routine of every member of the family is tinged by ceremonial observances as well as avoidances. The weaver uses songs and prayers. The tanner places a turquoise or white shell bead on his pole in order to protect his joints from becoming stiff. A squirrel's tail should be tied to a baby's cradle so that the child will be protected in case of a fall. Every family has a number of "good luck songs" which are believed to bring protection to family members and their property, to aid in the production of ample crops, and to secure increase of flocks and herds. Such songs are regarded as important property which a father or uncle may transmit to son or nephew. . . .

The lore of dreams is complex and much discussed by the folk, for most dreams are thought to have prognostic value. A dream of anything sick or weak or deformed is a cause for anxiety. If bad dreams keep coming, the hogan will be torn down and a new one built some distance away, because the bad dreams are supposed to come from ghosts who are frequenting their old haunts and trying to draw their relatives into ghostland with them.

There are many folk rites connected with travel. There are songs for safe journey and for success on a trip undertaken for love-making or for trading. By the side of old trails all over the country of The People, there can be seen cairns three to five feet high made of stones, twigs, bits of turquoise, and shell. These objects have been deposited by individuals on a journey, uttering a prayer like this:

> Placing rocks, Male One.
> Placing rocks, Female One.
> Everywhere I go, myself
> May I have luck.
> Everywhere my close relatives go
> May they have their luck.

When Navahos go near sacred places they will visit the shrines and leave offerings. Some shrines lie on the summits of mountain peaks; others are found deep in canyons, in rock crevices, or by streams or springs. They are located wherever events of great mythological significance are thought to have occurred.

Many ritual practices are an everyday adjunct of agriculture. Seeds are mixed with ground "mirage stone" and treated in a variety of other ways. To prevent early frosts, stones from the sweathouses are planted in the fields or at the base of fruit trees. If the crop is being damaged by wind, the wind is called by its secret name and asked to leave the corn alone. Cutworms are placed on fragments of pottery, sprinkled with pollen, and given other "magical" treatment. When the harvest is stored, a stalk of corn having two ears is placed in the bottom of the storage pit to ensure a healthy crop for the next year.

If there is a long dry spell, a rainmaker may be asked to perform a ceremony of which this song is a part:

> I usually walk where the rains fall
> Below the east I walk
> I being the Talking God
> I usually walk where the rains fall
> Within the dawn I walk
> I usually walk where the rains fall (repeated after each line)
> Among the white corn I walk
> Among the soft goods I walk
> Among the collected water I walk
> Among the pollen I walk
> I usually walk where the rains fall . . .

One type of ceremonial participation is, in more than one sense, midway between the rites engaged in by all laymen and the more complex "priestly" ceremonials: the ritual occasions which mark passage of a particular milestone in the individual's life career. While some of them require the presence of a trained ceremonialist, they are relatively simple in character, and all Navahos—not just those who are "sick"—pass through them. . . .

The newborn infant is placed in the ceremonially defined position. It is at first fed only pollen, a ceremonial food. Naming the baby is a ritual act which may occur within a few days after birth or not for several months. The infant's first laugh is occasion for a ceremonial gift-giving.

Boys and girls are made recognized members of The People and are introduced to full participation in ceremonial life by a short initiation ceremony which usually occurs on the next to the last night of a Night Way. This ceremony and the whole of the Night Way are popularly known as Yeibichai, from the principal figures in their initiation ceremony, who represent *yei* divinities. . . .

We pass now from those "religious" activities which everyone knows how to do to those which are esoteric, known only by the gifted few. The simplest of these is divination. Although diviners may be instructed in certain details of their rites, they do not acquire the ability itself primarily through long training, as do other Navaho ceremonialists. It is a "gift" which suddenly descends upon them.

Disease is the result of violation of a taboo or of attack by one of the Holy People, a ghost, or a witch. But in a life where the possibilities of transgression and attack are so multifarious, how is one to discover precisely which possible cause needs to be treated? Sometimes the case seems plain to The People. If one has been bold enough to kill a bear or a snake (or has been under the unfortunate necessity of having to do so) and subsequently develops the symptoms of "bear sickness" or "snake sickness," then both cause and cure are clearly indicated. More often, however, the person who is ill is not sure which of the many things he has left undone which he ought to have done, or the things he has done which he ought not to have done, is responsible. The cause is determined by divination.

Divination is also employed to locate property which has been lost or stolen, to find water in unfamiliar territory, to discover the whereabouts of persons, to determine whether one's wife has been guilty of adultery, and to predict the outcome of a hunting party or (in the past) of a war raid. In short, divination is the Navaho way of finding things out. But its greatest function is that of determining the proper form of ceremonial activity to be employed when any Navaho is in difficulties. By divination the cause is discovered and the whole ritual treatment may be prescribed: the precise ceremonial, the time, the right practitioner to select. . . .

The rite called Blessing Way is, as English-speaking Navahos are wont to say, "for good hope." In other words, it places the Navaho in tune with the Holy People—particularly Changing Woman—and so ensures health, prosperity, and general well-being. The expectant mother whose pregnancy is proceeding perfectly normally will have Blessing Way sung over her a short time before birth is anticipated. Navahos were given a Blessing Way by their families before they left for the Army or when they returned on furlough. There is a special Blessing Way for newly chosen headmen. The songs sung in the girl's puberty rite and in marriage are from Blessing Way. Blessing Way is thus precautionary, protecting, prophylactic—not a cure.

The People themselves say that Blessing Way, which is the ceremonial held by the Holy People when they created mankind and taught them skills and ritual, is the cornerstone of their whole ceremonial system. Changing Woman gave some of the songs, and the rite in general is most intimately connected with her. Father Berard Haile says the "legends, songs, and prayers are chiefly concerned with the creation and placement of the earth and sky, sun and moon, sacred mountains and vegetation, the inner forms of these natural phenomena, the control of he- and she-rains, dark clouds and mist, the inner forms of the cardinal points and like phenomena that may be considered as harbingers of blessing and happiness."

Blessing Way is given very frequently indeed. Seldom does a family go for six months without having Blessing Way sung at least once in their hogan. It is held to be peculiarly important that every member of the immediate biological family should be present. Despite the sacredness of the ceremonial and the rich, complicated, and beautiful ideas behind it, the rite has the dignity of great simplicity. There are a few songs one night, a ritual bath in yucca suds with prayers and songs the next day, an all-night singing that night. Cornmeal and pollen are prominently used throughout, and drypaintings of these materials and pulverized flower blossoms are sometimes prepared on buckskin spread upon the ground. Only in Blessing Way is Changing Woman ever represented in visible form in a drypainting. . . .

There are minor priestly rites as well as ones of common knowledge for salt-gathering, for trading with foreigners, for gambling. The hunting rites were complex but now, for obvious reasons, are falling into disuse. Deer, antelope, mountain lion, and bear could be hunted only in ceremonial fashion. These rites, like some of the war rites, are continued to some extent with new functions—to prevent or control epidemics, for example.

For victims of witchcraft the treatment most highly valued is one of the several prayer ceremonials. For four days, long prayers are said without singing. There may be the ceremony of the bath, and drypaintings may be made on buckskin.

Enemy Way, though used as a curing ceremonial, has probably enjoyed its continual popularity because of one associated feature, the "squaw dance." The social aspects of this dance will be discussed later, but here it should be pointed out that the curative functions of Enemy Way are in demand for those who, according to the diviner, have received their sickness from non-Navahos. In the old days the prime purpose was to protect warriors from the ghost sickness threatened by ghosts of enemies they had slain. Today the patients are often those who have married into other Indian tribes or have used white prostitutes in Gallup or some other town. Sometimes men or women who have worked in the laundries at Indian agencies, where they handle clothes of white people and of sick people, are advised to have this rite. . . .

All Navaho rites have secondary social functions. People are drawn to them not only because they wish to acquire "religious" benefits or because they are under pressure to assist; they come also because the rite offers a chance to see and be seen, to talk and to listen. Increasingly, it must be admitted, ceremonial gatherings are occasions for drinking and violent behavior. This tendency is deplored by most Singers.

In no ceremonial do these secondary motivations loom so large as in Enemy Way. The Girls' Dance ("squaw dance"), at which marriageable girls ask young men to dance, was once only an incidental element in this ceremonial, but today it is the chief attraction for the great crowds which invariably attend. Most of the girls who dance are brought there to announce the fact that they have recently become, or still are, of the right age to marry. Young men come to sing and to hear the singing, and to look over the girls. The crowds gather to watch this public dance each night of the ceremonial and to enjoy the accompanying "sway-singing" of the men, which frequently embodies Rabelaisian quips at the expense of participants and bystanders.

The dance also has its serious side. The parallel to the debutante ball in white society is inescapable. Everyone—particularly members of families who are considering a marriage alliance—dresses as well as possible and appears with his best horse, wagon, or automobile. Putting up a front through borrowed jewelry and other finery is not unknown. Navaho mothers, a trifle franker than is usual among whites, literally push their daughters after a "catch," saying: "Go ask that boy. His mother has two thousand sheep." At last even the shyest girl is induced to choose a man, and the dance goes on until morning.

Skill in all the ceremonial arts—singing, dancing, making dry-paintings, telling stories—is highly valued by The People. Experts are richly rewarded in prestige as well as money, and not without reason. Prodigious memory is demanded of the ceremonialist. The Singer who knows one nine-night chant must learn at least as much as a man who sets out to memorize the whole of a Wagnerian opera: orchestral score, every vocal part, all the details of the settings, stage business, and each requirement of costume. Some Singers know three or more long chants, as well as various minor rites.

But ceremonial life gives opportunity for personal expression to more than the small group of Singers. Lay folk can show their skill in dancing and singing and in making drypaintings. They can win plaudits for their adroitness in helping with the tricks and other "vaudeville acts" which make up a great part of the public performance on the final night of Mountain Top Way. They can show off their good memory and oratorical skill in telling myths.

The giving of a rite—particularly an elaborate one—also confers prestige. It shows not only that the family are doing their duty by one of their number but that they have the wherewithal to pay for it. Hence rites are sometimes given primarily as gestures of affluence rather than because some one of the family is really ill or disturbed. They seem to be the Navaho form of conspicuous spending. To give an unusual ceremonial with elaborate equipment—to summon a famous Singer and invite guests from miles away—is perhaps the best way for a family to show the world that they have "arrived." . . .

It is difficult for many white people to understand why, when the resources of white medicine are available to Navahos in government hospitals and dispensaries, The People continue to patronize "ignorant medicine men." The answer is that native practice brings good results—in many cases as good as those of a white physician or hospital. . . . There can be no doubt that the main effects are "psychological." There is nothing too mysterious about this. . . . Illness often gives the sufferer the suspicion that he is disliked or unprotected. During the chant the patient feels himself personally (rather than impersonally) being succored and loved, for his relatives are spending their substance to get him cured, and they are rallying round to aid in the ceremonial.

Then there is the prestige and authority of the Singer assuring the patient that he will recover. In his capacity as Singer, gifted with the learning of the Holy People, he is more than a mortal and at times becomes identified with the supernaturals, speaking in their voices and telling the hearers that all is well. The prestige, mysticism, and power of the ceremonial itself are active, coming directly from the supernatural powers that build up the growing earth in spring, drench it with rain, or tear it apart with lightning. In the height of the chant the patient himself becomes one of the Holy People, puts his feet in their moccasins, and breathes in the strength of the sun. He comes into complete harmony with the universe and must of course be free of all ills and evil. Finally, it is very likely that he has seen the ceremonial work with others and may have had it before himself; in this case there will be an upswing of reawakened memories, like old melodies bearing him on emotional waves to feelings of security. . . .

The old beliefs have uses for The People as a tribe, as well as for The People as individuals. Some of these are the functions of "religion" in any group without a written language, but others are specifically Navaho. In both secular and sacred spheres, myths serve as statements of the right way to behave and the reasons therefor, somewhat as the Bible does (or did) in Christian societies. Women must sit with their feet in a certain position because the female Holy People sat that way. When questioned as to why almost anything is done in a particular way, Navahos will usually reply, "Because the Holy People did it that way in the first place." Even when children are asked why they play Navaho games according to certain rules, they almost invariably make this response.

Thus to some degree the myths are The People's code of manners and morals and their law books as well. But myths, legends, and folk tales are also their literature, which serves ends from intellectual and moral edification to simple entertainment. . . .

Rites also play a significant role in interpersonal relationships among The People. One important contribution of the curing chants to good group relationships comes from the informal chat that goes on between the Singer and the patient and other members of the family. Since the Singer is usually an intellectual, who often knows the habits and tendencies of his clientele in the same manner as the family doctor in white society, it is very likely that, like the family doctor, he often gives sound practical advice based on his knowledge of his people. Probably many personal and interpersonal problems come nearer to adjustment at the time of a ceremonial. Indeed, certain passages in the myths indicate that The People have a more or less conscious realization that the ceremonies act as a cure, not only for physical and mental illness, but also for antisocial tendencies. For example, the myth of the Mountain Top Way chant says: "The ceremony cured Dsiliyi Neyani of all his strange feelings and notions. The lodge of his people no longer smelled unpleasant to him." Today ordinary lay Navahos speak of being "changed" so that they are better men and women in their relations with their families and neighbors. For instance, an English-speaking Navaho who had just completed a jail sentence for beating his wife and molesting his stepdaughter remarked: "I am sure going to behave from now on. I am going to be changed—just like someone who has been sung over.". . .

But myths and rituals contribute to the equilibrium of the society in other ways than by "curing" individual members of the society. In the first place, the centering of rites upon disease and upon the individual serves social purposes beyond that of helping individuals adjust more amicably to their relatives and neighbors. Furthermore, to describe the rites of The People as purely "individualistic" and purely for curing is an oversimplification. . . .

In sum, myths and rituals jointly provide systematic protection against supernatural dangers, the threats of ill health and of the physical environment, antisocial tensions, and the pressures of a more powerful society. In the absence of a codified law and of an authoritarian chief, it is only through the myth-ritual system that the Navahos can present a unified front to all these disintegrating pressures. The all-pervasive configurations of word-symbols (myths) and of act-symbols (rituals) preserve the cohesion of the society and sustain the individual, protecting both from intolerable conflict.

. . . Let us now turn to those attempts to manipulate the supernatural by word and deed which are done furtively and which come under strong social disapproval. The cost of witchcraft belief is obvious: there is the addition of just that many more things to be feared; there are occasional acts of violence; guiltless individuals are made to suffer mildly or tragically. . . . Even though The People themselves abhor the deeds which witches are believed to do, still their having these fears and talking about them and acting upon them plays a part in easing the strains in the social structure, in keeping Navaho society a going concern. . . . Belief in witches is universal and . . . there are deep fears, much gossip, and countless and widely current anecdotes.

These tales are the medium through which witchcraft touches the lives of all The People. Together with the myths about witchcraft, they have the effect of plugging up certain holes in the ideological system. If chants don't work, the Navaho doesn't have to say, "Well, that ceremonial is no good." He is encouraged to say, in effect, "I am certain that that chant is wonderfully powerful, but naturally you can't expect it to prevail against the evil strength of witches." In this and in other ways, witchcraft conceptions supply a partial answer to some of the deeper uncertainties.

. . . The crucial question for understanding the psychological outlets which The People get through witchcraft tales is always: does the
person see himself as the witch or as the victim? If he imagines himself the witch, presumably he gets hostile impulses out of his system
vicariously; if he takes the victim's role, some of his uneasiness is allayed.
The main contribution which this complex of acts and ideas makes to
the steadiness of Navaho society are in handling the anxiety problem
and in serving as a safety valve for and control over aggressive tendencies. . . .

It is no accident that a high proportion of those who suddenly
show symptoms of being bewitched (such as fainting or going into a
semi-trance) at "squaw dances" or other large gatherings are women
or men who are somewhat neglected or who occupy low social status.
In most of these cases it is probably not a matter of consciously capi-
talizing on the credence of their fellows in order to get the center of
the stage for themselves. It is unlikely that Navahos often deliberately
complain of the symptoms of witchcraft as a device for getting attention. The process normally takes place at an altogether unconscious
level: those whose uneasiness goes beyond a certain point have to do
something; and if they are believed to be at the mercy of witches they
are likely to get help.

Especially in a society where the social units are small, the disturbance of any person's daily routines constitutes a danger to the
smooth functioning of the whole social organization, and Navaho society
could ill afford not to support its members who are "witched." The
rare references to abandonment of such individuals always specify that
the case was hopeless. Being "witched" normally calls forth the very
maximum of social support, and the writers know of more than one
family impoverished from paying for one "cure" after another.

The expensive prayer ceremonials, demanding the presence of the
patient's family and of practitioners who represent the wider social
organization, symbolically affirm that the victim is succored by the
whole social structure. The importance of the near presence and support of one's fellows as the surest protection against witches is attested
by the facts that were-animals are almost always seen by lone individuals and that going about alone at night is considered peculiarly dangerous. Moreover, if exaggerated fear of witches arises in a person
partly because he feels aggressive and thus suspects that others feel the
same way toward him, witchcraft "illness" is to this extent dependent
upon a loss of rapport with the society—the penalty for giving way to

feelings the society does not permit. The most efficacious reassurance for victims of witchcraft is provided, therefore, by the unusual, complicated, and costly prayer ceremonials, with many relatives and friends in attendance, lending their help and expressing their sympathy.

The important thing for the adjustment of the individual is that witchcraft is a focus of anxiety which The People recognize as valid. . . .

Nothing is more intolerable to human beings than to be persistently disturbed without being able to say why or without being able to phrase the matter in such a way that some relief or control is available. Witchcraft belief allows one to talk about his anxiety in terms that are acceptable and which imply the possibility of doing something about it. Much of the tension among The People may actually be traced to the uncertainties of making a living in a difficult environment with the technological means at their disposal. Since the caprices of the environment are not controllable by the society, the worry related to this is attributed to witches who, as living individuals, can be dealt with. A correlation between the amount of fear and talk about witches and the general state of tension prevailing among the Navahos is evidenced by the fact that during the recent difficult years of controversy over the stock reduction program there has been appreciably more witchcraft excitement than for some time past, and a number of murders of supposed witches have occurred. There have also been several well-documented attempts by Navahos to "witch" government employees concerned with stock reduction.

Witchcraft patterns supply many releases, direct and indirect, actual and imaginative, for hostile impulses. The most obvious of these is actually becoming a witch. It is quite possible that the kind of temperament which in the old days found an outlet through organizing and leading war parties finds witchcraft the most congenial substitute available today. Direct aggression is also expressed, of course, through attacks upon "witches." These range from hushed gossip to public accusation or even physical assault.

The classes of persons accused and gossiped about most frequently, and the relationships between accused and accusers, constitute a revealing commentary on the stresses in Navaho social organization. Rich people, ceremonial practitioners, "political" leaders, the old—these make up the vast bulk of those whom gossip singles out. Sons-in-law spread stories about their fathers-in-law; nephews permit themselves a sly innuendo in referring to their maternal uncles. A brother will sometimes express doubt about a sister, real or clan; but brothers very seldom gossip about brothers or sisters about sisters, and talk against parents is virtually unknown. Very often the expression of aggression is disguised and indirect. For example, a young man will not name his own actual maternal uncle or even imply that he might be a witch. He will, however, evidence much relish in telling a tale laid in a distant locality where the evil hero just happens to show all sorts of resemblances in age, appearance, and personality traits to his own tyrannous uncle.

More significant than the release of direct aggression is that of displaced aggression. That is, Navahos "take out" on witches by word and by deed the hostility which in fact they feel against their relatives, against whites, against the hazards of life itself. Talk about witches commonly has a violent quality completely out of proportion to the involvement of the speaker in that particular case. The killing of witches is characteristically messy and brutal, even on the part of those who are not avenging some near relative or close friend. Witches, in other words, are scapegoats.

In this very general sense of scapegoats "witches" have probably played some part in all social structures since the Old Stone Age.

57. Magical Practices among the Nacirema

HORACE MINER

The distinction between magic and nonmagic is not so clear as we sometimes think. Nor is the distinction between belief and disbelief. Who among us has not from time to time had the fleeting thought that he caused the rain by washing the car or stopped it by carrying an umbrella. This essay not only reminds us of our own tendencies to think in magical terms but also makes it clear that when we use the anthropological concept of religion in our own society, we must include other elements in our behavior than those associated with our formal religious beliefs.

Horace Miner, whose ironic essay originally appeared in the *American Anthropologist* (Volume 55, No. 3, 1956), received his Ph.D. from the University of Chicago in 1935 and is Professor of Anthropology and Sociology at the University of Michigan. He has published *St. Denis, a French-Canadian Parish, Culture and Agriculture,* and *The Primitive City of Timbuktu.* The last of these was based upon extensive field work just before the outbreak of the second world war. The essay is printed with the kind permission of the editor of the *American Anthropologist* and the author.

The anthropologist has become so familiar with the diversity of ways in which different peoples behave in similar situations that he is not apt to be surprised by even the most exotic customs. In fact, if all of the logically possible combinations of behavior have not been found somewhere in the world, he is apt to suspect that they must be present in some yet undescribed tribe. . . . In this light, the magical beliefs and practices of the Nacirema present such unusual aspects that it seems desirable to describe them as an example of the extremes to which human behavior can go.

Professor Linton first brought the ritual of the Nacirema to the attention of anthropologists twenty years ago, but the culture of this people is still very poorly understood. They are a North American group living in the territory between the Canadian Cree, the Yaqui and Tara-humare of Mexico, and the Carib and Arawak of the Antilles. Little is known of their origin, although tradition states that they came from the east. According to Nacirema mythology, their nation was originated by a culture hero, Notgnihsaw, who is otherwise known for two great feats of strength—the throwing of a piece of wampum across the river Pa-To-Mac and the chopping down of a cherry tree in which the Spirit of Truth resided.

Nacirema culture is characterized by a highly developed market economy which has evolved in a rich natural habitat. While much of the people's time is devoted to economic pursuits, a large part of the fruits of these labors and a considerable portion of the day are spent in ritual activity. The focus of this activity is the human body, the appearance and health of which loom as a dominant concern in the ethos of the people. While such a concern is certainly not unusual, its ceremonial aspects and associated philosophy are unique.

The fundamental belief underlying the whole system appears to be that the human body is ugly and that its natural tendency is to debility and disease. Incarcerated in such a body, man's only hope is to avert these characteristics through the use of the powerful influences of ritual and ceremony. Every household has one or more shrines devoted to this purpose. The more powerful individuals in the society have sev-eral shrines in their houses and, in fact, the opulence of a house is often referred to in terms of the number of such ritual centers it possesses. Most houses are of wattle and daub construction, but the shrine rooms of the more wealthy are walled with stone. Poorer families imitate the rich by applying pottery plaques to their shrine walls.

While each family has at least one such shrine, the rituals associated with it are not family ceremonies but are private and secret. The rites are normally only discussed with children, and then only during the period when they are being initiated into these mysteries. I was able, however, to establish sufficient rapport with the natives to examine these shrines and to have the rituals described to me.

The focal point of the shrine is a box or chest which is built into the wall. In this chest are kept the many charms and magical potions without which no native believes he could live. These preparations are secured from a variety of specialized practitioners. The most powerful of these are the medicine men, whose assistance must be rewarded with substantial gifts. However, the medicine men do not provide the curative potions for their clients, but decide what the ingredients should be and then write them down in an ancient and secret language. This writing is understood only by the medicine men and by the herbalists who, for another gift, provide the required charm.

The charm is not disposed of after it has served its purpose, but is placed in the charm-box of the household shrine. As these magical materials are specific for certain ills, and the real or imagined maladies of the people are many, the charm-box is usually full to overflowing. The magical packets are so numerous that people forget what their purposes were and fear to use them again. While the natives are very vague on this point, we can only assume that the idea in retaining all the old magical materials is that their presence in the charm-box, before which the body rituals are conducted, will in some way protect the worshipper.

Beneath the charm-box is a small font. Each day every member of the family, in succession, enters the shrine room, bows his head before the charm-box, mingles different sorts of holy water in the font, and proceeds with a brief rite of ablution. The holy waters are secured from the Water Temple of the community, where the priests conduct elaborate ceremonies to make the liquid ritually pure.

In the hierarchy of magical practitioners, and below the medicine men in prestige, are specialists whose designation is best translated "holy-mouth-men." The Nacirema have an almost pathological horror of and fascination with the mouth, the condition of which is believed to have a supernatural influence on all social relationships. Were it not for the rituals of the mouth, they believe that their teeth would fall out, their gums bleed, their jaws shrink, their friends desert them, and their lovers reject them. They also believe that a strong relationship exists between oral and moral characteristics. For example, there is a ritual ablution of the mouth for children which is supposed to improve their moral fiber.

The daily body ritual performed by everyone includes a mouth-rite. Despite the fact that these people are so punctilious about care of the mouth, this rite involves a practice which strikes the uninitiated stranger as revolting. It was reported to me that the ritual consists of inserting a small bundle of hog hairs into the mouth, along with certain magical powders, and then moving the bundle in a highly formalized series of gestures.

In addition to the private mouth-rite, the people seek out a holy-mouth-man once or twice a year. These practitioners have an impressive set of paraphernalia, consisting of a variety of augers, awls, probes, and prods. The use of these objects in the exorcism of the evils of the mouth involves almost unbelievable ritual torture of the client. The holy-mouth-man opens the client's mouth and, using the above mentioned tools, enlarges any holes which decay may have created in the teeth. Magical materials are put into these holes. If there are no naturally occurring holes in the teeth, large sections of one or more teeth are gouged out so that the supernatural substance can be applied. In the client's view, the purpose of these ministrations is to arrest decay and to draw friends. The extremely sacred and traditional character of the rite is evident in the fact that the natives return to the holy-mouth-men year after year, despite the fact that their teeth continue to decay.

It is to be hoped that, when a thorough study of the Nacirema is made, there will be careful inquiry into the personality structure of these people. One has but to watch the gleam in the eye of a holy-mouth-man, as he jabs an awl into an exposed nerve, to suspect a certain amount of sadism is involved. If this can be established, a very interesting pattern emerges, for most of the population shows definite masochistic tendencies. It was to these that Professor Linton referred in discussing a distinctive part of the daily body ritual which is performed only by men. This part of the rite involves scraping and lacerating the surface of the face with a sharp instrument. Special women's rites are performed only four times during each lunar month, but what they lack in frequency is made up in barbarity. As part of this ceremony, women bake their heads in small ovens for about an hour. The theoretically interesting point is that what seems to be a preponderantly masochistic people have developed sadistic specialists.

The medicine men have an imposing temple, or *latipso*, in every community of any size. The more elaborate ceremonies required to treat very sick patients can only be performed at this temple. These ceremonies involve not only the thaumaturge but a permanent group of vestal maidens who move sedately about the temple chambers in distinctive costume and headdress.

The *latipso* ceremonies are so harsh that it is phenomenal that a fair proportion of the really sick natives who enter the temple ever recover. Small children whose indoctrination is still incomplete have been known to resist attempts to take them to the temple because "that is where you go to die." Despite this fact, sick adults are not only willing but eager to undergo the protracted ritual purification, if they can afford to do so. No matter how ill the supplicant or how grave the emergency, the guardians of many temples will not admit a client if he cannot give a rich gift to the custodian. Even after one has gained admission and survived the ceremonies, the guardians will not permit the neophyte to leave until he makes still another gift.

The supplicant entering the temple is first stripped of all his or her clothes. In every-day life the Nacirema avoids exposure of his body and its natural functions. Bathing and excretory acts are performed only in the secrecy of the household shrine, where they are ritualized as part of the body-rites. Psychological shock results from the fact that body secrecy is suddenly lost upon entry into the *latipso*. A man, whose own wife has never seen him in an excretory act, suddenly finds himself naked and assisted by a vestal maiden while he performs his natural functions into a sacred vessel. This sort of ceremonial treatment is necessitated by the fact that the excreta are used by a diviner to ascertain the course and nature of the client's sickness. Female clients, on the other hand, find their naked bodies are subjected to the scrutiny, manipulation and prodding of the medicine men.

Few supplicants in the temple are well enough to do anything but lie on their hard beds. The daily ceremonies, like the rites of the holy-mouth-men, involve discomfort and torture. With ritual precision, the vestals awaken their miserable charges each dawn and roll them about on their beds of pain while performing ablutions, in the formal movements of which the maidens are highly trained. At other times they insert magic wands in the supplicant's mouth or force him to eat substances which are supposed to be healing. From time to time the medicine men come to their clients and jab magically treated needles into their flesh. The fact that these temple ceremonies may not cure, and may even kill the neophyte, in no way decreases the people's faith in the medicine men.

There remains one other kind of practitioner, known as a "listener." This witch-doctor has the power to exorcise the devils that lodge in the heads of people who have been bewitched. The Nacirema believe that parents bewitch their own children. Mothers are particularly suspected of putting a curse on children while teaching them the secret body rituals. The counter-magic of the witch-doctor is unusual in its lack of ritual. The patient simply tells the "listener" all his troubles and fears, beginning with the earliest difficulties he can remember. The memory displayed by the Nacirema in these exorcism sessions is truly remarkable. It is not uncommon for the patient to bemoan the rejection he felt upon being weaned as a babe, and a few individuals even see their troubles going back to the traumatic effects of their own birth.

In conclusion, mention must be made of certain practices which have their base in native esthetics but which depend upon the pervasive aversion to the natural body and its functions. There are ritual fasts to make fat people thin and ceremonial feasts to make thin people fat. Still other rites are used to make women's breasts larger if they are small, and smaller if they are large. General dissatisfaction with breast shape is symbolized in the fact that the ideal form is virtually outside the range of human variation. A few women afflicted with almost inhuman hypermammary development are so idolized that they make a handsome living by simply going from village to village and permitting the natives to stare at them for a fee.

Reference has already been made to the fact that excretory functions are ritualized, routinized, and relegated to secrecy. Natural reproductive functions are similarly distorted. Intercourse is taboo as a topic and scheduled as an act. Efforts are made to avoid pregnancy by the use of magical materials or by limiting intercourse to certain phases of the moon. Conception is actually very infrequent. When pregnant, women dress so as to hide their condition. Parturition takes place in secret, without friends or relatives to assist, and the majority of women do not nurse their infants.

Our review of the ritual life of the Nacirema has certainly shown them to be a magic-ridden people. It is hard to understand how they have managed to exist so long under the burdens which they have imposed upon themselves. But even such exotic customs as these take on real meaning when they are viewed with the insight provided by Malinowski when he wrote:

> Looking from far and above, from our high places of safety in the developed civilization, it is easy to see all the crudity and irrelevance of magic. But without its power and guidance early man could not have mastered his practical difficulties as he has done, nor could man have advanced to the higher stages of civilization.

XI.

ETHICS

The Guides to Human Conduct

Human existence requires that each person recognize the rights of others; that at times he forego his own interests in recognition of other people's interests. Without such behavior, the parent would not nurture the child. Without such behavior, group life as it is found among humans everywhere would be impossible. We need not be surprised, therefore, that ethical concepts are universal to human societies.

Some social philosophers, notably Prince Kropotkin, have argued that man is innately cooperative. Others, especially under the influence of Darwinism, have asserted that man is innately competitive. Neither extreme position is tenable. Man is dependent by his very nature on others, not only for his own physical well-being but for those very responses which give him a satisfactory feeling about himself. He grows up in an environment of people and can hardly escape having a strong sense of attachment to others. Yet each person must also meet the demands for survival and the satisfaction of his own appetites; no one can entirely escape these concerns with his own requirements. Conflict between these two interests may therefore be expected as a recurrent element in every social system. The cultural mode may place emphasis upon individual self-help or upon subordination of the individual to group harmony, but it cannot entirely avoid the dilemma. Indeed, we may say that the fundamental task of an ethical system is to provide a standard means for the resolution of the conflict between individual interests and public welfare; between the self and other beings.

In this sense, then, every people has an ethical system, for every people recognizes that the individual must subordinate his own interest and conduct his own business in such a way as to protect the interests of some group. But how that interest is defined, what constraints are demanded, and, above all, the nature of the group toward which the individual has responsibility, all vary from one culture to another. It is only on such a broad level of generalization that we can find commonality among the ethical patterns of behavior in society.

Consider murder, for example. All societies recognize that murder is wrong. But in most societies there is a distinction between murder and killing an enemy. The former is killing somebody who belongs to one's own society, who comes under a common code of ethics. Very few societies view all killing as wrong—only a century ago we condoned the killing of native populations, and we still accept the necessity of killing as a part of warfare. The point here is that an ethical system applies to a limited sphere; to the group within which one recognizes a sense of responsibility. Only rarely do ethical systems transcend this limitation.

This discussion of murder leads to a further consideration, for we (and other people, as well) recognize circumstances in which killing a person of our society is justifiable. One of these is, of course, punishment for a capital crime. Most societies recognize circumstances of this kind, and not a few, as we have already seen, place the responsibility for such punishment in the hands of the person who has been wronged. An ethical system must provide for a definition of just when the act of killing is considered wrong and when it is considered proper. But when we get to such details, we find that cultures vary widely. In some cultures, a man is justified in slaying the man who has cuckolded him; in others he may slay his wife; in some both, and in others neither.

Other elements of ethical systems—property rights, sexual relationships, mutual aid, and so on—are similarly varied. That is, though all peoples recognize the rights of others, what these rights are and how they may be evoked will differ from one culture to another.

Ethics must be viewed as separate from religion, though closely related to it. Our own ethical attitudes are so rooted in our religion that we consider ethics as a part of religious philosophy. Elsewhere, religious belief and practice are not so closely associated with morality. That is to say, the religious system does not itself involve a code of moral conduct. Yet it seems probable that moral attitudes are everywhere supported by the conceptions of supernatural phenomena. We have already seen that the strong urge toward family solidarity among the Chinese was supported by family shrines and the spiritual importance of family ancestors. We have seen that initiatory rituals among primitive people normally contain an explicit communication of the moral rules the initiate should follow. Religious prescriptions and proscriptions of many primitive peoples can be shown to carry general moral imperatives. What is often—but by no means always—lacking, is the codification of these moral rules into an ethical system. A people without writing will find it difficult, though not impossible, to systematize their ethics.

Beyond this, we can say that the notion that the gods have handed down a system of moral rules, is foreign to most primitive peoples. They more frequently see ethical behavior merely as customary procedure, and do not philosophize about it. Yet an anthropologist can examine the moralistic expressions of a people and find them to be relatively consistent and self-contained, as Paul Radin did for the Winnebago

Indians. But no Winnebago ever drew these elements together in this way, as theologians and religious leaders have at various times and places in the history of Western civilization.

Our ethical system has long been influenced by the idea of good and evil as moral opposites. Such dualistic philosophy is infrequently found among primitive peoples, yet, the Ba-Ila of Northern Rhodesia have a whole array of dualistic terms distinguishing the light (worthless) from the heavy (valuable), the good from the bad. Dualism may be found in the philosophy of primitive peoples.

Ethics and values are close and interlocking concepts. We make a distinction between values, which are desirable and satisfying, as opposed to ethics which deals with what is proper and right. The distinction can be seen in some of our own behavior. It is ethically proper in our culture for a person to work hard and achieve success, but it is not ethically proper for a person to achieve success—which clearly is one of our values—by subterfuge, brutality, or wanton unconcern about what happens to others. Some of the values enumerated by Robin Williams in Section IX are not matters of ethics at all (for example, efficiency and progress), while he considers the fact that we see things in ethical terms as itself being a value. It does not seem worthwhile to try to differentiate the meaning of these two concepts any further; though they overlap and interlock, they are not the same; and it is necessary to see how each operates in human society.

In earlier sections of this book we showed that as culture progressed to higher levels of economic efficiency and more complex modes of social organization, the topic under discussion also underwent characteristic changes. That is to say, broadly and generally, there has been an evolutionary growth in most areas of social life. This does not seem to be the case with respect to ethics, which is the more surprising because we tend to think that it is precisely in the field of morality that we are superior to the savages. However much it may please us to think in these terms, the data of anthropology and sociology do not bear it out. For instance, the Yurok Indians of northwestern California, which are described in this section, had a very strict moral code. It was surprisingly much like that developed in the early Protestant movement, with strict rules of self-denial (specifically with respect to gluttony and sexuality), a strong imperative to work hard, and a vigorous condemnation of what they and we would consider immoral behavior. In some ways, as a matter of fact, the Yurok went further than Calvinist philosophy. Thus, for instance, sexual intercourse was viewed as evil and even married couples were supposed to restrain their sexual drives, for having many children was viewed as vulgar, if not actually wicked.

The Yurok ethic was strictly grounded in religious conviction, for the wealth that the Yurok achieved was goods which had their sole use as equipment for religious rites. As a matter of fact, all the ethical precepts of the Yurok had such religious involvement, though we cannot here go into the details. The point is worth noting, however, for it shows that quite different religious systems (we could certainly call the Yurok animistic) can lead to the same set of ethical convictions.

The Yurok emphasis upon individualism is quite unusual in primitive societies. More frequently, the individual is subordinated to a group, with a definite emphasis upon group solidarity. To see how strong this ethical demand may be, re-examine the essays by Benedict on the Kwakiutl and Oberg on the Tlingit. These two tribes are neighbors along the northwest coast of America, and have similar cultures. Here the sense of subordination of the individual to the clan or household is a dominant motif. Though the Hopi also expect the individual to subordinate himself to the group, the behavior that is expected is quite different, as the essay by Richard B. Brandt in this section shows. The Kwakiutl and Tlingit share the Yurok concern with status and tend to be suspicious and hostile toward others; no proper member of these societies is quiet, unobtrusive, or modest. The Kwakiutl and Tlingit differ from the Yurok in that they emphasize a group solidarity with clan or lineage, and this they share with the Hopi. But among the Hopi this emphasis upon group unity suffuses to a general concern with peaceableness and cooperativeness. The ethical standards of the Hopi way of life demands "a good heart," and full restraint of aggressive impulses, while on the Northern Coast it demands only that aggressive action be channeled into group interests.

Perhaps one aspect of ethics has undergone evolutionary development. This is that codified and self-conscious ethical systems appeared somewhat recently in human history, as a product of advanced culture. Advanced cultures tend to have more centralized organization, they often have a priestly class with time for the consideration of cosmological and philosophical problems, and above all, with the advent of civilization came that great accomplishment writing, which makes the codification of ideas so much easier. Such development does not necessarily make for a stricter sense of morality, but it does enable man to give more conscious thought to its basis and to compare his own ethical system with his neighbors'. Though more advanced civilizations regularly have ethical codes, these are by no means uniform. Even within the broad framework of Christianity there has been a wide variation in ethics.

No change within the Christian system has been more significant than the development of Protestantism. While much of the belief, philosophy and doctrine of Catholicism and Protestantism are similar, the kind of behavior which leads to, or demonstrates, a state of grace varies widely. The two kinds of Christianity place emphasis upon very different elements of character. Weber tries to show that the Protestant ethic was a necessary condition for developing a capitalist society; that is, an economic system built upon industry, trade, and credit. Whether or not it is a necessary condition, an ethic which exhorts the individual to work and to improve himself fits a social system based upon free opportunity for self improvement, as opposed to a fixed class society. It appears to be no accident that the more industrialized countries of the world, those where capitalist economic systems prevail, are the predominantly Protestant ones. For, in contrast, the spirit of Catholic teaching places far greater emphasis upon satisfaction with one's lot and with a more passive relationship toward the world.

Our country has been influenced by many cultural sources, and its citizenry adhere to many religions. It would not be proper to assert that our country is molded entirely in the spirit of the Protestantism that Weber describes. But the mainstream of intellectual attitudes at the time of the foundation of our government, and even more vigorously in the pioneer phase of our western expansion, owed more to this source than to any other. If any one tradition remains dominant in America today, it is the tradition that stems out of this religious and intellectual movement. What is more to the point, the ethical attitudes toward work, self-denial, the concept of calling, and proof of oneself remain the dominant motifs irrespective of religious affiliation—for ethics are substantiated in religion, but are not tied to it.

A broad gap often exists between the oughts of an ethical code and the daily life of the people. In all societies, there are persons who act contrary to law, and who do not obey the specific dictates for its ethical demands. Ethics may be considered the ideal of behavior, rather than the actuality. No population ever fulfills the ideals its culture holds as proper. It was precisely this difference between moral code and actual behavior which created the public shock when the Kinsey report on sexual behavior first appeared. Instances of a similar kind are not easy to find in the literature of primitive peoples. This does not mean that such divergence from the moral code does not exist, but rather that we lack this kind of information about primitive cultures. The fact that primitive people do not usually have a clearly verbalized code of ethics means that we must discover it, as Radin has done, from statements made and behavior observed. But we can reasonably assume that ethical standards are not always reflected accurately in behavior. For instance, the Zuni Indians (like their neighbors, the Hopi) believe that a person should be self-effacing, never seek personal aggrandizement or use his position in society as a means of exerting pressure on others. Yet ethnologists have reported instances where the priests, who are also the secular authorities, connived to improve their position and exerted strong pressures on others to force them to conformity.

Ethical attitudes are acquired through that subtle process of cultural indoctrination which we have already discussed at length. The individual uses them more as unspoken assumptions than as directly expressed fact. To the individual, his ethics are not properly a subject for debate; insofar as they are brought to his awareness, they are thought to be more or less self-evident. A comparison between different ethical systems inevitably seems like a comparison between right and wrong to those who adhere to one of the systems compared.

Our task here, however, is to understand how ethical attitudes vary and what elements remain constant. We do not have sufficient studies to give a sure answer, but this much seems evident: all ethical systems recognize that the individual has a community of interest with a group of fellow beings, and that within that group he should act in such ways as to preserve its integrity.

58. Universal Ethical Principles

RALPH LINTON

Comparative ethics rarely includes the data from primitive people. The essay included here is a unique effort to set forth what elements in the ethical systems of peoples of all kinds and conditions are held in common. It offers us a valuable guide to an obscure area of human behavior.

Ralph Linton's discussion first appeared in *Moral Principles of Action; Man's Ethical Imperative*, edited by Ruth Nanda Anshen, New York: Harper & Brothers, 1952. This volume is part of the Science of Culture series. The essay is printed by kind permission of the publisher.

The problem of whether there are universally applicable ethical principles has been debated by philosophers for centuries, but recent world developments make it of much more than academic interest. . . .

All human societies are composed of members of the same mammalian species. . . . Every culture has to provide for the same basic physiological and psychological needs of individuals. Moreover, the organization, operation, and perpetuation of societies involve the same basic problems whether the society is in Australia, Africa, or Arkansas. Children have to be produced, fed, sheltered, and trained. The diversified activities by which the various members of a society contribute to the well-being of the whole have to be assigned to individuals who must, in turn, be reimbursed for their services. Leadership in communal activities has to be provided and disputes have to be settled or at least circumscribed before they can disrupt the community.

Each of these things can be done in any one of several different ways, but all of them have to be done if the society is to survive. Moreover, the actual range of variation seems to be strictly delimited. As the social scientist's acquaintance with a large number of cultures improves, he cannot fail to be more impressed with their similarities than with their differences. This is especially the case where his acquaintance extends to continuous first-hand contact with the societies involved. Any individual who is willing to observe and imitate can orient himself in any human society. A Cortez or a Pizarro, confronted by a complex civilization most of whose overt behavior patterns were completely alien to his experience could still grasp the social and political picture and apply the same principles of statecraft which he would have used in Europe. . . .

One of the first requirements of a scientific approach to the problem of universal ethical principles is a clear delimitation of the frame of reference within which the comparative studies are to be made. *It must be stressed that the significant units are societies, not individuals.* . . .

Not only is the society the unit for ethical studies but *ethical systems function only in terms of in-groups.* Since the structure of societies is reminiscent of those Chinese sweetmeat boxes filled with smaller fitted boxes which contain still smaller ones, it is often difficult to determine the limits of the group to which ethical systems apply. Thus every society contains a number of family groups which are organized into communities. The communities are, in turn, organized into larger units, tribes at the "primitive" level, which may form part of still larger groupings such as confederacies or states established by conquest. Lastly, the concept of social membership may be extended to include the whole of mankind, as in some Messianic religions, or even, on the basis of a pantheistic philosophy, to include the whole of nature. Needless to say, at this point the emotional affects on which ethics depends for behavioral expression become so diluted that ethical concepts are rarely applied in practice. . . .

It seems that in spite of the common social phenomenon of groups within groups the same ethical system applies to all forms of social interaction within the society. In general, the smaller and more closely knit the unit within the society, the greater the emphasis on ethical considerations in the dealings of the unit's members with each other. Thus all societies reprehend unethical behavior between the members of nuclear families, i.e., parents and children, more severely than any other sort. Next in importance come more distant kindred and members of the same village, the relative emphasis differing with the culture. Ethical rules apply with still less vigor to dealings with members of other communities within the society and with least vigor to interaction with socially marginal individuals such as foreign traders or tolerated refugees. With these last two groups, length of association seems to be the most important factor: the longer the association, the stronger the tendency to recognize ethical principles in social interaction. . . .

To conclude, it seems probable that the extent to which ethical standards are recognized and adhered to in the social interactions of individuals is primarily a function (in the mathematical sense) of the closeness and continuity of association between the individuals involved. This might be explained in psychological terms of identification, but it can also be explained in terms of practical, informal sanctions. To cheat or abuse a person with whom you have to go on interacting afterward is much more likely to bring reprisals than is the same sort of behavior toward a comparative stranger. An excellent example of this principle is seen in the different patterns of treatment of field slaves and house slaves in all slave-holding societies. House slaves are always dealt with more leniently but a much higher level of honesty is expected from them. . . .

To return to the problem of universal ethical principles, ethical relativists seem to be particularly intrigued by the differences in the patterns of sex behavior approved in different societies. In fact, many of them seem to follow our own colloquial practice of making "morals" and "sex behavior" equivalent. Different societies do differ more in their attitudes toward sex than in any other activity within the field of ethics, but all of them have very definite rules governing sex behavior, and these rules have much in common. Thus all societies prohibit incest and punish it with great vigor. The same holds for rape, although there may be differences in the exact definition of this offense. The main differences in sexual mores lie in attitudes toward pre-marital chastity and toward exclusive possession of spouses.

Many societies do not expect pre-marital chastity from either boys or girls. Their attitude toward adolescent affairs is much like our own amused tolerance of "puppy love." Thanks to the period of adolescent sterility, such affairs rarely result in pregnancy, so have little implication for the society as a whole. Nearly all societies frown on promiscuity, in the sense of entertaining a large number of partners. In most "primitive" societies the extension of incest taboos to remote relatives, and the comparatively small size of the adolescent group, limit the possibilities severely. In all societies which permit pre-marital affairs, it is taken for granted that they will result in the formation of permanent matings and the establishment of new nuclear families.

With one or two doubtful exceptions, marriage is a universal institution. Moreover, the lifelong union of spouses is everywhere the ideal no matter how easy and frequent separations may be in practice. The rights and duties between parents, between parents and offspring, and between children of the same parents are always culturally defined and enforced by ethical sanctions. Thus each parent must make certain contributions toward the economic life of the family. Loyalty to the spouse is expected in most societies and those which permit exceptions limit these to situations in which there is a conflict between the claims of one spouse and those of the other spouse's kindred.

The marriage relation always limits the sex activities of both parties. Although sex relations with more than one individual may be permitted, the available partners and the conditions under which they may enjoy a spouse's favors are always culturally established and ethically sanctioned. Even in polygynous and polyandrous societies, the rights of plural wives or husbands are clearly defined. Thus in many polygynous societies, each wife is entitled to her husband's company for one day in turn. For a husband to spend another wife's day with a favorite is regarded as adultery and more severely reprehended than ordinary adultery, since it strikes at the very roots of the family system.

Permitted sex relations by married people outside marriage are found in about the same number of societies and frequently in the same societies as those which permit pre-marital experimentation. However, the possible partners are socially designated and the affairs are arranged in such a way as to avoid either disruption of the family unit or ego injury to the spouse. Thus in wife-lending the borrower is, with few exceptions, either a close relative, such as a younger brother, or a friend who does not live in the same community. In either case the man who receives the favor is expected to reciprocate in kind when he is able to do so. Conversely, the wife may have sexual rights in some of the husband's male relatives, but culture patterns establish which ones and the arrangement is thoroughly understood at the time of the marriage.

Both permitted adolescent love-making and permitted non-monogamous sex behavior in marriage reflect a lowered evaluation of sex per se. Where the sexual act is regarded as a normal, pleasurable exercise, like eating, and where parentage is a matter of social ascription rather than biological relationship, the claims of kinship or even friendship are given precedence over those of exclusive possession. At the same time, practically all societies recognize adultery as unethical and punish the offenders. The same man who will lend his wife to a friend or brother will be roused to fury if she goes to another man without his permission.

Turning to the rights and duties between parents and children, the only point at which sex enters is in the almost universal prohibition of sex relations between parent and offspring. As far as known, no society permits sex relations between mother and son while only two or three permit it between father and daughter, and even in these it is limited to royal or sacerdotal groups. The comparative study of other parent-child relations is complicated by the fact that societies differ greatly in the emphasis they place on the nuclear family. In several matrilineal societies, what are ordinarily the paternal functions are shifted from a woman's husband to her brother. In such cases the ethical obligations between a child and his maternal uncle are practically the same as those between a child and his father in patrilineal societies.

In all societies the parents are expected to care for and train children while the children in turn will care for them in old age. In connection with the training, different societies permit differing disciplinary techniques which vary greatly in severity. However, no society approves sadistic behavior on the part of a parent or any sort of discipline which results in permanent injury. With few exceptions, children are expected to accord both parents respect and obedience. Violence against a parent is a major crime in nearly all societies. Since the care and training of children is the primary function of the family as an institution, failure of either side to live up to its obligations in the parent-child relationship is severely reprehended. Supernatural sanctions are invoked more frequently here than in any other type of social interaction.

The obligations between siblings show more variation than those between parents and offspring. In all cases, some degree of loyalty and mutual assistance is prescribed, but the extent of these claims differs enormously in different societies. The rivalry of half-siblings is recognized and allowed for in the ethical systems of most polygynous societies but violence, treachery, and deceit are disapproved. Even in monogamous societies there is always some conflict between the claims of the sibling group and those of the new nuclear families established by its members' marriages. Various societies lay stress on one or the other of these groups as the focus for individual loyalties. Patterns vary from societies which expect the wife to sever all relations with her siblings at marriage to those which regard spouses as only peripherally attached to the functional family. This is, in such cases, a group of real or classificatory siblings. The most nearly universal regulation governing sibling interaction is the prohibition of sex relations, but even here the exceptions are much more numerous than for the parent-child incest rule.

In addition to its basic function of child-rearing, the family is normally an economic unit for both production and consumption. This pattern tends to break down under modern urban conditions, but throughout most of the world ethical sanctions are invoked to ensure that each family member contributes to the family economy and also receives an adequate return for his services. In cases where some member seems to receive a disproportionate share of the family income, investigation usually shows that this share is not used for personal benefit but is disbursed to increase the family prestige.

Lastly, the family everywhere is expected to support its members' interests and to present a united front to outsiders. Particular members may be sacrificed for the good of the whole, but to side with another family against one's own is everywhere regarded as wrong. The only cases in which it might be adjudged right for a man to ignore the interest of his own family are those in which there is a clash between this and the interest of some larger social unit to which the family belongs. In such cases of conflicting loyalties, some cultures prescribe that the family be favored, some the larger group. The significant point is that loyalty to any social unit to which the individual belongs is always regarded as a virtue, disloyalty as a vice.

So much for the ethical patterns governing sex behavior and family life. It can be seen that the similarities far outweigh the differences. The same seems to hold true for another aspect of culture, i.e., property, although here also there is considerable difference in the behavior patterns which implement the common values. To understand the ethical values involved, it is necessary to give a brief description of property concepts in general.

All societies recognize personal property in tools, utensils, ornaments, and so forth. The only exceptions are a few completely communistic societies established by sophisticated individuals as a part of religious movements, and no society of this sort has ever had a long duration. The concept of personal property is easily explained in terms of the individual's identification with objects he has made or habitually uses. Similar identification can often be seen in domestic animals. Products of hunting and food gathering, domestic animals and crops, either garnered or in the field, are universally owned by either individuals or the smallest family groupings operating as organized economic units. The principle involved seems to be that the products of skill or labor belong to the individual or group which has exercised these qualities. Private ownership of means of production is mainly a phenomenon of civilization, especially modern mechanized civilization, but it is not unknown in simpler societies. Individuals, families, or even corporate groups often own such productive appliances as canoes or nets and permit others to use them for a fee.

With respect to land or other irreplaceable natural resources all societies retain the right of eminent domain. The differences lie in the point at which the society recognizes a threat to its well-being and takes over. However, subject to this right, there is a universal tendency toward individual or family ownership of land or resources which possess continuing value. Even at the simplest levels of technological development, family hunting territories are usual in regions where game is nonmigratory. More advanced societies recognize ownership of such resources as winter pasture, fishing places, and improved land. With respect to the last, it is a general rule that crops belong to the individuals or groups who have planted them, but the land itself reverts to the society's common holding when it is no longer in use. Most societies have, in addition to individual holdings, waste land of little value whose products can be exploited by any society member.

There are no economically equalitarian societies. Even among nomadic food gatherers the good hunter with a clever wife has more food, better equipment, and more ornaments. Among food-raising peoples the inequalities in wealth may be striking. It is not uncommon in such societies to have natural resources preempted by wealthy families to such a degree that poor individuals are almost excluded from access to them. However, all societies have culturally recognized patterns for the care of the poor or unfortunate. Extension of family ties and disgrace attaching to failure to care for relatives are usually enough to provide food and shelter at a survival level. Charity, as distinct from the fulfillment of family obligations, is also common. In fact, in most uncivilized societies the main incentive for the accumulation of property seems to be the desire to disburse the surplus at public functions, thus acquiring prestige. The principal alternative to this practice is the destruction or interment of surplus property at funerals but this form of ostentatious waste is highly developed in only a few cultures.

Societies living under conditions that preclude any large accumulation of property nearly all have patterns for sharing food and lending surplus tools and weapons. This is quite different from genuine communal ownership, since the owner of the things shared gains prestige and expects reciprocal favors. Under such conditions theft becomes ridiculous and is so regarded. It is said that the Eskimos do not punish thieves but whenever a thief's name is mentioned everybody laughs. In societies where accumulation is possible, theft is everywhere regarded as a crime and is severely punished. Actually, it is rare in most uncivilized communities. This may be due less to ethical considerations than to the ease with which objects which are not mass-produced can be recognized. Only a kleptomaniac would steal something which he could not use or profitably dispose of without immediate detection. It is worth noting in this connection that with the introduction of money into uncivilized societies both hoarding and theft of money usually appear even though attitudes toward theft of other types of property remain unchanged.

All societies recognize economic obligations of the sort involved in exchange of goods and services and the individual who fails to live up to them is punished simply but effectively by exclusion from future exchanges. Attitudes with respect to sharp practices show more diversity but each society defines the areas in which such practices are permitted and usually has rules as to what techniques are or are not permissible. Thus the Yankee of the horse-trading era regarded it as quite legitimate to hide the faults of a horse as long as he could do so without a direct lie. The trading was regarded as a sport, a battle of wits waged according to mutually recognized rules. However, once the parties agreed that it was a trade, neither side could withdraw without complete loss of reputation.

. . . Attitudes toward lying differ greatly in various societies. The North European is almost unique in regarding verbal truth as an ethical value per se. Most societies regard lying as quite permissible under most circumstances and ability to detect the truth regardless of what is said as a legitimate test of intelligence. The judgments of Solomon brought him great credit but it is not recorded that the litigants were embarrassed at being caught in untruth. However, all societies demand truth in at least certain areas of personal interaction, and a great many of them seek to insure it by invoking supernatural sanctions, i.e., oaths.

Attitudes on offenses against the person appear highly variable at first sight. It would seem that the only offense which is universally reprehended is killing or maiming without justification. All societies recognize and punish the crime of murder as distinct from justifiable homicide, but their definitions of murder differ considerably. Some of the complications disappear when it is recognized that many societies place ego injury through insult on a par with bodily injury. Such injury justifies physical retaliation, often by culturally delimited techniques, as in the *code duello*. However, it is only with the development of government in the modern sense that the problem of preventing physical aggression can be solved. Where blood revenge is a culture pattern, it may serve as a deterrent to initial acts of violence, but once the act has been committed the consequences are an increasing number of violent acts. The most effective technique for preventing violence in the absence of centralized authority is the institution of *wergild* by which the offender has to pay a fine so heavy that he can rarely meet it without the assistance of his relatives. The knowledge that they will have to part with property if one of the kindred maims or kills a member of another kin group insures that they will do their best to prevent the crime from taking place.

It is interesting to note that no society has successfully solved the problem of preventing psychic aggression. The practice of malevolent magic must not be classed under that head since, to societies which believe in it, it ranks as a form of physical attack. Most societies distinguish between justifiable and unjustifiable use of malevolent magic and punish the latter with great severity, since the insidious nature of the magician's attack makes him a potential threat to the whole community. Psychic aggression either directly through curses or indirectly through slander is actionable in many societies. However, the form which such aggression takes varies greatly from one society to another. Many factors are involved in an individual's insult reaction. Even in Europe where the *code duello* had been elaborated for generations, courts of honor had to be convened to pass on doubtful cases of insult.

Information is now available on a large number of cultures which are so widely distributed in time and space that they provide an adequate sample for comparative studies. There is no society on record which does not have an ethical system. Apparent exceptions are due to the observer's failure to recognize the social limits within which the system is expected to apply. By an ethical system we mean definite ideas regarding what constitutes right or wrong behavior in most situations involving social interaction with a high degree of consistency in the values which these ideas reflect. Whether the society's members consciously generalize from their specific judgments of right and wrong to an abstract ethical system is a different matter. However, a certain amount of generalization is inevitable. There must be agreement on general principles governing the interaction of individuals since the actual situations which may arise are extremely variable. Even in our own law courts, after thousands of years of accumulated experience, every year produces cases for which there are no precedents.

The values reflected in ethical systems seem to be much the same everywhere. However, the relative importance attached to particular values differs considerably from one society to another and even at different points in the history of the same society. Thus one society may attach great importance to chastity per se and organize wide areas of behavior about it while another regards it as secondary to such a value as hospitality. Contrast the British attitudes toward sex during the Regency with those of a generation later under Queen Victoria. Again, human life may be held so cheap relative to honor that no man is counted as really adult until he has fought a duel, or so dear that killing under any circumstances is punished by death or exile. The important point is that in spite of such variations in the value hierarchy, there is no society which does not have adverse attitudes toward killing society members or in which sexual selectivity is not approved.

Among the values involved in ethical systems, that of insuring the perpetuation and successful functioning of the society always takes first place. Acts which threaten the group are condemned and punished with greater severity than those which threaten only individuals. Note our own attitudes toward treason and toward murder. All societies also recognize that there is a point beyond which the interests of the individual must be made subordinate to those of the state. Note the universality of property regulations comparable to our own right of eminent domain. Within the limits set by the priority given to a society's needs, all ethical systems also seek to provide for the physical and psychological needs of individuals. All societies guard persons in the marriage relationship from both physical deprivation and ego injury by recognizing and enforcing their mutual rights and duties. They also provide a high degree of security in all the other relationships within the family group by approving all forms of cooperation and condemning acts which threaten family solidarity. The recognition of personal property militates against both actual deprivation and ego injury while all societies have developed techniques for the distribution of economic surplus to those who are in want. Violence, allowing for the cultural differences in definition of that term, is everywhere condemned and techniques are present to prevent its outbreak and minimize its consequences. This list could be extended considerably in terms of less fundamental values which are common to a very large proportion of the world's cultures if not to all.

The resemblances in ethical concepts so far outweigh the differences that a sound basis for mutual understanding between groups of different cultures is already in existence. The present difficulties seem to stem from two main sources: the first is that societies which share the same values often differ considerably in the relative importance which they attach to them. To judge from historic evidence on the changes which have taken place in various cultures, such differences are by no means insurmountable. A greater difficulty lies in the age-old tendency of every society's members to assume that ethical systems apply only within their own tribe or nation. This attitude is difficult to overcome but the modern world is witnessing a rapid expansion of social horizons. When people learn to think of themselves as members of a single world society, it will be easy for them to agree on a single ethical system.

59. The Ethical Prescriptions of Yurok Society

WALTER GOLDSCHMIDT

Yurok ethics reflect our own. The comparison between the ethical system of this primitive tribe and that of Protestantism is a surprising one in view of the vast differences in religious beliefs as well as in economic modes of life. This puritanical attitude is not only expressed in the stern restraint of sexuality and mundane pleasures but, more importantly, involves the idea that each individual must prove his own worth through self-denial and hard work. In the original essay, the author shows how these virtues relate to a social system in which the individual may advance his own status through the free exercise of his own will. The essay was first printed in the *American Anthropologist*, Volume 53, No. 4, 1951, and is printed here with the kind permission of its editor.

The structure of Yurok society may be briefly stated. On the economic side there are the following: The universal application of the concept of property, privately and individually held; the use of money as a universal means of exchange; the existence of wealth and its accumulation for purposes of prestige. On the social side these characteristics are paramount: The organization of the tribe into villages and households; the general but not universal patrilineal descent; absence of clans or any other inalienable group affiliations; absence of any vested authoritarian position, and the maintenance of power through control of wealth with social stratification not clearly marked into classes, but of overweening importance. More broadly, Northwest California society was an open class system in which prestige and power rested fundamentally with the possession of goods.

All property, whether natural resources, money, or items of wealth, is privately (and for the most part individually) owned. By resource property is meant fishing, hunting and gathering grounds. Like no other hunting-gathering people of which I have knowledge (and very few primitive peoples generally), these resources are held as private property by individuals for their own use and control, and not in trust or as titular head for some larger group. This ownership was individual. The sharp definition of title includes such considerations as:

(1)   The separation of title to separate types of products such as right to stranded whales along a specified segment of seacoast; or the right to the flippers off all sea lions that are killed by hunters along a section of coastline.

(2)   The ownership of property rights within the territory of an alien tribe, such as a Hupa family's ownership of a rock on the Yurok coast area from which they obtained clams, and the possession by Yurok of a seed-gathering area in Chilula territory.

(3)   The division of title to a fishing place between two or more persons by measured time-spans; so that one uses it one day, another the next, etc.

Ownership was complete, with free right of alienation. Land holdings were readily transferred, either in legal disputes or for a consideration. The degree of freedom in this right is indicated by the fact that an owner might transfer his share to a person who was stranger or enemy to his co-owner so that a piece of property might be co-owned by persons with unfriendly relationships.

Where private property is recognized among primitive peoples, its importance is frequently vitiated by the mandatory generosity with respect to goods. Not so among the Northwest Californians. Generosity with food is expected as a general thing, but not to the impairment of one's own interests. Poachers, for instance, were shot. This was not a matter of territoriality, but of the transgression of individual rights. Or again, Waterman reports with respect to oak groves that "when acorns were plentiful no one worried much about his 'rights' or 'other people's rights' for that matter. In seasons of scarcity, when the acorn crop fell short (which often happened), or when it failed in certain sections, ownership of places became a very important matter. Permission to pick up acorns in a given spot might in that case be bartered for Indian money." If a man allowed another to fish at his place, the owner received the bulk of the catch. If only one salmon was taken, the "tenant" kept merely the tail. Such rental and restriction of the usufruct can hardly be compared to western economic exploitation, but it does show the relationship of ownership to the relative well-being of the individual. Waterman indicates that there is a direct relationship between resource ownership and wealth status.

The close identification of the individual with his property is another feature of the ownership pattern that must receive attention. This is manifested in attitudes toward the more personal forms of property (careful storage, tabus on handling, and the like), but it also appears in respect to real property. This is shown by laws of liability, where harm which befalls one on the property of another is treated as the direct responsibility (indeed the will) of that person.

So developed a concept of property requires the use of money, and in Northwest California money buys everything—wealth, resources, food, honor, and wives. As a form of behavior it is more uniformly applied than it is with us, though not so frequently. The dentalium shell served this purpose, the denominational value varying with its length. This was so much a matter of concern that every man of substance had standardized measurements tattooed on his forearm. This money was carefully preserved in elkhorn purses, each dentalium of value individually wrapped and decorated. Such decoration did not enhance the value of the object, but was merely care, lavished for its own sake, upon a treasured thing.

The third category of property is wealth—goods which served as the recognized goal of the individual, the possession of which marked his social position. Wealth consisted chiefly of paraphernalia used in one or another of the religious ceremonials of the people. These include the skins of albino or other off-color deer, large flint or obsidian blades (both used in the White Deerskin dance), woodpecker crest headbands and a host of lesser items of attire and personal decoration. These are not things which have utilitarian value in any direct sense. But they were used in the transfer of resource property, in legal disputes, and in the purchase of brides, as well as being displayed in the important ceremonial activities. Above all, the amount and value defined the social status of the owner, and his position of power in the community. We will return to this later.

The structure of the Yurok social system had an amorphous quality. Though there were functioning social groups to which each person belonged, and though status distinctions were of greatest importance, still the most significant characteristic of the structure was the general absence of preordained group membership and ascribed social position. All social affiliation contained a measure of individual consent, and all social position a measure of personal achievement. Groups to which the individual was attached included the family or household unit, the sweathouse group, the village, and the tribe. The household unit was crucial. It was a moderately extended patrilineal family consisting of man, wife, children, married-in in-laws, and their children. Such families shared a dwelling house, about which their activities centered. The sharp delineation of the constitution of a family was prevented by the custom of "half-marriage," a second-rate marital practice in which the man joined the family of his bride, and their children became members of the house of the bride's father. These marriages took place in one out of five cases, so that nearly half the households must have been involved in such a marriage each generation. This custom, more than any other, prevented the family from taking on a crystallized structure because it prevented the juridical definition of family constitution, so frequent among primitive peoples.

Furthermore, a person might break with his family without social disapproval. Thus Spott and Kroeber report one case of a man who left his father's household and set himself up independently across the river, because his father had been niggardly in refusing to assist in the purchase of a bride—and this with public approval and no recrimination. This does not mean that the family was unimportant or that family ties were loosely regarded (the contrary is clearly the case), but only that there was a measure of personal consent and lack of preordained identification even in this basic institution.

The sweathouse group formed a clique of men from three or so neighboring houses who shared the use of a subterranean sudatory. This structure served as sleeping, working, and lounging quarters for the men, as well as a sudatory for the semi-ritualized sweating activity. The personnel at any one time was fixed, and there were clearly marked status positions within the group. Boys about the age of puberty joined the group, presumably that to which the head of their household belonged. Membership of this group was not, therefore, a fixed matter. It was subject to the same vagaries that affected membership in the household. In addition, the data obtained on sweathouse membership suggests that a person was free to join any nearby group, so long as it was mutually agreeable.

These sweathouse cliques appear to have formed the unit (or the nucleus) for two separate, though related functions: (1) a body of men who acted in mutual support in case of dispute or fight, and (2) a group to support an individual presenting a unit of the White Deerskin dance. These political and religious functions are frequently performed by clans in the simpler societies. But significantly the groups were not structured like clans; not merely because they did not have unilinearity of descent, but because an individual's membership was neither foreordained nor eternal, but always contained an element of personal choice.

We may dismiss the village and tribe with a word. Though persons were identified by their village of residence and their tribe of origin, neither of these groups had any direct claim upon the action of the individual; there was no village nor national government, no village or tribal action in wars. Significantly, the affiliation could effectively be broken by moving to a distance or to one of the other tribes within the orbit of the culture.

Social status distinctions were an essential element in the structuring of Yurok society. Certain statuses ascribed position to a small minority. Bastards had no social standing by virtue of their illegitimacy. Slaves were held, but their position was not quite so hopeless. Aside from these, there were the rich and the poor, class differentials which represent a continuum of status, not unlike that of the middle class in Western society. Since class status depended upon wealth, which was heritable, class affiliations followed closely according to the parents. Indeed, there was a clear distinction between the man of rich family background and the parvenu. Thus class position was not entirely open.

But in Yurok theory it was open. Myths contain repeatedly the element of movement from poverty to riches. The youth is told that he can achieve by proper effort. At least one case is recorded of an individual independently attaining wealth, and his behavior was approved and his position accepted. The situation appears to have been as with us: in theory everyone might achieve status; in actuality models for such movement existed but in fact only a small proportion of persons significantly altered their social position. There is some evidence that the Yurok class differentiation was more sharply defined and mobility less realizable than among the Hupa or the Tolowa. But it seems to me this is a crystallization which will naturally take place in an open class system because of the tendency of persons of status toward such a definition. . . .

The third facet of Northwest California society was the systems of power and authority. Here again the situation was unstructured, for there were no persons vested with authority by virtue of station or public office. There were religious leaders or priests, whose official powers were limited to the ceremonial situation or the religious rite. Kroeber considers the go-betweens selected to negotiate settlements as functionaries since they were entrusted with judicial authority. But they were selected and employed by the disputants, and had no powers beyond that which the disputing parties allocated to them. Government was strictly *laissez faire,* with order prevailing through the consistent effort of each person to serve his own self interest. Authority rested on a continual threat and show of force by the quick recognition of offense and the insistent demand for retribution. In Northwest California law all offense was against the person—it could hardly be otherwise in the absence of any formalized social unit. A great range of offenses was recognized: murder and adultery, theft and poaching, curses, minor insults.

For each offense there was a more or less clearly indicated fine or indemnity to be paid by the offender to the plaintiff, after proper adjudication through a neutral go-between. Not only were liability, intent and value of damage done recognized in determination of indemnity, but the status of the offended party was also considered, particularly in matters of murder. In view of these variables, it is not surprising that each case was the subject of prolonged litigation and negotiation, in which other considerations than the purely legalistic were brought to play.

For, in final analysis, the only ultimate sanction for legal settlement was the threat of physical force. The constant threat and show of force (remarkably ineffective, it would appear) is indicated in a Yurok war reminiscence reported by Kroeber. The community was concerned with justice and its pressures were brought to bear for settlement according to established precedents. But it had no machinery to enforce a peaceful settlement, and an offended person might resort to, and always implicitly threatened to bring, physical retribution. In this use of force the individual counted on the support of his associates—his household group, his sweathouse clique, and a widening circle of supporters. It follows from the nature of the group affiliations that this was no absolute call, but an expectation of support which was subject to the willingness and consent of the supporters. This consent must have been a function in part of the righteousness of the cause and the appropriateness of the conduct of the principal. It was also a function of the social position and system of obligation that he had established.

It follows further that authority rested in large measure with the strong, and that this strength was fiscal strength. It was not merely the differential fines that worked to the advantage of the wealthy, or the higher bride price for their daughters, nor even that the wealthy were in a better economic position to push the limits of propriety and the demands for retribution. These were real but secondary by-products. It was that the owners of resources and of wealth could surround themselves with a greater body of persons willing to stand by them at times of crisis. Directly, the owner of resources could support a larger family. Indirectly, a wealthy man was central in a system of mutual obligations, and lesser persons found it useful to stand with him. Among these obligations might have been economic assistance and support (with his resources) in legal disputes. The pattern of allegiances was established in the presentation of the White Deerskin Dance. In these ceremonials, leadership was taken by several individuals of substance, each of whom presented a set of dances utilizing his own paraphernalia. They were aided by their household and sweathouse-group fellows, and by others who felt sufficient obligation or allegiance. These ceremonials were public displays, not only of wealth, but also of power and the ties of mutual obligation. They were institutionalized and canalized expressions of individuated aggressive behavior which served to demonstrate fiscal strength, public power, social allegiances and social status.

The capitalist structure of the society may be summarized as follows: a system in which the individual was placed chiefly by personal acquisition of wealth which in theory was freely attainable by all, with both status and power resting upon the ownership of property.

The ethical pattern in Northwest California may be examined under its three fundamental features: the moral demand to work and by extension to the pursuit of gain; the moral demand of self denial; and the individuation of moral responsibility.

There is a strong compulsion to work heavily emphasized in child rearing, supported by the religious beliefs and demands, and expressed as a basic element in behavior. Northwest Californians were a busy and creative people. Wallace writes "Both a man and his wife are constantly busy. . . . Some seasons of the year are marked by more activity than others, but during none of them is anyone idle for long. The life is one of continuous routine work, although not necessarily of drudgery." Even in pregnancy a woman is expected to work: . . . "if a woman took it easy before she had her baby, the other women figured she was lazy and talked about her." "Old people continue their economic activities as long as possible; only when they become too feeble to endure hard work do they give up." In societies living close to the minimum level of subsistence, the emphasis upon industriousness is not surprising. But poverty was not found here. The important thing about the evaluation of industriousness is not that there was such a value; but the moral involvement of the value: work as a moral end.

The gathering of sweathouse wood demonstrates this fact. All men, particularly the youths, were exhorted to gather wood for use in sweating. This was not exploitation of child labor, but an important religious act, freighted with significance. Special wood was brought from the mountain ridges; it was used for an important purification ritual. The gathering itself was a religious act, for it was a means of acquiring "luck." It had to be done with the proper psychological attitude of which restrained demeanor and constant thinking about the acquisition of riches were the chief elements. The job became a moral end rather than a means to an end, with both religious and economic involvements.

The second commandment of the Northwest Californians was worldly asceticism. The Yurok was exhorted to abstain from any kind of over-indulgence—eating, sexual gratification, play or sloth. The evidence here is definitive. For instance, sexuality was unclean. The sex act might not be committed in the dwelling house but was performed on the beaches. Youths were exhorted to be continent, and a woman particularly to preserve her virginity until married. Even after marriage, a man was expected to restrain himself: . . . "It's not good to be with a woman all the time. It's bad luck in getting money or hunting deer. A man weans himself from doing that as much as he can. . . . Most men have strong minds and good control . . ." and again, "If a man has too many kids, he is thought to be hoggish, like a dog."

Again big eaters were viewed as vulgar, and a person of good manners always ate slowly and in moderation, leaving food in his baskets to indicate self control as well as economic well-being. These patterns are clearly articulated by every student of these cultures and need no further elucidation. "There seems to be no end to the emphasis given to the restraint in eating. When the young Yurok visits friends and is offered food, he speaks much and acts as if he did not see the food until it has been urged so much that not to eat would be affront. As an adult, he will begin his day's work without breakfast and have his first meal only after the major work is done."

But these behavior patterns were not purely secular. Sexual indulgence was not only bad, but sinful. And sin had a peculiarly economic definition. Sexual intercourse was bad because seminal fluid drives out dentalia and other wealth, to which it is abhorrent. Put another way, objects which at one and the same time demonstrated secular power and were associated with sacred ritual were the focal point in the taboo against intercourse. The rejection of sexuality was a religious aversion. It was religious yet it is important to appreciate how closely it was tied to economic well-being. There was constant economic evaluation of moral acts—with the custom of bride purchase, the wages of sin became subject to strict cost accounting.

The sweathouse ritual offered a daily test of other forms of self-indulgence for the men. The subterranean sweathouse had two doors. One was a hatchway in the roof for easy entrance and ordinary use. After sweating, however, the men had to leave through a narrow oval opening at the floor level and climb out a cobble-lined flue. Only a lithe, naked, sweaty body could work its way through this opening. It is obvious that any indulgence in food or sloth would make egress impossible. Here was a test that was daily and absolute, and carried with it the full force of religious sanction. Furthermore the sweathouse activities and sweating itself were attached to the wealth-acquisition pattern, for the overt purpose of the sweating ritual was to insure luck for the individual in his economic pursuits.

Asceticism like work therefore was moral behavior which came to be an end itself; an end closely connected with economic and social success on one hand, and with deep religious meaning and sanction on the other. Though it had these moral aspects, the "practical" implications of asceticism were recognized. The Yurok youth was told what our own fathers have told us, that if you want to be rich you must leave the women alone.

The third feature of the Protestant ethic of Northwest California society is the individuation of moral responsibility; that is, the placing of responsibility for the individual's worth and his acts upon the individual himself. He was neither the creature of some unseen power nor the product of circumstance, but the master of his own fate. To this there were exceptions, such as bastards whose circumstances of birth determined their character, and shamans, whose possession of power was viewed as lying beyond their individual will. But the normal citizen was held personally responsible for his acts, and so conceived of himself.

Consider again the nature of the wood-gathering act, in which the youth sought power not by subjecting himself to the will of some unseen spirit, but by directing his thoughts along consciously chosen channels.

Closely associated with this individuated self are the concepts of sin and guilt, which were to be found among the Northwest Californians. Present tribal members regularly use the word "sin" to describe morally disapproved behavior. The White Deerskin Dance is specifically designed to rid the world of the contaminating influence of the cumulative sins of individuals of their community. Descriptions of child rearing practices indicate that "rules of conduct are inculcated by parents eager to see their progeny grow up in the 'right way' and anxious to avoid litigation which juvenile action might cause, as parents are held responsible for acts of their children from the age of eight or nine on." Imitation is not enough; inculcation of morality is consciously taught. The evidence for the internalization of this pattern of responsibility, and its expression in the form of guilt, is somewhat nebulous, but not entirely wanting. . . .

Finally, this pattern of individuation is expressed in the personality characteristics of the people. The Yurok is extremely aggressive in his interpersonal relations; he is hostile to his fellow men and expects hostility toward himself; he never relaxes his barriers of suspicion. The myths demonstrate these components which may be observed in the real world—aggressiveness, bickering and drive toward personal success. They also demonstrate certain reaction patterns—compulsive demand to work, withdrawal in the geographic sense, and obedience and submission to the absolute powers of the creator gods.

Other personality traits were also involved. There was a constant theme of loneliness running through the mythology, and loneliness is an expected concomitant of individuation and hostility. More remote, perhaps, is the notion of romantic love, so familiar to us but so rare among primitive peoples. Here again individuation is implicit, for romantic love involves both the individuated self and the individuated other.

In summary, Yurok ethics placed the focus of moral responsibility upon the individual, a moral responsibility which internalized the command to industriousness, self-denial and personal aggrandizement; a moral demand which produced a pattern of individual guilt and the concept of sin.

60. Hopi Ethics

RICHARD B. BRANDT

The Hopi stand in sharp contrast to the Yurok. Where the Yurok emphasize individualism, the Hopi emphasize the subordination of the individual to the common good. It is important that we appreciate the contrast, for it indicates how widely divergent ethical attitudes can be among primitive people. Just as Goldschmidt points to the comparison between the Yurok and Protestant ethics, observers have noted similarities between Hopi religious and ethical orientations and those of Catholicism.

Richard B. Brandt is Professor of Philosophy at Swarthmore College; he studied in England, Germany and at Yale University. With the encouragement of A. L. Kroeber and assisted by a Guggenheim Fellowship, he turned to the implications of primitive material for ethical theory. He studied the Hopi from 1946 to 1948 and published his book, *Hopi Ethics, A Theoretical Analysis* with the University of Chicago Press, Chicago, 1954. The essay is published by kind permission of The University of Chicago Press. Copyright 1954 by The University of Chicago.

The Hopi conception of the ideal man has only a few main themes. The good Hopi, in outline, is approximately as follows:

A good family man: is industrious and thrifty, works to provide more material comforts for his family, is concerned for his children and has affection for them, is prudent and cautious.

Agreeable in his social relations: is polite and kind, does not hurt others' feelings, does not get into disputes, does not complain, does not get angry, does not gossip, is not grouchy or mean, heeds valid criticism without taking offense, is cordial, does not cause trouble by having affairs with others' wives.

Not dangerous: he is peaceable, does not get drunk or into brawls.

Cooperative: helps in community enterprises, does what he is asked to do, gives time and effort for the group and especially for relatives, can be counted on for advice, is reliable.

Generous: is generous with his help and food; is sympathetic, hospitable, and unselfish.

Honest: pays his debts, keeps his promises, respects property rights.

Modest: is not a snob but not bashful.

Quiet and unobtrusive: does not try to be important, has no political ambitions.

Cheerful: does not worry, is not vengeful or jealous, maintains his mental equilibrium, is indifferent to unjust criticism.

Manly and brave (but on the submissive side in social relations).

A good worker: is persistent, foresighted, and careful.

In all societies most of the foregoing traits are beneficial to the group, to a man's family, or to a man himself, and we shall therefore expect a large measure of intercultural agreement in appraisal of them. Nevertheless, there are differences on details and emphases. In order to see how this works out, let us consider points of disagreement with . . . white Americans (the segment with which the writer is acquainted). . . .

White Americans would be more sympathetic with aspirations to a position of economic and political influence. They would see no point in being submissive or accepting life. They would approve of a man's standing up vigorously for his rights. I believe they would not think it a bad thing to get angry on occasion—especially if other persons attempted to take advantage of one. They would admire initiative and ingenuity, even in a bad cause. Americans would be less interested in a man's concern for his relatives, except for his immediate family. At least residents of large cities would not demand as much community spirit as is expected by the Hopi, although they would approve of it strongly. . . .

Another difference between Hopi and white American ideals arises from the fact that Hopi apparently do not discriminate clearly certain traits which figure quite importantly in white American thinking: conscientiousness, fair-mindedness and impartiality, tolerance, dependability, discipline of the "lower" impulses, self-confidence, independence in thought and action. . . .

The Hopi regard themselves as a distinctively peaceable people; in fact, "Hopi," in one of its senses, means "peaceable." And Hopi are probably correct in supposing that their disapproval of aggressive behavior is developed to an unusually high degree. At least their behavior suggests that it is, when compared with behavior in comparable situations of adult men from among the Philippine Ifugao, the Bontok Igorot, the Eskimo, or even, probably, various white groups in the United States. For it may be fairly said that Hopi emphasize relatively highly the avoidance of violence and disputes and being affable and inoffensive. They seldom engage in physical violence of any sort. They approve and practice nonaggression in circumstances where the provocation is extreme and where nonaggression would not be practiced or even approved by other groups. And Hopi are concerned about and require control of even mildly aggressive impulses, to which other groups, by all accounts, are rather indifferent. . . .

[Informant:] A man with a good heart would pay no attention if he found his wife misbehaving with another man. He would just take his things and go back to his own home. . . .

[Informant:] People who commit adultery can't control themselves. You must let them go. Yes, it makes the husband angry. But he just lets her go. There are no murders here. The Hopi are told not to injure the bodies of persons, even if a man catches them in the act. There'll be some punishment for them later. . . . Injury of the body in any way is against the rules; you might hurt a person. . . .

[Informant:] (Q.: Is it ever all right to argue?) No: you are never justified in arguing. Because it warms you up inside, and the good Being you are to worship doesn't help you that day. You get nothing out of it. When I think of this, I know I am wrong, and I stop right away. . . .

[Informant:] If an innocent man doesn't get angry, he'll live a long while. A guilty man will get sick because of bad thoughts, a bad conscience. . . .

These statements, in conjunction with ones cited earlier, suggest that certain Hopi beliefs support their attitude toward aggression: that a malefactor is likely to be paid off by sickness; that nonaggression is the way to avoid trouble . . . ; that nonaggression makes for the mental serenity required for health; that fighting serves no purpose; that peaceableness helps get good luck in general and preserves the atmosphere necessary for cooperation.

61. Winnebago Ethical Attitudes

PAUL RADIN

Ethical statements are found embedded in the oral literature of primitive peoples. Though they themselves may not synthesize their ethical attitudes into a systematic statement, these attitudes can be discovered by a careful examination of the literature. It is precisely that which Paul Radin has done for the Winnebago Indians.

Radin took his doctorate in anthropology from Columbia University in 1911, and was a student of Franz Boas. He did extensive field work among the Winnebago and published widely on these people. Radin is known for his contributions to anthropological theory; in addition to *Primitive Man as Philosopher,* from which the present essay is taken, and a general theoretical treatise, *Method and Theory of Ethnology,* he has analyzed the literature of various primitive peoples. More than any other scholar, Radin represents the humanistic approach to the understanding of preliterate societies. From: *Primitive Man as Philosopher* by Paul Radin. Copyright, 1927, D. Appleton & Company. Reprinted by permission of the publishers Appleton-Century-Crofts, Inc.

On no subject connected with primitive people does so much confusion exist in the mind of the general public and have so many ill-considered statements been made as on the nature of their behavior to one another. The prevalent view today among laymen is that they are at all times the plaything of their passions, and that self-control and poise are utterly alien to their character, if not, indeed, quite beyond their reach. . . . Actually the situation is quite different.

Briefly stated, the underlying ideal of conduct among most primitive tribes is self-discipline, self-control and a resolute endeavor to observe a proper measure of proportion in all things. I am well aware that in some tribes this is more definitely expressed than in others and that not infrequently certain excrescences in their ceremonial life seem to contradict this assertion. Yet I think most field ethnologists would agree with me. Since in the face of so formidable a body of opinion apparently to the contrary, incontrovertible evidence will be demanded of me to substantiate so broad and explicit a statement, I shall confine myself in my presentation of the facts to a tribe which I know personally and where the material which I use can be definitely controlled. The data upon which I rely come from the Winnebago Indians of Wisconsin and Nebraska and are to be found in two monographs published by me. Only statements made by the Winnebago themselves in accounts either actually written by themselves or contained in verbatim descriptions of the rituals obtained in the original Winnebago are used in order to obviate all inaccuracy.

I can think of no better method of introducing the subject than by quoting appropriate passages from the Winnebago texts secured and then discussing them in the light of the knowledge they throw upon the system of ethics enunciated and, more specifically, upon the type of self-control implied. For facility of reference I shall number these passages:

1. It is always good to be good.
2. What does life consist of but love?
3. Of what value is it to kill?
4. You ought to be of some help to your fellow men.
5. Do not abuse your wife; women are sacred.
6. If you cast off your dress for many people, they will be benefitted by your deed.
7. For the good you do every one will love you.
8. Never do any wrong to children.
9. It is not good to gamble.
10. If you see a helpless old man, help him if you have anything at all.
11. If you have a home of your own, see to it that whoever enters it obtains something to eat. Such food will be a source of death to you if withheld.
12. When you are recounting your war deeds on behalf of the departed soul, do not try to add to your honor by claiming more for yourself than you have actually accomplished. If you tell a falsehood then and exaggerate your achievements you will die beforehand. The telling of truth is sacred. Tell less than you did. The old men say it is wiser.
13. Be on friendly terms with every one and then every one will love you.
14. Marry only one person at a time.
15. Do not be haughty with your husband. Kindness will be returned to you and he will treat you in the same way in which you treat him.
16. Do not imagine that you are taking your children's part if you just speak about loving them. Let them see it for themselves.
17. Do not show your love for other people so that people notice it. Love them but let your love be different from that for your own.
18. As you travel along life's road, never harm any one or cause any one to feel sad. On the contrary, if at any time you can make a person feel happy, do so. . . .

Obviously we are here in the presence of a fairly well elaborated system of conduct. To those who consistently deny to primitive man any true capacity for abstract thinking or objective formulation of an ethical code—and their number is very large both among scholars and laymen—the injunctions given above would probably be interpreted as having a definitely concrete significance. That is, they are not to be regarded as attempts at generalization in any true sense of the word but merely as inherently wise saws and precepts of a practical and personal application. Now there is sufficient justification for such a view to warrant our discussing it before we proceed any further.

A number of the precepts given avowedly allow a concrete practical and personal application. In 5, for example, we are told, "If you abuse your wife you will die in a short time. Our grandmother Earth is a woman and in abusing your wife you will be abusing her. Since it is she who takes care of us, by your actions you will be practically killing yourself." To precept 10 is added the following: "If you happen to possess a home, take him (the old man) there and feed him for he may suddenly make uncomplimentary remarks about you. You will be strengthened thereby."

We thus do indeed seem to obtain the impression that a Winnebago in being good to a helpless old man is guided by motives secondary to those implied in the precept as quoted. And what follows would seem to strip our apparently generous precept of whatever further altruistic value still attaches to it, for there it is stated that perhaps the old man is carrying under his arm a box of medicines that he cherishes very much and which he will offer to you. Similarly in precept 11 we find, "If you are stingy about giving food some one may kill you." Indeed I think we shall have to admit that in the majority of cases none of the Winnebago virtues or actions are extolled for their own sake, and that in every instance they have reference to and derive their validity from whatever relation they possess to the preponderatingly practical needs of human intercourse. "Don't be a fool," precept 5 seems to imply, "and treat your wife badly, because if you do, you'll run the risk of having the woman's protecting deity, the Earth, punish you." I should not even be surprised if, in concrete instances, the moral was further emphasized by giving examples of how men were punished who had abused their wives. We are fairly obviously told to be guided by the practical side of the question, i.e., take no risks and get the most out of every good action you perform. . . .

There are, however, in our list certain precepts where the abstract formulation is undeniable, where, in fact, reference to the particular context in which the precepts occur not only shows no secondary concrete significance, but, on the contrary, a reenforcement of their abstract and general connotation. In precept 1 the full statement is this: "If you hear of a person traveling through your country and you want to see him, prepare your table and send for him. In this manner you will do good, and it is always good to do good, it is said." Similarly in precept 2. Here it is in the course of a speech delivered at a ceremony that the phrase occurs: "what does life consist of but love?" "All the members of the clan have given me counsel," the speaker says, "and all women and children have pleaded in my behalf with the spirits. What love that was! And of what does life consist but of love?"

Here we have no concrete practical implications. The statements are meant to be taken as general propositions. They are very remarkable enunciations and we may legitimately draw from their existence the inference that even in so-called "primitive" tribes, certain individuals have apparently felt within themselves the same moral truths that are regarded as the glory of our great moralists, and that they have formulated these truths in general terms.

62. The Ethical Basis of Modern Capitalism

MAX WEBER

Max Weber was a German sociologist whose researches, insight, and theoretical orientation have had increasing influence on sociological and anthropological theory over the past half century. His approach to sociology involved the analysis of historic phenomena and the comparison of social systems in various civilizations. Widely trained and informed on economic, social and legal history, political and military development, religious and intellectual evolution, Weber was instrumental in founding the Deutsche Gesellschaft für Soziologie and was editor of the *Archiv für Sozialwissenschaft und Sozialpolitik*. He taught first at Freiburg and subsequently at the Universities of Heidelberg and Munich. His most important work was *Wirtschaft und Gesellschaft*, published posthumously, but his most widely read essay probably is *The Protestant Ethic and the Spirit of Capitalism* which was first published in Germany in 1904–5 and was translated by the American sociologist Talcott Parsons and published in New York in 1930. It is from this volume that the present essay is taken. Reprinted with the permission of George Allen & Unwin, Ltd. and Charles Scribner's Sons from *The Protestant Ethic and the Spirit of Capitalism* by Max Weber.

"Remember, that *time* is money. He that can earn ten shillings a day by his labor, and goes abroad, or sits idle, one half of that day, though he spends but sixpence during his diversion or idleness, ought not to reckon *that* the only expense; he has really spent, or rather thrown away, five shillings besides.

"Remember, that *credit* is money. If a man lets his money lie in my hands after it is due, he gives me the interest, or so much as I can make of it during that time. This amounts to a considerable sum where a man has good and large credit, and makes good use of it.

"Remember, that money is of the prolific, generating nature. Money can beget money, and its offspring can beget more, and so on. Five shillings turned is six, turned again it is seven and threepence, and so on, till it becomes a hundred pounds. The more there is of it, the more it produces every turning, so that the profits rise quicker and quicker. He that kills a breeding-sow, destroys all her offspring to the thousandth generation. He that murders a crown, destroys all that it might have produced, even scores of pounds."

"Remember this saying, *The good paymaster is lord of another man's purse.* He that is known to pay punctually and exactly to the time he promises, may at any time, and on any occasion, raise all the money his friends can spare. This is sometimes of great use. After industry and frugality, nothing contributes more to the raising of a young man in the world than punctuality and justice in all his dealings; therefore never keep borrowed money an hour beyond the time you promised, lest a disappointment shut up your friend's purse for ever.

"The most trifling actions that affect a man's credit are to be regarded. The sound of your hammer at five in the morning, or eight at night, heard by a creditor, makes him easy six months longer; but if he sees you at a billiard-table, or hears your voice at a tavern, when you should be at work, he sends for his money the next day; demands it, before he can receive it, in a lump.

"It shows, besides, that you are mindful of what you owe; it makes you appear a careful as well as an honest man, and that still increases your credit.

"Beware of thinking all your own that you possess, and of living accordingly. It is a mistake that many people who have credit fall into. To prevent this, keep an exact account for some time both of your expenses and your income. If you take the pains at first to mention particulars, it will have this good effect: you will discover how wonderfully small, trifling expenses mount up to large sums, and will discern what might have been, and may for the future be saved, without occasioning any great inconvenience."

"For six pounds a year you may have the use of one hundred pounds, provided you are a man of known prudence and honesty.

"He that spends a groat a day idly, spends idly above six pounds a year, which is the price for the use of one hundred pounds.

"He that wastes idly a groat's worth of his time per day, one day with another, wastes the privilege of using one hundred pounds each day.

"He that idly loses five shillings' worth of time, loses five shillings, and might as prudently throw five shillings into the sea.

"He that loses five shillings, not only loses that sum, but all the advantage that might be made by turning it in dealing, which by the time that a young man becomes old, will amount to a considerable sum of money."

It is Benjamin Franklin who preaches to us in these sentences, the same which Ferdinand Kürnberger satirizes in his clever and malicious *Picture of American Culture* as the supposed confession of faith of the Yankee. That it is the spirit of capitalism which here speaks in characteristic fashion, no one will doubt, however little we may wish to claim that everything which could be understood as pertaining to that spirit is contained in it. Let us pause a moment to consider this passage, the philosophy of which Kürnberger sums up in the words, "They make tallow out of cattle and money out of men." The peculiarity of this philosophy of avarice appears to be the ideal of the honest man of recognized credit, and above all the idea of a duty of the individual toward the increase of his capital, which is assumed as an end in itself. Truly what is here preached is not simply a means of making one's way in the world, but a peculiar ethic. The infraction of its rules is treated not as foolishness but as forgetfulness of duty. That is the essence of the matter. It is not mere business astuteness, that sort of thing is common enough, it is an ethos. . . .

Now, all Franklin's moral attitudes are colored with utilitarianism. Honesty is useful, because it assures credit; so are punctuality, industry, frugality, and that is the reason they are virtues. A logical deduction from this would be that where, for instance, the appearance of honesty serves the same purpose, that would suffice, and an unnecessary surplus of this virtue would evidently appear to Franklin's eyes as unproductive waste. And as a matter of fact, the story in his autobiography of his conversion to those virtues, or the discussion of the value of a strict maintenance of the appearance of modesty, the assiduous belittlement of one's own deserts in order to gain general recognition later, confirms this impression. According to Franklin, those virtues, like all others, are only in so far virtues as they are actually useful to the individual, and the surrogate of mere appearance is always sufficient when it accomplishes the end in view. It is a conclusion which is inevitable for strict utilitarianism. The impression of many Germans that the virtues professed by Americanism are pure hypocrisy seems to have been confirmed by this striking case. But in fact the matter is not by any means so simple. Benjamin Franklin's own character, as it appears in the really unusual candidness of his autobiography, belies that suspicion. The circumstance that he ascribes his recognition of the utility of virtue to a divine revelation which was intended to lead him in the path of righteousness, shows that something more than mere garnishing for purely egocentric motives is involved.

In fact, the *summum bonum* of this ethic, the earning of more and more money, combined with the strict avoidance of all spontaneous enjoyment of life, is above all completely devoid of any eudæmonistic, not to say hedonistic, admixture. It is thought of so purely as an end in itself, that from the point of view of the happiness of, or utility to, the single individual, it appears entirely transcendental and absolutely irrational. Man is dominated by the making of money, by acquisition as the ultimate purpose of his life. Economic acquisition is no longer subordinated to man as the means for the satisfaction of his material needs. This reversal of what we should call the natural relationship, so irrational from a naïve point of view, is evidently as definitely a leading principle of capitalism as it is foreign to all peoples not under capitalistic influence. At the same time it expresses a type of feeling which is closely connected with certain religious ideas. If we thus ask, *why* should "money be made out of men," Benjamin Franklin himself, although he was a colorless deist, answers in his autobiography with a quotation from the Bible, which his strict Calvinistic father drummed into him again and again in his youth: "Seest thou a man diligent in his business? He shall stand before kings" (Prov. xxii. 29). The earning of money within the modern economic order is, so long as it is done legally, the result and the expression of virtue and proficiency in a calling; and this virtue and proficiency are, as it is now not difficult to see, the real Alpha and Omega of Franklin's ethic, as expressed in the passages we have quoted, as well as in all his works without exception.

And in truth this peculiar idea, so familiar to us today, but in reality so little a matter of course, of one's duty in a calling, is what is most characteristic of the social ethic of capitalistic culture, and is in a sense the fundamental basis of it. It is an obligation which the individual is supposed to feel and does feel towards the content of his professional activity, no matter in what it consists, in particular no matter whether it appears on the surface as a utilization of his personal powers, or only of his material possessions (as capital). . . .

. . . The spirit of capitalism, in the sense in which we are using the term had to fight its way to supremacy against a whole world of hostile forces. A state of mind such as that expressed in the passages we have quoted from Franklin, and which called forth the applause of a whole people, would both in ancient times and in the Middle Ages have been proscribed as the lowest sort of avarice and as an attitude entirely lacking in self-respect. It is, in fact, still regularly thus looked upon by all those social groups which are least involved in or adapted to modern capitalistic conditions. This is not wholly because the instinct of acquisition was in those times unknown or undeveloped, as has often been said. Nor because the *auri sacra fames,* the greed for gold, was then, or now, less powerful outside of bourgeois capitalism than within its peculiar sphere, as the illusions of modern romanticists are wont to believe. The difference between the capitalistic and pre-capitalistic spirits is not to be found at this point. The greed of the Chinese Mandarin, the old Roman aristocrat, or the modern peasant, can stand up to any comparison. And the *auri sacra fames* of a Neapolitan cab-driver or *barcaiuolo,* and certainly of Asiatic representatives of similar trades, as well as of the craftsmen of southern European or Asiatic countries, is, as anyone can find out for himself, very much more intense, and especially more unscrupulous than that of, say, an Englishman in similar circumstances. . . .

One of the technical means which the modern employer uses in order to secure the greatest possible amount of work from his men is the device of piece-rates. In agriculture, for instance, the gathering of the harvest is a case where the greatest possible intensity of labor is called for, since, the weather being uncertain, the difference between high profit and heavy loss may depend on the speed with which the harvesting can be done. Hence a system of piece-rates is almost universal in this case. And since the interest of the employer in a speeding-up of harvesting increases with the increase of the results and the intensity of the work, the attempt has again and again been made, by increasing the piece-rates of the workmen, thereby giving them an opportunity to earn what is for them a very high wage, to interest them in increasing their own efficiency. But a peculiar difficulty has been met with surprising frequency: raising the piece-rates has often had the result that not more but less has been accomplished in the same time, because the worker reacted to the increase not by increasing but by decreasing the amount of his work. A man, for instance, who at the rate of 1 mark per acre mowed 2½ acres per day and earned 2½ marks, when the rate was raised to 1.25 marks per acre mowed, not 3 acres, as he might easily have done, thus earning 3.75 marks, but only 2 acres, so that he could still earn the 2½ marks to which he was accustomed. The opportunity of earning more was less attractive than that of working less. He did not ask: how much can I earn in a day if I do as much work as possible? but: how much must I work in order to earn the wage, 2½ marks, which I earned before and which takes care of my traditional needs? This is an example of what is here meant by traditionalism. A man does not "by nature" wish to earn more and more money, but simply to live as he is accustomed to live and to earn as much as is necessary for that purpose. Wherever modern capitalism has begun its work of increasing the productivity of human labor by increasing its intensity, it has encountered the immensely stubborn resistance of this leading trait of pre-capitalistic labor. And today it encounters it the more, the more backward (from a capitalistic point of view) the laboring forces are with which it has to deal. . . .

. . . Benjamin Franklin was filled with the spirit of capitalism at a time when his printing business did not differ in form from any handicraft enterprise. And we shall see that at the beginning of modern times it was by no means the capitalistic entrepreneurs of the commercial aristocracy, who were either the sole or the predominant bearers of the attitude we have here called the spirit of capitalism. It was much more the rising strata of the lower industrial middle classes. Even in the nineteenth century its classical representatives were not the elegant gentlemen of Liverpool and Hamburg, with their commercial fortunes handed down for generations, but the self-made parvenus of Manchester and Westphalia, who often rose from very modest circumstances. As early as the sixteenth century the situation was similar; the industries which arose at that time were mostly created by parvenus. . . .

Until about the middle of the past century the life of a putter-out was, at least in many of the branches of the Continental textile industry, what we should today consider very comfortable. We may imagine its routine somewhat as follows: The peasants came with their cloth, often (in the case of linen) principally or entirely made from raw material which the peasant himself had produced, to the town in which the putter-out lived, and after a careful, often official, appraisal of the quality, received the customary price for it. The putter-out's customers, for markets any appreciable distance away, were middlemen, who also came to him, generally not yet following samples, but seeking traditional qualities, and bought from his warehouse, or, long before delivery, placed orders which were probably in turn passed on to the peasants. Personal canvassing of customers took place, if at all, only at long intervals. Otherwise correspondence sufficed, though the sending of samples slowly gained ground. The number of business hours was very moderate, perhaps five to six a day, sometimes considerably less; in the rush season, where there was one, more. Earnings were moderate; enough to lead a respectable life and in good times to put away a little. On the whole, relations among competitors were relatively good, with a large degree of agreement on the fundamentals of business. A long daily visit to the tavern, with often plenty to drink, and a congenial circle of friends, made life comfortable and leisurely.

The form of organization was in every respect capitalistic; the entrepreneur's activity was of a purely business character; the use of capital, turned over in the business, was indispensable; and finally, the objective aspect of the economic process, the bookkeeping, was rational. But it was traditionalistic business, if one considers the spirit which animated the entrepreneur: the traditional manner of life, the traditional rate of profit, the traditional amount of work, the traditional manner of regulating the relationships with labor, and the essentially traditional circle of customers and the manner of attracting new ones. All these dominated the conduct of the business, were at the basis, one may say, of the *ethos* of this group of business men.

Now at some time this leisureliness was suddenly destroyed, and often entirely without any essential change in the form of organization, such as the transition to a unified factory, to mechanical weaving, etc. What happened was, on the contrary, often no more than this: some young man from one of the putting-out families went out into the country, carefully chose weavers for his employ, greatly increased the rigor of his supervision of their work, and thus turned them from peasants into laborers. On the other hand, he would begin to change his marketing methods by so far as possible going directly to the final consumer, would take the details into his own hands, would personally solicit customers, visiting them every year, and above all would adapt the quality of the product directly to their needs and wishes. At the same time he began to introduce the principle of low prices and large turnover. There was repeated what everywhere and always is the result of such a process of rationalization: those who would not follow suit had to go out of business. The idyllic state collapsed under the pressure of a bitter competitive struggle, respectable fortunes were made, and not lent out at interest, but always reinvested in the business. The old leisurely and comfortable attitude toward life gave way to a hard frugality in which some participated and came to the top, because they did not wish to consume but to earn, while others who wished to keep on with the old ways were forced to curtail their consumption. . . .

In order to understand the connection between the fundamental religious ideas of ascetic Protestantism and its maxims for everyday economic conduct, it is necessary to examine with especial care such writings as have evidently been derived from ministerial practice. For in a time in which the beyond meant everything, when the social position of the Christian depended upon his admission to the communion, the clergyman, through his ministry, Church discipline, and preaching, exercised an influence (as a glance at collections of *consilia, casus conscientiæ,* etc., shows) which we modern men are entirely unable to picture. In such a time the religious forces which express themselves through such channels are the decisive influences in the formation of national character.

. . . We can treat ascetic Protestantism as a single whole. But since that side of English Puritanism which was derived from Calvinism gives the most consistent religious basis for the idea of the calling, we shall place one of its representatives at the centre of the discussion. Richard Baxter stands out above many other writers on Puritan ethics, both because of his eminently practical and realistic attitude, and, at the same time, because of the universal recognition accorded to his works. . . .

Now, in glancing at Baxter's *Saints' Everlasting Rest,* or his *Christian Directory,* or similar works of others, one is struck at first glance by the emphasis placed, in the discussion of wealth and its acquisition, on the ebionitic elements of the New Testament. Wealth as such is a great danger; its temptations never end, and its pursuit is not only senseless as compared with the dominating importance of the Kingdom of God, but it is morally suspect. Here asceticism seems to have turned much more sharply against the acquisition of earthly goods than it did in Calvin, who saw no hindrance to the effectiveness of the clergy in their wealth, but rather a thoroughly desirable enhancement of their prestige. Hence he permitted them to employ their means profitably. Examples of the condemnation of the pursuit of money and goods may be gathered without end from Puritan writings, and may be contrasted with the late mediæval ethical literature, which was much more open-minded on this point.

Moreover, these doubts were meant with perfect seriousness; only it is necessary to examine them somewhat more closely in order to understand their true ethical significance and implications. The real moral objection is to relaxation in the security of possession, the enjoyment of wealth with the consequence of idleness and the temptations of the flesh, above all of distraction from the pursuit of a righteous life. In fact, it is only because possession involves this danger of relaxation that it is objectionable at all. For the saints' everlasting rest is in the next world; on earth man must, to be certain of his state of grace, "do the works of him who sent him, as long as it is yet day." Not leisure and enjoyment, but only activity serves to increase the glory of God, according to the definite manifestations of His will.

Waste of time is thus the first and in principle the deadliest of sins. The span of human life in infinitely short and precious to make sure of one's own election. Loss of time through sociability, idle talk, luxury, even more sleep than is necessary for health, six to at most eight hours, is worthy of absolute moral condemnation. It does not yet hold, with Franklin, that time is money, but the proposition is true in a certain spiritual sense. It is infinitely valuable because every hour lost is lost to labor for the glory of God. Thus inactive contemplation is also valueless, or even directly reprehensible if it is at the expense of one's daily work. For it is less pleasing to God than the active performance of His will in a calling. Besides, Sunday is provided for that, and, according to Baxter, it is always those who are not diligent in their callings who have no time for God when the occasion demands it.

Accordingly, Baxter's principal work is dominated by the continually repeated, often almost passionate preaching of hard, continuous bodily or mental labor. It is due to a combination of two different motives. Labor is, on the one hand, an approved ascetic technique, as it always has been in the Western Church, in sharp contrast not only to the Orient but to almost all monastic rules the world over. It is in particular the specific defence against all those temptations which Puritanism united under the name of the unclean life, whose rôle for it was by no means small. . . .

. . . Baxter holds most emphatically that wealth does not exempt anyone from the unconditional command. Even the wealthy shall not eat without working, for even though they do not need to labor to support their own needs, there is God's commandment which they, like the poor, must obey. For everyone without exception God's Providence has prepared a calling, which he should profess and in which he should labor. . . .

The phenomenon of the division of labor and occupations in society had, among others, been interpreted by Thomas Aquinas as a direct consequence of the divine scheme of things. But the places assigned to each man in this cosmos follow *ex causis naturalibus* and are fortuitous (contingent in the Scholastic terminology). The differentiation of men into the classes and occupations established through historical development became for Luther, as we have seen, a direct result of the divine will. The perseverance of the individual in the place and within the limits which God had assigned to him was a religious duty. This was the more certainly the consequence since the relations of Lutheranism to the world were in general uncertain from the beginning and remained so. Ethical principles for the reform of the world could not be found in Luther's realm of ideas; in fact it never quite freed itself from Pauline indifference. Hence the world had to be accepted as it was, and this alone could be made a religious duty.

But in the Puritan view, the providential character of the play of private economic interests takes on a somewhat different emphasis. True to the Puritan tendency to pragmatic interpretations, the providential purpose of the division of labor is to be known by its fruits. On this point Baxter expresses himself in terms which more than once directly recall Adam Smith's well-known apotheosis of the division of labor. The specialization of occupations leads, since it makes the development of skill possible, to a quantitative and qualitative improvement in production, and thus serves the common good, which is identical with the good of the greatest possible number. So far, the motivation is purely utilitarian, and is closely related to the customary viewpoint of much of the secular literature of the time.

But the characteristic Puritan element appears when Baxter sets at the head of his discussion the statement that "outside of a well-marked calling the accomplishments of a man are only casual and irregular, and he spends more time in idleness than at work," and when he concludes it as follows: "and he [the specialized worker] will carry out his work in order while another remains in constant confusion, and his business knows neither time nor place . . . therefore is a certain calling the best for everyone." Irregular work, which the ordinary laborer is often forced to accept, is often unavoidable, but always an unwelcome state of transition. A man without a calling thus lacks the systematic, methodical character which is, as we have seen, demanded by worldly asceticism.

The Quaker ethic also holds that a man's life in his calling is an exercise in ascetic virtue, a proof of his state of grace through his conscientiousness, which is expressed in the care and method with which he pursues his calling. What God demands is not labor in itself, but rational labor in a calling. In the Puritan concept of the calling the emphasis is always placed on this methodical character of worldly asceticism, not, as with Luther, on the acceptance of the lot which God has irretrievably assigned to man. . . .

. . . The Puritan's ferocious hatred of everything which smacked of superstition, of all survivals of magical or sacramental salvation, applied to the Christmas festivities and the May Pole and all spontaneous religious art. . . .

The theatre was obnoxious to the Puritans, and with the strict exclusion of the erotic and of nudity from the realm of toleration, a radical view of either literature or art could not exist. The conceptions of idle talk, of superfluities, and of vain ostentation, all designations of an irrational attitude without objective purpose, thus not ascetic, and especially not serving the glory of God, but of man, were always at hand to serve in deciding in favor of sober utility as against any artistic tendencies. This was especially true in the case of decoration of the person, for instance clothing. That powerful tendency toward uniformity of life, which today so immensely aids the capitalistic interest in the standardization of production, had its ideal foundations in the repudiation of all idolatry of the flesh. . . .

Although we cannot here enter upon a discussion of the influence of Puritanism in all these directions, we should call attention to the fact that the toleration of pleasure in cultural goods, which contributed to purely esthetic or athletic enjoyment, certainly always ran up against one characteristic limitation: they must not cost anything. Man is only a trustee of the goods which have come to him through God's grace. He must, like the servant in the parable, give an account of every penny entrusted to him, and it is at least hazardous to spend any of it for a purpose which does not serve the glory of God but only one's own enjoyment. What person, who keeps his eyes open, has not met representatives of this viewpoint even in the present? The idea of a man's duty to his possessions, to which he subordinates himself as an obedient steward, or even as an acquisitive machine, bears with chilling weight on his life. The greater the possessions the heavier, if the ascetic attitude toward life stands the test, the feeling of responsibility for them, for holding them undiminished for the glory of God and increasing them by restless effort. The origin of this type of life also extends in certain roots, like so many aspects of the spirit of capitalism, back into the Middle Ages. But it was in the ethic of ascetic Protestantism that it first found a consistent ethical foundation. Its significance for the development of capitalism is obvious.

This worldly Protestant asceticism, as we may recapitulate up to this point, acted powerfully against the spontaneous enjoyment of possessions; it restricted consumption, especially of luxuries. On the other hand, it had the psychological effect of freeing the acquisition of goods from the inhibitions of traditionalistic ethics. It broke the bonds of the impulse of acquisition in that it not only legalized it, but (in the sense discussed) looked upon it as directly willed by God. The campaign against the temptations of the flesh, and the dependence on external things, was, as besides the Puritans the great Quaker apologist Barclay expressly says, not a struggle against the rational acquisition, but against the irrational use of wealth.

But this irrational use was exemplified in the outward forms of luxury which their code condemned as idolatry of the flesh, however natural they had appeared to the feudal mind. On the other hand, they approved the rational and utilitarian uses of wealth which were willed by God for the needs of the individual and the community. They did not wish to impose mortification on the man of wealth, but the use of his means for necessary and practical things. The idea of comfort characteristically limits the extent of ethically permissible expenditures. It is naturally no accident that the development of a manner of living consistent with that idea may be observed earliest and most clearly among the most consistent representatives of this whole attitude toward life. Over against the glitter and ostentation of feudal magnificence which, resting on an unsound economic basis, prefers a sordid elegance to a sober simplicity, they set the clean and solid comfort of the middle-class home as an ideal. . . .

One of the fundamental elements of the spirit of modern capitalism, and not only of that but of all modern culture: rational conduct on the basis of the idea of the calling, was born—that is what this discussion has sought to demonstrate—from the spirit of Christian asceticism. One has only to re-read the passage from Franklin, quoted at the beginning of this essay, in order to see that the essential elements of the attitude which was there called the spirit of capitalism are the same as what we have just shown to be the content of the Puritan worldly asceticism, only without the religious basis, which by Franklin's time had died away.

63. The Operation of Ethics in the Underworld

DAVID W. MAURER

"Honor among Thieves" is an expression recognizing that even the underworld has a code of ethics. In this essay we examine some aspects of the behavior of pickpockets in their relation to one another. We find that they do, in fact, have a strong sense of honor in their dealings with one another, and that their mode of life depends upon the fact that their fellows will live up to this code. Of course, this ethic applies only to others of the underworld; the members of dominant society are not accorded any consideration—except, perhaps, those who are really hard up.

David W. Maurer, Professor of English at the University of Louisville, is primarily interested in criminal argot and the linguistic usages of the underworld. He has published a number of works on criminal argots and is currently collaborating on a modernization of H. L. Mencken's *The American Language*. The material presented here is excerpted from a work designed to show how language relates to behavior among a certain class of pickpockets and, though it does not deal with the total range of pickpocket subculture, it provides revealing aspects of their "business ethic." It is taken from *Whiz Mob, A Correlation of the Technical Argot of Pickpockets with Their Behavior Pattern*, Publication of the American Dialect Society, No. 24, University of Florida, Gainesville. It is printed by kind permission of The Society and the author.

The subculture of thieves has a rather full set of mores which govern—or are supposed to govern—their behavior. In some cases—kindness to children or animals, for instance—these mores may be identical, or nearly so, with those of the dominant culture. In others—the belief, for example, that a man who does not protect his money from theft has no right to it—there is a considerable distance between the subculture and the dominant culture. . . .

Probably the heart of the ethics of pickpockets involves the relationship between partners, or among members of a mob. This has evolved throughout the ages, and manifests itself in our own times in the form of different ethics for different levels. . . .

First, among *class cannons* [high-class pickpockets], each pickpocket owes complete loyalty to the mob. If he is not prepared to support them, he has no business *hustling* with them. This support is moral, personal, and—with some limitations—financial. His financial obligations go only as far as his *fall dough* [money held by the mob in case of arrest] would indicate; that is, if he has put up an equal share of $4500 *fall dough* with two other *guns,* he is obligated to the extent of $1500 if any of the three—including himself—has a *fall* [arrest]. When that amount of money is spent, he is free of financial obligation, though of course he still owes his moral support. Even though he is known to have more cash in reserve, or with him, he has no obligation to spend that money to fight the case of another member of the mob. . . .

If a *class mob* agrees to *fill in* a third (or fourth) member, not because he is needed, but because he has just had some bad luck and needs help, each would specify in advance how much *fall dough* he is willing to risk on this *pick up* who will, presumably, be filled in without *fall dough* of his own. Some mobs might refuse to put up any *fall dough* for him, but this is not likely among *class cannons.* They would calculate the risks and estimate what a *fall* might cost. Then they would agree to *go for* him up to a certain conservative limit thought to be sufficient to cover him in any ordinary difficulty. If he should *take a fall,* however, and the fall dough was inadequate, he would have no additional claim against the other members; in fact, he would have received a gift from heaven. If he *beat the rap,* he would recognize an obligation to pay back the *fall dough* put up for him—when he was able to do so; he would owe this money to the mob and would repay it to the men who put it up, or *stood for* it. Even if he got *settled,* he would still have this obligation after he got out of *stir.* While debts of this kind are not always paid, the obligations are there; a *class cannon* recognizes them and pays them; if he does not, his reputation suffers; if he ignores enough of them, he loses his standing as a *class cannon.*

> If you're with a class mob, it's a different thing. Here's another thing. For instance, you pick a guy up. Here's a guy that just got out of stir and you say, "Well, I'll give you a couple days' work." You're already three-handed, and you fill him in and so you're four-handed. Maybe this mob has got six thousands dollars fall dough, two grand

apiece. Now this guy you fill in, this fourth man, he fills in and you fill him in with an understanding to this extent. We'll say, "We're pretty fat, doing all right. We'll give you a couple days' work and we'll fill you in to this extent, we'll go for you as far as $500 apiece. Now you ain't put up your two grand fall dough, you understand. . . ."

Class mobs are almost legalistic in their insistence that all arrangements be understood in advance. Some mobs have a permanent, standing arrangement which all members know and respect. Others vary this arrangement from day to day or even from *score* [act of theft; money or wallet stolen] to *score*. However, the variation must be stated and understood in order to avoid trouble. For instance, some mobs operate permanently under this succinct contract: *in with the grief, in with the gravy,* which means that anyone with *fall dough* up is entitled to his share of all *touches*—even though he may have been delayed, or sick, or otherwise unable to participate in the *action* of the mob. These maxims are also used in the negative. . . .

But what about those times when they are working on their own, *single o?* Those occasions are taken care of by an advance arrangement. One says to the other, "I'm going out for breakfast; want to go along?" "Yes," says his partner, and they go together, knowing that anything they *take off* is to be split equally. But if the partner says, "No," that leaves a problem. Is he *in with the pokes and in with the pinches?* He hasn't said. So the first pickpocket will ask "Well, are you in?" "Yes," he answers, "I'm in." That means that he can lie in bed and sleep while his partner goes down the street to breakfast; if the pickpocket going to breakfast makes a *single o score* on the way, he must give his partner half of it. If, on the other hand, he *rumbles* [alerts] a mark who *beefs gun* [calls the police] and has him arrested, the pickpocket lying upstairs in bed is responsible for his entire share of the *fall dough* if it is needed to *spring* his partner. . . .

Likewise, certain members of any *class mob* may *declare themselves out* on any type of touch which they do not like, or which in their judgment may lead to disaster. A Jewish pickpocket may *declare himself out* while a rabbi is being robbed; he does not collect any share of the proceeds, neither does he risk his *fall dough* if the *fur* should pounce just as the *touch comes off.* A Roman Catholic can do the same when a *buck,* or Catholic priest, is robbed. He avers that he is *not in with the pinches and not in with the pokes.* This ability to *declare* oneself *in* or *out* at will extends throughout the fraternity on a *class* basis, and such *declarations* are respected as binding contracts. However, it should be understood that these clear-cut arrangements do not extend throughout all levels of pickpockets. . . .

Women who are not working with a mob may sometimes travel with them, each girl joining her man after the day's work. (Pickpockets who work together often do not live together, nor do they associate after working hours, except in the case of a man and woman working and living together.) However, this is not common; if a male pickpocket has a nonworking wife, or children, he leaves them somewhere in a house or apartment when he travels out from that center. In the case of *locals,* a house or apartment is maintained more or less permanently in that city. Male pickpockets of the better class—like thieves in general —are very possessive about their women and insist on monogamy—on the woman's part. . . .

Once a woman is recognized as belonging to a certain pickpocket, this relationship is respected by others (excepting those Lotharios who would like to steal her) and if her man *falls* and goes to prison, or cannot work during a considerable period of trial or probation, his partners feel a certain sense of responsibility for supporting her. If the man is broke, his partners or his friends may *pass the sheet* for him. This means that someone circulates through the hangouts and solicits money; sometimes there is an actual *sheet* of paper on which names and amounts are recorded; again, the solicitors simply remember who contributes and tell the man how much was taken and who contributed it.

Among better-class thieves, these *sheets* are considered loans and are repaid if the thief wants to maintain his standing. Among low-class thieves, a *sheet* may be unheard of. Of course there is no legal means of collecting the debt, nor is there any desire to do so, but "bad news travels fast" as the saying goes, and, if a man does not pay back such loans when he is able, they will not be forthcoming again. This is true likewise of money loaned outright from one thief to another, or to a thief by a *fixer* or professional gambler or any other person. To a thief, then, credit is more important than it is to the legitimate citizen, and he tries to keep it in good repair; thieves who do not cannot raise any money when it is needed.

A *sheet* is sometimes passed for a man without dependents if he takes a *wrong rap* (is convicted for a theft he did not perform) or a particularly *rough one* (one carrying an unusually stiff penalty, or giving him an undue amount of trouble and expense). Also, several mobs may *throw a night* for some unfortunate thief, which consists of a beer party or raffle to raise funds. This money may make things easier for him in prison, or it may be used to help defray heavy *fixing* expenses or legal costs. Recipients of such largesse must be duly observant of the code of the *grift,* however, or they lose standing. For instance, a woman or woman with children will be supported if her man is a *class cannon* and goes to prison. This support may come to her from one of several different sources at irregular intervals, usually in the form of money orders or cash. It will continue as long as she does not have anything to do with men; as soon as she "steps out" and the fact becomes known, her support stops, and if her new-found friend does not take over her support, she may have a hard time of it. Fortunately for marital felicity, prison terms for pickpockets are not often long.

Here is an example of how a formerly famous thief lost standing by his behavior following a *sheet passing* which might have been repeated now and then; he is getting old and arthritis has crippled his fingers.

> I don't suppose you have heard of him. He was hanging around and they took up a collection every time he come around. All the guns that were there would throw in a sawbuck or a fin, and he'd say, "My bloody bloomin' fingers is stiff and I can't do no good." And he says, "I'd do the same for you." He'd been all over the world. So he come down there one night, and, son, here's what cooked his goose. And so one gun started off with a quip. He says, "Aw, let's put the ding on him." So they passed the hat around and the guy must have gotten three or four G's. Tens and twenties in the pot. And so they took it and gave it to him. And he goes down on Charity Street or one of those zigaboo neighborhoods. And some gal clipped him for the dough. So what do you think happened? He fingered her and goes to court and testifies against her. And he come down there, and he must have come down there a thousand times after that and he didn't get a dime. Not a dime."

These obligations on the part of professionals are not charity; they are part of the mores of the subculture. Charity is taught toward people in distress (members of the dominant culture included), and thieves feel strong obligation to help crippled persons, blind persons, or others who have had disasters which handicap them in the making of a living. No pickpocket with any principle whatever would rob a cripple or a blind man. One informant told me that he had once inadvertently robbed a blind man. It was in a heavy crowd and he had already *taken off the score* and passed the man when he caught a *flash* of the man's white cane. By the time he found him again, it was impossible to return the wallet without being seen, so he went his way much disturbed. This incident continued to bother him for some years afterward. This attitude toward cripples and other handicapped people is strongly reenforced by superstition, so that the motivation for showing them consideration is not so thoroughly altruistic as it might seem at first glance. . . .

. . . The thief is taught both by precept and example never to *throw his mob,* that is, to betray any of his confederates to the police, or to leave mob members in the hands of the *law* without giving them assistance. There is a strong sentiment against *tipping off* any *touch,* even though it might have been *taken off* by one's enemies, to the *fuzz.* In fact, a thief learns that it is frowned upon to *cop a plea* (plead guilty in return for a light or suspended sentence). Likewise, one should never *tip off the racket,* or tell anyone, especially a member of the dominant culture, how pickpockets operate. "Never wise up a sucker," is the way it is put, and this aphorism is repeated over and over again. It is a cardinal sin to be a *fink* (stool pigeon). . . . If you are going to buy anything, buy something *hot;* it shows solidarity against the dominant culture and, at the same time, helps some struggling thief to stay in business for himself; besides, it is much cheaper, as many a member of the dominant culture has discovered. . . .

XII.
ART

Man's Special Satisfactions

Humanity is never satisfied with the mere practical, however much people must be guided by it. Man everywhere embellishes his life activities with special flourishes which give esthetic satisfaction. Art takes many forms, and in one form or another it is universal.

Why this should be so is not clear. It is not our task here to undertake a psychological or physiological explanation of the universal impulse to create rhythms in sound, movement, or form, or the universal concern with the outer appearance and tonal quality of events. Efforts at such explanations have not taken us very far, and we will be better off if we direct our attention to examining the various aspects of art and to the understanding of the social contexts in which art forms occur.

Nor is there any need to enter into a debate as to what art is. We may simply say that we include here those activities in which man engages (and the product of such activities) because he feels that the shape, sound, color, smell, taste, or movement is particularly satisfying irrespective of its practical usefulness.

We cannot define as art that which we think is beautiful, for no two of us would agree. Nor can we include only those things made simply for their decorative effect, for most products of the artist serve other purposes as well. A practical instrument like a spear or an automobile contains an esthetic element if the maker has endeavored to create it in forms that are satisfying to him and which are not merely a requirement of the instrument. A sacred object like an amulet or an ikon is artistic, though it also serves a religious purpose. A thing is an artistic creation whether we ourselves are pleased by it, so long as it affords esthetic pleasure to those who made it. For art must be seen in terms of the culturally formed esthetic values out of which it stems.

Man has embellished all his sensory experiences: his taste, smell, tactile and kinesthetic, as well as his auditory and visual ones which are given more emphasis. Probably every culture devotes some time to each of these.

Whether or not there are universal canons of taste is a problem for the student of esthetics. Since art relates closely to life activities, one might assume that common human experiences tend to make for recurrent artistic expressions. The basic similarity of the human figure, the recurrent human biological needs for food and sex and the natural rhythms of life activities should call forth a measure of uniformity in esthetic expression. The natural aspects of color—the red of blood, the changing colors of the seasons—might also be expected to have a fairly constant effect upon esthetic meaning.

Art forms from various parts of the world do exhibit the influence of the natural elements. But they are not the essence of art. For esthetic judgments are much more influenced by cultural than by natural experience. Man, as we have repeatedly said, is a symbol-using animal, and the meaning of symbols is always a cultural product. And art is always symbolic: it always expresses more than its explicit content. Since both the cultural experiences and the symbol systems vary from one people to another, artistic expression varies widely. With art, as with life, the basic natural man is submerged in the cultural circumstances in which it appears.

The symbol systems of an art form may be so clear and direct that even a person from another culture can understand them. The *pietà* as an expression of the suffering of Christ (and of humanity) does not require interpretation. The fertility figurines of paleolithic man and the phallic representations of much Australian art often communicate with symbols that are readily understood. But symbols more frequently require some indoctrination, so that they are meaningless to an outsider but clear and seemingly self-evident to those who have grown up in the culture. The totem poles and other conventional art forms of the Northwest Coast are examples of clear but culturally delimited symbols. The serpent and apple in Christian art relate to an elaborate structure of meaning available only to those who know the Book of Genesis.

There is a third level of symbolism, a level of meaning which never reaches explicitness even to those who participate in the culture. Alan Lomax shows that there is a deep-seated, culturally derived meaning in the folk songs that a people sing; that the very pitch and rhythm express deep emotional feeling derived from circumstances in the culture, though the singer is not himself aware of the fact. Freudian psychology sees such latent expression in all art forms. We need not go this far, yet there is reason to believe that artistic expression does appeal to the basic human urges and unconscious culturally derived attitudes. Since the judgment of people with respect to art forms differs, and since cultures tend to hold on to their ideals of beauty, we may well assume that the unconscious aspect in the transmission of culture plays an important role in determining a person's attitude toward art forms. In this sense, esthetic expression is a release of those emotional elements that spring from the culturally conditioned experiences related to basic human needs.

It is perhaps this very element in art that not only makes us respond with emotion to artistic expressions which conform to our own esthetic tastes, but also to condemn those which are alien to our experiences. This is particularly the case with respect to music, and it applies not only to the music of other peoples, but with remarkable frequency to the music of the younger generation. Much of the condemnation of modern popular musical style is expressed in moral terms, as if the latent symbolic content of that music were being responded to and rejected by those generations who do not share the emotional attitudes that the music expresses. To paraphrase: One man's music is another man's noise.

We must conclude, therefore, that whatever universal canons of esthetic virtue may exist are heavily overlaid with the more specific culturally derived sentiments which provide the diversity of tastes and the variety of artistic styles.

There is a further important point here. Our tastes in art are often thought of as mere custom—we like what we are used to and reject the new. While there is truth in this, it is not the whole truth, for we do not merely *like* the customary; we respond to it with emotional conviction that rests upon deep-seated feelings which derive from our cultural experience.

For every art there is both a creator and a public. When we look at a Pueblo Indian pot and see how much it is like other pots from the same village, we tend to think that tradition has created the form and the style; that the individual plays only the role of craftsman. But we must remember, as E. R. Leach points out, that the distinction between craftsman and artist is not meaningful in primitive cultures. To be sure, Pueblo culture, like many folk and primitive cultures, places less emphasis upon the new than we do. Yet Ruth Bunzel makes it clear that the Pueblo potter is an artist who makes every effort to create an esthetically pleasing object; who feels each new vessel as a separate creative act.

Normally the artist and the public stem from the same culture, so that these feelings of esthetic satisfaction have the same basis. Not only do they share underlying emotional orientations of the kind that Lomax describes, but they are attuned to the same symbols and accustomed to the same elements of design. This fact furthers the conservatism of artistic tradition in primitive communities, for the artist is not only limited by his own imagination and perception, but also by the expectations of his public. We have only to consider how new artistic concepts have been greeted in the Western world (even though it is attuned to a wide variety of artistic expressions) to appreciate what force such conservatism can exert.

Despite this conservatism, styles continuously change. This is clear from our own history, but it appears to be true of primitive people as well. For when we dig up the remains of old cultures where there is pottery, which does not deteriorate in time, we always find gradual changes in design elements and forms even when the population has not changed. As a matter of fact, gradual change is so characteristic that merely by counting the proportion of vessels of various kinds in a particular collection one can determine its place in a sequence. In the southwestern United States these changes are so marked that it is possible to distinguish pottery collections only ten years apart.

Cultures differ not only in the nature of their esthetic values, but also in the emphasis they place upon artistic expression. As Covarrubias shows, the Balinese emphasize art in many forms. Carving and painting, dancing, poetry, and drama are extremely important in the everyday life of the ordinary Balinese. Other cultures place far less emphasis upon artistic expression of any kind. The Masai of Africa have practically no plastic arts, though they do decorate their bodies, but have music and dancing. We can see this variation in Western society. For instance, the periods of great French painting and of great German music were periods when these two arts were particularly emphasized in these two cultures. For a long time, esthetic creativity was viewed as unmanly in large sectors of the American culture, so that artists tended to migrate to European centers not only to learn from established masters, but also to dwell in an environment where these activities met with approval. Clearly artistic creativity—or a particular kind of artistic creativity—may or may not be highly valued in a culture. This means that the "artistic temperament" of a people stems from cultural forces, and is not to be viewed as a "racial" attribute, as it once was.

What can be said about the development of art in the course of human history? A century ago, there was a tendency to see art as growing increasingly representational. Though most primitive art does not endeavor to represent reality as seen, and though one might reasonably assume a gradual perfection of the artist's ability to be representational, the stubborn fact remains that one of the most realistic depictions of life forms is found in the oldest-known art style—that of the paleolithic caves of France and Spain. At the same time, these peoples made highly stylized statuettes of the human female. The movement between abstract and realistic representation must therefore be seen as a cultural matter of style and not as an evolutionary development, and certainly not as an evidence of ability to copy nature.

The following artistic activities are found at the most primitive level of culture: dance, song with at least percussion instrumentation, body decoration, oral literature, painting, and carving. All the basic arts are found among preliterate peoples of more advanced culture within the limits of their technical abilities. This again suggests that the development of art is not an evolution of artistic ability as such nor of esthetic sense, but that it is dependent upon other technological advances. Instrumentation requires the knowledge for making the instruments; ceramic arts, the knowledge of pottery making; bronze casting, the metallurgical crafts; monumental architecture, the tools and manpower for handling massive stone. While such requirements are self-evident, we must remember that having the technical knowledge does not necessarily lead to the artistic activity, and that, though all these arts are found on the primitive level, not all peoples engage in these artistic enterprises.

Beyond this, we may also say that the great arts are usually built upon a general cultural advancement that will enable adequate surplus goods to support full-time artistic specialists who can be freed from the daily tasks of food production. Occasionally such specialization appears on the primitive level. Most archeologists believe that the level of craftsmanship in the cave art of Europe was possible only to specialists who were supported as full-time magician–artists. Something close to full time specialization was found among the Indians of the Northwest Coast, who also had a remarkable well-developed art.

The arts of high civilization are built upon craft specialization. This is clearly true of architecture in both the ancient world and the New World; it is true of the statues of Greece, the gold work of the Incas and Aztecs, and the fine bronze and gold casting of West Africa. The artist as a separate category of person, as a man who has a long apprenticeship and then spends his lifetime following the pursuit of his art, may be seen as a relatively late development in human culture; he is a product of high civilization of both the Old World and the New, with occasional forerunners on a more primitive level.

This point about the artistic specialization in high cultures leads us to a classification of the kinds of artistic production which will be useful for understanding art in relation to society; namely, between folk art, professional art, and popular art. By folk art we mean the traditional artistic products made by men specially gifted but created strictly according to ancient (though continuously changing) patterns. It is the art that comes from the people. Among Europeans, it is the native ceramics, weaving, embroidery, and the like that is found in the villages; the dancing in the square and the music that accompanies it. Bunzel, Lomax, and Covarrubias are all describing aspects of folk art.

By professional art we mean the products of the specialist, who has mastered his craft, has devoted a great deal of time to its perfection, and who sees himself as an artist by calling. He will build on traditional patterns, but he makes them his own. He makes conscious innovations, so that the culture's art is changed by his having been there. Though he builds upon tradition, the traditional is for him the starting point rather than the ultimate goal. And his public tends to be a special public of sponsors and connoisseurs. It is the professional artist whom we normally think of as artist (as opposed to craftsman), and it is his products that we usually think of as art with a capital A.

The popular artist is also a professional, but a professional whose work is designed specifically for mass appeal. He is concerned less with influencing the art (and through his art the perception the public has of the world), than he is with the public appeal of his product. He may be thought of as a kind of synthetic folk artist for mass society.

While the distinctions between these categories are not absolute, they do help us to understand and relate different kinds of artistic products. Perhaps this can be made clear with an example or two. The stories collected by Hans Christian Andersen, the brothers Grimm and subsequent folklorists since their time are folk art. They are the product of a culture. Certainly somebody invented them, some tellers embellished them, and some told them better than others. But they were depersonalized; they grew out of the culture and express cultural attitudes. Such folk tales have been built upon by professional artists. Shakespeare, Wagner, Goethe, Sibelius, and most great artists and composers have borrowed from the common stock of folklore, but their rendering is the work of a professional craftsman. It has an individual stamp; its authorship is known; the author's treatment transforms these things into something different.

But the endless output of stories in popular magazines, stories that play minor variations on a recurrent theme—written to sell and publish because the editor knows what his public wants—these are popular art. The stories written by Horatio Alger, which Wohl has analyzed for us, are classic examples of popular art. Religious prints, calendars, *Saturday Evening Post* covers, the design of tract houses, and many other things are popular art of a comparable kind. While popular art is characteristic of modern Western culture, it is by no means limited to it. However, popular art requires a cheap means of mass reproduction by printing, recording, and the like. Cheap religious pictures were printed in Europe before the technique was applied to writing by Gutenberg. (It is said that the theatre is a vulgar art form, for it must appeal to the masses— and it was long the only professional art product that had a mass audience.)

Primitive and folk art have wide appeal today, especially among those very intellectuals who take the view that popular art is not art at all. Yet we must appreciate the fact that popular arts are also important to society and its members, as Wohl makes quite explicit.

The functions of art are both individual and social. What functions it performs depend upon the kind of art and the circumstances in which it appears, and we cannot here enumerate all of its potential functions. To say that art gives esthetic satisfaction is true, but tautological. To the artist, certainly, it gives a sense of creativity and often recognition by his fellow man. To the public, art often gives a sense of new experience, a refreshed view of some aspect of his environment, a sense of communication with others, a release from tension, or erotic stimulation.

Analyses of such popular arts in America as, for example, soap operas indicate that they give the listeners strength to meet their own problems, a feeling that they understand human behavior, an escape from the confinement and dissatisfactions of their own lives.

Art also has a function in society. The cohesive effect of group singing and dancing is an obvious example of the social effect of artistic activity. The symbolism of unity and community provided by the arts has certainly always been one of its major purposes. This is especially true of religious art—as much for primitive man, as Leach makes clear, as it is for modern man. The symbolic importance of architecture for strengthening national ties is equally great.

Art is also involved in the differentiation of status. The totem poles of the Kwakiutl and Tlingit Indians, the carved house fronts of the New Zealand Maori, and the elaborate head-dresses of the Plains Indians each symbolize the status of the owners in their primitive societies. The Egyptian temple, pyramid, and tomb art are examples of conspicuous display, and the whole of Western art has expressed social distinction. It is the prestige of commissioning art for personal or group monuments that seems to have led to the development of professional artists, supported by the largess of their patrons.

Art in all societies is also associated with religious beliefs. Archeologists believe that the cave art of the paleolithic was created as acts of magic to increase game, while the statuettes were concerned with fertility magic. The Australian carves elaborate totem designs which have mystic symbols, he tells elaborate stories of mythical import, and has songs and dance ceremonies of a deeply religious character. And so it goes, from one society to another. In our own history, painting, sculpture, music, architecture, and literature all developed in the context of the Christian church.

Yet, beyond these functional aspects of art, it is difficult to escape the feeling that man engages in artistic production for the satisfactions that it gives him, both in the creating and in the beholding. At least this much must be said: in being an artist man has made something special of himself; has, so to speak, partaken of the gods and enriched his mundane existence.

64. Art in Its Social Context

E . R . L E A C H

The social meaning of primitive art has rarely been examined. Though hundreds of books dealing with the art of one or another people or area have been written and much has been said about their esthetic values, few people have treated the arts from a truly anthropological point of view. Fewer still have examined them in relation to social life. The present essay by E. R. Leach was prepared as a broadcast on the Third Programme of the British Broadcasting Corporation. It was part of a series on social anthropology which has been published under the title *The Institutions of Primitive Society* by The Free Press, Glencoe, Illinois, 1954. It is reprinted here by kind permission of the author, the Free Press, and Basil Blackwell & Mott, Ltd.

Leach received his doctoral degree from the London School of Economics in 1947 having studied cultural change among the hill tribes of Burma and Siam. He has also done research in Ceylon and has concerned himself with a wide variety of problems ranging from kinship organizations and political systems to such matters as primitive time reckoning, as well as primitive art. He is Lecturer at the University of Cambridge.

My primary concern is not "What does primitive art mean to *us?*" but rather "what does it mean to the people for whom it is made?" I want to discuss how far the substance of what the primitive artist "says" and the way he says it to his own community correspond to something with which we are ordinarily familiar with regard to the art of our own society.

First of all: what is primitive art? Even if we ignore altogether the vast field of music and dancing and poetry, and confine our attention to the plastic arts alone, primitive art must certainly still include such varied objects as Bushmen rock paintings, Eskimo drawings on ivory, Fijian prints on bark-cloth, and decorated ancestral skulls from New Guinea; and that is without arguing whether *primitive* is a proper adjective to apply to such relatively sophisticated products as the stone carving of ancient Mexico, the pottery of prehistoric Peru, or the cast metal work of West Africa. Altogether, the variety before us is immense and bewildering.

Now, obviously, up to a point, the form and content of any plastic art is conditioned by the medium through which it is expressed; and in primitive society the medium of artistic expression is partly determined by environment. People who live in tropical deserts are not likely to be expert wood carvers but they may have an elaborate aesthetic of sand drawing. The fact that primitive peoples in different parts of the world have entirely different forms of art must not then be taken to imply that there are fundamental differences of artistic temperament in the different branches of the human race.

However, our European reactions to Primitive Art depend a good deal upon what sort of art it is. When the medium of a primitive art is a substance like sand or bark-cloth which is not an ordinary medium for art in Europe the effect of the finished product upon ourselves is largely neutral; we have no preconceived notions of what the things *ought* to look like, and are not tempted to make judgments as to whether it is good or bad of its kind—we do not expect such art to "say" things which we can understand. But with sculpture it is different. When you or I first encounter a carving from New Guinea or West Africa or British Columbia we automatically see it *as if* it were a work of European art. One may like it or dislike it, but in either case judgment is based on an assumption that the primitive artist is trying to "say" the same sort of thing as European artists try to say. There is also an assumption that the symbolic conventions which a primitive artist uses are essentially the same as those which form the core of European tradition. . . . We tend to fit the concept "Primitive Art" into the traditional European Fine Art categories of painting and sculpture. We expect to be able to understand primitive art as a variant of European art in this restricted sense. Well, let us have it that way. When I talk about *primitive art* you can take me to mean mainly carving in wood, and when I talk about *primitive people* you can take me to mean people who live in the forest and have plenty of wood to carve.

But with this qualification, please. In our society the various arts are conceptually separate—painters and sculptors and poets and musicians and dancers only occasionally integrate their activities as in the staging of a ballet or grand opera. We have come to think of both the practice and the enjoyment of the arts as private pursuits. But in primitive society privacy is seldom valued; the arts are an adornment for public festivity, and on such occasions music, dancing, poetry, and the plastic arts all come together in a single complex. Even if you think of my primitive artists primarily as wood-carvers you must realize that they are poets and dancers as well.

As for the word "artist," I mean by this simply the individual who makes the things which European critics describe as works of art. But you need to remember that the notion of artist is a European one.

With us the artist tends to be a professional specialist. A work of art, even if it is a very bad one, is readily distinguishable. We think of the artist and the craftsman as distinct individuals with quite different technical functions. Even the most hostile critic would hardly describe Henry Moore as a stonemason.

For primitive society this clear distinction does not apply. Among the forest peoples, houses and boats and equipment of all kinds are mostly made of wood. But since saws and iron nails are lacking, the tools and skills required to make a piece of furniture are much the same as those required to make a "work of art." In primitive society the master carpenter and the master sculptor are often one and the same individual. Besides which, such manual skills are often very widely distributed among the population.

One important characteristic which distinguishes primitive society from our own is the relative self-sufficiency of local communities. With us, most of the things we use in everyday life—clothes, furniture, utensils, gadgets of all kinds—have been made elsewhere by people we do not know and by processes we do not understand. But in primitive society trade is much less important; most of the things which people use have been made by local craftsmen by processes familiar to everyone. In a North Burma village in which I lived every adult woman without exception was an accomplished weaver of elaborately brocaded cloth, while every adult male knew all the multifarious techniques of housebuilding. In other words, in this village, weaving for women and housebuilding for men were considered normal and essential requirements, just as reading and writing are normal and essential in *our* society.

Let me pursue this analogy. With us, reading and writing are technical skills used in communication. Writing in particular calls for long training and a kind of precise muscular control which to the illiterate appears uncanny. We have this muscular control because we have been handling pencils and pens since we were about four years old. In contrast, at the age when a European infant starts to play with a pencil, a Borneo Dyak boy starts to play with a knife. By the time the European can express himself reasonably well by writing conventional symbols on paper, the Borneo Dyak can do the same by carving conventional shapes out of wood. In such societies nearly every adult male can carve after

a fashion. Master carvers, of course, are just as rare as are master callig-
raphers in our own society.

The illiteracy of primitive peoples is also significant in another
way. Whereas we are trained to think scientifically, many primitive peoples are trained to think poetically. Because we are literate, we tend to
credit words with exact meanings—dictionary meanings. Our whole
education is designed to make language a precise scientific instrument.
The ordinary speech of an educated man is expected to conform to the
canons of prose rather than of poetry; ambiguity of statement is deplored. But in primitive society the reverse may be the case; a faculty
for making and understanding ambiguous statements may even be cultivated.

In many parts of Asia, for example, we find variants of a courtship game the essence of which is that the young man first recites a
verse of poetry which is formally innocent but amorous by innuendo.
The girl must then reply with another poem which matches the first
not only in its overt theme, but also in its erotic covert meaning. People
who use language in this way become highly adept at understanding
symbolic statements. This applies not only to words but also to the
motifs and arrangements of material designs. For us Europeans a good
deal of primitive art has a kind of surrealist quality. We feel that it
contains a symbolic statement, but we have no idea what the symbols
mean. We ought not to infer from this that the primitive artist is intentionally obscure. He is addressing an audience which is much more
practised than we are at understanding poetic statement.

At this point I must say something about the attitudes adopted by
European art critics, for a number of popular misconceptions derive
from this source.

In any work of art there are, roughly speaking, three distinguishable elements—firstly, the sheer technical skill with which the work is
accomplished; secondly, the qualities of form and overall design; and
thirdly, the metaphysical content of what is expressed. European critics
when they consider a *European* work of art take all three elements into
account; when they consider a *primitive* work of art both the language
of communication and the subject matter of what is communicated are
so strange that they find themselves at a loss. Some writers have assumed
that since they cannot understand what the primitive artist has to say
the primitive artist must be talking gibberish. For example, Worringer,
the German aesthetician whose views are often endorsed by Sir Herbert
Read, has described Primitive Man as "a creature who confronts the

outer world as helplessly and incoherently as a dumbfounded animal," and again "artistic creation means for primitive man the avoidance of life and its arbitrariness, it means the intuitive establishment of a stable world beyond the world of appearances. . . ."

For Worringer, apparently, the idea is that the semi-imbecile primitive produces works of art instinctively without consciously trying to convey anything coherent at all. Clive Bell was once quite explicit on this point. "Primitives," he wrote, "produce art because they must. They have no other motive than a passionate desire to express their sense of form."

Given a romantic hypothesis of this kind the tendency is to idealize the primitive artist as a practitioner of Art for Art's sake. To quote Clive Bell again, "In Primitive Art you will find no accurate representation; you will find only significant form. . . ."

Critics of this school tend to see the primitive artist as an exponent of twentieth-century abstraction after the manner of Paul Klee or Barbara Hepworth.

Others less favorably impressed are equally mystified as to what the primitive artist may be trying to say, but they suspect the worst. Thus Eric Newton, reviewing a London exhibition of African sculpture some years ago, declared: 'The spirit behind it is always the same. It is that of a trapped animal trying to escape by means of magic.'

All that I can say about such opinions is that they are wrong. The primitive artist is in every way as rational and sensible a being as his European counterpart. The great bulk of primitive art is definitely representational rather than abstract. It is intended to be understood. And in the ordinary way it will be understood by the audience for whom it is designed. For the audience for which a primitive artist works is composed of members of his own community steeped in the same mythological traditions as himself and familiar with the same environment of material fact and ritual activity; the primitive artist can therefore afford to communicate in shorthand; symbols have the same basic significance and the same range of ambiguity for artist and audience alike.

It is very different for the European critic who tries to understand primitive works of art. He knows nothing of the religious and mythological background of the objects he is examining. He is therefore forced to concentrate his attention upon form alone. It is this which leads to the kind of misapprehension which I have quoted.

As a by-product of the notion that primitive artists are inspired by instinct, it is sometimes supposed that primitive art is characterized by a startling originality. The reverse is the case. The forms of primitive art are original only in the sense that they are alien to the European tradition; in their own context they are often in the highest degree conventional and academic—originality is an admired virtue among modern European artists; in most primitive contexts it is a vice.

Even as regards our own society, although we value originality so highly, we recognize that individual artists operate within the conventions of an established style, Byzantine, Gothic, Baroque, and so on. But in European art such conventions are unstable, there is always local development which produces further special styles in chronological sequence. Thus in the history of Italian painting Venice comes *after* Florence; Florence comes *after* Sienna. In the European scheme of values each generation of artists is temporally outmoded by the innovations of the next, and this is consistent with the high value which we set upon originality. Analogy with primitive art can be deceptive. All European art styles are, despite their differences, historically related. Even the most revolutionary innovator is, technically speaking, very close to his immediate predecessors; thus today, for example, even the greatest experts are not sure whether they can distinguish a painting by Masaccio from one by Masolino. Thematically also, all European art is related to the common mythological background provided by the Iliad and the Christian Bible. Broadly speaking, the same kinds of symbolism and the same kinds of metaphysical statement recur again and again in every phase of European art. There is no such common background to the innumerable local art styles of primitive peoples. There are regional types; it perhaps makes sense to speak of African Negro art in the same way that one can talk of European art; but it is plainly useless to look for historical connections between the arts of West Africa and those of the New Zealand Maori. In other words, the opposition that I have been making between European art and primitive art is a false opposition. European art ranging over the whole continent of Europe and through a time span of 3,000 years has an essential unity. Primitive art is not a unity at all. Among primitive peoples all over the world each local cultural group has its own esthetic traditions which are peculiar to that group and to that group alone. Just as the European aesthetic is linked with the mythology of Christianity and classical Greece, so the aesthetic of any primitive society is linked with the mythology of its own peculiar religion. It follows that any discussion of primitive esthetic values can only be in most general terms.

In general terms, then, why is the primitive artist an artist? The

answer, I suppose, is "Partly for fun and partly because the public provides a market for his work." Can we say anything about the relation
of the primitive artist to his market? In European societies there have
been, broadly speaking, two kinds of market for the artist's products—
the Church and the private patron, the sacred and the profane. The
two outlets may vary in importance and sometimes partly overlap but
we can think of them separately. In Italy down to about the middle of
the fifteenth century the Church was virtually the only buyer of art,
and art was required to make statements about universal truth. The
Renaissance grandees who later dominated the market had little interest
in universals, but were much concerned with their own reputations. Each
patron endeavored to commission work which would outshine that
sponsored by his rivals. It is clear that this shift in patronage had a
marked influence not only upon the content, but also upon the style
of what late Renaissance artists produced.

Similar factors operate under the conditions of primitive society.
A work of primitive art is much easier to understand if one knows
whether it was designed to display the unity of some religious group or
to assert the prestige of an individual patron.

The principal markets for the primitive artist's products are three:
firstly, the furnishing of religious ceremonial; secondly, the decoration
of the houses, boats, and personal equipment of wealthy and important
persons; and thirdly, the provision of memorials for the celebrated dead
—the last being a category that combines both secular and sacred functions.

Up to a point I think it is possible to distinguish the influence of
these several factors. Take the religious element. Primitive peoples do
not have church buildings that need to be decorated. Primitive religious
art is largely associated with ritual dances and dramas in which the
principal performers represent deities who are identified by traditionally
established costumes. Masks are nearly always intended to be seen by
a crowd of people at a distance, the statement therefore is strident not
intimate, the representation has the stark simplicity and exaggeration
of a poster; its content is heraldic—obvious to the initiated, obscure to
everyone else. It is fatuous to comment on such work as if it were
intended to decorate the corner of a fashionable drawing-room. The
extraordinary forms of many of these masks, the weird combinations
of human and inhuman characteristics, become comprehensible enough
once it is understood that they are intended as representations of supernatural beings. All deities necessarily have some human attributes, for

man cannot conceptualize a divine personality except in terms of his own. But if gods are like men they are also unlike men, and if gods have personalities they are not individual but generalized personalities. The god, it has been said, is a collective representation of the people who make offerings at his shrine. Religious masks are thus an attempt to express an abstract idea in material form.

If we are to go further than that and try to understand the symbolism at all completely, we shall need to know something about the form of the society to which it relates.

Thus many primitive societies are what the anthropologist describes as "segmentary." They consist of a number of distinct groups each of which resembles any other except that each group has a different name, a different territory, and a different set of religious rites. Each such group tends to have its own gods which differ from the gods of the other groups in the system only in name and seemingly minor ritual attributes. In much the same way each English parish has its own patron saint which serves to distinguish it from other parishes. In such a case, then, the significance of the masked dancers is not simply that they represent particular gods; it is further that each particular god also represents the special interests of a particular group of people.

To generalize satisfactorily about the profane aspects of primitive art is much more difficult for there are glaring exceptions to every rule. Yet I think that there is something in the proposition that style in non-religious art serves to express current ethical ideals about the proper relations between man and man. For example, there are societies in which it is asserted as an ideal that all men are equal; there are others where it is taken for granted that men are unequal and that each individual acquires at birth a peculiar unalterable status, and again there are other societies in which although differences of rank are emphasized this is not felt to be inconsistent with a good deal of mobility up and down the social scale. I maintain that there are characteristic differences of artistic expression which go along with such differences of ethical ideal.

Let me try to illustrate the sort of thing I mean. Some of you will be familiar with the totem poles of British Columbia. . . . Covered all over from top to bottom with grotesque and intricate carving. Or perhaps you know the wood-carving style of the New Zealand Maori with its extraordinary elaboration of circular and spiral ornamentation covering everything from canoe prows to door posts. In cases such as these, value seems to be attached to size and complexity and elaboration for its own sake; also there is a tendency to produce decorated versions of everyday objects which are not only flamboyant but technically useless. The adjective "ostentatious" sums up the whole complex. From this point of view these primitive art styles from the Pacific area have much that was characteristic of the artistic taste of mid-nineteenth-century England.

I believe that such correspondences are not altogether accidental. The resemblances in artistic taste reflect common moral values, in this case the moral values of the socially ambitious. For as in Victorian England, the primitive societies of British Columbia and New Zealand were characterized by notions of a class hierarchy coupled with much social competition.

Everywhere there is some intimate relationship between ethics and esthetics and, since ethical systems vary from one society to another, so esthetic systems must vary too. The esthetic values of any primitive work of art are only to be understood in the light of a knowledge of what is thought to be right or wrong or socially desirable by the artist concerned and the patrons who employed him.

65. The Primitive Artist at Work

RUTH L. BUNZEL

An insight into how primitive artists work is provided by Ruth Bunzel in this essay. A student of art before she turned to anthropology, Bunzel worked closely with the Pueblo potters, studying their methods, discussing their problems, and inquiring into their feelings and attitudes about their work. Such intimate knowledge of the primitive artist is not easily gained, and her insights are of particular value. Not only did she pioneer this kind of work, but few have yet followed in her path.

Bunzel took her doctorate in anthropology from Columbia University, where she studied under Franz Boas. Her dissertation was an analysis of pottery making among the Pueblo Indians of the American Southwest and was published as *The Pueblo Potter: A Study of Creative Imagination in Primitive Art*, Columbia University Contributions to Anthropology, Columbia University Press, New York, 1929, from which the present essay is taken. The essay is printed with the kind permission of the publisher.

We are now ready to return to our potter holding in her hands the carefully molded and polished vessel, ready to receive its painted decoration. What will she do with this gleaming white or yellow or black surface? What is in her mind as she turns the vessel over in her hands, studying its proportions with reference to the style of decoration traditional in her group? Up to this point she has been guided wholly by sense and intuition. Her appreciation of form and surface is non-intellectual and non-analytical. But the manipulation of design involves something more. "Anyone can make a good shape, but you have to use your head in putting on the design," as the pueblo potter naively remarks. This same comment has been heard from many women in many different villages and is their recognition of mental processes of different orders. The relative importance of rational and non-rational functions in the creation of these artistic products will become clearer in the following pages. Whether the potter actually constructs her designs intelligently, or merely rationalizes about them, the tendency to analyze is always present. She can always give an *ex post facto* explanation of design, but never of form.

The frame of mind in which the artists approach the problem of decorating a pot may best be described in their own words:

> While I am making a jar, I think all the time I am working with the clay about what kind of a design I am going to paint on it. When I am ready, I just sit and think what I shall paint. I do not look at anything but just think what I shall draw and then when the pot is dry, I draw it. . . . I think about designs all the time. . . . I always know just how it will look before I start to paint. (Zuni.)

> I always know the whole design before I start to paint. (Zuni.)

> When I have finished with the shape, my thoughts are always on the design that I shall put on. Generally I have the whole design in my head before I begin to paint. (Laguna.)

> Whenever I am ready to paint, I just close my eyes and see the design, and then I paint it. (Hopi.)

. . . Only one informant did not "see just how it will look" before starting to paint, although several admitted that their achievements often fell short of their original plan. Of course we must not take too literally the statements of the artists that they never deviate from the chosen plan.

We need only examine pottery to see numerous examples of asymmetries, cases where the original plan is not fully carried out. . . .

The care with which the general scheme of decoration is planned extends also to the adjustment of the design to the field and to the actual painting. Nothing could be further from the truth than the usual picture of the pueblo potter, sitting down and casually covering jars with free-hand designs, with only her instinct to guide her brush. The perfect spacing of decoration on pottery is not achieved in this hit or miss fashion. The potter is fully aware of the technical difficulties of her work, and the greatest care is taken to overcome them. All potters measure the surfaces of their jars in one way or another. They do not use tape-measures and dividers but with their ten fingers are able to take fairly accurate measurements.

> Before I start to paint, I measure with my thumb and finger all around the jar. First I measure for the large designs. If it doesn't come out right, I measure again, putting a small design between the large ones. I know just how it will look before I start. Then I measure with my fingers flat against the jar for the spaces between the different parts and for the thickness of the designs. If I start to paint before it is all measured, then I get nervous that it may not come out right. (Zuni.)

. . . There is a considerable individual variation in the amount of measuring that is done. Some women, such as the one quoted above, measure their designs with great care. She is an old woman,—an expert potter who has been making pottery for about forty years and is thoroughly familiar with all designs. Her method of decorating a water jar was as follows:

First she studied carefully for some minutes the undecorated form, turning it around in her hands. Then she measured hastily with her thumb and middle finger the greatest circumference of the jar. Then she drew in the outlines of the first design, which was to be used four times around the jar. After the first element was completed, she measured it and the remaining space and drew in the second element. The two together occupied a little more than half the space, so the remaining two had to be slightly crowded, but this was hardly perceptible in the finished object. After drawing in outline the fillers and the design on the neck, she went over the whole jar, putting in the detail, such as hatchure, red fillings, etc.

This is the usual procedure among the potters of Zuni, Laguna and

Isleta. At Acoma where a more intricate decorative scheme prevails even more care is used in the planning of the design. Here the usual method is to sketch the designs on the jar in charcoal, erasing whatever fails to please and correcting any errors in spacing.

> First I draw in the design with charcoal, and if it does not look right, I rub it out and draw it over again and if it is not right, I rub it out again and do it over. Sometimes I rub it out two or three times before it is right.

I have seen this method in use, and wherever I inquired, I found it to be the common practice of Acoma potters.

The Hopi women frequently draw their designs somewhere before painting them on pots. The more sophisticated women use pencil and paper, the others use the more primitive implements of finger nails on adobe floors. When I asked one woman whether she first drew her designs on paper, she was rather offended. "No. We draw them in our heads." But further questioning elicited the fact that she drew them on the floor first, "just to see how they will look."

The seriousness of these potters goes deeper than concern with the technical excellence of their products. . . . The importance which they attach to the purely esthetic aspects of pottery design is greater than is ordinarily assumed. Most of these women display the same symptoms which are common to creative artists among more sophisticated people. They all speak of sleepless nights spent in thinking of designs for the pot to be decorated in the morning, of dreams of new patterns which on waking they try and often fail to recapture, and above all, the constant preoccupation with decorative problems even while they are engaged in other kinds of work. The following quotations from a number of different women all illustrate this earnestness. That this is not a pose assumed before a foreigner and a prospective buyer is indicated in a remark made by an expert Zuni potter to me,—the potter being a very matter-of-fact person who was not blessed with the artistic temperament. She laughed heartily at the idea of dreaming about designs. "I never dream about designs. I know some women dream about them, but only the women who don't know how to paint dream about it. I always know just what I want to paint, and so I don't dream about it, and I don't worry about it."

Regarding the sources of design women speak as follows:

> I am always thinking about designs, even when I am doing other things, and whenever I close my eyes, I see designs in front of me. I

often dream of designs, and whenever I am ready to paint, I close my eyes and then the designs just come to me. I paint them as I see them. (Hopi.)

One night I dreamed and saw lots of large jars and they all had designs on them. I looked at them and got the designs in my head and next morning I painted them. I often dream about designs, and if I can remember them, I paint them. (Hopi.)

I think about designs all the time. Sometimes when I have to paint a pot, I can't think what design to put on it. Then I go to bed thinking about it all the time. Then when I go to sleep, I dream about designs. I can't always remember them in the morning, but if I do, then I paint that on the pot. (Zuni.)

I get all my ideas from my thoughts. I think of my thoughts as a person who tells me what to do. I dream about designs too. Sometimes before I go to bed, I am thinking about how I shall paint the next piece, and then I dream about it. I remember the designs well enough to paint in the morning. That is why my designs are better than those of other women. Some people do not think that pottery is anything, but it means a great deal to me. It is something sacred. I try to paint all my thoughts on my pottery. (Laguna.)

I never copy other women's designs. I use all the old Laguna designs. . . . I used to watch my aunt while she made pottery because she was such a good potter. That is how I learned to paint. (Laguna.)

When I am ready to paint, I think how I am going to paint. I pick out pieces from the old village where I have my peach trees and try to get the line of the design and think how it went. I put the pieces together and pick out the best. That is how I learned to paint, from copying the old designs. When I first started to paint, I always used the designs from the old pottery, but now I sometimes make up new designs of my own. I always think about pottery even when I am doing other things. When I dream about designs, I paint them the next day. Whenever I close my eyes, I see the designs right in front of me. When I dream about designs, they are always new designs. When I am ready to paint, I just close my eyes and see the design and then I paint it. The designs just come to me, and I paint them as I see them. Every woman paints differently. (Hopi.)

It is apparent from these few extracts that not only does a great deal of thought go into the creation of these objects, but also there seems to be a definite attempt to make them a vehicle for personal experience. To say, "We paint our thoughts," is common in the villages where designs are clothed with symbolic meaning. But even where symbolism plays no role in decoration, as for instance, among the Acoma and the Hopi, there is nevertheless a strong feeling that each pot is an individual and a significant creation. The condemnation of copying the designs of other women is unanimous. All women denied copying from other potters, and most of them disclaimed repetition of their own designs. Even at Zuni where the inventive faculty is at a low ebb and where choice of design is narrowly circumscribed by prevailing taste, in spite of all this, each pot is approached as a new creation, the decoration of which is evolved only after much thought and inner communings. However much theory and practice may be at variance, there can be no doubt concerning the theory. And strangely enough, it is at Zuni where the ideal is stated with the deepest conviction that it is most frequently violated. This discrepancy between theory and practice in the invention of designs might be paralleled in our own and other civilizations.

The psychological implications of this very simple and rather amusing condition are profound and far-reaching, and rather disconcerting in the light they throw upon the workings of the human mind. There are other factors besides sterility of imagination involved. A woman in all sincerity reproduces a familiar type of ornament, believing it to be something derived from her own consciousness. The decorative content and treatment are long since familiar to the ethnologist; he can analyze the whole pattern into definite well known motives which regularly appear together, and the details of arrangement are those already noted for these motives. An analysis of the material with the potter is illuminating. She is puzzled and somewhat chagrined to have it pointed out that she has used three designs on the jar, although she has frequently expressed a decided preference for four designs. She can offer but one explanation: "We always use three when we make this design." They always *do* use three in this particular design, but of this fact, so striking to the ethnologist, she has never before thought. She is also much interested to have pointed out to her that the particular rim design chosen is invariably used with this body design and one other of similar character, but is never used in association with the very different deer and sunflower design. "Yes, that is right. We always do it that way, but I never thought about it before." As a matter of fact, however much she may rationalize, she has probably never thought about the design, its structure, or its elements, at all. She has experienced it unanalytically as a configuration, just as she has experienced the forms of her vessels.

The design is a constellation of which the essential part is a relationship. The various elements may later be abstracted, as words may be isolated from the sentences of a naive speaker, who for many years has been correctly speaking his native tongue, though innocent of the simplest rules of grammar. In art, as in language, it is not difficult to bring into consciousness these unexpressed feelings for formal relationships.

One important point that is implicit, rather than explicitly expressed in the statements of the women, is the importance of the visual image in the creation of design. Only one woman speaks of shutting her eyes and seeing designs, but it seems safe to infer that all the women who speak of seeing "just how it will look" have a perceptual rather than an intellectual approach to the artistic problem. At Zuni, where principles of design are clearly recognized and where, furthermore, religious ideas are associated with designs, we might expect to find a strengthening of the intellectual point of view at the expense of the more purely esthetic, but so far as our information goes, this does not seem to be the case. Here as elsewhere, sensation and intuition play a larger role than intellect in the creation of design. The very inarticulateness of the artists on all general problems of expression favors a conclusion which cannot be documented.

66. Art and Artist in Bali

MIGUEL COVARRUBIAS

Miguel Covarrubias was both artist and anthropologist. He first made his name as an illustrator and caricaturist and subsequently made an extended visit to the Island of Bali and published a book which he profusely illustrated with his own drawings and with photographs taken by his wife. He later turned his dual interests to a part of his native country and published *Mexico South,* a study of the Isthmus of Tehuantepec.

Bali is an ideal place for an ethnographer—artist. No people known to history or ethnology seem to have placed a greater emphasis upon artistic creativity. Nor are they selective with respect to their arts, for they enjoy dance, drama, and poetry as well as sculpturing and music. Covarrubias, who could see with the eye of the artist and who prided himself on his primitive Indian background, captures the spirit of a Balinese art and its meaning for

Everybody in Bali seems to be an artist. Coolies and princes, priests and peasants, men and women alike, can dance, play musical instruments, paint, or carve in wood and stone. It was often surprising to discover that an otherwise poor and dilapidated village harbored an elaborate temple, a great orchestra, or a group of actors of repute.

One of the most famous orchestras in Bali is to be found in the remote mountain village of Selat, and the finest dancers of *legong* were in Saba, an unimportant little village hidden among the ricefields. Villages such as Mas, Batuan, Gelgel, are made up of families of painters, sculptors, and actors, and Sanur produces, besides priests and witch-doctors, fine story-tellers and dancers. In Sebatu, another isolated mountain village, even the children can carve little statues from odd bits of wood, some to be used as bottle-stoppers, perches for birds, handles, but most often simply absurd little human figures in comic attitudes, strange animals, birds of their own invention, frogs, snakes, larvæ of insects, figures without reason or purpose, simply as an outlet for their creative urge. In contrast to the devil-may-care primitive works of Sebatu are the super-refined, masterful carvings from Badung, Ubud, Pliatan, and especially those by the family of young Brahmanas from Mas who turn out intricate statues of hard wood or with equal ability paint a picture, design a temple gate, or act and dance.

Painting, sculpture, and playing on musical instruments are arts by tradition reserved to the men, but almost any woman can weave beautiful stuffs and it is curious that the most intriguing textiles, those in which the dyeing and weaving process is so complicated that years of labor are required to complete a scarf, are made by the women of Tenganan, an ancient village of six hundred souls who are so conservative that they will not maintain connections with the rest of Bali and who punish with exile whoever dares to marry outside the village.

The main artistic activity of the women goes into the making of beautiful offerings for the gods. These are intricate structures of cut-out palm-leaf, or great pyramids of fruit, flowers, cakes, and even roast chickens, arranged with splendid taste, masterpieces of composition in which the relative form of the elements employed, their texture and color are taken into consideration. I have seen monuments seven feet in height, made entirely of roasted pig's meat on skewers, decorated into shapes cut out of the waxy fat of the pig and surmounted with banners and little umbrellas of the lacy stomach tissues, the whole relieved by the vivid vermilion of chili-peppers. Although women of all ages have always taken part in the ritual offering dances, in olden times only little girls became dancers and actresses; but today beautiful girls take part in theatrical performances, playing the parts of princesses formerly performed exclusively by female impersonators.

The effervescence of artistic activity and the highly developed esthetic sense of the population can perhaps be explained by a natural urge to express themselves, combined with the important factor of leisure resulting from well-organized agricultural cooperatism. However, the most important element for the development of a popular culture, with primitive as well as refined characteristics, was perhaps the fact that the Balinese did not permit the centralization of the artistic knowledge in a special intellectual class. In old Balinese books on ethics, like the *Niti Sastra,* it is stated that a man who is ignorant of the writings is like a man who has lost his speech, because he shall have to remain silent during the conversation of other men. Furthermore, it was a requirement for the education of every prince that he should know mythology, history, and poetry well enough; should learn painting, woodcarving, music, and the making of musical instruments; should be able to dance and to sing in Kawi, the classic language of literature. There is hardly a prince who does not possess a good number of these attributes, and those deprived of talent themselves support artists, musicians, and actors as part of their retinue. Ordinary people look upon their feudal lords as models of conduct and do not hesitate to imitate them, learning their poetry, dancing, painting, and carving in order to be like them.

Thus, not only the aristocracy can create informal beauty, but a commoner may be as finished an artist as the educated nobleman, although he may be an agriculturist, a tradesman, or even a coolie. . . .

Until a few years ago the Balinese did not paint pictures or make statues without some definite purpose. It has often been stated that there are no words in the Balinese language for "art" and "artist." This is true and logical; making a beautiful offering, and carving a stone temple gate, and making a set of masks are tasks of equal esthetic importance, and although the artist is regarded as a preferred member of the community, there is no separate class of artists, and a sculptor is simply a "carver" or a figure-maker, and the painter is a picture-maker.

A dancer is a *legong,* a *djanger,* and so forth—the names of the dances they perform.

The artist is in Bali essentially a craftsman and at the same time an amateur, casual and anonymous, who uses his talents knowing that no one will care to record his name for posterity. His only aim is to serve his community, seeing that the work is well done when he is called to embellish the temple of the village, or when he carves his neighbor's gate in exchange for a new roof or some other similar service. Actors and musicians play for the feasts of the village without pay, and when they perform for private festivals they are lavishly entertained and banqueted instead. Foreigners have to pay a good amount for a performance: from five to thirty guilders according to the quality of the show and the pretensions of the actors; but a Balinese who calls the village's orchestra or a troupe of actors for a home festival provides special food, refreshments, *sirih,* and cigarettes for them. If he pays a small amount besides, from a guilder to five, it is not considered as remuneration, but rather as a present to help the finances of the musical or theatrical club. Whatever money they receive goes to the funds of the association to cover the expenses of the feasts given by the club or to buy new costumes or instruments.

Nothing in Bali is made for posterity; the only available stone is a soft sandstone that crumbles away after a few years, and temples and reliefs have to be renewed constantly; white ants devour the wooden sculptures, and the humidity rots away all paper and cloth, so their arts have never suffered from fossilization. The Balinese are extremely proud of their traditions, but they are also progressive and unconservative, and when a foreign idea strikes their fancy, they adopt it with great enthusiasm as their own. All sorts of influences from the outside, Indian, Chinese, Javanese, have left their mark on Balinese art, but they are always translated into their own manner and they become strongly Balinese in the process.

Thus the lively Balinese art is in constant flux. What becomes the rage for a while may be suddenly abandoned and forgotten when a new fashion is invented, new styles in music or in the theatre, or new ways of making sculptures and paintings. But the traditional art also remains, and when the artists tire of a new idea, they go back to the classic forms until a new style is again invented. They are great copyists and it is not surprising to find in a temple, as part of the decoration, a fat Chinese god or a scene representing a highway hold-up, or a crashing plane, events unknown in Bali, that can only be explained as having been copied from some Western magazine. Once a young Balinese painter saw my friend Walter Spies painting yellow high-lights on the tips of the leaves of a jungle scene. He went home and made a painting that was thoroughly Balinese, but with modeling and high-lights until then unknown in Balinese painting. Artistic property cannot exist in the communal Balinese culture; if an artist invents or copies something that is an interesting novelty, soon all the others are reproducing the new find. Once a sculptor made a little statue representing the larvæ of an insect standing upright on its tail; a few weeks later everybody was making them and soon the statue market was flooded with Brancusi-like little erect worms on square bases.

Unlike the individualistic art of the West in which the main concern of the artist is to develop his personality in order to create an easily recognizable style as the means to attain his ultimate goal—recognition and fame—the anonymous artistic production of the Balinese, like their entire life, is the expression of collective thought. A piece of music or sculpture is often the work of two or more artists, and the pupils of a painter or a sculptor invariably collaborate with their master. The Balinese artist builds up with traditional standard elements. The arrangement and the general spirit may be his own, and there may even be a certain amount of individuality, however subordinated to the local style. There are definite proportions, standard features, peculiar garments, and so forth to represent a devil, a holy man, a prince, or a peasant, and the personality of a given character is determined, not so much by physical characteristics, but rather by sartorial details. . . .

The Balinese obtain their artistic standards of beauty from ancient Java, and for centuries there has been only one way to treat a beautiful face; which they have, curiously enough, come to identify with themselves. Once, discussing the facial characteristics of various races with the Regent of Karangasem, a man of high Balinese education, he asked me how I drew a Balinese. He disagreed with my conception and proceeded to draw one himself, a face from the classic paintings and a type that could not be found on the whole island. Within these conventions, Balinese art is realistic without being photographic—that is, without attempting to give the optical illusion of the real thing. Thus there is no perspective and no modeling in painting, and sculpture is highly stylized. They admire technique and good craftsmanship above other points, and when I showed a Balinese friend a beautiful sculpture

I had just acquired, he found fault with the minute parallel grooves that marked the strands of hair because in places they ran together.

Balinese art is not in the class of the "great" arts like great Chinese painting—the conscious production of works of art for their own sake, with an esthetic value apart from their function. Again, it is too refined, too developed, to fit into peasant arts; nor is it one of the primitive arts, those subject to ritual and tribal laws, which we call "primitive" because their esthetics do not conform to ours. Their art is a highly developed, although informal Baroque folk-art that combines the peasant liveliness with the refinement of the classicism of Hinduistic Java, but free of conservative prejudice and with a new vitality fired by the exuberance of the demoniac spirit of the tropical primitive. The Balinese peasants took the flowery art of ancient Java, itself an offshoot of the aristocratic art of India of the seventh and eighth centuries, brought it down to earth, and made it popular property.

Although at the service of religion, Balinese art is not a religious art. An artist carves ludicrous subjects in the temples or embellishes objects of daily use with religious symbols, using them purely as ornamental elements regardless of their significance. The Balinese carve or paint to tell the only stories they know—those created by their intellectuals, the religious teachers of former times.

67. The Cultural Context of Folk Songs

ALAN LOMAX

Alan Lomax has collected, studied and sung folk music for the past twenty-five years. He is famous for his discovery of Leadbelly, his books on folk musicians, and for contributing widely to the storehouse of recorded folk music. He served the Library of Congress for a while; but left it to collect and study songs in England and on the continent of Europe.

The present essay is more than a description of folk music. It analyzes folk songs in terms of the social context in which they are sung and shows that the intimate music of the folk is tied in with the elemental experiences provided them by their culture. The essay demonstrates the deep involvement of the artistic expression of a people with their cultural characteristics and social system. It is taken from "Folk Song Style," *American Anthropologist*, Volume 61, No. 6, 1959, and is published with the kind permission of its editor and the author.

A song is a complex human action—music plus speech, relating performers to a larger group in a special situation by means of certain behavior patterns, and giving rise to a common emotional experience. At the risk of going over elementary ground, I ask the reader to consider a series of familiar musical situations: The symphony hall, where the audience sits motionless and withdrawn into a rapture of inner contemplation, while on stage a man with a little stick directs the cooperative activity of a hundred musicians, each one with his attention riveted on a page of type; the bedding-ground of a Texas trail-herd, where two weary cowboys rode around the cattle, singing, crooning, talking, keeping up a steady stream of familiar sounds to reassure their nervous charges against the sudden noises and unknown terrors of the night; an African village dance, led by a battery of drums, where a dancing throng dramatizes erotic, hostile, and playful impulses, and one or two choirs sing well-rehearsed polyphony; a near-Eastern bard, his eyes closed, his face contorted with his inner vision, reciting a traditional epic for his village, while a small orchestra provides a repetitious musical ground for the thread of his solo voice.

Other examples would only further emphasize the point that musical reality is three-quarters composed of such materials, and it is therefore unscientific to focus our interest on formal musical patterns torn out of their context (as if music was intrinsically different from other human activities), or upon the precise measurement of particles of sound (as if musicology were a branch of physics). . . .

A musical style is learned as a whole and responded to as a whole by a member of any culture. If some familiar element is absent in a performance, the music gives far less satisfaction. Conversely, the very magic of music lies in the fact that its formal elements can conjure up the total musical experience. An Andalusian gypsy finds it difficult to sing well in his flamenco style unless he is in a bar with wine on the table, money promised, women to clap and dance the rhythms and fans to shout encouragement. Yet a melody hummed at work in an olive grove conjures up this experience to his imagination.

The child begins to learn the musical style of his culture as he acquires the language and the emotional patterns of his people. This style is thus an important link between an individual and his culture, and later in life, brings back to the adult unconscious the emotional texture of the world which formed his personality.

Thus, from the point of view of the social scientist, the primary effect of music is to give the listener a feeling of security, for it symbolizes the place where he was born, his earliest childhood satisfactions, his religious experience, his pleasure in community doings, his courtship and his work—any or all of these personality-shaping experiences. As soon as the familiar sound pattern is established, he is prepared to laugh, to weep, to dance, to fight, to worship, etc. His heart is opened. The amount or kind of rhythmic, melodic or harmonic material then offered him depends upon the musical inventiveness of his culture, but the quantity or excellence of all this does not affect his basic response, so long as it conforms to the musical style that formed him. I have been in villages where one or two tunes brought forth the satisfaction that dozens of melodies did in another place, or that a symphony produced in a city audience. Apparently the character and the variety of the music matters less than its conformity to tradition, which produces a sensation of security. The work of composers in the folk world is, so far as I have observed, limited by this stylistic security-bringing framework.

An art so deeply rooted in the security patterns of the community should not, in theory, be subject to rapid change; and, in fact, this seems to be the case. Musical style appears to be one of the most conservative, if not the most conservative of culture traits. Religion, language, even many aspects of social structure may change; an entirely new set of tunes or rhythms or harmonic patterns may be introduced; but, in its over-all character, a musical style will remain intact. Only the most profound social upheavals—the coming of a new population; the acceptance of a new set of mores—or migration to a new territory, involving complete acculturation will profoundly transform a musical style, and even then the process takes place very slowly. . . .

When I left Spain, I had established in my own mind the possibility that a correlation exists between a musical style and certain social factors, most especially the position of women, the degree of permissiveness towards sexual love, and the treatment of children. I had also begun to see the importance of political and cultural history, but these still seemed of secondary importance to the more basic factors of social structure and sexual pattern. I then prepared to test these tentative conclusions in Italy. To say that the strident falsetto in Andalusia was

Arab and the open voice of the North was Nordic was merely to beg the question—to put it comfortably in the distance. Why then do the Arabs sing in strident falsetto, the Nordics in a more open, deeper-voiced style? A more provocative question posed itself—why was one style acceptable and another unacceptable in a given area?

The main questions that I proposed for my Italian research were: (1) What role did history play in the formation of musical style, and (2) what were the social and psychological mechanisms involved in implanting a musical style in all the individuals of a given region?

Italy proved to be an ideal laboratory for posing these questions. . . . Its equable climate, its fertility and its beauty had attracted invaders for thousands of years. Since the time of the Romans, however, no strong national culture had united Italy, and hundreds of cultural enclaves, some dating back to the dawn of European history, had been protected in the folds of her rough terrain. The early urbanization of Italy had worked for rather than against the preservation of a variety of folk patterns.

Since the high culture of the Italian city states of the Renaissance was based upon the culture of classical times, a high wall sprang up between the life of the townsfolk and that of the peasants, though each city was proud in a rather snobbish way of the peculiarities of its dependent villages. Thus the two-way exchange between city and country which gave unity to the emerging Spanish, French and English national cultures, scarcely disturbed the ancient variety of Italy until modern times.

Italy proved to be a museum of music, as it was of classical art during the Renaissance. For example, the pagan practice of the sung funeral lamentation, which has virtually disappeared in the remainder of western Europe, is still an everyday matter in most rural areas south of Rome. However, when the innumerable culture pockets hidden in the folds of the Italian hills had been taken into account, the main contours of Italy's stylistic map proved to have the same North-South orientation as that of Spain.

THE NORTH (including the Alpine arc, the province of Genoa, the Valley of the Po, and the Northern slopes of the Apennines) is Old European [category of folk singing style]. . . . Dancing and singing is choral, so strongly so, in fact, that song is virtually impossible without a harmonizing group. Polyphony exists in a wide variety of forms, from the seven-part longshoremen choruses of Genoa to the Slavic use of seconds and fourths to the East. Voices are open, clear, bell-like, and deep in pitch; in Genoa, again, basses are more common than tenors.

Singers stand with arms round their cronies' shoulders, or, leaning across a wine-soaked table, blend their voices, smiling at one another benignly over the pleasures of drink, sweet chords and the often bawdy or tenderly sexual verses of their songs. Most songs are short and lyrical in character, but even the ballads of Piedmont and Genoa are performed in chorus and with such a strong beat that it is plain they had once been danced as they were sung.

The open, comradely, tolerant spirit of the North is evident to any visitor who knows the whole of Italy. Where the people work in factories or on big estates, they sing together at work, organize powerful unions, and vote labor at the polls. The courtship patterns are closer kin to those of France or Switzerland or Croatia than of Italy to the South. Contact between men and women is relaxed and friendly, and children, especially in the mountains are treated with respect.

THE CENTER. The Apennines, running in a southeasterly direction to the Adriatic south of the Po Delta, form the most dramatic stylistic borderline that it has been my fortune to encounter. I criss-crossed this hundred-mile-wide mountain barrier at a dozen points, and always found that I passed from one musical style area into another. As one musician, who lived in Northern Tuscany, fifty miles south of choral Piedmont, remarked to me, "It is impossible to organize a chorus in my town. These people simply can't sing together."

Tuscany, Umbria, Lazio and parts of the provinces farther south— this is Italy's Modern European area. Here, song is predominantly solo in performance, with occasional harsh and unblended unison choruses. Singers stand or sit stiffly erect, their throats showing the tension of this vocal delivery, their expression withdrawn, and their eyes often closed— in other words, following a familiar Modern European folk song pattern. The singing voice is harsh or hard and clear, and notably higher in pitch than in the North. The function of the song is to mount the text, even more than in Central Spain, for Tuscan singers favor long, improvised, somewhat satirical verses (*stornelli* and *ottavi*) or present long, melodically dull folk operas (*maggi*). A generation ago, most marriages were arranged between the families of these small land-holders; girls were closely supervised until marriage, and illegitimacy was severely stigmatized. The texts of the countless *stornelli* consist of an allusive, ironic fencing with the opposite sex. One woman told me, "South of the Apennines, the men are wolves, and they wish only to eat you once."

THE SOUTH. The old kingdom of Naples, together with Sicily and Sardinia, is another Italy, and is so regarded by many Italians of the

North. From the point of view of musical style, it is indeed another world. The norm of Southern Italian singing is in solo, in a voice as pinched and strangulated and high-pitched as any in Europe. The singing expression is one of true agony, the throat is distended and flushed with strain, the brow knotted with a painful expression. Many tunes are long and highly ornamented in Oriental style, and in Lucania are often punctuated with shrieks, like the cries of the damned. The universal subject is love, the beauties of women, the torments of courtship, and the commonest song-type is the serenade, of which there are two kinds —the serenade of compliments and the serenade of insults, if a suitor is refused. Laments for the dead are common to the whole area, and a singer from Lucania (which is the area of greatest isolation) moves from a lament to a lullabye to a love song without change of emotional tone. Here, too, sexual jealousy reaches a peak unique in Southern Europe. The presumption is that a man and a woman left alone together for five minutes will have sexual contact, and thus the smallest violation of courtship taboos may stain a woman's reputation so that she will never find a husband. For a person sensitive to the treatment of children, travel in the South is a torment, so slapped and pushed and mistreated are the young people of this Arabicized world.

However, the poverty, isolation and political retardation of Southern Italy have also permitted the survival of many cultural enclaves of varying musical style. Most of these cultural pockets, in which one can hear various types of polyphony, were formed when one or another group of invaders came into the area, and took over a region or built their villages on hilltops. Thus we find chordal singing in the villages where Byzantine Greek is still spoken along the Eastern Coast of Puglia, and again in the Albanian-speaking villages of Abruzzi, Lucania and Calabria. But there may be survivals of a more ancient level of Old European singing style in the strange, shrieked chords of Lucania and Calabria, as in the case of Sardinia, to which we will presently come.

In Italy, as in Spain, history and the social patterns seem to work together. For over two thousand years the South has been dominated by classical (Eastern) culture and exploited by imperialistic governments. The principal invaders, after the Romans, came from Eurasian musical areas—the Byzantine Greeks, the Saracens, the Normans, the Spaniards.

The Center, between Rome and Florence, was formed by the Etruscans, an oriental people of high culture, who apparently brought the *saltarello* with them from the east. Later, the flowering of poetry in the Renaissance confirmed the folk of the Center in their attachment to solo lyric poetry, to improvisation and to the primitive solo-decked Maytime operas of the high Renaissance.

In pre-Roman times, the North was the domain of the Ligurians, who today, at least, are the most accomplished polyphonic folk singers in Western Europe. Celts from the North poured into the Po Valley in the Roman era, and later invaders — the Longobards, the Goths and the Slavs — all came from the heartlands of the Old European song style. Moving across the North, from west to east, one passes from Liguria into French Piedmont, the ballad country of Italy, where ballads are invariably sung in chorus, into an area of Tyrolese and Austrian song and finally into the eastern provinces where Slavic choral singing is found.

One of the most important discoveries of the trip showed a North-South line of Slavic influence which cut across these three Italian musical areas. In the mountains near the Austrian border are small enclaves of Slavic speaking and singing people. The whole province of Friuli has a Slavic cast to its song. In La Marche on the Adriatic coast facing Jugo-slavia, the dominant type of work song is in two parts, harmonized in seconds and fourths, sung with an open, far-carrying tone in the Slavic manner favored in Croatia and the mountains of Bulgaria and Rumania.

Anywhere in the mountains south of Rome one may come upon a community that sings part songs in a Slavic style. The province of Abruzzi, today an island of accomplished modern rural choruses in the Eurasian south, has a coastline closer to Jugoslavia than any other part of Italy, and its oldest choral songs, found on the coastal plain (rather than in the mountains which were once monodic) are Slavic in color. I believe it was by this avenue that the bagpipe and the custom of singing counter-melodically with the bagpipe entered Italy, for one finds this instrument and this practice all along the mountain routes of the shepherds from coastal Abruzzi into Calabria.

Many colonies of Albanians came to Italy as refugees from the Turks in the 13th century. In their villages, scattered through the hills of Abruzzi, Lucania and Calabria, old Albanian dialects are still spoken, and singing is, without exception, in the choral, open-throated, Old European style. Some non-Albanian villages in the South have apparently adopted Albanian style, but it is interesting to note that here the harmony is shrieked in high-pitched, agonized voices, and that the mood is one of torment and frustration as compared to the Albanian. This may be a case of the formal elements of a musical style failing to carry with them their emotional content.

The folk-song map of the South is further complicated by the colonies of Byzantine Greeks in Puglia and Central Sicily, who practice an antique harmonic vocal style that they imported with their Greek Orthodoxy many centuries ago. However, as these villages have been absorbed into the southern pattern of sexual jealousy, the singing is harsh-voiced and strident and so is the harmonic blend.

Finally, I discovered in the mountains between Naples and Salerno, colonies of Saracen origin, people who had fled into the hills when their coastal cities were recaptured by the Christians, and who have preserved intact the music of their North-African forebears. This is, I believe, the only occurrence of purely Arab music in Europe.

To return to the main theme, in every case which I had the opportunity to examine, there is a positive correlation between the musical style and the sexual mores of the communities. The Slavic enclaves of the North are open-voiced and permissive, those of the Center less markedly so, and finally, in the South the Albanian and other Slavic communities stand like islands of feminine independence in the sea of southern jealousy and frustration, though the Eurasian social and musical patterns have altered the Albanian style considerably.

There remains the question of the mechanism which links a musical style to the preference pattern of the individual, and to community mores. I found one answer in an examination of Italian lullabies, some two or three hundred of which are recorded. Southern-Italian lullabies are agonized, sorrow-ridden wails, often hard to distinguish from funeral lamentations. Northern-Italian mothers sing playful baby-bouncing songs, or wistfully tender sleep-songs. An apparent exception seems to emphasize the pattern: in the coastal areas round about Venice, there is a treasure of lullabies in the Southern Italian manner. The Venetian fisherfolk have harsh singing voices and are positively unable to sing polyphonically or to blend their voices. The existence of this Eurasian musical island in the north is explained by the isolated position of this people who took refuge in their pile villages in the lagoons during the invasions from the north. Later, Venice, as the Queen of the Mediterranean, faced east toward its Oriental trading empire.

The distribution of lullabye types in Spain conforms to this north-south pattern, but with a precision that would delight a linguist. From the Andalusian sleep-producing refrain vocable—a high-pitched, nasalized ay-ay-ay—the refrain vowel gradually grows rounder as one moves towards the Old European area, until, in the Basque country, the women signal their babies to sleep with a low-pitched, liquid—oo—oo—oo.

The child in Southern Italy and Southern Spain has its first musical contacts with its mother and its other female relatives. Their voices, as they rock him to sleep or move about their housework, accompany his waking and sleeping hours. And what he hears is a high-pitched voice and a wailing melody, expressive of the tragedy of Southern Italian life, its poverty and its frustrating sexual pattern. The lullabies call on the Saints to protect the little one, born into a harsh and menacing world, and they threaten the irritable child with the wolf who often comes to eat the lambs of the flock.

Lullabies for an Italian woman have direct sexual connotation. At first, unmarried girls flatly refused to perform them for me, overcome with embarrassment at having to sing them to a strange man. The reason for this is clear. The Catholic church virtually interdicts sexual relations except for the purpose of procreation, and since, in theory at least, no unmarried girl has sexual experience and no married woman permits intercourse without childbearing in mind, lullabies are intimately associated with love-making in the mind of the Italian peasant woman.

Now what is the quality of the sexual experience of the Southern-Italian woman? In the first place, as a young girl, she has feared the father and brothers, who jealously protected her and would drive her from the house if they so much as suspected her of making love to a man. In her period of courtship, she feared all men. Carlo Levi says about the peasants of Lucania that they "consider love or sexual attraction so powerful a force in nature that no power on earth can resist it. If a man and a woman are alone in a sheltered spot, no power on earth can prevent their embrace; good intentions and chastity are of no avail. If by chance nothing comes of their propinquity, it is just as bad as if something had come of it, because the mere fact of being together implies love-making. . . ."

The Southern-Italian girl knows that there is no trick or deceit to which her hungry and predatory admirer will not descend for a sexual contact. She also knows that he will regard her as a whore if she yields to his sexual desires, and that her chances of marriage, her only career, may thus be forever closed.

In the minds of a Southern Italian there are two idealized feminine categories—the madonna, the virginal mother figure, and the prostitute. If he has any actual sexual experience in his youth, it is likely to be with the prostitute. He comes to the bed of his inexperienced madonna flushed with wine and the repressed passion of a long engagement—a feeling that is closely akin to anger. Little wonder that so many Southern Italian marriages are sexually infelicitous, and that the man goes back to his cards and to his prostitutes, after dutifully siring his children, leaving his nagging madonna to wail out her frustration in her lullabies, and add her sorrowful feminine notes to the love songs she heard on moonlit nights. For now she is in prison. Even though unfulfilled sexually, worn out by hard work and childbearing, she will seldom attempt to escape her marriage. Divorce is forbidden and separation in this patriarchal community means condemnation to concubinage or slavery as a servant. Is it any wonder that the women of this land wail their children to sleep? The women bear the heaviest burden of pain in this Southern-Italian world, bled white by the Romans and exploited since then by corrupt and rapacious feudal systems.

This is the social and psychological background of the singers who shape the musical preference pattern of the babies of Southern Italy. Their wailing voices blend with the child's first experiences of love and affection, the satisfaction of his need to be fed, cleaned, kept warm and cuddled. When he grows up, he finds no reason to change his emotional perspective. The mother, who is pressed by church law into a succession of exhausting pregnancies, has a new baby in her arms and refuses the older sibling. When the child is obstreperous, he is severely punished or slapped and then may be covered with passionate caresses by a mother to whom he represents the whole of life's satisfactions. I have never seen children so harshly treated as in Southern Calabria and in Sicily, nor have I ever encountered such timorous little girls and such mischievous, maddening little boys.

Girls from an early age must stay at home to help their mothers. The idea of free play or long schooling for them is unthinkable. As soon as they begin to mature, they are housebound and guarded like so many potential criminals. The boys, on the other hand, have little or no organized sport, and spend their time standing in the streets and piazzas with the older boys, being cuffed and tormented and, in turn, cuffing and tormenting the smaller ones. During their adolescence they burn with frustrated desire, for contact is forbidden with the girls they yearn for. There are no dances, no parties, and unless a girl is engaged, she cannot even go to the movies with her young man. Thus Southern Italy has become famous for the beautiful eyes of her women, eyes which can say everything in a glance. Thus your young Italian, summoned by the burning glances of the girls, stimulated by wine, by the sun, by a culture whose only folklore deals with love in the most passionate and romantic terms, is left to burn in the piazza. He becomes a silent hunter, waiting and hoping for the moment when he can catch a girl unaware, or briefly reach a haven in the arms of some complaisant married woman. In this culture, no man can really trust his friend, for to leave one's wife or fiancée alone with another man is far too risky.

Thus the whole society of Southern Italy comes to share in varying degrees the sorrows and frustrations of its housebound women. And there is almost literally nothing else in the folk poetry of this area but yearning for unattainable love, love songs which the males sing in voices almost as high-pitched and falsetto as their mothers', sending through the barred windows a vocal sign of their identification with the emotional problems of their imprisoned sweethearts.

But, you may ask, is high-pitched, strident singing necessarily a musical symbol of the burning pain of sexual starvation? It appears to me that this is so, for people sing in this fashion in all the areas in which women are secluded, owned, exploited, and thus never can trust or be trusted completely by their men. . . .

. . . When a human being, especially a female, is given over to agonized grief, she emits a series of high-pitched, long, sustained, wailing notes. Even grown men sound like little children when they howl in sorrow. Then the head is thrown back, the jaw thrust forward, the soft palate is pulled down and back, the throat is constricted so that a small column of air under high pressure shoots upward and vibrates the hard palate and the heavily charged sinus. An easy personal experiment will convince anyone that this is the best way to howl or wail. Then, if you open your eyes slightly (for they will automatically close if you are really howling), you will see the brows knotted, the face and neck flushed, the facial muscles knotted under the eyes, and the throat distended with the strain of producing this high-pitched wail.

This is quite an accurate picture of the Southern Italian or Andalusian folk singer. This is what the Southern Italian or Spanish child learns in the cradle and in the kitchen, and later uses for abstract expressive purposes, recalling feelings of infant love and security. The proof is that everyone in the culture sings or tries to sing in this way. Not only do mature women howl or wail when they sing, but also do most of the men, especially the most highly esteemed singers. It is rare to find a low singing voice among Southern Italian men. Tenors with a falsetto quality are the rule. And this is the tale of Tunis, Egypt, Arabia, Persia, of the raga singers of India and of all the lands where women are the chattel slaves of high culture.

I come now to a final example which sharpens this cartoon of Italian musical styles. In the central mountains of Sardinia there is a small area said never to have been conquered by the Romans. The population live a quasi-tribal life, pasturing their flocks on communal land, resisting the modern Italian government, as they did Imperial Rome. In fact, they are celebrated brigands who make travel on the roads unsafe after dark, and frequently carry out raids on neighboring villages. Yet I was told that passion murders due to jealousy rarely occur amongst them. Women, as clan members, are not the slaves of their husbands, and infidelities and sexual irregularities are talked out between families.

Sard lullabies often run to the lilting rhythm of the *ballo tondo,* the primitive Sardinian circle dance, and even in the funeral lamentations, the voices of the mourning women are low-pitched and husky. The men, who practice the art of song to the exclusion of every other art and whose songs transmit the tribal lore, sing and dance together in a line with arms linked round each other's shoulders. Their voices are pitched so low that, in the Italian context, you think at once of Zulu singing style. All songs are choral and the choruses are composed of baritones, and basses, sounding a polyphonic, lively bass figure as their song-leader (sometimes a tenor) tells his story. Their harmonic system is unique in Italy and in Europe, and indeed, seems to be one of the genuine prehistoric musical traits that has survived intact in modern Europe.

Coastal Sards sing in modified Hispano-Arabic style, in high-pitched strident voices, mostly in solo, even though their accompaniment is the most elaborate polyphonic instrument produced in the Mediterranean—the Greek *aulos,* called in Sardinia the *launneddas,* which is in effect, a triple clarinet.

The bassy song style of Central Sardinia is linked, in my mind, with the polyphonic music of Liguria, and in both areas one finds a permissive attitude towards sex, more equality for women, tenderness for children, and many mementos of a primitive communal life. Indeed, I have come to feel that these areas belong to an Old European culture pushed back into the mountains and surrounded by the onrush of Oriental civilization, which overwhelmed and shattered most of the older tribal societies, and made chattels of the women, and brought in its train a folk-art of strident monody. The Catholic church, also oriental in origin and in musical preferences, sustained this monodic pattern, indeed for centuries resisted polyphonic influences from the North with all its strength. In the mountain Sard we have, perhaps, an indication of the kind of life and the kind of music that existed in Europe before high culture came from the East.

68. The Function of Myth in Modern Society

R. RICHARD WOHL

Myth is a form of art. It is the oral folk literature of preliterate societies. Like other forms of art, it conveys the attitudes and feelings of a people; but because it is formulated in words it can convey these sentiments more directly. Modern man also has his myths. We have come to want each story to be—or appear to be—new, but the basic elements in our popular stories tend to be the same. In this essay, Wohl finds two Horatio Alger myths: the nineteenth-century one created by Alger himself, and the current one created by modern businessmen. In the very differentiation of these two myths, we can see how popular literature performs a function in society.

R. Richard Wohl was Associate Professor of the Social Sciences in the College of the University of Chicago and an Associate on the Committee on Human Development in the Department of Sociology, when he died in 1957. He had been trained at New York University and at Yale in economics and took his doctorate in social science at Harvard. He initiated a study of the social history of Kansas City under a Rockefeller grant. The essay, which appeared in *Class, Status, and Power* (Reinhard Bendix and Seymour M. Lipset, eds.) published by The Free Press, Glencoe, Ill. (1953), is printed with the kind permission of the publisher.

Every year, the American Schools and Colleges Association polls thousands of "college leaders" to select a few men for public acclaim who have risen from humble origins to great success. When the final tally discloses the names of these fortunate few, they are summoned to New York City to receive the Horatio Alger award. Great businessmen and potent industrialists interrupt their affairs to gather for the ceremony. They are tendered a banquet in the course of which each is presented with a bronze plaque testifying that he has "climbed the ladder of success through toil and diligence and responsible application of his talents to whatever tasks were his." Newspaper photographers snap their pictures, press releases are handed out, and the next day's newspapers hold up the winners as the cynosure of a nation's admiring eyes.

Horatio Alger, in whose name these honors are dispensed, is himself not described in the newspaper accounts. His title to fame is casually taken for granted, although his reputation rests on a long shelf of books written for children, all forgotten, all out of print, all of them often and roundly condemned by literary critics and historians. To the continued bafflement of these accredited intellectuals who regard the preservation of literary reputations as their special province (and who, incidentally, have been expecting Alger's reputation to exhaust itself for the past fifty years) his glory will not down.

Of Alger's many works, not one survives to be widely read today. Contemporary opinion has judged them all to be dull, vulgar and trashy. Alger himself had never claimed them as works of art or great discernment but he had hoped, at least, that they would be edifying. Present day adult opinion condemns them as positively pernicious to right-thinking boys and girls. The children for whom these books were intended have no opinion in the matter: they have not read Alger, could not easily obtain a copy of one of his books even if they wished to do so. When they get one, they are bored with it. . . .

Yet, Alger found fifty million readers for his books in the United States, and labored all his life to keep pace with an insatiable demand for more of his novels. When he died, in 1889, he left behind him a Horatio Alger industry: New York publishers kept hacks at work turning out successful imitations of his stories as long as the market demanded them. (The last such book was copyrighted in 1904.)

This, it might be thought, from the standpoint of hindsight is paradox enough for one man; but Alger's greatest glory awaited him when he had died and his works had disappeared from the nation's bookshelves. Just as he was mocked and execrated by the literary men as a trifler and bungler, another set of intellectuals elevated him to the status of philosopher and moralist. As recently as 1948, Harold Laski, in analyzing American democracy, found this country's workers "living in a state of psychological coma embodied in Horatio Alger," so hypnotized by his optimistic creed that they could not properly define or adequately struggle for what was held to be their class interests. David McCord Wright, writing in 1951, selected "the Horatio Alger 'rags to riches' story" as one of the small bundles of beliefs which, he felt, formed the underlying faith of American capitalist democracy. This trite plot formula, frozen into a host of clumsily written novels, has many times been picked out by shrewd observers as characterizing a fundamental and crucial aspect of American culture.

What, then, is the Alger "rags to riches" saga? Like every proper legend, recalled in nostalgia, transmitted by hearsay, and buffeted by changing circumstances it exists in two versions: its present form (much altered from the original) and its first version.

In its latter-day phrasing it is solemnly reported in textbooks as a national by-word. The Horatio Alger hero is described as

> A boy who was born in the slums of a great city with a very low social position, becomes a bootblack, works hard, applies himself to his studies, saves his money, and rises through sheer effort to a position of social, economic and occupational importance.

Yet a careful study of Alger's novels shows that the message of the stories he wrote, and the deeds he commemorated, do not follow this pattern at all.

With few exceptions (the memory of which faded as the list of Alger's works grew longer) his heroes are not slum children. On the contrary, they are well-brought-up, comfortably nourished middle-class boys, the sons of property owners with substantial social reputation. Originally, the heroes come from farms and rural villages to the city to seek their fortunes; they are country-bred. They are rendered physically and socially mobile by person or family misfortune. Typically, the father of the hero has died recently and the boy is devoting himself to supporting his mother. An evil, merciless "squire" holds the mortgage on the family home and threatens to foreclose and dispossess the widow. The hero, thrown on his mettle, goes off to the city to earn enough to forestall this unfortunate outcome.

While purposefully ambitious, he surrenders none of the careful middle-class socialization by which he has been reared to boyhood. He is conspicuously clean and courteous (many of the city boys he meets are dirty and rude); he speaks perfect English with irreproachable diction (he never picks up city street slang); unlike city boys, particularly unambitious city boys, he does not drink, smoke, or indulge in frivolous pastimes. He helps the weak, is as charitable as it is in his power to be, and contrives to keep his disposition sunny and winning.

He is, however, strong enough to stand up to a bully; shrewd enough successfully to match wits with the sharpers and scoundrels with which the city teems.

Established in the city, the hero proves his resolution and self-reliance by finding a low-status job, with poor pay, by which he barely manages to maintain himself. Alger with a rare faithfulness to reality portrays the hero's plight with sympathy and accuracy. The boy makes enough to live on and no more: the slightest extravagance or indulgence is punished by immediate want. Alger heroes, like good middle class boys, improve their minds with good books and live in clean, moral boarding houses, but they save no money; it is impossible for them to accumulate enough to form a little capital that might be pregnant with fortune, because they have no money to save.

For a time, the hero continues to work hard, keeps clean and cheerful, courteous and calm. He is firm in his belief that honesty is the best policy and ambition is sensible; but he remains poor. In Alger's world, success and redeemed ambition depend on proper sponsorship, and our hero makes no headway at all until he finds a benefactor. And, unwittingly, without planning or foresight, he is suddenly rewarded. He performs a noble deed. Down a busy street a pair of maddened runaway horses will come careening, in the carriage behind lies a terrified little girl. Our hero will rush out, drag the horses to a halt, and restore the sobbing child to her father. Or, he will leap (like *Ragged Dick*) from a ferry-boat into New York harbor and save a child from drowning in the bay; or he will catch a thief (like *Frank the Bond Boy*). Alger's expedients are inexhaustible.

The noble deed accomplished the grateful parent (or the affluent merchant, often the sponsor is both) will confront the hero swearing eternal gratitude. "My brave boy," says Mr. Roswell to Ragged Dick when his daughter is restored to him, "I owe you a debt I can never repay." Trained Alger readers will immediately recognize this for the rhetorical flourish that it is. Immediate, tangible evidences of this acknowledged obligation are forthcoming. The hero will invariably get a job in his patron's business where, under his watchful and grateful eye, the reader is assured that he will progress upward and onward to fame and fortune. When the hero is in dire financial straits (most are) there may also be an outright gift of money (usually $5,000 or $10,000) which serves to lift him and his kin out of the reach of want until he can make his way to permanent prosperity. (One of the first things the hero usually does to celebrate his good fortune is to buy a nice, new suit and a watch.) In many of the stories the reader is assured in a final, editorial paragraph that the hero and the sponsor's daughter will one day marry—and presumably inherit.

Alger himself admitted the quandary into which such solutions thrust him. The moralizing, the resolute virtue, and the steady application did not bring reward (and as a good Puritan moralist, it was perhaps necessary for Alger that pay-off and virtue should be decently separated) but rather unpredictable and unearnable luck. Alger avoids the logical dilemma raised up by this turn of events by admitting it in a puzzled and bemused fashion. Frank the Bond Boy after much unrewarding and dreary work as a messenger, with a pittance for wages, captures a thief and reaps a rich reward. "Frank did not exaggerate his own merits in the matter," Alger reports. "He felt that it was largely due to luck that he had been the means of capturing the bond robber." "However," concludes Alger gravely, "it is precisely to such lucky chances that men are often indebted for their advancement."

In final contradiction to the modern version, the original form of the Alger story stops significantly when the hero has his foot on the first rung of the ladder to success. Having employed a *deus ex machina* to give his hero the needed leg up, Alger leaves room open for the continued exercise of virtue to make the initial success permanent and to justify its ultimate consummation.

We may now address ourselves once again to the involved paradox of Alger's literary reputation: how to account for his great, initial success with an audience of millions, the subsequent disappearance of this audience, and the puzzling phenomenon of his resurgent fame after his books had disappeared from view.

The period of Alger's greatest popularity coincided with the filling up of the nation's cities. Farm boys by the millions, seeking wider horizons and enlarged opportunity, left the farms on which they had been born to take up an urban existence. Alger became the apostle of this migration.

Alger helped define the aspirations of those boys—to make money, to get ahead, to make good—he described for them the experience which they were bracing themselves to undertake. His city (he mainly wrote about New York) was accurately described with a loving attention to authentic detail. It teems with people and traffic. It is a busy place, full of strange and various sights: colorful, noisy and knowing. His heroes may have always triumphed over the villains; but the tricksters, the criminals and confidence men, the drunkards, loafers and urchins were all truly and fully depicted. Their jargon was faithfully rendered; their follies and bad habits exactly catalogued.

His books, in addition, were full of practical and minute information about how one lived and worked in a city once one got there. One could learn from such a novel what kinds of boarding houses there were, and what was fair value in shelter; there were careful lists of the prevailing prices of food and clothing, utensils and amusement; an audience eager for just this kind of practical counsel snapped up these books as fast as they were printed.

Even if we did not know from other sources that Alger's books were addressed to youngsters in the hinterland, we might fairly infer it from an inquiry of what city life meant to the urban boy who actually lived in a slum because he was born there, had low status, and worked as a bootblack or match boy. Even in Alger's day there were too many such boys already in the cities for even that sanguine age to promise much opportunity or hope for advancement. These city boys—the unredeemed gamins in his novels—were systematically encouraged by benevolent urban philanthropists to forsake city life, to go West, and try to set up as independent farmers! . . .

The city boy, wry, hardened and wise in the ways of the seamy side of slum life found no prophet at all in Alger. Had they been asked, they would have told Alger that his image of the city's life was already obsolete for many of those he was inspiring.

For Alger's audience at large, living away from the metropolis and not knowing the true state of affairs there, Alger's message was reinforced by some of the most potent and irreproachably respectable public opinion of the day. Protestant ministers had for decades addressed the fathers and mothers of the young people for whom Alger wrote and their message was identical with his. Sound morals in a sturdy character was the whole equipment for success in life, it was urged. The imputation of poverty or failure to social conditions or prevailing institutions was a wicked falsehood, a positive evidence of evil. So persistent was this message that, 1889, the very year in which Alger died, heard the first voices of exasperated protest against this dogma. "If you tell a single concrete workman on the Baltimore and Ohio Railroad," wrote Richard T. Ely, economist and reformer, "that he may yet be president of the company, it is not demonstrable that you have told him what is not true, although it is within bounds to say that he is far more likely to be killed by a stroke of lightning."

The press, like the pulpit, echoed the same message that Alger sent out to his young folk. Popular novels, like pulpit oratory, reflecting metaphors which were fast growing obsolescent, preached the gospel of thrift, hard work, and endurance. In one such novel, representative of many, a young lady of unblemished character noted for her delicate sentiments finds occasion to say (and to be applauded for saying): "In the laboring class, property is a sign of good morals. In this country no one sinks to deep poverty except by vice, directly or indirectly." The ambiguities in the qualifying phrases for long escaped careful scrutiny.

Alger's original contribution to this tired controversy was to inject it into a new dimension. While the other great juvenile writers of his day—Oliver Optic, Edward Ellis and Henry Castlemon—were producing adventure tales full of pirates, cowboys and Indians, and war heroes Alger cut down this adult theme to fit the needs and understanding of children. In doing so, he had behind him the combined efforts not only of much articulate and expounded public opinion, but he geared his tales in with the very injunctions that many parents were giving their children to fit them for life as grown men and women.

His success was founded, too, in the solid example afforded by the many men who had started with nothing and built a fair fortune by their own exertions. In Alger's native Massachusetts, a list of rich men was published in 1852 when Alger was himself a young man, which described the 1,257 men in the state who possessed property worth $50,000 or more. The origin of their wealth could be traced for some 1,092 of these rich men. No less than 775 are described as having begun poor or nearly so; 342 inherited their wealth or gained it through marriage; 140 farmers are listed of whom many were self-made but precise details are not given by the author.

Alger reported a common fact from the time of his own youth to an age already markedly different from the one in which he had grown up. For many opportunity was narrowing, industrialization and wage work offered a slim base for advancement for those employed in the shops and factories, although even then much room was left for the determined and the canny. It is revealing, however, that Alger dragged in luck rather than occupational strategy, not to explain success, but to explain how an aspirant got a foothold on the upward path. Alger's patrons interestingly enough are merchants not industrialists, another obsolete element in his outlook. His boys are not child laborers in factories but street-traders, messengers, shop-clerks.

As the cities filled, and a realistic picture of urban life became more general; as the face of industrialization was discerned in unfettered, un-controlled growth, Alger's audience fell away in disbelief. By this time, millions of his books had been sold and read: the popular magazines had scattered his stories broadcast through the land. His name, his catchy titles, the skeleton of the plot he had endlessly repeated in his novels, remained behind in the memories of those to whom he had once been an inspiration. By word of mouth they carried his fame further than even his books could reach.

The Alger saga, it has been remarked, "is almost too simple to believe, but oddly moving too." It is this capacity to inspire and excite which has kept Alger's name and fame alive even after his stories have collapsed under their simplicity—their uncritical, naive optimism. Their theme has universal appeal. In all ages, the disadvantaged hero struggling against odds, bearing witness to aspiration, but finally redeemed by success is a folk figure everywhere rejoiced in. It is not surprising, there-fore, that a story cognate to this universal theme survives. All that was required for it to survive in association with Alger's name was that it be edited and revised to fit new conditions. In its modern version, the snug congruity between the altered legend and the changed circum-stances is achieved. The new hero is a slum boy making his way in the modern world.

69. The Esthetic Experience

FRANZ BOAS

Franz Boas was the dominant figure in anthropology for many years and his concept of the field and his theoretical writings remain a major contribution to anthropology. Having trained in his native Germany, he early turned to anthropology and as a young man made a field investigation of Eskimo cul-ture. Most of his research, however, was devoted to the Northwest Coast and particularly to the Kwakiutl Indians. His voluminous writings cover practically every field of anthropology from art and folklore to the nature and meaning of race. Most of the first generation of American anthropologists were trained by him, so that he influenced anthropology as much through teaching as by his writings.

Boas was one of the first anthropologists to make a detailed study of the artistic outlook of native peoples. His volume, *Primitive Art*, was first published in 1927 and has recently been reissued by Dover Publications, Inc., New York. In this book he deals with the formal elements in art, representative art, symbolism and style, and then turns to a detailed analysis of the art of the Northwest Coast of North America and the character of primitive literature, music and dance. In the essay reproduced here he deals with the meaning of art and character of esthetic appeal in man; it is reprinted by kind permission of Dover Publications, Inc.

No people known to us, however hard their lives may be, spend all their time, all their energies in the acquisition of food and shelter, nor do those who live under more favorable conditions and who are free to devote to other pursuits the time not needed for securing their sustenance occupy themselves with purely industrial work or idle away the days in indolence. Even the poorest tribes have produced work that gives to them esthetic pleasure, and those whom a bountiful nature or a greater wealth of inventions has granted freedom from care, devote much of their energy to the creation of works of beauty.

In one way or another esthetic pleasure is felt by all members of mankind. No matter how diverse the ideals of beauty may be, the general character of the enjoyment of beauty is of the same order everywhere; the crude song of the Siberians, the dance of the African Negroes, the pantomime of the Californian Indians, the stone work of the New Zealanders, the carvings of the Melanesians, the sculpture of the Alaskans appeal to them in a manner not different from that felt by us when we hear a song, when we see an artistic dance, or when we admire ornamental work, painting or sculpture. The very existence of song, dance, painting and sculpture among all the tribes known to us is proof of the craving to produce things that are felt as satisfying through their form, and of the capability of man to enjoy them.

All human activities may assume forms that give them esthetic values. The mere cry, or the word does not necessarily possess the elements of beauty. If it does so it is merely a matter of accident. Violent, unrestrained movements induced by excitement; the exertions of the chase and the movements required by daily occupations are partly reflexes of passion, partly practically determined. They have no immediate esthetic appeal. The same is true of all products of industrial activity. The daubing of paint, the whittling of wood or bone, the flaking of stone do not necessarily lead to results that compel our admiration on account of their beauty.

Nevertheless, all of them may assume esthetic values. Rhythmical movements of the body or of objects, forms that appeal to the eye, sequences of tones and forms of speech which please the ear, produce artistic effects. Muscular, visual and auditory sensations are the materials that give us esthetic pleasure and that are used in art.

We may also speak of impressions that appeal to the senses of smell, taste and touch. A composition of scents, a gastronomical repast may be called works of art provided they excite pleasurable sensations.

What then gives to the sensation an esthetic value? When the technical treatment has attained a certain standard of excellence, when the control of the processes involved is such that certain typical forms are produced, we call the process an art, and however simple the forms may be, they may be judged from the point of view of formal perfection; industrial pursuits such as cutting, carving, moulding, weaving; as well as singing, dancing and cooking are capable of attaining technical excellence and fixed forms. The judgment of perfection of technical form is essentially an esthetic judgment. It is hardly possible to state objectively just where the line between artistic and pre-artistic forms should be drawn, because we cannot determine just where the esthetic attitude sets in. It seems certain, however, that wherever a definite type of movement, a definite sequence of tones or a fixed form has developed it must become a standard by which its perfection, that is, its beauty, is measured.

Such types exist among mankind the world over, and we must assume that if an unstandardized form should prove to possess an esthetic appeal for a community it would readily be adopted. Fixity of form seems to be most intimately connected with our ideas of beauty.

Since a perfect standard of form can be attained only in a highly developed and perfectly controlled technique there must be an intimate relation between technique and a feeling for beauty.

It might be said that achievement is irrelevant as long as the ideal of beauty for which the would-be artist strives is in existence, although on account of imperfect technique he may be unable to attain it. Alois Riegl expresses this idea by saying that the will to produce an esthetic result is the essence of artistic work. The truth of this assertion may be admitted and undoubtedly many individuals strive for expression of an esthetic impulse without being able to realize it. What they are striving for presupposes the existence of an ideal form which the unskilled muscles are unable to express adequately. The intuitive feeling for form must be present. So far as our knowledge of the works of art of primitive people extends the feeling for form is inextricably bound up with technical experience. Nature does not seem to present formal ideals, — that is fixed types that are imitated, — except when a natural object is used in daily life; when it is handled, perhaps modified, by technical processes. It would seem that only in this way form impresses itself upon the human mind. The very fact that the manufactures of man in each and every part of the world have pronounced style proves that a feeling for form develops with technical activities. There is nothing to show that the mere contemplation of nature or of natural objects develops a sense of fixed form. Neither have we any proof that a definite stylistic form develops as a product purely of the power of the imagination of the workman, unguided by his technical experience which brings the form into his consciousness. It is conceivable that elementary esthetic forms like symmetry and rhythm, are not entirely dependent upon technical activities; but these are common to all art styles; they are not specifically characteristic of any particular region. Without stability of form of objects, manufactured or in common use, there is no style; and stability of form depends upon the development of a high technique, or in a few cases on the constant use of the same kind of natural products. When stable forms have been attained, imaginative development of form in an imperfect technique may set in and in this case the will to produce an esthetic result may outrun the ability of the would-be artist. The same consideration holds good in regard to the esthetic value of muscular movements used in song and dance.

The manufactures of man the world over prove that the ideal forms are based essentially on standards developed by expert technicians. They may also be imaginative developments of older standardized forms. Without a formal basis the will to create something that appeals to the sense of beauty can hardly exist.

Many works of art affect us in another way. The emotions may be stimulated not by the form alone, but also by close associations that exist between the form and ideas held by the people. In other words, when the forms convey a meaning, because they recall past experiences or because they act as symbols, a new element is added to the enjoyment. The form and its meaning combine to elevate the mind above the indifferent emotional state of every-day life. Beautiful sculpture or painting, a musical composition, dramatic art, a pantomime, may so affect us. This is no less true of primitive art than of our own.

Sometimes esthetic pleasure is released by natural forms. The song of a bird may be beautiful; we may experience pleasure in viewing the form of a landscape or in viewing the movements of an animal; we may enjoy a natural taste or smell, or a pleasant feeling; grandeur of nature may give us an emotional thrill and the actions of animals may have a dramatic effect; all of these have esthetic values but they are not art. On the other hand, a melody, a carving, a painting, a dance, a pantomime are esthetic productions, because they have been created by our own activities.

Form, and creation by our own activities are essential features of art. The pleasure or elevation of the mind must be brought about by a particular form of sense impression, but this sense impression must be made by some kind of human activity or by some product of human activity.

It is essential to bear in mind the twofold source of artistic effect, the one based on form alone, the other on ideas associated with form. Otherwise the theory of art will be one-sided. Since the art of man, the world over, among primitive tribes as well as among civilized nations, contains both elements, the purely formal and the significant, it is not admissible to base all discussions of the manifestations of the art impulse upon the assumption that the expression of emotional states by significant forms must be the beginning of art, or that, like language, art is a form of expression. In modern times this opinion is based in part on the often observed fact that in primitive art even simple geometrical forms may possess a meaning that adds to their emotional value, and that dance, music and poetry almost always have definite meaning. However, significance of artistic form is neither universal nor can it be shown that it is necessarily older than the form.

XIII.

SOCIETY

A Summing Up

Having begun with the concept of culture, we close with a discussion of society. If man lives by culture, he lives in society. And his living in society dictates what must be a part of his culture.

Society may be defined as the community of persons who share a culture and feel themselves in some important way to be a unit. It is through this association among men that man gets his strength, for society is necessary to preserve culture, as culture is necessary to maintain society. Though the terms culture and society are often used interchangeably, they refer to different things: culture is the way of acting, the body of tradition, the learned behavior of a society; a society is the body of personnel who interact with one another in a regular manner and who share a culture that sets this mode of interaction. Though they are separate things, they are interdependent.

This interdependence is of such a kind that each influences the character of the other. Surely what the boundaries of any society are is set by its tradition, while cultural modes influence the interaction that takes place within the boundaries of each society. Yet the fact of social life not only requires that there be tradition but places specific demands that require elements in that tradition.

What are these requirements? Broadly, they are the need for those elements discussed in the several intervening chapters—or most of them. There must be communication and specifically the communication of behavior to the oncoming generation; there must be groups, among which must be groups for nurturing the young; there must be definitions of status and role, particularly roles which allocate the responsibility for control of community action; there must be a common sense of values, a system of understanding the world and man's relationships in it, and there must be ideas of right and wrong as general guides to conduct.

Social existence requires these elements, though it does not require that they take one form or another. Families may, as we have seen, place emphasis upon the marital couple or the lineal descendants, upon the maternal line or the paternal; but the regulation of intersexual relationships and the orderly care of the immature is demanded of all social systems. A society may place emphasis upon individualism or cooperation (though it must leave room for both) in its value system, but it must have a set of values which orient and give meaning to life. And so on.

The general characteristics of all social systems are set forth in the essay by Redfield which follows in this section. It offers a summary of what we have covered in this volume, placing each part in an orderly presentation of the character of social life.

Though we can see these elements of commonality among all social systems, clearly not all societies are alike.

Every society operates within a set of conditions, determined basically by the physical environment in which it exists and the technical knowledge it has at its command, with which to cope with that environment. In academic terms, it operates in an ecologic setting. This ecological setting places further demands on the society; that is, places limitations on the way in which the society operates. Some of the examples presented below make this point, but it is worth developing here. Where a tribe lives by hunting and food gathering in an extremely poor environment, food-sharing institutions are necessary. Without them, the man who killed an animal could not use it up before it spoiled, while others would be starving. Since such peoples have a hard time getting enough to sustain life as it is, they cannot afford this waste. Though food-sharing institutions exist, they take different forms. Among the Andaman Islanders there is such a strong emphasis upon generosity that no man would fail to give away the large and better part of the pig or dugong he has killed. Among the Arunta of Australia there is no value placed upon generosity but, by customary law, a man is simply expected to give certain parts of the animal to particular relatives. On the other hand, societies with large populations do not need such institutions—they can afford to let people starve to death if it is within their ethical system to do so.

The Eskimos, the Bushmen of the Kalahari, the Australians, or many other peoples who live in bleak environments where it is necessary to be constantly on the move in search of food, practice infanticide. It is quite clear that they do this because they have to. The description of this practice among the Bushmen of the Kalahari desert given by Elizabeth Marshall Thomas in her *The Harmless People,* makes it quite clear that this infanticide is necessary and that, though it is sanctioned by custom, it is a painful experience for those mothers who become pregnant while still carrying a child in their arms.

Such examples are not limited to the most primitive circumstances. For instance, wherever political states have come into being, they have certain general features which appear to be necessary for the maintenance of a political system under relatively primitive circumstances. Thus, among preliterate people, and often among peoples with writing, states always are supported by religious institutions and the belief that the ruler has a special relation to the gods which legitimizes that rule. He also has an army at his command. Only after political systems are firmly established can they forego the former of these organizational devices, while apparently they can never entirely escape the latter. As I have also pointed out, modern industrial society requires elaborate training institutions to develop and maintain the complex equipment of its highly technical economy. We need not multiply examples.

Despite the different demands of various economic conditions and social circumstances, despite the great variety of cultural forms that are found throughout the world, there is nevertheless a common core of cultural uniformity. It is this universal element in human behavior which Murdock discusses. To what degree these must be viewed as a product of basic human needs and human psychology, to what degree they are a product of the fact of social existence and the requirements of social life, and to what degree they stem from the common core of human history, is a matter not yet fully known. They do, however, suggest the basic unity of mankind.

70. How Human Society Operates

ROBERT REDFIELD

Robert Redfield combined anthropological and sociological research, though his early training was in the law. At the time of his death he was Robert Maynard Hutchins Distinguished Service Professor at The University of Chicago, where he had taught continuously since he took his doctorate there in 1928. He is chiefly known for his study of the folk cultures of Mexico—his dissertation was on the village of Tepoztlan—and of Guatemala. In later years he increasingly gave attention to problems in the development of civilization. He has written widely on the character of folk societies and the relation of the primitive community to the larger society. Much of his writing has been in the philosophical vein, though always closely rooted to detailed anthropological knowledge.

In this essay he presents a general outline of all social systems, indicating the functions they must perform and their characteristic elements. The essay is from *Man, Culture, and Society,* edited by Harry L. Shapiro. © copyright 1956 by Oxford University Press, Inc. Reprinted by permission.

A society is people with common ends getting along with one another. A brawl in a barroom is not a society, nor is there yet a society when ten exhausted shipwrecked sailors clamber up on a lonely beach— at least there is none until they begin to work out their common problems of getting a living and of living together. A society has, then, organization. It is people doing things with and to and for each other to the interests of each and all in ways that those people have come to accept.

In this sense a group of boys organized to play baseball or to exchange postage stamps is a society, but here we have in mind those societies in which people are organized not for some special purpose or interest, but for all the business and pleasure of living. The societies that are the subject of this chapter are composed of men and women and children living together, generation after generation, according to traditional ways of life. Such societies are whole societies, in that they exist for all human needs and interests. They are enduring societies in that children are born and raised to become adults with ways of life much like those of their parents and grandparents. A nation is such a society, and so is an Indian tribe. So, too, is a town or village, and even a single family in so far as its members have traditions that are transmitted to each succeeding generation and make that family, through time, distinguishable from other families. On the other hand groups of nations taken together are great societies; one speaks of Western society in contrast to Oriental society. In some sense all the people of the world taken together constitute a single society. But it is of the separate tribes and nations that we are chiefly thinking here. Because there have been and still are so many and so various primitive societies, one learns a good deal about society in general by referring, as will be done in this chapter, to one or another of these simple societies.

A society is easily seen as people doing work. It has other aspects, too. A society is also people sharing common convictions as to the good life. This is to say that it is not merely a system of production and of services—an anthill is that—but that a human society exists in the fact that its members feel that certain conduct is right and other conduct wrong, and act more or less accordingly. And a third aspect of human society is to be recognized in the sentiment its members have of belonging together as against other people who do not belong. A society is people feeling solidarity with one another.

In every society the work is divided. Everyone takes advantage from work done by others of a kind which he does not do and in exchange serves those others by doing useful things that are not done by them. The division of labor between men and women is universal, in that everywhere what women do is on the whole different from what men do; on the other hand what each sex does varies with the society: in Polynesia the men did the cooking; among the Hidatsa Indians the women did the farming. Equally obvious is the division of labor that goes with differences in age. Beyond these bases for the organization of work, there are those which depend on differences in temperament, or on training, or on the accidents of opportunity, or on the variations in demand.

In some small, isolated, primitive societies there is almost no division of labor except between the sexes and the age-groups, and except for some individuals who act as magicians or as leaders of ceremonies. Every adult man does about what every other does, and so it is with women. With the development of tools and techniques, with increase in population, and with the advancement of communications and transportation, the division of labor has become far more complete and complex. In the Guatemalan village of San Pedro de la Laguna, fifty-nine different kinds of specialists are to be recognized in a population of less than two thousand. A classified telephone directory suggests but by no means completely lists the thousands and thousands of kinds of specialists that make up a modern city.

An obvious result of this increasing division of labor is the increasing ease in the number and kinds of commodities and services which people can enjoy. But another effect is to limit the view which any one individual has of the operations and goals of his society to a very small segment of the whole, with corresponding difficulties for industrial management, for democratic government, and for personal happiness. Another result is greatly to extend the number and distribution of people who divide labor with one another. Millions of people, from China to the Congo to Akron, come to depend upon one another for services and products exchanged, and yet these people have no common purposes and understandings; they hardly know that one another exist. The organization of work tends to become worldwide while national and other local groups distrust, dislike, or fear one another. So men come to depend upon one another while yet without common sentiments and values.

The organization of work takes place in ways other than the mere division of labor. Slavery is a way of organizing work. The market, to be discussed below, is another way. And a third, perhaps the basic form of the organization of work, arises from the fact that in a society people share common sentiments and beliefs as to what it is good to do. People work, not only because in most cases they are uncomfortable or even starve if they do not, but because work is a part of the meaning of life. To the primitive agricultural Indian, farming is a necessary part of decent and appropriate human existence, an essential way of maintaining relationship with the supernaturals, a test and duty of honorable manhood. In such a society one prays as one works, and work is, in part, religion. In aristocratic societies of recent times on the other hand, work was appropriate only to the underprivileged masses; while in modern Western society work is again a general positive value, and men work for wealth and power and to excel their neighbors.

The more general statement to make about society is that it consists of a plan of life. Society operates because its members have around them a universe which to them makes sense. Moreover, this plan is not merely a pattern without moral meaning: it is a plan for right conduct, an organization of conceptions as to the good, the true, and indeed the beautiful. The body of conventional meanings that are made known to us through acts and artifacts is by anthropologists called "the culture" of a community. In the primitive societies the "wholeness" of these meanings is more easily seen than in the case of large, complex, and rapidly changing societies. The customs and institutions fit together to make a single moral representation of the universe. The Papago Indians, for example, carry on warfare not as an opportunity for exploit separate from their other interests. The Apache scalp taken in a foray is the symbol of the supernatural power brought to the Papago camp by the warrior who killed, a source of spiritual strength, a form of divine power, solemnly to be welcomed into the camp, into the home of the killer. When the men are away on the expedition, the women and children, by abstaining from noisy or indecorous conduct, in effect share in the making of war, just as, in some primitive societies, men share in the importance and responsibilities of childbirth by "lying in"—by restricting their behavior for the welfare of the newborn child. Labor is divided, but all members of the society act in terms of common conceptions and ideals. Commonly the myths of such a society are narrative representations of its moral values, as its ceremonies are dramatic expressions that correspond. So every culture is a provider of a course of action for the individual, a source of his motives, and validater of his convictions.

This is the way a simple and isolated society operates. But as societies have become larger and rapidly changing, with many different kinds of people in them, the customs and institutions no longer preserve this unity and harmony. There is then no single culture for all, even in one nation or town, but rather a great many incomplete cultures, so that what a man does at his office or in his factory is not always closely related to what he does when he plays or goes to church or visits the neighbors—if he does visit them. And what his children do and believe may be notably different from what he himself was brought up to do and believe. Then the sense of the meaning of life tends to be lost; men experience uncertainty, insecurity, and confusion. On the other hand as this happens men more and more come to think rationally and critically about the life around them and to act intentionally to change and to guide it. Science develops, along with rational administration and planning. The basis for the operation of society thus tends to shift, over the course of human history, from tradition to deliberate social invention and thoughtful choice.

A society also operates by virtue of the confidence its members feel in one another and of the loyalty they have to their own group. It is said that the dangers of a great war between the present great powers of this earth would be quickly averted if Mars would attack this planet. Perhaps it would be sufficient for us earth-dwellers merely to know that there were Martians. We would feel a new sense of solidarity for all fellow earth-beings as contrasted with those inferior or iniquitous Martians. At any rate it appears that the members of every society, small or great, think very well of themselves as contrasted with the members of comparable societies. What is seen on a small scale in gangs, appears again in nations. Every tribe and nationality, in some parts of the world every valley or cluster of hamlets, refers to itself in favorable terms and to others unfavorably. Many primitive tribes reserve the term for "people" or "human beings" to themselves alone, while everywhere the terms used to refer to neighboring peoples are contemptuous, derogatory. It would seem, indeed, that the resentment and scorn shown toward other peoples are strongest with regard to neighboring people, as though, as Sigmund Freud remarked, one could least well bear to see what is so much like oneself and yet so different.

In cases where one society is divided into subgroups, each with its own loyalty, but yet a loyalty subordinated to that of the entire tribe or nation, this fact of appreciation of the lesser in-group and depreciation of the out-group contributes to the effective operation of the society. There is a special kind of strength in a tribe divided into clans, for each clan is a warm and supporting intimate group for every individual within it; its limited solidarity is intensified by the contrast and competition with other clans. A similar effect is brought about by the grouping of colleges within a university, and perhaps was realized among the nations of Europe in the nineteenth century, when all the nations were held together by a degree of common tradition and by common commercial and banking interests, so that national pride flourished while wars were limited to moderate destructiveness.

This sense of common membership, pleasant in itself and often referred to as *esprit de corps,* increases the effective operation of the society by making it possible for its members to withstand difficulty and defeat and to act together powerfully for the common good. Then we know it as morale. The sentiments are unifying when they attach to the same single society, or are qualified by limited attachments to balanced component units, as just indicated. The sentiments may, however, attach to groupings which cut across societal lines, and then may have a divisive effect. In-group sentiments may attach to religious group-ings, or to racial groupings. When Christendom was a political and regional community as well as a religious community, the loyalties to the brotherhood of Christians as contrasted with infidels, however un-christian these loyalties were, may have served the solidarity of that part of the world that was Christian, as corresponding sentiments united the Islamic world, but the prejudice and conflict between Jew and Chris-tian within a modern nation is disruptive of that nation. The disposi-tion of a society or part-society to seek a basis for a revived solidarity in an intensification of hatred of some other group than itself is illus-trated by the anti-semitism, anti-Catholicism, or anti-foreignism of groups threatened or insecure in many a land in modern times. As a technique of waging war on an enemy, thus to be weakened by intensi-fying the ethnic and religious hostilities within it, the general principle was well understood by Hitler and Goebbels, as it is also employed for special advantage by occasional rousers of the masses everywhere. In peacetime also a nation may suffer when the in-group sentiment ex-cludes some of a man's fellow citizens and neighbors, as appears in the racial prejudices of modern times, and especially in the prejudice and intolerance directed by white Americans or South Africans to Negroes. In these cases a large minority or even majority of fellow citizens are excluded in great measure from both the privileges of citizenship and from the sense of group solidarity corresponding to the nation. The result is a loss in man power, material and spiritual, for the dominating group is itself weakened by the unresolved inconsistency between its professed ideals and its evident practices. In these cases, then, the restriction of group-sentiments to only those racially qualified is to be recognized, in appraising the working of the society, as unfavorable to the effective operation of the nation. . . .

. . . The division of labor was emphasized as a universal method for organizing work. This aspect of the operation of society may now be examined more fully. The division of labor does bring it about that the whole society realizes the advantages of having some people do some things well through their freedom from necessity to do other things. But this is not all there is to the social organization of economic activity. In every society it is also necessary to determine, somehow, what resources shall be used in producing what products. How shall products and consumable commodities be distributed, and to whom? Who shall consume what commodities? The organized ways of accomplishing these ends may be called the economy of that society. The technology is the tools and techniques for producing and making useful things; the economy is the institutions and customs that get raw materials into products and that get both distributed and consumed. . . .

The basic form of economy in human societies is a status economy. In primitive societies most of the production—whether by hunting or by farming or by raising cattle or by handicraft manufacture—is brought about not because somebody sees a chance to make a profit in some market, but because it is part of the traditional status of that man or woman to hunt or farm or make baskets. And what is made is shared with others according to status. In many South Pacific societies a man works, not to feed his own children, but to feed his sister's children; his own children will be fed by his wife's brother. In certain hunting tribes it is usual for the hunter to give certain parts of the slain animal to just certain relatives—perhaps eight or nine different parts go, respectively, to eight or nine different relatives. So goods are distributed and consumed. These are reciprocal exchanges according to status: what a woman's brother gives to his sister's son is balanced by what that same man, as sister's son, gets from his own mother's brother, in the long run, and on the average. It is also common for goods to be distributed in status economies by the gathering of these goods in one place and by their distribution to all from this center. In a certain Melanesian community every gardener brings some of his best yams and puts them into the chief's yam house. They are "given" to the chief. As the large and beautiful yams pile up, the villagers take satisfaction in the richness and industry of their own community; the abundance of the chief's yams redounds to the credit and glory of all. At a certain festival, the chief distributes these yams, some to visitors, and some to the villagers themselves. So everyone participates, in both the pride and the eating. In many simple societies there is neither money nor market. The whole society is, in respect to this matter of the economy, like a family; the status relationships determine production and distribution. The medieval manor had an economy which was largely a matter of status.

In contrast with this is that economy which depends upon the market. For the beginnings of the market economy in primitive societies we must look outside of the local society to its relations with other societies. The beginnings of human social living must be thought of as taking the form of small groups scattered over a territory and pretty much isolated from one another. The relation between such groups is not ordinarily one of warfare. Organized aggressive violence against a neighboring society is not characteristic of the very simplest societies. Many such societies get along with one another in a more or less friendly way: both societies recognize customary visits, without hostile intention, from one to another. An occasional invader from the outside may be killed, but the formal visit is expected and is received without violence. Many such visits are the occasion of the exchange of goods.

More commonly, in primitive societies, people from one community pay a visit to another community, taking with them goods produced by the visitors and wanted by those visited. Then goods are exchanged, partly by barter, and partly by exchange of gifts. Something is given in the expectation that something will be given to the giver by the one to whom he gives. It is an equivalence of good will, rather than of precise market value, that determines the transaction. So in such a market personal relations, and the status of guest and host, affect the exchange. In larger communities, where people do not know each other personally, and more goods and more kinds of goods appear, the market may be more fully a matter of an effort to sell at the highest price and to buy at the lowest; then buyer and seller alike "shop around," and who the man is who buys or sells does not matter as compared with the opportunity to get the best price. Such a market can to some degree operate by the exchange of one sort of good for another, but money, as a universal measure of value, is an enormous help in facilitation of market exchanges. In some societies incomplete money appears: in some Melanesian communities certain strings of shell beads are used only in payment for pigs or wives. But in other places metal hoes or copper axes or coined metal or engraved certificates of promises to pay both serve as tokens of value that measure the value of one article against all others in the market, and also provide a way of temporarily holding buying power from one market or opportunity to buy to another.

In most societies of the world, and through most of human history, the production and distribution of goods has taken place chiefly as an aspect of the status relationships of the society: the market has been not the central mechanism for making society work, but a special or peripheral part of it. In modern times, and especially in the western world, the market became much more important. In our society the effort of the laborer is to a considerable extent bid for and offered to the highest bidder and the use of land, paid for as rent, also enters into market competition. Now markets are very wide; for some goods, like wheat and rubber and tin, the market is worldwide; and, with rapid and universal communication, and with the machinery of banking and credit, what goes into production where and what goes where to what consumer are matters that the market "decides," rather than status and moral custom. So, in our society, the operations of the market have a principal and even determining influence on all sorts of affairs. Many a worker must live where the opportunity to get a job determines, and if suddenly the produce he makes ceases to be wanted, he may have no livelihood at all, and perhaps cannot keep his family together; in parts of the world men starve because the market no longer needs their labor. Where a family goes to live, perhaps its own solidarity, perhaps even whether its members live at all, follow from what happens in an immense impersonal market, and the actions of a nation, from its form of government to its remaining at peace or its going to war, may be shaped by what happens in markets. . . .

Among the common understandings which constitute the ultimate basis of society are those which attach to things that may be used, enjoyed, or disposed of. Where the understandings limit or otherwise define such rights and obligations of one individual or one group as to others, we speak of "property." Property operates to keep use and enjoyment and disposal in expected channels; it contributes to the working of society in wide and far-reaching ways: to confer and to limit power and the basis for getting more power; to serve as a criterion for status; to provide motives for effort. Wanting to own things, men may work, steal, or go to war. Owning things, men may enter social groups otherwise barred to them, exercise influence over political decisions, or assume correspondingly great responsibility for serving the common good.

Property is thought of most immediately in connection with such tangible goods as tools, automobiles, houses, and land. It exists also, with respect to such intangibles as magical spells, power-inducing songs addressed to supernaturals, hunting and fishing rights, patents and copyrights. In some societies personal names are owned in that they may be disposed of by sale or gift; in our society, a trade name may be registered and so owned. On the whole, the conceptions of ownership have become more complex with the developing complexity of society. Land, in particular, has become subject to private and exclusive ownership, with rights of sale and disposition by will; in most primitive societies such precise and exclusive rights to land are not recognized; nevertheless, individual or familial rights over hunting and fishing territories may be sanctioned in custom in some very simple societies.

In primitive societies, and to an extent in modern society that is not always recognized, property does not consist of a single all-embracing bundle of rights held by one man as against all the world. On the other hand, thoroughly communal ownership of important goods, in the sense that every individual has the same right in most goods as has every other, is not to be found. What is usual, rather, is that every species of ownership turns out to be the exercise of certain rights as to the thing owned subject to other rights in that thing held by others, at least in possibility. The Melanesian canoe-maker does not completely "own" his canoe: he is expected to share it with certain others, and to share the catch it helps to bring about. The owner of land on Main Street may own it subject to zoning regulations, and to the right of the state to take it from him for certain public uses. Beyond this, furthermore, are the claims on property which are made outside of the law, but through expectations resting on custom. The primitive fisherman may share his catch with the whole settlement, as a matter of course. The rich American is expected to do something useful and generous with his riches; and everywhere the claims on the nearest of kin constitute a real limitation on ownership of many kinds of goods. And still further it is to be recognized that property rights are deeply associated with attachments that are sentimental and outside of the rights of control and disposal. It is not so much that the aborigine, long established on the desert or in the forest, owns the desert or the forest; he is attached to it, is a part of it, almost "is owned" by it. And the reader of these pages may feel similarly about his home, if he happens to live in a home and not simply in a house, or about an heirloom of tender memories, or about a familiar old garment. . . .

Society may . . . be seen as a system of status relationships. Many of these take the form of relationships of kinship. . . . Also mentioned already is the status of the members of the in-group as contrasted with that of the out-group. And easily added are the differences in status of a man as contrasted with a woman, or a priest, policeman, or potentate as contrasted with a man who is none of these things. Conduct is expected of the one, and is due to him, different from that expected of or due to the other. In every society there are status-groups connected with differences in age. Any school reveals them, where they are connected with the grades through which the child passes. In many primitive societies this sort of classification in terms of status is made without schools; boys and men pass through a series of ranked groups, each perhaps with its name, its rights and duties, its growing prestige. In many cases certain of these age-groups enjoy a special clubhouse, or have special secrets or ceremonies. Such a ladder of attainment defines what is expected of everyone according to successive categories, from birth to death.

The attitudes that make up the status of any one individual, or group, in a society include, it will be noticed, authorization of various degrees of approach and intimacy. If someone has the status of "best friend" I may go close to him and claim his sympathies as he may claim mine. They also include attitudes of superiority and inferiority. A cat— or a commoner—may look at a king, but he must look up when he looks at him. The "place" in which an American Negro is thought by most white men to be "all right" is a place that is down, not up, with reference to the white man. These differences of ranked status, of "vertical" social position, are apparent as one individual is compared with another. In any gang or small school group the individuals with superior prestige are well known as such, and it may be possible even to rank all the members in an order of "up-or-down." There is no society in which the relative vertical status of the individual does not depend in some degree on himself—on his own conduct and personal chances. . . . All these organizations of society into persisting layered groups are ways of defining the rights and obligations of people with regard to one another, and so contribute to its operation. In most cases, there are special kinds of occupations appropriate to each of the classes in a society so organized; thus classes constitute an aspect of the division of labor. In India the correspondence between inherited social position and the kind of work or useful function performed is very close. In America it has been the immigrant or latest arrival who has done the most unpleasant work. And also social classes are ways of maintaining an unequal distribution of wealth and power that is to the advantage of the dominant classes. The upper layers get more than their share of prestige, social influence, and wealth. At the same time, in societies where class or caste is well established, the glories of the privileged provide a certain second-hand satisfaction to the less privileged. In many societies that include conspicuously different racial groups, relative vertical social positions correspond with the racial groupings, and as the skin color or other racial mark is permanent, the racial classes become caste-like, with the taboos against contact and the ceremonial separation of the racial groups which are characteristic of castes.

The simplest answer that can be made to the question, how does society operate, is that it operates because on the whole people do what is expected of them. But why do people do what is expected of them? To this question there are many true answers. It is easier to do what one has done before than to do something else; a habit that everyone in a society has we call a custom. Further, the things that one has done, and that one's father's father has done, as well as some things that have been thought over and struggled for, have come to be so rooted in sentiments and in explanations and justifications that they have the force of what we speak of as conscience; they are felt to be right, ultimately and necessarily right. And still further, one does what is expected of one because it is often extremely inconvenient, even dangerous, if one does not. That is why I do not start out tomorrow to drive on the left-hand side of an American road. There is an efficiency, an ease, about doing what is expected of one. In a more special form, the expediency of doing what other people expect appears in the exchanges of services and benefits which help us all to get along. I do a thing helpful to another knowing that he is then more apt to do something helpful to me. If I pay my bills, lend my lawnmower, keep out of those of my neighbor's affairs which correspond to those of mine that I want him to keep out of, and yet listen to enough of his troubles so that I may tell him mine, we all get along pretty well. It is, however, to be emphasized that it is the nature of human society to regard these considerations of expediency, important as they are, as less worthy than those which are rooted in conscience and the sense of duty. Society is not, basically, so much a body of traffic rules and favors exchanged as it is a system of moral convictions.

At a more obvious level society operates because conduct is sanctioned. A sanction is a consequence, pleasant or unpleasant, that follows the doing of something and is known to follow it. Some such consequences are internal—the pangs of conscience—but others fall upon the transgressor from without. Of those that so fall, many are imposed by almost anybody in a diffuse and generalized way, as is illustrated by the looks I receive from the people who know me if I do something of which they disapprove. Perhaps what I do is not otherwise punishable. If a specific consequence follows through the exercise of some centralized authority, we begin to think of the transgression and its consequence as an affair of the law. Legal sanctions have a quality of preciseness about them: the misconduct is defined in advance in clear terms, and the consequence is also precisely known. Commonly the procedure for matching the transgression to its appropriate consequence—complaint or arrest, charge, hearing, trial, judgment—is specific and formal. Also, for the matter to be one of law and not just custom, the consequence that is the sanction is carried out not entirely if at all by the particular person that suffered from the transgression, but by someone or some body that stands for the society as a whole and acts for it. Law is the whole society settling a local dispute or punishing or redressing a wrong in the interests of the whole society and according to its common conscience. When in a Plains Indian tribe a society of warriors finds a wrongfully wounded man and sees to it that the wrongdoer heals the wound and pays horses as a fine, law has begun. One may recognize law-making and law-administering in groups smaller than the whole society: there is something like law in some families; and there is certainly law in many gangs. But there is a tendency for that group which is the principal in-group, the tribe or the nation, to insist on its chief or exclusive power and right to make and enforce law. So law appears more clearly in the centralized and monopolizing force of the state.

In the simplest societies there is nothing that is "political" if we use that word for institutions to express or enforce the common will or the ruler's will formally and publicly. In the Andaman Islands the natives lived in small bands without chief, council, law, or administrative regulation. If a man lost his temper and smashed things, the rest of the people just let him alone till he got over it. No one exercised any general authority to rule or to decide or to negotiate on behalf of the community. In such a society there is no state, no political government. Political institutions do clearly appear, however, in many tribal societies; there is a chief who has power to decide issues or to lead in the making of decisions; there may be a council; there may be groups to police the people.

The dependence of modern complex societies upon political institutions for their operation is obvious. The making, enforcing, and interpreting of law is the manifold business of thousands of individuals and hundreds of bodies: from legislatures, courts, and executives to the citizens who vote or obey orders, bring law suits or defend them, pay taxes, and discuss public issues with their neighbors or write a letter to some newspaper. These political institutions keep people's behavior more or less within the rules. They also are a means to the reconsideration of the rules and for the changing of the rules. They operate in that frontier of rule-making and rule-observing where conflicts occur, or at least differences of opinion, and the enforcement and interpretation of the rules helps to keep at least some of the people conscious of them, and so pushing to change them. Formal political institutions not only keep societies going in the good old ways; they also provoke a challenge of those ways.

What is, then, not so obvious is that political and administrative acts have an effect upon moral custom. It is commonly said that the laws express the customs and grow out of them. This is true, but it is also true that the passage of a law or the making of an administrative decision has an impact upon the sentiments and convictions of the society. To punish a criminal is to make a solemn gesture renewing the collective moral judgment with regard to the conduct for which the criminal is punished. Sometimes the law stands for a sort of theoretical or ideal norm which the society does not really mean to have realized, at least without exception, as when a Southern jury of white men find confessed lynchers of a Negro not guilty. Then the decision expresses a moral judgment that is inconsistent with the letter of the law. At the same time such a decision sharpens the conflict between the general principles and the exception, and helps either to remove the exception, or to weaken the principle. The decision and act whereby American citizens of Japanese descent were locked up during the war had one effect in strengthening the prejudices of those who were prejudiced against Orientals, for by conspicuous and effective public action a discriminatory act was performed. On the other hand, it aroused or strengthened sentiments of condemnation of the act. It is true that the customs make the law. It is also true that legal and administrative acts help to change the moral judgments of the society.

Some of the sanctions that keep men doing what is expected of them are neither the exterior sanctions of the law or of public opinion, nor the wholly interior sanctions of conscience. The sentiments that arise within a man that prevent him from doing that of which he would be ashamed, or that condemn him for doing it, in certain situations seem to come from outside him, yet not to come from this earthly world. Then it is a religious sanction that affects him. The convictions about the good are associated with unseen powers; these powers *are* the good, or represent it. A man's relationships to them have a unique quality; they are supremely critical for his ultimate welfare; and before the powers or their symbols he feels awe. The consequence of his action that is the sanction in this case may be a punishment, a suffering here on earth or a suffering in some other life. It may be a hand withered, or a soul damned. The suffering—or the reward, should his conduct be right, not wrong—may be simply the sense that the unseen powers are satisfied or dissatisfied, the feeling that one is or is not in harmony with ultimate goodness, final and unearthly authority.

Religion has been briefly defined as the adoration of goodness. It is goodness that is its essence; religion is not concerned with the trivial, nor with the morally neutral. It is about what most matters. But though an aspect of the moral life, it is not the same as morals. There are peoples—and many of these are primitive, uncivilized—whose religions are the worship or propitiation of supernatural beings who do not enforce the rules of good conduct among men. In such religions it is the worship and the propitiation, the ritual and the relationship between man and god, that matter; earthly morality is supported by conscience and the interplay of reciprocal obligations among people. In other religions, of which Christianity, Islam, and some primitive ones are examples, what a man should do to or for another *is* a matter of divine concern. On the whole, the ethical aspects of religion have grown stronger in the course of human history.

Religion is, moreover, activity; it is something going on in mind and in overt act; it is belief and rite. The power that is beyond men and that holds the welfare of men, mundane and spiritual, is thought about, conceived in certain forms and powers, and approached in prayer and offering and sacrifice. Commonly the power is conceived with qualities that are personal; the god may be angered, appeased, gratified. But in some religions, as in forms of Buddhism, the rites and beliefs have to do with conduct and with spiritual qualities. A religion is yet a religion even though it does not center about a god or gods.

Religion thus contributes to the operation of society through the power and authority and sacred meaning which it provides to the support of man's conduct and to his understanding of his place in the universe. In the totemic societies of aboriginal Australia groups of men carry on rituals at water-holes in their arid land to bring about the multiplication of the wild animals which the natives hunt for food. These rituals act out events and evoke sacred beings that were there before man was, and that were man's ancestors and benefactors. So the life of today is, through religion, conceived as an outcome of powers mysteriously greater than men's powers; they are greater, and yet men today share in that power through the goodness of these beings and the effectiveness of the rites. Similarly, the heavenly hierarchy of Christian faith is a version, in religious thought, of the hierarchies of earthly power of medieval times. These divine beings provide help to the worshiper; and the rite of the Mass, solemnly commemorative of the great act of sacrifice of God become man, is effective in bringing to the worshiper a benefit and strength which only religion can give.

In many of the preceding pages the operation of society has been described as a matter of work and discipline. It has been suggested how people become and continue as a society by virtue of the fact that they labor together for common ends, and how they are kept at it by the convenience of cooperation and by the rewards and penalties which are provided by law, the general opinion, or the conscience of the individual. In this account the sober, the practical, and the constraining have perhaps been too strongly emphasized. Perhaps the impression has been given that society gets along wholly or chiefly because people do what they are compelled to do, or that work is the sole or the basic form of activity.

As a matter of fact, a very great part of human social behavior is quite the opposite of work. In work one does what a particular end demands in just the way it demands it and when the end requires it. To hoe corn effectively is usually work because one must move the hoe just so, one must do the hoeing just when the weather and the weeds make it necessary, and one may not stop when one would care to. But a very great deal of human activity is simply expressive. It is activity which responds to the impulse of the individual to be active; it is activity which takes a form that shows what the individual is thinking and feeling; it is a fruit of the human impulse to create. Some expressive activity takes place when it occurs to the individual to express himself; much takes place at times fixed by the expectations and rhythms of society, but even then without having to meet the demands of practically useful effort.

Laughing, joking, improvising with language, storytelling, praying, arranging flowers, painting pictures, enjoying or playing a ball game or Beethoven, and dancing are all forms of expressive activity. The expressive forms of behavior in large part give each society its own special character as they give special flavor to each personality. Different societies may have the same tools and the same work habits, but if their art and storytelling are different, the societies are then different. "What do you dance?" is the first enquiry a man of a certain Bantu tribe puts to a stranger. What a man dances in that part of Africa is the key to a man's whole life, the way to ask about a foreign society. . . .

Art is like play in that it has its justification in itself, not in getting something done by its means. In art the limitations set around what is done are not rules for contestants and make-believe goals, as in play; the limitations that give art its character are the expectations and satisfactions of a technique mastered, a creation made or appreciated. There are standards, as in play; but in art they are the standards of craftsmanship and the conceptions of the beautiful that prevail in that society and as they are modified by the creative artist. . . .

All these forms of expressive action help in the operation of society by providing opportunities for carrying out the expectations which are the basis of society and by depicting to its members the related conceptions and ideals. Games involve the ideas and ideals as to sportsmanship which the society entertains; playing them disciplines player and audience toward these ideals and tests each player by them. In many primitive societies some games are representations of religious ideas. A game played by the ancient Maya represented the movement of the divine sun through the heavens; yet the game was sport too. "Pure art" is a relatively new and unusual conception; in most times and places art is or has been a form for the expression of the religious conceptions, or for the earthly ideas and ideals. The totem poles carved by Indians of the Northwest Coast proclaimed the social position and divine connections of the family connected with the pole.

In ceremony and in mythology the expressive side of life appears in forms plainly related to the persistence of society. A ceremony is a meaningful formal act that signalizes an occasion of special importance. It is a little drama to underline the significance of a person or a moment that is out of the ordinary and that the society wishes to recognize. Some ceremonies are in ancient forms of deep religious meaning, like the Mass; others are unconnected with the church but yet are public and solemn, like the pledge of allegiance before the national flag; still others are domestic matters and not solemn at all, like the merry little ceremonies of a birthday party. All of them are representations of beliefs that the people hold; they are ways in which people together show that they care about something. Although not every society has well-developed myths and also well-developed ceremonies, myths are the stories that correspond to the ceremonies. Myths are ways in which the institutions and expectations of the society are emphasized and made dramatic and persuasive in narrative form. Myths show that what a people has to enjoy or endure is right and true—true to the sentiments the people hold. It does not so much matter whether or not little George Washington really cut down the cherry tree and told his father about it; what matters is that the story expresses some ideas the tellers had about telling the truth when it goes against you. The religious myths are true to the moral and sacred ideas that inspire them; they need not be true as legal evidence must be true. Myths and ceremonies, like much of art and some of play, are collective and traditional forms in which people of a society remind themselves of what matters to them and why it matters. They are gestures made by a people to itself. Work and sanctions alone do not suffice to keep a society in operation. It is also needful that the tendencies of people to leap, move, shape, and tell fall into representations that satisfy and intensify the conceptions which, held in common, make that people a society.

This chapter suggests some of the answers to the question expressed in its title: How does a human society operate? In its first pages the answer given was that a society is kept in operation by arrangements whereby a number of people can do the work that needs to be done to keep them going and whereby they can feel that they belong together and share a kind of life which they believe to be good. There is a world of necessity into which people are born; to survive they must live together; to live together they must have tacit agreements as to who does what, and is what. They must, in short, regulate their common life. The regulation is a matter of conventional understandings partly as to what each one should do, and partly as to what is, generally and for everybody, the good life. The plan of the good life finds expression, it was then added, in religion, myth, and art. We can think of the operation of society as machinery for social control and also as a sort of charter or drama of a scheme of all things.

But there is another way to think of the operation of society that is, probably, implicit in what has been written here. We may also think of society as operating so as to realize impulses and meet needs of human beings. Instead of asking, as we have, What operations keep this society going? we can ask, What is there about society that keeps human beings going? Any human being must have protection and food, and we can see society as providing for these necessities. Human beings have also sexual demands or needs, and every society provides some arrangement for meeting these. Moreover, beyond this, human beings have characteristics that are not shared with the animals but are peculiarly human. The foregoing discussion of the "Expressive Life" rests on the assumption that there is an "impulse of the individual to be active," that it is the nature of human nature to use the imagination and to shape things that please themselves. While it is perhaps not possible very definitely to describe the human impulses and needs beyond those that are shared with animals, it is hardly possible to deny that there are some; and society may thus be seen as a way of providing for the development and expression in everyone of human nature. In this sense, society operates by doing for us what our natures, given society, demand.

71. Universal Aspects of Culture

GEORGE PETER MURDOCK

Uniformities are found among the cultures of the world, as well as variation. An understanding of those elements which are universal in human societies is as important as an appreciation of the differences, for they tell us about the nature of humanity and of social life. In this essay George Peter Murdock discusses the common denominator of culture.

Murdock is Professor of Anthropology at Yale University, where he took his doctorate in 1925 and has taught since 1928. He has done ethnographic field work on the Northwest Coast and in Micronesia, but he is chiefly known for his continuing effort at the scientific comparison of cultures. Murdock began this interest with his widely used *Our Primitive Contemporaries* and subsequently established the Human Resources Area Files, which endeavors to classify cultural information on all known cultures. This research project has been widely used by governmental agencies as well as serving as a basis for many contributions to the science of anthropology. The essay reproduced here first appeared in *The Science of Man in the World Crisis* (Ralph Linton, ed.), New York: Columbia University Press, 1945, and is reproduced here by kind permission of the publisher and the author.

Most of anthropological theory has revolved about the interpretation of the similarities and differences between the various cultures of mankind. Cultural differences, perhaps because they are more immediately obvious, have received especially close attention. They have been variously explained in terms of distinct stages of postulated evolutionary series, of allegedly disparate racial endowments, of diverse geographic or economic conditions, of nonrepetitive historical accidents, of endlessly varying social contexts, of unique configurations of like or unlike elements, of divergent personality characteristics created by differential childhood training, and so on. Cross-cultural similarities have received theoretical consideration, in the main, only when they have been confined to a limited number of particular cultures, in other words, when they could be regarded as exceptions in a universe of cultural diversity. Such instances of similarity have been explained in terms of the transplantation of culture through migration, of cultural diffusion through contact and borrowing, of parallel development from similar cultural backgrounds, of convergent development from unlike backgrounds, of the independent burgeoning of hereditary potentialities, or of the allegedly determining influence of like geographical factors. In comparison, universal similarities in culture, the respects in which all known cultures resemble each other, have received relatively little theoretical treatment. It is this subject—the common denominator of cultures—with which the present paper will be exclusively concerned.

Early reports of peoples lacking language or fire, morals or religion, marriage or government, have been proved erroneous in every instance. Nevertheless, even today it is not generally recognized how numerous and diverse are the elements common to all known cultures. The following is a partial list of items, arranged in alphabetical order to emphasize their variety, which occur, so far as the author's knowledge goes, in every culture known to history or ethnography:

age-grading
athletic sports
bodily adornment
calendar
cleanliness training
community organization
cooking
cooperative labor
cosmology
courtship
dancing
decorative art
divination
division of labor
dream interpretation
education
eschatology

ethics
ethnobotany
etiquette
faith healing
family
feasting
fire making
folklore
food taboos
funeral rites
games
gestures
gift giving
government
greetings
hair styles
hospitality

housing
hygiene
incest taboos
inheritance rules
joking
kin-groups
kinship nomenclature
language
law
luck superstitions
magic
marriage
mealtimes
medicine
modesty concerning
    natural functions
mourning

music	pregnancy usages	soul concepts
mythology	property rights	status differentiation
numerals	propitiation of super-	surgery
obstetrics	natural beings	tool making
penal sanctions	puberty customs	trade
personal names	religious ritual	visiting
population policy	residence rules	weaning
postnatal care	sexual restrictions	weather control

Cross-cultural similarities appear even more far-reaching when individual items in such a list are subjected to further analysis. For example, not only does every culture have a language, but all languages are resolvable into identical kinds of components, such as phonemes or conventional sound units, words or meaningful combinations of phonemes, grammar or standard rules for combining words into sentences. Similarly funeral rites always include expressions of grief, a means of disposing of the corpse, rituals designed to protect the participants from supernatural harm, and the like. When thus analyzed in detail, the resemblances between all cultures are found to be exceedingly numerous.

Rarely if ever, however, do these universal similarities represent identities in specific cultural content. The actual components of any culture are elements of behavior—motor, verbal, or implicit—which are habitual, in the appropriate context, either to all the members of a social group or to those who occupy particular statuses within it. Each such component, whether called a folkway or a cultural trait or item, can be described with precision in terms of the responses of the behaving individuals and of the stimulus situations in which the responses are evoked. Eating rice with chopsticks, tipping the hat to a woman, scalping a slain enemy, and attributing colic to the evil eye are random examples. Any such specifically defined unit of customary behavior may be found in a particular society or in a number of societies which have had sufficient contact to permit acculturative modifications in behavior. It is highly doubtful, however, whether any specific element of behavior has ever attained genuinely universal distribution.

The true universals of culture, then, are not identities in habit, in definable behavior. They are similarities in classification, not in content. They represent categories of historically and behaviorally diverse elements which nevertheless have so much in common that competent observers feel compelled to classify them together. There can be no question, for example, that the actual behavior exhibited in acquiring a spouse, teaching a child, or treating a sick person differs enormously from society to society. Few would hesitate, however, to group such divergent acts under the unifying categories of marriage, education, and medicine. All of the genuinely widespread or universal resemblances between cultures resolve themselves, upon analysis, into a series of such generally recognized categories. What cultures are found to have in common is a uniform system of classification, not a fund of identical elements. Despite immense diversity in behavioristic detail, all cultures are constructed according to a single fundamental plan—the "universal culture pattern" as Wissler has so aptly termed it. . . .

Most attempts to explain the universal culture pattern have started with the "psychic unity of mankind"—with the assumption, now firmly grounded in social science, that all peoples now living or of whom we possess substantial historical records, irrespective of differences in geography and physique, are essentially alike in their basic psychological equipment and mechanism, and that the cultural differences between them reflect only the differential responses of essentially similar organisms to unlike stimuli or conditions. In its broader aspects this position is probably not open to serious challenge. However, the great majority of theorists have sought the unifying factor in a single facet of man's fundamentally similar psychology, namely, in the common impulse factors in behavior. All cultures are said to resemble one another because men everywhere are driven to action by an identical set of inborn impulses which direct their behavior along parallel lines. . . .

[But], in the first place, the impulses or drives that have been scientifically established do not account for all parts of the universal pattern in an equally satisfactory manner. It seems reasonably safe to attribute the food quest to the hunger drive, shelter to heat and cold avoidance, war to aggression, and marriage to the sex impulse. To what recognized impulses, however, can we assign such equally universal cultural phenomena as the arts and crafts, family organization, and religion? Defenders of the interpretation in question are prone to invent hypothetical impulses to meet such cases, postulating, for example, an instinct of workmanship, a parental drive, or a religious thrill. Such inventions, however, find no shred of support in physiological or psychological science. On the contrary, a fully satisfactory alternative explanation of the underlying motivations is available in the psychological theory of acquired or derived drives.

It is common knowledge that only a small proportion of men's actions in any society spring directly from any of the demonstrable basic drives. In most human behavior the motivation is exceedingly complex and derivative. Even in the case of eating, the widespread prevalence of food preferences and taboos reveals the importance of acquired appetites as contrasted with the inborn drive of hunger. We eat what we like, at hours to which we are habituated, in surroundings which we enjoy. Daily in our habitual eating behavior we satisfy appetitive cravings, but rarely in adult life are we driven by actual hunger pangs. In obeying the dictates of an acquired appetite we incidentally satisfy, of course, the hunger drive, and thereby reinforce the appetite, but the actual incentive is the derived and not the basic impulse.

What is true of eating is even more characteristic of other forms of behavior. Many of our sexual responses, for example, are also appetitive in character; acquired drives impel us to seek the company of persons of opposite sex on the basis of age, appearance and garb, social congeniality, and other factors irrelevant to physical sex, and to engage in conversation, dancing, and divers other activities short of copulation. In still other aspects of social behavior—for example, in religious ritual and the fine arts—the factor of basic-drive reduction shrinks to relative insignificance by comparison with derivative motivations, and may even become impossible to identify. In the case of those elements of the universal culture pattern which cannot readily be attributed, at least in part, to some recognized basic drive, it seems more scientific to ascribe them to derived or acquired drives, which naturally vary from society to society, than to invent hypothetical new drives for which no factual evidence can be advanced.

A second substantial reason for rejecting the impulse factor in behavior as the sole explanation of the universal culture pattern is the fact that most social institutions or culture complexes actually give satisfaction to several basic impulses as well as to a variety of derived drives. To attribute marriage to sex alone, for example, is greatly to oversimplify a complex social phenomenon. As Lippert was the first to point out clearly, the economic factor in marriage is at least as important as the sex factor. The latter can really account only for copulation; it is the conjunction of the former that produces an enduring marital association. The relation of the hunger drive to marriage is seen, for example, in the division of labor by sex, which characterizes marital unions in all societies and, in most of them, demonstrably increases, diversifies, and stabilizes the food supply available to each spouse. Even our own society, which emphasizes the sex factor in marriage to an exceptional degree, has enshrined the hunger factor in a proverb about the most direct way to a man's heart. Marriage gives expression to still another basic impulse in various forms of relief from anxiety; for example, escape from the social disapproval commonly encountered by celibates, economic security gained through union with a wealthy spouse or a good provider, and the personal solace achievable in an intimate relationship. . . .

Cultural behavior may be related to rewards in various ways. In some instances it leads directly and almost exclusively to the reduction of a basic drive. Thus the food quest leads directly to hunger satisfaction, the use of fire and clothing in northern latitudes to cold avoidance, and various sex practices to sexual gratification. The behavior must conform to conditions set by human physiology and psychology for the reduction of the drive in question, and the variant customs of different societies have in common the fact that they all meet these conditions. They can be regarded as alternative solutions to identical problems posed by original human nature. . . .

Many cultural habits, however, instead of gratifying basic drives directly, serve only to facilitate their eventual satisfaction. Cultures contain an immense number of so-called "instrumental responses" which of themselves reduce no basic drives but merely pave the way for other acts which have rewarding results. Instrumental acts acquire in time, of course, the support of learned or derived drives, but they are seldom innately rewarding in themselves. Making a spear or a pot, for instance, gratifies no basic impulse, although at some future time the result may serve to lessen the interval or the expended effort between the onset of the hunger drive and its reduction. The reciprocal habits embodied in social and economic organization represent another outstanding example of instrumental behavior. Through interpersonal relationships and organization, individuals are enabled to use other individuals as instruments to facilitate eventual impulse gratification in much the same way as technology enables them to use artifacts. . . .

A like situation prevails with respect to a third and very large category of cultural habits, namely, those in which behavior is followed by rewards that bear no relation, or only an incidental one, to the impulses prompting the behavior. A gambling spell may be followed by a lucky fall of the dice, or rain-making magic by a providential thunderstorm, and thus become entrenched as a habit. Neither action, however, either produced the rewarding situation or facilitated it in instrumental fashion. . . .

Another example is seen in instances where behavior motivated by one drive results in the gratification of other drives not actually involved in the particular response. A superstitious fear of blood may motivate a tribe to isolate its women after childbirth, but this action may incidentally achieve the fortunate results of assuring postparturient mothers of a needed rest period and of preventing the spread of puerperal fever or other infections, and these may be at least as rewarding as the effect in relieving anxiety. Similarly, even though marriage may often be prompted in large measure by the sex drive, the matrimonial relationship brings other rewards—food, physical comforts, and security—without which, as we have seen, the institution would be difficult to explain.

All cultures, moreover, exhibit numerous adaptive responses which are not directly supported by primary impulse satisfactions. Some authors have attributed these to "social needs," which are defined as depending not upon drives but upon requirements which must be met if groups of individuals and the cultures they bear are to survive in competition with other societies bearing other cultures. One example is the so-called need of education. A culture cannot persist unless it is transmitted from generation to generation, and a society cannot survive without culture, which embodies in the form of collective habits the successful experience of past generations in meeting the problems of living. Hence every society is said to be characterized by the need of educating its young. Unlike reproduction, which is assured in large measure by the sex impulse, education is supported by no primary drive. The immense effort which must be expended by parents and teachers over so many years to inculcate in the young the full cultural equipment of adults is not in itself rewarding but must be bulwarked with auxiliary rewards.

Similarly every society is said to have a "need" for government—for a political organization sufficiently developed to provide for effective common action against potential enemies, to maintain internal order against dangerous interferences with the routine of social living, and to furnish necessary social services not achievable in other ways. Public service is not self-rewarding. Men cannot be depended upon to devote themselves to the common weal through altruism alone. Every society consequently surrounds the holders of political positions with prerogatives and dignities.

The concept of social needs, though useful as a first approximation, is a loose and not wholly satisfactory solution of the scientific problem presented by the universality of certain social institutions or culture complexes which are not directly maintained by specific primary impulse gratifications. It seems preferable to state rather that they have their origin in the ordinary processes of cultural change and their support in the gratification of complex and derivative impulses. Under the pressure of frustration and nonsuccess, behavior is altered. Certain responses, either random in their origin or borrowed from contiguous societies which appear to have achieved greater success, are tried out. If they chance to be followed by rewards of any sort, or even by a lesser degree of discomfort than attends alternative responses, they tend to be repeated and to become established as habits. The situations under which they arise acquire increasing power to evoke them. Learned or derivative impulses develop in support of them, and primary impulses which chance to be satisfied incidentally are pressed into their service, until they are amply fortified with auxiliary rewards.

In the case of education, acquired drives such as pride, prestige, identification, and parental love spring to the support of instruction. The primary drives of pain and anxiety are mobilized in the form of social sanctions for nonconformity. The children themselves, as they become socialized and acquire skills, reciprocate with materially rewarding behavior in ever increasing measure, and in many societies become actual economic assets at an early age. In divers ways an adjustment is evolved whereby the effort expended in education is balanced by a complex system of commensurate rewards.

In the case of government, through a similar process of adaptive cultural change, chiefs are induced to assume war leadership, maintain public order, and perform other social services by according them deference, the right to exact tribute, the privilege of polygyny, or other rewards. Feudal lords receive rents and services, municipal officials enrich themselves by graft, legislators secure jobs for their relatives or special favors for themselves and their business associates, and so on. Actually, of course, the power and pelf of political office are usually sufficiently great to attract a plethora of applicants, and the social problem is more commonly that of keeping exploitation within moderate limits—by revolution or "voting the rascals out"—rather than that of finding somebody who will assume the responsibilities. Only the naïve expect good government at no cost. . . .

The essentially psychological character of the processes and products of culture change suggests that we look into the principles of learning for an interpretation of the universal culture pattern. One factor, that of basic drive or impulse, has already been isolated and found helpful, though not sufficient in itself to provide a complete explanation. A second factor is that of stimulus or cue. Any recurrent element or pattern of elements in the situations in which particular responses occur and are rewarded may acquire the power to evoke those responses, even in the absence of the original impulse. Any prominent stimuli that are of worldwide occurrence might thus be expected to be associated with cultural responses in numerous societies. Among the stimuli of this type are night and day, the heavenly bodies, widespread meteorological and geographical phenomena, certain animals and plants, and the features of human anatomy and physiology. As a matter of fact, nearly all peoples have cultural beliefs about, and cultural responses to, such phenomena as the sun and moon, darkness, rain, thunder, the ocean, mountains, streams, blood, hair, the heart, the genitals, sneezing, breathing, menstruation, childbirth, sickness, and death. Although these culture forms need have nothing in common save their stimuli, the principle of limited possibilities and the psychological factor of generalization, not to mention cultural diffusion, often result in striking similarities among different populations. In any event, widely occurring natural stimuli provide a useful auxiliary basis for classifying and interpreting cultural universals.

A third important factor in learning is that of prior habit. Since pre-existing habits greatly affect behavior in a learning situation, experimenters in animal learning always use naïve subjects, that is, those as free as possible from unknown prior habits that might predetermine their behavior. It is perhaps for this reason that the psychologists themselves have been so uniformly unsuccessful in their attempts to interpret cultural behavior, for no adult human being in any society ever enters naïve into a situation of cultural learning; on the contrary, men carry into every learning situation a battery of cultural habits in comparison with which the prior conditioning of the most maze-wise experimental rat appears infinitesimal.

From the point of view of the universal culture pattern, prior habit becomes important especially in connection with the psychological factor of generalization, by which is meant the tendency of any learned response to be repeated under similar conditions of drive and stimulus. In consequence of generalization, a response adapted to one situation will tend to reappear in another in proportion to the elements of similarity between the two situations. Cultures provide innumerable examples. Supernatural beings are regularly anthropomorphized and dealt with in ways that have proved successful in human relations—by supplication (prayer), gift (sacrifice), aggression (exorcism), flattery (laudation), self-abasement (asceticism), or etiquette (ritual). Political organization commonly follows the model of the family, with which it has an authoritarian element in common. Departed spirits are often assimilated to the breath, which also leaves the body in death. Menstrual and lunar phenomena are frequently equated because of their similar periodicity. Numerous indeed are the cross-cultural similarities which result from generalization.

A final important factor in learning is that of limitation in the range of potential responses. In any learning situation the number of possible responses an organism can make is always limited. No animal can respond with an act for which it is not physically adapted. A man cannot jump or fly to the top of a tree to gather its fruits; his responses are limited to such acts as climbing, cutting down the tree, or employing a pole or a missile. Prior habits or their lack sharply limit the range of possible behavior. Familiar situations tend to evoke familiar responses and inhibit novel ones, and complex responses, like speaking a new language or making an important invention, are impossible until a whole series of prerequisite habits has been acquired. Limitations are also set by the structure of the situation in which behavior occurs. Under identical conditions of drive, reward, and prior conditioning, an experimental rat will behave differently in two mazes of different shape, and a human being in two differing social situations. The limiting conditions of geographical environment have often been pointed out; a Samoan cannot build an igloo or an Eskimo prepare kava.

The most important of limitations on the possibilities of response are probably those set by the nature of man himself and of the world in which he lives, as these are known to science. Technological activities must conform to the physical and chemical properties of the materials with which men work. There are relatively few ways, for example, in which fire can be generated or a pot constructed. Customs in hunting and animal husbandry must conform not only to the physical but also to the biological and behavioral characteristics of the animals concerned. Human physiology and psychology set limits to the ways in which disease can be cured or a child brought into the world. Habit and custom must be observed in social relations. Successful responses—and all established cultural responses are successful, that is, normally rewarded—must cope with all the conditions under which they take place. These conditions introduce into culture the principle of limited possibilities, which is of extreme importance in determining the universal culture patterns.

72. Anthropology and the Modern World

WALTER GOLDSCHMIDT

The understanding of anthropology is important for the conduct of modern society. In this essay Walter Goldschmidt shows that the basic social and cultural processes continue to operate in the modern world and that an understanding of them is requisite for intelligent action. The essay is taken from the last chapter of his *Man's Way, A Preface to the Understanding of Human Society*, and is reproduced here by kind permission of his publishers, The World Publishing Company, Cleveland, Ohio, and Henry Holt and Company, New York.

Human society may be viewed as a system of interpersonal relationships. These operate in a real world made up on the one hand of the needs and capacities of its human components, and on the other of the recalcitrant elements of an environment, out of which these needs are supplied. This is neither biological nor environmental determinism, for the significant elements in our viewpoint are social and cultural. Yet the social and cultural needs are limited and channeled by these elements which are external to the system.

For purposes of our analysis, the focal point is man's commitment to social existence, a commitment that is perduring and inexorable, and in terms of which all further elements of social behavior are to be seen. It is an old assumption, having variously been expressed as man's being a political animal or being possessed of a social instinct akin to the instinct of bees. While endeavoring to avoid such biological terminology, we nevertheless find it necessary to predicate that this commitment lies behind culture; that it is a tendency in man (however he has come by it) which is outside the cultural system and everywhere present. To consider it a product of culture and then proceed to explain cultural behavior in terms of it is a narrow circle of argument. We postulate that this quest is central in human behavior, drawing men everywhere into the vortex of the demands their cultural environment makes of them, rendering them willing to submit to the hardships and indignities that such cultural life often imposes.

No claim is made for a predominant urge to love; rather, man is seen as self-seeking. But his efforts to meet his selfish interests cannot operate except in the context of others through whom his personal satisfaction may be had. Society is the recurrent, the inevitable answer. And society must be organized to balance off the pull of individual self-seeking against the demands of social harmony.

Useful scientific generalization requires both a taxonomy of events and a theory of relevance. Anthropology has too much avoided both. Early evolutionary theory provided anthropology with a classification of societies on a hierarchical level of development. The rejection of this schema led to the tendency to lump together all peoples outside Western civilization under the term *primitives*. Actually, this came to include all those people who were normally the subject of anthropological inquiry. The Aztecs and the Incas were in (since we knew them largely by means of archeology), but the Greeks and Romans were out (because they were early the province of history and classics). The result was that massive African and Southeast Asiatic kingdoms enter into our theories along with, and taxonomically (and therefore conceptually) undifferentiated from, the Arunta and the Andaman Islanders. Consider, for instance, Paul Radin's classic and creative *Primitive Man as Philosopher,* which includes references to many peoples (provided they lack writing) or the only broad contemporary analysis of economic life by Melville Herskovits, *The Economic Life of Primitive People,* as its first edition was called. In neither instance does the author regularly investigate whether the elements of his analysis vary with different kinds of primitive peoples—different in evolutionary stages or according to any other relevant criteria.

The underlying rationale of this procedure is that after all, human beings are all really alike. This statement is true only when the "really" refers to man's innate average capacities and needs; and as far as this is true, it renders the distinction between *primitives* (i.e., the usual subject of anthropological inquiry) and *moderns* (i.e., the usual subject of sociological inquiry) entirely useless as well. Actually, of course, the subject of our study is not man as such, but aspects of his culture and his social institutions. And these, quite clearly, are not alike. Nor is it any more appropriate to lump the Ashanti with the Arunta than to lump them with modern Americans. To me, it seems much less appropriate. The discomfort in the procedure has been demonstrated by those who engage in it, for they have placed a tabu on the word *primitive* (though it is too useful to be entirely avoided). The circumlocutions that

have developed, words such as *preliterate* or *nonliterate,* do not resolve
the problem because they avoid the true issue, which is the rejection of
efforts to categorize into significant entities the broad and disparate
phenomena that are the societies with which anthropologists deal. In the
final analysis, *primitive* is a comparative rather than an absolute word,
and by any reasonable use of it, the Arunta are more primitive than the
Ashanti, the Ashanti than modern Americans. It must be emphasized
that the term has no reference to virtue or morality or to the intellectual
capacities of the peoples involved; it is a statement of the condition of
their technical apparatus and the social institutions. *Good* and *bad* are
terms properly left to the philosophers; *simple* and *complex, primitive*
and *advanced* are crass but useful scientific expressions.

This leads us to face the problem of cultural relativity and the
evaluation of social systems. The dominant mode of anthropological
thought has been relativistic. This seems to stem from the essentially
liberal tradition out of which anthropology has grown, a tradition which
recognizes human worth in whatever circumstances it is found. In part
it is a rejection of the bigotry and cupidity that has characterized, until
recently at least, the public attitude toward native peoples, and it specifically expresses a desire to protect these subordinated populations
from the discrimination and plundering of a dominant people. It stems
in part, too, from a love of the exotic and not a little from the anti-
quarian interests that drew so many of its practitioners to the anthropological arts. In great measure, it stems from the generic affection and
respect that most of us have felt for the natives we meet in the field.
Finally, of course, it stems from the fact that as reporters of behavior
our descriptions must not be apperceived—in so far as possible—by
our prejudices.

In naïve form, cultural relativism asserts that all peoples, all cultures, are equally good: if they be cannibals, well, that's not for me,
but *de gustibus.* . . . In more sophisticated form it asserts that each
culture must be valued in its own terms: does it satisfy the people themselves? If they are cannibals, what satisfactions does eating human flesh
supply in terms of native values? There is much to be said for this point
of view; the evaluation of infanticide in the Arctic or the eating of grubs
by the Arunta cannot be judged through the love we feel toward our
children or by our culinary predilections. For this is a judgment of good
versus bad, and the good is defined in terms of the conditioning that
each of us has had, in terms of our own cultural values.

The problem, however, is not that evaluation is wrong, but, rather, that the basis of evaluation is faulty. It was precisely here that early evolutionists were wrong; they were freely comparing against their own cultural standards. What we need to seek, therefore, is a standard of judgment which is not a product of our own culture. Actually there is but one which is entirely culture-free, but there may be others of sufficient breadth to be useful. That one, of course, is survival value. The history of life itself is predicated on the assumption that life, whether sweet or not, is desirable; desirable not merely for the individual but for the group of which he is a part. The evaluation of cultural behavior then must be made in relation to its viability; and it must be made in terms of the adequacy for continued existence, rather than in terms of moral value or ethical good. (Of course we can—and frequently do—judge some cultures as good and bad because we like or dislike them; but this is frankly a different kind of judgment.)

Underlying such a view is the assumption that social forms are instrumentalities—i.e., that they serve a purpose for life continuation of the group. In an earlier chapter we asserted that the techniques of a culture are instrumentalities that carry the basis for their own evaluation, inasmuch as the technical apparatus is used for specific recognized ends. Institutions, on the other hand, do not have this built-in evaluation. Now, however, we must point out that this is not because they are not actually end-oriented. Rather, it is because the persons in a culture cannot ordinarily view them as such. As social analysts we may note that the flag serves as a symbol of national unity and acts as a reminder and a stimulus to patriotic behavior. So, too, do the totem poles of the Northwest Coast. Both are institutional instrumentalities for the promotion of social cohesiveness. But neither we nor the Tlingit think of the flag or the raven crest as an instrumentality in the sense that we think of the U.S.S. *Nautilus* or a sinew-backed bow. Those living in a culture can make judgments about the physical instrumentality that they cannot make about the social one.

Time, however (and perhaps social analysts), can make different evaluations. Those who participate in a culture may not be perturbed by the inadequacies of its institutions to provide a coherent and viable mode of life. Nero is not the only one to have fiddled while a way of life was being destroyed. Yet in the long run, a social system cannot survive if institutions for cohesion, order, and the maintenance of physical needs are wanting. Here lies the essential dynamic for social evolution and the essential basis for evaluating cultures. If institutions are instrumentalities, they are in fact subject to evaluation.

Let us observe this through a favorite anthropological example: Eskimo infanticide. Cultural assumptions in our society place a great premium on the preservation of human life so that we find such a practice repugnant. But Eskimo infanticide is a necessary institution to protect the group, for the proportion of infants to adults in each social unit cannot rise too high. As an instrumentality, it is a useful pattern of behavior even though the people themselves might very much prefer other forms of action despite their cultural conditioning. Significantly, the pattern also appears in desert areas where similar economic conditions prevail. Primitive communism is another example. All the more sparsely populated hunting and gathering cultures share the land, and all, I believe, have institutions for sharing the kill. We cannot see how such institutions could be avoided at the margins of subsistence, but the recurrence of this phenomenon at such a level is entirely beside the point in any effort to justify communistic institutions at any other.

Adequate social institutions do not grow of themselves, however much they appear to, but must first be conceived in the minds of men and promulgated by them. They are not the product of a tropism; they do not develop out of some sure instinct, such as determines the status hierarchy or the proportion of workers in a colony of bees. To be sure, sapient beings can foretell consequences and can seek to avoid those that they fear as harmful—to the degree that habit and cultural conditioning has not blinded them. Therefore, it is only in the selective processes, only in the crucible of time, that the fitness of an institution or a cultural pattern can be tested. Unfortunately, like all clinical tests, these can never provide a sure answer. No group of American historians can long converse without raising the question as to what might have happened had Lincoln not been elected, had the Civil War not occurred, and so on. Or again, was social security legislation a product of the New Deal, or was it a necessary institution forced upon a public by circumstances of an industrial society awakened by the disaster of 1929?

The answer is equivocal. Circumstances do create needs, but the needs may be variously met. Even where old conditions manifestly cannot prevail, new solutions are not necessarily sought, nor are the solutions sought necessarily adequate. But because people can act instrumentally, they can preserve a situation. This is not only true of modern societies but of primitive ones as well.

Two anthropologists, John Adair and Evon Vogt, had the opportunity of examining the attitudes of Zuñi and Navaho toward returned veterans of World War II. At Zuñi these men were viewed as a threat to the social order, and through such informal pressures as ridicule and gossip were forced to give up white patterns and return to Zuñi ways. It was a conscious technique on the part of the political and religious leaders to preserve their culture and the integrity of their community. The Navaho were not subjected to this treatment; indeed, they were welcomed as returned warriors and obtained a considerable degree of leadership. While several cultural factors and other circumstances are involved, it is clear that Zuñi leadership saw a threat to a way of life and conscientiously took action to ward it off.

Yet for one reason or another, people cannot always act nor can they foresee all the consequences for the future of their present actions. Where institutional adjustment is lacking, the society falls apart or disappears. We can only wonder how many hunting and food-gathering peoples may have perished because they did not develop customs such as sharing and infanticide. We can only wonder whether social systems were engulfed or destroyed by their neighbors because they lacked the integrative devices necessary to protect themselves. We do know that throughout recorded history nations have disappeared because of inadequate institutions to protect their integrity and maintain their social order.

Man is one, but cultures vary. If this is so, then modern man is one with the primitive, and any theory of his behavior must take into account our own society along with that of the Andaman Islanders and the Australians. If we are to do this, however, we must do it with the realization that our culture is operating in the framework of evolution and the social imperatives; further that our institutions are instrumentalities for the preservation of a people and a nation.

An examination of the formulation of the American system of government impresses one with the sociological sense that entered into the documents, creating a system of governance sufficiently rigid to provide a frame of action, yet flexible enough to meet the exigencies that prevailed during a period of unprecedented growth and change. Some of the insights show profound understanding of social forces: the dangers inherent in the provision of authority along with the equal dangers in anarchy, the problem inherent in providing for the general welfare combined with the need for recognition of individual freedom. The result was not a fortuitous one, for those who framed the Constitution did so in the light of history. Their careful analysis of the political systems of contemporary Europe and of antiquity guided them in forming our own institutions. Social planning is not a twentieth-century invention.

Their work was but a beginning, for the progress of technical evolution has not ended; the problems of institutional adjustment continue. Thus the problems of institutional adjustment are not always resolved by man consciously formulating plans to meet future exigencies; more often they are the more or less unanticipated consequences of specific acts designed to meet particular needs. We can illustrate this from current events.

Our first example has to do with the institutions of higher learning. The postwar era has seen a remarkable advancement of education at all levels, but especially among the universities. Communities, states, and the Federal Government have been pouring money and concrete into the improvement of our college facilities. Major foundations have added to these riches, and a new phenomenon—the provision of educational facilities by big business—is coming into being. The press, which was recently decrying the universities as hotbeds of radicalism, seems now to be thoroughly in favor of an increased investment in our educational plant. It may, during a political campaign, build on ancient prejudices and decry the eggheads, but by and large it is supporting higher learning. This is neither a fad nor a response to prosperity and the economic need to consume. It is manifestly related to the functional needs of our society. It takes a great deal of skilled manpower to staff our modern technology, and the educational institutions are necessary to replenish and enrich this supply of skill. Emphasis may be upon the technicians, but not so much as one would expect, for the managerial talents are also requisite.

Meanwhile the same thing is happening elsewhere with great regularity, and this can hardly be explained as merely a matter of diffusion, though diffusion it is. Indonesia borrows our techniques and manpower to provide higher learning for its own personnel; India sends students to this country by the thousands and invites our scholars to further their training in India; England has extended educational opportunity ever more widely, because class differentials were depriving her of talent; and beyond the Iron Curtain, the great skyscraper that is the University of Moscow was raised to meet the technical needs of a growing industrialization.

That great Moscow skyscraper is relevant to the emerging attitude toward higher education in America. Popular articles supporting the need for furthering our universities and colleges, for revamping our program of general education, for improving the standing and salaries of professors, have repeatedly rested their case upon this development abroad. Such articles view with alarm the fact that the Soviet Union is producing doctorates (and especially physicists and engineers) at a

faster rate than we are, for they know that a technological society requires an army of technicians. It has been said that our national budget
is drawn up in the Kremlin, and the point is relevant, for the institutions
of a society are not merely a matter of the internal structure but are
responsive to the environment—and that environment includes potential threats from beyond the borders.

The international scene is a factor in shaping the institutions of
each nation. (Something similar took place among the Indians of the
Great Plains during the period when some tribes received the gun,
others horses, and their neighbors had to adjust their methods of warfare
—and presumably other aspects of their behavior—to these new external
conditions.) To speak of education thus instrumentally and its current
boom as a product of geopolitics would seem to be a denial of the
cultural background out of which it grew. We are not unmindful of the
historical forces that shape our present institutions of higher learning.
We are fully aware of an old and deep-seated tradition in America which
favors intellectual pursuits and the virtue of knowledge. But we are also
aware that there has always been a contrary philosophy running along
with it, decrying learning as a perversion of man's purpose on earth.
The Greek revival and the Chautauqua circuit have as their counterbalance the Know-Nothing Party and the mucker pose; the popular
image of a brain trust is counterbalanced by snide references to eggheads. Both sets of attitudes remain, but the situational demand gives
potency to the one over the other. It is not just tradition and not merely
the threat to our society from the growing power beyond our borders
that have brought about the recent interest in education, for the very
problem of operating an industrial society makes this higher learning
a necessity.

A further illustration will show how tradition can be manipulated
to fulfill institutional requirements. An examination of the history and
practices of American patent law by Walton Hamilton demonstrates the
potential flexibility of institutions. Hamilton shows that in the realm of
patents, where customs go back to the very beginning of modern national
organization and where these customs have been written down and
specified in the law books, actual practice can range to the polar extremes. Comparing the glass-container industry with the automobile
industry, Hamilton shows how the one was built on the authority and
close control of patents while the other was built on the free exchange
of such rights, so that two sets of highly self-conscious institutional
practices operate within one closed cultural system. Furthermore, he

shows, through an analysis of the historical development and economic circumstances of each industry, why and how these patterns came into being. The glass industry would be chaotic without control of patents, for the manufacturer of glass containers requires little specialized skill and generally available resources. It was through the control of patents that organization was provided to an otherwise amorphous and uncontrollable economic and social situation. The automobile industry also started out with an effort to maintain carefully controlled patent rights— the famed Selden patents. Very quickly, however, there developed a free licensing of patents and to this day the use of this law has little to do with divergent advantages of one automobile company over another. In the automobile industry, organization could more easily and effectively be maintained through the control of scarce material, technical skill, and developed organization, whereas the limitation on patents would only hamper expansion. The important point is that cultural background is amenable to the forces of institutional requirements, requirements which must be met if an organization is to flourish, whether it be an industry or a nation.

In our view, man is no more guided in his actions by "the dead hand of custom" than by the hand of God. The dead hand of custom is a faulty figure of speech, no longer heard in anthropological circles. Man is guided by the hand of custom, but the hand is not dead. It is rather a living, changing, and growing thing. Its viability is less easy to demonstrate from societies lacking historic records, but there is sufficient evidence to indicate its existence on the primitive as well as the civilized levels. We have already suggested the existence of such institutional adjustments on the Great Plains, and we could find examples in a variety of places.

A nice example of cultural processes that relate to the maintenance of the social order is found among the Tiv of central Nigeria. Paul Bohannan points out that in Tiv history over the past fifty years or so there have been a number of social movements which might be called antiwitchcraft. According to Bohannan these movements have taken place as a counterbalance against the concentration of power—a concentration made possible through the use of witchcraft. They are thus more or less conscious corrective movements, each one separate but all sharing the same basic pattern, serving to maintain the orderly processes of Tiv society.

Let us turn to another example from our own times to further the matter of institutional adjustment. We are nearing the centenary of the

Civil War, but the years since 1943 have seen more advancement in the position of Negroes in America than did the preceding seventy. The Congress of the United States has drawn up civil legislation of a kind not written since Reconstruction days, and the Supreme Court rulings on desegregation in the years 1954-1958 have revolutionized the legal basis for race relations in this country. Such changes can hardly be accounted for by any renewed vigor of morality, in as much as in days of prosperity man traditionally lays aside moral virtue and turns to the satisfaction of his appetites. These changes can hardly be accounted for by the influence of anthropology and sociology, which have given far less consideration to such problems in the post-war years than they did during the depression years and earlier. To some extent they may be viewed as a process of accumulated influence of earlier action, and we do not belittle the service of scholarly knowledge or the actions of moralists. Yet to see merely inertia as the force bringing about these changes is to deny the validity of another figure of speech—the swing of the pendulum.

There is actually little doubt that a major impetus for improving the condition of the Negro and for slacking discriminatory practices is a conscious reaction to pressures from abroad. The growing influence of colored groups in Asia and Africa and their role in the geopolitics of the future are not remote contingencies to the policy makers; they are the real and ever-present concerns of those who must take action. If an anthropologist among a primitive tribe on the slopes of Mt. Elgon in Uganda can feel the repercussions of a Supreme Court desegregation act, what would a journalist at Bandung, an ambassador at New Delhi, or a representative to the United Nations feel? In the context of international relations, the continuation of age-old, deeply-rooted cultural practices are dysfunctional, just as anti-Semitism was dysfunctional to Nazi Germany. American institutions are being forced to change to meet new conditions. The scholars and the moralists may rationalize the new patterns as well as provide the impetus for their development, but the institutions must change to meet the exigencies to which they are subject or the society will not long endure. It is the recognition of these needs and the appropriate action to implement them which establishes the reality of "far-sighted leadership"—and that is a judgment which can be rendered only by the historian.

The institutions of modern America, like those of all peoples everywhere, are a product of the past, having their sources deep in history. They are subject to forces that change them to fit new situations, both internally and externally. But these forces are not merely forces for change. They tend to direct the character of the transformation, to set the pattern and the style of the transformed society. Whether or not the transformation is viable depends upon the accurate calculations of those who minister to the changes and upon the flexibility of the society to make the adjustments.

Such circumstances and such actions have produced the evolutionary development of the human condition, raising man to ever greater control of his environment, to ever larger aggregates of population, to ever more complex social systems. They have taken place unrecorded and unsung in earlier eras; they continue to take place. For modern society is not the end product of such evolutionary development; it is merely at some stage along man's way.

Bibliography and Suggestions
for Further Reading

Questions for Discussion

Index

Bibliography and Suggestions for Further Reading

Note: This bibliography offers suggestions for further reading on topics in this book. Works from which the essays have been derived are usually not included here. For the most part, the works cited below are directed to the nonspecialist, though written by scholars who are specialists. Where possible, reference is made to the most readily available material.

I. CULTURE

To understand the nature of culture, the best approach is to live for a time with a people having a different culture from one's own. The next most advantageous method is to read detailed accounts of their customs. A series of brief accounts of a few are available in a series published in paperback by Henry Holt and Company and edited by George D. Spindler: C. W. N. Hart and Arnold R. Pilling, *The Tiwi of North Australia*, E. Adamson Hoebel, *The Cheyennes: Indians of the Great Plains*, Oscar Lewis, *Tepoztlán: Village in Mexico*, John Beattie, *Bunyoro: An African Kingdom*, and Homer G. Barnett, *Being a Palauan*. Robert H. Lowie's *The Crow Indians* (Rinehart) is also an excellent account of a tribe, available in paperback. There are literally hundreds of ethnographic accounts of particular peoples.

Another way to understand culture is to examine some studies on the culture you are most familiar with, namely, that of the United States. There have been many studies of particular communities, starting with Robert and Helen Lynd's, *Middletown* and their subsequent *Middletown in Transition* (Harcourt Brace). Other community studies are: James West, *Plainville, U.S.A.* (Columbia), Hortense Powdermaker, *After Freedom* (Viking), Walter Goldschmidt, *As You Sow* (The Free Press), Allison Davis, B. B. Gardiner, and Mary Gardiner, *Deep South* (Chicago), and a number of studies by W. Lloyd Warner and his associates. General accounts of American culture include Margaret Mead, *And Keep Your Powder Dry* (Morrow) and W. Lloyd Warner, *American Life* (Chicago).

A final way to see what culture means is to examine what has been written about the concept. A detailed analysis of the use of the term has been developed in a monograph by A. L. Kroeber and Clyde Kluckhohn, *Culture, A Critical Review of Concepts and Definitions*, Papers of the Peabody Museum, XLVII. Popular analyses of culture may be had in Ruth

Benedict, *Patterns of Culture* (Houghton Mifflin) and Clyde Kluckhohn, *Mirror for Man* (McGraw-Hill).

II. LANGUAGE

Many excellent books have been written on this subject, which is forever fascinating. Most of the following are available in paperback. A basic and standard textbook is Edward Sapir, *Language* (Harvest Books). A classic discussion of semantics is C. K. Ogden and I. A. Richards, *The Meaning of Meaning* (Harvest Books). Stuart Chase popularized these ideas in *The Tyranny of Words* (Harvest Books). A more general work on language is Margaret Schlauch, *The Gift of Language* (Dover). From a more philosophical standpoint are the following: Ernst Cassirer, *An Essay on Man* (Doubleday Anchor Books) and Susanne K. Langer, *Philosophy in a New Key* (Pelican Books).

Some more scholarly works, especially dealing with the relation of language to culture are *Language, Thought and Reality, The Selected Writings of Benjamin Lee Whorf* (Wiley) and Harry Hoijer (editor) *Language in Culture* (Memoir No. 79 of the American Anthropological Association). Edward T. Hall's *The Silent Language* (Doubleday) reminds us that we still communicate a good deal in other ways than by the use of our voices.

III. TECHNOLOGY

A magnificent five-volume encyclopedic *History of Technology* (edited by Singer, Holmyard, Hall, and Williams) has recently been published by the Oxford University Press. It is made up of articles dealing with various aspects of man's technical accomplishment up to the beginning of this century, starting with a consideration of animal tool using in contrast to the human (a portion of which is published in this volume). It is authoritative, well written, and profusely illustrated.

The evolution of technology is discussed by V. Gordon Childe in *Man Makes Himself* (Mentor Books), *What Happened in History* (Pelican Books), and *Social Evolution* (Scherman's College Paperbacks). A view of social evolution is also discussed by Leslie A. White, *The Evolution of Culture* (McGraw-Hill). A. R. Ubbelohde discusses the relation of man's technical knowledge to human affairs in *Man and Energy* (Braziller).

The relation between technology and the social character of a population is examined in a number of works, most of which deal with problems inherent in the modernization of underdeveloped areas. Among these are *Human Problems in Technological Change* (Russell Sage Foundation) edited by Edward H. Spicer, from which the contribution by Lauriston Sharp was taken, and *Cultural Patterns and Technical Change* (Mentor Books), edited by Margaret Mead. A more theoretical study of this subject is provided by Homer Barnett, *Innovation, the Basis of Culture Change* (McGraw-Hill). A voluminous literature on change as a result of European contact (acculturation) has been developed, only part of which deals with technology as such.

The sociological study of cultural change as a result of technological development has been developed by William Fielding Ogburn, who edited *Technology and International Relations* (Chicago), and by W. F. Cotrell, *Energy and Society* (McGraw-Hill).

IV. EDUCATION

A general treatise on primitive education has yet to be written. George Pettitt's work, *Primitive Education in North America* (California), from which the conclusions have been reproduced here, deals with the formal processes among American Indians. Some detailed studies of the educational processes in American tribes have been made, notably by Laura Thompson and Alice Joseph, *The Hopi Way* (Chicago), Dorothea Leighton and Clyde Kluckhohn, *Children of the People* (Harvard), and Alice Joseph, Rosamond B. Spicer, and Jane Chesky *The Desert People* (Chicago). Gregory Bateson and Margaret Mead studied the informal training aspects of the Balinese, recorded in *Balinese Character* (New York Academy of Sciences), and Eric Ericson studied several tribes in America from a psychoanalytic point of view and summarizes his data in *Childhood and Society* (Norton). Margaret Mead's studies are also pertinent, particularly *Growing Up in New Guinea* (Morrow), *Coming of Age in Samoa* (Mentor), and *Sex and Temperament in Three Primitive Societies* (Mentor). She summarizes some aspect of child training in her *Male and Female* (Morrow). Summary statements regarding the influence of culture on the character of the individual are to be found in Ralph Linton, *The Cultural Background of Personality* (Appleton-Century-Crofts), John J. Honigman, *Culture and Personality* (Harper), and Clyde Kluckhohn and Henry A. Murray (editors), *Personality in Nature, Society, and Culture* (Knopf). Sociological studies of education in America include W. Lloyd Warner, R. J. Havighurst and M. B. Loeb, *Who Shall be Educated?* (Harper), A. B. Hollingshead, *Elmtown's Youth* (Wiley), and Wayne Gordon, *The Social System of the High School* (The Free Press).

V. FAMILY

While perhaps more has been written on the family and kinship by both anthropologists and sociologists than on any other single topic, there is no good modern summary offering an understanding of family life. Every specific study of a particular people includes a section on this subject. The influence of family life on the individual is treated in books referred to in the preceding section.

The subject of kinship has been particularly important in anthropology since Louis Henry Morgan wrote *Systems of Consanguinity and Affinity of the Human Family* (Smithsonian Institution) in 1871. A modern analysis of kinship is the highly technical work of George Peter Murdock, *Social Structure* (Macmillan).

Specific studies of family and kinship include Meyer Fortes, *The Web of Kinship among the Tallensi* (Oxford) and Oscar Lewis, *Five Families* (Basic Books). The latter offers vignettes of family life among a peasant people. Ruth Nanda Anshen, editor, *The Family, its Function and Destiny* (Harper) discusses family life in various modern societies.

VI. GROUPS

An effort to develop a theory of social groups was made by George C. Homans in *The Human Group* (Harcourt Brace). Laboratory analysis of small-group behavior has recently been initiated, and is summarized in *Social Group Studies in Social Interaction* (Knopf), edited by A. Paul Hare, Edgar F. Borgatta and Robert F. Bales. These developments build upon earlier work, especially that of J. L. Moreno, *Who Shall Survive?* (Nervous and Mental Disease Publishing Co.) and by F. J. Roethlisberger and William J. Dickson, *Management and the Worker* (Harvard), a selection from which appears in this book. The researches of Moreno and his associates appeared in *Sociometry* for many years, and a selection of their essays has been published under the title *The Sociometry Reader* (The Free Press).

Though all anthropological and sociological community studies inevitably involve themselves with groups, perhaps the best studies dealing specifically with this aspect are William F. Whyte, *Street Corner Society* (Chicago), Raymond Firth, *We, the Tikopia* (American Book Co.) and Douglas Oliver, *A Solomon Island Society* (Harvard).

VII. STATUS AND ROLE

The best statement on the general comparative nature of status and role is the chapter by Linton selected for this section. The subject is also discussed in Walter Goldschmidt, *Man's Way* (World). A comparative approach to social status has not been developed since the highly theoretical and dated book by Gunnar Landtman, *The Origin of the Inequality of the Social Classes* (Chicago). Recent, more limited, studies are Marshall Sahlins, *Social Stratification in Polynesia* and Munro S. Edmonson, *Status Terminology and the Social Structure of North American Indians* (both published by the American Ethnological Society). Every thorough study of a primitive tribe will discuss the system of status differentiation, and many will discuss the social roles, though not necessarily using this term. Status differentiation has been emphasized in most studies of American communities, such as those listed under Section I. One point of view has been expressed by W. Lloyd Warner, Marchia Meeker, and Kenneth Eells, *Social Class in America* (Chicago). The literature on social class in America and other modern countries is voluminous; an introduction is provided in a reader edited by Reinhold Bendix and Seymour Lipsett, *Class, Status and Power* (The Free Press). A good popular account of status problems in modern middle-class society is developed in William H. Whyte, Jr., *The Organization Man* (Anchor).

VIII. AUTHORITY

The structure of power and the character of legal institutions was introduced into anthropological literature by Sir Henry Maine in his *Ancient Law* (Murray) in 1861. The most recent and thorough discussion of the problem of primitive law is found in E. Adamson Hoebel, *The Law of Primitive Man, A Study in Comparative Legal Dynamics* (Harvard). Studies of political organizations have been more highly developed for Africa than elsewhere among primitive people; see particularly *African Political Systems,* edited by Meyer Fortes and E. E. Evans-Pritchard (Oxford) and I. Schapera, *Custom and Conflict in Africa* (The Free Press). A more popular discussion of the subject may be found in Walter Goldschmidt, *The Ways to Justice* (Fund for Adult Education). Detailed studies of particular political systems and legal processes have been developed in the following: Karl Llewellyn and E. Adamson Hoebel, *The Cheyenne Way* (Oklahoma), Max Gluckman, *The Judicial Process Among the Barotse of Northern Rhodesia* (The Free Press), and Lloyd A. Fallers, *Bantu Bureaucracy* (W. Heffner).

From the sociological point of view, in addition to the work by MacIver from which one selection was drawn, there are a number of readers summarizing aspects of authority, including *A Study of Power* (The Free Press) by Harold D. Lasswell, Charles E. Merriam, and T. V. Smith, *Reader in Bureaucracy* (Free Press) edited by Robert K. Merton and others, *Studies in Leadership* (Harper) by Alvin Gouldner and the book cited in the previous section edited by Bendix and Lipsett. Broad and useful studies in the nature of authority include Lord Acton, *Essays on Freedom and Power* (Meridian Books) and Harold Lasswell, *Who Gets What, When, How* (The Free Press).

IX. VALUES

A compendium on this subject has recently been published by Ethel M. Albert and Clyde Kluckhohn, *A Selected Bibliography on Values, Ethics and*

Aesthetics in the Behavioral Sciences and Philosophy (The Free Press). Charles Morris has endeavored to study values objectively in his *Varieties of Human Value* (Chicago). A discussion from a more psychological orientation is provided by Gordon Allport, Philip E. Vernon and Gardner Lindzey, *The Study of Values* (Houghton Mifflin). The most detailed and analytic discussion of values from an anthropological point of view is offered by Clyde Kluckhohn in *Toward a General Theory of Action,* edited by Talcott Parsons and Edward A. Shils (Harvard). There is no popular discussion of comparative values available.

X. RELIGION

Early theoretical treatment on the nature and origins of religion include Sir James Frazer, *The Golden Bough* (Macmillan), Edward B. Tylor, *Primitive Culture* (Harper), and Emile Durkheim, *The Elementary Forms of the Religious Life* (Allen & Unwin). A recent book of reprinted essays edited by William A. Lessa and Evon Z. Vogt, *Reader in Comparative Religion* (Row, Peterson) not only offers a broad treatment of the subject but also lists several dozen excellent specific studies of primitive religion. There are no popular books dealing with primitive religion but a number of textbooks including W. W. Howells, *The Heathens* (Doubleday), Robert H. Lowie, *Primitive Religion* (Liveright), Paul Radin, *Primitive Religion* (Viking), and William J. Goode, *Religion Among the Primitive* (The Free Press). An excellent treatment of the religion of several primitive people in a broad context is provided by *African Worlds,* edited by Daryll Forde (Oxford).

The literature on modern religions is far too voluminous to present here, but some sociological studies are worthy of note, particularly Joseph Henry Fichter, *The Urban Parish* (Chicago) and Liston Pope, *Millhands and Preachers* (Yale). Studies of modern American communities such as those listed in the bibliography for Section I, have sections dealing with the social aspects of religious life.

XI. ETHICS

The study of ethical systems of primitive peoples was first attempted by Paul Radin in *Primitive Man as Philosopher* (Appleton). A recent work is *Anthropology and Ethics* by May Edel and Abraham Edel (Thomas). Specific studies among primitive peoples have been made by Richard B. Brandt, *Hopi Ethics* (Chicago) and John Ladd, *The Structure of a Moral Code; a Philosophical Analysis of Ethical Discourse Applied to the Navaho Indians* (Harvard). *African Worlds,* cited above, also provides a basis of understanding the ethical systems of a number of peoples.

XII. ART

The two major anthropological works dealing broadly with the art of primitive people are available in paperback: Franz Boas, *Primitive Art* (Dover) and Leonhard Adam, *Primitive Art* (Pelican). More specialized works, popular accounts, and art books are numerous; about two dozen were reviewed in the February, 1957, issue of the *American Anthropologist*. Among the more important works are André Malraux, *The Voices of Silence* (Doubleday), Herbert Read, *The Grass Roots of Art* (George Wittenborn), Irwin O. Christensen, *Primitive Art* (Crowell), Miguel Covarrubias, *The Eagle, The Jaguar, and the Serpent: Indian Art of the Americas* (Knopf).

The treatment of primitive oral traditions as art is rare; the subject matter has been studied by folklorists from an entirely different point of view. The dominant exception to this is found in Radin's *Primitive Man as Philosopher,* already cited. Some more detailed efforts at esthetic appreciation are Melville Jacobs *The Content and Style of an Oral Literature: Clackamas Chinook Myths and Tales,* Viking Fund Publications in Anthropology No. 26 (Wenner-Gren Foundation), Katharine Luomala, *Voices on the Wind* (Bishop Museum Press), dealing with Polynesian literature, Radin's *The Evolution of an American Prose Epic, A Study in Comparative Literature* (Bolingen Foundation) and, his *African Folklore and Sculpture* (Pantheon).

The science of ethnomusicology has been more concerned with the distribution of musical styles and instruments than it has with the character of the esthetic expression. Perhaps the best recent work on this subject is *Music in Primitive Culture* by Bruno Nettl (Harvard).

XIII. SOCIETY

A summary of the current state of anthropology will be found in *Anthropology Today* (Chicago) edited by A. L. Kroeber and others. A similar volume for sociology is *Sociology Today,* edited by Robert K. Merton, Leonard Broom, and Leonard S. Cottrell, Jr. (Basic Books). A summary of conditions in the less developed areas of the world is presented in *Most of the World, The Peoples of Africa, Latin America and the East Today* (Columbia), edited by Ralph Linton. A broad history of primitive man has been set forth by Ralph Linton in *The Tree of Culture* (Knopf). A philosophical statement of the character of primitive society is provided by Robert Redfield in *The Primitive World and Its Transformations* (Great Seal Books).

Questions for Discussion

1. Try to name things that you and others do that are not influenced by culture. Are the following *always* free of cultural forces: heart beat, feelings of hunger, attitudes toward your mother, dreams? Indicate how and to what degree they may be influenced by culture. What does such influence mean for the relation between biology and culture?

2. What is meant by culture pattern? Can you name some patterned aspects of American behavior? Compare the father-son relationship of today with the same relationship fifty years ago. Can you see similar patterns between senior and junior men in other kinds of relationships such as preacher-congregation member, boss-employee or teacher-student?

3. What elements in American culture discussed by Lynd are found among the Kwakiutl? How would some of these elements be different from behavior in France, Germany or England? Do the differences in cultural elements have an influence on the position of these nations in international relations?

4. How do you react to other cultures? Can you justify these feelings? In doing so, what assumptions do you make with respect to the basic purposes in life? Do you think your assumptions have been influenced by your own culture?

II. **LANGUAGE**

1. List the "vocabulary" of your pet: what expressions does he seem to understand; what ones can he imitate? How does this communication differ from human language?

2. Consider some aspects of life that you learned about through being told, before you actually experienced them: what college is like, what marriage is like, how to behave at a party. Did these set your attitudes? Consider other elements in your experience as the products of learning through words: attitudes toward foreigners or toward other races; were these first formulated in terms of words? What attitudes were learned still earlier in childhood?

3. If you have had experience with a foreign language, discuss some of the problems of translation. Do you frequently find words that mean almost, but not exactly, the same as their equivalent word in English?

4. The capacity for symbol making and using is considered basic to

language. Does this capacity appear in other aspects of cultural behavior? What problems does it raise? Would culture be possible without using non-linguistic symbols?

III. TECHNOLOGY

1. How does the most primitive human technology differ from that of the most advanced animal tool-using capacity?

2. Consider what a modern man and a primitive man must "carry in his head"? How are they different? Why? Which do you believe must carry more?

3. Discuss the proposition: inventions beget inventions. How is this a factor in the difference of modern and primitive technology. Consider here the crucial importance of such a basic invention as the clock.

4. Do you think "Necessity is the mother of invention"? Always? Sometimes? Never?

5. List some of the fundamental inventions in human prehistory and discuss how they probably affected other aspects of life.

6. List some basic inventions of recent years, such as the internal combustion engine and discuss (1) how they have proliferated into other, secondary developments, and (2) how they have affected other aspects of modern culture.

IV. EDUCATION

1. What parts of your learning did you acquire in schools? What kinds of groups, other than your parents and teachers, do you feel contributed to your understanding (or misunderstanding) of the world? Did you ever learn by simply trying to conform to unspoken group norms?

2. Examine current newspaper articles, or the best-selling book on child rearing by Dr. Spock, and compare the type of advice there with the attitudes early in the century. Where does child training in Plainville seem to fit? What differences does this make, in your opinion, in the kinds of adults that will be produced? What are the advantages and disadvantages?

3. What form of punishment is best for a child? Why? What do you think of having an impersonal outside force like Hopi katchinas frighten children?

4. In view of our rapidly advancing technology, what changes do you foresee in modern education as an institution, and in teaching practices?

V. FAMILY

1. What different meanings do you attach to the phrase "my family"? Are the kinds of ties different when used in one sense than when used in

another? Are there ways you act toward (and actions you expect from) relatives different from the way you act towards friends. If so, how?

2. Do you sometimes act toward friends as if they were kin and address them by a kinship term? Are these different kinds of friends from those which you do not treat this way, and if so, what is the difference?

3. What functions does the modern family perform in society? Are there some functions which were once taken care of by the family that other institutions now share or have taken on? If so what are they?

4. Characterize the difference between the Chinese and the American family system. What are the advantages and disadvantages of each? How do the advantages of each relate to other aspects of the social system in the two places?

VI. GROUPS

1. Can a person really be alone? Culturally?

2. What do you mean when we say a group is structured? Describe the structure of a clique or informal group you belong to. How are the leaders determined?

3. What functions does the group perform for the individual? Describe these for some group you know or have read about.

4. What is the difference between the Dahomey work group and the work groups in the Hawthorne plant described by Roethlisberger and Dickson with respect to cultural support, formality of organization, and functional usefulness? What are the similarities.

5. What is meant by group responsibility?

VII. STATUS AND ROLE

1. Consider the various social statuses that you have. How do they relate to the *groups* you belong to? How do they set your relations to other members of the same group? Do you find that as a result you sometimes behave one way in one situation and differently in another?

2. The role conflicts of the African chief are an effect of Westernization. What does this analysis tell us about social roles in native Soga culture? Have there been changes within American society which have brought about role changes?

3. How do symbols of status determine the social position of the individual? How do persons of status determine the symbols used? Are these two effects really in conflict or do they just appear to be? Why? Discuss in terms of the New Guinea situation and Fischer's technique for predicting status symbols.

4. What changes do you think have taken place with respect to social status (in the hierarchical sense) since the beginning of this century? In

view of modern developments, what changes do you expect in the future? How will status be symbolized by the end of the century? Will there be more or less status differentiation?

VIII. AUTHORITY

1. From your knowledge of American history, what were seen as the major problems in the establishment of authoritative roles by those who formulated our Constitution? How were they met? Why is the President of the United States also Commander in Chief of the Armed Forces?

2. Is the existence of an authority role contrary to democratic principles?

3. What is the relationship between custom and law? What is the relation between law and government? How can laws be enforced without government?

4. Criticize the statement: "The savage is ruled by the iron law of custom." (Consider the selections by Oberg, Fallers and Barnett, as well as the items in this section.)

5. Does authority always rest on force. If not, what other bases exist for the use of power?

IX. VALUES

1. Compare the values of New England and the South in the first half of the 19th century. How do these relate to the different modes of life in each? Is there a relation (however indirect) between environment and values in this comparison? Could you therefore say that environment determines values?

2. If values relate to basic life modes of the society, what changes in our values do you think will take place between now and the end of the 20th century? Consider work, leisure, possessions, family background, ethnic background, education, creativity, along with the value orientations discussed by Williams.

3. One definition of class-organized societies is that different social strata have different values. Comment in terms of Ruanda and Athens? Is the same thing true in modern America? To the same extent?

4. Are there any values that are common to the several societies discussed in this section? Do you think these are universal values? What ones? Why are they universal?

X. RELIGION

1. What is meant by the distinction between the social and the individual function of religion? Which do you think is responsible for the universality of religious belief and behavior?

2. If we include superstitions, magical practices, and commitment to unprovable assumptions as religion (as we tend to do with primitive people), do you think there is such a thing as an irreligious person? Is "faith," belief in an after-life, or belief in a Supreme Being necessary to a religious system? Can one have a "personal religion"?

3. In what ways does religious belief enter into secular life in modern America? In what ways do social relations enter into our religious practices?

4. Do you believe that the "household shrines" among the Nacirema involve magical practices? Do we make a religion of science?

5. What elements appear to be common to all systems of religious belief and practice?

6. The "Great Religions" emerged in a fairly limited part of the world and appeared (as anthropologists calculate history) rather close together in time. Is there any anthropological explanation for this?

XI. ETHICS

1. Compare the ethical system of the Yurok and that described as "The Protestant Ethic." Does this comparison tell us anything about the relation of ethics to religion? About the relation of ethics to the degree of cultural advancements?

2. Compare Hopi ethics with the ethical attitudes on the northwest coast of North America, as indicated in the earlier essays by Benedict and Oberg. Which seems closer to your own attitudes? to general ethical patterns in the United States?

3. There is a close interrelation between ethics, values and status. Show the distinction between these terms and indicate how they are related to one another.

4. Some scholars have pointed to a distinction between ethics in a society and regular practices of the people. Give illustrations of this distinction from our own society. Where there is a clear case of disagreement between regular practices and ethical systems, does this disagreement mean that the ethics are inconsequential to behavior? If not, why not?

XII. ART

1. Discuss the proposition: There are no universal cannons of esthetic judgment.

2. Define art. Does your definition include things which you would not yourself like to see or hear? Does it include things made primarily for use, such as an automobile? Does it include primitive as well as modern; popular as well as classic? If it does not, how can you justify the exclusion?

3. Does the primitive artist following closely a traditional style (such

as described by Ruth Bunzel) act as a creator or a copyist? If she is a copyist, how do you account for style changes?

4. In the light of what Alan Lomax says about the influences of childhood training and sexual attitudes on the style and character of folk songs, what would you say about the changing styles of popular music over the past few years?

5. What basic cultural influences do you see at work changing other aspects of our esthetic tastes such as in home decoration, literary style, pictorial art? Can you see any reason why modern artists have been influenced by primitive art, while a century ago they were influenced by classical art?

XIII. SOCIETY

1. What is the difference between "culture" and "society"?

2. List the features of society and the aspects of culture that seem to be universal. How do you account for these? Do they tell us anything about "human nature"? Do they tell us anything about the demands that social life makes upon the forms that culture may take? Might they be survivals of an extremely ancient tradition?

3. Go back over the essays dealing with modern America to see if any general themes emerge. Consider for instance, American family patterns, the social aspects of religion, Weber's analysis of the Protestant ethic or Wohl's discussion of the Horatio Alger myth in the light of what Lynd and Williams have written about our culture and its values.

4. In the light of what Goldschmidt says about the forces at work in America, what changes in our culture do you foresee?

Index